J. N.
LOUGHBOROUGH

To order additional copies of *J. N. Loughborough*, by Brian E. Strayer,
call 1-800-765-6955.

Visit us at **www.reviewandherald.com** for information on other
Review and Herald® products.

J. N. LOUGHBOROUGH

The Last of the Adventist Pioneers

BRIAN E. STRAYER

REVIEW AND HERALD® PUBLISHING ASSOCIATION
Since 1861 | www.reviewandherald.com

Published by Review and Herald® Publishing Association, Hagerstown, MD 21741-1119

Review and Herald® titles may be purchased in bulk for educational, business, fund-raising, or sales promotional use. For information, e-mail SpecialMarkets@reviewandherald.com.

The Review and Herald® Publishing Association publishes biblically based materials for spiritual, physical, and mental growth and Christian discipleship.

The author assumes full responsibility for the accuracy of all facts and quotations as cited in this book.

This book was
Edited by Gerald Wheeler
Copyedited by Jeremy J. Johnson
Cover design by Ron J. Pride/Review and Herald Design Center
Interior Design by Derek Knecht/Review and Herald Design Center
Typeset: Berkeley

PRINTED IN U.S.A.

16 15 14 5 4 3 2 1

Library of Congress Cataloging-in-Publication Data
Strayer, Brian Eugene.
J. N. Loughborough : the last of the Adventist pioneers / Brian E. Strayer.
p. cm.
ISBN 978-0-8280-2662-8
1. Loughborough, J. N. (John Norton), 1832-1924. 2. Seventh-Day Adventists—Biography. I. Title.
BX6193.L65S87 2014
286.7092—dc23
[B]
2012024157

ISBN 978-0-8280-2662-8

DEDICATED

to the memory of
Richard W. Schwarz,
whose 1974 invitation to collaborate
in the research and writing of the
first edition of *Light Bearers*
transformed a graduate student into a
passionate scholar of Adventist history

Acknowledgments

John Donne's famous statement "No man is an island, entire unto itself" certainly applies to the process of researching and writing a book. Although the cover bears my name, a host of people assisted in the search for artifacts, books, buildings, newspapers, periodicals, photographs, and other sources concerning J. N. Loughborough.

I am grateful to Merlin Burt, director of the Center for Adventist Research (CAR) in the James White Library at Andrews University, for granting me access to source material in the file cabinets, bookshelves, and vault. In addition, Merlin loaned me his copies of minutes regarding M. E. Cornell's case (1871-1873) at the San Francisco Central SDA Church. Jim Ford, associate director of CAR, helped me locate hard-to-find materials and artifacts, such as two rare books on the Loughborough family that proved helpful.

Also at CAR, reference specialist Carol Williams (retired) and cataloger Camille Kurtz-Clayton demonstrated unflagging patience in helping me find letters, manuscripts, and other rare sources in the files. Special programs manager Katy Wolfer solved several technical glitches so that rare photographs of Loughborough family members could be scanned into CAR's digital images collection and made available to scholars around the world. Joe Nesbit, digitization project manager, who can find anything anywhere on the Internet, tracked down rare letters and J. N. Loughborough's previously unknown connections with British temperance, vegetarian, and antivaccination societies. Muritha Mutale, interlibrary loan manager for the James White Library, secured on microfilm the only copy of the Victor, New York, Methodist-Episcopal Church Record Book that shows the roles John's father and grandfather played in that congregation during the 1840s.

In Rochester, New York, Larry Naukam, coordinator of historical services (retired) of the Central Library of Rochester and Monroe County, New York, gave invaluable assistance both online and on-site in locating rare newspapers, books, letters, city directories, and maps concerning early Adventists in Rochester in the 1840s and 1850s. In Canandaigua, Mary Jo Lanphear, retired assistant records management officer at the Ontario County Records and Information Management Services Archives, provided a cornucopia of rare materials (maps, deeds, jury lists, atlases, court records, etc.) documenting the pre-1850 history of the Loofboroughs and Nortons in the region. At the nearby Ontario County Historical Society, librarian Linda Templer Alexander supplied me with local histories, letters, maps, and a three-century-old book bearing the signatures of John and his grandfather Nathan Loofborough.

Then, in Victor, New York, three immensely talented and charming women guided my search for Loughborough links. Babette Huber, historian of the Village and Town of Victor, showed me old maps, photos, deeds, and histories, and spent hours of her time tracking down Loughborough properties. Local genealogists Dianne Parks and Bonnie Waters directed me to the sites of several Loofborough graves and provided invaluable tips regarding the Norton and Loofborough family connections.

George and Ruth Ann Tyler (herself a descendant of John's older brother, William K. Loughborough) invited me to their lakeside cottage northwest of Battle Creek, Michigan, to share old photos, rare family artifacts, genealogical information, and delightful stories about her nineteenth-century ancestors. I am grateful to them for allowing the staff at CAR to scan the only extant photo (a four-generation portrait) of Minerva Loughborough, John's mother, with her son William and his daughter and granddaughter. Stanley Hickerson, pastor of the Stevensville, Michigan, Seventh-day Adventist Church, generously allowed me to mine his Ancestry.com membership for Loughborough genealogies, provided useful insights into nineteenth-century architecture, and helped locate William Loofborough's 1840s farm in East Bloomfield, New York.

I am also grateful to David Trim, director of the General Conference Archives, and his associate Shauna Spink for providing me with copies of 20 Loughborough letters of which I was unaware. Likewise, Lori N. Curtis, chair of the Department of Archives and Special Collections at Loma Linda University, supplied copies of several Loughborough letters not available at CAR, and gave me permission to examine the minutes of the San Francisco Central Seventh-day Adventist Church concerning the case of Merritt E. Cornell in the 1870s.

For their critical reading of the original manuscript (in whole or in part) and many helpful suggestions, I owe a great debt to Benjamin McArthur, professor of history at Southern Adventist University in Collegedale, Tennessee; Russell Staples, professor emeritus of the Seventh-day Adventist Theological Seminary at Andrews University; David Trim, director of the General Conference Archives; Babette Huber, Victor, New York, Town historian; and Bonnie Waters, Victor genealogist.

Finally, I want to thank George Knight, editor of this series, for inviting me to begin an exciting journey that has gained me so many friends across the country and culminated in the first biography on the life of John Norton Loughborough. I hope that this book will both inform and inspire those who read it.

—Brian E. Strayer
Andrews University

LIST OF ABBREVIATIONS

AUG	*Atlantic Union Gleaner*
BC	Battle Creek
BTS	*Bible Training School*
CAR	Center for Adventist Research, James White Library, Andrews University
DF	Document File
EGW	Ellen Gould White
GC	General Conference
GCB	*General Conference Bulletin*
GH	*Good Health*
HR	*Health Reformer*
JHK	John Harvey Kellogg
JNL	John Norton Loughborough
JSW	James Springer White
LUH	*Lake Union Herald*
m.	microfilm
ms.	manuscript
NPUG	*North Pacific Union Gleaner*
PHJ	*Pacific Health Journal*
PPPA	Pacific Press Publishing Association
PTB	*Present Truth* (British edition)
PUR	*Pacific Union Recorder*
RH	*Second Advent Review and Sabbath Herald*
San	Sanitarium
SB	Systematic Benevolence
ST	*Signs of the Times*
ST-A	*Signs of the Times* (Australian edition)
ST-M	*Signs of the Times* (monthly edition)
SWUR	*Southwestern Union Record*
T&M	Tract and Missionary Society
VMS	Vigilant Missionary Society
WCW	William Clarence White
WHRI	Western Health Reform Institute (became Battle Creek Sanitarium)
YI	*Youth's Instructor*

Contents

A WORD TO THE READER

John Norton Loughborough is a well-known name to anybody familiar with Seventh-day Adventist history. A small man with large ambitions for God's cause, his ministry touched every phase of Adventist endeavor, including the pastorate, evangelism, foreign missions, church administration, education, medical programs, and writing. And sandwiched in between his activities in those various fields, Loughborough managed to publish the first two book-length histories of Seventh-day Adventism—*The Rise and Progress of Seventh-day Adventists* (1892) and *The Great Second Advent Movement* (1905)—along with extensive historical sketches in various periodicals.

Loughborough's ministry was as long as it was broad and ambitious. He began ministerial activity as "the boy preacher" in 1849 at the age of 17, and continued in various ministerial roles until his death at the age of 92 in 1924.

As a result, his work for the church included the denomination's formative period and the years of its early maturity. While J. N. Loughborough was not one of the founders of Seventh-day Adventism (a class restricted to Joseph Bates and James and Ellen White), he was by the time of his death, in a very real sense, the last of the Adventist pioneers. In the pioneering realm, he was one of the earliest ministers to be ordained in the budding denomination. His 1853 ordination credential was signed by Bates and James White nine years after the Millerite disappointment and eight years before the formal organization of the Seventh-day Adventist denomination. Yet that first among ordinands managed to be the last to die of what might be thought of as the first generation of Adventist preachers and leaders.

By the time of his death he had become something of an icon among the church's members and clergy. It was "Elder Loughborough" who had known all those individuals who had served the church in its early days. It was "Elder Loughborough" who had witnessed the major events in the denomination's development. And it was "Elder Loughborough" who could tell the story of Adventism as a first-person witness. Thus it is no wonder that people clamored to hear him speak of the "old days" at camp meetings and other Adventist gatherings.

No one can doubt the man's significance to Adventism. Yet, surprisingly, up to this time there has never been a major biography of him. The only book on his life and work was a brief, undocumented biography published for young people by Ella Robinson in 1954. Her *Lighter of Gospel Fires: John N. Loughborough* was a helpful sketch by a person who had known him personally, but it hardly provided the kind of treatment that the man deserves or the denomination needs.

Thus the significance of Brian Strayer's *J. N. Loughborough: The Last of the Adventist Pioneers.* Strayer, a diligent researcher, has spent several years seeking to uncover every bit of information extant on the man. Given our current resources, it is difficult to imagine a more complete biography of this individual who did so much to build up the church he had devoted his life to.

Strayer is well qualified for the task. He has taught history, including Seventh-day Adventist history, at Andrews University for three decades and is the author of books and scholarly articles that cover a broad range of topics extending from historical studies of the Huguenots, Jansenists, Convulsionnaires, and eighteenth-century French penal history to several significant books and articles on the development of Adventism.

J. N. Loughborough is the eighth volume in an unprecedented series of Adventist biography. Thus far the series has seen treatments of James White, Joseph Bates, W. W. Prescott, John Harvey Kellogg, E. J. Waggoner, Lewis C. Sheafe, and A. T. Jones. Upcoming volumes already scheduled for publication include Uriah Smith, S. N. Haskell, Arthur G. Daniells, Dudley Canright, and J. N. Andrews. And those contributions are merely the beginning of the volumes projected for the Adventist Pioneer Series, which will eventually include some 30 titles. Each book will focus on the individual's major contribution to the church and will be written by a person well versed in his or her topic.

Meanwhile, we are indebted to Brian Strayer for enabling us to understand better the story of J. N. Loughborough and the church he dedicated his life to. I trust that reading this book will be a fascinating and profitable journey.

—George Knight
Series Editor
Rogue River, Oregon

PREFACE

It was a hot summer afternoon in 1916. Leaning heavily on his cane, an old white-haired man in a black Prince Albert suit cautiously made his way down the gravel path toward the large canvass camp meeting tent in Stockton, California. Suddenly, a woman rushed up to him, her face flushed with excitement.

"Elder Loughborough!" she exclaimed. "Aren't you *thrilled* that *you* are going to live to see Jesus come!"

Startled, the old man stepped back. "But sister," he asked, "how would *you* know anything about that?"

"Well, Elder Loughborough," she explained, "somebody told me that Ellen White told you and several ministers on the platform of the Battle Creek Tabernacle that 'Some of you ministers will live until the Lord comes.' Then pointing directly at *you*, she declared, 'And you, Brother Loughborough, will be one of them.' "

A gentle smile playing across his face, Loughborough replied, "Well, sister, this is the first time I ever heard of it."

Eyes wide with amazement, the woman asked, "Then is it just hearsay? Didn't Sister White *really* say you would live until the Second Advent?"

"Quite to the contrary, sister." The old gentleman stroked his Vandyke beard. "You see, back in 1858 my wife Mary and I traveled with Sister White to visit the scattered Advent band in southern Michigan. One day as Charley, the White's chestnut horse, pulled the buggy along, we three began talking about what conditions would be like just before the Second Coming. Suddenly, a solemn look crossed Sister White's face. Touching my arm and gazing into my eyes, she said, 'Brother John, the Lord has shown me that the early pioneer preachers who have labored and sacrificed for the cause will *all* be laid to rest before that time when the people will have to flee.' "

Wiping a tear from his eye, the stooped octogenarian whispered, "And sister, that prophecy has been fulfilled. They're gone—*all* the pioneer ministers who once preached the third angel's message in the 1840s and '50s are gone—except for me."

Then, grasping the woman's hand in farewell, Loughborough looked into her eyes and exclaimed, "Nevertheless, sister, I hope to be among those who will be *resurrected* to everlasting life and see my Lord come in the clouds of glory!"*

This anecdote, which first appeared in the pamphlet *Questions on the Sealing Message*, reveals several underlying themes concerning the life, work, and beliefs of John Norton Loughborough. An Irishman to the core, he loved hearing, sharing, and writing stories. Indeed, for him, history—especially that of the Seventh-day Adventist movement—was not analysis or interpretation or statistics, but a fascinating narrative. Although Loughborough possessed a sharp memory for details and often went to great lengths to verify the facts in his books, his historical interpretations, as we shall see, sometimes fell short of complete accuracy, especially when the facts clashed with his optimistic view of "the rise and progress" of "the great Second Advent Movement."

For more than seven decades Loughborough loved hitting the sawdust trail. Attending camp meetings, revival efforts, evangelistic crusades, General Conference sessions, and Bible institutes brought him deep personal satisfaction. He enjoyed meeting old friends and making new ones, teaching others how to give Bible studies, and preaching the distinctive Advent message. Well into his 80s, this pioneer preacher continued sharing his fascinating stories about the "rise and progress" of the church and its institutions across the United States and in Europe, Australia, New Zealand, and South Africa. His 60 diaries and hundreds of letters reveal the thrill he felt in public evangelism, baptizing new believers, and swapping memories with old friends around the world.

While Loughborough could be harsh at times (several letters from Ellen White rebuked him for the trait), in his relationships with women—even confused ones as in this story—he was invariably courteous, even courtly. His diminutive size, Irish charm, and optimistic spirit charmed them wherever he traveled. Loughborough is the only pioneer minister to have been married three times: to Mary J. Walker (1851-1867), Margaret ("Maggie") Newman (1868-1875), and Mary Anna ("Annie") M. Driscoll

(1875-1907). Even in his 80s, retired at St. Helena Sanitarium (1916-1924), he enjoyed a close friendship with Edith Barnes, a nurse in her early 40s who assisted him in many ways and saved all of his diaries after his death.

Another special woman in his life for more than 60 years was Ellen G. White. Loughborough's sermons, articles, books, and pamphlets reveal how much he respected and even revered her, not only as his personal friend, but also as God's messenger to the Adventist Church. Never once from 1852 (when they first met) until his death in 1924 did he question the veracity of her writings or her divine inspiration. Instead, he constantly quoted her testimonies, upheld her reputation, and defended her visions (claiming to have been present for 50 of them). Indeed, toward the end of his life, he spent several years typing up exhaustive indexes to all of Ellen White's then extant books and *Review and Herald* articles.

As the preceeding anecdote has shown, Loughborough enjoyed the popularity of a celebrity within the world church. Having outgrown his earlier reputation of being "the boy preacher" and the "little preacher" (he was only five-foot-four-inches tall and never weighed more than 125 pounds), after World War I Adventists widely hailed him as "the oldest minister among us" and "the last of the original pioneers." Since John had been only 12 years old in 1844 and did not begin preaching until 1849 at 17, one could argue that he was not a "pioneer" in the same sense as such older church founders as Joseph Bates, Hiram Edson, and James and Ellen White. However, since Loughborough *outlived* all of them, by the time of his death at 92 in 1924, his contemporaries thought of him as the last remaining pioneer.

For more than 80 years he firmly believed in, preached, wrote about, and prepared for the imminent second advent of Jesus Christ. Indeed, Loughborough wrote more books, tracts, and articles about the Second Coming than on any other topic. One could argue that, while he was not a theologian, his hundreds of articles in the *Review, Signs of the Times,* and *Bible Training School* did more to publicize the prophetic insights of James White, J. N. Andrews, and Uriah Smith than any other preacher or writer. Although later in life he clashed with some church theologians concerning minor teachings such as "the daily," Loughborough never wavered in his loyalty to the cardinal doctrines of the Seventh-day Adventist Church.

Indeed, in many significant ways, J. N. Loughborough helped to shape the future of the church. He was present in Battle Creek in 1863 when its leaders established the General Conference and again in 1901 at its reorganization. Loughborough poured half a century of organizational expertise into his 1907 book *The Church, Its Organization, Order, and Discipline*, which served as a manual for forming new churches until the official *Seventh-day Adventist Church Manual* in 1932.

His two published histories—*Rise and Progress of Seventh-day Adventists* (1892) and *The Great Second Advent Movement* (1905)—shaped the popular view of the church's history as a divinely led prophetic movement destined to expand around the globe. Near the end of his life, Loughborough's frequent chats with church historian Arthur W. Spalding, *Review* editor Francis M. Wilcox, and theologian LeRoy E. Froom inspired them to write the same kind of uplifting stories about the Adventist heritage that he had done for half a century.

While Adventist pioneer and missionary to Europe J. N. Andrews is justly famous for having memorized the entire New Testament and much of the Old Testament as well, it was Loughborough who is credited with having read his Bible through the most times—76 to be exact. Likewise, it was Loughborough in the 1920s—not Glenn Coon in the 1970s—who actually tallied up 3,573 divine promises in God's Word. His faithful Bible study habits inspired the General Conference to form the Loughborough Devotional League in the 1950s. Moreover, for half a century his book *The Great Second Advent Movement* served as a textbook on church history at Adventist academies and colleges. In addition, Missionary Volunteers from 1908 into the 1950s studied that book to pass exams in denominational history and thus receive the coveted Standard of Attainment Award.

Four times a year Seventh-day Adventists celebrate the Lord's Supper—and the Communion bread they eat follows a recipe that Loughborough adapted from the Jewish Passover bread in 1906. In addition, church musicians owe him a huge debt of gratitude for his successful efforts during the 1880s to introduce pump organs in local Adventist churches and at camp meetings and other public venues. Against stiff opposition from some church members and leaders, he consistently quoted Psalm 150 to justify the presence of organs and other musical instruments in Adventist services.

Yet despite his many contributions, no one has ever written a scholarly biography of John Norton Loughborough (1832-1924). It is the hope of this author that those who as young people enjoyed reading Ella Robinson's *Lighter of Gospel Fires* (1954) about Loughborough's childhood will find the rest of his life's story equally as fascinating.

—Brian E. Strayer
Andrews University
Berrien Springs, Michigan

---

*Portions, including Ellen White's words, adapted from JNL, *Questions on the Sealing Message* (Bakersfield, Calif.: B. F. Gregory, 1916), pp. 23, 24.

J. N. Loughborough

CHAPTER I

THE BOY FROM VICTOR, NEW YORK (1832-1842)

"The J. N. Loughboroughs were more or less obsessed with the idea that they were descended from 'Lord' Loughborough."[1]

For generations John Loughborough's family had been "obsessed" with the notion that they had descended from Alexander Wedderburn, the chancellor of George III, whom the king had ennobled as Lord Loughborough in 1780.[2] To the end of his life, John, who spent much time poring over genealogical charts, maintained that his ancestors had come from good English stock.[3]

WHAT'S IN A NAME?

It is more likely, however, that the family had roots in Ireland. While the English word for a small body of water is "lake" and the Scots call it a "loch," the Celtic word is "luf" or "lough." Maps of Northern Ireland show Belfast Lough, Lough Fayle, Lough Swilly, and Lough Neagh, for example. "Borough" means neighborhood, town, or manor.[4] Therefore, at some time in the distant past, John's ancestors probably came from an Irish town near an inland lake (a lough). It could explain, in part at least, why John's spot-on imitation of Irish brogue left listeners convulsed with laughter, particularly when he regaled camp meeting crowds with his one-man rendition of "Mike and the Saloonkeeper."[5]

Even after John's ancestors left Ireland for England sometime during the High Middle Ages, it took centuries for the family name to evolve. They appear as "Lucteburnes" in the Domesday Book (1088) and as "Lucteburgs" under Henry II (1154). By the seventeenth century, creative spellers rendered the family moniker as "Lickbara," "Lifbarra," "Loufborough," "Lufbrough," "Lovebourough," and "Loughborrow." A notoriously poor speller himself, perhaps Loughborough took comfort in knowing that his ancestors struggled with their surname as well.[6] As for the family's claim to noble blood, genealogical research reveals that the famous Lord Loughborough, although twice married, had no children and hence no heirs.[7]

In fact, John's immediate ancestors—John and Hannah Loofbourrow—left England for America in 1684 where they settled in New Jersey and raised a large family (a Loughborough characteristic well into the nineteenth century). Three generations later, several of John's New Jersey relatives fought for the Patriot cause in the American Revolution.[8] Although John claimed years later that his grandfather Nathan had told him stories of fighting beside General George Washington in the Revolution, the fact that Nathan was only 8 years old when the war commenced makes it highly unlikely. Military records prove instead that the 27-year-old Lieutenant Nathan Loofborough served three months in the Third Regiment of Middlesex County Infantry under Captain Ezekiel Pierce during the less glamorous Whiskey Rebellion in Massachusetts in 1794.[9]

GRANDFATHER NATHAN LOOFBOROUGH

While shingling a house in Perth Amboy, New Jersey, 13-year-old Nathan had experienced the Dark Day of May 19, 1780. When it became so dark that he could no longer see the chalk line and pounded his fingers (instead of the iron nails) with the hammer, the boy quit working and fled home, dodging terrified horses and citizens who were certain that the final day of judgment had arrived. Decades later Grandpa Nathan would tell John about seeing the stars fall (meteorite shower) on November 13, 1833, and about his conviction that both events signified the imminence of the second coming of Christ. To his dying day, Nathan Loofborough qualified every promise he made with the words *"if the Lord does not come."*[10]

Eleven years after the Dark Day, Nathan wed Sarah Morford of Cranbury, New Jersey, and between 1791 and 1809 they raised nine children, including John's father, Nathan Benson Loofborough (born 1802) and John's favorite aunt, Sarah Morford (born 1804). Sometime about 1804 or 1805 the family moved near Albany, New York. They probably watched Robert

Fulton pilot his steam-driven paddle wheel boat *Clermont* up the Hudson River. Years later, when Nathan told his grandson about it, John shouted, "Three cheers for Fulton!" In 1806 Nathan and Sarah, perhaps seeking a quiet rural environment for their children, migrated to western New York. They settled near Canandaigua Lake, where land was cheap and Nathan could support his family by farming and carpentering.[11]

THE LOOFBOROUGHS IN UPSTATE NEW YORK

Prior to the completion of the Erie Canal between Albany and Buffalo in 1825 and the building of railroads in the 1830s and 1840s, the Finger Lakes region of upstate New York was truly a rough and rugged frontier where wolves, bears, and panthers roamed the woods. Highways consisted of Indian trails or split-plank (corduroy) roads over which wagons, buggies, and stagecoaches traveled with bone-rattling effects through swamps and thick forests. To improve travel and communication, some entrepreneurs began charging tolls, and the Farmington Toll Road (which still exists east of Victor) was one of the first of these primitive highways that carried the mail coaches through the tiny hamlet.[12]

Seeking peace and quiet, the Loofboroughs built a farmhouse on East Bloomfield Town Line Road. Then a narrow dirt road, it is today paved and known as Cherry Street (possibly named by Nathan himself, who, as a boy, had lived on Cherry Street in Woodbridge, New Jersey).[13] Following the destructive campaign of Generals Sullivan and Clinton to defeat and remove the Iroquois from central New York during the American Revolution, the government sold the Indian lands to army veterans. Victor and Bloomfield townships, formerly inhabited by the Seneca Nation (whose 150 longhouses at nearby Ganondagan the French had destroyed in 1687), now fell into the hands of English, Scottish, and Irish Yankees from New England, many of them Revolutionary War veterans.[14] As their plows broke the soil for planting wheat, corn, and potatoes, farmers such as Nathan, his son Nathan Benson, and his grandson John Loofborough frequently unearthed Indian arrowheads, French silver coins and crosses, and iron bullets.[15]

Of the many military veterans with whom the Loofboroughs became well acquainted, the most prominent were the Nortons. Like the Loofboroughs, the Nortons had left England for America in the seventeenth century and settled near New Haven, Connecticut. After the American Revolution, however, they too had moved to Bloomfield Township, where Eber Norton helped establish the town of Canandaigua in 1791. By 1806 the family had grown rich from their saltworks on the lake. Their offspring became prosperous farmers, millers, and merchants as well as judges, clergymen, and assemblymen.[16] While the Loofboroughs embraced Methodism, the Nortons remained staunch Baptists. Yet their religious differences did not interfere with business and pleasure. During the next half century, the Loofboroughs would trade with and purchase dozens of acres of prime farmland in East Bloomfield and Victor townships from their Norton neighbors. The two families grew even closer when John's father Nathan B. Loofborough married Minerva Norton. The couple would name their second son John Norton Loofborough.[17]

Although the Loofboroughs lived on a farm in East Bloomfield Township, they worshipped and traded a few miles north in Victor Township. Boughtontown, named by its founders Enos and Jared Boughton in 1789, remained a tiny hamlet of scattered cabins until after the War of 1812, when the settlers renamed it Victor in honor of Claudius Victor Boughton, a local war hero.[18]

As a prosperous farmer, skilled carpenter, and highly respected citizen, Nathan Loofborough contributed to the development of Victor in many ways. Soon after the family's arrival, settlers asked him and another local carpenter to design and build a wood frame building to function as a town meeting hall and church. With box pews, a gallery on three sides, a servants' pew, and a high pulpit, the Proprietors' Meeting House served as a place of worship for Christians of all denominations from 1806 to 1821.[19] Here in 1807 Methodist circuit-riding preacher Joseph Jewel appointed Nathan as class leader. As such, he supervised the spiritual welfare of seven class members who met in quarterly meetings in barns and fieldstone schoolhouses to sing hymns, pray, and study the Bible. A gifted speaker, Nathan was soon elected an "exhorter" (lay preacher). In 1808 he served as a delegate to the first quarterly conference of the Methodist Church in Ontario County. His star was rising. By 1810 the popular exhorter with a Sunday school class of 40 members was widely known as "the Reverend Loofborough"—one of only 14 men in the county granted that title as Methodist "circuit stewards."[20]

Popularity, however, provided no antidote for sorrow when in February 1810 Nathan and Sarah's 10-month-old baby William Lacy Loofborough died. Their first child born in upstate New York, little William would become the first person buried in the new community cemetery behind the Methodist Church in Victor. As the years passed, however, seven other Loofboroughs would join him.[21]

Nathan's growing reputation within the Methodist Church widened his sphere of influence in commerce, society, and politics as well. In 1810 he purchased the Trask place, an even larger farm wedged between those of Sereno and Eber Norton. Here he established a cabinet-making shop with a handful of employees.[22] From 1811 to 1816 his name appeared regularly on the jury lists for East Bloomfield.[23] Yet (as his grandson John would later assert) court records show that Nathan himself was a model citizen. For more than half a century no Loofborough appeared before the Court of Oyer and Terminer (charged with hearing cases of treason, felonies, and misdemeanors), the Court of Sessions (the criminal court), or the Ontario County Supreme Court (the court of appeals). When contentious neighbors forced Nathan to sue in the Court of Common Pleas (dealing with civil matters), the judge ruled in his favor all three times.[24]

His reputation as a peaceable man and a talented preacher led to his appointment in 1817 as one of four trustees for the Methodist Circuit that included Bloomfield, Victor, and Canandaigua. In 1818 the Methodists in Canandaigua hired him to build their new church on Chapel Street.[25] As the Reverend Loofborough's wealth grew, so did his personal library. His collection of books included *The Confession of Faith, the Larger and Shorter Catechisms With the Scripture Proofs at Large . . . of Publick Authority in the Church of Scotland* (1745)—a rather dry theological tome he later gave to his grandson, the boy preacher John Loofborough.[26]

Thanks in large part to the Reverend Loofborough's evangelical zeal, Methodism grew rapidly in Ontario County. On some Sundays the Proprietors' Meeting House had standing room only. So at the quarterly meeting in January 1820, members voted to erect a new Methodist church in Victor. The board of trustees commissioned five men, including the Reverend Loofborough and his carpenter son Nathan Benson, to build it. To complete the structure before winter set in, Nathan Benson actually worked, ate, and slept inside the building. Dedicated in August 1821, this impressive 32' x 45' wooden chapel served the Methodists for nearly half a century. Its completion sparked a revival that witnessed the conversion of more than 100 persons. Here three generations of Loofboroughs would worship and grandson John would receive his early education. [27]

VICTOR, NEW YORK, AND IMMIGRATION

The decade prior to John's birth in 1832 witnessed rapid changes in Ontario County and in the village of Victor, which more than doubled in size from about 100 inhabitants in 1810 to more than 250 by 1830. A few miles to the north near the growing city of Rochester, Irish and German immigrants in 1817 began digging the Erie Canal, a 363-mile, four-foot deep channel (nicknamed "Clinton's ditch" after the New York governor) between Albany and Buffalo. Long days with pick and shovel made such laborers thirsty, and Victor's 14 distilleries helped supply them with the whiskey they craved. But local citizens, who, like most Americans, were White Anglo-Saxon Protestants, despised the Irish as dirty, illiterate, Roman Catholic interlopers. While some business establishments posted signs declaring "No Dogs or Irishmen Allowed," others eventually organized the Sons of Temperance and the Total Abstinence Society to reform them or exclude them from polite society.[28]

But when the immigrants discovered that the clay and loam soil around Victor grew magnificent potatoes, many chose to buy land and begin farming after the completion of the canal in 1825. During the 1830s and 1840s even more Irish (fleeing the potato famine of 1845-1846) and Germans (escaping political upheavals across Germany in 1830 and 1848) arrived to build New York's railroads. Within a few years they had erected St. Patrick's (Roman Catholic) Church. Because local Whites refused to let them bury their dead in Victor's cemeteries, they opened St. Patrick's Cemetery. Their tombstones testify that during John Loofborough's boyhood in Victor, he was surrounded by Mahoneys, McCarthys, and McCalls as well as O'Sullivans, O'Learys, and O'Byrnes speaking the Irish brogue he would later imitate so perfectly.[29]

Despite ethnic tension, the immigrants soon made themselves indispensable to the local economy. In addition to building the Erie Canal, they laid the track for the three railroad lines that passed through Victor, and erected several of the 22 cobblestone buildings (14 of which survive today) using fieldstones, lime, and sand. They also built some of the 20 mills on the surrounding creeks. As a child, John attended classes in one of those cobblestone schools. Then as a preacher, he also rode the local railroads, counting fence posts as the train sped past them at 15 miles per hour.[30]

Despite such changes, Victor remained a quiet little village. During the 1830s cows wearing bells and accompanied by their owners still wandered the dirt streets. In warm weather members of the Seneca tribe came to town to sell their basket wares and beg for food. Occasionally, though, politics stirred deeper feelings. Throughout the early part of the century most of Victor's citizens were staunch Democratic-Republicans, but their neighbors in Canandaigua usually voted for the Federalists—the main opposition. So the election of Andrew Jackson as U.S. president in 1828 witnessed some vigorous debates.[31]

BIRTH OF JOHN NORTON LOOFBOROUGH

As a partner in Nathan Loofborough's growing carpentry and cabinetry business, his son Nathan Benson had by the 1820s grown rich enough to invest in land. In 1824, at 22, Nathan Benson paid Alfred Norton the impressive sum of $350 for some prime farm land in East Bloomfield. During the next five years, he invested $334 in further land purchases in East Bloomfield and Victor townships.[32] While Nathan Benson was by no means a wealthy farmer, the tax rolls for 1829 assess his net worth at $75 in real estate and show that he paid about 32 cents monthly in taxes. As a successful middle-class farmer and skilled tradesmen like his father, Nathan Benson's reputation soon led to his being appointed to the petit jury and then to the grand jury—one of only six men from Victor to share that honor.[33]

Feeling financially secure, Nathan Benson, at 24, decided the time had come to start a family. Sometime in 1826 he married Minerva Norton, the 25-year-old daughter of a prosperous local family. During the next 14 years they would be blessed with five children: William Kerr (1827), Minerva Jane (1829), John Norton (1832), Eber C. (1837), and Sarah Diantha (1840).[34] As the family grew, so did the need for more living space. In 1828, four years before John's birth on January 26, 1832, the Loofborough's moved into the village of Victor and built a house on the south side of East Main Street (then the old mail stage line between Albany and

Buffalo and now Route 96) a few rods from the growing Methodist church where John's father and grandfather served as licensed ministers.[35]

In February 1832 Minerva Loofborough took her 3-week-old son to church for a solemn service: first, she consecrated him to the Lord; then she dedicated him to God (as biblical Hannah had done with Samuel), asking that someday he might become a preacher. Two years later, when Mr. Boughton, a family friend, visited their home, Nathan told him that while he wanted his son William to become a good mechanic (he did) and his daughter Minerva to become a teacher (she didn't), he hoped that 2-year-old John would someday "help sound the gospel trumpet" as a minister (he did). In such a pious home, it was only natural that John's earliest memories were religious ones. Every morning and evening Nathan gathered the family and hired hands around the dining room table for worship. After reading a chapter or two from the family Bible, he led in the prayers that followed as everyone knelt. Each Sunday morning the family walked down the block to the Methodist church where John's grandpa Nathan often preached. Tiny though he was, John heard the musical cadences of his grandfather's voice and sought to imitate him. At the age of 3, when he and his 8-year-old brother William and 6-year-old sister Jane played church at home, they asked John to do the preaching. "I can not remember [a time] when I did not want to be a Christian," he wrote decades later.[36]

While still an infant, however, John suffered a crippling setback. He contracted scarlet fever, and when a maid held him too long near an open window, the cold wintry air caused severe congestion in his ear. According to Loughborough's recollection decades later, it ulcerated, leaving him deaf in his right ear for the next half century (until he experienced what he believed to be a miraculous healing in 1882 while he was in England).[37]

Despite this handicap, his parents, believing Christian education paramount, sent William, Jane, and John to attend Miss Bibbins' class for tiny tots in the basement of the Methodist church. Here kindergartners learned to read and write and memorized Bible verses and poems which they recited before their peers. At 4, John could say:

"Were I so tall as to reach the sky,
    Or grasp the ocean in my span;
I must be measured by my soul;
    The mind's the standard of the man."[38]

In addition to giving John a lifelong love of poetry, Miss Bibbins inspired in him an enduring awe for astronomy. Although he preferred his friend's definition of stars as "holes cut in the sky to let the glory [of God shine] through," he dutifully memorized the scientific information his teacher shared. But "my childish mind had wished she had let this alone, and had not spoiled the 'glory holes' in the sky." However, the boy experienced some of this heavenly "glory" the day before his sixth birthday when he witnessed such a spectacular display of the aurora borealis that it filled him with "awe and wonder." Gazing up at the evening sky, he saw "a red flame, mingled with clouds of smoky vapor . . . [with] the appearance of an immense conflagration." Terrified, John's babysitter shrieked, "The world is coming to an end!" John's parents, thinking their house had caught fire, rushed back from a sleigh ride to comfort their boy. When the heavens staged a repeat performance in November, Minerva talked to her children about Joel's prophecy concerning "wonders in the heavens" at the end of time. In school, the teacher led them in singing a new song: "See the northern lights, the northern lights, plainly telling He [God] is great, who did all its beams create; never changing, never changing, source of life and light."[39] Remembering those fiery scenes seven decades later, John would write a book entitled *Last-Day Tokens* in which he vividly described other such "wonders in the heavens," seeing them as tokens of Christ's soon return.

Like kindergarten, Sunday school classes and church services in the 1830s emphasized piety, duty, order, and memorizing Scripture. Although many children probably found it boring, John enjoyed attending church. He especially liked the "love feasts" and Communion services at which he heard personal testimonies "moistened with tears" and "shouts of praise." Such meetings left him with a deep impression of the Holy Spirit's power working in the lives of humble people. At a tender age he also learned that Methodism required self-discipline, when the deacons denied one woman a ticket to attend Communion because she wore gold jewelry, and excluded her daughter as well for attending dances. Years later as a minister of the gospel, Loughborough would exemplify the same disciplined approach to church organization.[40]

When Miss Bibbins' class of toddlers outgrew their one-room school at the Methodist church in 1837, the kindergartners moved into more spacious quarters at the Presbyterian church. As in most one-room schoolhouses across nineteenth century America, their teacher, Joseph Hollister, taught multiple grades. Five-year-old John, however, sometimes refused to play with his kindergarten pals, preferring instead to listen to the elementary students' recitations so that he could better learn to read and write at their level. Once, observing a handwriting class in session, John scribbled a "composition" and asked his teacher to read it. "I can't make it out, Johnny; you read it yourself," the man replied. So little John "read" what he supposed he had written to the class.[41] His passion for reading, writing, and study (especially biographies, theology, and history) would remain with him his entire life.

As did children all across rural America in the nineteenth century, John had chores before and after school each day. Early in the morning he drove Brindle (their milk cow) a quarter mile to pasture outside the village, and every evening he brought her home again. When old enough to ride a horse, he enjoyed the task even more. But one morning he rode so long that he was late for school, so his mother kept him home all day, promising to punish him later. Promptly at 5:00, she took him into the bedroom, told him how much it hurt her to punish him, and then whipped him with a peach switch. "Of course, I cried," he admitted, "but she wept more than I did." It would be his last whipping, for he had learned lessons about obedience and punctuality that he never forgot.[42]

In addition to his love of Brindle and his horse, John early developed a fascination with all kinds of animals. Living on the old stage road gave him a front-row seat for all the animals that paraded through Victor. Such "animal menageries" (predecessors of Barnum and Bailey's Circus in the post-Civil War era) brought lions, tigers, leopards, bears, hyenas, and elephants to rural America for the first time. Occasionally they also included colorfully dressed clowns singing popular tunes. John never forgot the Van Amburgh parade of wild beasts in 1837. It sported a monkey dressed as a boy riding a pony, baby lion cubs in a basket, and a den of lions (that the director fearlessly entered). Van Amburgh also gave the children rides on the elephant. For a month afterward, William, Jane, and John talked of nothing else but this "great sight." Minerva used the occasion to teach her children a lesson based on Isaiah 11:6, which describes the new earth as a place where the wolf will dwell with the lamb. She appealed to them to be ready to go to heaven where they could play with such beasts in safety. Deeply impressed, John wanted to leave for that place immediately![43] Near the end of his life, he confessed that his mother's talk "made an impression on my mind which time has never effaced," leading to the firm resolve that "I must be there in that blessed state."[44] The local Sunday school superintendent, likewise recognizing the event as a teachable moment, led his pupils in memorizing Revelation 22, which describes the life of God's saints in the new earth. As John and his friends recited the chapter, he saw tears trickle down his teacher's face. The experience created in the boy's mind a deep desire to understand the symbolic beasts in the apocalypse, a subject that would fill many of his books and articles later in life.[45]

When John was 6 years old, a schoolmate died suddenly from an undisclosed illness. A 10-year-old friend informed him that because it took three days for the soul to reach heaven (based on Christ's spending three days in the tomb), this boy's funeral would be held three days after his death so that his soul had time to go to heaven and sing with the angels. As his friend could not find a Bible text to prove his theory, however, John had doubts about it. When an elderly Methodist woman died in 1838, John heard the minister at the funeral declare that the woman was sitting on the edge of a cloud singing psalm tunes. Deeply impressed, John stared at clouds to see if he could spot those saints. When a few months later another preacher told the congregation that souls were immaterial and so tiny that thousands could dance on the head of a needle, John was devastated. Years later, as an Adventist minister, he would more closely examine such "floating heresies" (as he called them) in his writings.[46]

Hollister's untimely death provided John's parents with an opportunity to find another school for him to attend. Although by the 1830s only about 2,300 people lived in Victor, the township boasted no fewer than 11 elementary schools. Every one of their teachers firmly believed that the only way "to fix the instructions in the treacherous memories of their pupils [was] by a physical application of birch or good apple tree sprout [switch]." Frequent visits by school inspectors made certain that they applied the rod of teaching to the seat of learning.[47] In 1838 and 1839 John began attending singing classes several evenings a week. His early vocal training provided the foundation for his lifelong efforts to improve choral singing among Seventh-day Adventists and also to introduce church organs among them.[48] Furthermore, when John read in his *Webster Spelling Book* that one should "eat slow [and] chew your food fine," such advice encouraged him to think more seriously about diet, health, and avoiding illness.[49]

DEATH OF NATHAN BENSON LOOFBOROUGH

By 1839 John's father had established his reputation as a dynamic lay preacher, a successful builder and carpenter, a prosperous landowner, and a respected civic leader. When 38 male members of the local Methodist Episcopal church met in 1838 to legally incorporate as a society, Nathan Loofborough and his sons, Nathan Benson and John Wade, signed the incorporation document.[50] Nathan Benson had spent two decades buying parcels of prime land in Ontario County, and by 1839 he was worth almost $1,000.[51] His cabinet shop employed 17 full-time workers and supplied the coffins for all of Ontario County. Yet perhaps Nathan worked *too* hard building houses, crafting furniture, and holding class meetings among scattered Methodist groups. On some days he returned home after 10:00 p.m. Thus, when typhoid fever swept the Finger Lakes region that summer, Nathan Benson, even in his mid-30s, had little vitality left to fight it off.[52]

Minerva summoned Dr. Elijah Sedgewick, who had practiced medicine in Victor since 1827. Although he had written a medical manual (*The Plain Physician*), Sedgewick had a reputation as a physician "full of theory, a scholar, but not very successful at the bedside."[53] He ordered Nathan's four-poster bed covered with heavy drapes and his windows sealed shut to prevent fresh air from entering. Then he bled the patient and administered generous doses of calomel and jalap (strong drugs), and when Nathan burned with fever, Sedgewick denied him the relief of water internally or externally for fear of "insalivating" him. Years later when the pain of this memory had receded somewhat, John told the story of a typhoid-stricken Irishman in Victor complaining to his brother Pat: "En' I was jist a burnin' with the faver sax wakes in the minth of August, en' me continual cry was *water! WATER!! WATER!!!*"[54]

On rare occasions when John was permitted to enter the darkened bedroom, his father spoke with him about Christ's second coming and the judgment, which he believed would occur sometime before 1860. He hoped that John would "help *blow the gospel trumpet*" and "have a great work to do in the cause of the Lord" when he grew to manhood.[55] On September 20, 1839, John talked with his father for the last time. The scene remained etched on his mind half a century later: "Well do I remember being called into the sick-room of my father [for] the last time I (a boy of seven years) ever saw him alive. A frame had been built around his bedstead, which was covered with thick blankets both at sides and top, to exclude the air and light. Through a small opening near the head of the bed, I was permitted to look at his shaded face. It left an impression on my mind that typhoid fever was something awful."[56]

To prevent others from suffering as his father had done, as an adult John would labor tirelessly to establish the Western Health Reform Institute (1866) in Battle Creek, Michigan, and the Rural Health Retreat in St. Helena, California (1878). He would also become editor of *The Pacific Health Journal*.

When Nathan Benson Loofborough died, about 2,000 mourners—including many prominent ministers—attended his funeral. Decades later John remembered that the preacher spoke from Daniel 12:13 regarding judgment and reward in the resurrection day. As the grave digger shoveled dirt on his father's grave, John wept openly, thinking to himself, *My father is dead, and I also must die.* He took little comfort from his friends' assurance that his father was now in heaven and that if he were good, he would join him there someday. "I passed many sad hours alone, and prayed earnestly that the Lord would make me good," he recalled. Throughout John's long life the grim reaper would pay frequent visits to his family, leading him to search his Bible often for promises of hope and resurrection.[57]

Nathan Benson died intestate (without a will), leaving behind a pregnant wife and four children: William (12), Minerva Jane (10), John (7), and Eber (2). Five months later in February 1840, Sarah Diantha was born. Faced with the impossible task of supporting five children by taking in sewing, Minerva made two decisions that would ensure her family's future: first in 1839 and again in 1841 she appeared before the Surrogate Court of Ontario County to make Caleb Boughton, a prosperous Victor landowner and family friend, the legal guardian of her family and the administrator of her late husband's estate. Second, she sent her son John to live with his grandparents three miles away in East Bloomfield. That decision would profoundly shape the boy's life.[58]

JOHN'S LIFE WITH HIS GRANDPARENTS

By 1839 Nathan (72) and Sarah (67) Loofborough had already reared nine children, most of whom had children of their own. Taking in their 7-year-old grandson John literally meant starting the process all over again. Nonetheless, they welcomed the shy, grieving boy into their home and raised him with what later generations would call "tough love." On the one hand they assured him that his father now lived in heaven with Jesus and the angels, but they also warned him that if he was not good, he would die and burn for all eternity. Although his uncle Norton, a Baptist, believed that the wicked would be "burned up root and branch," his Methodist grandfather prayed, "Lord, teach us each that we have a soul that must die, forever die, and [yet] never die" in the fires of hell.[59] Consequently, John developed a phobia of death and hell.

Hellfire became more real to him when, at the age of 10, he discovered "lucifers," the popular name for the newly invented matches. Deciding to make his own, John dipped whittled sticks into melted brimstone and wax. Miles Carter, an uncle figure visiting at the time, asked the boy if he knew how hot brimstone fire burned. When John replied that he did not, Carter told him that hell fire was 1,000 times hotter than melting a nailrod (a thin strip of iron that blacksmiths used in making horseshoe nails) over brimstone. John shuddered at the thought of fire that hot. "If grandfather's statement had shocked me, this statement had doubled the dose," he recalled years later. He began having nightmares about being suspended in a pulleylike device over hell's fire pits, then would awaken in a cold sweat and screaming. Regaining his composure, he would kneel and thank God that he was still alive. When their Dutch neighbor, Mr. Van Vechten, died suddenly of a heart attack, his grandparents attended the funeral, leaving John behind to hoe 10 acres of corn. Every time he neared the dark woods, he imagined the devil emerging with pitchfork in hand and snatching his soul to hell. The scared boy knelt and prayed to God to help him be a good boy. Yet he could not escape the feeling that God hated him. Two years later, when he read the Millerite preacher George Storrs' tract "Six Sermons on Future Punishment" (about conditional immortality), John learned that no one goes to heaven or hell at death. Instead, the Bible teaches that the dead sleep in their graves until Jesus' second coming. "I wished many times they would tell me how to be good, instead of telling me so much about the terrors of hell," he said. In 1850 at Chautauqua, New York, Uncle Miles would listen with "breathless attention" as his 18-year-old nephew preached on the state of the dead. Carter took notes on the Bible texts John quoted, and later in family worship he prayed that God would help him receive truth "from whatever source it might come."[60]

For the most part, however, John enjoyed living with his grandparents. His days began and ended with family worship. Frequently, he saw his grandfather's face bathed in tears as he prayed for his wife, for John, and for his two employees. Nathan even prayed for his Universalist neighbors who had harassed him for opposing their doctrine of universal salvation. Occasionally while the Loofboroughs attended church, the Universalist believers would strip their cherry and pear trees, break their fences, and let cattle flatten their wheat field. Nathan's only response was to pray for them. But when bad harvests drove the price of wheat on the Erie Canal up to $2 a bushel, Nathan sold wheat to his nearby laborers for $1 a bushel. Soon the Universalists became his friends, ready to defend Reverend Loofborough as an honest man. "Many of my early religious impressions were doubtless deepened by the example of that man of God," John later admitted.[61]

In addition to modeling lessons in forgiveness for his grandson, Nathan provided him with useful labor, thereby teaching him diligence and self-reliance. In antebellum America farm labor meant arduous work from dawn to dusk prior to the advent of labor-saving machinery. Although their neighbor, Mr. Collins, had purchased a new McCormick reaper in 1842, Nathan and his hired hands continued harvesting wheat by hand using scythes with cradles for another decade. He did, however, later purchase a "vibrator" (threshing machine), paying John 25 cents a day to shovel away the chaff that fell into the separator. To the end of his life, John remained convinced that such "older methods," though more arduous, developed better bodily strength and endurance and provided boys greater satisfaction from a job well done.[62]

But during the late fall and winter months, John attended school, where his mind absorbed knowledge like a sponge. Reading especially delighted him. He spent some of his allowance on the *Sunday School Advocate*, whose cartoon lessons on the evils of playing marbles for keeps and card games left him with a lifelong fear that gambling would lead to intoxication, suicide, or murder. Seven decades later he told an Australian audience: "To this day I know no more about the cards [than] a four-year-old child knows of Latin." Instead, he found ways to earn money at school by fetching wood, sweeping classrooms, ringing the bell for recess, building fires, and selling the ashes to local businessmen.[63] Somewhat of a show-off, John loved spelling bees, declamations, and recitations when he could stand in front, arms folded, and give his speeches in a high-pitched voice.[64]

Arithmetic particularly intrigued him, for he saw in numbers the empowerment to increase and multiply. When the class studied the decimal system, John learned that 10 mills made one cent; 10 cents made one dime; 10 dimes made one dollar; and 10 dollars made one "eagle" (a silver coin with an eagle minted on its surface). It fascinated him to realize that adding a zero to any number increased its value tenfold. For the rest of his life John would employ numbers and statistics to demonstrate the "rise and progress" of Seventh-day Adventism around the world.[65]

His childhood education at home, church, and school also reinforced his love for music. The Loofboroughs sang at family worship, in Sunday school, and at church services. In addition, John attended evening singing classes at the Methodist church where, despite deafness in one ear, he learned to sing various pitches with a tuning fork. Called shape-note or sacred harp singing in the Appalachian South, the choir would sing up or down a scale until they reached the note for the next song. When someone brought a violin to keep them in tune, certain members objected, arguing that the fiddle was a dance instrument. The minister, quoting Psalm 150, countered that the violin improved the quality of their singing by helping them remember the tune and the words better. The incident deeply impressed John. Three years later at 13 he made a violin from beech wood and sold it to a local physician. In the 1870s, as California Conference president, he too would cite Psalm 150 to justify introducing pump organs into Adventist churches.[66]

Sharing the memories of his school days with later generations, John explained that in the 1830s writing was done with goose-quill pens, which each student learned to make and repair in handwriting class at the beginning of each day. Not until 1840 did he see his first steel pen. Teachers loved them because now they could devote more time to teaching penmanship. They enclosed letters with sealing wax melted over candle flames until the advent of the "wafer" (made from a thin paste of flour, egg whites, isinglass, and yeast spread with water and gum, then dried). Not until he was 16 did John see his first envelope. When it grew dark, the Loofboroughs lit oil lamps (filled with sperm whale oil), beef tallow candles, or (in the 1840s) coal oil lamps. Usually, however, John studied his lessons lying flat on his stomach before the fireplace.[67]

Laborious farm work and diligent study gave John an appetite for his grandmother's cooking. Although throughout his life he resembled a leprechaun, he could devour mountains of food. Despite the fact that contemporary health reformers such as Jackson, Trall, and Shew preached vegetarianism, the Loofboroughs preferred a "hearty" farmer regimen. "I was a great lover of animal flesh as food," John confessed. For breakfast he ate fried pork with rich gravy spread over thick slices of homemade bread; at dinner he swallowed boiled pork or corned beef with beans and potatoes; for supper he devoured dried beef or ham with pie, shortcake, or pastries saturated with lard. At every meal he drank tea or coffee. The vegetables usually came to the table covered with black or red pepper or horseradish, garnished with pickles, mustard, ketchup, and sharp cheese. Salads dripped with cider vinegar. The family consumed seven barrels of fermented cider and half a barrel of vinegar each year. Every fall John helped his grandfather and the hired hands slaughter one beef cow and three hogs to supply meat for the table throughout the winter. In the spring, when everyone suffered from languor (or had "a poor spell"), they ate sharp pickles, horseradish, mustard, and black pepper to "sharpen the appetite" and "tone up the system." The Loofboroughs also summoned the local physician to administer various tonics (strong drugs such as calomel) and to bleed bowlfuls of blood from their arms.[68]

Such a diet heavy in fats and carbohydrates naturally took its toll on their health. John's grandmother often lay prostrate for weeks until the doctor could "build up her strength" with tonics. The boy himself suffered from half a dozen painful boils and a persistent cough. For the former, the physician recommended "poor man's plasters," and for the latter, he suggested John try smoking cigars to soothe his lungs.[69]

A VISIT TO ROCHESTER, NEW YORK

One of the highlights of John's childhood was a train trip with his grandfather to Rochester, 18 miles north near Lake Ontario. During the 1820s, Rochester, "America's first inland boomtown," was the fastest growing community in the United States. In 1823 the Erie Canal had come through; in 1830 residents killed the last wolf in town; and two years after John's birth, Rochester was incorporated as a city. By 1840 both the Tonawanda and the Rochester and Auburn railroads threaded their way through the city, making it possible two years later for the Loofboroughs to travel from Victor to downtown Rochester in about two hours (at seven miles per hour).[70] Between 1830 and 1840 the village became a city of more than 20,000 people—nearly 100 times the population in the village of Victor. Nearly 75 percent were under 30 years of age. For John, it was like visiting another planet. He stared in awe at the packet boats plying the 17-foot-wide Erie Canal, the 20-foot-long railway cars leaving the station every hour, and the colorful red stagecoaches rumbling through town twice a day. Sharing his grandfather's interest in mechanics, they visited several of Rochester's 137 factories, including 24 flour mills that produced half a million barrels of flour every year. John saw why the city was nicknamed "The Flour City of America."[71]

Textile manufacturing was another of Rochester's leading industries. In fact, it ranked first in the number of employees, wages paid, and profits. At 30 shops, tailors measured and cut the cloth, then sent it out to 1,000 seamstresses for them to sew it into garments. Given the scarcity of inns and hotels along the city's dirt streets, many of those single females took in boarders to make extra money on the side. One seamstress who did so—Mary J. Walker—in 1851 would marry the young visitor from Victor, and together they would set up house in the city.[72]

Given the building boom along the Erie Canal and New York's expanding railroads, yet a third thriving industry was the manufacture of window sash locks. In 1827 the first water-powered sash factory was built in Rochester. Another followed in the 1830s. But when Nathan and his grandson visited in 1842, the most popular brand in town was Arnold's Patent Sash Locks. A decade later John and Mary would live one block from the factory, and John would become one of a growing team of successful salespeople for their varied products.[73]

At the time Nathan and John came to Rochester, the city was beginning to attract a colorful variety of reformers. In fact, it had become a microcosm of upstate New York's "burned-over district" as ultraist reform groups gravitated to the city like moths to a lantern. Thurlow Weed, one of the founders of the Whig Party in 1834, edited the *Anti-Masonic Enquirer* in Rochester, a newspaper whose attacks on Masons and Catholics and immigrants fomented nativist riots across America as Protestant mobs attacked Irish, Italian, and German Catholics.[74] Rochester also boasted five of the six Fourierist colonies in New York State in which followers of the French utopian socialist Charles Fourier lived in communities called phalanxes and shared all work equally irrespective of gender.[75]

By 1839 Rochester had also become a stronghold of William Ladd's American Peace Society and the American Anti-Slavery Party. The abolitionist Frederick Douglass started his newspaper, *The North Star*, here in 1847 and made the city a hub on the Underground Railroad, funneling Black fugitives to Canada. In addition, citizens formed the Society for the Promotion of Temperance and other groups to enforce Sunday observance, encourage Bible study, promote moral reform, and advance women's rights. The fiery orator Susan B. Anthony often lectured on women's suffrage to enthusiastic crowds in the city. Here also the teenagers Margaret and Kate Fox of nearby Hydesville wowed audiences with their demonstrations of "spirit rapping" in Corinthian Hall.[76] During the 1840s, and indeed throughout their lives, John Loofborough and Mary Walker would be profoundly changed by their exposure to many of the reforms they encountered in Rochester between 1840 and 1852.

TROUBLED BY RELIGIOUS QUANDARIES

Shortly after John's tour of Rochester, an elderly man visited their schoolroom. During the course of his presentation, he asked the pupils, "What is the beginning of all wisdom?" Some students thought it was the ABC's while others suggested nature. "No," he replied, "the fear of the Lord is the beginning of wisdom."[77]

Sometimes, however, the fear of God conflicted with human opinions, forcing John to make choices that he was not entirely comfortable with. In Sunday school, for example, the superintendent urged the class to learn the Ten Commandments during the coming week and recite them together the following Sunday. John, who had memorized them that afternoon, found himself puzzled by the statement in Exodus 20:8-11 that the Sabbath was Saturday, the *seventh* day. He had always considered Sunday the seventh day, because everyone he knew referred to it as the Sabbath. But when his day school teacher had them recite the days of the week, he noticed that she called Sunday the first day—and she threatened him with the birch rod for saying otherwise! Confused, he went to his aunt Susan, who told him that Christ had changed the day of worship from Saturday to Sunday in the New Testament. Ten years later in 1852 when John encountered Sabbatarian Adventists in Rochester, he asked a cousin to inquire whether his aunt had scriptural proof for any transfer of worship from one day to another. Instead, she said, "You tell John I would rather he kept the seventh day of the week than not to keep any day."[78]

When the Millerite movement swept the "burned-over district" in 1843-1844, 11-year-old John Loofborough—troubled about the Sabbath, fearing death and hell, and anxious concerning the day of judgment—would finally get the answers he sought. But they would change his life forever.

---

[1] Milton R. Lufborrow, "A History of the Loofbourrow, Loughborough and Lufburrow Families" (Tampa, Fla.: typewritten manuscript, 1952), p. 5.

[2] *Ibid.*, pp. 2, 5.

[3] *AUG*, Aug. 21, 1929, p. 6; JNL, in *PUR*, June 4, 1908, p. 1.

[4] Claude Manceron, *The Wind From America, 1778-1781*, in *Age of the French Revolution* (New York: Simon and Schuster, 1978), vol. 2, p. 5; Lufborrow, "Families," p. 1.

[5] Diary, June 21 and 28, 1914. Elder Loughborough reported that his comedic act sometimes "caused a revolution" or "brought down the house" at such gatherings.

[6] Lufborrow, pp. 1, 2.

[7] *Ibid.*, p. 2.

[8] DAR Patriot Index, Centennial Edition, Part 2, p. 1853. These men included John's great-uncles David, John, and Elias Loofbourrow of Hunterdon County, Amboy, and Middlesex County, New Jersey.

[9] Daniel M. Weinstock to Mrs. Fagan, May 9, 1982 (handwritten letter on file with Babette Huber, town historian, Victor, N.Y.); "Eighteenth-Century Loofbourrows" (typewritten manuscript on file with Babette Huber, town historian, Victor, N.Y.); JNL, in *PUR*, June 4, 1908, p. 1; Nathan Loofborough's military record can be found on www.ancestry.com (accessed Aug. 25, 2009).

[10] *PUR*, May 21, 1908, pp. 1, 2; Ella Robinson, *Lighter of Gospel Fires, John N. Loughborough* (Mountain View, Calif.: Pacific Press Pub. Assn., 1954), pp. 20, 21; *RH*, Jan. 1, 1884, p. 12.

[11] Leona G. Hawkins to Juan Carlos Atencio, c. September 2008 (letter in possession of the author); www.ancestry.com (accessed July 12, 2009); Lufborrow, p. 55; JNL, in

PUR, June 4, 1908, p. 1.

[12] Rose Marie Fagan, Ann Guiffre, and Mary Joan Snyder, *A History of Victor, New York* (Victor, N.Y.: The History Committee of the Victor Bicentennial Commission, 1976), pp. 7, 9; George S. Conover, ed., *History of Ontario County, New York, With Illustrations and Family Sketches of Some of the Prominent Men and Families* (Syracuse, N.Y.: D. Mason, 1893), p. 365.

[13] Milton R. Lufborrow, "Loughborough Family History" (handwritten manuscript, March 1953, in the author's possession); Hawkins to Atencio (c. September 2008).

[14] Conover, ed., *History of Ontario County, New York, With Illustrations and Family Sketches*, pp. 121, 365, 366; J. Sheldon Fisher and Lewis Fisher, *A Victor Album* (Pittsford, N.Y.: Wolfe Publications, 1981), p. 8.

[15] W. H. McIntosh, *History of Ontario County, New York, With Illustrations Descriptive of Its Scenery, Palatial Residences, Public Building, Fine Blocks, and Important Manufacturies* (Philadelphia: Everts, Ensign, and Everts, 1876), p. 198.

[16] Conover, ed., p. 128; see the Nortons in the U. S. Census Reports for 1790, 1800, 1810, 1820, and 1830 in New York; Orsamus Turner, *History of the Pioneer Settlement of Phelps and Gorham's Purchase, and Morris Reserve* (Rochester, N.Y.: William Alling, 1851), pp. 169, 184-189, 399, 525, 530.

[17] John Ray and Samuel Kempton, *Northfield on the Genesee . . . Early Times in Monroe County, N.Y.* (Rochester, N.Y.: County of Monroe, 1981), p. 241; typewritten manuscript on file with Babette Huber, township historian, Victor, New York; Loofborough family land purchases (1811-1862), found in the Ontario County Deeds Records, pp. 1404, 1408, 1420. Although the number of acres bought or sold are never listed in land purchases, the lot numbers sometimes appear in the record and the prices paid are always given. From 1811 to 1862 the Loofborough family bought and sold $6,994.28 worth of land, a figure probably exceeding the purchasing power of $250,000 today.

[18] Marlene O'Keefe, "History of Victor [New York]" (loose-leaf notebook, 1976), pp. 173, 354.

[19] Charles F. Milliken, *A History of Ontario County, New York, and Its People* (New York: Lewis Historical Publishing Company, 1911), p. 491; Williams/Schreibner File 3333, Ontario County Historical Society and Museum, Canandaigua, New York.

[20] McIntosh, pp. 60, 203; O'Keefe, pp. 93-95; and Fisher and Fisher, pp. 14, 100.

[21] Loughboroughs in Victor (N.Y.) Cemeteries, www.usgennet.org/usa/ny/county/ontario/cems/victorvillage.html (accessed July 25, 2009).

[22] McIntosh, p. 207. The Federal Census of 1810, p. 7, shows a Nathan Loffborough with three employees, but the Federal Census of 1820, p. 370, indicates that he had four workers engaged in manufacturing.

[23] Jury lists, 1811-1816, Ontario County Records and Archives Center, Canandaigua, New York.

[24] Court of Oyer and Terminer (1793-1866), Court of Sessions (1816-1870), Court of Common Pleas (1794-1838), and Ontario County Supreme Court (1821-1852) records found at the Ontario County Records and Archives Center, Canandaigua, New York. Nathan Loofborough was the plaintiff in three civil cases before the Court of Common Pleas in 1815, 1816, and 1817.

[25] McIntosh, p. 113.

[26] This book, containing both the signatures of Nathan Loofborough and John Loughborough, can be found at the Ontario County Historical Society and Museum in Canandaigua, New York.

[27] McIntosh, p. 203; Lewis F. Fisher, *Victor: The History of a Town* (San Antonio, Tex.: Maverick Publishing Company, 1996), pp. 28, 29.

[28] Fagan et al., p. 70; L. F. Fisher, *Victor*, pp. 32, 33, 82; and Douglas Brinkly, "A Boy From Tampico," *American Heritage* (Winter 2011), p. 55.

[29] Fagan, et al., p. 70. Both the U. S. Census of 1850 for Ontario County and the New York Census of 1855 for Ontario County show a sharp increase in Irish and German names. The gravestones in St. Patrick's Cemetery (established 1856) on High Street northwest of the village of Victor are filled with Irish names even today.

[30] Fagan et al., pp. 23, 39, 40; L. F. Fisher, *Victor*, pp. 22-26. The railroad pump station adjacent to the post office is today the oldest cobblestone building in New York. The Auburn to Syracuse (1837), Auburn and Rochester (1838), and New York Central (1851) railroads all passed through Victor in those days, and J. N. Loughborough rode them all.

[31] Harry C. Buell, "Historical Gleanings: Origin and Naming of the Village Streets" (typed manuscript, 1907), p. 4; L. F. Fisher, *Victor*, pp. 24, 25.

[32] See land purchases by grantee Nathan B. Loofborough in the Ontario County Deeds Records (1789-1845). In 2011 purchasing power, $684 would probably exceed $16,000.

[33] Assessment roll for Victor (1829); jury lists for Victor (October 1838).

[34] See children of Nathan Benson and Minerva Norton Loughborough on www.ancestry.com (accessed July 12, 2009).

[35] JNL, "Apostolic and Adventist Experience Compared" (typewritten manuscript, Aug. 10, 1919 [internal evidence suggests an earlier version c. 1892]), p. 47. Nathan B. Loofborough's name appears on a land deed—Liber 62/470—for March 4, 1834, indicating that the trustees of the Methodist church in Victor had recently purchased "several parcels" of land totaling approximately 12 square rods, or 3,267 square feet, along Victor's main street for the use of the Methodists (Bonnie Waters, e-mails to Brian Strayer, February 12 and March 24, 2011).

[36] *PUR*, Oct. 17, 1907, p. 1; Robinson, pp. 1, 2, 48, 49. Fourteen years later in 1848, Mr. Boughton reminded 16-year-old John of his father's dream for him and gave him $3 to encourage him to preach.

[37] Robinson, pp. 3, 12. Unfortunately, Loughborough's explanation does not make good medical sense today.

[38] *PUR*, Oct. 31, 1907, p. 1; Robinson, p. 3; DF 230, CAR, Andrews University.

[39] *PUR*, Oct. 31, 1907, p. 1; *PUR*, Dec. 12, 1907, pp. 1, 2.

[40] *Ibid.*

[41] DF 230; *PUR*, Nov. 28, 1907, p. 1; Robinson, p. 6.

[42] *PUR*, Nov. 7, 1907, p. 1; Robinson, p. 3. Near the end of his life, Loughborough would also devote many articles to the subject of proper child rearing. As an example, see *PUR*, Nov. 14, 1907, p. 1; *PUR*, Nov. 21, 1907, p. 1.

[43] Fagan et al., p. 97; *YI*, June 1863, p. 43; *PUR*, Jan. 9, 1907, p. 1.

[44] *PUR*, Jan. 9, 1907, p. 1.

[45] *Ibid.*

[46] *PUR*, Nov. 28, 1907, p.1; *PUR*, Dec. 19, 1907, p. 1.

[47] Fagan et al., p. 58; L. F. Fisher, *Victor*, p. 82. Surprisingly, eight of those 11 schools—two of them cobblestone buildings in excellent shape—survive today, 180 years later. Seven are currently private dwellings.

[48] DF 230.

[49] *PHJ*, July 1889, p. 195.

[50] Minutes for April 10, 1838, in Methodist Episcopal Society at East Bloomfield and Victor, New York, Miscellaneous Records-D (1829-1839), Ontario County Records and Archives Center, Canandaigua, New York.

[51] Surrogate Records, File 87, Reel 30-17, Book G, p. 50; Book 22, pp. 45-50; Book

23, p. 64; Book 25, p. 61.

[52] Robinson, pp. 10, 11.

[53] Fagan et al., p. 80.

[54] *PHJ*, February and March 1887, p. 133; *PHJ*, November 1890, p. 321; Robinson, pp. 10, 11.

[55] *YI*, October 1863, p. 80.

[56] *PHJ*, November 1890, p. 321.

[57] *YI*, October 1863, p. 80; Robinson, p. 11. Nathan Benson Loofborough's tombstone in the Village of Victor Cemetery gives his age as 37 years 3 months 3 days. Unfortunately, the severely aged and weather-beaten stone makes it impossible to read the message chiseled below. However, as one enters the cemetery, one can see engraved on a granite marker the following words (from John 5:28, 29) with which he would wholeheartedly agree: "Jesus said that the hour is coming in the which all that are in the graves shall hear His voice and shall come forth; they that have done good unto the resurrection of life and they that have done evil unto the resurrection of judgment. O Earth, Earth, Earth, hear the word of the Lord."

[58] "Settlement of Estate" for Nathan B. Loofborough, Surrogate Court Records for Ontario County, Sept. 21, 1839, vol. G, p. 53, and Feb. 16, 1841, vol. 22, p. 45; *BTS*, May 1918, p. 11.

[59] *YI*, June 1862, p. 45; *PUR*, Mar. 26. 1908, pp. 1, 2; JNL, *The Great Second Advent Movement*, pp. 555, 556.

[60] *YI*, December 1863, p. 90; *PUR*, Mar. 5, 1908, p. 1; PUR, Mar. 12, 1908, pp. 1, 2; Robinson, p. 22.

[61] *RH*, Jan. 1, 1884, p. 12; *PUR*, May 7, 1908, pp. 1, 2; *PUR*, May 14, 1908, pp. 1, 2; Minerva Loofborough family and Nathan Loofborough family members, U.S. Census (1840). During the 1840s Victor's three religious congregations—Presbyterians, Methodists, and Universalists—often quarreled over issues of unconditional election, free grace, and universal salvation, demonstrating that, if they did not all agree, they at least took their religion seriously.

[62] *YI*, Jan. 7, 1913, p. 12; *PUR*, Feb. 6, 1908, p. 1; *PUR*, Apr. 2, 1908, pp. 1, 2.

[63] *Central Union Outlook*, July 22, 1919, p. 2; *ST-A*, Apr. 13, 1908, p. 237; Robinson, pp. 17, 18.

[64] *YI*, Apr. 22, 1913, p. 6.

[65] *ST*, Aug. 8, 1878, p. 237.

[66] Robinson, p. 7; DF 230.

[67] *PUR*, Mar. 19, 1908, p. 2; DF 230.

[68] *Gospel of Health*, October 1899, p. 175; *PUR*, Apr. 9, 1908, p. 1; *Life and Health*, March 1915, p. 109; Robinson, p. 11.

[69] *PUR*, Apr. 9, 1908, p. 1; Robinson, p. 11.

[70] Edward R. Foreman, comp. and ed., *Centennial History of Rochester, New York* (Rochester, N.Y.: Rochester Public Library, 1931), p. 272; Robinson, p. 20; Paul E. Johnson, *A Shopkeeper's Millennium: Society and Revivals in Rochester, New York, 1815-1837* (New York: Hill and Wang, 1978), pp. 16-18, 37, 40. In the 1830s, while Albany's population grew at a rate of 96 percent, Utica at 183 percent, Syracuse at 282 percent, and Buffalo at 314 percent, Rochester's population skyrocketed by 512 percent. See Whitney Cross, *Burned-over District* (New York: Harper Torchbooks, 1950), p. 56.

[71] Jenny Marsh Parker, *Rochester—A Story Historical* (Rochester, N.Y.: Scrantom, Wetmore, and Co., 1884), pp. 193-197, 391; Blake McKelvey, *Rochester on the Genesee: The Growth of a City* (Syracuse, N.Y.: Syracuse University Press, 1973), p. 14; *idem*, "Rochester in Retrospect and Prospect," *Rochester History* 23, no. 3 (July 1961): 7.

[72] McKelvey, *Rochester on the Genesee,* pp. 23, 48; Ruth Rosenberg-Naparsteck, "Two Centuries of Industry and Trade in Rochester," *Rochester History* 51, no. 4 (Fall 1989): 17-19.

[73] Rosenberg-Naparsteck, p. 6; McKelvey, p. 7.

[74] Jerome Clark, *1844* (Nashville: Southern Pub. Assn., 1968), vol. 1, pp. 103, 203, 204, 217; Cross, *Burned-over District*, pp. 71-73, 116, 233; Johnson, *Rochester*, pp. 20, 62, 63, 128.

[75] Cross, *Burned-over District*, p. 331.

[76] McKelvey, *Rochester on the Genesee,* p. 59; Parker, pp. 254, 257, 261, 267-269, 346; Jerome Clark, *1844,* vol. 2, pp. 88, 107; Johnson, *Rochester*, pp. 79, 81, 84; Jon Butler, *Awash in a Sea of Faith: Christianizing the American People* (Cambridge, Mass.: Harvard University Press, 1990), pp. 252-256, 282; Alice Felt Tyler, *Freedom's Ferment* (New York: Harper and Row, 1944), p. 82.

[77] JNL, "Some Individual Experience" (Takoma Park, Md.: Review and Herald Pub. Assn., 1919), p. 22.

[78] *BTS*, May 1918, p. 11.

CHAPTER II

FROM MILLERITE TO BOY PREACHER (1842-1852)

"Oh, how I prayed to the Lord that I might be ready [in 1844]!" [1]

During John's childhood three groups dominated Victor's religious landscape: Methodists, Presbyterians, and Universalists. Occasionally their members quarreled about free grace, unconditional election, and universal salvation, thereby demonstrating that, if they did not all agree on the path to salvation, they at least took their religious beliefs seriously. After 1842, however, they confronted another religious movement sweeping across the burned-over district of upstate New York. As Millerite agents came to Rochester and Victor preaching their end-of-the-world message, members of these three churches circled the wagons to meet the perceived threat to orthodoxy and church unity.

MILLERISM IN VICTOR

In 1842 the evangelical preaching of the Reverend Zina Buck sparked a revival in Victor. Seeking ways to cement this spiritual reform in the hearts of his parishioners, Buck invited a Millerite lecturer named Adams from Lowell, Massachusetts, to deliver a course of lectures on Adventism. Contrary to Buck's anticipation, however, the meetings brought schism to Victor's congregations. Years later, one writer described the "wild, universal excitement" and "disorders" engendered by Millerite preaching as "injurious to the church" and "a warning for all coming time."[2]

Apparently some trustees of the local Methodist-Episcopal church disagreed, for in 1843 they invited Millerite evangelist James Barry to hold a series of meetings in town. For two months Barry preached on the first angel's message of Revelation 14:6, the great image of Daniel 2, and the prophetic beasts of Daniel 8. He also taught attendees a new chorus: "I Am Bound for the Land of Canaan." During the course of his meetings, a stunning display of the aurora borealis lit up the skies over Victor. Many saw it as a fulfillment of Joel 2, wherein the Old Testament prophet had predicted flaming "fire" in the heavens just before the coming of the "great and terrible day of the Lord."[3]

As good churchgoing Methodists, the entire Loofborough family traveled by sleigh to attend the winter meetings night after night, listening spellbound as Barry explained how the 2300-day prophecy of Daniel 8:14 would culminate in Christ's second coming sometime before the spring of 1844. Three years earlier, the Loofboroughs had been stunned at the fulfillment of Millerite lecturer Josiah Litch's prediction that the Ottoman Empire would fall in August of 1840, according to Bible prophecy (the sixth trumpet of Revelation 9). Therefore, they studied the "new light" diligently.[4]

Barry's meetings in December 1843 left an indelible impression on 11-year-old John, who, to the end of his life, could vividly recall the preacher's sermon: "The Hour of His Judgment Is Come." Little John, perched atop a friend's shoulders in the back bench, listened intently to the service, fascinated by the mathematical precision of prophecy demonstrated on Charles Fitch's 1842 chart. Responding to the call for sinners to confess and repent of their sins, he pressed his way to the front of the church, pleading for special prayer. "So you've decided to be a good boy," one elderly member remarked; "I'm glad of it." An older playmate invited John to join a young people's prayer group meeting daily in the nearby woods. A Methodist steward whose 12-year-old daughter had been converted during the meetings loaned John some religious books and tracts to nourish his growing spiritual experience. John also began reading copies of the Millerite newspapers the *Signs of the Times*, *Midnight Cry*, and *Voice of Truth*. Eager to spread the Advent message, John volunteered to peddle the papers to the neighbors and invite them to the meetings.[5]

His involvement in the controversial movement did not go unnoticed, however. Objecting to his spreading such "heretical" literature throughout Victor, the son of the local Presbyterian pastor threatened John's life. A bully at school boasted that he would "kill instantly" any boy who publicly stated that Christ would return in 1843. Standing up before his classmates, John replied, "Well, begin here, for I believe it." Instantly several friends surrounded him, providing protective cover until the bully's anger cooled. One woman who claimed to receive the "blessing of perfect love" (sanctification) at the meetings, later repudiated her experience. When John spoke in favor of the Millerite message, she angrily hit him on the head with her fist. John's sister Minerva Jane wondered out loud if "the blessing of perfect love" had made her angry. "I guess that was the blessing of perfect hatred," John replied. Local opponents also spread rumors against the Millerites, accusing them of donning white "ascension robes" and gathering on "Piety Hill" on October 22, 1844, to await the Lord's return. Employing racist humor, the *Christian Advocate* ridiculed those "come outers" who believed in "Massa Miller's day of judgment." John's 17-year-old brother William (along with 20 friends) endured a "Bible trial" in 1844 for believing in Miller's "follies." When the pastor lost this case, he demanded a second trial following Methodist-Episcopal rules. Rather than allow his grandfather's church to expel him, William asked to have his name removed from the church books.[6] It required great courage to profess one's convictions in Christ's imminent return.

Yet many did so, and the impact on the community was profound. Allegedly, about 500 citizens in Victor Township accepted Millerism in 1843 and 1844. Barry's converts included Nathan and Sarah Loofborough and their entire family, including their grandsons William and John, and at least one of John's Presbyterian uncles. Victor's saloon closed its doors; local infidels (atheists) converted in droves; and Ki Lippit, a drunken Irish ruffian who frequently galloped his pony through the streets shouting obscenities, now testified of God's saving grace. Nevertheless, in the face of rising opposition, Nathan Loofborough made what must have been a painful decision: he withdrew from the Methodist church he himself had founded and built. Sometime during 1843 he constructed a simple wooden meetinghouse on the northeast corner of Main and Church streets—directly across the street from the Methodist church—where local Millerites held their services.[7]

REVIVALS IN ROCHESTER

When Barry began a new series of meetings in Rochester in December of 1843, the Millerite seeds he planted grew rapidly in the rich soil previously plowed by religious reformers of the burned-over district. After the nationally famous evangelist Charles G. Finney had preached perfectionism, millennialism, and free will in the city in 1830-1831, church membership doubled, and Rochester became "the most thoroughly evangelized of American cities," the "spiritual capital of western New York's burned-over district." Finney's revival shook the very foundations of Rochester society. Bible study, prayer, and filling out temperance pledges supplanted drinking and theater and circus attendance.[8] Shortly thereafter, Joseph Smith, Jr., a young dreamer and treasure hunter who worked in a blacksmith's shop in Rochester for a while, wrote the *Book of Mormon* following instructions allegedly given him by the angel Moroni. Soon his sect, the Latter-day Saints (or Mormons), would clash with American Protestant denominations across New York and the Midwest, leading to religious and armed conflicts.[9]

Another reason why Barry's preaching led to revivals in Rochester is because William Miller, Charles Fitch, Josiah Litch, and Joshua V. Himes (among other Millerite lecturers) had already evangelized the city in 1843. Himes' monthlong series of meetings in June drew 3,000 citizens into his tent. Even more crowded the edges of the tent when Fitch and Miller joined him in preaching later that fall. Their heart-stirring messages planted the seed that Barry harvested weeks later when more than 1,000 of Rochester's citizens converted to Adventism. Himes began editing *The Voice of Truth and Glad Tidings* in the city to nurture the new converts and further propagate the first angel's message.[10]

In the winter of 1843-1844 Nathan took his grandson by train to the big city to hear the message of Christ's soon return. There, before a capacity crowd with standing room only in the back, Barry expounded the scriptures regarding the 1260- and 2300-day/year prophecies in Daniel 8 and 9 while the people listened with "almost breathless silence" for hours. "A solemn awe pervaded the place," John recalled years later. The preaching and the prayers brought tears to many eyes, but what impressed the boy even more was the singing. Half a century later John could still recite the words of several Millerite hymns from memory. One described heaven as the "land of Canaan":

"O, Canaan, bright Canaan,
I am bound for the land of Canaan.
O, Canaan, it is my happy home;
I am bound for the land of Canaan."[11]

Another portrayed the faithful band who would soon sing Zion's songs:

"See Gideon marching out to fight
(O, I love God! glory! Hallelujah!)
He had no weapons but his light
(O, I love God! glory! Hallelujah!)
Hallelujah, hallelujah!
Who will be in this band? Hallelujah!
"King David on his throne of state
Did belong to this band. Hallelujah!
And Lazarus at the rich man's gate
Was numbered in this band. Hallelujah!
Hallelujah, hallelujah!
I will join this band. Hallelujah!
"Sweet music in heaven is beginning to ring
(O, I love God! glory! Hallelujah!)
If you touch one string,
The whole will ring,
(O, I love God! glory! Hallelujah!)
Hallelujah, hallelujah!
I belong to this band. Hallelujah!"[12]

Once again, at the close of the meeting, 12-year-old John, with tears streaming down his face, pressed to the front to sit on the "anxious seat" and ask for prayer.[13]

But conviction did not bring conversion. Although John firmly believed the Millerite doctrines and resolved to "be a good boy," he felt no assurance of salvation. "I longed for someone to tell me *how* to seek the Lord," he recalled decades later. "How much earlier in life might I have found peace with God, had there then been such encouragement given and efforts made to reach the youth as are now made."[14] But if the boy found little support from his earthly companions, he received Divine reassurance. Several nights later he had the first of many dreams he would record throughout his life. In the dream he met an angelic being who, bowing and smiling, beckoned him to follow him. Seeing this as a token of God's love, John sang at work for a week thereafter.[15]

His cheerful spirit, however, faced a severe test on October 22, 1844, when Christ did not return to earth in fulfillment of the "Midnight Cry" preached by Joshua V. Himes, Samuel S. Snow, Joseph Bates, and scores of other Millerite agents. The passing of that fateful day (known among believers as "the Great Disappointment") fulfilled for many the words of Revelation 10:9, 10 that their experience would be "sweet" in the mouth but "bitter" in the stomach.[16] Subsequently, the majority of Adventists in Victor returned to their original churches—including Nathan Loofborough, who served once again as a trustee on the Methodist-Episcopal church board. When they died, both Nathan and Sarah would be buried in the cemetery behind the church.[17]

Evidence suggests, however, that some of Nathan's children and grandchildren—including William and John—continued worshipping across the street in the Millerite meeting house after the fall of 1844. Years later, John remembered that during worship services there, the son of the local Methodist-Episcopal pastor would sneak around under their windows howling: "O-o-oh! This awful hole! Oh, I wish I had never been a Millerite! O-o-oh! Help me out of this hole!"[18]

The First-day Adventists (or Advent Christians as they would later be known) experienced persecution in many forms, ranging from scolding and verbal ridicule to physical violence. John himself was sharply scolded by a nonbelieving minister whose horse he curried. Another time some men scoffed and swore at him as he helped make maple syrup.[19] In the periodical *The Midnight Cry* he read of mob violence against Adventists in some cities.[20] Former friends mocked him as he passed. Some shouted, "I thought you had gone up! When are you going up now, John?" Others pointed at him and taunted, "There, there he goes, a regular every day go upper!"[21] Seeking to bury their disappointed hopes in pleasure, a few former believers now staged bazaars, parties, oyster feeds, festivals, and other Sunday entertainments.[22]

ADVENT CHRISTIANS IN ROCHESTER

In 1843 and 1844 Rochester, New York, became one of several hubs of Millerite Adventism (others included Boston, Philadelphia, Cincinnati, and Cleveland). Following in the wake of the anti-Masonic craze that gripped the "Flour City" in the 1830s, the arrival of Advent lecturers such as William Miller, Josiah Litch, Charles Fitch, and Joshua V. Himes in the 1840s created "not a little excitement" in Rochester's staid old church circles. While Baptists furnished the largest number of converts, all religious groups, to some degree or other, felt the impact of the Millerites' premillennial message. Fervent preaching, emotional singing, and religious publications stirred deep interest among the city's 25,000 citizens, one quarter of whom were Irish, Scottish, or English.[23]

In the late fall of 1844 Rochester became the headquarters for one of the groups that survived the Great Disappointment. Known at different times as "The Congregation of Advent Believers," "Advent Christians," "Advent Harbingers," and the "Premillennial Advent Church," the tiny group would incorporate in 1867 as the Second Advent Church of Rochester. In 1870 they would merge with the Christadelphian Ecclesia whose 60 local members preached primitive Christianity, opposed war, and anticipated the establishment of a future millennial kingdom in Palestine. During the 1840s their spiritual leader was Joseph Marsh, who edited *The Voice of Truth*, a religious paper published at 17 Arcade Street in Rochester.[24]

According to John Loofborough (who joined the group in 1849), their church polity represented a kind of "Christian anarchism." They opposed church organization, did not elect or ordain church officers, kept no membership records, and had no systematic method of raising funds. Consequently, their lay ministers did manual labor to support themselves. Furthermore, believing that on October 22, 1844, a door in the heavenly sanctuary had been closed, they interpreted it as signifying that after that date there was "no more mercy for sinners." Consequently, they saw no need to proselytize except among those Christians who, like themselves, had previously accepted the first and second angels' messages of Revelation 14 and had survived the Great Disappointment with faith intact. The names of "true Christians," they maintained, were registered in the "Lamb's book of life" kept by Jesus in heaven.[25]

JOHN LOOFBOROUGH'S CONVERSION

Despite his firm belief in the Advent message, John had no assurance that his name was registered in heaven's books in the fall of 1844. Facing ridicule and rejection from his peers, he returned to school that winter determined to drown his disappointment in study and work. Perhaps to disprove the accusations that he had been a fool for believing in "Miller's folly," the 12-year-old boy immersed himself in his studies. With mechanical abilities inherited through four generations, he amazed his teachers and friends by creating a host of useful implements. From beech wood he crafted a violin so exquisite that a local physician immediately offered him money for it. Poring over his copy of Comstock's *Natural Philosophy* (a science textbook), he resolved to make every machine pictured in its pages. In short order, he created an electrical machine with a glass cylinder; a Leyden jar with thunder tongs, insulating stools, and jacks; and a galvanic battery from copper and zinc with rasp electric coils. To satisfy his curiosity, he attended public lectures on electricity and telegraphy to understand how the telegraph operators forced the dots and dashes down the wires and past the wooden poles. His schoolmates, who paid him for the privilege of receiving electric shocks from his machines, dubbed him "The philosopher." Their parents filled the schoolroom to watch John demonstrate his amazing contraptions.[26]

After eight years of living with his grandparents, John decided the time had come for him to spread his wings. Moreover, prior to Horace Mann's public school reforms, his education did not come free. He wondered how he would be able to pay for his books, tuition, and school supplies. Since he loved working with his hands, John, then 15, decided to join his older brother William (20) in opening a blacksmith and carriage shop in Victor. In the spring of 1847 he moved in with William, who had recently purchased some property on Cherry Street between Hog Hollow Creek and Fish Creek in East Bloomfield.[27] For the next seven months the slender boy labored at the forge and anvil, hammering nails, shoeing horses, and making wheels for wagons. But the hot, dirty smithy proved too much for a lad barely five feet tall and weighing no more than 100 pounds. Decades later, reminiscing about those days, he confessed, "I have scars on my hands that were wounds [from the blacksmith shop] thirty years ago."[28] Arduous though it was, his practical experience in working with wood and metal would serve him well throughout his life, enabling him to build bookcases, tables, chicken coops, and even houses well into his 70s.

Despite the brothers' best efforts, however, their blacksmith enterprise apparently failed to reap the revenue they had anticipated. In September, when William married the 20-year-old Eliza Norton, daughter of Alfred Norton, a prosperous Bloomfield farmer and close family friend, the couple moved 30 miles away to Adam's Basin, where William worked for another carriage maker. So for the first time in nearly a decade, John returned home to live with his widowed mother and her three children: Minerva Jane (18), Eber (10), and Sarah Diantha (7). Instead of sweating at the smithy, he swept classrooms, built fires, and rang bells to pay for his education. Grateful for the opportunity to attend an "uncommonly good" district school, he resolved to "study night and day" to gain all the wisdom he could.[29] He even joined the advanced students in forming a literary society. Every two weeks its members read their compositions in public. Soon they elected John secretary and then president of the society, and he became the editor of their newsletter. His early experience of giving speeches in public removed his "natural timidity," he later confessed. Although he did not know it at the time, public speaking and writing also prepared him for his later career as a minister of the gospel.[30]

However, in 1847-1848, the 16-year-old boy confessed, "I had but little thought of religion." Disappointed at the indifference toward spiritual matters exemplified by Victor's Methodist pastor, John stopped going to church with his mother and siblings for months at a time. Instead, he and William regularly attended Advent Christian services in the area. On one occasion, a sermon on the second coming of Christ "touched my heart anew." Noticing this, the preacher spoke with John about his eternal salvation, extracting from him a solemn promise to "serve the Lord." Seeing himself as a great sinner, John longed for true conversion. He decided to leave Victor and move to Rochester to work in his brother's new blacksmith shop so that he could attend some religious meetings. "I turned away from teachers, scholars, friends, and even my own mother," he recalled years later. Yet because he "had not made much progress in finding the peace of mind I desired, . . . I was still longing for truth, light, and pardon."[31] To a degree he could never have imagined, during the next four years John would find all three—and much more—in Rochester.

BEGINNING A NEW LIFE IN ROCHESTER

When these meetings, sponsored by the Advent Christians, commenced in the spring of 1848, John and William attended every night. "I hungered for the truths contained in the Word of God," he declared. Having neglected Bible study for months, he now bought a pocket Bible, carried it with him everywhere, and in spare moments at the blacksmith's shop devoured its contents. To spare himself the embarrassment of his fellow workers' teasing, he retreated to the coal shed out back, where he knelt in prayer, pleading for forgiveness of his sins and for grace to be ready for heaven. His daily study of the scriptural evidence for Christ's second advent often gave him vivid dreams depicting that event. "I thought it was [a matter of] life or death with me," he said. He also longed to be baptized, but knew in his heart that he was not yet a converted Christian. His brother William, who empathized with his spiritual struggles, encouraged him to attend some meetings with him in Brockport. There on June 1 John took his stand to serve God. Following a powerful conviction that "to be *free* I must be baptized," he was immersed by Elder Phinehas Smith at Clarkson on July 4. "When I came out of the water I was as happy as I desired to be. It seemed that all nature praised the Lord. I was now free and could say, 'I *know* the Lord loves me.'" In fact, for two days thereafter, "my soul was [so] full of glory," he exclaimed, that he walked 10 miles to the meeting place and "sang and praised the Lord all the way." For the first time in his young life he also found the courage to pray in public. "I obtained a great blessing from the Lord in so doing," he added. He now began a lifelong habit of studying the Bible and Christian literature daily. But when he tried sharing his faith with his fellow workers and customers, many ridiculed or swore at him. Despite such rejection, John had a deep impression "that it was my duty to make known to others, in a public manner, the great truths I had learned concerning the coming and kingdom of our Lord."[32]

Unfortunately, John found more than the Spirit of God while working in his brother's blacksmith shop. Months of shoeing Erie Canal horses near a mosquito-infested pool infected him with malaria. His tiny frame, already weakened by the arduous labor, surrendered to the illness. Returning home once again, John's body shook with fever and chills for the next two months. Haunted by memories of his father's death nine years before and sensing that his illness could be a "chastening from the Lord," John made a bargain with God: cure me and I will become a preacher. Immediately, the chills ceased.[33]

Preaching, however, required physical strength, financial support, and open doors, but John had none of them. Rising from his sick bed, he tried chopping wood and digging potatoes to earn money, but the labor proved exhausting. A country boy typically dressed in rough linsey-woolsey shirts and pants, he lacked the proper attire for public ministry. Friendly neighbors gave him a vest and a pair of pants seven inches too long. William loaned him a double-breasted overcoat and handed him $5 worth of tracts to sell or give away. When Caleb Boughton, a family friend, heard of his desire to preach, he exclaimed, "Thank the Lord, Bro. John!" and handed him $3. Other friends, wishing to encourage him, also gave him money. But when a local minister heard that he intended to propagate Advent Christian teachings, he admonished, "*Oh!* Now! John, I would *get out* of that *moonshine*." John quietly replied that in his opinion, he had already left "the moonshine" behind and was now entering the light of gospel truth.[34]

Hoping not to "disgrace my friends who had so kindly helped me," he decided to hold his first meetings far from the censorious eyes of local opponents. He rode the train to Rochester and then walked 12 miles to Adam's Basin to spend the night with William and Eliza. The next morning, following his brother's pep talk and prayer, he walked 12 more miles to the tiny hamlet of Kendall's Corners and knocked at the door of the Thompson family. "I had never spent any time among strangers," he confessed, "and was exceedingly bashful." But he need not have worried. The Advent Christian family took him in and fed him, and to his relief, they did not ask about his preaching experience.[35]

On January 2, 1849—three weeks before his seventeenth birthday—John Loofborough preached his first sermon, on the fall of man and God's restitution, at a Baptist meetinghouse. The trustees had promised him it would be available for three evenings, and since he had only five sermons prepared, that suited John just fine. "I went into the meeting with much fearfulness, sang a hymn and prayed," and "had a good heavenly time talking to the people," he recalled years later. As word of mouth had spread the news that a "boy preacher" had arrived, the meetinghouse became packed. John had reason to be fearful, however, for in the audience sat *seven* pastors, one of whom decided to hold a singing class at the church two nights later, hoping thereby to terminate John's preaching. Unfazed, he moved his meetings to Rice's Schoolhouse nearby. Praying "not [to] wound my friends with my failure," he opened the meeting to a full house. Feeling more relaxed this time, "I began to take courage a little that I had not mistaken my duty."[36]

JOHN LOOFBOROUGH, THE "BOY PREACHER"

Half a century later in his book *Rise and Progress of the Seventh-day Adventists* (1892), J. N. Loughborough called his early days of preaching for the Advent Christians "a school of over three years' privations" that prepared his mind for receiving the third angel's message in 1852.[37] In a rare accolade to his former coreligionists, he praised the Advent Christians for teaching him to find scriptural evidence for every doctrine he preached. Between 1849 and 1851, John frequently heard J. B. Cook, Joseph Marsh, O.R.L. Crosier, and other leading ministers preach in the Rochester area. With his brother William he studied anew the biblical evidence for a heavenly sanctuary in Hebrews 9, the nature of the two-horned beast of Revelation 13, and all the New Testament texts relating to Christ's second coming. Following weeks of study, John developed 11 sermons covering biblical history from the Fall of humanity in the Garden of Eden to the Second Coming and restoration of the new Earth. Filling the roles of preacher, marketer, and booking agent, the teenager posted announcements for his lectures, secured lodgings for himself, arranged the benches or chairs in the meeting place, built the fires to warm the hall, and led the singing. Once, despite all his hard work, no one came to the meeting. Discouraged, he sat beside the road and wept. Another time, after winning debates with a Methodist pastor on the state of the dead and with a Universalist pastor on his view of hell, John faced a group of angry rowdies who pelted him with corn, shot, and hickory nuts during the service. Although he sustained no injuries, their projectiles hit the blackboard behind him "with considerable force," breaking listeners' concentration on his message. "By the Lord's grace," he wrote, "I took it all pleasantly." When his hosts, the Thompsons, offered to prosecute the delinquents, John asked them not to do so.[38]

Sensing his discouragement, Joseph Marsh's wife encouraged John to apprentice himself to an older, experienced minister. As a former blacksmith's apprentice, John recognized the wisdom in the suggestion. When he shared his troubles with Elder Phinehas Smith, the trusted counselor who had baptized him, Smith agreed to travel with him for three weeks. That winter they walked or rode horses to preach in colorful hamlets all around the Finger Lakes and along the Southern Tier region of New York and Pennsylvania. Encouraged, John began preaching alone once again. When he met opposition to his teachings, he would "study hard all day on their objections, and preach and battle them in the evening," then cry himself to sleep at night.[39]

At one house meeting he encountered a Baptist minister who had bragged to the host, "Get that boy to come in here, and I will use him up in about two minutes." The pastor disagreed with John's view concerning human mortality, asserting that one could clearly prove the immortality of the soul from Revelation 25, which he quoted as saying, "These shall go into everlasting punishment, the death that never dies." John quietly informed the man that while Revelation 25 was three chapters outside the Bible, the first half of his text did appear in Matthew 25 and the second half in the Methodist hymnbook. Suddenly, the pastor remembered that he had an urgent appointment and abruptly left as his listeners laughed in astonishment at his ignorance of the Bible.[40]

When his brother fell ill with malaria, John, growing increasingly homesick, interrupted his ministry for six months to help William run his blacksmith shop in Adam's Basin. Although suffering from chills and fever, William cheered his brother "with words of sympathy and encouragement, as well as pecuniary aid." When William recovered, John teamed up with Sullivan Heath for a preaching tour along the Southern Tier area of New York during the fall and winter of 1849-1850. Sixty years later, he recalled that "it was a valuable experience to [me]." The men saw "some substantial results" in souls converted. In the spring of 1850, when some friends loaned him a horse and wagon, John preached across western New York for several months.[41]

While speaking to an audience in Morganville, New York, John for the first time encountered mesmerism (a form of hypnotism called "animal magnetism" first introduced by F. A. Mesmer in late-eighteenth century France). He witnessed a young man who, under normal circumstances, could not carry a tune suddenly sing an Advent hymn melodiously under the spell of hypnotism. John watched fascinated as this young man either sang or stopped in midnote depending on how the hypnotist raised or lowered his hand behind the subject's head. "I came near the point of learning the art," he later admitted, "but [I] got my eyes open to the nature of the thing as I saw its close connection with modern spiritualism. I concluded the safest way for me was to let it alone."[42] His early experience with mesmerism would fortify John years later when his preaching partner, Moses Hull, apostatized because of his involvement in spiritualism.

When John's money ran out, he found odd jobs to replenish his funds. Since all kinds of businesses advertised for workers in Rochester, opportunities abounded. Because he boarded with the carter Jonathan Orton and his family on the corner of Monroe and Union streets near downtown Rochester, he could walk to most of his jobs. Frequently between 1849 and 1852 he painted houses and did carpentry work. When John de Mersman opened a new business on State Street in 1851, John became one of the six experienced workmen hanging 25,000 colorful pieces of wall paper printed in Boston, Philadelphia, and New York City.[43]

But family death and illness forced him to suspend his ministry temporarily. In September 1849 John's beloved grandmother, Sarah Loofborough, had died in Victor at the age of 77. Writing in the *Northern Christian Advocate*, E. Wood, noting that "many have witnessed her pious example and [have] been blessed by her Godly counsels," hoped that her aged husband Nathan (82), "a veteran of the Cross, [might] be supported by grace, and finally meet her in heaven."[44] Devastated by his grandmother's death, John had hurried back to Victor. After the funeral, relatives, citing 1 Timothy 5:8, impressed on him his duty to care for his mother, whose own health was failing. During the months that followed, he returned to blacksmithing to support the family. Yet he could not shake the conviction that he should be preaching. Depressed, the sensitive 18-year-old passed "awful hours of gloom." He began to neglect praying and Bible study, mingled with partygoers, and tried to drown his sorrow with mirth. But such activities merely awakened "an awful stinging of conscience, and a horror of darkness" in his life. Fortunately for him, Brother Lamson, a family friend, visited their home, and after listening to John share his feelings, Lamson spoke encouraging words.[45]

Recognizing that part of John's depression could be related to his poor diet, his uncle Norton shared with him copies of Sylvester Graham's lectures, articles on healthful living by O. S. and L. N. Fowler, and a subscription to Dr. James Caleb Jackson's *Water-Cure Journal.* In 1849 and 1850 John began drinking more water, getting more exercise, and eating graham bread and hot mush made from unbolted wheat flour. While he did not give up meat, he tried eating more fruits and vegetables. However, although nearly every health reformer of that era recommended taking a *daily* cold bath, John would continue taking a *monthly* hot bath for the next half century. Moreover, because he suffered from "slight hemorrhages of the lungs," a physician advised John to take up smoking to soothe his lungs. So for a short time he smoked cigars.[46]

JOHN LOOFBOROUGH AND MARY WALKER

However, the 19-year-old cigar-puffing preacher found that he could not support himself in the gospel ministry on the donations of relatives and friends. Although his grandfather's will in 1849 had given John and his four siblings a few acres of land in East Bloomfield Township, John had no desire to return to farming.[47] So when William E. Arnold opened a sash lock factory on the corner of Main and Alexander Streets in Rochester and advertised for 1,000 "energetic and persevering men" to sell his new invention, John applied for a job. Arnold bragged that, while most laborers made a dollar a day, his salesmen earned two or three times that amount—at least $50 to $100 a month! He also offered an award of $300 to any man who could invent a better window lock than his Arnold's Patent Sash Locks, which he produced in six varieties.[48] During 1851 John proved himself a super-salesman of sash locks. On some days he sold as many as $5 worth, far more money than he had ever earned in his life farming, blacksmithing, painting houses, or hanging wallpaper. By the end of the summer he had saved $35, a small fortune in those days.[49]

Yet even better opportunities beckoned. Two years after the discovery of gold at Sutter's Mill in California in 1849, newspapers all across America notified readers that even richer deposits of gold had recently been found there. On October 16, 1851, the Rochester *Daily Advertiser*'s headlines screamed: "Hurrah for California! Great Excitement! Now for a Fortune! The last arrival brings astounding intelligence of the new discovery of immense and exhaustless fountains of Gold!! No time to be lost!" Agent Daniel Wood urged gold-seekers to buy their life insurance policies at his Rochester office before going west.[50] Soon a wave of "gold fever" swept the city, and one wealthy entrepreneur who approved of John Loofborough's initiative and success asked him to join a business partnership to seek gold nuggets in California.

Politely, John declined the man's offer, for he had already discovered his "nugget" right there in Rochester. Attracted by newspaper ads for seamstresses, 17-year-old Mary J. Walker of Troy, New York, had come to Rochester in 1849 to try her hand at dressmaking. She found lodgings with the mason Alanson Curtiss and his wife, Caroline. Mary's sewing work in their home permitted her to babysit their two children: Charles (9) and baby Walstein (8 months).[51] After hearing Elder E. R. Pinney preach, she gave her heart to the Lord. Although it remains a mystery how John Loofborough and Mary Walker first became acquainted, it is likely that they met while attending Advent Christian services in Rochester. As the number of believers was relatively small, they could hardly avoid each other, especially since they were about the same age (19) at the time. Seeing in Mary a deeply Christian girl who was cheerful under difficulties, John proposed, and Mary accepted. With little fanfare and no newspaper announcements, they were married on October 14, 1851.[52]

When he changed his marital status, did John also alter his surname? In the absence of written records (a marriage certificate, newspaper announcements, etc.), it is impossible to say with certainty. What is certain, however, is that while the United States Census for 1850 records the name "*Loof*borough" for John's Grandfather Nathan (83), his aunt Susan (44), and his uncle Elias (54), as well as his younger brother Eber (13), it lists the surname of his mother, Minerva (49), and sister Diantha (10) as "*Lough*borough." Was it a clerical error, or perhaps a conscious effort by some members of the family to replace their Irish-sounding name with a more respectable English one? As the offensive nickname "Mick" for an Irishman gained popularity in the 1850s, did John and Mary decide that Loofborough—with its onomatopoeia of loafing and clumsy oafishness—tied them too closely to the dirty, lower-class Irish laborers all around them? Perhaps in their minds, "Loughborough" sounded more English, more sophisticated, more suitable for the middle-class life to which they now aspired.[53]

Whatever their reason, when John and Mary joined the tiny Sabbatarian Adventist band who worshipped at 124 Mount Hope Avenue in Rochester in 1852, John, writing his first letter to their paper *The Advent Review and Sabbath Herald*, would sign his name "J. N. Loughborough." That signature would remain unchanged until his death seven decades later.

---

[1] *YI*, January 1864, p. 2.

[2] W. H. McIntosh, *History of Ontario County*, pp. 60, 61, 203; *YI*, January 1864, p. 2.

[3] *PUR*, June 18, 1908, pp. 1, 2; E. Robinson, *Lighter of Gospel Fires*, pp. 24-26.

[4] Robinson, p. 28; *PUR*, Aug. 6, 1908, pp. 1, 2.

[5] *YI*, January 1864, p. 2; JNL, *The Great Second Advent Movement*, pp. 516-519; *PUR*, June 11, 1908, p. 1; Robinson, pp. 27, 28. Loughborough apparently retained copies of *Advent Herald, Signs of the Times,* and *Midnight Cry,* because 60 years later he often quoted directly from them. See, for example: *PUR*, Oct. 8, 1908, p. 1; *PUR*, Oct. 15, 1908, pp. 1, 2.

[6] *YI*, January 1864, p. 2; *YI*, February 1864, p. 11; JNL, *The Great Second Advent Movement*, pp. 518-522; "Apostolic and Adventist Experience," pp. 48, 52; and L. F. Fisher, *Victor*, p. 29.

[7] *YI*, p. 2; JNL, *The Great Second Advent Movement*, pp. 139, 517-519; J. S. Fisher and L. F. Fisher, *A Victor Album* (Pittsford, N.Y.: Wolfe Publications, 1981), p. 22; R. M. Fagan et al., *A History of Victor*, p. 68; Robinson, pp. 30, 31. Although Loughborough several times asserts that 500 citizens of Victor converted to Millerite Adventism, the village had only about 250 inhabitants while the township had about 2,000 people. If 25 percent of the latter initially believed in Adventism, most quickly returned to their local congregations after the Great Disappointment of October 22, 1844, as historical sources attest. Although the current structure at 105 East Main Street, sheathed in yellow vinyl siding and divided into four apartment dwellings, resembles a nineteenth-century meetinghouse (minus the front porch) with its peaked roof and two front entrances, the property deed shows that it does not go back far enough to be the original building, which was probably torn down after its Advent members returned to the Methodist church across the street.

[8] Johnson, *Rochester*, pp. 3-6, 13, 14, 100-102, 108; W. Cross, *Burned-over District*, p. 75.

[9] Butler, *Sea of Faith*, pp. 242-247.

[10] Cross, *Burned-over District*, pp. 293, 298-303; J. Clark, *1844*, vol. 1, p. 31.

[11] *PUR*, June 11, 1908, p. 1.

[12] JNL, quoted in *GCB* (1899), p. 153.

[13] *RH*, July 30, 1914, p. 4.

[14] *RH*, Jan. 1, 1884, p. 12.

[15] *YI*, February 1864, p. 11.

[16] *PUR*, Nov. 5, 1908, p. 1.

[17] Fagan et al., p. 68; Victor, New York, Methodist-Episcopal Church records (1844 and 1845). According to these records, Nathan was still a church trustee in April 1844 and served as cochair of a meeting of Methodist-Episcopal male trustees held on April 8, 1845. Sarah died four years later at 77 on September 28, 1849, while Nathan passed away on July 17, 1854, at 87. See www.ancestry.com (accessed Aug. 25, 2009).

[18] JNL, "Some Individual Experience, a Companion to the Book *The Great Second Advent Movement*" (Takoma Park, Md.: Review and Herald, 1919), p. 50; Fagan et al., p. 68. Fagan states that most Victor area Millerites eventually returned to the Methodist Church, but "among the exceptions were the children of Nathan Loughborough who maintained the Advent belief." However, she does not indicate which of Nathan's six living children remained Millerites.

[19] *YI*, March 1864, pp. 21, 22; *PUR*, Sept. 17, 1908, p. 1.

[20] *Church Officers' Gazette*, July 1916, pp. 1, 2.

[21] JNL, "Apostolic and Advent Experience," p. 56; Robinson, p. 37.

[22] JNL, *Rise and Progress* (Battle Creek, Mich.: General Conference of Seventh-day Adventists, 1892), p. 68; *PUR*, Sept. 10, 1908, p. 1.

[23] E. R. Foreman, ed., *Centennial History of Rochester,* vol. 3, p. 284; Williams, "Sketch" (1846), p. 578.

[24] JNL, "Individual Experience," p. 87; Foreman, pp. 306, 307; J. Parker, *Rochester—A Story Historical,* pp.251-253.

[25] *Church Officers Gazette*, July 1916, p. 2; *The Great Second Advent Movement* (Washington, D.C.: Review and Herald Pub. Assn., 1905), pp. 234, 500; JNL, *The Church: Its Organization, Order, and Discipline* (Washington, D.C.: Review and Herald Press, 1907), pp. 89, 90. From 1848 to about 1855 John (and after 1851 his wife Mary) lived on Union Street, one block away from Joseph Marsh's home on Alexander Street. We should bear in mind, however, that Loughborough wrote his description of the Advent Christians decades after he left the group and joined the Sabbatarian Adventists in 1852. Throughout his writings, Loughborough disparages the Advent Christians (whom he insists on calling "First Day Adventists") and always compares them unfavorably with Seventh-day Adventists. Further chapters on his books *Rise and Progress* and *The Great Second Advent Movement* will examine this and other biases more closely.

[26] *PUR*, Dec. 3, 1908, p. 1; Robinson, pp. 42, 43.

[27] *YI*, July 1864, p. 49; *PUR*, Dec. 10, 1908, p. 2; 1852 Gillett Map of East Bloomfield Township.

[28] JNL, *Hope of the Gospel: or Immortality the Gift of God* (1860), in *S. D. Advent Library* (Battle Creek, Mich.: Steam Press of Review and Herald Office, 1860-1880), p. 39; Robinson, p. 43.

[29] Robinson, p. 43; *YI*, July 1864, p. 49; Rochester *Daily Advertiser,* Sept. 21, 1847, p. 3; Rochester *Republican,* Sept. 28, 1847, p. 3. Although Robinson states that John attended the local high school in Victor, Loughborough himself never mentions it. In fact, during the 1840s Victor did not have a high school, so John would have had to commute to Canandaigua, approximately nine miles each way—too far to walk, as he had previously done. When Loughborough states that he attended "the upper grades" in a "district school," he most likely meant grades seven and eight, what we today call "junior high."

[30] *PUR*, Dec. 10, 1908, p. 2; Robinson, pp. 43, 44.

[31] *YI*, July 1864, pp. 49, 50.

[32] *YI*, August 1864, p. 62; *YI*, October 1864, pp. 74, 75; *YI*, December 1864, p. 90; *RH*, Jan. 29, 1884, pp. 74, 75.

[33] *YI*, December 1864, p. 90; *RH*, Jan. 29, 1884, p. 75.

[34] *RH*, Jan. 29, 1884, p. 75; *YI*, December 1864, p. 90; *YI*, January 1865, p. 4; *PUR*, Dec. 24, 1908, p. 1.

[35] *YI*, December 1864, p. 90; *YI*, January 1865, p. 4; *PUR*, Dec. 31, 1908, pp. 2, 3; *PUR*, Jan. 7, 1908, p. 1.

[36] *RH*, Jan. 29, 1884, p. 75; *YI*, December 1864, p. 90; *YI*, January 1865, p. 4; *PUR*,

Feb. 11, 1909, p. 1.

[37] JNL, *Rise and Progress*, p. 147.

[38] *YI*, July 1865, pp. 52, 53; *RH*, Feb. 12, 1884, p. 106; PUR, Feb. 11, 1909; PUR, June 17, 1915, p. 1; Robinson, p. 55. John's 11 lectures covered such topics as the Fall, restitution, the nature of humanity, the state of the dead, the future punishment, the saints' inheritance, the Second Advent, and various signs of the end of time.

[39] *YI*, May 1865, pp. 36, 37; *YI*, July 1865, p. 52; *RH*, Feb. 12, 1884, p. 106; *PUR*, Mar. 11, 1909, p. 1. Many of the charming rural hamlets no longer appear on current maps.

[40] *YI*, March 1865, pp. 20, 21; *PUR*, Jan. 28, 1909, pp. 1, 2.

[41] *YI*, May 1865, pp. 36, 37; *PUR*, Mar. 11, 1909, p. 1.

[42] *YI*, August 1865, p. 58.

[43] Rochester City Directories (1849-1855); Gary Land, *Historical Dictionary of the Seventh-day Adventists* (Lanham, Md.: The Scarecrow Press, 2005), p. 179; Rochester *Daily Advertiser*, Oct. 17, 1851, p. 1; "Orton, Jonathan T.," *Ellen G. White Encyclopedia* (Hagerstown, Md.: Review and Herald Pub. Assn., 2013), p. 484.

[44] E. Wood, *Northern Christian Advocate* (1849), p. 156.

[45] *YI*, September 1865, pp. 69, 70.

[46] Ronald L. Numbers, *Prophetess of Health: A Study of Ellen G. White* (New York: Harper and Row Publishers, 1976), p. 79; Ellen G. White Estate, *A Critique of Prophetess of Health* (Takoma Park, Md.: General Conference of Seventh-day Adventists), p. 48.

[47] Nathan Loofborough's Will (1849), vol. L, p. 58, Ontario County Court Records, Canandaigua, New York.

[48] "One Thousand Men Wanted," ad in the Rochester *Daily Advertiser*, Oct. 16, 1851, p. 1.

[49] JNL to C. E. Holmes, Apr. 29, 1920, C. E. Holmes Collection 142-2, CAR.

[50] Rochester *Daily Advertiser*, Oct. 16, 1851, p. 4.

[51] See www.ancestry.com (accessed July 12, 2009); Rochester City Directory (1849), Monroe County Library System; U.S. Census of 1850.

[52] *RH*, July 2, 1867, p. 8. The only extant record of their wedding date occurs in the flyleaf of J. N. Loughborough's 1915 diary, wherein he lists the names, wedding dates, and death dates of all three of his wives. Unlike his older brother William, who announced his marriage to Eliza Norton in two of Rochester's newspapers, John and Mary apparently did not do so. Prior to 1870, New York State did not require couples to legally register their marriages, so no civil records exist of the Loofboroughs' wedding. While most mainstream churches maintained marriage registries, the Advent Christians kept no records of any kind.

[53] U.S. Census of 1850; "mick" in *Merriam-Webster's Collegiate Dictionary*, tenth edition (1993), p. 734; M. Lufborrow, "Families," p. 65; Robinson, p. 58.

CHAPTER III

CONVERSION TO SEVENTH-DAY ADVENTISM (1852-1853)

"What am I going to do with this light I have received?"
"I was like a wounded bird."[1]

Although John continued preaching in the fall of 1851, the fact that the Advent Christians did not pay their preachers a salary necessitated his finding additional resources. Now that he had a wife to support, monthly bills to pay, and growing travel expenses, he needed a steady income. Selling Arnold's patent sash locks proved to be a highly lucrative solution to his cash flow problem. As the 1850s witnessed a building boom in Rochester (now a city of 44,000 people) and across upstate New York, he saw a ready market for selling homeowners the newly patented window "sash-fasteners" produced by William E. Arnold in Rochester's downtown Seeley Building.[2] The fact that by 1852 three new railway lines intersected Rochester also made it easy for John to travel to outlying towns in the Genesee Valley.[3]

The 7,000 Irish citizens living in the "Flour City" also constituted a ready market of consumers for his products. Combining business with gospel work, John sold sash locks during the week and preached on weekends. With his genial, sprightly nature, ready Irish wit, and glib tongue, he soon became a super-salesman and a popular preacher. Given his youthful looks and leprechaun-like frame, congregants dubbed the little man who smoked the big black cigars "the boy preacher." His wife Mary converted their tiny house on 78 Union Street (adjacent to Jonathan and Caroline Orton's home) into a seamstress shop in which she sewed shirts and dresses for a growing clientele of middle and upper class patrons.[4]

JOHN'S DOCTRINAL QUANDARIES

To his friends and clients, no doubt John Loughborough personified success. He had a pretty teenage wife who adored him, a lucrative position in marketing, and a growing ministry to the scattered Advent Christian congregations in Canandaigua, Auburn, and Geneva. Yet outward appearances could be deceiving, for by 1852 John entertained serious doubts concerning certain doctrinal positions held by his sect. Although he remained convinced that the soul was not immortal (indeed, he won a four-hour debate with a Universalist pastor that summer involving that doctrine), he questioned the Advent Christian position that the Ten Commandments as well as the ceremonial law had been abolished at the cross. By way of illustration, he filled a pitcher full of water to show that in Matthew 5:17, 18, Christ had "filled the law full" and now offers grace through the gospel. But the phrase "till heaven and earth pass" troubled him, for he knew that part of the promise had not yet been fulfilled. "I was like a wounded bird," he later recalled, and so he decided not to preach on that subject until he received further insight.[5]

Another subject that had been puzzling the 19-year-old preacher for seven years was the location of the sanctuary mentioned in Daniel 8:14. While most Advent Christians still believed that the earth was the sanctuary, John did not accept this view, reasoning that if the earth had been the sanctuary, God would have cleansed it with fire on October 22, 1844. He also disagreed with his friends who advocated the new age-to-come views espoused by Joseph Marsh in the *Advent Harbinger* (for example, that the Jews would be converted and return to Palestine). Also he had questions regarding which day should be kept holy as the Sabbath (the first or the seventh), what the third angel's message of Revelation 14:9-12 meant for believers today, and the identity of the two-horned beast of Revelation 13.[6]

Then, sometime during the summer of 1852, Loughborough attended an Advent Christian meeting in Rochester at which he heard Elder J. B. Cook preach "a tirade" against two Sabbatarian Adventist leaders John knew nothing about—James and Ellen White—with James listening in the audience. He found the whole matter "a curious mess." Shortly thereafter, however, he faced a "mess" of his own when certain Advent Christian leaders treated him dishonestly, causing him to lose confidence in them. Then news reached him that some of his congregants in Parma and Clarkson, recently exposed to Sabbatarian Adventist preaching, had changed their views on the sanctuary, the Sabbath, and the third angel's message—the same topics that puzzled him.[7] As he prayed about what he should do, he had two dreams that shaped his course of action.

In the first dream he entered a dingy, ill-ventilated, poorly lit room with a low ceiling where four age-to-come Adventists (Joseph Marsh, J. B. Cook, O.R.L. Crozier, and J. C. Bywater), looking sad and discouraged, argued doctrinal issues among themselves. They attempted to prevent him from opening another door and entering a second room. But he barged past them into a clean, spacious, well-lit, and well-ventilated room. Here he saw a group of happy people studying pictures of the heavenly sanctuary and the two-horned beast hanging on the wall. In a second dream he saw a tall, thin young preacher wearing spectacles and standing before an audience with open Bibles studying the very issues that had long confused him. "It seemed as though angels accompanied him," John wrote. Suddenly a feeling of relief and joy engulfed him, and he awoke with the impression that he would soon receive light.[8]

Shortly thereafter, Jonathan Orton, the Loughboroughs' good friend and neighbor, invited John to attend some meetings being held in a hall at 124 Mount Hope Avenue.[9] A Sabbatarian Adventist preacher named John Andrews was concluding a series focusing on the very issues that puzzled the Loughboroughs. Since some of Loughborough's Advent Christian members had joined the group, Orton told him, "You have a duty there. . . . You ought to get them out of this heresy. They will give you a chance to speak in their meeting. So get your texts ready, and you can show them in two minutes that the Sabbath has been abolished."[10]

Recent rumors concerning the Sabbatarian Adventist group had prejudiced John's mind against them. He had heard that "they get together and scream, and yell, and have a great demonstration, and a noisy, fanatical time."[11] Nonetheless, he resolved to attend the last meeting in the series on September 26, 1852. In preparation, he drew up a list of Bible texts regarding the ten-commandment law, the ceremonial law, the sanctuary, the Sabbath, and the three angels' messages. As he entered the hall with seven of his Advent Christian friends, he was surprised to discover a testimony meeting in progress. Although the attendees sat on hard wooden chairs, he observed the "calm, heavenly atmosphere" in the room as men and women joined in giving "calm, sensible testimonies, wet down with tears."[12]

John's biggest surprise, however, came when the 23-year-old John N. Andrews rose to speak. He was the same man that he had seen in his second dream! Andrews told the audience that although he had originally planned to speak on another topic, he felt impressed to lecture instead on whether the cross had abolished the law. To Loughborough's astonishment, Andrews cited every single Bible text in the precise order that John had written them down on his sheet of paper![13] Loughborough recalled that Andrews' lecture was "the most consistent of anything I ever heard on the law question." It had "straightened them [the confusing texts] all out to my perfect satisfaction." He now understood that it was the ceremonial law and not the ten-commandment law that Christ had fulfilled (and abolished) at the cross.[14] "Father" J. B. Lamson, a Sabbatarian Adventist, asked him after the meeting, "Brother John, does not that subject look pretty clear?"

"Yes, it does," John replied.

"Then you will have to keep the [seventh day] Sabbath, won't you?" Lamson inquired.

"Brother Lamson, unless I can find something stronger than what I had supposed teaches the abolition of the law of the Ten Commandments, I shall have to keep the Sabbath," Loughborough admitted. He confessed that "the third angel's message seemed to me to be so far in advance of the matters I had preached that I thought I could not preach, but would try to help those who were preaching."[15]

During the following week, Andrews met with the Loughboroughs and their seven Advent Christian friends for Bible studies concerning the Sabbath, the ministry of Christ in the heavenly sanctuary, the "mark of the beast," the "two-horned beast," and the third angel's message. All of them accepted the new understandings as "light from heaven."[16] After further studies with Andrews and Hiram Edson, their neighbors the Ortons also accepted them, though not without a struggle. "We cried unto the Lord, with broken hearts and contrite spirits, to show us the truth, which, praise his name, he has done," Jonathan's daughter Drusilla wrote in the *Advent Review and Sabbath Herald*.[17]

When John and Mary and their friends joined with the Mount Hope Avenue group for worship on the first Sabbath in October, they found there a warm, caring fellowship. Members prayed for them, studied the Bible with them, and even fed them. "We could not doubt but that the third angel's message was God's message to us, and [that] we must obey it, let what would be the result," John resolved.[18]

LOUGHBOROUGHS WITNESS MIRACULOUS HEALINGS

Although John and Mary found most of the Sabbatarian Adventist worship services calm and deeply spiritual, a few included supernatural phenomena that amazed them. As nineteenth century medicine was primitive and unreliable at best and harmful if not life-threatening at worst, Americans turned to home remedies (and sundry quack doctors) to cure their aches and pains. But some religious sects—including Advent Christians and Sabbatarian Adventists—relied on prayer instead. During the summer of 1852 an epidemic of the ague (malaria) struck upstate New York. Loughborough's Uncle Norton, racked with fever and chills, summoned John and two other Advent Christians named Morehouse and Boughton to his bedside. After reading the promise in James 5:14, 15, they placed their hands on him and prayed for him. He experienced instant healing. "The fever was immediately rebuked," John wrote, "and he arose healed and praised God. What a sensible presence of the Spirit of God filled the room!"[19]

During J. N. Andrews' last meeting on September 26, John and Mary had watched as Sabbatarian believers placed their hands on Harvey Cottrell, an Advent Christian also suffering from the ague. After they anointed him with oil and prayed over him, claiming the promise in James 5 Cottrell too, was healed immediately.[20] On the first Sabbath in October the Loughboroughs met church leaders James and Ellen White, who had just returned from a preaching tour of New England. At that meeting, the Whites invited John to join them in kneeling around the bed of Oswald Stowell, a press compositor dying of pleurisy. Once again, after anointing and prayer, Stowell experienced instant healing. Two days later he was operating the printing press. On that occasion John felt "a sensible presence of the Spirit of God."[21] We find this aspect of primitive Christianity in early Adventism further illustrated in the instant healings of many others, among them Mrs. Penfield, Frances Howland, William Hyde, Clarissa Bonfoey, Anna White, and Luman Masten.[22]

Why this frequent recourse to faith healing in the 1850s? Loughborough explained:

"When there was sickness among us, we had not the light on the treatment of disease by the use of nature's remedies, but were requested to bring our sick ones to the Lord in prayer, following the rule of the fifth chapter of James. In the Rochester church for many months every case thus brought to the Lord was healed."[23]

Yet not *every* case resulted in healing, as Loughborough later acknowledged. James White's brother Nathaniel, suffering from consumption (TB) in 1853, died in his rocking chair despite the believers' prayers and anointing. Ellen White reassured his disappointed friends that although God had heard their prayers, "He gives us the things that are for our best good and [for] His own glory." God had allowed Nathaniel to fall asleep, she said, "while [he was] in a well-prepared state of consecration."[24]

In 1853 Mary herself witnessed an astonishing case of exorcism during a women's prayer meeting in Rochester. A certain Mrs. Riggs, who had attended several spiritualist séances, claimed to be afflicted by a demon in the shape of an old woman dressed in black. The evil spirit visited her every night, threatening to choke her to death if she told anyone about it. Having seen Mrs. Riggs' predicament in vision, Ellen White counseled her to seek deliverance through group prayer. Days later, during a prayer meeting at the Orton home, the demon again attacked Riggs, choking her so severely that her face turned black and she could barely whisper, "Pray!" The women, led by Mrs. White, did so, rebuking the evil spirit in God's name. Instantly, the demon released its hold and fled from the room. "Thank the Lord," Riggs gasped, "[for] He has given me the victory." For the rest of her life, Riggs remained untroubled by demonic visits. As a result of this experience, Mary and John resolved never to go near "the circles of spirit mediums."[25]

JOHN WITNESSES ELLEN WHITE'S VISIONS

But if previous experiences had prepared the Loughboroughs to accept faith healings and exorcism as divinely inspired, Ellen White's visions were something totally beyond anything they had previously encountered. Indeed, at the Albany Conference in 1845, Advent Christians had repudiated modern visionary phenomena as fanaticism, claiming that the genuine gift of prophecy had ended with the apostolic church. But at the same service in which Oswald Stowell had been healed, Loughborough saw Mrs. White in vision for the first time. Unlike spiritualist mediums who closed their eyes as they entered a trancelike state, White's eyes remained wide open and unblinking, seemingly unaware of her immediate surroundings. John expressed amazement that during the 80 minutes her vision lasted, she never took a single breath.[26]

If the physical phenomena of her ecstatic experience amazed him, however, her message surprised John even more. Although she had never met the man, White described in great detail the immoral course of a certain Sabbatarian Advent businessman from Rochester, who, during a recent trip, had committed adultery with a woman in Paw Paw, Michigan. When he returned six weeks later to worship with the Mount Hope Avenue group, Ellen confronted him with his adultery. Bursting into tears, he dropped to his knees, confessed his sin, and asked his wife for forgiveness before the entire congregation. In a subsequent conversation with the Whites, he discovered that Ellen's vision had occurred on the same day as his immoral act 600 miles away.[27]

In that same vision, however, White received a message for John himself. She told him that she had seen three (unnamed) Advent Christian ministers "trying hard to keep you from joining the Sabbathkeeping Adventists." White then related the very thoughts that had been going through his mind while he was deciding whether or not to observe the Sabbath—thoughts he had not even shared with his wife, Mary. Stunned, he declared, "Surely there is a power more than human connected with this vision."[28]

Although John was convicted that the Sabbathkeeping Adventists preached biblical truth and, with Mary, had begun observing the seventh-day Sabbath, he was not yet fully convinced that he should preach the new message. When he told his Advent Christian congregants that he could no longer minister to them, he apparently intended to sell Arnold's patent sash locks full-time. From a few months' sales he had saved $35 in the bank. Nevertheless, as he boarded the train every Monday morning, he felt impressed that God wanted him to be an Adventist preacher instead of a window-lock peddler. But with tears in her eyes Mary begged him not to preach full-time, reminding him that gospel ministers received no salaries other than the free-will gifts people offered them.

However, at a subsequent Sabbath meeting, Ellen White warned John that God had shown her in vision that he was "holding back from his duty to preach the message, waiting to secure means for his support." She assured him that if he would "decide to obey the Lord and go out to preach the message, the Lord will open the way for your support."

Consequently, when he failed to sell a single sash lock for several weeks, he felt like Jonah running away from God's call. Spending several hours on his knees in prayer alone in the bedroom, he finally submitted to God's will. When Mary objected to his decision, asking what they would live on, he assured her that God would provide. She too entered the bedroom to weep for an hour. Within minutes after she had left to buy matches and thread with the last silver three-cent piece John possessed, however, an elderly man from Middleport knocked at the door and asked Loughborough to sell him $80 worth of window locks (John's commission amounted to $26 on the sale) so that he could establish a business in Ohio. When Mary returned, John shared the news of his good fortune, and both accepted it as a sign from God that He would indeed provide for their needs. A subsequent vision by Ellen White further convinced him to become a full-time Sabbatarian Adventist preacher.[29] During the course of his public ministry, Loughborough would see Ellen White in vision between 40 and 50 times, convincing him that her special prophetic gift came from God.[30]

To help John understand how Sabbatarian Adventist theology had developed, James White loaned him back issues of the sect's papers: *Present Truth* (1849) and the *Advent Review and Sabbath Herald* (1850-1852). Ellen White also gave him a copy of her recent autobiography, *Christian Experience and Views*. Near the end of his long life, Loughborough would boast that he had read every issue of the church paper *Review and Herald* for 75 years (1850-1924).[31] After John and Mary had studied their Bibles and Adventist materials for three weeks, they officially joined the Sabbathkeeping Adventist group in Rochester. To the end of his life more than seven decades later, John celebrated two birthdays each year: January 26 (his natural birth day) and September 26 (the date of his conversion)—and gave a thank offering to God on each occasion.[32]

Several members of John's family—including his mother, Minerva, his brother William and William's wife, Eliza, and his sister Minerva Jane—would eventually join the tiny Sabbatarian Adventist movement, which in

1852 numbered perhaps 200 members.[33] That same year two other future preachers also converted to Sabbathkeeping Adventism—John Harvey Waggoner in Wisconsin and Merritt E. Cornell in Michigan—and both would eventually join Loughborough in holding evangelistic meetings throughout the United States. As John's circle of Adventist friends grew in the 1850s, it would also include pioneer preachers Hiram Edson, Samuel Rhodes, Joseph Bates, Frederick Wheeler, Uriah Smith, and W. S. Ingraham, among others.[34]

PRESS WORKER AND ADVENTIST PREACHER

After he quit selling sash locks, John needed some other form of regular income to pay the monthly bills. Consequently, James White invited him to join the tiny staff of the press that operated out of the Whites' home at 124 Mount Hope Avenue in Rochester. From their cramped first-floor shop, Adventists printed a growing number of tracts, pamphlets, and books until the fall of 1855, including the movement's official paper *The Advent Review and Sabbath Herald.* During the winter of 1852 the group assembled J. N. Andrews' new tract, *The Sanctuary.* Lacking sophisticated machinery, they gathered for a work bee. While John perforated the pages with a shoemaker's pegging awl, Uriah Smith trimmed them with his pocketknife and a straight edge, Mary Patten glued on the covers, Ellen White wrapped the copies, and her husband James addressed them for the post office.[35] "We blistered our hands in the operation," Smith later recalled, "and often the tracts in form were not half so true and square as the doctrines they taught."[36] Despite the long hours, low pay, and physical discomforts, John described the group as "a happy company together."[37]

The same optimistic spirit pervades John's first letter printed in the *Advent Review* of October 28, 1852, in which he reviews his Christian experience from 1847 to the present. After explaining how he and Mary had gradually accepted new light on the two-horned beast, the Sabbath, and the two laws, he confessed: "I see my duty. My heart is full. And God helping [me], I will do my duty." He exhorted readers to "be strong in faith, giving glory to God, for what he has promised, he will perform." He signed the letter, "J. N. Loughborough," providing the first documentary evidence that John Loofborough, the former Irish blacksmith's apprentice, would henceforth be remembered as J. N. Loughborough of English ancestry, a

Review and Herald press employee and preacher of Sabbatarian Adventist truth. He had planted the first seed of a growing legend that would follow him to the day of his death in 1924.[38]

Despite his optimism, however, the path John had chosen to walk sometimes proved rocky and uncertain. Like other Millerite offshoots, Sabbath-keeping Adventists witnessed numerous instances of fanaticism within their ranks. Church leaders in Rochester dealt with several bizarre individuals during the early 1850s. One man, claiming to have holy flesh, urged Adventists to "come up on the high platform that I am on . . . and you will never be tempted anymore, [you will] never have another wrong thought!" John heard James White rebuke the man, informing him that "you are giving up the warfare against temptation, and are sitting down on the 'easy stool of Satan'; and if you continue thus to do, you will make shipwreck of [your] faith, and be led into gross sins." Six weeks later when the man brought a young woman into his home, ordering his wife and their 2-month-old baby to leave, the police intervened to prevent him from evicting his family. A second Rochester Adventist, convinced that he too had attained perfect sanctification after observing the seventh-day Sabbath five or six times, felt that henceforth he could keep Sunday with impunity. Another man whom Loughborough visited believed that since he was under grace and not law, he no longer needed to do work. Instead, he spent his days indoors with his feet propped up, singing, "We'll have nothing at all to do but to march around Jerusalem, when we arrive home." Meanwhile, his wife chopped wood for the family stove. Disgusted, John ran into the yard, took the axe from her hands, and finished cutting the wood.[39] Such early experiences helped prepare him for his later roles as evangelist, church founder, conference organizer, administrator, and global missionary, for in each position he would face fanaticism, apostasy, and dissidence in every imaginable form.

Expressing confidence in the 27-year-old preacher's abilities, James and Ellen White decided to send him on an evangelistic tour around New York and Pennsylvania in the winter of 1852. Unwilling to have him go alone, however, they enlisted the help of Hiram Edson, a seasoned veteran whose understanding of Hebrews 9 had helped Adventists grasp Christ's ministry in the heavenly sanctuary following the Great Disappointment of October 22, 1844. For years, Edson had trained such beginning preachers as

Joseph Bates, J. N. Andrews, G. W. Holt, Frederick Wheeler, and Samuel Rhodes, "breaking them in" (as he liked to phrase it) on preaching forays across the Empire State. Although he had not intended to go to the December 1852 meeting at which Loughborough received his preaching call, Edson (who lived near Centerport on the Erie Canal) heard an inner voice telling him to go to Rochester, for "you are needed there." When he arrived, he asked James White, "What do you want of me?" White instructed him to take Loughborough, the Whites' horse old Charley, and a carriage on a six-weeks' preaching tour.[40]

Before leaving, Edson bought John a heavy winter overcoat, as they would spend most of their time walking, riding horseback, or sitting atop a carriage in the chill wintry air. With nearly all of the mainstream churches closed to them, they held their meetings in scattered homes and schoolhouses. To advertise such gatherings, they prepared printed handbills and distributed them several days ahead. One such handbill, illustrating John's flair for the melodramatic, stated: "J. N. Loughborough, of Rochester, will speak in the schoolhouse on Sunday at 2 and 7 p.m. Come and hear, for 'these that have turned the world upside down are come hither also.' . . . And these do all contrary to the decrees of the pope, saying that there is a better way—the commandments of God and the faith of Jesus."[41]

As the Southern Tier (southern New York and northern Pennsylvania) had very few roads and no railroads or canals in the 1850s, traveling conditions could test the mettle of even the most determined preachers, especially in midwinter. When old Charley could no longer pull their carriage through the drifted snow, the men turned the carriage bed into a "pung" (a primitive box sled with runners) and plowed ahead through blinding snowstorms. Further north, they preached their message to curious crowds along the Erie Canal from Buffalo in the west to Rochester in central New York before heading south again into the gently rolling Allegheny Mountains of northern Pennsylvania, covering hundreds of miles during a month and a half.[42]

Reflecting on the experience half a century later, Loughborough declared: "I had now received an introduction into preaching the third angel's message, and was soon in the field for the fulfillment of a call which had been given directly by the Lord's testimony through Sister White."[43] Judging by the accolades pouring into the *Advent Review* from new converts, the evangelistic tour had been a great success. J. Hamilton of Fredonia, New York, exclaimed: "We feel that the labors of Brn. Loughborough, and Edson, have been blessed among us. The faith of God's children have [*sic*] been greatly strengthened." Hamilton specifically praised John's preaching: "The blessing of the Lord rested upon his labors, while the position of the remnant was set forth with clearness."[44]

Over in Laona, Eliza Miller stated: "It was truly refreshing to hear the word preached. We were strengthened and encouraged by the meat given in due season."[45] During one series of meetings in the Wesleyan Chapel in Olcott, New York, Loughborough's preaching converted the entire Lindsay family to Sabbathkeeping Adventism—including Mrs. Lindsay's mother, the granddaughter of the legendary Puritan divine Cotton Mather. Their children, Mary and Harmon Lindsay, would later become Adventist missionaries to Africa.[46]

Not content to remain home sewing, Mary Loughborough also witnessed to her friends and neighbors. During the winter of 1853 she and Caroline Orton studied the Bible with the Woodhull family of Olcott, New York. Former Advent Christians and close friends of the Loughboroughs, the Woodhulls accepted Sabbatarian Adventism and became staunch believers for the rest of their lives.[47] Over in Lorraine, John and Mary's ministry converted Lorenzo Lowrey and his pregnant wife, Jane. Later, when the Whites and Loughboroughs visited their home, Ellen had a vision as they all gathered around Jane's bed. When Jane gave birth to a baby girl, she named her Ellen Marion Lowrey in honor of Ellen White and Mary (nicknamed Marion) Loughborough.[48]

Although at 21 John Loughborough had barely reached the legal age of adulthood, church leaders James and Ellen White, Hiram Edson, and Joseph Bates had witnessed his talent for preaching, his reliable service at the Review and Herald press, and his calm steadfastness amid fanaticism. The time had come, they concluded, for him to stretch his ministerial wings. During the 1850s Yankee farmers and mechanics from New England and New York were moving west to Michigan, Ohio, Illinois, Indiana, and Wisconsin. The previous four years (1849 to 1852) the ex-sea captain and former Millerite agent Joseph Bates had been breaking new ground in the Midwest, establishing scattered churches among the transplanted Yankees. Having survived the Great Disappointment of October 22, 1844, many were seeking answers to their spiritual dilemma—answers that Sabbath-keeping Adventists could now provide. In tune with newspaper editor Horace Greeley's famous call to "Go West, young man," the time had come for J. N. Loughborough to leave the Empire State and follow the American migration west.

---

[1] *PUR*, May 6, 1909, p. 2; *PUR*, July 1, 1915, p. 2.

[2] *PUR*, Mar. 25, 1909, p. 1; *PUR*, July 29, 1909, p. 1; E. R. Foreman, *Centennial History*, vol. 1, p. 262. The U.S. Census for 1850 shows that William E. Arnold (age 40), his second wife, Esther (24), and their children, Mary (18), Hobart (14), and Eugene (2) lived on the corner of Main and Alexander streets in Rochester's Seventh Ward. Rochester city directories for the 1850s show that his sash lock business was located at No. 10 Seeley Building, Rochester.

[3] J. Parker, *Rochester—A Story Historical*, p. 347. These new railroads were the Buffalo and Rochester Railroad Company (1850), the Rochester and Genesee Railroad Company (1851), and the Rochester and Charlotte Railroad Company (1852).

[4] B. McKelvey, *Rochester, A Brief History* (New York: The Edwin Mellen Press, 1984), pp. 23-25; *idem, Rochester on the Genesee*, pp. 56-58, 67; G. M. Hopkins, *City Atlas of Rochester* (1875), Rochester Public Library; *RH*, Apr. 27, 1950, p. 10; U.S. Census (1850). In 1855 Rochester also had 6,700 German-born and 4500 English-, Scottish-, and Canadian-born citizens.

[5] *PUR*, Mar. 18, 1909, p. 1; *PUR*, July 1, 1915, pp. 1, 2.

[6] *PUR*, May 20, 1909, pp. 1, 2; *PUR*, May 27, 1909, pp. 1, 2; E. Robinson, *Lighter of Gospel Fires*, pp. 58, 59.

[7] *RH*, Feb. 12, 1884, p. 106; *PUR*, Mar. 25, 1909, p. 1; *PUR*, May 6, 1909, p. 2.

[8] *RH*, Feb. 12, 1884, p. 107; *PUR*, June 17, 1915, p. 1; DF 230; Richard Schwarz and Floyd Greenleaf, *Light Bearers: A History of the Seventh-day Adventist Church* (Nampa, Idaho: Pacific Press Pub. Assn., 2000), p. 76.

[9] Because of the frequent renumbering of lots in Rochester between 1850 and 1875, 124 Mount Hope Avenue today could be either a parking lot, part of a home for the aged, or a corner store.

[10] Jonathan Orton, quoted in George Knight, *Lest We Forget* (Hagerstown, Md.: Review and Herald Pub. Assn., 2008), p. 138.

[11] *PUR*, Apr. 8, 1909, p. 1; DF 230.

[12] *PUR*, Apr. 8, 1909, p. 1; *RH*, Aug. 2, 1923, p. 6; Arthur W. Spalding, *Origin and History of Seventh-day Adventists* (Washington, D.C.: Review and Herald Pub. Assn., 1961), vol. 1, p. 211.

[13] *PUR*, Apr. 8, 1909, p. 1; *PUR*, Apr. 22, 1909, p. 1; *PUR*, Apr. 29, 1909, pp. 1, 2. The Bible texts included Colossians 2:14-17, Hebrews 7:11-13, Romans 7:24, Luke 16:16, Matthew 5:17-19, Leviticus 23:37, 38, Ephesians 2:13-15, Ezekiel 43:8, and Hebrews 9:1.

[14] *PUR*, Apr. 8, 1909, p. 1; *PUR*, Apr. 22, 1909, p. 1.

[15] JNL to C. E. Holmes, May 2, 1920, CAR; conversation also quoted in Robinson, p. 64.

[16] *PUR*, May 6, 1909, p. 2; Robinson, p. 64.

[17] *RH*, Nov. 25, 1852, pp. 111, 112.

[18] *PUR*, May 13, 1909, p. 1; JNL to C. E. Holmes, Apr. 29, 1920, m. 142-2, CAR.

[19] *PHJ*, May 1889, p. 130; *SWUR*, Dec. 14, 1915, p. 6; Robinson, pp. 60, 61. Decades later, Loughborough stated that nearly everyone in the 1850s took Brandreth's Pills for "a grand panacea for all human ills," especially "bilious fevers."

[20] *SWUR*, Dec. 14, 1915, p. 6; Robinson, p. 60.

[21] *RH*, Mar. 4, 1884, p. 154; *PUR*, July 8, 1909, pp. 1, 2; *PUR*, Aug. 12, 1915, p. 1; Arthur L. White, *Ellen G. White: The Early Years, 1827-1862* (Hagerstown, Md.: Review and Herald Pub. Assn., 1985), vol. 1, p. 237.

[22] EGW, quoted in Ellen G. White Estate, *A Critique*, p. 43. Although four different men named James White lived in Rochester during the early 1850s (a carriage maker on 49 Adam Street, two laborers at 13 Monroe Street and Grape Street, and the printer James Springer White at 109-111 Monroe Street), apparently neither Mary nor John had met James and Ellen White despite the fact that they lived nearby. See the Rochester city directories for 1853-1855.

[23] JNL, quoted in Ellen G. White Estate, *A Critique*, p. 43.

[24] *PUR*, Sept. 16, 1909, p. 1.

[25] *PUR*, July 22, 1909, p. 1; JNL, *Rise and Progress*, pp. 173-175.

[26] *RH*, Mar. 4, 1884, p. 154.

[27] *RH*, Mar. 4, 1884, p. 154; *RH*, Nov. 5, 1914, p. 6.

[28] *RH*, Mar. 4, 1884, p. 154; Robinson, p. 67.

[29] Several slightly different versions of the story appear in *RH*, Mar. 25, 1884, pp. 201, 202; *PUR*, Aug. 12, 1909, p. 1; DF 230; *Rise and Progress*, pp. 176-179; JNL to C. E. Holmes, Apr. 29, 1920, m. 142-2, CAR; JNL to C. E. Holmes, May 2, 1920, CAR; Robinson, pp. 74-77. In his May 2 letter to Holmes, Loughborough stated: "I have never been down to three cents since that experience."

[30] *RH*, Oct. 20, 1921, p. 7.

[31] *RH*, July 31, 1919, pp. 14, 15; Robinson, pp. 70-72.

[32] *RH*, Feb. 12, 1884, p. 107; E. T. Lloyd, "Memories of Elder J. N. Loughborough," *RH*, Nov. 8, 1962, p. 6.

[33] Loughborough originally gave this estimate of Sabbatarian Adventists at the 1913 General Conference session. W. A. Spicer repeated it at the 1946 General Conference session. See *Eastern Tidings*, Aug. 15, 1946, p. 1, and *RH*, June 7, 1946, p. 20.

[34] *Atlantic Union Conference Record*, May 1, 1905, p. 1; JNL, in "Apostolic and Adventist Experience," drew up a list of 21 pioneers (19 men and two women) with whom he became acquainted during the 1840s and 1850s.

[35] *RH*, May 27, 1890, p. 335; *RH*, July 31, 1919, p. 15.

[36] Uriah Smith, quoted in *RH*, June 19, 1966, p. 4.

[37] JNL, "Early Experiences in the Publishing Work" (typed manuscript, c. 1908); Loughborough, quoted in Merlin D. Burt, *Adventist Pioneer Places: New York and New England* (Hagerstown, Md.: Review and Herald Pub. Assn., 2011), p. 137.

[38] *RH*, Oct. 28, 1852, p. 101.

[39] *RH*, Oct. 18, 1898, p. 663; Robinson, pp. 80, 81.

[40] *PUR*, Aug. 12, 1909, p. 1; Robinson, pp. 77, 78; Burt, p. 132. It was on this tour that Edson told Loughborough about his insight regarding Christ's work in the heavenly sanctuary that came to him in the cornfield on October 23, 1844, a story that Loughborough would later make famous in his books *Rise and Progress* and *The Great Second Advent Movement*. See JNL to R. M. Kelley, Dec. 23, 1919, m. 006529, CAR.

[41] JNL letter to 1922 General Conference delegates, printed in *RH*, Apr. 27, 1922, p. 24; Robinson, p. 79.

[42] *PUR*, Aug. 19, 1909, pp. 1, 2; Robinson, pp. 78, 79.

[43] *PUR*, Aug. 19, 1909, p. 2.
[44] J. Hamilton, quoted in *RH*, Mar. 17, 1853, p. 174; *RH*, May 26, 1853, p. 7.
[45] Eliza A. Miller, quoted in *RH*, Apr. 14, 1853, p. 191.
[46] Robinson, pp. 92, 93.
[47] Robinson, pp. 91, 92.
[48] Obituary for Ellen Marion (Lowrey) Ballou, *AUG*, May 22, 1929, p. 6.

Chapter IV

PIONEERING IN THE AMERICAN MIDWEST (1853-1856)

"The wide western field is opening, and there is a call for much labor there. . . . [Pray for] those who have to travel long journeys in a new country, and often meet with prejudice, and a cool reception, and error in many forms."[1]

Before John left for Michigan in the spring of 1853, he had some unfinished business to attend to in western New York. The opposition he met from his former Advent Christian friends weighed heavily on his heart. As he traveled westward, he stopped in several small towns near the New York-Pennsylvania border to hold meetings among them. For the most part, he "found their minds somewhat prejudiced" against Sabbatarian Adventism due to the negative articles they had read in Joseph Marsh's *Advent Harbinger*. Sometimes John spoke until almost midnight, seeking to persuade his listeners that Marsh was spreading "false reports." At one meeting, he wrote, "The Lord was with us in power by his Spirit, and we were made to rejoice." When he reached Ohio, however, the battle against error intensified, and he "had an earnest struggle for liberty."[2] Yet in the end, he declared, "we vanquished Satan there."

ADVENTISM IN THE MIDWEST

At times, defeating spiritual evils proved easier than conquering the obstacles to travel and communication in America's Midwest before the Civil War. During the 1850s Michigan, Wisconsin, Indiana, Illinois, and Ohio were all fairly new states. With scattered settlers and limited resources, the Midwest had few railroads or decent highways. Instead, across its many swamps and mud sloughs citizens built corduroy roads by laying down split logs,[3] filling the spaces between with dirt and stones to create bone-rattling rides in stage coaches and wagons.

Consequently, when John and his preaching partner Merritt Cornell reached Michigan, they either rode horseback or walked to scattered schoolhouses in rural villages and towns. To their delight, however, they found the local settlers deeply interested in spiritual matters. Following services in Locke, for example, John baptized 23 converts, and while in Hastings he baptized four more among "a class of intelligent minds." Equally successful meetings in Plymouth, Tyrone, Jackson, and Bedford led Loughborough to conclude that "the interest in the West is increasing, and the cause rising." He exhorted the new believers "to live humble, and watchful, and be ready to move forward as the message rises."[4]

Yet a spreading message did not always result in large congregations. When James and Ellen White joined the two men in May (their first trip west of Buffalo), Loughborough reported that the number of worshippers meeting at David Hewitt's home in Battle Creek—eight—equaled the number who escaped the biblical Flood in Noah's ark.[5] At that time, Hewitts' home was one of only 10 houses in a heavily wooded section of the village known as "Canaan." With the Whites in attendance, Loughborough preached several times at general meetings in Battle Creek, Jackson, and Bedford, prompting James White to praise him for his clarity and "edification of the brethren." At one meeting James began speaking on 2 Thessalonians 2 but nearly fainted, so Loughborough stepped to the podium and finished the sermon for him. Although he had never preached on that text, he believed that God provided both an outline and the words to speak.[6]

Outbreaks of fanaticism among several new converts, however, soon challenged the clarity of Loughborouh's message. In Tyrone some Adventists who claimed that God had bestowed the prophetic gift upon them began prophesying "whenever they felt an icy sensation on their backs." The Whites rebuked them as deluded souls. Another man claimed to have the gift of healing but had little love for lost souls. James White warned him that it was not God's Spirit who inspired his actions, and he accepted the rebuke. Other Pentecostal-like Adventists sought the gift of tongues, working themselves into frenzies by babbling gibberish.[7]

By her hasty temper and sharp tongue, Abigail Palmer even sparked a dissident movement. The wife of Jackson blacksmith Dan Palmer (Joseph Bates' first convert in the city in 1849), Abigail lived next door to a woman who considered Sabbatarian Adventists "Jews" in disguise. One day Abigail caught the neighbor throwing pails of dirty mop water onto the Palmer's freshly laundered sheets. Rushing outdoors, Abigail shouted, "You old *witch*! Your heart is so cold that butter won't melt on your tongue!" Unfortunately, the teenaged daughter of lay preacher Hiram Case, who had been visiting with Mrs. Palmer at the time, thought she had heard her hostess call the woman a "bitch" instead. When she reported this to her father, Case demanded that Abigail confess to employing the vile word and seek forgiveness. But Mrs. Palmer denied using that word.

Incensed, Case and his friend C. P. Russell summoned Mrs. Palmer before a church hearing at the Cyrenius Smith home in June 1853. James and Ellen White and Loughborough attended the trial. During a period of three days, Ellen had two visions concerning Abigail's case that led her to declare that although Mrs. Palmer needed to bridle her tongue and gain control of her temper, she had never said "bitch" as Case and Russell charged. White further admonished the two accusers for their "unmerciful course" toward Abigail. While Mrs. Palmer admitted using the word "witch" and asked for forgiveness, Case and Russell repudiated White's second vision. Instead, they withdrew from the Jackson church and formed a dissident movement called the *Messenger* Party (after their paper the *Messenger of Truth*). John, who read several copies, declared that their assertions against Mrs. Palmer and the Whites "had no foundation in truth." But when he asked the Whites for permission to refute the slanders in print, Ellen told him that such a course would please Satan and have a deleterious effect on the Sabbatarian Adventist cause. Instead, she counseled him to ignore their charges and soon the movement would disintegrate. Within a year, infighting had scattered the *Messenger* Party, while during that same period, the number of Sabbathkeepers in Michigan had doubled.[8]

Loughborough drew several conclusions from the embarrassing experiences. First, he had even more confidence in James and Ellen White's administrative abilities to lead a unified movement forward despite doctrinal challenges from within. Second, his admiration for Ellen White's prophetic ministry grew enormously as he saw her visionary predictions fulfilled during the course of the *Messenger* Party's demise. Third, he learned a lesson regarding the dangers of unbridled growth. Citing Christ's parable regarding the net that brings in "both good and bad fish," he concluded that evangelistic efforts in Michigan had increased church membership "too rapidly for a healthy growth." Somehow, the movement needed to combine the preaching of gospel truth with the imposition of gospel order.[9]

While on a preaching tour of central Michigan with James and Ellen White that spring, Loughborough witnessed another dramatic instance in which the Whites' leadership—and particularly Ellen's prophetic role—were vindicated. A certain married woman (Loughborough calls her "Sister A") who claimed to have holy flesh and the gift of tongues left her husband at home and traveled about the country with her lover (Mr. Pearsall) shouting, threatening, and babbling what she called "Highland Garlic Indian" in barns, homes, and schoolhouses. Although Mrs. White had never met the woman, she had apparently received a vision concerning the ménage à trois, and she asked Loughborough to make a copy of that vision. Days later while James White was preaching at Vergennes (with Ellen, John, and Merritt Cornell sitting behind him on the platform), the woman entered the meetinghouse with her lover and stepson. Turning to John, Ellen pointed at "Sister A" and told him exactly what she would say when Ellen confronted her with her sinful course. Sure enough, when Mrs. White charged the woman with adultery, she replied, "God knows my heart." After the meeting, however, her stepson and her lover confessed that Ellen's vision had been accurate. Furthermore, after the woman spoke in tongues before a local Indian who knew a number of tribal languages, the man exclaimed, "Very bad Indian that," and claimed that he could not understand a single word she said.[10]

Deeply impressed by what he had seen and heard, Loughborough concluded: "In this experience, and the developments that followed, our people in the state of Michigan had a most striking demonstration that the visions of Mrs. White were above human agency, and from a source that in no easy terms was in the line of rebuking sin wherever developing."[11]

LOUGHBOROUGH ORDAINED

If John Loughborough was impressed with the Whites' leadership abilities, they expressed growing confidence in his ministerial talents. Having proved his reliability under fire in New York, Ohio, and Michigan, John was now a candidate for ordination to the gospel ministry. Although in later years he claimed to have been the first Seventh-day Adventist minister to be ordained, the facts speak otherwise. In 1851, for example, George Washington Morse was ordained by George Holt. During three separate services in 1853, seven men (Horace Lawrence, J. N. Andrews, A. S. Hutchins, C. W. Sperry, E. P. Butler, Elon Everts, and Josiah Hart) also received ordination by the laying on of hands.[12]

Typically, such men (Ellen White was the only woman to receive ordination credentials in nineteenth-century Adventism) received a card or certificate to carry with them on their preaching tours. Signed by James White, Joseph Bates, and other "leading ministers" (in the 1850s), the card recommended the bearer "to the fellowship of the Lord's people everywhere."[13] When did J. N. Loughborough receive his first ministerial certificate? The question is not an easy one to answer. Near the end of his life, Loughborough claimed that he had been ordained at Grand Rapids, Michigan, by James White and Merritt E. Cornell in January 1853, and that thereafter, he carried a card signed by White and Bates "recommending [him] to the fellowship of the Lord's people everywhere."[14] In the flyleaf of his Bible in 1914, however, he asserted: "I was ordained at Grand Rapids, Mich. June 19, 1853."[15] A quarter century later, General Conference president William A. Spicer stated that he had seen Loughborough's 1853 ministerial credentials, signed by White and Bates, and that it stated: "Brother Loughborough, of Rochester, New York, is one whom we recommend to the brethren where he may travel."[16]

Two months after Loughborough died in April 1924, however, the official church paper, the *Review and Herald,* carried a summary of his life with several tributes regarding the impact of his worldwide ministry. This article gave the date of his ordination as June 18, 1854 in Grand Rapids, Michigan.[17] In his book *Founders of the Message*, church historian Everett Dick supports this latter date.[18] Because Loughborough's original ministerial certificate no longer exists, it may never be possible to establish with absolute certainty whether he was ordained in 1853 or 1854. However, the fact that Loughborough was not only preaching but also baptizing converts in the Midwest during the winter and spring of 1853 makes it probable that he was ordained in January of that year.

At a general meeting in Jackson, Michigan, in June, 1853, delegates voted to send Cornell and Loughborough on an extended preaching tour through Illinois, Wisconsin, and Indiana. Jackson church members supplied them with a horse and wagon and paid their expenses for the next three months. In addition to strengthening the faith of "the scattered [Sabbathkeeping] brethren," their summer circuit focused on converting Seventh Day Baptists. "We sought the Lord much in prayer, and his blessing was with us at every point," John declared.[19]

The preaching pair faced several challenges, however. Because of storms on Lake Michigan, their steamer took 20 hours to sail from Grand Haven, Michigan, to Chicago (then a town of 16,000 people). Disembarking, they found the "Windy City" engulfed in a foot of mud. Hitching horse to buggy, they plodded through "a mud prairie" for meetings in scattered northern Illinois hamlets. To stretch their food budget, the men picked quarts of wintergreen berries and strawberries along the way.[20]

Despite physical obstacles, the pair experienced spiritual victories everywhere they went. In Wisconsin they recruited John H. Waggoner, a Baptist newspaper editor, who despite his eye problems would become a leading Adventist evangelist during the next three decades. Likewise, their preaching converted J. M. Stephenson and D. P. Hall, two Advent Christians who joined Loughborough and Cornell for evangelistic meetings across the state. They lectured in schools, courthouses, churches, private homes, and barns. On one occasion they nailed their prophetic chart to a corn crib and preached in the adjacent shed. At one place their prayers led to the instant healing of a boy racked by malarial fever. Everywhere they went, people packed their meetings and baptisms followed.[21] Some former Millerites found their questions concerning the heavenly sanctuary, the investigative judgment, and the fulfillment of the 2300-day prophecy amply answered. Brother Hawkins of Sandusky, Ohio, sat in his rocking chair listening as John presented the third angel's message. Suddenly he shouted, "Glory to God! . . . I have found my moorings. It is all right and plain now, glory to God."[22]

At the end of the summer Loughborough and Cornell returned to Michigan physically exhausted but satisfied that they had laid a solid foundation in the Midwest. "The wide western field is opening, and there is a call for much labor there." "God is moving on the hearts of men in the West and preparing the way for the truth," Loughborough stated. "Let us cry mightily that laborers may be raised up to go forth into the harvest."[23] Refusing to rest, the men traveled to Plymouth and Detroit, where Loughborough preached for two days despite intense pain and sleepless nights from a badly swollen finger after hitting his hand on the carriage wheel. But when he reached the Orton's home in Rochester, New York, special prayers led by Drusilla Orton and Mrs. Woodhull brought instant relief.[24]

Loughborough's evangelistic efforts in western New York that fall brought further rewards. His grove meetings in Clarkson converted three families—the Lindsays, Lamsons, and Amadons—who would become pillars in the Adventist cause for generations to come. George Amadon, a horse driver on the Erie Canal, began setting type at the Review and Herald office in Rochester. He would follow the press to Battle Creek in 1855.[25] Reports to the *Review* regarding Loughborough's preaching abilities were uniformly positive. "My heart was cheered to see him," J. B. Frisbie wrote, and to hear him "tell of the prosperity of the cause [in the] West."[26]

Although the Loughborough's home remained in Rochester, John's mind was clearly focused on the progress of the Advent cause in the Midwest. So after only a few days visiting with Mary, he returned to Michigan. During the winter and spring of 1854, he and Joseph Bates pioneered the Adventist message across Ohio, despite snow, sleet, and rain that made the roads nearly impassable. In Milan he debated the Sabbath/Sunday question with a Methodist Episcopal minister who insisted on using the church Fathers (rather than the Bible) as his chief sources. Loughborough pointed out to him that the men "blow hot and cold" (disagreed) on a number of doctrinal issues, making them totally unreliable to settle the true day for worship.[27] Following months of backbreaking labor, however, Loughborough rejoiced that "the way opens here in every direction, and souls are inquiring after truth. Lord, speed the work, is my prayer."[28] That spring, when the number of Sabbatarian Adventists (40) in Ohio had more than doubled, church leaders described it as "a promising field."[29]

Delighted with the 22-year-old preacher's success, the Whites invited John to join them for preaching forays across southern Michigan. Their conferences at Sylvan and Locke brought together the largest gathering of Sabbatarian Adventists in the state up to that time. Witnessing the attendees' enthusiasm, James suggested that believers should regularly "come together something on the plan of a camp-meeting, bringing a trunk of provisions, and a few bedclothes."[30] Despite facing "Satan's mischief-makers," they succeeded in baptizing several converts, including a local pastor.[31]

The experience of traveling all around the Midwest with the Whites would leave an indelible imprint on John Loughborough's ministry and writings. Years later he recalled that "from 1853 to 1868 there was no minister in our ranks who traveled from State to State with Brother and Sister White more than myself." During such preaching tours he witnessed Ellen White in vision more than 40 times and heard her make dozens of important predictions concerning individuals and future events (Loughborough compiled a list of more than 100 of her fulfilled prophecies). As his future career would demonstrate, his apprenticeship shaped his approach to church order (as he faced apostasies), preaching (as he listened to the Whites, Bates, and Cornell), Ellen's prophetic role in the church (as he saw her in vision), and God's leading in the "rise and progress" (Loughborough's favorite theme) of the Adventist movement.[32]

ADVENTISTS' FIRST TENT MEETINGS

In May 1854 so many people crowded the schoolhouse in Locke, Michigan, that James White and his preaching team removed some of the windows so they could preach to the even larger crowd sitting in carriages and scattered across the lawn. Pressed by similar crowds at meetings in Washtenaw, Ingham, and Jackson counties, James suggested that in a year or so they should probably buy a tent. "Why not now?" Merritt Cornell asked. When the group stopped at C. S. Glover's home, Glover handed James $35, adding, "I'll venture that much on it." In Jackson, farmer Cyrenius Smith, blacksmith Dan Palmer, and broom-maker J. P. Kellogg each gave $35. In addition, Kellogg loaned White another $60 to equal the expected cost of $200.[33]

Although pitching tents for revivals and evangelistic meetings would become standard procedure among Adventists for 150 years, during the 1850s only circuses, animal menageries, and shows of various types featured tents. Perhaps because the Millerites, whose predictions concerning the end of the world in 1843-1844 had failed to materialize, had used a "Great Tent," America's mainstream denominations avoided them as something from a disreputable past.[34]

Indeed, finding someone who could make a tent large enough for public meetings presented a formidable obstacle in itself. Merritt Cornell, learning that some Advent Christians in Detroit had tried tent meetings a year before and failed, decided to go there and purchase their tent. When he arrived, however, he discovered that they had already sold it. So he took the train to Rochester, New York, and found the perfect tent at the shop of Advent Christian E. C. Williams. Almost new, the 60-foot circular cotton tent had briefly been pitched on the New York State Fairgrounds. Williams sold it to Cornell for $160, tossing in a 15-foot banner with the motto "What Is Truth?" With the remaining $40 Cornell purchased benches, lamps, and other paraphernalia needed for holding meetings.[35]

But when Loughborough and Cornell pitched this large tent on a vacant lot at the corner of Tompkins and Van Buren Streets near the Hewitt home in Battle Creek that June, they had no assurance that anyone would show up for their scheduled three days of meetings. They asked *Review* readers to pray for them, "for without [God] our efforts will be in vain."[36] To their astonishment, God's blessing and John's booming voice (that reportedly could be heard nearly half a mile away) filled the tent on the first night and drew 1,000 listeners for Sunday services. Throughout the weekend, the two men alternated in speaking on a variety of topics, with Loughborough focusing on Bible prophecies.[37] Although John did not know it at the time, some of the spiritual seed sown at this first tent series would bear fruit decades later in the lives of several who heard him preach. At his evangelistic meetings in Reno, Nevada, in 1878, two individuals who had heard him preach in Battle Creek took their stand for Adventism. Another woman who had given no serious thought to religion was converted in 1914 when at the outbreak of World War I she recalled the sermons on end-time prophecy that Loughborough had given 60 years before.[38]

Encouraged by the public support at the Battle Creek meetings, Loughborough and Cornell set up their tent in groves or on vacant lots in Grand Rapids, Jackson, Delhi, and Rochester for further weekend services that summer. Uncertain whether they could sustain public interest for more than a week, the men crafted their sermons to cover the essential Adventist doctrines in as short a time as possible so that they could move the tent to a new location. Years later Sands Lane commented: "We used to run the tents . . . that is, we kept them on the run." Rather than present "all the minutiae of the truth," they "preached the thing, clear, straight, plain and direct."[39] Moreover, with no reliable financial support either from the public or fellow Adventists, Loughborough and Cornell paid their expenses (between $15 and $25 per series) by helping farmers harvest their wheat and hay four days a week so that they could preach on the weekends. For John it must have been exhausting labor.[40]

Recognizing the team's desperate need for money, James White made a radical suggestion: Why not at the next weekend meetings sell some of the tracts and pamphlets published by the Review and Herald press in Rochester? Given the prevailing public prejudice against Millerites, most Advent Christian and Sabbatarian Adventist preachers had counted themselves lucky if they succeeded in *giving* tracts away. No one had ever considered *selling* them. Indeed, some believers felt that after 10 years of getting them free, the public would refuse to pay cash for them now. But Loughborough agreed to give the plan a trial run at his tent meetings in Shelby. Using his carpentry skills, he built a speaker's stand wide enough to display one copy of every Sabbatarian Adventist publication available—all 35 cents' worth of them.[41] John's two-week debate with Elder Russell, a local Methodist pastor, over the change of Sabbath to Sunday drew 246 wagonloads of listeners. To the amazement of Adventists everywhere, during the course of three Sundays that July, Loughborough and Cornell sold $50 worth of publications (equivalent to 143 complete sets at 35 cents each). Needless to say, their success inspired other preachers to follow their example, and soon, selling Adventist literature at evangelistic meetings became routine.[42]

Although pleased with the team's phenomenal sales success, Ellen White advised that if they would stay in one place longer, their spiritual success would also be greater. Following the pattern set by ex-sea captain Joseph Bates, however, most Adventist evangelists in the 1850s favored shorter series of meetings so that they could cover more ground geographically. For example, during the summer of 1854, Loughborough and Cornell pitched their tent 14 times in 11 different places for weekend services. Seeing tent meetings as the entering wedge for truth, they did not know how to plan daily lectures for an entire week so as to make a thorough effort rather than simply "scattering the seed" and allowing the Holy Spirit to make it grow in the hearts of listeners. While weekend meetings brought a buffet of new doctrines to the public's attention, they did not provide sufficient time for following up the preacher's efforts with Bible studies.

So Mrs. White counseled the two men to spend between one to six weeks nurturing their converts before moving to new locations. Following her advice brought amazing results as the number of converts grew exponentially. Then Robert Andrews, a recent Scottish convert, became their first tent master in 1855, relieving them of many physical burdens.[43]

Following a two-week series of meetings with J. B. Frisbie (a new preacher converted by Bates the year before) in Paw Paw and Hastings, Loughborough returned to Battle Creek, his mind troubled. He was convinced that his baptism at age 17 into the Advent Christian Church had been invalid. As a Sundaykeeper, he had been "treading underfoot the Sabbath of the fourth commandment." "Unconsciously I was [living] in sin, when I was buried [immersed]" and therefore could not be "dead to sin." Citing Leviticus 5:5 (one should confess sin as soon as it is discovered) and Romans 7:9 (the commandment law brings conviction of sin), John decided that rebaptism was the "proper thing to do." Following Christ's example, his preaching partner M. E. Cornell immersed him in the Kalamazoo River. The twice-born preacher had now been twice baptized as well.[44]

With renewed energy, he and Cornell commenced meetings in Delhi, Michigan, where "the intelligent portion" of residents soon filled the tent and mobbed his bookstand, purchasing more than $12 worth of tracts. One new convert exclaimed that they had "preached the truth with a commendable zeal, and in all candor" had presented "the fullness of the gospel."[45] Loughborough asked *Review* readers to pray for them "that we may be so guided that an effectual blow may be struck for the cause in Michigan." He concluded by reminding believers that the "day of trouble is near."[46]

JOHN AND MARY'S "TIME OF TROUBLE"

That "day of trouble" became deeply personal when John received news that his beloved grandfather and role model, the Reverend Nathan Loofborough, had died at age 87. Rushing to Victor, New York, John joined his mother, brothers William and Eber, and sisters Minerva Jane and Diantha for the funeral. Two months later when Nathan's will was read, John learned that his grandfather had left him a substantial amount of money and land in East Bloomfield.[47] The Eastern General Conference of Nathan's beloved Methodist Episcopal Church mourned his passing as well, noting that "Father Loofborough" had for half a century been "a bright and shining light" as an exhorter, steward, and spiritual leader, filling his offices "with a zeal and integrity and a devotion . . . equaled by few, and surpassed by none." His special ministry had included "confirming the wavering, admonishing the back-sliding, encouraging the fainting, and comforting all by earnest exhortation, by a godly conversation, and above all, by an example known and read by all." Conference officials urged members to "cherish his memory by cultivating his virtues, his meekness, humility, charity, and unaffected piety . . . following him as he followed Christ."[48]

While still grieving his grandfather's passing, John received yet another surprise: his mother told him that, after living as a widow for 15 years, she had decided to remarry. With two teenagers—Eber (17) and Diantha (15)—to raise, Minerva (now 53) consented to wed Andrew Rowley, a trustee and inspector of Victor's Methodist Episcopal Church. Rowley, a widower whose wife, Sarah, had recently died, leaving him with a teenage boy and an infant, needed a wife. Sometime in 1855 the two families merged.[49] The fact that John never mentions his mother's remarriage anywhere in his private letters or diaries may signify his disapproval of the match. At any rate, not until after Andrew Rowley's death in 1877 and Minerva's conversion to Seventh-day Adventism does her name reappear in his private correspondence.[50]

Deciding that family business required him to remain a while in New York, John returned to Rochester, which became his home base for preaching and bookselling forays around the Finger Lakes region for the next nine months.[51] No doubt Mary (now 22) was delighted to welcome her husband (whom she seldom saw for months at a time) home again. In fact, evidence indicates that she tried to charm, tease, and argue with him, hoping to persuade him never to return to the Midwest again.

But Ellen White believed that God had called John to do a special work in the West. In a letter to Mary sometime during the winter of 1854-1855, Ellen told her that Michigan had many "hungry sheep" that must be fed the spiritual food John had to offer them. Because his ministry would present her husband with many trials and burdens, Mary must be ready to show him sympathy, comfort, and encouragement. Then came the rebuke: instead of sustaining John with her prayers and compliments, Mary had been criticizing, complaining, and laying burdens on him. Her harsh words, Ellen asserted, "cause him deep sorrow." Rather than devoting her time to her friends, she should listen to his problems, sympathize with his sorrows, and comfort the one who "does still fondly love you."

Probing deeper into the cause of Mary's malaise, Mrs. White identified several spiritual and emotional factors Mary needed to adjust in her life. First, she should refocus her attention on heavenly things rather than earthly (materialistic) comforts. Second, she must "cut loose from relatives and acquaintances" (probably Advent Christians) whom she was trying to please too much. Third, she was not yet fully converted. "[You need to] have your eye single to the glory of God, and serve him with your *whole heart,*" Mrs. White admonished. "I saw that you were not half given up to God, not half consecrated to Him. Your will was not swallowed up in the will of God." Fourth, she needed to draw closer to John "and love him better than anyone on earth, and make his wishes your wishes." Then "you can live in harmony and happiness." Finally, she should relinquish her sewing work and partner with John in gospel ministry, and "cheer, encourage, and hold him up in your prayers." If Mary followed her advice, Mrs. White promised, "God will notice it and will reward you."[52]

Apparently Ellen White's boldness did not offend John and Mary. Instead, they saw the letter as a testimony from God providing them spiritual guidance. If anything, Ellen's frankness merely served to deepen their friendship. In another letter to the Loughboroughs, she begged them to pray for her. "I need your prayers," she confessed. She and James also cherished their letters. "Write us often," she requested. From time to time, the Whites lent their horse old Charley and their wagon to help the Loughboroughs transport their household goods.[53]

LOUGHBOROUGH'S ARTICLES AND TRACTS

J. N. Loughborough's articles began to appear in the *Advent Review and Sabbath Herald* barely one year after his conversion to Sabbatarian Adventism in the fall of 1852. Entitled "A Few Reasons Why We Are Not Under the Law," his first article set the pattern that John would follow for the rest of his life. He always began by quoting a Bible text (in this case Romans 6:14), then stated his argument (Christ's blood frees us from the law's condemnation). In the 1850s he, like other Adventist pioneers, quoted texts from the Old Testament, the New Testament, and even the

Apocryphal books of the Bible to support their theological points. While Loughborough's articles (like most in the early *Reviews*) read like Bible studies, they also show his familiarity with a wide range of sources. Frequently he cites Jewish, Methodist, Roman Catholic, and other religious authorities. He draws his explanations, anecdotes, and illustrations from current newspapers, poems, encyclopedias, and books on philosophy, history, geography and science. Occasionally, Loughborough quotes pagan authors (Ovid, Plato) and American writers (such as Thomas Paine). Since his preaching lifestyle required him to pack light and travel on foot or by horseback, he obviously could not have carried all those sources with him. Given the scarcity of libraries across the Midwest at the time, one might conclude that Loughborough consulted his own book collection at home or carried most of the information in his head. Consequently, although he may never have gone beyond the eighth grade, J. N. Loughborough would demonstrate throughout his life a breadth of knowledge that he could only have acquired from reading widely.[54]

Despite the fact that Loughborough cannot be considered a first-rate scholar like his contemporaries J. N. Andrews and Uriah Smith, he did make a few theological contributions to the corpus of Adventist doctrine in the 1850s. In 1854 *Review* editor James White published Loughborough's article linking the first angel's message to the pre-Advent judgment, telling readers that "it meets inquiries which have been presented to us."[55] In tandem with Bates, White, and Smith, Loughborough helped to develop the concept of an "investigative judgment" to explain the reason for the delay in Christ's second coming after October 22, 1844. His 1854 article also connected the cleansing of the sanctuary with the judgment-hour message of Revelation 14:6, 7.[56]

John's lifelong fascination with history and prophecy manifested itself in 1854 with another series of *Review* articles concerning the two-horned beast of Daniel 7 and Revelation 13. The bizarre creature, he asserted, was not pagan Rome, Papal Rome, or Napoleon Bonaparte (as other commentators believed), but the United States of America. Although at its founding it had been innocent like a lamb, it had since become a fire-breathing dragon, hypocritically condoning slavery, lynching, and Sunday blue laws in several states. In writing his articles, he relied heavily on contemporary newspapers, statistical reports, the U.S. Constitution, and the works of

American and French writers.[57] In 1857 Loughborough's articles appeared in pamphlet form as *The Two-horned Beast of Rev. XIII: A Symbol of the United States.* James White advertised the three-cent tract as "an excellent work for circulation."[58]

As a former Advent Christian, John had long been interested in the debate over the immortality of the soul. His commitment to conditional immortality found expression in his longest series of *Review* articles, one that ran from September through December 1855. The breadth of his research for this series is evident in his frequent citations not only to the Bible and a host of Christian writers, but also to Greek and Roman sources, modern philosophers, contemporary poets and historical authors, and even propagandists such as Thomas Paine (considered disreputable by most Victorians). While the style of his theological articles is somewhat dry, John introduces imaginary dialogues between Universalists and Spiritualists, question-and-answer catechism format, debating techniques, and direct appeals to the reader's emotions to enhance interest in his subject matter. His research led him to conclude that while humans are mortal at birth and remain asleep in the grave at death, they can receive immortality at the second coming of Christ.[59] The following year the Review and Herald published the articles as a book entitled *An Examination of the Scripture Testimony Concerning Man's Present Condition and His Future Reward or Punishment.*[60]

Like most other writers for the *Review* in the 1850s, Loughborough chose theological topics that he could argue convincingly in the form of Bible studies or debates. One exception was his article "Ye Are the Light of the World," which appeared in May 1854. Devotional in nature, it urged readers to let their "light shine that God's name may be glorified and his cause advanced." Rather than "partake of the spirit and merry laugh of the giddy," Adventists in this "solemn time" should "be more active in bending every energy of our being to the advancement of the cause of truth."[61]

During the winter and spring of 1855 Loughborough and his preaching partner Samuel Rhodes let their gospel lights shine all across upstate New York from Oswego in the east to Buffalo in the west. Soon a growing cadre of Adventist believers raised the money to purchase three more evangelistic tents from E. C. Williams in Rochester—one for New York, another for Wisconsin, and a third for Vermont.[62] That summer and fall Loughborough joined W. S. Ingraham as coevangelist and R. F. Cottrell as tent-master, and together they "ran the tent" all across New York and Pennsylvania. As the team attempted to ford a swollen stream, the swift current swept their wagon and the White's horse Old Charley downstream. John (who never learned to swim) held onto the buckboard for dear life, praying for deliverance. When the wagon hit a rock and stopped, John pleaded, "Charley, you must get me out of this!" After casting "a pitiful glance" toward the desperate man, the horse succeeded in pulling the wagon from the river as 20 onlookers cheered. For all their arduous labor, the two evangelists received about $4 a week and their tent-master about $3 a week from freewill donations of cash and produce.[63]

But the "little preacher" also endured much censure for "following the fashions of the day" by sporting a mustache and goatee. When she learned of the teasing, Ellen White sprang to his defense. "Brother Loughborough does not shave at all," she stated. "He lets all the beard grow that the Lord has given him. And I suppose when the Lord gives him any more he will let that grow, too." His detractors expressed themselves satisfied with this explanation. Perhaps fearing they might lose old Charley on another of Loughborough's preaching tours, James White also started a fund in the *Review* to buy John a horse of his own.[64]

Despite numerous hardships, Loughborough felt that his evangelistic tour had been a great success. In a letter to Mr. Dodge (who was looking after Mary and the children in Rochester), John declared, "The blessing of the Lord has been with me, and I have had some excellent times in striving to speak the word of truth to the people. I think the cause is rising somewhat in central New York."[65] His preaching efforts had also strengthened John's faith, for he saw the third angel's message as a godsend "to purify us, wean us from the world, prepare us to work for him in the spread of his truth, and fit us for his heavenly kingdom." Alluding to Bunyan's *Pilgrim's Progress*, he resolved that with God's help, he would march "through the enchanted ground" and "keep free from the drowsy spirit of darkness."[66]

Loughborough especially faced a "spirit of darkness" from the *Messenger* Party. Its leaders in Wisconsin—J. M. Stephenson and D. P. Hall—purloined the new tent financed by Sabbathkeeping Adventists and published their paper *Messenger of Truth*. While John preached in Oswego, New York, he faced several of its adherents who taught "age-to-come" doctrines (temporal millennium, restoration of the Jews to Palestine, etc.), accused James White of mismanaging funds, attacked Ellen White's visions, and generally tried to destroy the veracity of the Sabbatarian Adventist message. Although Ellen called them "a lying and corrupt people" and compared their personal vendettas to the "biting of an adder," she counseled Loughborough not to answer their slanders. Instead, she said, he should let them alone, and they would destroy themselves. Within months, most of them had abandoned the seventh-day Sabbath, thereby losing their influence with Sabbatarian Adventists. According to Loughborough's recollections 60 years later, Stephenson divorced his wife, married a much younger woman, and later died an imbecile in a poorhouse. Hall, who tried selling real estate, went bankrupt and likewise lost his mental faculties, suffering under the delusion that if he left his house, the sky would fall on him.[67]

After combating this dissident group in New York, John returned to Michigan that summer with a sense of relief. He arrived just in time to help dedicate the first Adventist meetinghouse erected in Battle Creek. From 1852 to 1855 Sabbathkeepers had worshipped in the home of David Hewitt and his wife, but their numbers had outgrown the couple's parlor, so the believers had built a wooden chapel 18' x 24' on the corner of Cass and Van Buren streets. Here during the next three years Loughborough would preach many sermons, and Ellen White would have several visions.[68]

MOVE TO WAUKON, IOWA

During the first half of 1856, however, John (who had recently been appointed treasurer of the New York tent fund) returned to the Empire State for yet another extended evangelistic tour. Joining his preaching partners W. S. Ingraham and R. F. Cottrell, Loughborough once again "ran the tent" all over western New York and northern Pennsylvania. His modest comment that "our congregations were fair" contradicts the reality that at several meetings, between 400 and 700 listeners crowded their tent. Despite persistent competition from nearby Methodist meetings, the hay and wheat harvest, and inclement weather, sometimes attendance even exceeded 1,000.[69] Speaking to Adventists who for the past decade had observed the Sabbath from 6:00 p.m. Friday evening to 6:00 p.m. Saturday evening, Loughborough explained the biblical way of keeping the seventh day from sundown Friday evening to sundown Saturday evening. One woman wrote to the *Review* expressing gratitude for John's preaching and especially for the "light on the commencement of the Sabbath," adding, "I believe it is true."[70]

John and Mary Loughborough (who had kept the Sabbath according to this sunset plan since November 1855) likewise believed with all their hearts that the Sabbatarian Adventist message was true. But preaching it entailed many sacrifices, not the least of which was frequent separation from each other. To finance his preaching, John often worked four days a week helping farmers harvest their wheat, oats, and hay. But such backbreaking labor paid only a dollar a day. His "wages" as an evangelist consisted of whatever freewill offerings of cash, fruit, vegetables, or meat people gave him. By the summer of 1856, Mary, accustomed to John's previously steady income from selling sash locks, became despondent at their poverty. "This is too much," she exclaimed; "we can't live any longer in this way." John agreed with her that their "financially embarrassing circumstances" demanded a new plan of action. Since James White was encouraging preachers to take the third angel's message to Iowa, perhaps a brighter future awaited them there where land was cheap, the soil rich, and farming prospects bright.[71]

Already, six New England and New York families whose farms had failed and whose money had run out, had moved to Waukon in northeastern Iowa.[72] So that October the Ortons and Loughboroughs, "being somewhat discouraged as to finances" (as John phrased it), packed all their belongings into two lumber wagons and traveled to Buffalo, where they caught a steamship to Detroit and hopped aboard a freight train to Chicago. During the next two weeks they crossed Illinois. When they finally joined the tiny group of 30 Adventists at Waukon, John decided he could earn a living as a carpenter and cabinetmaker and preach to the scattered farmers on the weekends. However, as he and Hosea Mead were working on a storefront on Christmas Eve, something happened that changed the course of John's life.[73]

---

[1] *RH*, July 7, 1853, p. 32.
[2] *RH*, June 9, 1853, p. 15.
[3] M. Ellsworth Olsen, *A History of the Origin and Progress of Seventh-day Adventists*

(Washington, D.C.: Review and Herald Pub. Assn., 1925), p. 226.

[4] *RH,* June 9, 1853, pp. 15, 16; "Lamson, David Henry" and "Lamson, Drusilla Orton," *Ellen G. White Encyclopedia* (Hagerstown, Md.: Review and Herald Pub. Assn., 2013), pp. 445, 446.

[5] *ST*, Nov. 14, 1878, p. 344; *RH*, May 8, 1879, p. 145.

[6] *RH*, Sept. 1, 1868, p. 162; *PUR*, Nov. 18, 1909, pp. 1, 2; James White, quoted in Robinson, *Lighter of Gospel Fires,* p. 82.

[7] *PUR*, Oct. 28, 1909, pp. 1, 2.

[8] *RH,* July 22, 1884, pp. 472, 473; *PUR*, Nov. 4, 1909, pp. 1, 2; *PUR*, Nov. 11, 1909, pp. 1, 2; "*Messenger* Party," *Ellen G. White Encyclopedia*, pp. 974-976.

[9] JNL, *Rise and Progress*, pp. 194, 195.

[10] *RH,* May 6, 1884, pp. 299, 300; *RH,* June 10, 1884, pp. 378, 379; *PUR,* Nov. 25, 1909, pp. 1, 2; *PUR,* Dec. 23, 1909, p. 1; *PUR,* Dec. 30, 1909, pp. 1, 2. Although all of the versions of this remarkable story agree on the main points, some of the details get embellished during the 25 years in which John tells it. For example, the Indian in the story knew 12 tribal languages in the 1884 version but 17 in the 1909 version.

[11] *PUR*, Dec. 30, 1909, pp. 1, 2.

[12] Andrew G. Mustard, *James White and Seventh-day Adventist Organization: Historical Development, 1844-1881* (Berrien Springs, Mich.: Andrews University Press, 1987), p. 125. Since Loughborough was not yet a part of the Sabbatarian Adventist movement in 1851 when Morse received ordination, he apparently did not know this fact. But as he joined the movement in 1852, he could have known about the seven men ordained in 1853. This raises certain questions regarding Loughborough's historical reliability that we will treat in greater detail in chapters 14 and 18.

[13] JNL, *The Church*, p. 100; A. Spalding, *Origin and History*, vol. 1, p. 295.

[14] *PUR*, Apr. 14, 1910, p. 2; see also G. Knight, *Lest We Forget*, p. 144.

[15] JNL, diary (1914).

[16] W. A. Spicer, quoted in the *Atlantic Union Conference Record*, Sept. 2, 1940, p. 2, and in the *RH*, June 6, 1940, p. 9.

[17] *RH*, June 19, 1924, p. 17.

[18] Everett D. Dick, *Founders of the Message* (Washington, D.C.: Review and Herald Pub. Assn., 1938), p. 272.

[19] *RH,* Oct. 21, 1884, pp. 664, 665; *Rise and Progress*, pp. 191, 192.

[20] *RH*, May 12, 1891, p. 300; *PUR*, Jan. 6, 1910, pp. 1, 2.

[21] *PUR*, Jan. 13, 1910, pp. 1, 2; *PUR*, Feb. 17, 1910, pp. 9, 10.

[22] Brother Hawkins, quoted in JNL, *The Great Second Advent Movement*, p. 530; *RH,* Sept. 20, 1853, p. 87.

[23] *RH*, July 7, 1853, p. 32; *RH*, Sept. 20, 1853, p. 87.

[24] *PUR*, Mar. 3, 1910, pp. 1, 2.

[25] *RH,* Jan. 27, 1885, pp. 57, 58; *PUR*, Mar. 10, 1910, pp. 2, 3; *RH*, Aug. 2, 1923, p. 6; "Amadon, George W. and Martha," *Ellen G. White Encyclopedia*, p. 291.

[26] J. B. Frisbie, quoted in *RH,* Oct. 18, 1853, p. 119; *RH*, Nov. 29, 1853, p. 167.

[27] *RH*, Apr. 11, 1854, p. 94; Joseph Bates, quoted in *RH,* Apr. 26, 1854, p. 111.

[28] *RH*, Apr. 11, 1854, p. 94.

[29] *RH*, May 23, 1854, p. 141.

[30] JSW, quoted in *RH*, May 2, 1854, p. 120; *RH*, May 23, 1854, p. 142. This may indeed be the very first suggestion that Adventists should hold camp meetings, yet 12 years would pass before SDAs held their first camp meeting at Pilot Grove, Iowa, in 1866.

[31] A. C. Morton, quoted in *RH*, Aug. 22, 1854, pp. 14, 15.

[32] DF 230 (CAR), p. 27; JNL, *The Great Second Advent Movement*, p. 488.

[33] *PUR*, Mar. 24, 1910, pp. 5, 6; Arthur W. Spalding, *Origin and History of Seventh-day Adventists* (Washington, D.C.: Review and Herald Pub. Assn., 1962), vol. 2, pp. 7, 8.

[34] JNL, *The Great Second Advent Movement*, p. 327.

[35] *RH*, May 8, 1879, p. 145; *PUR*, Apr. 14, 1910, p. 2.

[36] *RH*, May 30, 1854, p. 152; *RH*, July 4, 1854, p. 174; Emmett K. Vande Vere, *The Wisdom Seekers* (Nashville: Southern Pub. Assn., 1972), p. 13.

[37] *RH*, July 4, 1854, p. 173; JNL, *The Great Second Advent Movement*, p. 562; *PUR*, Apr. 14, 1910, pp. 2, 3.

[38] *RH*, May 8, 1879, p. 145; *Field Tidings*, Dec. 2, 1914, p. 5.

[39] *GCB* (1899), pp. 169, 170; *PUR*, Apr. 14, 1910, pp. 2, 3.

[40] *PUR*, Apr. 14, 1910, p. 3; Dick, p. 274.

[41] *PUR*, Apr. 21, 1910, pp. 2, 3; *RH*, Nov. 2, 1911, p. 15; JNL to Howard May, Mar. 26, 1919, CAR; *Field Tidings*, May 17, 1916, p. 1. The tracts then available included J. N. Andrews' pamphlet on the sanctuary (10 cents), Loughborough's pamphlet on the United States in Bible prophecy (10 cents), and three of Andrews' tracts on Sabbath-Sunday issues (at five cents each).

[42] *PUR*, Apr. 21, 1910, pp. 2, 3. Coincidentally, the meetings at Shelby, Michigan, witnessed the conversion of several members of the Warren family, including both grandfathers of Luther Warren, the future General Conference MV and youth leader. All became SDA pastors.

[43] *RH*, Feb. 24, 1885, p. 122; Spalding, *Origin and History*, vol. 2, p. 8; "Andrews, Robert Frederick," *Ellen G. White Encyclopedia*, p. 296.

[44] *PUR*, Apr. 28, 1910, p. 1.

[45] Manning Curry, quoted in *RH*, Aug. 1, 1854, p. 204.

[46] *RH*, July 11, 1854, pp. 180, 181.

[47] Ontario County Surrogate Court Records, file 87, reel 30-15, book L, pp. 58, 59; book H, p. 423; book J, p. 173.

[48] Four Resolutions of the Eastern General Conference, Jan. 20, 1855, quoted in the *Northern Christian Advocate* (Auburn, New York), 1855, p. 28.

[49] New York Census (1855); Apr. 9, 1850, and Apr. 8, 1854, minutes of the Victor, New York, Methodist Episcopal Church; www.ancestry.com (accessed Aug. 11, 2009).

[50] In fact, not even when Elder Loughborough wrote his mother's obituary for the *Review* (Oct. 30, 1894, p. 15) did he mention the marriage to her second husband. As for Minerva's conversion to Seventh-day Adventism, he states only that it occurred "in her last days" while living with her daughter Minerva Jane Chapman in Battle Creek, Michigan.

[51] *RH*, Oct. 3, 1854, p. 64; *RH*, Oct. 10, 1854, p. 72; *RH*, Dec. 12, 1854, p. 136; *RH*, Dec. 19, 1854, p. 144; *RH*, Jan. 9, 1855, p. 158; *RH*, Jan. 23, 1855, p. 168; *RH*, May 22, 1855, p. 232; *RH*, May 29, 1855, p. 240.

[52] EGW to Mary Loughborough, winter 1854, letter 6, 1854, CAR.

[53] EGW to John and Mary Loughborough, Sept. 7, 1854, letter 7, 1854, CAR.

[54] See, for example, JNL's articles in the *RH*, Oct. 11, 1853, p. 108 ("A Few Reasons We Are Not Under the Law"); his series "The Two-horned Beast," *RH*, Mar. 21, 1854, pp. 65-67 and Mar. 28, 1854, pp. 73-75, 79; "Ye Are the Light of the World," *RH*, May 23, 1854, pp. 140, 141; his series "Is the Soul Immmortal?" *RH*, Sept. 4, 1855, pp. 33-36; Sept. 18, 1855, pp. 41-43; Oct. 2, 1855, pp. 49-52; Oct. 16, 1855, pp. 57-60; Oct. 30, 1855, pp. 65-68; Dec. 4, 1855, pp. 73-75; Dec. 11, 1855, pp. 81-83; Dec. 18, 1855, pp. 89-91; Dec. 27, 1855, pp. 97-100.

[55] *RH*, Feb. 14, 1854, p. 29, explicated by George Knight in *A Search for Identity: The Development of Seventh-day Adventist Beliefs* (Hagerstown, Md.: Review and Herald Pub. Assn., 2000), p. 81.

[56] Malcolm Bull and Keith Lockhart, *Seeking a Sanctuary: Seventh-day Adventism and the American Dream*, second. ed. (Bloomington and Indianapolis: Indiana University Press, 2007), p. 76; *RH*, Oct. 23, 1975, pp. 10, 11.

[57] *RH,* Mar. 21, 1854, pp. 65-67; *RH*, Mar. 28, 1854, pp. 73-75, 79. See also Bull and Lockhart, p. 59; Douglas Morgan, *Adventism and the American Republic: The Public Involvement of a Major Apocalyptic Movement* (Knoxville: The University of Tennessee Press, 2001), pp. 18, 19; Reinder Bruinsma, *Seventh-day Adventist Attitudes Toward Roman Catholicism, 1844-1965* (Berrien Springs, Mich.: Andrews University Press, 1994), pp. 94, 95.

[58] *RH*, Mar. 28, 1854, p. 80; JNL, *The Two-horned Beast of Rev. XIII: A Symbol of the United States* (Battle Creek, Mich.: Review and Herald Office, 1857). Originally a 52-page pamphlet in 1854, Loughborough revised and expanded it into an 80-page booklet during the summer of 1856. "For the labor of writing this work I received, as pay, the thanks of those who read it," he wrote in *Rise and Progress*, p. 212.

[59] *RH*, Sept. 4, 1855, pp. 33-36; *RH,* Sept. 18, 1855, pp. 41-43; *RH,* Oct. 2, 1855, pp. 49-52; *RH,* Oct. 16, 1855, pp. 57-60; *RH,* Oct. 30, 1855, pp. 65-68; *RH,* Dec. 4, 1855, pp. 73-75; *RH,* Dec. 11, 1855, pp. 81-83; *RH,* Dec. 18, 1855, pp. 89-91; *RH,* Dec. 27, 1855, pp. 97-100.

[60] See advertisement in *RH*, Dec. 4, 1855, p. 79; JNL, *An Examination of the Scripture Testimony Concerning Man's Present Condition and His Future Reward or Punishment* (Rochester, N.Y.: Advent Review Office, 1855). This booklet of 196 pages sold for 20 cents.

[61] *RH*, May 23, 1854, pp. 140, 141.

[62] *RH*, Mar. 3. 1885, pp. 137, 138; *PUR*, June 30, 1910, pp. 1, 2; *PUR*, July 7, 1910, pp. 1, 2.

[63] *PUR*, June 30, 1910, p. 2; *PUR*, July 7, 1910, p. 1; *RH*, Mar. 24, 1885, pp. 186, 187; JNL, *Rise and Progress,* p. 208.

[64] EGW, quoted in *PUR*, Feb. 16, 1911, p. 1; *RH*, July 24, 1855, p. 16.

[65] JNL to Bro. Dodge, 1855, microfilm 52, CAR.

[66] *RH*, July 24, 1855, p. 13.

[67] For a summary of the *Messenger* Party's demise, see *RH*, Dec. 26, 1854, p. 151; *PUR*, May 5, 1910, pp. 1, 2; *PUR*, May 12, 1910, p. 1; JNL, *The Great Second Advent Movement*, pp. 331-333.

[68] JNL, "The First Four Battle Creek Seventh-day Adventist Meeting-Houses," *Missionary Magazine* 13, nos. 5-8 (May-August 1901): 206-208; diary, Sept. 30, 1878.

[69] *RH*, Feb. 28, 1856, pp. 174-176; *RH,* May 8, 1856, p. 32; *RH*, May 29, 1856, p. 48; *RH*, Aug. 21, 1856, p. 128; *RH*, Aug. 28, 1856, pp. 133, 136.

[70] Sr. Drew, quoted in *RH*, Jan. 24, 1856, p. 135.

[71] *RH*, Mar. 16, 1886, pp. 168, 169; JNL, *Rise and Progress*, p. 208; A. Spalding, *Origin and History*, vol. 1, p. 282; Dick, pp. 274-277, 280.

[72] *RH*, Jan. 23, 1936, pp. 8, 9. They included the Edward Andrews and Cyprian Stevens families of Paris, Maine, as well as the Butlers, Lindseys, Meads, Hazeltines, and Lamsons. Most built log cabins for themselves and began farming.

[73] *RH*, Jan. 15, 1857, p. 84; *RH*, Mar. 16, 1886, p. 169; JNL, *Rise and Progress*, p. 208.

CHAPTER V

FAMILY TRIUMPHS AND TRAGEDIES (1856-1859)

"We are proclaiming Christ's second advent. Our walk should be sober; our conversation upon Jesus, upon the truth; and we should glory in the cross of Christ."[1]

Although later in his life J. N. Loughborough faced the accusation that he "once left the [gospel] work, and gave up preaching the message," he consistently denied the charge. He and Mary went to northeastern Iowa in 1856, he explained, because they had "grown discouraged as to finances"; because James White and J. N. Andrews urged him to go; and because he hoped to preach part-time among the settlers there. But when the Loughboroughs arrived in Iowa, they discovered that Waukon was surrounded by "raw prairie, with here and there a house, and these a great distance apart from each other." Consequently, as John put it, "the prospects of preaching . . . were rather dubious."[2] Instead, he and Hosea Mead took up cabinet making, carpentry, and construction work that fall to support their families. Loughborough viewed his decision "as a waiting position until further providence should indicate what I must do."[3]

REVIVAL IN WAUKON, IOWA

In mid-November the 30 Adventists in Waukon witnessed a stunning celestial phenomenon that they regarded as a providential sign. One morning a brilliant white light in the shape of a Maltese cross with rainbows at the edges of its four equal arms appeared in the sky. The iridescent cross shone for two whole days before disappearing. John (who had been fascinated with astronomy since childhood) interpreted it as a fulfillment of Joel 2:30 (God will work wonders in the sky) and Luke 21:11, 25 (strange and frightening things will appear in the sky). But what was God trying to tell them? Was it, they wondered, an omen of good or evil?[4]

The day before Christmas, as Mead and Loughborough were putting a roof on a store in downtown Waukon, they were startled to hear the voice of Elon Everts (an Adventist preacher supposedly 200 miles away in Round Grove, Illinois) shouting at them to come down immediately, for Ellen White wanted to speak with them. Unbeknownst to them, the Whites, Elon Everts, and Josiah Hart had come through three snowstorms, dug their way through countless drifts, and navigated their sleigh across the partially frozen Mississippi River as hundreds watched in astonishment—all because of a vision that Ellen White had had directing her to share a special message with the six families in Waukon.

When he reached the sleigh, Ellen (never one for small talk) asked John a direct question: "What *doest* thou here, Elijah?"

Missing the biblical allusion entirely, John responded, "I am working with Brother Mead at carpentry work."

Again she inquired, "What doest *thou* here, Elijah?" Uncertain how to answer, Loughborough remained silent.

But Mrs. White persisted a third time. "*What* doest thou here, *Elijah*?" she asked, clearly alluding to the time when the prophet Elijah had fled from the wicked Queen Jezebel into the wilderness and had hidden in a cave. Obviously, she did not approve of John's decision to move to Iowa. Years later he recalled that her strange "salutation most thoroughly convinced me that there was going to come a change . . . from the labor in which I was then engaged."[5]

While the Adventists in Waukon extended their visitors every courtesy, giving them lodging, bran bread, and boiled corn for a week (the drifted, ice-encrusted snow prevented them from buying groceries), they remained apprehensive and somewhat hostile. Those who had come from New York blamed James White for moving the press from Rochester to Battle Creek. Others denied that the Laodicean message (given to the seventh church in Revelation 3:14-22) applied to them. During meetings at the Andrews' home, James explained to everyone's satisfaction that the decision to relocate the press had been made, not by him, but by a committee with the sanction of a general conference gathering in 1855, and that Jackson, Michigan, Adventists had paid the entire cost for the move.[6]

As the group met for worship services, Hart, Everts, and the Whites explained why the Laodicean message especially applied to Adventists as part of God's last-day remnant church. Ellen White received three visions that week: one lasted half an hour, the other two for two minutes each. She appealed to her listeners to return to the Lord. Deeply convicted by the Holy Spirit, some shouted "Glory! Hallelujah!" others wept, and still others spoke in tongues. J. N. Andrews and one woman present were "prostrated by God's power," their bodies "limp as a piece of cloth." One after another confessed past errors, asked for forgiveness, and rededicated their lives to God's service. The meeting continued past midnight.[7]

One of the first to speak was Mary Loughborough. She told Ellen that she and John thought they had gone where the Whites could not find them, but now she was glad they had come. Admitting her lack of consecration, she confessed, "I have been wrong. I have sinned; and I have made my husband to sin. God forgive me! I clear away the rubbish. I open the door of my heart. Lord Jesus, come in!" Facing her husband, she told John to "go forth in the name of the Lord to do his work."[8]

The next day John declared, "I have laid up my hammer! I have driven the last nail! Henceforth my hand shall hold the sword of the Spirit, and never give it up."[9]

"These meetings were the most powerful we had witnessed for years," James White recalled, "and in many respects the most powerful we ever witnessed." "We parted with our dear friends in tears, feeling the sweetest union with them." For the first time, many of them saw "the wondrous beauty of the Laodicean message" that they had once despised. Recognizing that they were indeed spiritually "poor, blind, and naked," the Adventists in Waukon resolved to heed Christ's invitation to buy the gold, white raiment, and eye salve that He offered them.[10]

The Whites left Waukon on New Year's Day, taking Loughborough with them (Mary stayed behind in Waukon). During 1857 John trekked across Illinois, Iowa, Wisconsin, Michigan, Indiana, and Ohio, holding evangelistic services in schoolhouses, chapels, and private homes. His preaching partners included James and Ellen White, Elon Everts, Josiah Hart, A. S. Hutchins, and J. H. Waggoner. To protect the "little preacher" against the cruel prairie winds, one woman sewed him a buffalo robe. For his arduous labor that winter, Loughborough received bed and board and about $30 cash. "My case was not an exception," he explained. "Other ministers fared equally well, and we were all happy in the Lord's work."[11]

Sometimes, however, circumstances disturbed John's optimistic attitude. After three weeks' preaching in Dodgeville, Wisconsin, Loughborough received a gift of $60 from grateful listeners, only to have the entire amount stolen by his host. "That was the last I heard of the donation to me," he wrote ruefully.[12] Most of his rewards came in the form of converts rather than cash. Thanks largely to Loughborough's evangelistic efforts across the Midwest in 1857, future ministers and missionaries such as John G. Matteson, Moses Hull, and George I. Butler joined the fledgling Adventist movement. In the years ahead, John would work closely with each of the men.[13]

Even doctrinal debates with ministerial opponents could bring rich rewards in converts. Popular opinion during the nineteenth century held that no one loved a debate more than a Disciples of Christ preacher—unless it was a Sabbatarian Adventist minister. Thus public interest ran high in Heidleston, Illinois, when a local Disciples of Christ pastor challenged Hart, Everts, and Loughborough to a debate on the Sabbath/Sunday issue. For four straight nights the two sides battled until listeners signed a petition requesting the Adventists to discontinue the debates, because their opponent refused to answer their biblical arguments. Convinced that the seventh day is the true Sabbath, 10 citizens accepted Adventism. One wrote to the *Review* to say that Loughborough's evidence had been "irresistibly convincing." Another testified that John's efforts "have been blest of the Lord."[14]

During the summer as Loughborough and his colaborers traveled with the new Wisconsin tent, they faced rising public interest despite (indeed, perhaps because of) a growing national depression called the Panic of 1857. Amid fierce storms in Milwaukee, "some three or four hundred" people attended their meetings. "Here are fields white already to harvest," John exclaimed, "[but] we need laborers [preachers]."[15] Despite organized ministerial opposition in Dodgeville, Wisconsin, nearly 700 citizens flocked to their services, among them several "infidels" (atheists) who treated the team kindly. "As you teach the Bible," one skeptic admitted, "it looks clear and plain, and appears like a different book." Surprised that the Adventists did not ask for money, the unbelievers raised $22, insisting that Loughborough accept their gift because, if the gospel was free, their living expenses were not.[16]

LOUGHBOROUGHS MOVE TO BATTLE CREEK

The gift proved especially useful later that fall when John and Mary decided to move once again, this time from Waukon, Iowa, to Battle Creek, Michigan. Selling most of their household goods, they packed their few belongings in crates and boxes and once again made the long journey east by wagon, train, and steamship. When they arrived, James White surprised them with a gift of $250 donated by friends and benefactors. Added to the $150 John and Mary had saved, it purchased them a lot and a cottage free of any mortgage. Their new home on Champion Street in the west end of the city, while small by today's standards, proved large enough for Mary to take in several Review and Herald press workers as paying boarders. Here, during the next 10 years, the Loughboroughs would raise three of their children (Teresa, Mary, and Delmer) amid exciting developments in a rapidly growing Seventh-day Adventist church.[17]

The Loughboroughs had barely moved into their new home when church leaders asked John to participate in the dedication of Battle Creek Adventists' second meeting house. Measuring 42' x 28', the wooden chapel near the corner of Van Buren and Cass streets had cost $554 to build and was 10 feet wider and 20 feet longer than its 1855 predecessor. Using his carpentry skills, John built the benches and designed the unique windows (divided in the ratio of two thirds to one third on top and bottom glass sections). During a "general conference" held during the weekend of November 6-8, a standing-room-only crowd of 250 people packed the tiny church to hear Elder Loughborough preach a stirring dedicatory sermon entitled "Remember Lot's Wife."[18]

Despite its diminutive size, the whitewashed house of worship would witness many key events in Adventist history during the next decade. The fledgling movement would establish a system of "gospel order" for itself and adopt a systematic benevolence plan in 1859. Ellen White would speak for more than five hours concerning the great controversy vision given her at Lovett's Grove, Ohio, in 1858. Here also the Review and Herald Press would be legally organized and the church name Seventh-day Adventist adopted in 1860. In this chapel the idea of ministerial certificates of ordination would be voted and the Michigan Conference founded in 1861. Its walls would witness the organization of the General Conference and the first preaching of the Adventist health reform message in 1863. The year 1866 would see the establishment of the Western Health Reform Institute within its walls. Loughborough would play a key role in every development.[19]

Yet his untiring efforts to strengthen and unify a rapidly growing Adventist movement certainly did not make him rich in earthly goods. For three months of labor in Illinois in 1857 John received free bed and board, a buffalo skin overcoat, and $10 in cash. During another four-month stretch he garnered $15 in cash besides free bed and board. To save the train fare to Waukon, Iowa, he trudged about 26 miles through the drifted snow with a heavy satchel on his back. The winter of 1857-1858, as he perambulated around Michigan, John "earned" $4 in cash and received three 10-pound cakes of maple sugar, 10 bushels of wheat, five bushels of apples, five bushels of potatoes, one peck of beans, one ham, and half a hog. Yet thanks largely to the small profit Mary made from their three boarders, the Loughboroughs survived that winter "in better condition than other of our ministers."[20] The impoverished condition of so many Adventist preachers during the Panic of 1857 would during the next two years inspire renewed Bible study to find some sort of systematic giving plan to support the rapidly growing movement.

Unfortunately, a burgeoning religious movement often grew "tares" (dissenters) among the "wheat" (true believers), and prior to 1863 no organized church structure existed to deal with such problems. Thus, in addition to the physical and financial challenges John faced, he also had to cope with individuals who brought discredit to the Adventist cause. His previous experience with Case and Russell's age-to-come defection in Michigan and Stephenson and Hall's *Messenger* Party in Wisconsin prepared him to assist the Whites in confronting a certain Christian Connexion convert named Gilbert Cranmer. While preaching in Otsego, Michigan, Mrs. White had seen in vision that the man would be an effective Adventist preacher if he gave up his tobacco habit and prayed openly (instead of secretly in the barn) with his family. Cranmer promised to do both. Six weeks later when he attended a prayer meeting in Battle Creek, he asked James White for a "card of recommendation" to be a minister. When White discovered that he still used tobacco and prayed secretly, however, he refused to ordain him. Miffed, Cranmer decided to preach on his own. Within a few months, he had gained the support of the *Messenger* Party and started a newspaper called *The Hope of Israel*. Until its demise in 1863, it attacked Ellen White's visions, taught a second probation for the Jews and other age-to-come doctrines, and defended the use of tobacco. According to Loughborough, Cranmer went insane and smoked himself to death.[21]

Happily for John, most of his evangelistic efforts in the winter and spring of 1858 led to better results. Indeed, nearly everywhere he went, Loughborough baptized new members, established local congregations, and ordained deacons and elders to administer them. His preaching of the Laodicean message led to revivals in Hillsdale, Monterey, and Allegan, Michigan, as well as in West Liberty, Indiana. As his preaching reputation spread and demands for his services increased, John actually had to decline invitations to preach in Wisconsin and Ohio.[22] In May he helped organize a general conference in Battle Creek at which 400 attendees (including delegates from New England, New York, Illinois, Indiana, Michigan, and Ohio) packed the new meeting house to overflowing. Here Loughborough presented "a cheering discourse on the inheritance of the saints" based on Matthew 5 (a sermon he would later develop into a best-selling book in 1861) that inspired 13 listeners to request baptism in the nearby creek. During a business session, John suggested that the time had come to replace the original 1854 evangelistic tent: after four years of use it was "unfit for service." Delegates raised $400 to buy a new one.[23]

When the Whites and Loughborough finally reached Ohio that summer, spectacular results accompanied their ministry. Despite strong opposition from a motley crew of Methodist pastors (who called them "wolves in sheep's clothing"), spiritualists (who opposed their teaching on the state of the dead), and "Free Lovers" (advocates of free sex without marriage), the meetings in Republic attracted more than 100 people (including students from a boys' academy). At least 48 baptisms resulted.[24] That fall Mary joined John for the general conference in Lovett's Grove, where at a "spirited" social meeting (emotional testimony service) they saw Ellen White in vision. Weeks later, the Loughboroughs would be among the throng in

Battle Creek's meeting house listening spellbound for more than five and a half hours as Mrs. White shared the grand panorama of sacred history she had seen in this vision. During the next six years (1858-1864) she would transcribe it in the four-volume *Spiritual Gifts*, which in 1888 would become the greatly expanded book *The Great Controversy*.[25]

The preaching team's spectacular success in Ohio and Mrs. White's vision of how God had led in the triumph of truth throughout history inspired John to renew his commitment to God. He wrote to the *Review*: "Never since I professed to follow the light of the Third Angel's Message have I felt more as though an ALL POTENT arm was under it, than I have since I have been in Ohio. God's Spirit has at times rested on me in a powerful manner. . . . I never have seen a greater stir made in so short a time. . . . This message is rapidly rising in power. . . . The message is onward."[26] Testifying that he felt like "a bird loosed from a cage," John resolved, "I hope ever to remain *God's free man*."[27]

Impressed with Loughborough's testimony, James White released this "loosed bird" from all responsibilities in the Midwest and sent him on a preaching tour of New York and New England in the fall and winter of 1858-1859. With the newly converted 21-year-old Seymour Bangs Whitney (a former Methodist) as tent master, John and the Whites took the train for Rochester, New York. There a vision warned Mrs. White that Satan would personally attack her body and that her husband and John should intercede for her deliverance. Sure enough, at Mannsville (near Watertown), as Ellen attempted to preach, severe pain racked her body and her face swelled up and sealed her eyes shut. James and John knelt by her side and prayed for her recovery. About 10 minutes later "God's power filled the room." Ellen sat up, ate some food, and within half an hour the swelling had disappeared. While she was preaching that evening, she had a vision concerning the use of swine's flesh. Although excessive use of ham and pork were harmful, she advised against making their use a test of church fellowship at that time.[28]

During the team's tour of New England, Loughborough took some time from his preaching duties to talk with several individuals who had been associated with the Whites during the Millerite movement. The information he gleaned from those interviews in 1858-1859 (and later ones conducted between 1863 and 1865) shaped his views of Millerism, the early Adventist pioneers, and especially of Ellen White's prophetic gift. He would rely heavily on those notes decades later when he wrote his historical surveys *Rise and Progress* (1892) and *The Great Second Advent Movement* (1905).[29]

That J. N. Loughborough knew that two competing views of Adventist history existed we find revealed in this rare reflection penned in 1921: "What they [the pioneers] told me differs in many respects from what some persons are now [in 1921] relating. Some of these persons were not born until this side of that movement. In calling attention to these things, I do not claim that they are intentionally misrepresenting matters, neither am I challenging [them] for [the sake of] a controversy, but [I] merely desire to show that they have been misinformed. In these [*Review and Herald*] articles I shall note the points under the form of questions, with matter-of-fact replies."[30] As we will see in chapters 14 and 18, however, some of Loughborough's own facts and interpretations would be incorrect.

If competing views of Adventist history left the sanguine preacher undisturbed, one incident on his momentous tour ruffled his theological feathers somewhat. Discovering that the only affordable meeting place in Boston was a hall where spiritualists met for séances, John gave his lectures there, trying to ignore their "Banner of Light" emblazoned on the floor. Although he assured *Review* readers that this experience "did not mar our peace," he also confessed that "it did seem to us that we were very near to one of Satan's forts."[31] Returning by the scenic Southern Tier route to Michigan, Loughborough stopped in Ulysses, Pennsylvania, where his preaching converted the former Methodist farmer Nathan Fuller. Unfortunately, during the next decade the greed, immorality, and heresy of this future president of the New York-Pennsylvania Conference would bring church leaders even closer to "Satan's forts." Fortunately, neither Loughborough nor the Whites could foresee that dark future.[32]

Instead, during 1859 Loughborough faced a more mundane crowd of opponents as he preached the Adventist message across Michigan. Frequently, Methodist, Episcopal, Baptist, and Disciples of Christ pastors challenged him to debates on the Sabbath/Sunday issue, whether the cross had abolished the law, or the immortality of the soul, while Universalists argued that God would save everyone. When Elder Dorrity, a Methodist-Episcopal pastor in Marshall, debated with J. B. Frisbie on human mortality, Loughborough praised Dorrity's "talent" but found his presentations short on biblical "facts." "We had good liberty in replying to this discourse," he asserted, "and endeavored to set forth the scripture doctrine of [eternal] life only through Christ."[33]

Protracted meetings and debates (that could last several weeks) often left John exhausted and impoverished. When he and J. N. Andrews gave 38 lectures in 25 days in Parkville, they converted 20 listeners but sold only $52 worth of books and prophetic charts. The team had only $15 left to cover their expenses. At the time, the Loughboroughs had only $36 to their name—and every penny of it they owed to their friend J. P. Kellogg for the groceries he had bought them. Yet believers in Detroit insisted that John hold meetings there soon. Where was the money to come from? Frustrated, James White appealed to *Review* readers to send in funds to pay for Loughborough's trip to Detroit. Shortly after reading the notice, John dreamed that when he returned to Battle Creek, he would find 10 letters with $25 total inside them. Sure enough, when he entered their home on Champion Street, Carrie (a hired girl) handed him 10 letters containing exactly $25. So he and James White boarded the train for Detroit and held meetings there, enjoying "a glorious time all the way around."[34]

DEVELOPMENT OF A SYSTEMATIC BENEVOLENCE PLAN

Although Adventist pioneers frequently enjoyed "glorious times" while preaching, the harsh economic realities of the Panic of 1857 (with bank failures, mortgage foreclosures, and rising indebtedness) forced them to recognize that while the gospel was free, they had no reliable method of paying for their travel, living, and preaching expenses. Many Adventist evangelists supported themselves by working part-time at farming, carpentry, broommaking. and other trades so that they could preach on the weekends. Even so, some (such as J. N. Loughborough) became discouraged and temporarily left the ministry.

Given the Loughboroughs' near bankrupt situation, therefore, it should come as no surprise that John and Mary in February 1859 hosted the first study group to seek a biblical method of systematically supporting the gospel ministry. The gathering included J. N. Andrews, J. H. Waggoner, J. B. Frisbie, M. E. Cornell, James White, John Byington, and several others. Apparently the group chose Loughborough to present their findings to the general conference held at Battle Creek in June, because he preached the first of several sermons on offering thanksgiving to God, paying one's vows to Him, and returning tithes to His storehouse. Following John's moving sermon, 11 individuals were baptized. James White then gave the keynote address on "Systematic Benevolence." Challenging his listeners to avoid the follies, jesting, and materialism of the world, he called upon the women present to abandon their fashionable hoops and bonnets and for the men to avoid hoarding their riches. If Seventh Day Baptists could spend more than $4,000 each year on foreign missions, he said, then why shouldn't Adventists support their missionary-ministers who suffered hardships, cares, and deprivations for want of means as they gave 200 to 300 discourses each year? White closed by proposing a new plan of giving called "Systematic Benevolence" (also known as the S. B. plan).[35]

After White's address, Loughborough and seven other ministers spoke in favor of adopting the new concept to alleviate the "painful statements of the want of means which are a blot on the cause." They argued that it would work efficiently; that its tithing principle promoted equality in giving; that it introduced order and system into the fledgling movement; and that it demonstrated believers' faith by their good works (James 2:18). Furthermore, those who gave from cheerful hearts would not deem it a sacrifice but a blessing to help spread the third angel's message. Based on Paul's counsel in 1 Corinthians 16:2 (Sunday offerings to assist the impoverished Jerusalem church), the S. B. plan (or "Sister Betsy" as nicknamed later) called for men to give between two and 25 cents a week, for women to donate one to 10 cents a week, and for property owners to provide an additional one to five cents a week for every $100 in property owned. Although based on the tithing *principle*, S. B. basically assessed believers on their *increase* (or profit) from one year to the next (which White estimated to be 10 percent annual growth of one's assets). Thus giving 10 percent of that estimated increase amounted to only one percent of one's total *income*. Alluding perhaps to the current economic depression as much as to the Adventist doomsday scenario at the end of time, Loughborough informed listeners that in this "time of trouble," God was "weighing His people," but those who paid their vows would enjoy blessings, power, truth, renewal, and joy in the Spirit. "Brethren, throw open the floodgates, and let the Spirit fill your hearts," he appealed.[36]

In another article entitled "Yearly Meetings," White argued that boosting the S. B. plan would also promote "gospel order" (efficient organization). Systematic giving would pay the expenses of holding one or two annual conferences in each state; it would establish a system of efficient ministerial labor; and it would strengthen the cause of truth. Adventists needed to adopt gospel order (although without a creed) to promote "systematic action of the entire body," White declared. He called for further study of the apostolic church to discover how its officers, councils, and witnessing methods promoted unity in the fledgling movement. During the next four years James White and J. N. Loughborough would take leading roles in shaping this new church organization despite stiff opposition and financial struggles.[37]

In the meantime, however, the Loughboroughs faced struggles of a more personal nature. Despite Mary's heartfelt confession three years before in Waukon, Ellen White knew that she had not dedicated herself totally to God by helping John in his ministry. As Lot's wife looked longingly back at Sodom, so Mary longed to return to Rochester, New York. Nostalgic for old friends and deprived of the financial security John's sash lock sales and her sewing had guaranteed them, she grew fretful and frequently complained. Then in March 1858 she received a long letter from Ellen White relating a vision given in Green Springs, Ohio. As she broke the sealing wax and opened the letter, Ellen's blunt words stunned her.

"Mary, you must die to Rochester," Mrs. White warned. If she had returned to the city in the fall of 1857 as she had planned, "it would have proved your ruin" and that of her husband, for John would have left the ministry to please her. Satan had been "harassing her mind about going to Rochester." The thought had become for her "a snare of Satan," for God had nothing for either of them to do there. Instead, Mary needed to submit her will to God, for if she chose her own way, she would "lose eternal life, lose heaven." From a spiritual perspective, therefore, she stood on the edge of a precipice. "Mary, I fear for you greatly," Ellen said. "I saw that you were a slave, yes, a slave, to your own unsubdued will. You are in complete bondage. It holds control and cruel power over you." Mrs. White described her friend as having "a rebellious spirit," making an idol of her will, "murmuring against God," grieving the Holy Spirit, yielding to "childish feelings," and indulging "jealous thoughts." Either her will or her hopes for eternal life must die, for "both cannot live at the same time." "I saw that it was time that Sister Mary was alarmed about her own salvation, that unless she was diligent now she could not redeem the time."

Even more serious, however, Mary was undermining her husband's ministry. Her strong will had "often pulled John one way, when God directed him in another." While she could have known the joys of being his partner in ministry after their conversion in 1852, she had instead "murdered your way along, making yourself miserable by your lack of consecration and often embittering John's life and making him miserable" as well. "Mary, dear Mary, I have seen that God's providence has placed John and you where you are. God has been working for you both that you, Mary, may be left without excuse." Her husband had a God-ordained work to do, and "he must perform it." Therefore, "if John should follow as you wish, follow your will, your pleasure, he is no longer a servant of Jesus Christ." Rather than sharing her complaints and frustrations with him, Mary needed to be an affectionate companion and advisor to her husband. She should "watch over him, study to ease his burden," pray with and for him, and then she would "share the [eternal] reward."

In light of John's recent evangelistic successes, Ellen advised him to give God the glory. "I saw that Brother John must keep humble, must watch, and must live very near to God," for Satan's "darts [temptations] are flying thick and fast" all around him. "Watch your words," she counseled. "Let your words be solemn." At the same time, however, she rebuked John (and J. N. Andrews) for their failure to give "a plain, pointed testimony" at Parkville, Michigan, for fear of offending their listeners. Moving "with perfect restraint" while preaching the gospel, she explained, "will never do the work that God designs to have accomplished." On the other hand, bearing "a pointed testimony" (rebuking sins) "will cut the natural heart, and develop character."[38]

Despite the letter's forthright tone, Mary and John accepted Ellen White's counsel as sent by God. Moreover, as they had after the confrontation in Waukon in 1856, the Loughboroughs remained close friends of the Whites. Indeed, during the winter of 1859, James and Ellen invited John, Mary, and their 10-month-old daughter Teresa to accompany them on a preaching tour of central Michigan. When baby Teresa cried out for milk (which apparently Mary could not always supply), Ellen did not become upset. Instead, she penned a spiritual application in her diary: "Oh, that we may be as earnest for the bread of life as she is for temporal food. She will not be satisfied."[39]

In January 1860 as the nearly 2-year-old Teresa lay dying of tuberculosis, James and Ellen sat up late, keeping vigil with her parents. When the child took her last breath, Ellen wept. "Oh, how sad the sight, a mother [Mary] witnessing the last agonies of her loved one, her only child. We prayed for sustaining grace for the father [John] and mother, that they might be perfectly reconciled to the will of God, that the little one's name was enrolled in the Lamb's book of life, to be called forth immortal at the resurrection of the just. We witness[ed] the dying struggle. The little eyes are closed, no more to look on earthly things. The little prattling tongue has ceased. Her troubles are ended. Quietly will she rest until the Life-giver calls her from her dusty bed."[40] When the White's 3-month-old baby John Herbert died in December 1860, Mary left her housework to sit and weep with Ellen on that "black Friday."[41]

Mary Loughborough did learn to be less selfish and more kind and benevolent toward others. In March 1859 Ellen White commended her for sharing some of her clothes with Mrs. Ratel, an impoverished neighbor. "Oh, that all knew the sweetness of giving to the poor, of helping do others good and making others happy."[42] Perhaps the bittersweet memories of their shared losses drew both women into a tighter bond of friendship and helped transform Mary into the loving, committed Christian wife she became.

J. N. LOUGHBOROUGH'S DIARIES

Although not all nineteenth-century Adventist ministers kept diaries, Loughborough early on developed that habit. From 1854 (when he was only 22) until 1923 (when he was 91), John scribbled all kinds of fascinating information in his pocket diaries. Despite the fact that as he lay dying in 1924 he asked that they be destroyed, his close friend Edith Barnes (a teacher at Lodi Academy) saved them. Although several of them have disappeared,[43] those that remain are carefully preserved in a climate-controlled vault in the Center for Adventist Research at Andrews University. Those who take the time to decipher their faded scrawl will be rewarded with invaluable insights into John and Mary's private lives.

For example, throughout his life, Elder Loughborough kept a meticulous financial record of every penny earned and spent. During 1859 their income ranged from $23 to $52 a month (including the $6-$10 monthly rent that their boarders such as George Amadon and their maid Carrie Carpenter contributed). With rare exceptions the Loughboroughs lived within their means, despite heavy expenditures for meat, horse feed, wood, and travel.

Like most rural Victorians of the era, their diet included plenty of fresh fruits and vegetables from their orchard and garden, as well as lots of meat consumed three times daily. As we have seen, John's "salary" on the road was often paid in kind: apples, potatoes, pork, and buffalo robes, to mention a few items. Behind their home on Champion Street in Battle Creek they planted beans, cabbage, and other vegetables that required much hoeing and weeding in the summer months. Their tiny orchard supplied grapes, cherries, and Northern Spy apples (John's favorite), which made succulent juice, pies, and applesauce. The Loughboroughs also ate large quantities of meat—especially beef, turkey, and fish (which John caught in the nearby river).

Like many other Adventist ministers, Loughborough remained a lifelong learner, and his diary reflects his wide-ranging interests. Beginning in 1847, when he was 15, John read his Bible through every year. Like Uriah Smith, J. H. Waggoner, and M. E. Cornell, John taught himself shorthand (then called phonography) and used it occasionally in his diaries to summarize his sermon topics (and thankfully for not much else). During the 1850s he also studied Greek, although we have no samples of his writing that ancient language. Doubtless it helped him understand the New Testament better. Preparing sermons (which he called "discourses") and notes for debates also kept his mind sharp. Frequent references to packing his books indicate that Loughborough possessed a rudimentary library, although we do not know the titles of many of his books because (paradoxically for such a list maker) he never compiled a catalogue of them. References to the New York *Tribune* indicate that he read at least one newspaper regularly, finding in its reports of murders, bank failures, and natural disasters evidence of fulfilled prophecies. Nonetheless, his wide reading did not seem to improve his spelling, for J. N. Loughborough never met a new word he could not misspell in several different ways. He spelled Indiana as "Indianna," telegram as "tellegram," and the name of the Polish Adventist evangelist Michael B. Czechowski comes across as "Czehowsky" and "Czehouski" (even as late as 1911).

John was handy around the house—when he was home. Trained in carpentry, cabinetry, and masonry, he built the chimney for their new house, laid down its flooring, and put on its roof. As previously mentioned, he also constructed the benches and designed the windows for the 1857 meetinghouse. In addition, he often helped Mary make soap and do the laundry (with a scrub board in large wash tubs)—what he called "choring about home." When he went "choring about town," he often bought groceries for the Whites as well as for his family.

Friendship ties between the two families were strong. They often ate dinner in each other's homes, occasionally dropped by for short visits, and constantly traveled together by carriage and sleigh over Michigan's bumpy roads. Although weary and sore from the buffeting, they sang together, "The road may be rough, but it cannot be long." Ellen and Mary went to the milliner's to shop for bonnets together. When the Whites needed his help, John painted their carriage and put a new water pump in their cistern. During Mrs. White's frequent illnesses, James summoned the two Johns—Loughborough and Andrews—to pray for her healing.

Most of all, Ellen White loved to hear Loughborough preach and debate the Adventist message. When John bested one of Cranmer's followers, she boasted, "They seemed displeased. We felt freer." Another time when he "[gave] the election [predestination] doctrine a rub," she rejoiced. Her greatest praise for John's oratorical style is summed up in her oft-used phrase "He had freedom [in preaching]." Sometimes Loughborough's discourses helped her gain new perspectives on gospel truth. When he preached in the Battle Creek meeting house on the message to the Laodicean Church, Ellen wept. "Light seemed to break into my mind that since the message to the Laodiceans has gone forth the delay that we are now in is to develop character, to bring out what is in the heart, and separate the precious from the vile."

Loughborough's 1859 diary reveals, however, that despite his evangelistic success, the 27-year-old preacher sometimes suffered from spiritual doubt and depression. "I feel some disconsolate. When shall I get complete victory over self?" he wrote on January 10. "Shall I fight my way through the conflicts of this life and reach Mt. Zion?" he asked himself on January 19. "I say

Oh! When shall I overcome?" (January 22). "When will I get so I can trust God?" (January 28). "This was one of my dank days," he confessed on March 4, adding two weeks later, "[I am] sad at heart. Oh! What slow progress towards the kingdom I am making. I must lay aside worldliness" (March 17). In the flyleaf of his diary, John admitted, "I should trust in the Lord for all things which he grants us richly to enjoy. I should be content with such things as I have, and ever realize that every good gift comes from him in whom there is no shadow of turning." Occasionally, however, he walked in the sunshine of God's love. On such days, he rejoiced that "I have kept my mind more on heavenly things to-day" (February 14).

No doubt Michigan's long, dark winters as well as his Irish penchant for melancholic brooding contributed somewhat to John's occasional bouts of depression. His solution was to seek out congenial company—and not always among Adventist believers. Perhaps to a greater extent than his contemporaries, Loughborough enjoyed visiting with individuals of different races and ethnic backgrounds. During a snowstorm in January 1859 he and Ellen White spent the night at the home of the Hardys, a Black family who lived near Battle Creek. Mrs. Hardy fed them simple but nutritious food, and they had "a fine time" visiting with the children and their parents. In April, John spent a Sabbath evening chatting with Sister Gibbs, a Black woman who lived in Laporte, Indiana. Loughborough often dropped in on Brother Pero, another Black friend, and Philip Felker, a German immigrant. His frequent association with Irish, German, Black, and (in California) Chinese citizens no doubt contributed to his spot-on imitations of their distinctive speech patterns in the dialogues he inserted in his articles and in his amusing skits at camp meetings. While today we might consider them insensitive and even politically incorrect, it appears that, in sharing these dialogues, Loughborough never intended to demean the racial or ethnic groups he imitated. In fact, his most popular camp meeting monologue—"Mike and the Saloon Keeper"—that repeatedly "brought down the house" was a parody of an Irishman, John's own ethnic background.[44]

LOUGHBOROUGH'S ARTICLES AND TRACTS

Despite Loughborough's hectic preaching schedule, he somehow found time to write occasional articles for the *Review*. Like those submitted by his ministerial colleagues, John's contributions tended to be sermonic in tone and focused on key Adventist doctrines. Indeed, many Adventist evangelists simply polished up their sermons and transformed them into lengthy articles. Most of the longer articles that filled several issues of the *Review* would get recycled as tracts or pamphlets or even books. Between 1857 and 1859 Loughborough sent the *Review* several articles dealing with the two-horned beast of Revelation 13, the seven churches of Revelation 2 and 3, the papacy's change of Sabbath to Sunday, the judgment, and the nonimmortality of the soul. In addition, he penned three articles ("The Anchor," "The Race," and "The Christian Warrior") for the *Youth's Instructor*, a slim newspaper for Adventist young people. His series on heaven and the new earth also came out as a booklet entitled *The Saints' Inheritance*, in 1859.

In the articles on the two-horned beast in 1857, Loughborough basically recycled his 1854 *Review* series with updated statistics and a few more historical and newspaper sources. Yet his tone is bolder: he predicts that within a few years Adventists will be at war with the United States (the two-horned beast), which, despite its democratic pretentions, is guilty of enforcing Sunday blue laws and "slave-ocratic practices." To dramatize his point, he stages a conversation between Slave Jim and Master George during a typical July 4 celebration:

Slave Jim: "What for you make all de noise?"

Master George: "Why, Jim, don't you know? This is independence day."

Slave Jim: "Massa George, tell me more bout um."

Master George then attempts to explain the Declaration of Independence and its assertion that "*all men* are created *equal*" to his slave. Obviously, Slave Jim does not feel equal to his master. Loughborough explained that those who helped such slaves escape could be fined $1,000 for their efforts.[45]

His article (and later pamphlet) "Who Changed the Sabbath?" is less remarkable for its conclusion (the pope, or "Man of Sin," changed it) than for its pretext and research base. Annoyed that an anonymous author in the Allegan (Michigan) *Record* would introduce "heresy" in his article "What Day is Holy?" (especially after John had made the matter clear in 16 lectures at Allegan), Loughborough wanted to "set the record straight." In addition to citing several Bible texts, he quotes from a wide variety of Church Fathers, papal edicts, encyclopedias, and history books—most of which probably came from his personal library.[46] Likewise, when another writer argued in favor of the immortality of the soul without citing a single Bible text in the Warren (Illinois) *Independent*, John published a five-page rejoinder in the *Review* against the man's "sophistries" and "uninspired philosophy."[47]

Consequently, when editor Uriah Smith proposed inserting a "Liar's Department" in the pages of the *Review*, Loughborough strongly supported the proposal. "I am much pleased with the idea," he wrote in 1858. "It is always of great interest to me to learn the position of our enemies, as well as the strength of the weapons with which they fight." Too many opponents, he added, rely on "slang, raillery, and lies to attack us," but such tactics usually increased public interest in gospel truth. He sent Smith a recent copy of the Perrysburgh (Ohio) *Journal* in which the editor (who had not attended Loughborough's Bowling Green meetings) "reported" that Adventists predicted the end of the world in seven or eight years.[48]

In his three short articles for the *Instructor*, the contentious Irishman adopted a more paternal, devotional tone. "The Anchor" presented Christ and the Bible as the Christian's anchor to the bedrock of gospel truth.[49] Whereas only one runner could win "the race" in the ancient Greek Olympics, he assured boys and girls that each of them could receive the prize of eternal life if they would set aside "every sin and folly" that hindered them.[50] Every youth who wanted to be a "Christian warrior," he wrote, needed to don the "'whole armor of God'" that Paul described in Ephesians 6:11.[51]

Without a doubt, however, Loughborough's favorite topic was heaven and the new earth. In 1859 the seed planted by Mr. Hollister, John's grade-school teacher who had his pupils memorize Revelation 22, bore fruit in the publication of his booklet *The Saints' Inheritance*. Employing Bible texts, poetry, anecdotes, and illustrations drawn from nature, history, and a wide variety of writers, in a mere 88 pages Loughborough manages to refute the arguments of the Universalists, dispensationalists, temporal millennialists, spiritualizers, and Whitbyites regarding eternal life. At the same time, he paints a picture of heaven and the restored earth so appealing that any reader would want to be there. During the next three decades the popular little work would get republished many times.[52]

---

[1] EGW to Mary Loughborough, letter 1, 1858, CAR.

[2] *PUR*, Aug. 4, 1910, pp. 6-8.

[3] *Ibid.*

[4] *Ibid.*

[5] *PUR*, Aug. 4, 1910, p. 8; *PUR*, Aug. 18, 1910, pp. 4-6; A. L. White, *Ellen G. White: The Early Years*, vol. 1, pp. 348, 349.

[6] JSW, "Western Tour," in *RH*, Jan. 15, 1857, pp. 84, 85; *PUR*, Aug. 18, 1910, pp. 4-6.

[7] JSW, "Western Tour," in *RH*, Jan. 15, 1857, pp. 84, 85; *RH*, Nov. 30, 1886, p. 745; *PUR*, Aug. 18, 1910, pp. 4-6; *PUR*, Aug. 25, 1910, pp. 1, 2.

[8] Mary Loughborough, quoted in A. Spalding, *Origin and History*, vol. 1, pp. 286, 287; JSW, "Western Tour," *RH*, Jan. 15, 1857, pp. 84, 85; Ellen G. White, *Spiritual Gifts* (Battle Creek, Mich.: James White, Steam Press, 1860), vol. 2, p. 220.

[9] JNL, quoted in Spalding, *Origin and History*, vol. 1, p. 289; E. G. White, *Spiritual Gifts*, vol. 2, p. 220.

[10] *RH*, Jan. 15, 1857, p. 85; C. Mervyn Maxwell, "The Loughboroughs," misc. m. 000741, CAR. See Revelation 3:17, 18 for the symbols.

[11] *PUR*, Aug. 25, 1910, pp. 1, 2; JNL, *Rise and Progress*, p. 212. See JNL's reports in *RH*, May 28, 1857, p. 32; *RH*, June 4, 1857, p. 40; *RH*, June 25, 1857, p. 64.

[12] *PUR*, Sept. 1, 1910, pp. 1, 2.

[13] *PUR*, Sept. 1, 1910, p. 1; *PUR*, Sept. 8, 1910, pp. 1, 2.

[14] *RH*, Feb. 26, 1857, p. 133; R. M. Thurston of Marquette, Wisconsin, quoted in *RH*, July 23, 1857, p. 95; John Lindsey of Round Grove, Illinois, quoted in *RH*, Mar. 12, 1857, p. 151.

[15] *RH*, July 2, 1857, p. 69.

[16] *RH*, July 16, 1857, p. 85.

[17] *PUR*, Sept. 8, 1910, pp. 1, 2; E. Dick, *Founders of the Message*, p. 279; Robinson, *Lighter of Gospel Fires*, p. 114.

[18] *RH*, Oct. 22, 1857, p. 200; JNL, *Rise and Progress*, p. 213; diary, Sept. 30, 1878; *RH*, Nov. 12, 1857, pp. 4, 5; *RH*, Jan. 7, 1858, p. 71; JNL, "Four Battle Creek Meeting-houses," pp. 266, 267; *Southern Tidings*, October 1999, p. 35. Exactly what this second meeting house cost is somewhat disputed. The *Review* for Nov. 12, 1857, pp. 4, 5, states that at a business meeting members voted to pay $327.41 of the total cost of $553.98. But JNL asserts in both *Rise and Progress*, p. 213, and "Four Battle Creek Meeting-houses," *Missionary Magazine*, June 1901, p. 266, that the second building cost $881. Perhaps we can explain the difference between the two figures by the fact that James White made a loan of $300 to complete the structure, asking that it be refunded in "gold, silver, good bills, wheat, corn, oats, butter, cheese, deerskins, or good promises of help soon" (see *RH*, Oct. 22, 1857, p. 200). The 250 listeners who packed this chapel would have had about four square feet each, amounting to a standing-room only crowd.

[19] JNL, "Four Battle Creek Meetinghouses," p. 267.

[20] E. K. Vande Vere, comp., *Windows* (Nashville: Southern Pub. Assn., 1975), p. 133; JNL, *Rise and Progress*, pp. 212-214; R. Schwarz and F. Greenleaf, *Light Bearers*, p. 86; A. White, *Ellen G. White: The Early Years*, vol. 1, p. 383; *PUR*, Oct. 6, 1910, pp. 1, 2.

[21] JNL, *PUR*, Dec. 15, 1910, pp. 1, 2; JNL, "Experience of Mr. Cranmer," typed manuscript, 1910, m. 007532, CAR; JNL, *The Great Second Advent Movement*, pp. 563, 564. Although it is possible that Cranmer died of cancer from excessive tobacco use, this author questions whether he went insane as Loughborough alleges. A close reading of J. N. Loughborough's writings regarding dissidents and apostates—especially those who

opposed Ellen White's prophetic gift—reveals that he nearly always has them becoming atheists, going insane, or dying soon. The pattern appears, for example, in his treatment of William Foy, Hazen Foss, Case and Russell, Stephenson and Hall, and Cranmer. The fact that Foy did not die soon after refusing to relate his third vision (though Loughborough clearly asserts several times that he did) begs the same question regarding the later apostates.

[22] *RH,* Jan. 14, 1858, p. 80; *RH,* Jan. 21, 1858, p. 85; *RH,* Feb. 18, 1858, p. 120; *RH,* May 20, 1858, p. 5.

[23] *RH*, May 27, 1858, pp. 12, 13.

[24] *RH*, July 15, 1858, p. 72; *RH*, Oct. 21, 1858, p. 173; *PUR*, Dec. 22, 1910, pp. 1, 2.

[25] *RH*, Sept. 2, 1858, p. 128; Sept. 30, 1858, p. 148; *PUR*, Sept. 28, 1911, pp. 1, 2; "Social Meeting," *Ellen G. White Encyclopedia*, pp. 1176-1178. An outgrowth of the early Methodist class meetings, social meetings met believers' emotional and spiritual needs just as the Sabbath school and Bible study met their cognitive ones.

[26] *RH*, Sept. 23, 1858, p. 141.

[27] *Ibid.*

[28] *RH,* Apr. 1, 1858, p. 160; *AUG,* Aug. 25, 1920, p. 6; *PUR*, Dec. 29, 1910, pp. 1, 2; *PUR*, Jan. 26, 1911, p. 1.

[29] *PUR*, Feb. 23, 1911, pp. 1, 2; *PUR*, Apr. 13, 1911, pp. 1, 2; *PUR*, Aug. 17, 1911, pp. 1, 2; M. Burt, *Pioneer Places*, p. 71. The individuals included, among others, Elizabeth Haines, Otis Nichols, Joseph Bates, Uriah Smith, and Rebekah Smith among others. Elizabeth Haines (in whose home Ellen Harmon had her first vision in December 1844) assured JNL that Ellen "had not been a part of the fanaticism after 1844." Otis Nichols told him about Ellen's holding a 10-pound Bible during a six-hour vision in Randolph, Massachusetts, and rebuking the dissidents Sargent, Robbins, and French who opposed her there.

[30] *RH,* July 28, 1921, pp. 7, 11.

[31] *PUR*, Aug. 17, 1911, pp. 1, 2.

[32] *RH*, Feb. 17, 1859, p. 103. For a detailed narrative of the nefarious career of Elder Nathan Fuller, see Brian Strayer, "The Triumph and Tragedy of Nathan Fuller," *Adventist Heritage* 4 (Summer 1977): 3-12.

[33] *RH,* Feb. 10, 1859, pp. 89, 90; *RH,* Feb. 24, 1859, p. 112.

[34] *RH*, Sept. 15, 1859, p. 136; *RH,* Sept. 29, 1859, p. 152; *RH,* Nov. 24, 1859, p. 8; JNL to D. A. Parsons, Oct. 27, 1916, DF 230, CAR. Although J. N. Loughborough never claimed the gift of prophecy for himself, throughout his life he believed that when he prayed for divine guidance, God sometimes chose to lead him through dreams. As future chapters will illustrate, John received many dreams in which he saw himself traveling to California (in 1868) and to England (in 1878) before he had even decided to go there. In some cases Ellen White herself validated Elder Loughborough's dreams and requested written copies of them. Toward the end of his life John wrote down the experiences and they were posthumously published in the book *Miracles in My Life: Autobiography of Adventist Pioneer J. N. Loughborough* (Payson, Ariz.: Leaves-of-Autumn Books, 1987), 107 pp.

[35] *Union Conference Record*, July 14, 1980, p. 12; *RH,* June 9, 1859, pp. 20, 21; JNL, "Report of General Conference Held at Battle Creek, Michigan, June 3-6, 1859: Containing an Address on Systematic Benevolence, Also Practical Discourses" (Battle Creek, Mich.: Steam Press of Review and Herald Office, 1859), pp. 1-23.

[36] JNL, "Report of General Conference" (1859), pp. 5, 6, 18-32. A detailed explanation of the Systematic Benevolence Plan can be found in Brian E. Strayer, "Adventist Tithepaying—the Untold Story," *Spectrum* 17 (October 1986): 41-43.

[37] JSW, "Yearly Meetings," cited by JNL, "Report of the General Conference" (1859), pp. 44-47.

[38] EGW to John and Mary Loughborough, Mar. 3, 1858, letter 1, 1858, CAR; EGW, ms. 3, 1858, CAR; A. L. White, *Ellen G. White: The Early Years,* vol. 1, p. 436.

[39] EGW, diary, Jan. 19, 1859; see also A. L. White, *Ellen G. White: The Early Years,* vol. 1, pp. 396, 397.

[40] EGW, quoted in A. L. White, *Ellen G. White: The Early Years,* vol. 1, p. 410; obituary for Teresa C. Loughborough, *RH,* Jan. 12, 1860, p. 7.

[41] A. L. White, *Ellen G. White: The Early Years,* vol. 1, pp. 427, 430, 431.

[42] EGW, quoted in *RH,* June 14, 1951, p. 7; *RH,* Nov. 23, 1972, p. 5.

[43] No longer extant are Loughborough's diaries for the years 1854-1858, 1860-1866, 1869, 1877, and 1884-1886. In his 1917 diary Loughborough states: "I [am] restoring the faded diary of 1854." Sadly, it has not survived.

[44] The preceding paragraphs are based upon daily entries in the diaries of J. N. Loughborough and Ellen G. White from January to December 1859 as well as on EGW, *Testimonies for the Church* (Mountain View, Calif.: Pacific Press Pub. Assn., 1948), vol. 1, p. 185; Loughborough's misspelling of Czechowski's name also appears in *PUR,* Nov. 23, 1911, pp. 1, 2. In 1940 W. A Spicer described Loughborough, Smith, Waggoner, and Cornell as "stenographers" who could write "phonography," or shorthand. See *Union Conference Record,* Sept. 2, 1940, p. 2.

[45] JNL, "Two-horned Beast," *RH,* June 25, 1857, pp. 57-60; *RH,* July 2, 1857, pp. 65-68; *RH,* July 9, 1857, pp. 73-76; *RH,* July 16, 1857, p. 81. The series was also published as a pamphlet in 1857. See also D. Morgan, *Adventism and the American Republic,* p. 26; Jerry A. Stevens, *Vicarius Filii Dei: An Annotated Timeline* (Berrien Springs, Mich.: Adventists Affirm, 2009), p. 39.

[46] *RH,* Sept. 17, 1857, pp. 153, 154; JNL, "Sabbath Controversy in Allegan, Michigan" (Battle Creek, Mich: n.p., 1858), pp. 1-14.

[47] JNL, "Immortality of the Soul," *RH,* Apr. 15, 1858, pp. 169-171; *RH,* Apr. 22, 1858, pp. 177, 178.

[48] *RH,* Sept. 23, 1858, p. 141.

[49] *YI,* January 1859, p. 5.

[50] *YI,* February 1859, p. 13.

[51] *YI,* April 1859, pp. 29, 30.

[52] JNL, *The Saints' Inheritance* (Battle Creek, Mich.: Steam Press of the Review and Herald Office, 1859).

CHAPTER VI

EARLY ADVENTIST ORGANIZATIONAL EFFORTS (1859-1863)

"If the church were in a position to hold property by law, we readily see that the property might then be insured, and business be transacted in the name of the church, or institution, whatever it might be called." We need "a properly organized institution" so that "we can hold church property legally." "I am in favor of organizing by law."[1]

As logical as those words sound today, in March of 1860, when J. N. Loughborough wrote them in a *Review* article entitled "Legal Organization," he was swimming against the current of nearly two decades of Millerite and Sabbatarian Adventist opposition to organization. During the Millerite movement, George Storrs had declared that when a church organized and adopted a creed, at that moment it became "Babylon" (a biblical symbol for apostasy). Many of Loughborough's fellow ministers—including R. F. Cottrell and Nathan Fuller of New York—vehemently opposed legal incorporation.

In the 1860s, as Americans in blue and gray fought a bloody Civil War over states' rights and slavery, James and Ellen White and John Loughborough (among others) engaged in a series of bloodless (yet often contentious) battles to organize legally the Review and Herald press, local churches, conferences, and the General Conference of Seventh-day Adventists. During the protracted process Loughborough would demonstrate his remarkable ability to use theology, reason, and Irish charm to persuade Sabbathkeeping Adventists to replace "Christian anarchy" with "Gospel Order."

THE NECESSITY OF LEGAL ORGANIZATION

Several inconveniences spurred the campaign for church organization. Since 1844, scattered families of Sabbathkeeping Adventists had worshipped together in wooden meetinghouses. But who actually owned those buildings? From a legal standpoint, the person on whose property they stood. In three notorious cases, when property owners apostatized, one man in Cincinnati, Ohio, turned two meetinghouses into vinegar factories, while another near Charlotte, Michigan, converted his into a chicken coop. Adventists had no legal recourse to repossess their former places of worship. Likewise the Review and Herald press in Battle Creek (worth $5,000 in 1860) technically belonged to James White, who strongly supported legal incorporation to remove such a fiscal burden from his shoulders.[2]

The lack of legal incorporation presented Adventists with several other conundrums. For example, how could they separate the "wheat" (orthodox teachings) from the "chaff" (heresy) unless they had a clear list of fundamental beliefs that defined what a Sabbathkeeping Adventist professed? Loughborough's personal experience with several dissident individuals and groups (including Case and Russell's attack on the Whites in Michigan, Stephenson and Hall's age-to-come group and Isaac Wellcome's sanctification movement in Wisconsin, and later Snook and Brinkerhoff's Marion Party in Iowa) convinced him of the necessity for doctrinal clarity while avoiding any set creed.

Yet between 1844 and 1860 the Sabbatarian Adventist Millerite splinter group did not even have an official name by which to herald its beliefs, much less an ecclesiastical form of organization. While believers called themselves "the remnant" or "the church of God," nonmembers referred to them as "the Sabbathkeeping Advent people," "Advent Sabbathkeepers," or the far less flattering "Shut Door Seventh Day Sabbath and Annihilationists." Again, Loughborough's experience proved helpful in selecting an appropriate name. In 1856 during his lectures at Waldron's Hall in Hillsdale, Michigan, John had seen a handbill advertising his meetings that referred to the "Seventh-day Advent people." When delegates met in October 1860 to select a name for the fledgling church, Loughborough asserted that the name "Seventh-day Advent people" had been used in the advertisement "because everybody would know at once who it meant." After a vigorous discussion, delegates voted to adopt the name Seventh-day Adventist.[3]

Although in the 1850s James White and Joseph Bates had begun signing certificates of ordination for Adventist ministers, the movement had developed no system for distributing its preachers among the local churches. Consequently, larger urban congregations such as Battle Creek and Jackson, Michigan (where blacksmith Dan Palmer gave $5 gold pieces to every visiting preacher) might attract two or three ministers on the same Sabbath, while smaller congregations in rural Indiana or Iowa might never see an Adventist minister for months on end. Not until June of 1860 when a "council of ministers and laymen" (including Loughborough) met in Battle Creek to "divide up the preaching territory" for the coming year did the problem get solved. Later, when state conferences organized, constituents elected three or four ministers to serve on a committee that annually assigned preachers to their districts.[4]

The impetus for ecclesiastical organization, however, sprang from the need to find a way to relieve James White from legal responsibility for the Review and Herald press's $1,500 indebtedness. "No worldlyman would wish to assume such a responsibility," Loughborough argued. Indeed, gossips were spreading rumors charging White with speculation. But if the church had a name, it could incorporate the press under the laws of the State of Michigan, form an association to own it as property, insure it against fire, and borrow money with the press's assets as collateral. To fulfill all these purposes, Loughborough proposed forming an association as a legal body to hold the press according to clear biblical principles ("let all things be done decently and in order" [1 Cor. 14:40]) and state laws. Although a handful of Adventist ministers wrote articles to the *Review* supporting incorporation, historian A. W. Spalding asserts that Loughborough was "about the only one with a clear-cut conception of the issue, its distinctions, and its proper solution."[5] Subsequently, at a meeting held in Battle Creek in October 1860, delegates voted to establish the Advent Review Publishing Association. Following the vote, they selected a committee (which included Loughborough) to write a constitution for it. Then John and six other ministers presented the constitution to the Michigan House of Representatives. In May 1861 the new Seventh-day Adventist Publishing Association emerged as a stock company (primarily because Michigan laws did not allow for nonprofit corporations at that time).[6]

The next logical step, of course, was for local churches to secure incorporation so that they could legally hold the property on which their meetinghouses stood. Yet some delegates resisted taking such a step. With infinite patience and clear logic Loughborough's speeches and articles helped them see that the state differentiated between churches that organized themselves for religious purposes and church associations that formed to own property. Adventists could organize "on the Bible" (and not own land) or they could incorporate "by the law" (and own property). "Legalizing the [SDA] association," he argued, "has nothing to do with our organizing into a church." While the former involved adopting "articles of association," the latter entailed drawing up "articles of faith" (which were not a creed). Following the discussion, Loughborough moved "that this Conference recommend to our individual churches so to organize as to hold their church property or church buildings legally." The motion passed.[7] Less than three weeks later Loughborough led the Adventists in Hillsdale, Michigan, in electing trustees to hold their church property legally—the first church after Battle Creek to do so.[8]

In the spring of 1861, when delegates at another Battle Creek conference appointed nine ministers to develop a paper on church organization, it was a foregone conclusion that Loughborough would be among them. Published in June, the document "Order in the Churches" outlined a fairer representation of local constituency at Adventist district and state conferences where church business was transacted. It called for a more thorough organization of local congregations with membership lists, letters of transfer, disciplinary action, and the appointment of church officers (deacons and elders). Bemoaning "the low state of many of our churches," the ministers' object was "to call your attention to the necessity of a more thorough organization." Hoping that no "distrust" would greet their proposal, its writers suggested that "any just and proper means of avoiding difficulty and trial in the churches are worthy of your most earnest consideration."[9] During the next half century J. N. Loughborough would facilitate the legal incorporation of scores of churches in the United States and the British Isles.

Such efforts naturally led to the formation of new committees, and John's growing reputation as an "organization man" got him appointed to several of them. One committee issued circulars and sold $10 shares in the publishing association; another oversaw the circulation of Michigan's evangelistic tents; a third laid plans to build a new brick headquarters for the publishing association in Battle Creek. John's fiscal conservatism doubtless influenced delegates to appoint him the first auditor of the publishing association. In addition, his clear, logical writing style came in handy whenever the church needed new documents or legal forms prepared. He wrote the covenant under which local Adventist churches organized for decades: "We, the undersigned, hereby associate ourselves together, as a church, taking the name, Seventh-day Adventists, covenanting to keep the commandments of God, and the faith of Jesus Christ." Once John persuaded delegates that such a simple statement of identity did *not* constitute a creed by which members could be tried and persecuted as heretics, they voted unanimously to adopt it. He also helped revise the wording in the certificates of ordination and ministerial credentials given to Adventist preachers.[10]

Yet despite his administrative expertise, church leaders did not accept every proposal he made. While he had suggested in 1861 that local elders should be able to baptize new converts in the absence of a minister, the Michigan Conference executive committee a year later decided that local elders and nonordained pastors should not perform baptisms.[11] Likewise his proposal (based on Malachi 3:8-10) that Adventists should tithe their *income* (rather than giving 10 percent of their annual *increase*) fell on deaf ears. Although James White supported the idea, most Adventists saw such a tithing plan as rooted in the old covenant and the Mosaic Code (whereas the Systematic Benevolence plan, based on 1 Corinthians 16:2, followed the covenant of grace in the New Testament). Not until 1878, when the economic suffering imposed by the Panic of 1873 gripped America, would Adventists adopt the tithing plan proposed by Loughborough and elaborated by Dudley M. Canright.[12]

Loughborough's efforts at public evangelism and ecclesiastical organization throughout the Midwest sought to bring unity to the scattered believers. Changing the focus of his discourses, John preached about "the splendor and loveliness" of heaven as "a happy smile lit up his countenance." One observer who saw "the tears of joy that coursed down the cheeks of nearly all present, and the heartfelt responses of amen and glory to God," testified that "a thrill of joy pervaded my heart."[13] Anguish over personal sins and shock at the horrors of war led farmers, tradesmen, and shopkeepers to fill home, schoolhouse, and tent meetings to overflowing. While Loughborough and his team preached, people listened "with breathless attention."[14] As the number of baptisms surged upward, John declared "that the truth when heartily embraced has power to hold its converts," because God's power lay behind it.[15]

Yet if one part of Loughborough's mission was "to instruct and encourage," he occasionally needed "to reprove" the wayward and restore order in local churches.[16] Particularly in Wisconsin, where the age-to-come dissidents led by Stephenson and Hall had created havoc among Sabbathkeeping Adventists, J. N. Loughborough and Isaac Sanborn set about restoring order and legally incorporating local congregations.[17]

FURTHER TESTIMONIES OF REBUKE

Loughborough's growing popularity as a successful evangelist and church organizer, however, did not spare him or his wife from Ellen White's reproofs. Believing her testimonies came from God, John and Mary took them very seriously. One such testimony in April 1860 rebuked them for catering to the whims of their hired helpers (Carrie Carpenter and her brother George). They relied too much on Carrie's judgment; spent far too much money on her; and by taking her to Ohio boosted Carrie's ego and brought "trials" to the church members there who had to deal with her misbehavior. Ellen warned Mary that she had become far too attached to Carrie for her own good. Moreover, Carrie's and Mary's "firm unyielding wills" had "proved a grief to herself and a sorrow to others."

Reiterating a theme of previous testimonies to Mrs. Loughborough, Mrs. White admonished her for her lack of consecration, her "listless, restless, lonesome feelings," and most of all, for trying to dictate John's course of action. "Mary, you have lacked greatly in making yourself useful, and your life is but a cipher, and that often tells on the wrong side," Mrs. White declared. She attributed the woman's "lack of friends" to the "lack of religion" in her life. Her homesickness and unhappiness reflected the "lack of the spirit of God" in her life. Indeed, the spirit of criticism had replaced God's Spirit as Mary frequently complained about what she found wrong in the church.

The lengthy letter addressed some of John's shortcomings as well. Ellen chastised him for being "too much influenced by others' notions and wishes." As a result, his "usefulness is crippled." She called on him to "rise above these hindering influences and shake himself from them." Then, in what must have been particularly painful to read, Mrs. White informed John and Mary that they were partly responsible for their first daughter's death. They had "violated the laws of health" by taking Teresa to bed with them. This "frail flower" caught a fatal disease, withered, and died when she might have lived. Nonetheless, Ellen hoped that they would receive her testimony "and make straight paths for [their] feet" in the future.[18]

A year later, when Mary wrote to Mrs. White seeking advice about wearing hooped skirts (a popular women's clothing fad in the 1860s), Ellen advised her not to wear them. "Do not put on hoops by any means," she declared, for by doing so, Adventist women erased that "uniqueness" and "peculiarity" that distinguished them from the world. Calling hooped skirts "this ridiculous fashion," Mrs. White urged her not to wear even the smallest of hoops. "Stand clear from this disgusting fashion," she added, and "let your influence tell for God."

Then, taking advantage of the woman's fashion query to give her advice on other matters, Mrs. White once again stepped into the role of marriage counselor. "I wish in all sisterly and motherly kindness to kindly warn you. . . . I have often noticed before others a manner you have in speaking to John in rather a dictating manner, the tone of your voice sounding impatient," she wrote. "Mary, others notice this and have spoken of it to me. It hurts your influence." Fearing lest her words offend, Ellen hastened to add, "I am not reproving you, remember, but merely cautioning you. Never talk to John as though he were a little boy. [If] you reverence [i.e., respect] him . . . others will take an elevated position [regarding him], Mary, and you will elevate others." Moving from marital to spiritual advice, she urged Mary to "seek to be spiritually minded." "Let your influence tell for God." "Be an example." In closing, she assured her friend that "we love you as one of our children, and I wish so much that you and John may prosper. . . . Please write me, Mary, fully. Tell me all your joys, trials, disappointments, et cetera."[19]

When Mary answered two weeks later, she agreed to abandon hooped skirts but suggested a compromise: wearing quilted dresses instead. Ellen White apparently approved of her suggestion, stating that she was "glad to hear directly from you" and calling her letter "welcome." Once again, however, Mrs. White focused Mary's attention on the larger spiritual issues at stake. She begged her friend to "covenant together to earnestly seek the Lord and learn wisdom of Him. . . . I am very desirous that you should continue to enjoy the free Spirit of God. Do not be content without it." Then, addressing her as only a best friend would, Ellen pleaded with Mary to "fear not to speak to me freely and fully [about] your feelings. . . . Let us be faithful to each other. Your letter cheered and encouraged me. Love to yourself and John."[20]

Then Ellen White added some advice for John. Two years before, while holding meetings at Parkville, Michigan, he had failed to preach Adventist truth boldly. Instead, he had "smoothed over" some of the objectionable points of his message so as not to offend some of the influential members of the community. Responding in the *Review*, Loughborough confessed: "I deeply mourn that I have ever been left to thus cripple my testimony, and bring leanness into my own soul. I trust I shall have strength from God in [the] future to bear the straight testimony required by the third angel's message. In hope of overcoming, J. N. Loughborough."[21] Pleased with John's humble response, Mrs. White wrote: "I saw that if he took a straight forward course, and put his whole confidence in God, he would make him a triumphant conqueror. I was shown that God lays out the work for John, and he must perform it, just as long as he remains a servant of the Lord. He must do His bidding."[22]

CIVIL WAR FEVER

But doing God's bidding as "war fever" raged around him demanded all the tact that John could muster. As a Yankee raised in upstate New York, related to several Loofboroughs who had fought with Washington in the American Revolution, his sentiments were strongly pro-Union and antislavery. During the summer of 1860 he had avidly followed the Lincoln-Douglas debates in the newspapers, taking Abraham Lincoln's side on most issues. Yet he had to admit that reading Hinton R. Helper's book *The Impending Crisis of the South* had "deceived" him (and many Northerners) into believing that Southerners were "a pusillanimous race" unable to compete militarily with the North. "He [Helper] forgot to say that their young men of sporting turn were well skilled in bringing down the bird on the wing every time," Loughborough observed. Following Lincoln's election as United States president, the attack on Fort Sumter, and the secession of one Southern state after another, those same Confederate sportsmen began killing Union soldiers as skillfully as they had once brought down wild game. John reflected on how wrong Horace Greeley, editor of the New York *Tribune*, had been when he bragged that old women armed with broomsticks could defeat the rebel army![23]

A classic example of such an overconfident attitude occurred in Parkville, Michigan, when on January 12, 1861, Ellen White related a 20-minute vision she had just received regarding the war's bloody carnage yet three months away. Three Adventist ministers—James White, J. H. Waggoner, and J. N. Loughborough—sat in the audience, spellbound by the incredible scenes she described. Two leading Republicans in the county—Mr. Osborne, a judge on the police court, and Mr. Shelhouse, owner of a local woolen factory—also attended that meeting. But as Ellen spoke, they both shook their heads vigorously, indicating their disbelief in what she was saying. "A most terrible war is coming," she declared. "There are those in this house who will lose sons in that war." Given the prevailing opinion on both sides that the war would be of short duration, hardly anyone was prepared to believe Mrs. White's dire predictions. Yet within a year's time, at least five families in Parkville had lost sons. Judge Osborne's only son was killed, and one of Mr. Shelhouse's sons died in the war while another wound up in a Southern prison camp. When Loughborough revisited the Parkville Seventh-day Adventist Church in 1883, the local church elder told him that by 1865 the sons of 10 families had perished in the Civil War.[24]

After the Confederates fired on Fort Sumter in Charleston, South Carolina, on April 12, 1861, President Lincoln called for recruits. From their home on Champion Street, John and Mary saw hundreds of "raw volunteers" mustering at the railroad station in Battle Creek. Mingling among them, he heard many of them brag that they would be returning home in six weeks after "whipping Johnny Reb." Deeply worried, Loughborough joined a delegation with two other Adventist ministers to present a petition to the governor of Michigan asking for exemption from armed combat on behalf of Adventist young men. The State of Michigan recognized the Seventh-day Adventist noncombatant position just days before the First

Battle of Bull Run (or Manassas) occurred on July 21. Two weeks later church leaders called the faithful to observe a day of fasting and prayer that in God's mercy, the war might end soon.[25] But the war continued for another four years, taking the lives of what is now estimated as more than 750,000 Americans.

Consequently, wherever Adventist preachers pitched their tents, they faced diminished attendance between 1861 and 1865 due to "war fever." Although the vast majority of citizens in the Midwest supported the North and hated slavery, in some parts of Loughborough's four-state district (especially southern Indiana and Illinois), sympathies for the Confederate cause ran high (particularly among a faction known as the the Copperheads). During their meetings in Illinois, J. N. Loughborough and Isaac Sanborn, desiring to make their loyalties abundantly clear, began flying "Old Glory" above their tent, knowing that Lincoln had given orders for Union soldiers to protect properties over which the Stars and Stripes floated. They also invited soldiers waiting for the trains to rest in the shade of their tent. As they did so, the two ministers prayed for them and gave them encouragement. In some cases soldiers on parade drill nearby would visit the tent and listen to the preaching. On one occasion, when a rowdy man interrupted their meetings, a captain asked John three times for permission to "pitch [him] out" of the tent. Smiling, Loughborough assured the officer that "that man is not hurting us. He is only helping us as fast as he can."[26]

But John made certain concessions to the U.S. Army that ran counter to the Adventist Church's noncombatant position. To please two pro-war Republicans (one of whom owned the land where he had pitched his tent and the other who had loaned the seats inside it), Loughborough permitted Army officers to use his tent for "war meetings" (recruiting rallies), some of which took place on Saturday. He even offered prayers for "the preservation of those liberties for which our fathers fought" and for the soldiers "who were risking their lives in this war." A grateful Captain Cain sent two armed sentries to patrol the grounds and protect the tent day and night. Consequently, in several Midwestern towns spiritual converts and military recruits were harvested beneath the same canvas tent.[27]

While no one in John's immediate family died fighting in the Civil War, his younger brother Eber C. Loughborough passed away during the conflict. Born and raised in Victor, New York, Eber had remained behind to care for their mother, Minerva. Sometime in 1860 he began studying Seventh-day Adventist teachings. Then, shortly after the war broke out, he caught tuberculosis. The day before he died in September 1861 at age 24, however, he told his brother William "that he felt that he was all ready." When John penned his brother's obituary for the *Review*, he affirmed, "Blessed are the dead that die in the Lord."[28]

FORMING THE MICHIGAN CONFERENCE

With a sad heart John left his brother's grave in the Victor cemetery and returned to Michigan, where he soon discovered that his rapidly growing church expected him to bear new responsibilities. At a conference held at Battle Creek on October 5 and 6, 1861, he served on the business committee that prepared the agenda for the session. The session adopted his motion that ministers and lay delegates in each state should organize statewide conferences administered by "chairmen" and "clerks" who served one-year terms. Likewise, his resolution recommending that a new Adventist hymnbook be compiled met with unanimous approval. When asked where he preferred to labor during the coming year, Loughborough chose to remain in Michigan, because he sensed less "excitement . . . on the war question" there than in Wisconsin.[29] Joseph Bates and Uriah Smith issued him his first ministerial certificate from Michigan: "This is to certify that Elder J. N. Loughborough of Battle Creek, Michigan, is a Minister in good standing in the Michigan Annual Conference of Seventh-day Adventists," it read. "This recommendation is good for this Conference year."[30]

A year later J. N. Loughborough, M. E. Cornell, and Moses Hull summoned delegates from the 17 Adventist churches throughout Michigan to gather at Monterey to organize the Michigan Conference. Meeting from October 4 to 6, 1862, the delegates chose William Higley (a layman) as president and elected James White, John Byington, and J. N. Loughborough as the Michigan Conference Committee. In addition, they reappointed Loughborough auditor of the SDA Publishing Association (for which he received $15) and reelected him to its board of trustees. As the Michigan Conference supervised evangelistic outreach in other "mission fields" (states not yet organized as conferences), the Conference Committee assigned Cornell to work in Iowa for the coming year. From New York, J. N.

Andrews asked the Michigan Conference Committee "to provide in due season a messenger to labor in this state."[31]

With conference organization, however, came the obligation to unify congregations, and, if necessary, to discipline wayward members. As one of three ministers on the Michigan Conference Committee, Loughborough took his responsibilities seriously. One church elder asked his advice regarding organizing a church in which some members used tea, coffee, and tobacco, a few women wore hoops, and others did not believe in the divine inspiration of Ellen White's visions. Loughborough's response provides a glimpse into the mind-set of the early Adventist Church in Michigan:

"We do not take in any who use tobacco, and reject the gifts of the Spirit of God, if we know it. One of the very objects to be accomplished by church organization is to lop off these things. . . . To take in those who are holding on to their sins and wrongs, would be to encourage the very things we are seeking to remedy. . . .

"[It is] better [to] let them [new converts] know the straightness of the way, before taking them into the church [rather than to have them] fill that with darkness . . . trial and confusion. . . . Let them stand outside till they can come in [to the church] right. . . .

"It will harm no one to remain outside our organization till he or she is prepared to come in harmony with us. . . .

"One dozen [members] in harmony and walking in the light are better than a hundred with confusion in their midst."

John asserted that evangelists should "speak plainly" to new converts about abandoning tobacco, tea, coffee, and hoops well before they baptized them into church fellowship. Likewise, ministers should never "hurry them into fellowship" unless they were certain that they believed in the divine inspiration of Ellen White's visions. He concluded that it was far better to secure their agreement to church standards "than to lower down the standard of truth for the sake of [increasing the] numbers [of members]."[32]

Seventh-day Adventists in the 1860s clearly saw themselves as God's "peculiar people," a "remnant called out of Babylon" to preach a unique message. Belief in the three angels' messages required one to follow a rather ascetic lifestyle that involved social, personal, and financial sacrifices. Although neither Loughborough nor his Adventist contemporaries believed that such "good works" brought them eternal salvation, their emphasis on obeying God's law, their penchant for self-denial, and their love of theological debates engendered within the early movement a pronounced strain of legalism that went largely unchallenged until 1888. The preceding letter (among his other writings) clearly indicates that Elder Loughborough shared that legalistic bent in his early ministry.

Yet in at least one respect, Loughborough's mind-set proved to be an asset when it came to organizing scattered companies of believers into legally incorporated churches. The Address on Organization" that he, Hull, and Cornell had shared with delegates at the October 1861 Battle Creek conference became in essence a manual on how to establish local congregations. It provided guidelines for writing church covenants, electing officers (elders and deacons), their duties, ordination services, and how to provide letters of commendation for members in good and regular standing who transferred to other congregations.[33]

The two ministers most in demand to help churches organize were James White and J. N. Loughborough. As administrative duties often required James' attention at church headquarters, he frequently asked John to go in his place because "[his] attention has been especially called to the organizing question."[34] Throughout 1862, J. N. Loughborough and John Byington traveled all over Michigan legally incorporating 23 Adventist congregations.[35] It kept John so busy that he neglected sending in written reports of his accomplishments to the *Review*. In late December, he wrote: "I presume many of the brothers and sisters have wondered what I am doing, as they have seen no report from me since the [October 1862 Battle Creek] Conference." He produced an encyclopedic summary of his organizing efforts to catch readers up to date on about two months' worth of activity.[36]

But Loughborough's activities included far more than organizing Adventist churches. He and his preaching partners also held revival services among the scattered believers. Moreover, whenever they had some "spare time," they pitched their tent and held evangelistic meetings that often continued for several weeks. By far the most spectacular series occurred at Charlotte from June 5 to July 13, 1862. This time the team (J. N. Loughborough and Moses Hull as preachers with Isaac Van Horn as tent master) tried something totally unprecedented in Seventh-day Adventism: newspaper advertising. Adventists had never attempted it before for several reasons. Prior to 1860 they had no official name to use in ads; before 1862 they had no recognized, legal form of organization; and evangelists had no budget for advertising.[37]

However, when William Saunders, the editor of the Charlotte *Republican*, began attending their meetings and taking notes, Loughborough and Hull soon discovered the benefits of free advertising. Attendance at their evening services doubled from 200 to 400 people in two nights. When the evangelists put ads in other county newspapers, the attendance doubled again to 800 as farmers and their families, despite being exhausted after a day of planting crops, drove up to five miles to the tent, seeking rest, shade, and entertainment. Stunned, John wrote to the *Review:* "This feature of advertising in the county papers we think will wonderfully add to the interest of tent meetings, especially in the fore part of a meeting. . . . If we act as though we had a message which we wanted the world to hear, they certainly will be induced to come if for no more [reason] than curiosity at first. Curiosity often leads to interest."[38]

When the editor of the Eaton County *Argus* weighed in, summarizing Hull's and Loughborough's sermons and telling his readers that "a good deal of interest is manifested [in them] by the hearers," attendance spiked to more than 900, many of them community leaders (whom Hull referred to as "the intelligence of the village"). But when the two preachers commenced a series of debates on the state of the dead question with a local Methodist-Episcopal pastor, attendance literally went through the roof, as more than 1,200 people packed the tent and the adjacent acreage. After the local pastor lost the debate, several of his parishioners converted to Adventism and were baptized in Battle Creek (a nearby stream) as 1,000 people watched.[39] Then the Rev. Joseph Jones and the Rev. E. Miller stepped forward and offered to debate the pair. James White informed *Review* readers: "Two educated, talented, and experienced ministers of the village [Charlotte] are about to open fire from their batteries upon these young and uneducated tent-preachers [Loughborough and Hull]." He therefore hoped that "these young Davids" would successfully vanquish them using "the pebbles of God's eternal truth."[40]

Following a weeklong marathon during which the two teams debated each other for 42 hours, Uriah Smith informed readers that "truth came off unscathed from the conflict." The unprecedented five-week evangelistic series resulted in 10 baptisms and the formation of the Charlotte SDA Church on October 25, when Loughborough and Hull returned to assist 17 members in "signing the covenant."[41] Hull's and Loughborough's evangelistic meetings and debates created enormous goodwill in the larger community as well. At the conclusion of their debates in nearby Lowell with the Rev. Clutz (a Baptist pastor) and S. P. Leland (an atheist), a local women's club gave them both family Bibles for their "able defense of its contents."[42]

LOUGHBOROUGH'S ARTICLES AND BOOKS

Loughborough upheld the Bible not only in his public discourses and sermons, but also in his articles and books. In his ever-popular *Youth's Instructor* articles he sought to make religion practical and appealing (if somewhat legalistic) to Adventist children. To help them understand why God placed the tree of the knowledge of good and evil in the Garden of Eden as a "test-tree" to develop the moral character of Adam and Eve, he shared a story about a father who put a mouse under a bowl on a table heaped with fruit, candy, and sweetmeats. Before leaving the house, he told his children that they could eat anything on the table, but they must not touch the bowl. When he returned, he discovered that they had disobeyed him and allowed the mouse to escape. God places similar tests before us, Loughborough concluded. Those who obey live eternally, while those who disobey become victims of "the second death."[43]

In another article, John told a story about poor children taken in by families and given love, shelter, food, and education to illustrate how God adopts us into His "family of heaven," making us "sons and daughters" and heirs of His kingdom. "If we are obedient to the Commands which our heavenly Father has placed for us, we shall finally become KINGS as well as king's sons. May this [realization] tend to purify the heart," he wrote.[44] After sharing a personal experience when a boy in a home where Loughborough was staying showed disrespect for his blind grandmother after she asked him to bring in the cows, he urged children to "always speak with respect and reverence to your parents and guardians" and "take a course that will not bring them shame." Instead, they should be like "olive trees" and "crowns of gold" to them.[45]

In still other *Youth's Instructor* articles, Loughborough employed storytelling techniques and biblical quotations to teach lessons about loving one's siblings ("Power of Kindness"),[46] learning gospel truth early in life ("Learning Right"),[47] remaining as close to Christ and their parents as a lamb to its mother ("Response"),[48] showing courage amidst life's battles ("Take Courage"),[49] and memorizing Bible stories ("A Question").[50]

His articles in the *Review*, on the other hand, relate few stories, refer to many Bible texts, and resemble the discourses and Bible studies that he shared from the pulpit during his evangelistic and revival meetings. They often addressed controversial issues that he encountered on his preaching circuit or read about in local newspapers. He devoted two articles to answering the question "Was Moses Literally on the Mount of Transfiguration?"[51] Three more articles addressed the queries of W. W. Giles of Toledo regarding the Trinity, the first angel's message, the Sabbath, the unpardonable sin, and what the Bible means by "this generation shall not pass" (he asserted that those who witnessed the falling of the stars in 1833 would live to see the second coming of Christ).[52] By 1862 Loughborough had become a sort of Adventist "Dear Abby" who fielded a wide variety of theological, lifestyle, and organizational questions handed to him by the editorial staff at the *Review*. Such queries ranged from the practical (how to keep the Sabbath holy)[53] to the esoteric (how could Philip be a deacon, a preacher, and an evangelist at the same time?).[54]

However, if John thought that his hectic schedule of writing, organizing congregations, debating contentious pastors, and holding evangelistic meetings could not possibly get any busier, he would shortly discover that his church still needed his expertise to organize a General Conference, establish a sanitarium, write a medical book, and promote the cause of health and dress reform among Seventh-day Adventists.

---

[1] *RH*, Mar. 8, 1860, p. 125.

[2] *RH*, Oct. 9, 1860, p. 162; *PUR*, Jan. 11, 1912, pp. 2, 3.

[3] JNL, cited by Gary Land, ed., *Adventism in America* (Grand Rapids: William B. Eerdmans Pub. Co., 1986), pp. 58, 59.

[4] *PUR*, Jan. 25, 1912, pp. 1, 2.

[5] *RH*, Mar. 8, 1860, p. 125; A. Spalding, *Origin and History of Seventh-day Adventists*, vol. 1, p. 300. Other supporters of incorporation included James White, J. N. Andrews, J. H. Waggoner, M. E. Cornell, W. S. Ingraham, Moses Hull, and Joseph Bates.

[6] *RH*, Oct. 16, 1860, p. 171; *RH*, Oct. 23, 1860, pp. 178, 179; *PUR*, Feb. 8, 1912, p. 2; Spalding, *Origin and History*, vol. 1, p. 303.

[7] *RH*, Oct. 16, 1860, pp. 170, 171.

[8] *RH*, Oct. 16, 1860, p. 176.

[9] *RH*, Apr. 30, 1861, pp. 188, 189; "Order in the Churches," *RH*, June 11, 1861, pp. 21, 22; George Knight, *Organizing to Beat the Devil: The Development of Adventist Church Structure* (Hagerstown, Md.: Review and Herald Pub. Assn., 2001), pp. 53, 54. The nine authors of the document were J. H. Waggoner, J. S. White, J. N. Loughborough, John Byington, Joseph Bates, J. B. Frisbie, M. E. Cornell, Moses Hull, and E. W. Shortridge.

[10] *RH*, Apr. 30, 1861, pp. 188, 189; *RH*, May 28, 1861, p. 16; *RH*, Oct. 8, 1861, p. 148; A. L. White, *Ellen G. White: The Early Years*, vol. 1, pp. 451-454; *PUR*, June 6, 1912, pp. 1, 2.

[11] JNL, Moses Hull, M. E. Cornell, "Conference Address," *RH*, Oct. 15, 1861, pp. 156, 157; A. Mustard, *James White and Seventh-day Adventist Organization*, p. 159.

[12] Spalding, *Origin and History*, vol. 1, p. 296-299; *RH*, Sept. 15, 1983, p. 4. It is worth noting that both the Systematic Benevolence Plan of 1859 and the tithing plan of 1878 originated during times of economic depression (the first during the Panic of 1857 and the second during the Panic of 1873). Although biblical foundations undergirded both plans (1 Corinthians 16:2 for the S. B. Plan and Malachi. 3:8-10 for the tithing plan), national economic hardships provided the spark that led church leaders to study their Bibles to find a better way to finance the church's mission outreach.

[13] *RH*, July 10, 1860, p. 60.

[14] For an overview of Loughborough's evangelistic success in the Great Lakes states during 1860-1861, see his reports in *RH*, Aug. 14, 1860, p. 104; *RH*, Aug. 21, 1860, p. 109; *RH*, Aug. 28, 1860, p. 117; *RH*, Nov. 27, 1860, p. 13; *RH*, Dec. 11, 1860, p. 32; *RH*, Dec. 18, 1860, p. 40; *RH*, Mar. 19, 1861, p. 144; *RH*, Apr. 30, 1861, p. 192; *RH*, July 30, 1861, p. 72; *RH*, Aug. 27, 1861, p. 104.

[15] JNL, quoted by R. F. Cottrell, *RH*, Nov. 6, 1860, p. 197.

[16] Sister R. C. Farrar of Kingston, Wisconsin, provided this description of JNL's roles in *RH*, July 2, 1861, p. 46.

[17] *RH*, Dec. 18, 1860, p. 38; *RH*, July 16, 1861, p. 56; *RH*, Sept. 24, 1861, p. 135.

[18] EGW to John and Mary Loughborough, Apr. 17, 1860, letter 6, 1860, CAR. However, Ellen White's explanation of Teresa's catching a "fatal disease" from sharing her parents' bed seems medically unlikely.

[19] EGW to Mary Loughborough, June 6, 1861, letter 5, 1861, CAR; Herbert E. Douglass, *Messenger of the Lord: The Prophetic Ministry of Ellen G. White* (Nampa, Idaho: Pacific Press Pub. Assn., 1998), p. 89.

[20] EGW to Mary Loughborough, June 17, 1861, Letter 6-1861, CAR. John apparently accepted Ellen White's condemnation of the hooped-skirt fashion in 1861. Decades later, in his book *Rise and Progress* (1892) he called them "one of the most ridiculous fashions in women's dress," an "immodest fashion," and "this shameful style" (p. 233). In his *The Great Second Advent Movement* (1905) he described the wearing of hoops as an "infatuation . . . the dimensions of which made many [women] look as if walking in an inverted balloon." He further attacked the "bloomer dress" (popularized by Amelia Bloomer) as an "extreme" fashion (pp. 361, 362).

[21] EGW, *Testimonies for the Church*, vol. 1, pp. 248, 249; *RH*, Apr. 30, 1861, p. 191.

[22] EGW's 1862 testimony to JNL, quoted in JNL to C. E. Holmes, May 2, 1920, m. 006529, CAR.

[23] *PUR*, Mar. 7, 1912, pp. 1, 2.

[24] *PUR*, Mar. 14, 1912, pp. 1, 2; JNL, *The Great Second Advent Movement*, pp. 338-340; Emma Howell Cooper, *The Great Advent Movement*, rev. ed. (Washington, D.C.: Review and Herald Pub. Assn., 1968), pp. 149, 150; Herbert E. Douglass, *Dramatic Prophecies of Ellen White: Stories of World Events Divinely Foretold* (Nampa, Idaho: Pacific Press Pub. Assn., 2007), pp. 13-15, 20.

[25] *PUR*, Mar. 21, 1912, pp. 9, 10.

[26] *PUR*, Apr. 25, 1912, pp. 3, 4.

[27] *PUR*, May 23, 1912, pp. 2, 3; H. W. Decker (JNL's tent master in the summer of 1861), *RH*, Oct. 9, 1924, p. 17.

[28] *RH*, Sept. 24, 1861, p. 7.

[29] *RH*, Oct. 8, 1861, pp. 148, 149.

[30] JNL's Michigan Ministerial Certificate, Oct. 6, 1861, DF 230, CAR.

[31] *RH*, Aug. 19, 1862, p. 96; *RH*, Sept. 30, 1862, p. 144; *RH*, Oct. 14, 1862, pp. 156-158, 160; *RH*, Nov. 4, 1862, p. 182; Spalding, *Origin and History*, vol. 1, p. 306.

[32] JNL to "Dear Brother L," Oct. 28, 1861, m. 015744, CAR; *RH*, Nov. 5, 1861, pp. 181, 182.

[33] JNL, Moses Hull, M. E. Cornell, in *RH*, Oct. 15, 1861, pp. 156, 157; JNL, "Reports of the New-York State Conference for the Years 1862, '63, and '64: Together With the Constitution for State Conferences and General Conference Address" (Battle Creek, Mich.: Steam Press of Seventh-day Adventists Pub. Assn., 1865), p. 24. The form for membership transfers stated: "This is to certify that _________ is a member of the Seventh-day Adventist Church of _________, in good standing, and one whom we can recommend to the brethren where his (or her) lot may be cast. By order of the Church at __________. (Signed): ___________, Church Clerk."

[34] James White, *RH*, Apr. 1, 1862, p. 144.

[35] *RH*, Mar. 25, 1862, p. 136; *RH*, Apr. 8, 1862, p. 148; *RH*, May 13, 1862, p. 192; *RH*, Dec. 2, 1862, p. 8; *RH*, Dec. 9, 1862, p. 12; *RH*, Dec. 23, 1862, p. 29; *RH*, Jan. 6, 1863, p. 48. They included the churches at Hillsdale, Hanover, Parkville, Charlotte, West Plains, Eureka, Fair Plains, Orleans, Newton, West Windsor, Convis, Vicksburgh, Penfield, Assyria, Bourne, Lowell, Caledonia, Greenville, North Plains, Owasso, St. Charles, East Thetford, and Oakland.

[36] *RH*, Dec. 23, 1862, p. 29.

[37] A. L. White, *Ellen G. White: The Progressive Years, 1862-1876* (Hagerstown, Md.: Review and Herald Pub. Assn., 1986), vol. 2, p. 54.

[38] *RH*, June 17, 1862, p. 21. In 1863 Saunders sold his newspaper and moved to California. There, in 1872, he attended meetings at Woodland, where he heard Loughborough, Merritt Kellogg, M. E. Cornell, William Healey, and James and Ellen White preach. After the meetings and reading all the books they offered for sale, Saunders converted to Seventh-day Adventism. See *ST*, Mar. 9, 1904, p. 149.

[39] *RH*, June 17, 1862, p. 21; *RH*, June 24, 1862, pp. 28, 29; *RH*, July 1, 1862, pp. 36, 37; *RH*, July 15, 1862, p. 52.

[40] *RH*, July 1, 1862, pp. 36, 37.

[41] *RH*, July 15, 1862, p. 52; *RH*, Dec. 6, 1962, p. 18.

[42] *RH*, Sept. 16, 1862, pp. 124, 125.

[43] JNL, "The Curious Dish—A Test," *YI*, February 1860, pp. 9, 10.

[44] JNL, "Adopted Children," *YI*, May 1860, p. 35.

[45] JNL, "Rebellious Children," *YI*, January 1862, p. 3.

[46] JNL, "Power of Kindness," *YI*, May 1862, p. 37.

[47] JNL, "Learning Right," *YI*, June 1862, p. 45.

[48] JNL, "Response," *YI*, October 1862, p. 79.

[49] JNL, "Take Courage," *YI*, February 1863, p. 13.

[50] JNL, "A Question," *YI*, March 1863, p. 19.

[51] *RH*, Oct. 16, 1860, p. 172; *RH*, Nov. 20, 1860, pp. 4, 5.

[52] *RH*, Nov. 5, 1861, p. 184; *RH*, Nov. 12, 1861, p. 192; *RH*, Nov. 19, 1861, p. 200.

[53] JNL, "Lessons for Bible Students," *RH*, Mar. 10, 1863, pp. 116, 117. It contained a catechism of 42 questions based on J. N. Andrews' new book *The History of the Sabbath*.

[54] *RH*, Jan. 7, 1862, p. 48.

CHAPTER VII

THE RISE OF ADVENTIST INSTITUTIONS (1863-1868)

"To Whom it may Concern:—This is to certify that Elders J. N. Loughborough and Moses Hull are appointed by the General Conference of Seventh-day Adventists to labor among the scattered brethren in New England. We commend these brethren to your sympathy and co-operation, and as men sound in the faith and able Ministers. And further, that, as Bro. Loughborough is a man of more extensive experience in tent labor, and financiering [sic], we commend him to the friends in New England as the Minister in charge of this work."[1]

This dual ministerial certificate, containing words of praise and commendation for two of Adventism's leading evangelists, was issued in July 1863 by the committee of the General Conference of Seventh-day Adventists—an entity that had not even existed two months earlier. As six state conferences coalesced in 1861 and 1862, many believed that a rapidly growing church (with approximately 3,500 members) needed a nationwide organization to oversee its evangelistic and institutional development.

Therefore, in May 1863, James White and John Byington (representing the Michigan Conference committee) issued a call for delegates from the state conferences to gather in Battle Creek to form a General Conference. Because of his growing reputation as an astute organizer of local congregations and conferences, leaders asked J. N. Loughborough to play a leading role in creating Sabbatarian Adventism's highest ecclesiastical body. As one of 49 representatives from the Michigan Conference, John joined his fellow delegates for four days of prayer, Bible study, and deliberation. He served on the committee on credentials, chaired the committee to draw up state conference constitutions, and became a member of the committee to draft the General Conference constitution. Recognizing his administrative expertise, the delegates asked Loughborough to write a pamphlet clearly explaining "the necessary legal steps to be taken in securing meeting-house property" and other matters related to incorporation. His tract "Religious Societies" explained Michigan and Indiana laws governing religious organizations, electing officers and trustees, handling church finances, and filling in the new report forms. When the time came to elect members of the General Conference (GC) Committee, delegates chose James White, John Byington, and J. N. Loughborough (thus the Michigan Conference committee doubled as the GC Committee, but nobody worried about conflicts of interest in those days).[2]

When the committee to draft state conference constitutions met, the five men spent several hours in prayer and Bible study, seeking divine wisdom. "If ever I felt the Spirit of God guiding, it was there," John recalled.[3] He was convinced that, despite differences of opinion on some issues, "God was in it [forming the General Conference]." While James White recognized God's leading, he also knew that without Loughborough's organizational abilities, the goal of achieving ecclesiastical unity would have been far more difficult to attain. Once again, he praised John in the *Review*: "His firm and persevering efforts on organization, systematic benevolence, et cetera, added to his preaching talent . . . make him, with the blessing of God, the man to build up churches, and have the especial oversight of the work in the East."[4]

MISSION TO NEW ENGLAND

Consequently, the GC Committee asked J. N. Loughborough and Moses Hull to strengthen the work in what was then called "the New England Mission" (Maine, New Hampshire, Rhode Island, Massachusetts, and Connecticut, states not yet organized into conferences as was Vermont). Their task was enormous: to organize new churches, legally incorporate them, establish state conferences, and persuade penny-pinching Yankees to adopt the Systematic Benevolence plan.[5]

In addition, James and Ellen White hoped that by working closely with the experienced Loughborough (now 31), Moses Hull (27) would grow stronger spiritually. A prolific writer, a formidable debater, and an eloquent and convincing preacher who attracted multitudes to his meetings, Hull had a penchant for engaging spiritualists in debates about the state of human beings after death. Winning such contests boosted his ego and made him trust in his own abilities. In 1862 Mrs. White had appealed to him to look away from self and depend on the Lord. Furthermore, she advised him never to befriend a spiritualist or debate with one alone. Ignoring her counsel, Hull had attended a convention of spiritualists at Paw Paw, Michigan, to debate the state of the dead with them. During one session in which spiritualists formed a "prayer circle" around him, he became confused, made certain doctrinal concessions, and lost the battle. Some said that he had confessed, "From now on I am a spiritualist."[6]

Observing that Moses Hull "seemed like a man half 'off his base,'" the Loughboroughs had earlier invited him and the Whites to their home in Battle Creek for a lengthy prayer session. There they made a decision to separate Hull from spiritualist influences by sending the two men to New England. Believing that Hull could be saved, Ellen wrote him and Loughborough a letter prior to their departure. "I saw that if Bro. Loughborough and yourself [Hull] make God your strength, a work will be accomplished by you for His poor people, for two can be a host. Come close to each other, pray together and separately, be free with each other. Bro. Hull should confide in Bro. Loughborough's judgment, and listen to his counsel and advice."[7] But submitting to a man only four years older did not agree with Hull's proud spirit.

During the summer of 1863, as the pair held meetings across upstate New York, Vermont, and New Hampshire, Loughborough noticed that Hull "seemed like himself again." While Loughborough's discourses dealt with "church order," the seven seals of Revelation 6, and the history of the Advent Movement, Hull's sermons focused on the state of the dead and end-time judgment. When citizens mistook the evangelists for "secessionists" and threatened to tear down their tent, John and Moses convinced them otherwise by flying the Stars and Stripes over it.[8] Despite being bedridden with malarial fever for a week, Loughborough promised *Review* readers that "we shall try to . . . do what we can for the cause in the east."[9]

Yet just when that cause seemed to be prospering, Moses Hull "raised his old doubts" again. So Loughborough took him on a long hike into the woods for "a praying season," after which Hull promised that "he would take hold again in earnest." During August and September, as the Whites and John's wife, Mary, joined them, they held meetings in Manchester, New Hampshire, pitching their tent in the park and filling it with settees loaned by civic leaders. When torrential rains prevented their using the tent (now riddled with 60 mouse holes), they transferred services to a hall where between 600 and 1,500 people listened "with almost breathless silence." A policeman patrolling the grounds grew bored and left, finding nothing to do. After four weeks Loughborough had preached every one of the 18 discourses in his portfolio. Soon 100 believers worshipped together every Sabbath.[10]

In spite of their success in Manchester, however, Loughborough detected that all was not well with Hull. At one service when Moses spoke about the future punishment of the wicked, only 100 people came. "He put in a great many turns peculiar to Moses Hull," Loughborough observed, "but there was not much Lord in it, and not one word of exhortation from beginning to end." Instead of visiting the new converts, Hull went shopping, spending $50 (more than a month's salary) on clothing for himself and his family. The penny-pinching Loughborough complained to James White that his partner was "so reckless with his money, when he don't know where the next [dollar] is coming from."[11] On September 21, the day after preaching his final sermon ("Hold Fast to the Truth"), Moses told John, "I am not going to preach [SDA doctrines] anymore." Instead, he returned home to Ligonier, Indiana, and within six weeks joined the spiritualist movement. "He has taken a 'final leap,'" Loughborough exclaimed.[12]

Realizing that John might blame himself for Hull's defection, Ellen White sent him and Mary a comforting letter. Loughborough thanked her for her "consolation to us [in] our trial at present." He was especially grateful for the Whites' prayers "in this breaking-up time" and for their generous pledge of $100 for the work in New England. With strength and wisdom from God, he would carry on the mission of spreading the "Blessed Hope" alone.[13]

When he reached Dartmouth, Massachusetts, Loughborough met Sister Russell, a woman living without hope. Although Joseph Bates had prayed for her and Ellen White had sent her a comforting testimony, she felt eternally lost for committing the unpardonable sin. Calling church members to observe a day of fasting and prayer in her behalf, John prayed for guidance. That night in a dream he saw 50 angels descending in ranks of two, dressed in garments like thin muslin shimmering with gold and silver threads. In unison they shouted, "Uncover, and we will take it." Interpreting the dream as a message from God that if Sister Russell confessed her sins, God would remove her guilt, Loughborough shared it with her the next day. She experienced release from her despair and died days later "happy in the Lord."[14]

Encouraged by the experience, Loughborough forged ahead. Facing unseasonably cold weather, he teamed up with Stephen Pierce and D. T. Bourdeau for meetings across Vermont, New Hampshire, Massachusetts, and Rhode Island in 1863 and 1864.[15] Their mission, he declared, was "to look after the welfare of the scattered brethren, organize [churches] where practicable, comfort the lonely ones, warn those who are in danger of fanaticism and error, and preach the word to those who have ears to hear."[16] After the first year's labor, he reported that "the ball of truth is getting well started here in the East. The cause is rising. . . . The angels of God are not only hovering over the East, but their influence is being felt by the Lord's people."[17]

In the *Review* James White repeatedly praised John as one of the "best men" the church had to "restore order" in areas where "fanaticism, rebellion, and confusion" reigned. Such situations, he added, "are no places for the boys." Instead, they demanded the services of "experienced men." Employing a popular Victorian phrase, White asserted, "We are happily disappointed [with] the present state of unity and activity in the cause." To further demonstrate his satisfaction, James sent John a box of lutes to enhance his congregations' singing. He also asked Loughborough to represent the New England Mission at the next General Conference session since he "has explored nearly the whole [of it]."[18]

J. N. Loughborough's legacy to New England included far more than sermons preached, books sold, and churches organized. Often he left behind artifacts of craftsmanship in wood, glass, and stone. In Vermont he gave advice concerning the blueprints and helped construct the benches, pulpit, and wainscoting for the Bordoville SDA Church, while in Massachusetts he organized and helped to build the South Lancaster SDA Church. Both churches, built in 1864, would withstand the ravages of time for the next 150 years.[19]

On his way to the 1864 General Conference session in Battle Creek, John stopped in Victor, New York, where he learned that his older brother, William (a recent convert to Seventh-day Adventism), had become a circuit-riding preacher like Grandfather Nathan before him. His Sabbath services in Rochester, Fairport, and Victor had brought about the conversion of "our dear father Norton [John's maternal grandfather]," who soon became "another fireside preacher, for which the Lord be praised." William arranged for John to speak to the Adventists in the area, and despite a driving rain, they "had a good gathering."[20] Soon at least five members of John's family (his mother, two brothers, a sister, and grandfather) became Seventh-day Adventists.

During the 1864 General Conference session Loughborough once again served on the GC Committee, the Committee on Nominations, and the Committee on Publication. His report indicated that during the previous year he had traveled 5,800 miles (about 110 miles a week), held 250 meetings (five a week), baptized 30 converts, and sold more than $500 worth of books, charts, and *Review* subscriptions. Following his summary of labors, he moved that Vermont be admitted as a conference within the General Conference, and delegates unanimously voted it in.[21]

PROGRESS IN HEALTH REFORM

Although an uncle had introduced Loughborough to Graham bread (coarse grain bread) and hydrotherapy (including cold baths and exercise) in his youth when John's lungs were hemorrhaging, he struggled to give up meat. While living with his grandparents on the farm, he had eaten it three times a day. But on June 6, 1863, Ellen White had received a vision regarding healthful living, disease and its causes, and the harmful effects of meat eating that led her to write the six pamphlets in the "How to Live" series. John and Mary read the tracts and believed they were light from God. Unable to dispense with meat all at once, however, they took a gradualist approach. They went from eating it twice a week for two months to once a week for a month to once a month for three months, and then after six months they quit eating meat altogether. They also adopted a two-meal daily regimen with a diet of fruit, vegetables, nuts, and grains with occasional use of milk and eggs. For the next 60 years Loughborough would remain a strict vegetarian except on rare occasions when traveling in areas of the world where such a diet was unavailable. To their surprise, giving up meat brought John and Mary immediate health benefits.[22]

"Never was sleep sweeter, or health better, or my mind more cheerful, since I first started in the service of God at the age of 17 years, than for the last two months. . . . I would not, for any consideration, go back to the meat, spice, pepper, sweet cake, pickles, mustard, headache, stomach-ache and gloom, and give up the good wholesome fruit, grain, and vegetable diet, with pure cold water as a drink, no headaches, cheerfulness, happiness, vigor and health."[23]

Returning to New England with Merritt Cornell for a second year of ministry in 1864-1865, Loughborough made health reform a prominent topic among his discourses.

Unfortunately, his own health was declining. When James White joined him at Manchester, New Hampshire, he found John coughing and spitting bloody sputum for an hour every day. At 31, Loughborough was already in the early stages of tuberculosis. "If you do not stop that coughing," White warned, "you will soon have to be looking for your coffin." Handing John a copy of Dr. James Jackson's book on consumption (TB), he advised him to follow its counsel regarding proper rest, ventilation, bathing, exercise, and diet. John did so, and a month later, his coughing spells ceased.[24]

During his second "Eastern Tour" Loughborough and Cornell ranged widely across New England. In addition to holding evangelistic meetings and establishing new churches, John conducted interviews, collecting information from those who had participated in the Millerite Movement and the Sabbatarian Adventist movement in its formative years. The material would prove invaluable when writing his two history books, *Rise and Progress* and *The Great Second Advent Movement*.[25]

Delighted with their success, James White praised them in the *Review*: "Brethren Cornell and Loughborough are toiling to the utmost, and God is with them. The openings to labor, and calls for help, are very many more than they can fill. Those men . . . should be well sustained."[26] James also commended both men for "putting things in order among Eastern Sabbath-keepers." He told them that "the best way to dry up the influence of fanatics is to let them alone, but [to] actively visit the scattered friends of the cause, and set things in order with them."[27] Following this counsel with a group of extremists in Maine led by a Mr. Hancock, Loughborough soon reported that fanaticism was "losing ground" there.[28] Yet the dividing line between fanaticism and enthusiasm could become a bit indistinct at times. In New Boston, Massachusetts, where a blizzard had piled up three-foot snowdrifts, three converts, unwilling to wait for spring, were baptized by Loughborough and a Brother Daniels in the river after a hole had been cut through the ice.[29]

In the spirit of primitive Christianity, however, some of Loughborough's meetings witnessed miracles. When the Whites joined Cornell and Loughborough that winter, they discovered that Marion Bourdeau, D. T. Bourdeau's wife, was dying of typhoid fever. They anointed her and prayed over her, and during a subsequent three-hour meeting she testified that God had completely healed her.[30]

One miracle Adventists prayed for was a swift end to the war. In August 1864 the GC Executive Committee (John Byington, George Amadon, and J. N. Loughborough) had sent Michigan governor Austin Blair a letter explaining the biblical reasons why Adventists objected to bearing arms in time of war. But they also asserted that "Seventh-day Adventists are rigidly anti-slavery, loyal to the government, and in sympathy with it against the rebellion." Then they asked the governor for congressional protection as conscientious objectors. The governor's reply assured Adventists that "they are entitled to all the immunities secured by law to those who are conscientiously opposed to bearing arms, or engaging in war." Five months later the GC Executive Committee called for a day of fasting and prayer on February 11, 1865. Loughborough hoped the war would soon end so that people would focus on spiritual matters again. When Grant and Lee met at Appomattox Court House to sign the terms of surrender in April, many saw it as an answer to prayer.[31]

Yet no sooner had the Civil War ended than another controversy—this time within the church itself—began. While attending the 1865 GC session at Battle Creek, B. F. Snook and W. H. Brinkerhoff (president and secretary of the Iowa Conference respectively) saw the wives of two or three prominent ministers dressed in worldly fashion and wearing jewelry. Back in Iowa they spread the rumor that Battle Creek Adventists were a proud bunch who allowed women to wear feathers and jewelry, contrary to the plain style of dress that most Adventists followed. Regarding church headquarters as "Babylon," Snook sought support from Wisconsin leaders in "striking out on the old plan of the independence of the churches." After both men began attacking James White's leadership and Ellen's visions, James condemned the rebellion in Iowa. To nip it in the bud, the Whites and Loughborough traveled to Pilot Grove, Iowa, to meet with loyal Adventists and form an investigative committee. Following an eight-hour meeting in which Snook and Brinkerhoff aired all their grievances and the Whites answered them, Snook and Brinkerhoff signed written confessions promising to cooperate with church leaders. To insure that they did so, the Whites asked Loughborough and George Butler to remain in Iowa a while to partner with Snook and Brinkerhoff in holding evangelistic meetings across the state.[32]

But Snook and Brinkerhoff's repentance "was of short duration." Within weeks both men had moved to Marion, Iowa, where they advocated Sundaykeeping and age-to-come ideas and attacked the Whites and other church leaders in *The Hope of Israel*. Feeling financially cheated, they raised their salaries to $15 a week (most Adventist ministers received $12 a week), which they collected in advance each quarter from the Systematic Benevolance funds they handled. In an attempt to treat them fairly, Loughborough persuaded the Iowa Conference Committee to compensate both men at $1 a week for the time they had served the church prior to their defection—provided they submitted written reports of their ministerial labors.[33]

While these negotiations continued, Loughborough summoned the seasoned Wisconsin evangelists W. S. Ingraham and Isaac Sanborn to Iowa "to encourage and strengthen the flock, to labor to hold the cause together while rebellion is ripening." He appointed two other trusted individuals to audit the conference treasurer's books and send a report to the *Review*. Meanwhile, in a clever rearguard maneuver, Snook and Brinkerhoff took control of the Adventist church in Marion, Snook's home town. If the Iowa Conference sued them, John felt certain that the "Marion Party" would win in a court of law. In letters to Thomas Hare (a friend in Iowa), he asserted, "May God bless his honest people, and let those determined to rebel speedily go their own way. Amen."[34]

Loughborough's prayer soon had its answer. B. F. Snook, whose theological beliefs had become more liberal, left Adventism and began preaching for the Universalists at $1,000 a year, confessing to a fellow pastor that he had abandoned Adventism because "there was not enough money in it." W. H. Brinkerhoff taught school awhile before practicing law. As James White gleefully expressed it: "The Age-to-Come [futuristic dispensationalism] has gone to seed [dispersed]!"[35]

As soon as Iowa could spare Loughborough, he hastened back to Michigan. The GC session of 1865 had elected him president of the Michigan Conference (with Isaac D. Van Horn, his former tent master, as secretary). It did not relieve him of other administrative duties, however. He continued serving on the GC Executive Committee; he represented the New England Mission in all deliberations; and he was assigned "to labor in the Western and Central divisions of the field"—a broad territory covering all of Michigan, Ohio, Illinois, Wisconsin, Minnesota, and Iowa.[36] Incredibly, in the summer of 1865, John covered nearly all of it. Occasionally the Whites joined him for evangelistic meetings. In La Salle, Wisconsin, the trio spent the night "in a Western rum-selling hotel" full of tobacco smoke, whiskey fumes, and loud cursing. The same situation faced them in Princeville, Illinois, a village where "about every fourth door is a dram shop [saloon], swarming with customers" and "drunkenness, profanity, and incivility" were the order of the day.[37] But when they reached Hundred Mile, Wisconsin, John's trained eye admired the broad, smoothly planed pews in the newly built Adventist meeting house, and he could not help contrasting them with the "rickety board seats" in Battle Creek's 1857 meeting house.[38]

Like those rickety pews, some of the church's leading ministers—through overwork, poor diets, stress, and lack of rest—were also showing signs of wear. By 1865 several of them lay flat on their backs at home or in sanitariums, too sick to write, preach, or travel. When Hiram Edson became so ill in 1864 that he was rushed to Dr. James Jackson's sanitarium ("Our Home on the Hillside") in Dansville, New York, James White started a campaign in the *Review* to pay his expenses. Grieved that his old mentor was incapacitated, Loughborough mailed $5 to the fund. When the same misfortune struck Daniel Bourdeau in 1865, the Whites sent him to "Our Home" and raised $100 to pay his medical expenses. This time John contributed $10.[39] Weeks later when James had his first stroke, he too was admitted to "Our Home."

But he did not go there alone. Loughborough's exhausting tour of the Midwest had left him little time for rest or sleep. Preaching at so many meetings, visiting so many people, and then staying up late writing articles for the *Review* and *The Youth's Instructor* by the feeble flicker of a candle or the faint glow of a kerosene lamp had strained his eyes and given him severe headaches. By August the pain had grown so bad that he tiptoed around to avoid the jarring caused by ordinary walking.[40]

A month later John joined the growing pilgrimage of pale pastors wending their way to Dansville. Included in the caravan were James and Ellen White, Uriah Smith, H. S. Lay, J. N. Andrews, and M. F. Maxson. After giving each of them a phrenological reading (the practice of mapping one's character and "propensities" by feeling the "bumps" on one's cranium), Jackson prescribed eight months of bed rest for the entire group (at $20 to $40 a week). However, differing rates of recovery soon altered that prognosis. In addition, Adventists everywhere joined in a day of fasting and prayer for their ministers' restoration. In Enosburgh, Vermont, Adventists prayed one hour every day for John's recovery. By the end of October, Loughborough told Thomas Hare, "I am gaining quite rapidly. [I] am in hopes to recover fully in three or four months, so as to be as strong as ever." He closed the letter, "Yours in haste and hope." His hopes were fulfilled by a hasty recovery, for within six weeks both *Review* editor Uriah Smith and Loughborough felt strong enough to leave.[41]

But John, who chose to remain behind to assist James in his recovery, wrote letters to his friends and sent regular reports to the *Review* keeping Adventists apprised of White's progress. He told Thomas Hare that "Bro. White is not able to write six lines. His nervous system is prostrated; [he] cannot even take upon him the care of himself." For several months, all articles appearing under White's name he dictated to Loughborough, who transcribed them for the *Review*. John thanked the many people who sent money to pay for his and the Whites' medical expenses.[42] After Adelia Van Horn brought the Whites' boys, Edson and Willie, for a visit, she told *Review* readers that "the rest and treatment . . . is doing a work for him [Loughborough] which he has so much needed. . . . Pray on, brethren and sisters."[43] When he learned of the Whites' and Loughboroughs' financial needs, J. M. Aldrich urged believers to "make donations for [these] invalid preachers" according to "the true principle of equality"—that is, send as much money for one family as for the other.[44]

When James White had recovered sufficiently to move to the Bradley Lamson home (Adventist friends who lived nearby), John took him baskets of fresh food from the sanitarium to save James the arduous climb up the hill to the dining hall. Every afternoon he joined Ellen White and four other friends in praying for her husband's recovery, and as James gained strength, "we shouted the high praise of God."[45]

Just before Christmas, the ministers whom Dr. Jackson had expected to stay eight months left Dansville after only four months. During the winter and spring of 1866 Loughborough remained in upstate New York preaching with R. F. Cottrell and Nathan Fuller.[46] Because so many church leaders and ministers had suffered "prostration and affliction" during the past year (six had been bedridden, five had lost children, and one had died), the GC committee called Adventists to observe a day of fasting and prayer. "Let us cry to the Lord to revive his cause, remove his rebuke from off his people, restore his servants, and lead on the message to its destined victory." After spending the day in Bible study, prayer, and meditation, Loughborough testified that it had been for him "a season of refreshing . . . and a deeper settling into the cause of God." He urged Adventists everywhere to continue praying for James White's recovery.[47]

Both White and Loughborough had recovered sufficiently to attend the next GC session in Battle Creek, which met in the new meeting house. The third wooden chapel, built in the spring of 1866, was 40' wide and 65' long with a gallery across the front. It had cost $8,100 to construct. Here Adventists would establish their first sanitarium (1866), elementary school (1867), and college (1874). From this sanctuary, they would send their first missionaries (J. N. Loughborough, J. N. Andrews, D. T. Bourdeau, and J. G. Matteson) to California, Switzerland, France, Scandinavia, and England between 1868 and 1878.[48]

At the May 1866 session, Ellen White called for the establishment of a new health institute in conformity with Adventist principles of wholistic living. Although she had approved of some of Dr. Jackson's methods (hot and cold baths, exercise, rest, and the vegetarian diet), she just as firmly opposed other practices at Dansville (card playing, dancing, mental inactivity). She argued that Adventists, by integrating their biblical beliefs and health principles, could do a much better job of operating a medical missionary institution.

In stunned silence, Loughborough listened to her speak. As Michigan Conference president, he knew that Adventists had neither the funds nor the trained personnel to operate such a sanitarium. Nonetheless, after the conference committee had prayed about the matter, he announced to the delegates: "We will pledge to the enterprise, venturing out on what is said in the testimony, though it looks to us like a heavy load for us to hold up."[49] Compiling a list of potential subscribers, he first approached broom shop owner J. P. Kellogg who donated $500 to the enterprise, "sink or swim." Ellen White also pledged $500. J. M. Aldrich pledged $250, James White pledged $100, and Loughborough pledged $50. By asking donors to support a health institute, John became in effect the first fund-raiser among Adventist pioneers. Because the State of Michigan did not recognize nonprofit enterprises, however, the Battle Creek law firm of Dibble and Rhine helped Loughborough organize the new Western Health Reform Institute (WHRI) as a business corporation following the same laws that governed mining companies, with each share of stock selling for $25. However, since Mrs. White insisted that all profits should either go to charity or be used to improve the institution, most investors returned their dividends.[50]

That summer J. N. Loughborough traveled extensively throughout the Midwest promoting the institute and urging Adventist ministers to act as agents for it in their districts. With some $11,000 in shares sold, the WHRI purchased Judge B. F. Graves' two-story home situated on nine acres in Battle Creek (near the railroad depot) and on September 5, the sanitarium opened its doors with two physicians (Drs. Lay and Byington), two helpers, and one patient (it would admit 12 by the end of the month).[51] Well-to-do patients paid $8 to $14 dollars a week for their care so that "the worthy poor" (charity cases) could receive free treatment. That fall the board purchased two more acres, which added a detached cottage and additional shade trees, and finished the hydrotherapy building. By Thanksgiving patients had arrived from New England, New York, across the Midwest, and even from Canada seeking cures. A news item boasted: "We are now prepared to successfully treat all curable diseases; . . . come to us and we will do you good." Loughborough wrote: "A person once fairly on the grounds will be loth [*sic*] to leave."[52]

Yet not all Adventists were as thrilled with the idea of starting a sanitarium as was Loughborough. In fact, many felt that such an institution was a denial of faith in the imminence of the Second Advent. To counter such criticism, John argued that since health reform was an integral part of the third angel's message, the WHRI was "a branch of this cause," because it healed people not only physically but also spiritually. Indeed, many grateful patients converted to Seventh-day Adventism following their cure. Consequently, far from being "a denial of our faith" in the soon Second Advent, the sanitarium demonstrated that "our faith is genuine," because its staff prepared people to be "clean vessels," fit for translation when Jesus returned to earth.[53] After hearing Mrs. White praise the work of Drs. Lay and Byington, Loughborough and Smith urged her to write down her speeches, for they would have tremendous public relations value for the WHRI. She did so in a 40-page testimony (no. 11), published in 1867.[54]

John's untiring efforts as fund-raiser and PR agent for the WHRI did not go unrewarded. In the spring of 1867, he (and nine other men) signed the Articles of Association legally incorporating the WHRI for 30 years (1867-1897). Two weeks later, stockholders elected him president of its board. Stockholder J. M. Aldrich, noting that Loughborough had raised $1,100 for the sanitarium, praised him as one "very apt to do just so when he goes out among the brethren."[55]

In addition to giving speeches and raising funds, John discovered another way to propagate the Adventist health message. In June of 1866 (when Adelia Patten Van Horn was appointed "Editress" of *The Youth's Instructor*),[56] Loughborough raised $775 in subscriptions to a new periodical entitled the *Health Reformer*. With the motto "Our Physician, Nature: Obey and Live" on its masthead, the first issue rolled off the press in August.[57] James White admonished his fellow preachers: "Every S.D.A. minister is not only requested but expected to act as agent for the Health Reform Institute, and the *Health Reformer*."[58]

In the first issue of the *Health Reformer* J. N. Loughborough wrote an article, "Rest," in which he argued that while farmers gave their beasts of burden rest, they made "overworked jades of themselves," ingesting 10-minute meals and wondering why they got sick. From personal experience, John knew that he could accomplish far more work if he took periodic naps than if he pushed himself too hard. At night he went to bed "free from care" to sleep in a well-ventilated room on a mattress of straw, husks, hair, or moss, awakening at 5:00 a.m. "with joy in the heart, and praise on the tongue."[59]

His article "Items of Observation" told the story of a woman addicted to drugs who had spent $500 a year on physicians whose medications (opium, morphine, strychnine, and calomel) left her "a mere skeleton" of 80 pounds. However, when she quit using drugs and adopted the health-reform regimen (eating graham puddings, rice, fruit, and vegetables), she quickly recovered. Six months later, Loughborough found her "comparatively rugged," weighing 120 pounds, and her house "filled with cheerfulness."[60]

In a two-part series on "Health Reform," John argued that it "is not . . . 'a narrow, contracted, nut-shell theory,'" but a comprehensive health plan for recuperation and "preservation of every part of the human system." True health reformers, far from making one idea "the whole Alpha and Omega of reform," followed a balanced lifestyle of adequate rest, moderate exercise, a vegetarian diet, and useful work. They also bathed regularly, not in cold water (which is "slow torture, if not martyrdom"), but in warm water in a well-heated room followed by a gentle rubdown. Such a regimen promoted health and mental cheer.[61]

Loughborough began his six-part series with "Diseases and the Treatment of Diseases" by confessing that he had no professional experience, "as I am not an M. D." Instead, he had condensed information gleaned from the writings of Drs. Trall, Jackson, Graham, and others. He had also submitted his manuscripts to the physicians at the new health institution for critical review. His articles countered the popular belief that disease was an unavoidable part of normal life. To the contrary, he declared, it resulted from bad air, improper lighting, impure food and drink, human laziness or overwork, and "unregulated passions" (too much sex), which brought about imbalances within the body's systems. The proper use of water, air, light, food, exercise, and rest promoted health. Following such a balanced regimen constituted the best way to avoid a host of life-threatening fevers (including typhus, typhoid, inflammatory, intermittent, ague, putrid, nervous, and remittent).[62]

In addition to serious medical articles, the *Health Reformer* also carried poetry and humor. Roswell F. Cottrell, an evangelist in the New York Conference, frequently submitted health-related poems to the paper. One night in a dream he had sung the refrain to his lengthy poem *The Health Reformer* so loudly that he awakened himself from a sound sleep! That night he composed two stanzas, and the following morning he wrote four more. The song-poem vividly portrays the progress that individuals make physically and spiritually as they incorporate health-reform practices into their life.[63] Taking a jab at American physicians, the *Health Reformer* readers were told that "China must be a satisfactory sort of place for one to die in, for, according to the laws of that strange country, the physician who kills a man has to support his family. It is a pity we do not have a law of that kind in this country [the United States]."[64]

Pleased with John's support and the growing success of the *Health Reformer*, Drs. Lay and Byington asked him to write a book on human anatomy and physiology to promote Adventist health principles. He consented on condition that both physicians serve as critical readers of the manuscript. Devoting an entire year (1867-1868) to research, he took extensive notes from medical treatises such as Dr. R. T. Trall's *Hygienic Encyclopedia*, Dr. Sylvester Graham's *Lectures on the Science of Human Life*, Dr. Lambert's *Physiology*, and Mrs. Taylor's "Know Thyself," plus other works on health. In the spring of 1868 John also attended Trall's weeklong lecture series at the institute. Designed for practical use by ordinary families in their homes, Loughborough's "catechism on health" followed a question-and-answer format. He had chosen such a style, he explained, "not because it is especially designed for a school book . . . but to impress [these truths] more forcibly [upon] the mind of the reader."[65]

Originally projected to have 130 pages and no illustrations, the manuscript eventually grew to 227 pages with 19 illustrations by the time of its publication. Involving intense research, the project left John little time for writing doctrinal articles in the *Review*.[66] Responding to the inquiries of impatient saints, he replied: "I am making some headway with it, but have not succeeded as rapidly as I [had] expected, having my attention called to other matters which could not be deferred." He begged members, "Be patient with me. I must try to be hygienic myself, while [I am] writing, or I might write faster. But I do not esteem it [my] duty to put the work of two days into one, as I have sometimes done in the past."[67]

Hand Book of Health appeared in 1868 with a strong endorsement from Dr. H. S. Lay: "Having carefully examined the manuscript of this work, I can cheerfully recommend it to the confidence of the public as being well adapted to the wants of the common people, and in accordance with the recognized principles of physiology, and of hygienic medication. It should be in every family, and read and studied by old and young. The chapter on the 'Nervous System' . . . is worth more than the price of the book."[68]

Its 10 chapters dealt with physiology and hygiene, the human frame, the muscular system, blood circulation, the lymphatic system, the nervous system, organs of external senses (ears, eyes, nose, mouth), the viscera (internal organs), diet, and "miscellaneous items." The book also contains an alphabetized glossary with 426 terms and a short index.[69]

As the reading audience for the *Hand Book of Health* included children as well as adults, it contains no chapter on the human reproductive system and no direct reference to human sexuality. However, buried deep in the glossary one can find one-sentence definitions of such terms as abortion, fetus, menses, menstrual, scrotum, syphilitic, uterus, and vagina. John also adds occasional warnings against "the passions," "lustful feelings and habits [which] debase man and undermine his health," and "the secret evil habits and vices of youth [masturbation, or "solitary vice" as the Victorians called it]." Such habits the youth should avoid "with the same dread that they would the bites of the most venomous reptiles. Do not sin against God and your own soul by destroying yourself," he advised.[70]

Loughborough also makes some interesting suggestions, many of them years ahead of his time. For example, in Chapter 2, he recommends not only brushing one's teeth after every meal, but also flossing them ("drawing a thread between them").[71] In chapter 7 he touts the benefits of bathing every other day (advice he did not follow) to avoid the common cold.[72] Chapter 9 contains his list of the best foods (milk, wheat, and apples) and substances one should avoid (tea, coffee, tobacco, mustard, hot pepper, and spices).[73] Like most Adventists at that time, he has nothing good to say about drugs and medications, calling them "necessary evils." In chapter 10 he declares: "That physician who uses the least medicine is the best friend to man's physical interests."[74] He is equally opposed to shaving one's beard because "nature requires its growth." Therefore, he tells men to "keep the razor off your face."[75]

Like Victorians of that era, John frequently borrows terms from phrenology. In chapter 6 ("The Nervous System") he refers to "the phrenological organs" of the brain's surface. He describes the cerebrum as "the seat of all the mental and moral powers" and the cerebellum as "the seat of the sexual impulse." Further, he emphasizes the need for the "moral faculties" to constrain the "organs of destructiveness, combativeness, acquisitiveness, and amativeness."[76]

Like his contemporaries, Loughborough also subscribed to the theory of vital force—"that power placed in the human body, at its birth, which will enable the body, under favorable circumstances, to live to a certain age." Known colloquially as one's "constitution," vital force resembled a bank account given at birth: one could make withdrawals from it but not place deposits in it. "Violations of nature's laws" (such as having sex too often) depletes the "original stock" of vital force and shortens one's life proportionally. Hence the need "to manifest the greatest care, lest we overtax our energies, waste our life force, and shorten our days."[77]

ADVENTISTS' FIRST CAMP MEETING

During the Second Great Awakening, the Presbyterians had convened the first camp meetings in Kentucky early in the nineteenth century. Soon the idea caught on among the Methodists, Baptists, and Disciples of Christ as well. Between 1842 and 1844 the Millerites held about 50 camp meetings throughout the Northeast, most of them located near prominent towns or cities connected by railroads. But few in number, widely scattered, and financially strapped, Seventh-day Adventists did not hold camp meetings until after the Civil War.[78]

The first to do so were the Adventists in Iowa. At the conference session held at Pilot Grove in June 1866, Jacob Hare (a former Methodist) suggested bringing all the believers in the state together for "a convocation meeting." Loughborough immediately embraced the idea. Combating the Snook and Brinkerhoff defection at the time, he felt certain that a general gathering would help unify loyal Adventists. In August hundreds of Adventists convened at Pilot Grove for what leaders billed as "a feast of fat things." Living in tents and holding twice daily services (9:00 a.m. to noon and 5:00-6:00 p.m.) in a large 50-foot tent, they gathered for "mutual religious improvement." For several days they listened to 12 sermons (four by Loughborough) and held seven social meetings with hours of testimonies "characterized by deep feeling, hearty confessions, sobs and tears." Loughborough told *Review* readers: "This Convocation Meeting [is] the first of the kind ever held among Seventh-day Adventists."[79] In 1867 Adventists in Wisconsin held their first camp meeting, then in 1868 Adventists in Michigan and Illinois convened camp meetings as well.

Following his historic camp meeting, Loughborough labored in Wisconsin, Minnesota, Illinois, and New York during the summer and fall of 1866, raising up new churches, organizing state conferences, and attending quarterly meetings. State leaders called on him to open conference sessions with prayer and to chair the committees on resolutions (that drew up session agendas), nominations (that suggested names for conference officers), and auditing (financial reports). Once new officials were elected, John held seminars to teach Systematic Benovelence treasurers, conference secretaries, ministers, and local church leaders how to fill out the new GC "blanks" (printed report forms) every month or quarter.[80] A Wisconsin member praised Loughborough for "his cheerful countenance, and his faithful testimony."[81] Indeed, according to his reports in the *Review*, John found delight in lunching on graham bread and strawberries, exploring a cave, and observing "the wonders and beauties of nature" as he traveled along.[82]

Following a brief visit with relatives in Victor and Canandaigua, John returned to Michigan in the winter of 1866-1867, where he not only faced "the worst [muddy] roads I ever saw in any State,"[83] but also a host of new responsibilities. The General Conference session of 1867 appointed him to the five-man hymnbook committee to prepare a new Adventist songbook.[84] As a member of the Committee on Publications, he drafted several new amendments and changes to the bylaws governing the Review and Herald press.[85] In addition, he was reelected Michigan Conference president, but because of demands for his expertise in organizing church structure and revising constitutions, he spent most of the year in Illinois, Ohio, Wisconsin, and Iowa while Mary remained at home in Battle Creek.[86]

But everywhere he went John introduced health-reform practices and promoted the new medical institution. Convinced that healthful living was "a matter of conscience . . . a means to help us in the great work of preparing to go and dwell with holy angels," he added "a physiological discourse on Temperance" to his sermon portfolio. A frequent sufferer from malarial fever since childhood, John learned to dispense with quinine and use water treatments instead. With God's blessing, he found them "a thousand times better" in relieving his pain.[87]

MORE TESTIMONIES FROM ELLEN WHITE

To ease his financial pain, John began selling photographs on the side. But Ellen White disapproved of Adventist ministers indulging in such distracting sidelines. When he received a letter of admonition from her, John confessed in the *Review*: "While others are making their acknowledgments of their error in the sale of photographs as a matter of merchandise, I would say, that I deeply regret that in this matter, I too, have been at fault. Brethren, forgive me, I will try to walk more circumspectly in the future."[88]

During the winter of 1866-1867, J. N. Loughborough, J. N. Andrews, and J. B. Frisbie had spoken against James White. Resentful of his unforgiving spirit toward those he felt had wronged him, they accused him of being the "reprover in the gate," "butting and slashing" all who disagreed with him.[89] But now convinced that he himself had been too harsh, John sent James an apology. It provides insights into the nature of their friendship and the depths of his repentance: I deeply regret what I have said or done or written that has wounded the feelings of yourself or Sr. White. . . . I am sorry that I have not always maintained that demeanor towards you that I felt when you were first taken sick [in 1865]. It seemed to me then that I could die if that would raise you up. I find on searching my own heart, that the talking over your course with a few here, while you was [*sic*] sick (although not designed to defame or injure you) has, in some measure, blunted those tender feelings I had towards you. In view of your enfeebled condition while sick I do not think I made that allowance I should for your infirmities. . . . I fear as Sr. White said to me that I have been led of the Devil instead of the Lord. . . . I need to be humbling myself instead of trying to lead others. Forgive me wherein I have wronged you. . . . May the Lord enlighten my mind to see clearly all my wrongs.[90]

Apparently the letter reconciled the two, because four months later Loughborough served on an investigative committee that cleared James White of all charges of financial mismanagement. Instead, the committee praised him for his many sacrifices and thanked his wife for her Spirit-led visions and testimonies.[91] Moreover, having seen Ellen White in vision dozens of times, John readily responded to Uriah Smith's request for specific incidents that demonstrated the divine fulfillment of her visions. His *Review* series "Remarkable Fulfillments of the Visions" recapped many of his personal experiences of Mrs. White in vision between 1852 and 1866 as well as his interviews with Adventists whose lives her visions had changed.[92]

If J. N. Loughborough accepted Mrs. White's visions as sent by God, she wrote in *Testimony* No. 13 that some of his dreams bore divine earmarks as well. She declared that two such dreams in 1867, "are as truly the fruits of the spirit of prophecy as [biblical] visions." In the first, John saw Battle Creek Adventists riding on a rickety train with low ceilings and poor ventilation barreling at top speed over rough tracks toward a railroad terminal. When it reached the turntable, James and Ellen White shouted, "This train is going all wrong. It must be turned square about." In his dream John helped James and Ellen with the crank that reversed the train's direction. Suddenly a transformation occurred: the cars grew larger, brighter, well-ventilated, and gilded, and the track became level and smooth. Groups of happy passengers boarded, "their countenances lit up with holy joy."[93]

Then in his second dream John found himself back in Victor, New York, searching for an "all-healing fountain." He followed a youthful guide past muddy bogs to a huge vat of fresh spring water. Drinking deeply, they found themselves "instantly revived." James White plunged into the vat three times, each dip making him stronger than before. With "melodious voices," the Whites urged everyone to drink from the spring. As Ellen filled a cup and brought it to John, he suddenly awoke, rejoicing that someday he would drink of that heavenly fountain and enjoy everlasting life. When he shared the dreams with Mrs. White, she assured him that they had brought her great encouragement.[94]

Within days, however, Loughborough's dreams turned to nightmares. Two weeks earlier his pregnant wife, Mary, who was already suffering from scrofula and canker sores in her mouth and on her stomach, had injured herself in a fall. John worried that "this crisis would not be passed in safety." Sure enough, after giving birth to two infant girls on June 24, 1867, Mary (age 35) expired in his arms hours later. One baby died, the other—named Mary after her mother—lived. "Thus suddenly was I separated from her to whom I had been happily united for sixteen and one half years," he wrote. Left with "a helpless babe" and 3-year-old "Dellie" (Delmer, born in 1864), Loughborough accepted the offer of Myron and Cornelia Cornell to care for baby Mary during the next year. His brother William and his wife, Eliza, moved from Rochester, New York, to Battle Creek to babysit Delmer so that John could finish writing his *Hand Book of Health* and meet his preaching appointments throughout the Midwest.[95]

Writing Mary's obituary in the *Review*, James White declared: "No affliction has for a longtime come so near this church. One of our best beloved members has been taken from our midst, one who held a warm and tender place in the affections of every heart." Prior to her death, Mary had given "fervent prayers and testimonies" at the Battle Creek church. Following the funeral there, she and her stillborn baby were buried in Oak Hill Cemetery, "a new treasure committed to the tomb, there to slumber with her little one sweetly pillowed on her arm till the Life-giver shall return to rescue his jewels from the dominion of the enemy [death]."[96]

Although "plunged into deep affliction," John declared, "God is good. . . . The afflictions he permits to come upon us are designed for our good, and to bring us nearer to him, where we can consecrate our energies more and more to his service." Finding comfort in his friends, who, he said, "have been very kind to me during my affliction," he thanked them in the *Review* for their "sympathy and acts of kindness."[97] James and Ellen White did what they could to console him, although Ellen feared that Mary had died ill-prepared to meet her Maker.[98]

J. N. LOUGHBOROUGH'S DIARIES

Loughborough's diaries provide ample proof that during their last year together John and Mary enjoyed a close companionship. While on the road, he mailed her weekly letters. He remembered her birthday (June 17) with special gifts. When together at home, they attended prayer meetings, Sabbath school, and church. While she cooked and cleaned, he tended the garden and orchard. Together they canned the fruit and vegetables they raised. As loving parents, they reared their children. When Mary died, he wrote, "Oh! How lonely, lonely!" next to the date of her funeral (June 26).

Although John kept busy writing, preaching, and organizing new churches and conferences, such activities could not fill the aching void in his heart. While he continued studying shorthand and reading many books (too many, Ellen White thought),[99] the lonely widower developed new interests as well. He started attending Philharmonic Society concerts in Battle Creek; rode horseback and split wood regularly; spent relaxing hours at Goguac Lake; and took more naps. While traveling, he enjoyed seeing natural wonders (such as Niagara Falls and caves). He even learned to sew well enough to make himself a pair of pants. Fascinated by machinery, he occasionally dropped by the Smith's home to see what new invention Uriah was tinkering with. Also he made pilgrimages to Oak Hill Cemetery to sit beside Mary's grave.

But in January of 1868 things began looking up when a new name appeared in his diary: Margaret ("Maggie") A. Newman. Both John (born in 1832) and Maggie (born in 1840) had grown up in Victor, New York, although we have no evidence that they knew each other there (when 17-year-old John moved to Rochester in 1849, Maggie was only 9). As a teenager Maggie enjoyed sewing samplers from multicolored cloth. Some portrayed birds on a nest, floral wreaths, and pink roses, while others focused on themes such as "Friendship" and "Sweet Home." Sometime around the Civil War her parents, Benjamin and Margaret Newman, moved the family to Lansing, Michigan. How or when John and Maggie first met we do not know, but certainly one advantage of being a peripatetic preacher was that Loughborough had many opportunities to meet eligible, attractive Adventist women on his Midwest circuit. On January 26, 1868, he celebrated his thirty-sixth birthday with the Newman family. By spring he was keeping the postal service in business sending her regular letters. Each time she replied, he wrote "M. A. N." in his diary. Even thunderstorms and hailstorms could not deter his visits to the Newmans'. Soon they were engaged, and on June 12, 1868, D. T. Bourdeau married them in the home of Maggie's grandparents near Victor. "I believe the Lord is in this union," Bourdeau said, and "may it alleviate the wound that has been made in our dear fellow-laborer, and may our present Sr. Loughborough be truly a help-meet to her husband, and to us in our important mission."[100]

Although Loughborough had (understandably) neglected to visit his vast Midwestern district for several months, Adventists in the hinterlands had not forgotten him. "When is Mr. Loughborough coming back again?"

one of them asked.[101] Could they have seen the future, his constituents would have been shocked to learn that the answer to their query was—*never*. Instead, John and Maggie were about to travel to the end of the earth—to California.

---

[1] John Byington, George W. Amadon, and J.N. Andrews for the General Conference Committee, July 26, 1863, DF 230, CAR.

[2] *RH*, May 26, 1863, pp. 204-206; *GCB* (1863), pp. 1-5; *GCB* (1899), p. 37; *PUR*, June 20, 1912, pp. 1, 2; A. Spalding, *Origin and History*, vol. 1, p. 308; *RH*, May 12, 1988, p. 9; JNL, "Religious Societies" (Battle Creek, Mich.: Review and Herald Press, 1863), pp. 1-16.

[3] JNL, *GCB* (1899), p. 37.

[4] JSW, *RH*, Oct. 6, 1863, quoted in A. L. White, *Ellen G. White: The Progressive Years*, vol. 2, p. 65.

[5] JNL, *BTS*, February 1916, p. 165.

[6] "Hull, Moses," *Seventh-day Adventist Encyclopedia* (Hagerstown, Md.: Review and Herald Pub. Assn., 1996), vol. 10, p. 718; "Hull, Moses," *Ellen G. White Encyclopedia*, pp. 417-420.

[7] EGW, *Testimonies for the Church*, vol. 1, p. 437; *RH*, Jan. 19, 1864, pp. 62, 63; JNL, *PUR*, June 13, 1912, pp. 1, 2.

[8] *RH*, May 26, 1863, p. 208; *RH*, June 30, 1863, p. 37; JNL, *PUR*, June 13, 1912, pp. 1, 2.

[9] JNL, *RH*, July 7, 1863, p. 48.

[10] *RH*, July 28, 1863, p. 72; *RH*, Sept. 1, 1863, p. 112; *RH*, Sept. 22, 1863, p. 133; *RH*, Oct. 27, 1863, p. 172; *RH*, Sept. 29, 1863, p. 140; JNL, *PUR*, June 13, 1912, pp. 1, 2; A. L. White, *Ellen G. White: The Progressive Years*, vol. 2, p. 63.

[11] JNL to JSW, Sept. 19, 1863, m. 52, CAR.

[12] *RH*, Jan. 5, 1864, p. 46; JNL, *Rise and Progress*, pp. 252, 253; *RH*, Jan. 22, 1895, p. 59; *PUR*, June 13, 1912, p. 2. From 1863 until he died in San José, California, in 1907, Hull gave lectures and wrote books seeking to prove that spiritualism was biblical.

[13] JNL to JSW, Sept. 19, 1863, m. 52, CAR; *RH*, Oct. 6, 1863, p. 148.

[14] *PUR*, Oct. 3, 1912, pp. 5, 6.

[15] See JNL's (and others') reports in *RH*, Nov. 10, 1863, p. 192; *RH*, Dec. 22, 1863, p. 32; *RH*, Feb. 9, 1864, p. 88; *RH*, Feb. 23, 1864, p. 101; *RH*, Mar. 8, 1864, p. 120; *RH*, Mar. 29, 1864, p. 144; *RH*, Apr. 5, 1864, pp. 148, 149; *RH*, Apr. 26, 1864, p. 176; *RH*, May 3, 1864, p. 184; *RH*, May 10, 1864, p. 188; *RH*, Apr. 6, 1916, p. 7.

[16] *RH*, Dec. 22, 1863, p. 32; *RH*, Feb. 16, 1864, p. 92.

[17] *RH*, May 17, 1864, p. 196.

[18] *RH*, Nov. 24, 1863, p. 204; *RH*, Feb. 2, 1864, p. 76; *RH*, Jan. 19, 1864, p. 64; *RH*, Mar. 8, 1864, p. 116; *RH*, Mar. 22, 1864, pp. 135, 136.

[19] *AUG*, Sept. 24, 1956, p. 5; *Southern Tidings*, October 1999, p. 35; *NPUG*, Apr. 3, 1989, p. 19.

[20] *RH*, May 24, 1864, pp. 206, 207.

[21] *RH*, May 31, 1864, pp. 1, 2, 6; *GCB* (1864), pp. 8-10; *RH*, June 28, 1864, p. 33.

[22] *RH*, Dec. 6, 1864, p. 14; *PUR*, Aug. 22, 1912, pp. 1, 2; H. Douglass, *Messenger of the Lord*, p. 289.

[23] JNL, *RH*, Dec. 6, 1864, p. 14; Ellen G. White Estate, *A Critique*, pp. 48, 49.

[24] JNL, *Life and Health,* March 1915, pp. 109, 110.

[25] See JNL's reports in *RH*, Aug. 2, 1864, p. 80; *RH*, Sept. 6, 1864, p. 117; *RH*, Sept. 20, 1864, p. 136; *RH*, Oct. 4, 1864, p. 152; *RH*, Oct. 18, 1864, p. 168; *RH*, Dec. 6, 1864, p. 16; *RH*, Jan. 24, 1865, p. 72; *RH*, Mar. 7, 1865, p. 112; *RH*, Mar. 14, 1865, p. 120.

[26] *RH*, Sept. 27, 1864, p. 141.

[27] *RH*, Feb. 2, 1864, cited by F. D. Nichol in *RH*, Apr. 21, 1960, p. 3.

[28] *RH*, Nov. 29, 1864, p. 6.

[29] *RH*, Mar. 1, 1865, p. 118.

[30] *RH*, Nov. 29, 1864, p. 5.

[31] GC Committee to Governor Blair (Aug. 2, 1864) and Blair's reply (Aug. 3, 1864), quoted in A. L. White, *Ellen G. White: The Progressive Years,* vol. 2, pp. 99-101; *RH*, Jan. 31, 1865, p. 80; *RH*, Mar. 14, 1865, p. 118.

[32] *RH*, July 25, 1865, p. 60; *RH*, July 17, 1866, p. 49; *PUR*, Oct. 10, 1912, p. 3; *PUR*, Nov. 21, 1912, p. 1.

[33] JNL to unknown [c. 1865], DF 349, CAR; *PUR*, Nov. 21, 1912, pp. 1, 2.

[34] JNL to Thomas Hare, Dec. 15 and 22, 1865, DF 349, CAR.

[35] JNL, *Rise and Progress*, p. 269; James White, quoted in JNL's pocket notebook, m. 006529, CAR; JNL, *PUR*, Jan. 9, 1913, pp. 1, 2. According to Loughborough, during Snook's last three years of life he suffered terribly from dyspepsia and died in December 1901 in great anguish of spirit. Brinkerhoff later told Elder Starr that "I am sorry I ever left them [SDAs]. . . . I am a lost man."

[36] *RH*, May 23, 1865, pp. 196-198; *RH*, May 30, 1865, p. 204; *General Conference Session Minutes* (May 17, 1865), pp. 10, 11; A. L. White, *Ellen G. White: The Progressive Years*, vol. 2, p. 116.

[37] See JNL's reports in the *RH*, June 6, 1865, p. 8; *RH*, June 13, 1865, p. 16; *RH*, June 20, 1865, p. 20; *RH*, June 27, 1865, p. 28; *RH*, July 4, 1865, pp. 36, 37; *RH*, July 11, 1865, p. 48; *RH*, July 18, 1865, p. 56; *RH*, Aug. 1, 1865, p. 72; *RH*, Aug. 15, 1865, pp. 84, 88.

[38] *RH*, June 27, 1865, p. 28. In fact, in 1866 Battle Creek Adventists built their third meetinghouse, this time 40' x 65', about 12' wider and 21' longer than the 1857 meeting house. See JNL, diary, Sept. 30, 1878.

[39] *RH*, July 26, 1864, p. 72; *RH*, June 6, 1865, p. 7.

[40] E. Robinson, *Lighter of Gospel Fires*, pp. 116, 117.

[41] *RH*, Sept. 26, 1865, p. 136; *RH*, Oct. 3, 1865, pp. 140, 144; *RH*, Oct. 31, 1865, p. 176; *RH*, May 1, 1866, p. 176; JNL to Thomas Hare, Oct. 29, 1865, DF 349, CAR; EGW, "Reminiscent Account of the Experience of James White's Sickness and Recovery" (1867), ms.1, 1867, CAR; A. L. White, *Ellen G. White: The Progressive Years*, vol. 2, pp. 119, 120, 123.

[42] JNL to Thomas Hare, Oct. 29, 1865, DF 349, CAR; JNL, *RH*, Nov. 14, 1865, p. 192.

[43] *RH*, Nov. 21, 1865, p. 200.

[44] *RH*, Dec. 5, 1865, p. 4.

[45] JNL, *Rise and Progress,* p. 269; *RH*, Jan. 14, 1937, p. 10; R. Numbers, *Prophetess of Health*, pp. 96-99.

[46] See JNL's reports in *RH*, Dec. 26, 1865, p. 32; Feb. 27, 1866, pp. 101, 104.

[47] *RH*, Apr. 17, 1866, p. 156; *RH*, May 15, 1866, p. 192.

[48] A. L. White, *Ellen G. White: The Progressive Years*, vol. 2, p. 136; JNL, "Four Battle Creek Meetinghouses," *The Missionary Magazine*, July 1901, p. 319.

[49] JNL, quoted in A. L. White, *Ellen G. White: The Progressive Years,* vol. 2, p. 141.

[50] *Ibid.*; Milton J. Murray, North American Division Committee, Oct. 11, 1981, p. 52; *PUR*, Jan. 2, 1913, pp. 2, 3; *PUR*, Feb. 20, 1913, pp. 1, 2.

[51] JNL, *RH*, June 19, 1866, p. 24; *RH*, July 10, 1866, p. 48; *PUR*, Jan. 2, 1913, pp. 2, 3; "Health Reform Institute," *Ellen G. White Encyclopedia*, p. 862.

[52] *RH*, Sept. 11, 1866, p. 117; *HR*, September 1866, p. 32; *HR* ad, November 1866, p. 64.

[53] *RH,* Aug. 14, 1866, pp. 84, 85.

[54] Ellen G. White Estate, *A Critique*, p. 59; see also E. G. White, *Testimonies*, vol. 1, pp. 456-495.

[55] *RH*, May 28, 1867, p. 279; *RH,* June 18, 1867, p. 16; *RH,* Mar. 31, 1868, p. 256. The WHRI Board included J. N. Loughborough, J. M. Aldrich, Uriah Smith, J. N. Andrews, N. N. Lunt, J. P. Kellogg, and E. S. Walker.

[56] The term *editress* was actually applied to Adelia Van Horn by the GC delegates at Battle Creek in their May 16-17, 1866, sessions. See *RH,* May 22, 1866, p. 198.

[57] *RH,* June 26, 1866, p. 32; Numbers, *Prophetess of Health*, p. 109.

[58] *RH*, Aug. 7, 1866, p. 80.

[59] JNL, "Rest," *HR*, August 1866, pp. 4, 5.

[60] *HR*, October 1866, p. 41.

[61] *HR,* December 1866, pp. 65, 66; *HR,* January 1867, pp. 85, 86.

[62] JNL's series on "Diseases and Their Treatment" appears in *HR*, November 1867, pp. 65-67; December 1867, pp. 81-83; January 1868, pp. 102, 103; March 1868, pp. 134, 135; April 1868, pp. 145, 146; May 1868, pp. 164-166.

[63] Roswell F. Cottrell, "Oh, Yes, I See It Is So," *HR*, February 1867, p. 105.

[64] *HR*, September 1867, p. 43.

[65] *RH*, Nov. 20, 1866, p. 200; *PUR*, Apr. 17, 1913, pp. 2, 3; *PUR*, June 19, 1913, pp. 2, 3; A. L. White, *Ellen G. White: The Progressive Years*, vol. 2, p. 176; JNL, *Hand Book of Health: Or, a Brief Treatise on Physiology and Hygiene, Comprising Practical Instruction on the Structure and Functions of the Human System, and Rules for the Preservation of the Health* (Battle Creek, Mich.: Steam Press of the Seventh-day Adventist Pub. Assn., 1868), pp. iii, iv. As Dr. David Paulson pointed out half a century later in *RH,* Nov. 6, 1913, p. 5, "The first health book among [SDAs] was not written by a doctor but by a minister."

[66] *RH*, Sept. 24, 1867, p. 240. Between 1864 and 1868 Loughborough wrote 10 articles for the *Review*: "Hope of the Gospel" (May 10, 1864, p. 192); his answers to Bible questions series (Sept. 6, 1864, p. 116; Dec. 20, 1864, pp. 25-27); "Sabbath on a Round World" (Oct. 11, 1864, pp. 157, 158); "Was Adam Ever Immortal?" (Jan. 24, 1865, pp. 68, 69); "Peace and Safety" (May 23, 1865, p. 200); a two-part series entitled "The Kingdom" (Dec. 11, 1866, pp. 1, 2; Dec. 18, 1866, pp. 13-15); "Pressing On" (Dec. 17, 1867, pp. 1-3); "Receive My Spirit" (Mar. 10, 1868, p. 208). He wrote only one in the *Youth's Instructor*, "Beginning of Wisdom" (September 1863, p. 69).

[67] *RH*, Sept. 24, 1867, p. 240; *RH*, Jan. 15, 1867, p. 72.

[68] Dr. H. S. Lay, quoted in JNL, *Hand Book of Health*, p. iv.

[69] JNL, *Hand Book of Health*, chapters 1-10.

[70] *Ibid.*, pp. 205, 214-227.

[71] *Ibid.*, pp. 19-42.

[72] *Ibid.*, pp. 125-142.

[73] *Ibid.*, pp. 179-198.

[74] *Ibid.*, pp. 98-205.

[75] *Ibid.*, p. 141.

[76] *Ibid.*, pp. 88-124.

[77] *Ibid.*, pp. 14, 15.

[78] "Camp Meeting," *Seventh-day Adventist Encyclopedia,* 2nd ed., vol. 10, pp. 281, 282.

[79] *RH,* Sept. 11, 1866, p. 117; *PUR,* Feb. 20, 1913, pp. 1, 2. Although Adventist historians have always considered the gathering held near Wright, Michigan, in September 1868 as the first official SDA camp meeting (indeed, the August 25, 1868, *RH* advertised it as "Our First General Camp Meeting"), the Pilot Grove, Iowa, camp meeting in August 1866 deserves to be considered as the church's first "general camp meeting."

[80] See JNL's reports in *RH,* May 29, 1866, p. 207; *RH,* July 24, 1866, p. 62; *RH,* July 17, 1866, p. 56; *RH,* July 24, 1866, p. 63; *RH,* July 31, 1866, p. 70; *RH,* Aug. 21, 1866, p. 54; *RH,* Sept. 4, 1866, p. 108; *RH,* Oct. 16, 1866, p. 158.

[81] *RH,* July 31, 1866, p. 69.

[82] *RH,* Aug. 14, 1866, pp. 84, 85.

[83] *RH,* Jan. 22, 1867, p. 79; *RH,* Feb. 12, 1867, pp. 114, 115; *RH,* Nov. 5, 1867, p. 321. After spending six hours slogging 11 miles through deep mud, he called Michigan's roads "literally awful."

[84] *GCB* (1867), p. 30; *RH,* May 28, 1867, pp. 284, 285.

[85] *RH,* May 28, 1867, p. 281.

[86] See JNL's reports in *RH,* June 18, 1867, p. 5; *RH,* June 25, 1867, pp. 20, 21; *RH,* Aug. 20, 1867, p. 156.

[87] *RH,* Feb. 19, 1867, p. 127; *RH,* Aug. 27, 1867, p. 171; *RH,* Oct. 29, 1867, p. 305.

[88] JNL, *RH,* Mar. 26, 1867, p. 192.

[89] JNL to J. B. Frisbie and J. N. Andrews, Oct. 18, 1867, m. 006529, CAR.

[90] JNL to JSW, May 21, 1867, m. 006529, CAR.

[91] EGW, *Testimonies*, vol. 1, pp. 609-612.

[92] JNL, "Remarkable Fulfillments of the Visions," *RH,* Dec. 25, 1866, p. 30; *RH,* Jan. 15, 1867, pp. 62, 63; *RH,* Mar. 12, 1867, p. 162; *RH,* Sept. 17, 1867, p. 224.

[93] EGW, *Testimonies*, vol. 1, pp. 600-602; A. L. White, *Ellen G. White: The Progressive Years*, vol. 2, p. 206-211.

[94] EGW, *Testimonies*, vol. 1, pp. 602-604.

[95] Obituary for Mary Loughborough, *RH,* July 2, 1867, p. 8; *HR*, November 1867, p. 67; *PUR*, Apr. 24, 1913, p. 3; diary, June 1867, pp. 23, 24; and Flora Cornell Tazer, *RH,* Mar. 12, 1925, p. 15. Mary had already lost three children, including Teresa and two unnamed infants. Her daughter Mary, "a lean skeleton of a child" that weighed only five pounds and whom her father believed "could live [only] a week," grew into a strong, capable woman who married John J. Ireland, a church auditor, and took care of J. N. Loughborough for 10 years in California after his third wife died in 1907.

[96] James White, *RH,* July 2, 1867, pp. 40, 41. Elder A. S. Hutchins preached the funeral sermon with Elders J. H. Waggoner and I. D. Van Horn assisting at the service. It is possible that both James White and Uriah Smith helped compose her obituary.

[97] *RH,* July 30, 1867, p. 105.

[98] EGW to George and Martha Amadon, July 7, 1869, letter A-009, CAR. In her frank letter, Mrs. White accuses George and Martha Amadon, Cornelia Cornell, and Harriet Smith of "working with the devil" to create "a terrible condition of things." "I know that you are all more or less accountable for Mary dying unready," she declares.

[99] In "For Ministers," Ms. 7, 1863, Ellen White admonished J. N. Loughborough, Moses Hull, and J. N. Andrews for being "greedy for too many books. They have read and studied more than they can retain, and I was shown that much study is a weariness of the flesh (Eccl. 12:12). They have not given the mind time to rest." By "crowding into one discourse so much and making so many points that minds cannot always appreciate or follow them," they "injure the effect of the truth that they would advocate." She urged

them instead to "rivet" one or two points in the minds of listeners, and then "urge [them] to [make] a decision." Instead of spending so much time in research, time would be better "spent in secret prayer" and "sacred meditation." If they would do this, "a tremendous . . . compelling power" would attend their preaching. Otherwise, "the theory of truth without the power of God will produce but little effect," she warned.

[100] JNL, diary, January 1867-May 1868; www.ancestry.com (accessed July 12, 2009); cloth samplers preserved in a tiny 3" x 4" diary for 1856 in the J. N. Loughborough collection at CAR; marriage certificate for John and Margaret (Newman) Loughborough, June 12, 1868, ASC m. 92, CAR; *RH,* June 23, 1868, p. 5; Bonnie Waters e-mail to Brian Strayer, May 16, 2011.

[101] *RH,* Mar. 24, 1868, p. 234.

CHAPTER VIII

PIONEERING THE WORK IN CALIFORNIA (1868-1872)

"[The] sea boils like a pot. All [are] sick nearly on board the ship. I [am] a little better to-day, [but] eat nothing all day."[1]

In 1851, as "gold rush fever" swept the country, a wealthy Rochester entrepreneur had offered to pay Loughborough's travel expenses to California if he would enter a business partnership with him. Together they would "mine the miners" who since 1849 had been panning gold near Sutter's Fort. But John had politely declined his offer because he had discovered a "nugget" in Rochester. Her name was Mary J. Walker, and he married her a few months later.[2] If John had gone to the West Coast in 1851, it is certain that his life—and the Seventh-day Adventist Church itself—would have been quite different in many ways.

But after the Panic of 1857 began to level off another Sabbathkeeping Adventist did go to California, and his pioneering efforts laid the groundwork for J. N. Loughborough's activities there. Merritt G. Kellogg of Battle Creek, half brother to the soon-to-be-famous Dr. John Harvey Kellogg, left Michigan with his wife and three children intending to mine gold in Colorado. Traveling by railroad to Iowa, the family purchased a team of oxen and joined a wagon train. During the next five months they faced hostile Indians, quicksand, poisonous snakes, wolves, cyclones, grizzly bears, food shortages, and sickness. Tired of the "Great American Desert" (as people then called the Plains), they changed course for California. When they arrived in San Francisco, Merritt got a job as a carpenter at the fabulous wage of $10 a day.[3]

Besides making good money, however, Kellogg shared his Adventist faith. He converted the lumber worker B. G. St. John (a former gold miner who had made—and lost—$100,000). In 1861 the two men held an evangelistic campaign that converted 14, including Mrs. Short, the wife of the chief of police. During the next two years, as the shoemaker J. W. Conkrite joined their evangelistic team and displayed his prophetic charts, the number of Adventists grew. Soon they organized a Bible class and Sabbath school that met in the Kellogg's home. In the mid-1860s, seeking qualified evangelists, they sent $133 in gold to Battle Creek to pay their expenses. But the General Conference had no one to send. James White reassured them: "Do not be discouraged. We believe that in due time the Lord will provide men and means for the proclamation of His truth in California." Two years later, M. G. Kellogg (then studying medicine at Dr. Trall's Hygieo-Therapeutic Institute in New Jersey) attended the 1867 GC session and pleaded for ministers to go to California. Loughborough even published a formal call in the *Review*. But no one responded.[4]

In those early days evangelists chose where they wanted to work for the coming year. During the winter of 1867-1868, as John labored in Allegan County, Michigan, he prayed for guidance regarding where God wanted him to go the following year. Then he began having dreams in which he saw himself boarding a ship in New York City, sailing to the Isthmus of Panama and from there up the coast to San Francisco, and holding tent meetings in a town whose name he did not know. The bizarre dream reoccurred not once or twice but *20 times* during the next few months. He had never seriously considered preaching on the West Coast, because prior to the completion of the transcontinental railroad in 1869, California (as John phrased it) "was away off, almost out of the world." Unbeknownst to him, Daniel Bourdeau had been having the same dreams up in Vermont. Convicted that God truly wanted them to go to California, Daniel and his wife, Marion, sold their property and household goods and converted the profits into bank drafts that they brought with them to the GC session of 1868.[5]

When the Loughboroughs and Bourdeaus reached Battle Creek, everything seemed to be business as usual at the session. As a member of the GC Committee, John served on the Committee on Preaching, the Committee to Help the Poor, and the Committee on Nominations. The delegates elected him GC treasurer and reelected him to the editorial board of the *Health Reformer*. But then events took an unexpected turn. Before assigning territories for the coming year, James White had urged the ministers to spend 10 days in prayer. After they had done so, he asked each one where they felt God wanted them to work. When most had chosen their fields, White asked, "Does no one feel impressed to go to California?" Loughborough rose to his feet. Moments later, Bourdeau also stood. White asked both men to spend two more days seeking divine guidance before giving the delegates their final answer. When they had done so, they declared, "[It's] California or nothing." Only then did James White tell them that he too had been convicted for weeks that they were the most suitable to be "missionaries" (the first use of that term at a GC session) on the West Coast. On May 31 John (the habitual misspeller) wrote in his diary: "This morning the matter [was] decided about my going to Calafornia."[6]

The previous 15 years James and Ellen White had spent a great deal of time observing John Loughborough at home and in the field. Together they had held evangelistic meetings, organized new churches and conferences, established thriving institutions, and fought fanatics from Maine to Iowa. As next-door neighbors, they had shared times of joy and grief. As we have seen, Loughborough was a firm believer in the divine inspiration of Ellen G. White, even when (perhaps especially when) she rebuked him in her testimonies. His close study of her writings and of the Bible convinced him that God was leading what he called "the Great Second Advent Movement" to prepare the world for Christ's soon coming. In speeches and letters to the *Review,* believers across the U.S. had praised his adventuresome spirit, ardor, optimism, intensity, devotion, and debating ability. J. N. Loughborough was also famous for his frugality, humility, time-management skills, and dependence on God. During the past two decades he had faced floods, epidemics, and assorted accidents of all kinds—and they had made him adaptable, an essential trait for any missionary. For all these reasons and more, the delegates agreed that Loughborough was the right man for the challenging enterprise.[7]

Before he left they issued him new ministerial credentials: "This is to certify that Elder J. N. Loughborough of Battle Creek, Michigan, is an ordained Minister, in good standing, in the Michigan State Conference of Seventh-day Adventists, and is sent as a missionary to California, under the direction of the General Conference of Seventh-day Adventists." His longtime colleagues J. N. Andrews, James White, D. T. Bourdeau, and Uriah Smith signed the certificate. White also promised to raise $1,000 from donations to help fund the "California Mission."[8]

Yet, as John confessed in the *Review*, he could not bear the burden alone: "[Preparing to go] has worn upon our strength, yet we feel that God blesses us at every step, and that holy angels are about us to protect us and help us. We believe if we trust in God, walk in the path of humility, and press on in the cross-bearing way, that God will go with us. We expect your prayers to follow us, dear brethren, as we go on this mission. It touches a tender chord in our hearts to part with our dear brethren, friends, and near relatives, but in the strength of the Lord we drink of the cup."[9]

As the Loughboroughs and Bourdeaus traveled by train to New York City, John and Daniel stopped along the way to preach at Adventist meetinghouses and say farewell to friends and relatives. At each place, they reported, "We had an affecting parting scene . . . leaving an impression which we expect to retain as long as memory lasts." As luck would have it, they met a man on the train who had visited California several times, and he gave them invaluable information about its people, climate, routes, and economy. When the train reached Rochester, John paid $415 for a new 60-foot tent, which was shipped to San Francisco.[10]

THE JOURNEY TO CALIFORNIA

Nineteenth-century travelers to America's West Coast would *not* have agreed that "going there is half the fun." Before the completion of the Union Pacific Railroad in 1869, pioneers had two choices: a 2,000-mile, five-month journey by ox-drawn wagon across the Great Plains and over the Rocky Mountains, or a 6,000-mile, monthlong voyage by sea. As we have seen, the Kellogg family chose the former in 1859 and nearly died in the attempt. The Loughboroughs and Bourdeaus decided on the latter because it was quicker, cheaper, and safer. Nonetheless, some Adventists in 1868 believed that their trip to California proved that "the end [of the world] was about due, because the farthest limits of territory were then being reached."[11]

Following the advice of Mr. Peters (a Battle Creek friend who had been to the West Coast three times), John and Daniel went to New York City early and, by comparative shopping, found that they could save $212.50 (about $5,000 in today's dollars) by buying tickets with the Pacific Mail Steamship Company rather than sailing on the more expensive American Steamship Line. Consequently, tickets for four adults (at $160 apiece) and one child ($40)—the Loughboroughs took Delmer and left Mary in Battle Creek—cost $467.50, including their luggage and freight for the tent. After purchasing tickets and selecting berths aboard ship, John returned to Victor and visited the cemetery to meditate beside the graves of his uncle, grandparents, father, and sister. Then on June 24—the anniversary of Mary's death—they left New York City on the *Rising Star.*[12]

Of the 5,875-mile journey ahead of them (John recorded every mile!), Loughborough told *Review* readers that "this cannot be [considered] a pleasure trip as some have supposed." True indeed, for within minutes of leaving New York Harbor, the rough winds and towering waves soon made everyone violently seasick (except 4-year-old Delmer, who vomited once and was just fine the rest of the trip). John, who ate nothing but an orange on some days, described seasickness as "a sort of living death," like being swung around until dizzy for days on end.[13]

Yet the trip provided some pleasures. Passengers who remained topside enjoyed watching the antics of half a dozen whales, scores of porpoises, and hundreds of flying fish. Despite the tropical heat, those who had recovered from mal de mer savored fresh bananas, citrus, mangoes, pineapples, and coconuts. The Loughboroughs also ate the graham crackers and canned peaches provided by Battle Creek friends. Below deck, John and Maggie attended Episcopal services at which they enjoyed singing the "Missionary Hymn," "Calvary," and "The Burial of Mrs. Judson." Although "much weakened," the two families assured *Review* readers that "our minds are clear, and we are of good courage, trusting in the Lord."[14]

As the train (following Balboa's 1513 route from east to west) chugged across 50 miles of jungle between Aspinwall and Panama City, Loughborough was shocked by the poverty and ignorance of the natives. Like Protestants everywhere, he blamed their condition on centuries of "Spanish cruelties" and Roman Catholic domination during which the Indians had been "deprived of the light of revelation." But it was not the natives who most disturbed his peace of mind. During the Pacific voyage, when the parties began below decks, drunkenness, dancing, carousing, and licentiousness turned the ship into "a regular Sodom," kept them awake past midnight, and proved that "Satan was on board the ship." With Bourdeau's help, John took his mind off the carousing crowds by studying French. He also read Joseph Bates' new autobiography and a novel entitled *The Old Red House*. Like tourists everywhere, he collected souvenirs along the way, including a block of wood from a railroad tie in Panama (a century later, it would be carved into a gavel and presented to GC president R. R. Figuhr in 1962).[15]

LIGHTING FIVE BONFIRES

When the *Golden City* docked at San Francisco (a city of 165,000 people) on July 18, the missionaries' 24-day journey finally ended. But now they faced new challenges: Delmer fell ill; then Maggie needed expensive dental work; and finally John (apprised of a smallpox epidemic nearby) decided to get vaccinated—and fainted dead away. The evangelist who had never paid a dime to rent land for his tent meetings now discovered that in California vacant lots did not come free. Indeed, the *only* lot available in San Francisco belonged to a Jew who wanted $40 a month for it. The two penny-pinching preachers, shocked at the idea of paying three weeks' salary just to rent a piece of ground, knelt in prayer, asking God to provide answers to their dilemmas. Then the miracles began.[16]

A New York City newspaper had picked up James White's appeal in the *Review* for $1,000 to send the Loughboroughs and Bourdeaus to California, and its editor reprinted it as a news item. A copy of the newspaper, which had reached California before the missionaries arrived, came to the attention of a group of Independent Christians (who had seceded from several mainstream churches) in Petaluma, a town of about 2,000 people 40 miles north of San Francisco. They began praying for the missionaries' safe arrival. One of them—Mr. Wolf—had a dream in which he saw the two men building five bonfires to "dispel the [spiritual] gloom and darkness." When leading ministers tried to extinguish the fires by beating them with brush and turf, they only burned brighter. In the dream a voice told Wolf that the two men were Adventist evangelists from Michigan and that the Independents should assist them.[17] As a result, they decided to send Mr. Hough, a member of their group, to San Francisco to find the two evangelists.

Meanwhile, on July 20—two days after their arrival—John and Daniel, sauntering along the wharfs, were surprised to see the sacks containing their tent. The tent was not supposed to be on that steamer! To save money, Loughborough had paid the slow freight rate at New York City, and thus he did not expect the tent to arrive in San Francisco until two weeks after the *Golden City* docked. But stevedores in Panama, to lighten the load on the next cargo vessel, had put the bulky tent on the *Golden City*, the same ship on which the missionaries sailed. Telling the men to deliver it to B. G. St. John's home on Minna Street, John and Daniel hurried away to buy side poles, ropes, lamps, and fixtures for the tent.[18]

One week later, when Hough reached the city, he too went to the Pacific Mail Wharf and asked a drayman for the names of the evangelists and the destination of their tent. Within half an hour, he knocked at St. John's door. Introducing himself to the two evangelists, he told them about his friend Wolf's dream and urged them to pitch their tent in Petaluma. Promising to give the matter serious thought, the two preachers prayed for guidance. Then Loughborough had a dream in which he saw Ellen White telling him to go to Petaluma where "a good work can be done." Confident that God was leading, the two Adventists packed their tent and headed north.[19]

But holding evangelistic meetings in Petaluma presented the men with several challenges they had never faced back East. First, although nearly two decades had passed since the Gold Rush of 1849, northern California still felt the effects of rampant inflation. Indeed, between 1849 and 1853, the state had produced 20 times more gold than all the rest of the U.S. since 1776. Unlike the penny-pinching Yankees of New England, the citizens of California were liberal—even prodigal—spenders. With wages and prices rising rapidly, they could not be bothered with the pennies, three-cent pieces, and nickels that filled the pockets of Americans east of the Rockies: the smallest coin in California was the dime.[20]

Loughborough informed Ellen White, "I have found a new situation here in California. I have never seen it before. Things are much more expensive." According to Loughborough, Mrs. White (herself a notorious penny-pincher) replied: "You can not labor in California as you did in New England. Such strict economy would be considered 'penny wise' by the Californians. Things are managed there on a more liberal basis. You will have to meet them in the same liberal spirit, but not in a spendthrift manner."[21] When offered a limited selection of tracts and pamphlets costing between one and five cents, Californians typically handed the men a dime or a quarter, telling them that in lieu of change, they could give the rest away to others. Furthermore, they paid with gold dust or silver coins, seldom using the cheaper paper money circulating elsewhere. Within weeks the evangelists had sold four boxes containing about 400 books and tracts—roughly $300 worth—more than the amount sold by all Adventist evangelists east of the Rockies during the same period. One Sunday they sold 17 copies of Uriah Smith's prophetic book *Thoughts on Revelation*, an unprecedented feat in Adventist evangelism.[22]

Second, although Loughborough occasionally suffered from malarial fever, he had never encountered smallpox epidemics. Shortly after the men began holding tent meetings in Petaluma, the local authorities placed the town under quarantine. Although many families—and all the ministers—fled to the country, Loughborough, Bourdeau, and Merritt Kellogg remained behind, carrying water, nursing the sick, giving vaccinations, and cooking nourishing food. They advised those who had not succumbed to the scourge to "use the milk and fruit produced on their own" farms. Their good Samaritan service garnered enormous public relations benefits once the quarantine ended and their meetings resumed. Furthermore, after word spread that Mr. Wolf had identified Bourdeau and Loughborough as those he had seen in his dream, crowds packed their tent every night, delighted with the men's preaching and enthralled at their ability to sing gospel duets in four-part harmony. While 40 people attended the opening meeting, 200 came the following night, and soon 400 overflowed their tent.[23]

Although the evangelists found such public support gratifying, they soon learned a third lesson about California: here they would meet some of the strongest opposition in their ministerial careers. For example, when Loughborough informed Mr. Rice, the local lumber dealer, that back East lumberyards customarily gave preachers wooden boards at no cost (except for what they cut or damaged), he was stunned when Rice grumbled, "Well, I don't know about trusting a minister with lumber. My experience with them has taught me that they are rather a risky set of men." Turning on the Irish charm, John replied, "Mr. Rice, you may not find them [preachers] all alike." After scrutinizing John, Rice agreed to give him

1,000 feet of lumber if Mr. Hough would provide security for it.[24]

Their first series of tent meetings attracted 20 new converts and 25 children, whom Loughborough and Bourdeau formed into a Sabbath school.[25] But it also produced growing opposition, and soon the evangelists had good reason to recall Mr. Wolf's dream about opponents trying to extinguish their gospel fires. When a Petaluma lawyer challenged their teaching on the Sabbath, they agreed to debate the subject with him for three days. But as he studied the Bible, he became convinced that his views were wrong. He confessed to the crowd: "I sincerely thought [this] was heresy, but I find that Mr. Loughborough is on the right side of this question. With his permission I'd like to join him and get on the right side of this Sabbath truth."[26]

But some confrontations turned violent. A certain Mr. Peugh, armed with a club and a huge butcher knife, hid along the road to the Piner Schoolhouse to waylay John as he went by, but Loughborough, who had left early, had already passed that stretch of road. When Peugh reached the school, a man named Oliver Skinner met him at the door with a revolver, declaring that Peugh could expel the preacher only "over my dead body." Attendees formed a protective cordon around John, Maggie, and Delmer. When Loughborough attempted to preach in the Monroe schoolhouse near Healdsburg, a certain Mr. Morton grabbed his arm and threw him out the front door, calling him a liar, thief, blasphemer, and Mormon ("lying Mormons" and "haranguing Millerites" were frequent epithets hurled at Adventist preachers on the West Coast). As Morton raised his cane to strike, John recalled years later, "I never felt calmer [than at any time] in my life." Refusing to let others fight Morton, John withdrew to an oak grove and held services there, asserting that Morton's actions were "helping more than hurting." Facing trial, Morton fled the county, but years later before his death he confided to his son, "The sorriest day of my life was the occasion at the Monroe schoolhouse."[27]

Such threats convinced Loughborough and Bourdeau that, just as they alternated preaching each evening, so they should take turns sleeping in the tent. Gradually the tide turned, especially when the editor of the Petaluma *Journal and Argus* began printing favorable reports of the discourses given by "Messrs. Loughborough and Bourdeau." The downside to such publicity, however, was that it attracted opponents like bees to honey. Soon

Loughborough had his hands full responding to charges of Mormonism and wearing ascension robes in 1844. He also debated the Sabbath-Sunday question with the Reverends Mock and Lippitt.[28]

Yet if favorable newspaper publicity drew the ire of skeptics, unfavorable publicity sometimes backfired, leading to conversions. For example, the editor of the *California Christian Advocate* attacked Adventist teachings, predicting that nothing would come from them. But when a copy of that issue reached the miner William Hunt in Nevada, he was so happy that someone was preaching the prophecies of Daniel and Revelation that he sent John $60 in gold dust to purchase everything the Review and Herald press published. Convinced that what he read was truth, he became an Adventist, immigrated to South Africa, and won more converts there.[29]

During the 10 weeks they spent in Petaluma, the preaching team had effectively "lit the first bonfire" that Wolf had seen in his dream. They had established a company of believers with a weekly Sabbath school, prayer meeting, and five Bible classes (two of them taught by Maggie Loughborough and Marion Bourdeau). "The cause [in California] is in its infancy," Bourdeau wrote in the *Review*, "[but] we will not despise the day of small things."[30]

The preaching team next pitched their tent at Windsor during November and December (something no evangelist would have tried back East) and, with the help of wood-burning stoves, held their meetings. Although Windsor was a center of spiritualism, Loughborough's and Bourdeau's reputation for defeating all opponents on the state-of-the-dead question brought them no challengers on that issue. Instead, a pastor from Santa Rosa requested a debate on the Sabbath-Sunday controversy. The night before the debate, Loughborough had a dream in which he saw himself hiking a treacherous mountain path to a railroad depot, where he boarded a luxurious train full of smiling people (including the Whites). After he heard James White call it "the California train," John awoke "thrilled from head to foot by the thought that the dream was a token of victory" for the Adventist cause in the state. Subsequently John so roundly defeated his opponent that the Santa Rosa *Democrat* printed his discourses. The team sold $40 worth of books and organized a church and a small Sabbath school. The second bonfire had been lit.[31]

Yet the team accomplished far more than they realized at the time, for one of their 12 converts was Abram La Rue, a transient shepherd and woodcutter. A kind old man with long white hair and beard, La Rue had been a sailor earlier in life and had seawater in his veins. After further education at Healdsburg College, he became a self-supporting missionary to Hawaii, Hong Kong, Singapore, and eventually to China, distributing tracts and books to literally hundreds of people throughout Asia.[32]

Favorable newspaper publicity soon brought an invitation to commence meetings in nearby Santa Rosa Creek. Because the heavy rains had washed out the bridge, the men crossed on a tree trunk "which nature had graciously bent over the stream." Eager listeners packed the local schoolhouse as the two men preached alternatively (with three discourses every Sunday). Once again, their fame attracted opponents, including Mr. Kirk Patrick (who debated the temporal millennium), Reverend Crawford (who argued in favor of Sunday observance), and Reverend McCorkal (whose specialty was ascension robes). According to Bourdeau's report in the *Review*, "Never did we see so great a revolution in so short a time. . . . The victory of truth was complete."[33]

Once again, the spiritual harvest proved rewarding. After three months' labor, the two men had 40 converts. One was Dr. Parrot, who lay near death after being crushed by a horse in a fall. Ignoring pleas from her friends to fetch a doctor, she summoned the two evangelists, who early the next morning came, along with Mrs. Loughborough. After Maggie anointed Parrot's forehead with oil, Loughborough and Bourdeau prayed for her. Suddenly she clapped her hands and said, "I am healed." She "assisted in getting the dinner" and then rode to their meetings in a lumber wagon with no pain of any kind. A similar experience occurred when the two preachers carried Mrs. Ferguson, a bed-ridden cripple, into the river to baptize her in a chair. Following her immersion, she shouted "Glory!" walked to the shore by herself, and prepared dinner for her family, completely healed. Yet a third convert was Mr. Rice, the lumberyard owner who had called preachers "a pretty risky set of men." Thanks to his lumber (and the generosity of members who gave more than $1,300), Adventists in Santa Rosa quickly erected a 30' x 60' meetinghouse that withstood several tremblers (including the famous 1906 San Francisco earthquake).[34] The third bonfire had been lit.

Loughborough and Bourdeau next moved their tent to Healdsburg.

Here, debates with the Reverends McCorkal, Hallam, and Jenks (on the Sabbath-Sunday question and the perpetuity of God's law) attracted crowds of eager listeners. Their preaching convicted Oliver Skinner, a notorious atheist, who testified that all his "cobwebs" of doubt had been "swept away." After 14 weeks the team organized a small company of 20 believers there.[35] The fourth bonfire had been lit.

They next responded to invitations to preach in Sebastopol that fall. After two months of evangelism, the two men organized a company of 10 Adventists.[36] The fifth bonfire had been lit.

But after preaching nonstop at 240 evangelistic services during seven months, Loughborough (with characteristic understatement) admitted in the *Review*, "We are somewhat worn."[37] For two years the Loughboroughs and Bourdeaus had "lived as one family," eating together, preaching together, and splitting the expense. Now it was time to go their separate ways. The Bourdeaus boarded a train on the recently completed Union Pacific Railroad and headed east to work among French-speaking people in northern New England.[38]

"RIGHTING UP THE PAST"

Before deciding where to go next, J. N. Loughborough sat down and read Ellen White's *Testimony* No. 18 (dealing with intemperance, immorality, and contentiousness within Adventism) and several of her recent letters to him and others. If his evangelistic success had aroused in him any feelings of pride and self-congratulation, the letters humbled him. In an August 15, 1869, testimony, Mrs. White admonished John (and three others) for their negative influence on a certain Mr. Rodgers of Battle Creek. By "sowing seeds of rebellion," they had reflected "the spirit of Satan." She urged John to "draw near to God. Live in Him and walk even as He walked [and then] God will bless you with freedom."[39] A September 24 letter accused John of "[building] himself up upon what he supposed was the ruin of my husband." In the presence of others, he had "talked and laughed and made himself jovial over the humiliating features of my husband's case [following James White's stroke]. My heart was nearly broken."[40]

After reading *Testimony* No. 18 John wrote James and Ellen White: "I see myself in the light of that testimony a poor, selfish, self-indulgent, self-conceited creature. . . . I want to get nearer to God. I want to right up the past." "I have greatly wronged you, injured you, and done a vast amount of mischief in Battle Creek and elsewhere," he confessed. To set things right, he had written letters to all those who had heard him make fun of James (by mimicking him), asking for their forgiveness and urging them "to get right in the sight of God." He closed his letter: "In hope of getting right. Your unworthy brother, J. N. Loughborough."[41]

A week later, responding to a harsh letter from James White, Loughborough adopted a conciliatory (if somewhat hyperbolic) tone. "I have no spirit to resent one word you have written, but [I] want to make clean work relative to the past so as to find the favor of Heaven. After being insulted and abused by me as you have, I marvel that you have patience to write me so long a letter." In reviewing the past, John admitted, "I have had but little idea of the wrongs I had done or the true way to get those wrongs right. . . . Truly I have been a tool of the Devil in this desolating work in Battle Creek. I don't know as I can ever make it right in this world, but I will try to do what I can by God's grace. . . . I fear at times I am a doomed man." Describing himself as "exalted" and "puffed up," John apologized profusely for "the wrong I have done. . . . I want to . . . clear up the wrong influence I have exerted in the past." In fact, he would like to return to Battle Creek and talk the matter over face to face with the Whites and others. Resolving to use his time and money in "righting up the past," Loughborough sent a bank draft for $100 to be split between the Michigan Conference and the General Conference. He also asked White to burn the will that John had deposited in the Review and Herald safe because honoring it would divert means from the gospel work.[42] Then in his diary Elder Loughborough penned the following New Year's resolution: "As I enter upon this year [1869] I must consecrate *my all* . . . wholly to the Lord. . . . Oh! Lord may I live this year more to thy glory than ever before."[43]

To fulfill that resolution, Loughborough teamed up with Merritt Kellogg in the spring of 1870 to hold revival services among the five recently established companies and to begin evangelistic meetings in new locales. When another smallpox epidemic interrupted their tent effort at Bloomfield, Kellogg nursed the sick as he had in Petaluma, and it won them many friends—and a $50 purse raised by grateful citizens.[44] At Petaluma, Santa Rosa, Healdsburg, Bloomfield, Green Valley, and other towns north of San Francisco, the two men baptized scores of converts (many of them children and youth), raised up congregations, designed and built new meetinghouses, and organized Sabbath schools, prayer meetings, and quarterly services. As John's preaching circuit drew him ever farther from Maggie, the Loughboroughs decided to rent a house in Healdsburg for the winter.[45]

The two preachers' optimistic reports in the *Review* attracted so much attention that soon Adventists all over the East and Midwest wanted to know how to move to California. Although Merritt Kellogg readily supplied them with information about the state's geography, climate, soil, fruits and vegetables, and costs, he urged the poor, the sick, and those wanting to get rich quickly to remain where they were. Admitting that viticulture (growing wine grapes) was the most remunerative business in northern California, he recognized that Adventists, as teetotalers, would never "engage in making liquid fire for people to drink."[46] To counteract the "relaxed" lifestyles of so many California Adventists, what the state really needed were more "earnest" Christians willing to labor for God.[47] Because California Adventists' liberal lifestyle differed significantly from that of Adventists in the East (especially regarding wine, dancing, and jewelry), Loughborough soon had his hands full from "seeking to correct wrongs in the churches" that he, Bourdeau, and Kellogg had organized.[48]

What these independent-minded Adventists really needed, Loughborough concluded, was some form of statewide organization. As early as January 1869 James White had foreseen the time when the California Mission would become self-sustaining. Three months later, 60 converts had convened at Santa Rosa for the first "General Meeting" of Adventists, at which, in addition to forming a statewide association, new believers received instruction on how to observe the Sabbath and hold Communion services. That summer D. T. Bourdeau (as president of the state association) wrote to the *Review* releasing eastern Adventists "from further assisting with their means . . . the cause in California because from this time onward [it] will be self-sustaining." In April 1870, 100 Adventists, meeting at Santa Rosa, elected Bourdeau as president and Kellogg as secretary of the California State Association. They also appointed a three-man committee (Bourdeau, Kellogg, and John Bowman) to supervise its business affairs. The following year delegates chose Loughborough as president and treasurer and Kellogg as secretary. Given his new administrative responsibilities on the West Coast, John resigned as GC treasurer, trustee of the SDA Publishing Association, and director of the Health Reform Association. He also asked the Michigan Conference to "transfer" (release) him to California.[49] By 1871 California had 130 Adventists contributing $1,140 annually to the Systematic Benevolence Fund, and the State Association was also completely free of debt. Its officers asked the General Conference to send another evangelist to California to replace D. T. Bourdeau (now working in New England) and M. G. Kellogg (now doing manual labor).[50]

That spring church leaders sent Merritt E. Cornell to labor with Loughborough. With the young J. L. Wood as their tent master, they commenced the first evangelistic meetings ever held in San Francisco—or in any American metropolis (Adventist preachers typically avoided big cities). All summer long crowds filled their tent. Losing church members to Seventh-day Adventism, local pastors called in Miles Grant (a nationally famous Advent Christian debater) to counter their influence. Grant drew 100 curious listeners but left too soon to have a permanent impact. B. G. St. John then rented a hall and invited Loughborough and Cornell to preach to Grant's old crowd. They gladly accepted the invitation, and by the end of the campaign they had baptized more than 50 converts, who not only paid more than $500 toward the men's expenses, but also pledged $1,100 toward the Systematic Benevolence Fund.[51]

With church membership skyrocketing and funds pouring in, Adventist leaders began laying plans for statewide camp meetings and Sabbath school conferences. They also started a California Tract and Missionary Society (an outgrowth of the Vigilant Missionary Society founded in 1868 by several women in South Lancaster, Massachusetts, to distribute literature at home and abroad) with auxiliary bands in local churches. To celebrate Independence Day, they organized a convention for 100 youth near Sebastopol in July 1871. In addition to providing singing lessons for Sabbath school leaders, this "spiritual feast" featured outdoor recreation, a baptism, and fervent preaching. Local Adventists provided attendees with a healthful dinner, although it was admitted that "all was not strictly hygienic" (following strict health reform recipes), but "the cake and pie were [made] of graham [flour]." As he savored the delicious food, no doubt Loughborough recalled the warning Adventists had given him three years earlier: "You cannot survive in California as a vegetarian!" But he and Maggie had proved them wrong.[52]

LOUGHBOROUGH'S DIARY AND WRITINGS

In fact, John's diary provides ample proof that the Loughboroughs were thriving on a cornucopia of fruits and vegetables. They picked gooseberries, plums, pears, nectarines, and peaches every summer; harvested tomatoes and beans from their garden in the fall; and canned pears, peaches, and squash in the midst of winter—something they could never have done in Michigan. The closest John came to meat occurred during a visit to a local slaughter house. He left it even more committed to vegetarianism. With a regular supply of fresh food year-round, they liked having friends over for meals.

Despite his hectic schedule, when he was home John also enjoyed "choring around the house" with Maggie. They did the laundry, canned fruits and vegetables, and reared the children as a team. They also took walks and went on mountain hikes, either by themselves or with Delmer. Both went horseback riding as well. Since they enjoyed visiting with friends, Maggie accompanied John on many of his pastoral calls. In the evenings they often read books together or sang duets. They obviously loved each other very much, although they never committed their feelings to paper. So it is more than a little curious that whenever John returned home from an extended absence, he wrote "At home overnight" and drew an ellipse with an X at each end in his diary. Did he enjoy extra hugs and kisses that night—or did they actually have sex that often? John's commitment to Vitalism raises doubts about the latter, for as he himself warned in his *Hand Book*, indulging the passions depleted one's vital force.

But reading books does not, and Loughborough was a bookworm who read voraciously. In 1871 he received a 350-pound box of books for his library. He and Maggie read many of them aloud in the evenings, including all the volumes of D'Aubigné's *History of the Reformation*. When a Latter-Day Saint gave him a copy of the *Book of Mormon*, John actually read it all the way through—something few Adventist pastors would have done—and then wrote an article about it for the *Review*. After reading Maclay's *Life among the Chinese*, he visited a Chinese (Buddhist) temple in San Francisco to observe their habits of worship. He also plowed through Gibbon's six-volume *Decline and Fall of the Roman Empire*. Recognizing his deficiencies in punctuation and spelling, John occasionally studied grammar books. However, he never nailed the use of the apostrophe in the possessive case and continued to be a "creative speller" all his life.

Loughborough regularly read the *Review*, the *Health Reformer*, and the *Youth's Instructor* (aloud to Delmer), and wrote articles for each periodical. His contributions to the *Review* focused primarily on doctrinal or controversial topics such as the final judgment, God's laws, the Sabbath, spiritual revivals, spiritualism, and dress reform (the latter reflects his growing concern with California Adventists' sporting gold chains, brooches, jewelry, and fancy cufflinks).[53] Even his articles in the *Youth's Instructor*, containing interesting stories and fascinating trivia, are heavily moralistic in tone, quite in contrast with his wife Maggie's more grace-oriented contributions and his brother William's upbeat, creative homilies.[54]

California's warmer climate influenced Loughborough to adopt more healthful habits as well. He began taking more frequent naps both at home and on the road to restore his energy. Also he bathed twice a month now rather than monthly as he had in the Midwest. In addition to the warm climate, perhaps hints from Maggie or John's wide reading in health reform literature inspired the change. Possibly the fact that Loughborough regularly rubbed shoulders with a higher class of people now and often boarded around with Adventist families as he traveled may have improved his hygienic habits.[55]

REDEMPTIVE DISCIPLINE FOR MERRITT CORNELL

When Merritt Cornell arrived at San Francisco on June 17, 1871, M. G. Kellogg met him at the train station and took him directly to the evangelistic tent where he began preaching immediately. Cornell informed *Review* readers, "I am glad to report that my courage is good; and I esteem it a happy privilege to unite once more with Bro. Loughborough, my former fellow-laborer, in this good work."[56] Nearly two decades earlier, Cornell had ordained John to the gospel ministry and signed his first ministerial certificate in 1853. A year later, the two men had held the first tent evangelistic series sponsored by Sabbatarian Adventists in Battle Creek. Subsequently, they had spent several months together spreading the Adventist message across Michigan, Illinois, and Wisconsin in the mid-1850s. As preaching partners, pioneer innovators, and personal friends, they bonded well as a team.

As their San Francisco meetings progressed, Cornell soon proved himself a first-rate evangelist. After he had given 35 discourses and sold $125 worth of literature, 250 attendees voted that he and Loughborough spoke the truth. Fifty of them (including Merritt Kellogg's wife, who reconverted) began keeping the Sabbath. When Cornell debated the famous Miles Grant on the Sabbath-Sunday issue, one man handed him a $10 roll of silver coins. While John and Maggie also helped with the tent meetings, Cornell was getting most of the attention in the daily press.[57] It was enough to make even a modest man swell with pride.

Unfortunately, Merritt Cornell was not known for his modesty or his discretion. His weakness in this respect had brought serious marital problems between him and his wife, Angelina, and possibly explains why he had traveled to California alone. Then his rising star as a successful debater had earned him the congratulations of Adventists in San Francisco. His intelligence, wit, and charm soon attracted a bevy of admirers, chief among them Sarah E. Harris, a divorcé with two children. Merritt and Sarah bonded immediately, and soon they began taking long walks along the city's scenic streets.

But in Victorian America society considered it scandalous for a married man to consort with a divorced woman in such a public manner. Soon tongues began to wag, and accusations split the 50-member church. Sarah's children added fuel to the fire by reporting that they had peeked through the bedroom keyhole and seen their mother in bed and Cornell with his pants off ready to join her. Later, however, they denied their story, claiming that they had "only made it up."

One can only imagine the personal anguish Loughborough felt as these events unfolded. His mentor, preaching partner, and best friend was possibly indulging in adulterous behavior. What should he do? His diary reveals that he chose the path of redemptive discipline. Rather than condemn Merritt outright, he followed a course of graduated therapy designed to lead him to repentance. In November 1871 John and Maggie invited Merritt over for dinner and a fireside chat. When that failed to get results, John began writing him letters of admonition—three in December alone. Deeply infatuated with Sarah, however, Merritt ignored his friend's counsel. So in January 1872 Loughborough began visiting with Cornell at his boarding house, warning him that if he did not stop seeing Sarah, the church would discipline him. Merritt replied, "I have a right to walk the streets of San Francisco as I please with whom I please. It is none of your business or anyone else's." Stunned, John played the only card he had left.

On Sabbath, January 27, he scheduled a public inquiry (or "church trial") the following day to examine the recent misconduct of Merritt Cornell and Sarah Harris. At first Cornell planned to attend that meeting and defend himself no matter what the consequences. Loughborough expected him to be there as well. But about 9:00 a.m., as John walked to the meeting place, he met Merritt standing outside his boarding house, weeping. "I am not going to the meeting," he said. "But the meeting relates to your case," John replied. "I know that," Cornell responded, "but I am all wrong." The night before he had received a lengthy testimony from Ellen White rebuking him for his immoral behavior. Convicted of his wrong course, he had penned a letter of confession to be read at the church trial. He handed both letters to Loughborough and then returned to the boarding house.

As he read Mrs. White's letter at the trial, Loughborough was amazed at the accuracy of her information, which no one in San Francisco could possibly have told her. While speaking at Bordoville, Vermont, on December 10, 1871, she had seen Cornell's case in vision. Not until January 18, 1872, however, did she write the vision out and mail it—and it arrived nine days later just in time to avert disaster.[58]

Describing Cornell as being "like a man thrown off balance," she advised, "Be careful how you are enticed to make women your confidants or to allow them to make you their confidant. . . . Keep aloof from the society of women as much as you can. [Otherwise] you will be in danger." In a subsequent testimony embracing both Cornell and Harris, she added, "I must speak plainly. Your conduct . . . has been highly censurable. You have taken liberties with each other which should never be between even natural brothers and sisters. You have sinned against God [and] you have brought a deep wound upon His precious cause and greatly burdened the work of God in San Francisco and Woodland." She urged both of them to seek God "with a broken heart and a contrite spirit" and find forgiveness and peace.[59]

Accepting White's counsel as light from God, Cornell confessed his indiscretions and apologized for the hurt he had caused at a public gathering of the San Francisco Central SDA Church in December 1872. Sarah

Harris, on the other hand, denying the accuracy of some of Mrs. White's statements, admitted only that "if she had committed an error, it was of the head and not the heart." Refusing to admit any wrongdoing, she justified her actions at a five-hour hearing with James and Ellen White and J. N. Loughborough present. Consequently, the church board disfellowshipped her. "A sad day for me," John wrote in his diary. "I prayed [for] an hour in [the] evening in the barn."[60]

If Sarah Harris's subsequent behavior (attacking Ellen White's writings and gathering sympathizers around her) brought many more "sad days" for the Adventists in San Francisco, Merritt Cornell's reformed life brought them joy. "My soul thirsts after God, and yields every idol," he wrote in the *Review*. "A genuine conversion and new experience, I must have. I think of it, and labor for it day and night. . . . I know that nothing short of an entire consecration to the work will fit me to take part in this holy work."[61] A few months later he rejoiced that "my physical and mental health is almost entirely recovered, and I again feel free from that gloomy, confused and unsettled state of mind which has so long oppressed me. . . . The truth looks brighter, and I love it more and more."[62] Soon Cornell was receiving frequent invitations to preach at the San Francisco Central church.[63] But he was too busy to do so often, for during the mid-70s, he and his preaching partner John Loughborough would once again hold evangelistic meetings, baptize converts, erect churches, and establish new institutions.

---

[1] JNL, diary, June 26, 1868.

[2] *RH*, Sept. 1, 1868, pp. 161-163.

[3] *PUR*, Dec. 14, 1905, p. 1; Harold O. McCumber, *Pioneering the Message in the Golden West* (Mountain View, Calif.: Pacific Press Pub. Assn., 1946), pp. 28-51; "Kellogg, Merritt Gardner," *Ellen G. White Encyclopedia*, pp. 438, 439.

[4] *RH*, Dec. 11, 1866, p. 12; *RH*, July 25, 1871, p. 45; *PUR*, Dec. 21, 1905, pp. 1, 2; *PUR*, June 19, 1913, p. 3; *RH*, Mar. 30, 1967, p. 15; McCumber, pp. 52-55; "Centennial: Pacific Union Conference of SDAs, 1868-1968," DF 230, CAR.

[5] *GCB* (1897), p. 202; *PUR*, Dec. 28, 1905, p. 1; *PUR*, July 3, 1913, p. 5; DF 230, CAR.

[6] *RH*, June 9, 1868, p. 400; *GCB* (1868), pp. 32-37; *GCB* (1897), p. 202; JNL, *PUR*, Dec. 28, 1905, p. 1; *PUR*, July 3, 1913, p. 5; JNL, diary, May 31, 1868.

[7] David Fong's short paper, "A Character Study of John Loughborough During the Early Growth of the Church in California" (typed manuscript, November 1975, DF 230, CAR), nicely summarizes Loughborough's qualifications for the California mission.

[8] JNL's ministerial credentials, June 1, 1868, DF 230, CAR; *RH*, June 2, 1868, p.

384; *RH,* June 23, 1868, p. 8. Actually, the General Conference would spend $1,875 on the California enterprise during its first year, including transportation expenses to send the two families there and startup costs to insure the success of their mission. See "Progress in Northern California," *RH,* Oct. 2, 1941, p. 19.

[9] *RH,* June 23, 1868, p. 13.

[10] *RH,* June 23, 1868, p. 5.

[11] *PUR,* Jan. 4, 1906, pp. 1, 2; *RH,* July 31, 1919, pp. 16, 17; *RH,* July 3, 1913, p. 20. J. O. Corliss recalled in 1913 that in 1868 many said, "'Surely the Lord will come now, for the message is going to the ends of the world.' We thought that was as far as it could ever go, to California."

[12] JNL, diary, June 15-24, 1868; *RH,* June 23, 1868, p. 5; *PUR,* Oct. 30, 1913, p. 1; E. Robinson, *Lighter of Gospel Fires,* p. 121.

[13] *RH,* June 23, 1868, p. 5; *RH,* July 14, 1868, p. 61; JNL, diary, June 1868.

[14] JNL, diary, June 27-30, July 1-17, 1868; *RH,* July 28, 1868, p. 89; *RH,* Aug. 25, 1868, pp. 150, 151; *PHJ,* February and March 1887, pp. 125, 126.

[15] *RH,* Aug. 18, 1868, p. 140; *RH,* Aug. 25, 1868, pp. 150, 151; JNL, diary, July 1-17, 1868; *YI,* Sept. 5, 1944, p. 11; *RH,* July 29, 1962, p. 29.

[16] JNL, diary, July 1868; Pacific Union Conference Centennial (1868-1968), DF 230, CAR; *PUR,* Feb. 12, 1914, pp. 5, 6; *RH,* Mar. 5, 1872, p. 96.

[17] *PUR,* Jan. 11, 1906, pp. 1, 2; *PUR,* Nov. 27, 1913, pp. 1, 2; McCumber, p. 73.

[18] *PUR,* Feb. 12, 1914, p. 6.

[19] R. Schwarz and F. Greenleaf, *Light Bearers,* p. 133; and JNL to JSW, Aug. 25, 1868, m. 52, CAR. Loughborough confessed to James White that he hoped he would not be considered "a dreamer" or "be led astray by dreams" for going to Petaluma.

[20] A. Spalding, *Origin and History,* vol. 2, p. 145.

[21] *PUR,* Mar. 19, 1914, pp. 2, 3; *RH,* July 29, 1962, p. 28.

[22] JNL to JSW, Aug. 25, 1868, m. 52, CAR; *PUR,* Jan. 25, 1906, pp. 1, 2; *PUR,* Feb. 1, 1906, pp. 1, 2.

[23] *PUR,* Jan. 18, 1906, pp. 1, 2; *YI,* Feb. 13, 1951, p. 7; *PUR,* Mar. 19, 1914, p. 3; G. Knight, *Lest We Forget,* p. 201. One assumes that the two men did not sing all four parts simultaneously, but demonstrated their ability to sing first and second tenor, baritone, and bass alternatively in different songs—anything else would have constituted yet another miracle!

[24] *PUR,* Jan. 25, 1906, pp. 1, 2; *PUR,* Mar. 19, 1914, pp. 2, 3.

[25] *PUR,* July 29, 1915, p. 4.

[26] Mr. Morton, quoted in *RH,* Sept. 25, 1958, p. 8.

[27] *RH,* June 24, 1873, p. 14; JNL, *Rise and Progress,* pp. 280, 281; *PUR,* May 24, 1906, pp. 1, 2; PUR, June 7, 1906, pp. 1, 2; McCumber, pp. 86-91.

[28] JNL, diary, August, September, and October 1868; *RH,* Sept. 22, 1868, p. 181; *RH,* Oct. 6, 1868, pp. 193, 194; *RH,* Oct. 13, 1868, p. 205; *RH,* Oct. 27, 1868, p. 224. Loughborough also states that he and D. T. Bourdeau prepared a special pamphlet entitled "Ascension Robes" for public distribution, but copies of it have not survived.

[29] *PUR,* July 5, 1906, pp. 1, 2; *RH,* Oct. 31, 1985, p. 12.

[30] *RH,* Nov. 3, 1868, p. 232; *RH,* Nov. 17, 1868, pp. 245, 246; *RH,* Dec. 8, 1868, pp. 269, 270.

[31] JNL, diary, November and December 1868; *RH,* Jan. 12, 1869, p. 23; *PUR,* Apr. 12, 1906, p. 1; *PUR,* Apr. 19, 1906, p. 1.

[32] *PUR,* Feb. 8, 1906, pp. 1, 2; *PUR,* Feb. 15, 1906, p. 1; Robinson, p. 135.

[33] *RH,* Feb. 23, 1869, p. 69; *RH,* Mar. 23, 1869, p. 104; *RH,* Mar. 30, 1869, pp. 108, 109; *PUR,* June 21, 1906, pp. 1, 2; *RH,* Apr. 27, 1869, p. 141; *RH,* May 25, 1869, pp.

169-171; *RH,* June 1, 1869, pp. 177-179. In fact, Loughborough and Bourdeau offered a reward of $500 for incontrovertible evidence supporting the existence of ascension robes in 1844, but no one provided any. Where the men would have obtained such a huge sum is not known.

[34] *RH,* Apr. 20, 1869, p. 136; *RH,* May 25, 1869, pp. 169-171; *RH,* June 8, 1869, p. 190; *PUR,* May 3, 1906, pp. 1, 2; *PUR,* May 10, 1906, pp. 1, 2; *PUR,* May 17, 1906, pp. 1, 2; *PUR,* May 31, 1906, p. 1; McCumber, pp. 82-84.

[35] *RH,* July 27, 1869, p. 37; *RH,* Aug. 10, 1869, pp. 53, 54; *RH,* Sept. 28, 1869, p. 110; *PUR,* June 28, 1906, pp. 1, 2; *PUR,* July 19, 1906, pp. 1, 2; *RH,* June 22, 1869, p. 207; *RH,* July 10, 1919, p. 30.

[36] *RH,* Sept. 28, 1869, p. 110; *RH,* Nov. 23, 1869, p. 174; Robinson, p. 145.

[37] *RH,* Nov. 23, 1869, p. 174.

[38] *RH,* Apr. 26, 1870, p. 149; *PUR,* July 26, 1906, p. 1.

[39] EGW to JNL, Aug. 15, 1869, letter 10, 1869, CAR.

[40] EGW to Harriet Smith, Cornelia Cornell, and Martha Amadon, Sept. 24, 1869, letter 13, 1869, CAR.

[41] JNL to EGW and JSW, Jan. 12, 1870, m. 52, CAR. JNL's diary reveals that he wrote other letters to James White and Cornelia Cornell in February 1870.

[42] JNL to JSW, Jan. 18, 1870, m. 52, CAR.

[43] JNL, diary, Jan. 1, 1869.

[44] JNL, *RH,* July 12, 1870, p. 30; *PUR,* Aug. 2, 1906, p. 1.

[45] See California reports in *RH,* Mar. 8, 1870, p. 96; *RH,* June 14, 1870, p. 207; *RH,* Sept. 27, 1870, p. 119; *PUR,* Aug. 9, 1906, p. 1.

[46] *RH,* Mar. 1, 1870, pp. 82, 83.

[47] *RH,* June 21, 1870, pp. 6, 7.

[48] *RH,* Oct. 25, 1870, p. 152.

[49] JSW, "California Mission," in *RH,* Jan. 12, 1869, p. 24; *RH,* May 4, 1869, p. 151; *RH,* June 29, 1869, p. 3; *RH,* Mar. 29, 1870, p. 120; *RH,* May 3, 1870, p. 158; *RH,* Jan. 10, 1871, p. 32; *RH,* Feb. 14, 1871, p. 69; *RH,* May 23, 1871, pp. 182, 183; *GCB* (1870 and 1873), pp. 44, 71. Interestingly, however, the Michigan Conference rather than the General Conference renewed Loughborough's ministerial credentials. The Michigan Conference also renewed the ministerial credentials of Canright (in Iowa), Cornell and Waggoner (in New England), Van Horn (in Ohio), and Lawrence (in Missouri). See *RH,* Mar. 22, 1870, p. 110; *RH,* Oct. 18, 1870, p. 140.

[50] *RH,* Feb. 7, 1871, p. 62; *RH,* Feb. 28, 1871, p. 85; *RH,* May 30, 1871, p. 190.

[51] *PUR,* Aug. 23, 1906, p. 1; Spalding, *Origin and History*, vol. 2, pp. 149-151.

[52] *RH,* May 23, 1871, pp. 182, 183; *RH,* June 20, 1871, p. 7; *RH,* Aug. 8, 1871, p. 62.

[53] See JNL's *RH* articles for Aug. 24, 1869, pp. 65-67, 71; *RH,* Jan. 3, 1871, p. 21; *RH,* May 2, 1871, p. 157; *RH,* May 9, 1871, p. 165; *RH,* June 20, 1871, p. 3; *RH,* July 18, 1871, p. 39.

[54] See, for example, JNL's "Without Natural Affection," in *YI,* June 15, 1871, p. 47, and "Giants," in *YI,* Sept. 1, 1871, p. 65; Maggie Loughborough's "Children Can Do Good," in *YI,* May 15, 1871, p. 40; and William K. Loughborough's "Home," in *YI,* Feb. 1, 1871, p. 16, and "Be Firm," in *YI,* Dec. 15, 1871, p. 94.

[55] JNL, diary, January 1870-February 1872.

[56] *RH,* June 27, 1871, p. 16.

[57] See JNL's and Cornell's reports in the *RH,* July 4, 1871, p. 22; July 25, 1871, pp. 44, 45; Oct. 3, 1871, p. 126; *PUR,* Sept. 6, 1906, p. 1.

[58] JNL, diary, November-December 1871, January-February 1872; *Rise and Progress*,

pp. 282-286; JNL to G. I. Butler, Mar. 23, 1875, m. 52, CAR; and Denton E. Rebok, *Believe His Prophets* (Washington, D.C.: Review and Herald Pub. Assn., 1956), pp. 110-112.

[59] EGW to M. E. Cornell, Dec. 18, 1871, and EGW, *Testimonies for the Church* (Mountain View, Calif.: Pacific Press Pub. Assn., 1948), vol. 3, pp. 227-243, cited by Merlin D. Burt, "Ellen G. White and Church Conflict" (typed manuscript, Apr. 22, 1996, CAR).

[60] Records of the San Francisco Central SDA Church, Dec. 3, 4, 1872, Collection #4996.088, University Libraries, Loma Linda University, Loma Linda, California; JNL, diary, December 1872; Burt, "Ellen G. White and Conflict," pp. 2, 3. Despite his confession, however, Elder Cornell did not escape unscathed. He allegedly paid a certain Mrs. Rowland $90 to keep her from telling his wife Angelina the sordid details of his behavior with Sarah Harris. See JNL to JSW, Mar. 27, 1873, m. 52, CAR; "San Francisco Central Church," *Ellen G. White Encyclopedia*, pp. 1125-1127.

[61] M. E. Cornell, *RH,* Dec. 31, 1872, p. 22; Burt, "Ellen G. White and Conflict," pp. 2, 3. The records of the San Francisco Central SDA Church for May 6, 1880, demonstrate that doubts concerning Mrs. White's divine inspiration ripped the church apart for at least another decade.

[62] *RH,* Apr. 8, 1873, p. 134.

[63] Burt, "Ellen G. White and Conflict," p. 3; records of the San Francisco Central SDA Church, Mar. 30, 1873.

CHAPTER IX

A MATURING WORK IN CALIFORNIA (1872-1875)

"The preaching has been about an even mixture of close, searching, practical discourses, alternated with the theory of the truth, presented in a clear, concise, solemn, and pointed manner, spiced with exhortation, and close appeals to the consciences with an endeavor to arouse the moral sensibilities of the people."[1]

With Merritt Cornell back on board, Loughborough anticipated that their joint ministry would soon reap a harvest of souls in the Golden State. "There seems, on the whole, to be a desire in the hearts of the Lord's people on this coast to get nearer and still nearer to the Lord," he wrote in the *Review*. "I will patiently and earnestly strive to labor, the Lord being my helper. Without Him, our efforts are [in] vain."[2]

Yet at times it must have seemed to both men that, even with God's blessings, Satan (and devilish weather conditions) was winning the battle in 1872. During the wettest winter in the state's recorded history, when 30 inches of rain fell in 26 days, they slogged over muddy roads to Green Valley, passing flooded fields and farms where water reached the cows' backs. Once the rains subsided and the mud dried up, the spring sunshine brought out California's beautiful blossoms—and a healthy dose of ministerial opposition. Loughborough and Cornell locked horns with Reverend Jenks and Professor Martin regarding Sunday sacredness; they debated the ubiquitous Miles Grant and his falsehoods in the *World's Crisis*; and they answered charges that Ellen White was demon-inspired. And everywhere they went, they faced Methodist pastors and spiritualist mediums eager to debate the Sabbath-Sunday question and the state of the dead.[3]

By the 1870s spiritualism had long outgrown its primitive roots, which stemmed from Mother Ann Lee (the self-declared female incarnation of Christ) who founded the Shakers in the eighteenth century. Shakers, who denied the bodily resurrection, atonement, and the Trinity, believed instead in communication and guidance from the spirits of the dead. At their "holy hills" they held religious services, dances, and séances during which mediums invoked the wisdom of the spirits of the famous dead. The followers of Friedrich Anton Mesmer, the German father of eighteenth-century mesmerism (later called hypnotism), soon introduced extrasensory perception, telepathy, and clairvoyance, a potent brew that Andrew Jackson Davis incorporated into American Spiritualism in the 1830s and 1840s. Soon subjecting oneself to hypnotic trances and attending séances became all the rage in some upper-middle class circles across America. Believing, however, that the spirits had "departed" in 1847, American Shakers and mesmerists welcomed their "return" in 1848 with the "rappings" introduced by the Fox sisters of Hydesville (a village northeast of Rochester, New York).[4]

Although the Fox sisters later repudiated the "rappings" as trickery, the number of their followers, called spiritualists, reached 1,500,000 by 1859, when New York had 71 mediums, Massachusetts had 55, and Ohio had 27. Perhaps because they advocated such radical beliefs as gender equality, free sex, and communication with the dead, most spiritualists (largely White, Anglo-Saxon, middle- and upper-class former Protestants) sought respectability by remaining within established churches, particularly of the Universalist-Unitarian variety. By the Civil War era, thanks to vigorous proselytizing abroad, spiritualism enjoyed an international flavor similar to Mormonism and Methodism. During the 1870s it became a self-consciously "alternative" religion in the United States, where its lecturers drew enormous audiences in America's expanding cities.[5]

Despite bad weather and exhausting debates with spiritualist mediums, Loughborough and Cornell found many reasons to rejoice. For one, California Adventists were beginning to part with their jewelry. Everywhere they held meetings, women thrust gold necklaces, earrings, and bracelets into their hands, while men brought gold cufflinks, tie pins, and old coins. One San Francisco offering netted $52 in gold jewelry. Members in Santa Rosa and Healdsburg contributed $56.50 to the "jewelry fund." And Adventists in Red Bluff gave more than $200 worth of their jewelry to the cause (women began wearing jet and ivory pins instead). Loughborough, who had never seen so much gold in all his life, had it all melted down into bullion.[6]

A second reason for optimism was that, for the most part, the local press supported their preaching efforts. William Saunders, the editor of the Yolo *Democrat*, published summaries of their discourses, praising Cornell and Loughborough as "close students of the Bible" and "experienced preachers" who presented their discourses "in a manner new and acceptable to the mass of their hearers." Journalists especially appreciated the evangelists' habit of providing time at every service for "questions and investigation." Other reporters described the two as "men of more than ordinary ability . . . more candid, more zealous, and at the same time more consistent, than those who are termed the popular preachers of the day." In one sense, however, the flattering reports backfired, for when newspaper editors in Woodland tried to stage debates with the preachers, they discovered that no one would confront them before an audience of 1,000. Despite the adverse reports in the *California Christian Advocate*, therefore, local citizens testified that "there is now more Bible reading than was ever before known" prior to the meetings.[7]

The Bible-studying citizens of Woodland, convinced that Cornell had won the debate about Sundaykeeping with Professor Martin (president of a local Disciples of Christ college), handed him a prize of $100 in gold coins (equal to more than two months' salary) in appreciation for his "services as a Biblical Lecturer." Suffering from heat stroke and physical exhaustion, Merritt pocketed his prize and returned to San Francisco to enjoy the sea breezes and get some much-needed rest. But Martin, refusing to admit defeat, followed Loughborough to Yountville, determined to beat him in a second encounter. When the debate ended and local citizens placed two hats on the front table, Professor Martin received $2.50 while Loughborough got about $30.00. Preaching biblical truth paid good dividends.[8]

The growing financial prosperity and rapidly increasing membership of the California State Association convinced many that Adventists there should form a regular conference. By 1872 northern California boasted 238 members in six organized churches contributing more than $2,000 in Systematic Benevolence funds each year. At a general meeting in Bloomfield in February 1873, delegates voted unanimously to form the California Conference. Then they elected Loughborough as president, S. B. Bresee as secretary, and T. M. Chapman as treasurer. They also raised another $2,000 in gold to support various General Conference projects and institutions. Loughborough drew up the first conference constitution, apparently all by himself.[9]

But if the cause in California was rising, John and Maggie faced a crisis at home. Their daughter Elizabeth ("Eliza") Eunice, born on St. Patrick's Day in 1872, had never been "a rugged child" (as John phrased it). She had fought for life from the very beginning, and by the end of the summer it was obvious that she was losing the battle. Her short life came to an end in August, only five and a half months after it began. A local Adventist woman sewed a shroud for the baby, and the next day John and Maggie buried her. Having now lost four children to the Grim Reaper (three by Mary and one by Maggie), Loughborough returned to his tent meetings in Woodland with a heavy heart.[10]

JAMES AND ELLEN WHITE VISIT CALIFORNIA

But John and Maggie would soon be comforted by a visit from their former Battle Creek neighbors James and Ellen White, who with Lucinda Hall arrived four weeks later and boarded with the family for two and a half months. Ellen described the Loughborough home as a story-and-a-half dwelling with large, well-lit chambers and huge bedrooms. She enjoyed playing with Delmer and Patience, calling them "the best children, the most quiet and peaceable, I ever saw." She approved of the manner in which Maggie controlled them "in a quiet way, without noise, severity, or bluster." Despite Ellen's bad cold, ulcerated tooth, and swollen face, she and James joined Loughborough and Cornell on the sawdust trail, preaching at Woodland, San Francisco, Petaluma, and Santa Rosa to huge crowds that sometimes exceeded 800 people. At Bloomfield, where Mrs. White spoke on Christ's sufferings on the cross, the congregation had hardly a dry eye. Even Ellen wept as she spoke.[11]

After listening to John preach, she wrote in her diary: "He was free and his subject [was] very interesting. He applied the text [Jeremiah 29:11] with considerable force to the preparation for the coming of the Lord." Many of San Francisco's elites attended the services in Excelsior Hall, including former California Governor Holden, who invited Loughborough and the Whites to his home for dinner afterwards. Following the meal, James and Ellen prayed for the Holden family.[12]

Everywhere the Whites saw peace, prosperity, and progress among the Adventist churches in California. They recognized, however, that achieving a "good state of things" occasionally meant dropping "two or three disorderly ones" from church membership, but in the long run it usually brought harmony in the ranks. The Whites were especially pleased to receive letters from Adventists in San Francisco's Central church expressing confidence in Ellen White's divine inspiration and thanking them for their unselfish ministry in the state.[13] With genuine enthusiasm, James told *Review* readers: "We are safe in California, and are happily disappointed in the country, and what we have seen of the strength of the cause in the State. . . . We feel very much at home." "Nothing but stern duty will ever call us from this country. We like the people of California, and the country, and think it will be favorable to our health."[14]

Indeed, the Whites' health improved considerably during their five-month sojourn in the Golden State. Having spent most of their lives in New England, with its rocky soil, frigid climate, and penny-pinching population, they took obvious delight in California's rich soil, warm temperatures, and extremely generous people, many of whom they met for the first time at the Windsor camp meeting. The conference-wide gathering, hastily planned and executed, featured a motley assortment of dwellings, including 33 regular tents plus sheets nailed to wooden frames, rag carpets thrown over wooden sticks, and posts and rails precariously fastened together. Fortunately, the weather cooperated, and for 10 days it did not rain, although the cool nights led some to bring wood-burning stoves inside their makeshift homes.[15]

At this first West Coast camp meeting the Whites preached 13 sermons, Merritt Cornell delivered two discourses, and Loughborough (doubtless occupied with administrative duties) made only one presentation. In addition to the 33 Adventist families attending, their audience included a deputy sheriff, a county treasurer, a bank official, a court crier, and a former member of the state legislature. Delighted with the preaching, the court crier passed his beaver hat among the crowd on two different occasions, collecting $93 toward expenses. Another spontaneous offering raised $100 in gold coins for the four preachers. Somewhat embarrassed, they invested it in the building fund instead. At the final service, the Whites and Loughborough ordained Merritt Kellogg to the gospel ministry.[16]

Grateful for the Whites' help in making the first statewide camp meeting a success, John thanked them publicly for their "self-sacrificing spirit" and "their preaching, exhortation, and counsel." By the same token, judging by the "excellent" order that prevailed, James judged John "an able manager."[17] Before returning to Michigan, the Whites joined Loughborough and Cornell for a series of meetings in San Francisco at which Ellen preached seven sermons, James gave six discourses, and John presented five talks. After attending meetings, a nearly 70-year-old man leaving for Valparaiso promised to distribute Adventist literature aboard ship and among English readers in Chile if John would provide him some, which he gladly did. Then, with mixed feelings, Loughborough took the Whites to the train station and bade them goodbye. For nearly half a year he had benefited from their godly counsel. Nostalgic for California's sunny climate and warmhearted people, the Whites would return two years later.[18]

In the meantime, however, Loughborough's expanding evangelistic efforts reaped a surprising harvest. Newspaper reports testified that with greater frequency, Adventist converts came from the upper-middle class ("well-respected citizens" and those "of considerable means"). After the Whites left, John discovered that Mrs. White had sown gospel seeds while riding on the train. While befriending Mrs. Horne, a fellow traveler, Ellen had given her a copy of the *Health Reformer*. Later, when Horne and her atheist son attended John's meetings in Red Bluff (150 miles north of San Francisco), they became convinced that Adventists taught the truth and were baptized. During the same series, William Healey, a surveyor, sheep rancher, and grain entrepreneur, also converted to Adventism. In time he would become John's partner in evangelism, a missionary to Hawaii, and president of the North Pacific Union Conference. Another time on a sweltering summer day, as Loughborough preached under canvass, his booming voice carried a quarter of a mile to where a postmaster and his wife rested on their veranda. Turning to his wife, the man said, "I am going down there and see what that fellow is hollering about!" Soon both attended the meetings and were baptized. In San Francisco a former Black slave affectionately called "Uncle Marshall" heard Loughborough and James White preach on Revelation 7. "I'ze gwine ter jine yo church," he told them. A successful newspaper salesman, before he died Marshall gave $2,700 to Adventist missions, telling church officials, "I'd lose my soul if I kept dis money. And yo mus' take it." Marshall became a pillar in the Laguna and McAllister Street SDA Church.[19]

Not all of John Loughborough's witnessing endeavors occurred under canvass, inside wooden meetinghouses, or at rented halls. As the parameters of his preaching expanded, he frequently rode the ferryboats between Oakland and San Francisco, a journey that took about 20 minutes. Seeing his fellow travelers as a captive audience, John would hang up his prophetic chart on a convenient nail and deliver an abbreviated discourse on the imagery of Daniel 7, 8, or 9. How many converts he won would be difficult to determine, but one little girl who watched him remembered his lecture and became an Adventist when she grew up.[20]

While Loughborough's heart remained in evangelism, increasingly his head was occupied with administrative details. As conference president, he coordinated the schedule of quarterly meetings (Communion and testimony services) held at six California churches. As new congregations built meetinghouses, John drew up the blueprints, thus insuring that most of California's early Adventist chapels followed the New England colonial style of architecture.[21]

Unfortunately, not all the 300 Adventists who worshipped in them led such neat and orderly lives themselves. While West Coast women anguished over giving up jewelry, their husbands and brothers struggled to abandon tobacco. The Adventist message of self-denial ran counter to the independent-minded spirit of some California converts: the result was rebellion. Before the Whites returned to Michigan, James had helped John "arouse" certain "unconsecrated ones" and "expel" some "dead members." "A church can afford to exchange five [spiritually] dead members who are past help, for one humble soul who is determined to live near to God; and it makes a good exchange every time," Loughborough said. While "amputation . . . is the last resort," if appeals failed to bring reform, then such offending members must be "cut off" so that they do not "poison the blood and injure the health and life of the whole [church] body."[22]

A growing crisis in the already contentious San Francisco Central Church provided John with the opportunity to apply his disciplinary model. Henry

Stipp, a church official angry at being removed from office, accused the Whites of leading "a revengeful crusade against this church." Seeing himself as an advocate for "independence of thought and action" on the part of "the oppressed," he accused the Whites of "oppression and intolerance." When James tried to convince him that various San Francisco members had "shamefully treated and abused" Ellen and himself, Stipp retorted that he had lost confidence in church leaders who needed to confess their wrongdoing and ask for forgiveness. Portraying himself as a martyr, Stipp recruited other disaffected Adventists. Eventually he had to be removed from church membership.[23]

PROMOTING HARMONY AND UNITY

In addition to bringing harmony to local churches, President Loughborough encouraged harmonious singing among Seventh-day Adventists. Probably no Adventist minister in the nineteenth century (with the possible exception of James White) accomplished as much to promote good music in the church as J. N. Loughborough. As a boy in Victor, New York, he had attended weekly singing classes at the Methodist church. Maggie and he often sang together at home. And in their evangelistic meetings, he and Bourdeau had sung duets together.

In a report to the *Review* in May 1872, he threw down the gauntlet, indicating that he (and others) "[deplored] the sad state of musical talent among us." He suggested that each of the six California congregations select one of their number as a "musical director" to lead them in singing. Furthermore, such directors should meet as often as once every quarter at musical conventions "to devise ways and means for the cultivation of church music."[24] The directors apparently concluded that the lack of musical talent in most churches warranted meeting more frequently than once every three months. So in 1872 they met for one day in May and for three days in July at Santa Rosa. The following year they returned to Santa Rosa for conventions in January and February. Each day featured three singing sessions. While James White attended the first musical convention and gave a lecture on singing, Loughborough attended all of them. At each one, participants practiced singing parts, "seeking to promote harmony and [to] correct some of our common errors in singing." The directors also supported White's proposal to prepare two hymnbooks: one containing simple hymns, the other with “rudiments and tunes.”[25]

In addition to promoting choral singing, Loughborough also fought an uphill battle to install pump organs in Adventist churches to help members sing harmoniously and rhythmically. But many of California's Adventists equated organs with parlor entertainment or the dance hall. Surely it was a sin to bring the “devil's instrument” into the Lord's house! In his diary John occasionally mentions being involved in “a fuss about the organ” with local congregations. He agreed that “expensive organs got up simply for show and strife, and the popular choir, opera style of singing, was a sin.” But since harmony and melody were “an important part of the worship of God,” purchasing a “plain organ . . . for the sole object of being a *help* in the worship of God” could hardly be wicked. He felt certain that, with a trained organist and music director in every congregation, church music would significantly improve.[26]

Likewise, displeased by the slapdash manner in which the Windsor camp meeting had been planned, conference president Loughborough resolved to bring harmony and efficiency to the 1873 camp meeting near Yountville—even if it meant getting no more than three hours' sleep each night. This time the 63 tents would be laid out in a grid pattern, with intersecting “streets” named after Adventist churches (except for “Law and Order street” and “Present Truth street”). When attendance peaked at between 1,500 and 2,000, the ministers held five simultaneous services in large tents scattered over the grounds. Visitors witnessed “no mirth or trifling.” Instead, “a holy calm [and] solemn cheerfulness” pervaded the meetings. At one social meeting, 117 attendees gave their testimonies in English, French, Danish, Swedish, and German in less than an hour. Following the meetings, 29 were baptized. One convert compared the occasion to the day of Pentecost in apostolic times. Loughborough himself exclaimed, “God and holy angels were there.” The Yountville gathering became the model for future California camp meetings.[27]

In addition to being a spiritual convocation with preaching, praying, and testifying, the weeklong gathering also featured business meetings that conducted the administrative and financial work of the church. Delegates pledged more than $500 for a state missionary fund, laid plans to establish a publishing house and a sanitarium somewhere in California, and discussed sending missionaries to Washington and Oregon. They elected J. N. Loughborough as president, William Saunders as secretary, and T. M. Chapman as treasurer of the conference, and elected John Judson as president of the new California Tract and Missionary Society (T&M). During the coming years, John would organize many branches of the Vigilant Missionary Society (the local units of the T&M Society) in Adventist churches.[28] When he heard rumors that "our enemies report . . . that the Advent cause is dead," he wryly remarked, "We do not so understand it."[29]

Indeed, when the powerhouse preaching team of James and Ellen White, Isaac D. Van Horn, and Dudley M. Canright arrived from Michigan, the pace of progress accelerated in 1874. During two days of consultation at Santa Rosa (then the conference headquarters), the Whites insisted that conference leaders needed to make "broader plans" that targeted California's large cities and the entire West Coast. Although Loughborough and Cornell preferred working in rural towns, Mrs. White told them that she had seen in vision that "the angels of God are moving upon hearts" and preparing the way for the truth to be heard in metropolitan areas.[30] Heeding her counsel, Isaac and Adelia Van Horn left for Walla Walla in Washington Territory, which would become the hub of an expanding missionary endeavor known as the "Northern Pacific Mission."[31]

Meanwhile, the evangelistic team in California split up to evangelize new areas. While the Whites preached in Napa and Canright debated Miles Grant in San Francisco, Loughborough began a seven-week series of tent meetings in Oakland, speaking every night and three times on Sundays. That summer Canright, Cornell, and the Whites joined him. Once again, the benefits of advertising became obvious when wide distribution of James's circular "The Tent Meeting" swelled the crowds from 75 people a night to more than 1,000 each evening. When the series ended, John organized a church of 50 Adventists in a city that had had only one believer months before.[32]

Following this successful series, the team once again fanned out across northern California to enter new towns and cities. While Loughborough combated Advent Christians in Vallejo, Cornell debated the state of the dead at San Jose with spiritualists who argued that even vegetables had souls. Here again, distributing 1,000 handbills attracted hundreds of listeners, some of whom agreed with Merritt when he described spiritualists and others as "uncivilized" and living "in heathenish darkness."[33]

If Loughborough and Cornell feared spiritualism was spreading in the Golden State, James White believed that Adventism was growing even faster. "The cause of present truth is presenting a brighter aspect on the Pacific Coast," he declared.[34] Indeed, by October 1874 when the second camp meeting convened at Yountville, the conference boasted about 500 Adventists (a 20 percent annual growth rate) contributing about $3,600 to the Systematic Benevolence Fund. Starting three days prior to the camp meeting, a team of men prepared the grounds, pitched 85 tents, filled hundreds of straw ticks (for mattresses), and platted the streets. With military precision Loughborough organized a brigade of horse-drawn wagons to bring 400 Adventists from the California Pacific Railroad depot to the camp. The next 12 days they heard more than 30 discourses, gave scores of testimonies, and conducted the business of the conference. In addition, they pledged more than $21,000 to establish a West Coast publishing house. Thrilled with the sermons given by the Whites, M. E. Cornell, D. M. Canright, G. I. Butler, and Lougborough, attendees called the session a "Feast of Tabernacles." Yet preparing for and preaching at this convocation had taken a toll on John's health. "I have feared," Dudley Canright said, "[that] Bro. [Loughborough] would break down under his earnest labors."[35]

Fortunately, John did not suffer a nervous breakdown. Instead, it appeared that keeping busy took his mind off his physical and mental exhaustion and focused it on the needs of others. Within days of the Yountville camp meeting, Canright and Loughborough commenced another four-month series of meetings in Oakland. This time they distributed 5,000 handbills, placed ads in all the newspapers, put up bulletin-board notices, and erected a "lighted transparency" sign (a first for Adventist evangelism) in front of the lecture hall. Discovering an intense interest in spiritualism, the men distributed another 5,000 circulars focusing on the state of the dead. Soon local citizens, including Russian, German, Swedish, Danish, and English listeners, packed the hall. Excited by the turnout, Loughborough exclaimed, "Our zeal is fired [up] and we buckle on the armor anew." The fact that 20 Advent Christians had also converted to Seventh-day Adventism during the past year especially pleased John.[36]

ESTABLISHING A NEW PUBLICATION AND PRESS

Yet what thrilled him even more was to witness the fulfillment of a long-held dream. For some time now, James White had been urging California Adventists to produce a newspaper that they could use both for in-house and evangelistic purposes. He and Ellen felt that Oakland would be the ideal place to publish such a periodical. Called "The Athens of the Pacific Coast" (for its sophisticated cultural life), the city had about 18,000 citizens. Before Loughborough's spectacular tent meetings ended, James purchased a printing press and started a campaign to raise $10,000 to build an Adventist publishing house similar to the one in Battle Creek. On June 4, 1874, the Whites (with son Willie), the Canrights, and Loughborough knelt on the floor of Canright's boarding room with the first issue of the *Signs of the Times* before them and asked God to bless the new journalistic venture. John recalled years later: "It was with trembling, with anxiety, and yet with faith in God that Bro. White moved out in this enterprise." When the Whites appointed him manager of the paper, John had good reason for anxiety. "I wasn't much of a printer," he admitted, "but . . . I did the best I could." To protect their investment, he slept on the floor of the press room for three months.[37]

If Loughborough made a poor printer, he excelled at fund-raising. At the Yountville camp meeting of 1874 his rhetoric so fired up the crowd of 500 Adventists that they pledged or contributed more than $19,400 worth in gold bars, gold wedges, gold coins, and bags of gold dust. When the news reached Battle Creek, GC president G. I. Butler exclaimed, "We think this is the largest sum ever pledged at any S. D. Adventist meeting. . . . Certainly we must believe our brethren in California mean business now." They certainly did. At the business session, delegates voted to form a legal publishing association under General Conference control, to establish a state book depository, and to make the *Signs* a weekly paper like the *Review*, but published in California rather than Battle Creek. In the *Signs* John called for men and women who could easily give $100 each. To motivate Californians, he added that eastern Adventists had already pledged $6,000-$8,000 for the new paper and press.[38]

Unlike the *Review*, which in its early days men had largely edited, printed, and mailed, women produced the *Signs*. For the most part, they donated their time and talents to keep costs down. During the first six months of their apprenticeship, Priscilla Canright, Clara Morrison, and Emma White received free room and board in the homes of Oakland Adventists, but no wages. The first meeting of the new Pacific SDA Publishing Association also took place at the home of Mrs. James in San Francisco. The six men and two women (including Mrs. Rowland) chose Loughborough as president, Annie Driscoll as secretary, and John Tay as treasurer of the Association (when Tay resigned, Mrs. Hall replaced him).[39]

Obviously, establishing a West Coast publishing center created more work for Loughborough. It meant attending more meetings, filling out reams of paperwork, and finding qualified employees. The day after forming the publishing association, John sent the Articles of Incorporation via Wells Fargo coach to California's clerk and secretary of state. Then, hunched over the kitchen table, he labored night after night on the bylaws. As president of the association, John was responsible for securing subscriptions (at $2 a year) for the paper, paying the bills, training the staff, and marketing it "from [the] Atlantic to [the] Pacific Oceans . . . everywhere that the English language is read." The association's other four directors (James White, John Tay, Wesley Diggins, and Knud Brossen) helped him sell 2,800 shares of stock. Loughborough himself bought 30 shares, an investment of half a year's salary.[40]

Besides being president of the California Conference and president of the Pacific SDA Publishing Association, J. N. Loughborough wore many other hats. In 1875 he was still a member of the three-man GC Committee that met in Battle Creek. As president of the California Tract and Missionary Society, he was responsible for teaching local church officers how to fill out the new forms the state T&M generated and for inspiring members to distribute more Adventist publications. That some of his articles seem more nagging and nit-picking than inspiring reflects, perhaps, the burdens he carried and the endless hours he devoted to such tasks.[41]

That spring, as James White worked on the blueprints, the directors voted to hire Orrin B. Jones of Michigan to erect the new publishing house. An Adventist architect and builder, Jones had already helped construct three buildings for the Review and Herald press and one for Battle Creek College. He was also building the San Francisco SDA Church, "the largest and best S. D. Adventist house of worship in the United States" (until 1878, when his "Dime Tabernacle" was erected in Battle Creek). Shortly after the directors purchased a lot on the corner of Twelfth and Castro, they advertised for Adventist carpenters and masons. By May the crew had the foundations in place. In June they finished the engine room and put up the walls. Then in August Willie and Edson White moved the staff into their offices. Weeks later workers installed the Cottrell and Babcock Four Roller Air Spring Drum Cylinder printing press, a Universal Job Press, a paper cutter, a book trimmer, and a standing press at a cost of $6,500—entirely paid for by Adventist donations.[42]

Despite the skepticism of one man who declared that "these people will not give enough [money] to buy the ink for the first edition," West Coast Adventists provided the money.[43] In fact, the *Signs of the Times* (first as a weekly and later as a monthly publication) would still be in print nearly 140 years later. While the first few issues basically reprinted news notes and articles appearing in the *Review*, by 1875 the paper was beginning to stand on its own feet by publishing West Coast news and articles by California Adventists. Editor Loughborough did his bit by recycling several of his earlier contributions in the *Review*, including a 15-part series on "The Saints' Inheritance" (which had become his first book in 1859), a 10-part series on the "Hope of the Gospel" (another book in 1860), and a two-part series on "Systematic Benevolence."[44] In addition, he penned articles promoting true courage and the third angel's message and others opposing spiritualism and Christmas tableaux (especially those that blended Jesus Christ with Santa Claus, dancing, and fairies).[45]

As he nursed Maggie during her final illness, John spent several weeks writing a lengthy series for the *Review* on the papal pretentions and false teachings of the Roman Catholic Church. His hard-hitting rhetoric attacked the church for its arrogance, immorality, pomp, plots, cruelties, and greed for power as well as for teaching the concept of inherent human immortality, blending paganism with Christianity, and promoting unbiblical practices.[46] If Loughborough opposed the practice of confessing to a priest, however, he felt it proper to confess to *Review* readers that, while working in his brother's blacksmith shop at age 16, he had short-changed a man who purchased some wagon wheels that John had made. In 1871, convicted that he should somehow make restitution for his $4 offense, Loughborough added a significant percentage to the amount and donated it to the Adventist health institution in Battle Creek. Desiring to have a conscience "void of offense toward God," he hoped the Lord would accept his belated attempt to rectify a wrong committed a quarter century earlier.[47]

LOUGHBOROUGH'S DIARY

We see the same sensitivity reflected in John's diary, especially in his caring attitudes toward family, friends, and others who needed help. Whenever Maggie "got a chill" during the night, John cared for her; when she bore Eliza, rather than hiring domestic help, he prepared their meals, did the laundry, and cleaned the house. And when his son, "Del" (Delmer), got the measles, John gave him sitz baths and injections and sat beside his bed.

Outside the house, John planted and weeded the garden, set out cherry trees and grape vines, fenced in the chicken yard, and put in a sidewalk. Utilizing his carpentry skills, he made a dining room table and built chicken coops. Even when at rest, he was usually writing: by-laws, sermons, articles, and scores of letters to relatives, California Conference officials, and GC leaders. In October 1872 he penned his 278th letter to the Review and Herald office in Battle Creek. A year later he recorded "Business Letter #349." While on the road, he regularly wrote to Maggie and 9-year-old Del.

In spite of heavy responsibilities at home, at the office, and in the field, Loughborough also maintained an ambitious program of study and reading for self-improvement. He read several West Coast newspapers; literary classics (such as Milton's *Paradise Lost* and *Paradise Regained*); history books (about ancient Rome, Tyndale, and the Catholic Inquisition), and occasionally storybooks (he liked the Irish writer Edith O'Gorman). Even Del had a library of 21 books that his father read to him. They included light reading such as *The Boy's Own Toy Maker*, *Gerard the Lion Trainer*, and *Ditties*; inspirational books such as *The Guiding Hand*, *Precept upon Precept*, and *Sabbath Poems*; and serious tomes such as Rollin's *History of Rome* and *Ancient Cities*.

When he entered his 40s, John changed some of his lifelong habits. As his workdays grew longer, he began taking naps two or three times a week at home, in his *Signs* office, or with the families with whom he boarded. In the hot summer months he bathed weekly now (instead of semimonthly), a positive change that Maggie probably encouraged. To counteract stress, he took long buggy rides, went horseback riding with Del, hiked into the mountains for "a precious praying season," or went camping near an open-pit mine to obtain "some recreation from the mental pressure of the past few months." After such excursions, he returned "with recuperated energies to take hold in the work."[48]

Maggie, however, could no longer accompany her husband on such excursions, because her health was failing. In 1872 she and John had welcomed a woman suffering from TB into their home, fully expecting that Maggie could nurse her back to health. Instead, Maggie caught the disease (then called "slow consumption") herself. During the winter of 1873-1874, as her lungs grew worse, the Loughboroughs rented their Santa Rosa home and moved 60 miles east to Woodland. Maggie's sister Eliza rushed from New York to care for her. Although sometimes she felt "decidedly better," Maggie did not recover. Despite Loughborough's disdain for drugs, during 1874 the Loughboroughs' medical bills rose sharply. John and two Adventist women nursed his wife around the clock, feeding her, giving her sponge baths, and wiping away the blood she coughed up at night. Maggie resigned herself to God's will "come life or death."[49]

Hoping for a chance at life, the couple moved once again in 1875, this time to a house near St. Helena. During his evangelistic series there, John settled Maggie comfortably in bed inside a small tent adjacent to his meeting tent so that she could hear him preach. When on the road, he wrote her faithfully every three or four days. But by February it was obvious that Maggie was failing fast, so John cancelled all his appointments and hurried home. In March he wrote letters alerting her parents and siblings that the end was near. He also purchased a burial lot in St. Helena Cemetery for Maggie and baby Eliza. On March 24, as John finished his *Signs* article "Patience," Maggie passed to her rest. Two days later, he buried her on the hillside in St. Helena Cemetery with little Eliza in her arms.[50]

Both Mary (John's first wife) and Maggie had grown up in New York State. Both had died at 35, and both had lost children shortly after giving birth. Yet whereas Mary, with her complaining, self-centered spirit, had sometimes undermined her husband's ministry and criticized his actions, Maggie often traveled with him, assisted him in his evangelistic meetings, and even wrote an article for the *Signs*. In her obituary James White praised her for enduring "the hardships and privations and trials of missionary life with her husband." Her last recorded words were "Tell all my friends . . .

to meet me in the Kingdom [of heaven]." With that in mind, White ended his encomium with a poem: "She sleeps in Jesus, soon to rise; When the last trump shall rend the skies; Then burst the fetters of the tomb, To wake in full immortal bloom."[51]

Yet until that last trump sounded, John once again faced the challenge of being a single parent with three children— Delmer (14), Mary (11), and Patience (6)—to care for. And once again, he would find help closer at hand than he could have imagined.

---

[1] *RH*, Dec. 3, 1872, p. 198.

[2] *RH*, Feb. 13, 1872, p. 70.

[3] JNL, diary, September 1872; *RH*, Feb. 13, 1872, p. 70; *RH*, Mar. 5, 1872, p. 94; *RH*, Mar. 12, 1872, p. 102; *RH*, Apr. 30, 1872, pp. 158, 159; *RH*, June 18, 1872, pp. 6, 7; *RH*, July 30, 1872, p. 54; *RH*, Aug. 6, 1872, p. 62; *PUR*, Sept. 27, 1906, p. 1.

[4] For a summary of Shakerism, Swedenborgianism, mesmerism, phrenology, and spiritualism in eighteenth- and nineteenth-century America, see J. Clark, *1844*, vol. 1, pp. 327-382.

[5] R. Schwarz and F. Greenleaf, *Light Bearers*, p. 16; W. Cross, *Burned-over District*, pp. 348-352; Butler, *Sea of Faith*, pp. 252-255.

[6] *RH*, Feb. 13, 1872, p. 70; *RH*, Mar. 5, 1872, p. 94; *RH*, May 13, 1873, p. 174; *RH*, July 8, 1873, p. 30.

[7] *RH*, June 18, 1872, p. 6; *RH*, July 2, 1872, p. 23; *RH*, Apr. 29, 1873, p. 158; *RH*, July 16, 1872, p. 38; H. McCumber, *Golden West*, pp. 111, 112. The Napa *Register* also ran favorable reports of their meetings in 1873, praising their "self-sacrificing zeal and earnestness and their genial, gentlemanly deportment." As mentioned in chapter 6, J. N. Loughborough first encountered William Saunders, now the editor of the Yolo *Democrat*, during his spectacularly successful evangelistic meetings in Charlotte, Michigan, in 1864. Saunders' favorable reports of the meetings in his newspaper had boosted attendance to more than 1,200. Later the Saunders family moved to northern California, and, as a result of attending Loughborough's meetings there, William, his wife and daughter, and his foreman and his wife all converted to Seventh-day Adventism in 1873.

[8] JNL, diary, November 1872; *RH*, Sept. 17, 1872, p. 111; *RH*, Oct. 15, 1872, p. 142; Robinson, *JNL*, p. 157.

[9] *RH*, Mar. 11, 1873, p. 102; A. L. White, *Ellen G. White: The Progressive Years*, vol. 2, p. 371; JNL, diary, June 1872. At least in his diary, John does not mention that anyone else helped him compose the constitution.

[10] JNL, diary, March and August 1872; *PUR*, Sept. 13, 1906, p. 1; *PUR*, Sept. 20, 1906, p. 1. Although John does not mention where he and Maggie originally buried Eliza, sometime before 1906 she had been reburied in St. Helena Cemetery beside her mother.

[11] EGW, diary, October-December 1872, ms. 5, 1872; January 1873, ms. 3, 1873; February 1873, ms. 4, 1873, CAR; EGW to "Dear Children," Feb. 6, 1873, letter 6, 1873, CAR; A. L. White, *Ellen G. White: The Progressive Years*, vol. 2, p. 357; *PUR*, Sept. 27, 1906, p. 1; *PUR*, Oct. 11, 1906, p. 1.

[12] EGW, diary, Jan. 11, 12, 1873.

[13] EGW, diary, February 1873; *RH*, Feb. 4, 1873, p. 62.

[14] *RH*, Oct. 15, 1872, p. 140, *RH*, Oct. 22, 1872.

[15] *RH*, Oct. 15, 1872, p. 140; *Atlantic Union Conference Record*, Oct. 31, 1977, p. 7.

[16] JNL, diary, October 1872; *PUR*, Oct. 4, 1906, p. 1; E. Robinson, *Lighter of Gospel Fires*, pp. 152-155.

[17] *RH*, Dec. 3, 1872, p. 198; EGW, quoted in A. L. White, *Ellen G. White: The Progressive Years*, vol. 2, p. 358.

[18] *RH*, Dec. 3, 1872, p. 198; *RH*, Apr. 1, 1873, p. 126.

[19] EGW, diary, April 1873, ms. 6, 1873, CAR; JNL to EGW, Apr. 13, 1873, m. 52, CAR; *PUR*, Aug. 19, 1968, p. 8; *YI*, Dec. 21, 1926, pp. 7, 14; McCumber, p. 112.

[20] *Atlantic Union Conference Record*, Sept. 2, 1940, p. 3; *RH*, Jan. 15, 1942, p. 9.

[21] *RH*, May 21, 1872, p. 184; *RH*, Mar. 4, 1873, p. 95; *PUR*, Oct. 18, 1906, p. 1; *RH*, Aug. 4, 1927, p. 21.

[22] *RH*, July 8, 1873, p. 30; *RH*, June 24, 1873, pp. 14, 15; *RH*, Dec. 24, 1872, p. 14.

[23] Henry Stipp to JNL, Mar. 9, 1873, m. 52, CAR; JNL to EGW, Mar. 17, 1873, m. 52, CAR; Stockton to JNL, Mar. 17, 1873, m. 52, CAR.

[24] *RH*, May 28, 1872, p. 190.

[25] JNL, diary, July 1872, January and February 1873; *RH*, Mar. 4, 1873, p. 94.

[26] JNL, diary, May 1875; *ST*, June 24, 1875, p. 264.

[27] *RH*, Oct. 21, 1873, pp. 149-151; *RH*, Nov. 4, 1873, p. 166.

[28] *RH*, Oct. 21, 1873, pp. 149-151; *RH*, Nov. 25, 1873, p. 190; JNL, diary, November 1873.

[29] *RH*, Dec. 16, 1873, p. 6.

[30] JNL, diary, January 1874; *RH*, Jan. 20, 1874, p. 46; *RH*, Jan. 27, 1874, p. 54; A. L. White, *Ellen G. White: The Progressive Years*, vol. 2, p. 401; EGW, "Work in California—1874," ms. 1a, 1874, CAR.

[31] *RH*, Apr. 7, 1874, p. 134; *PUR*, Nov. 8, 1906, p. 1.

[32] *RH*, May 5, 1874, p. 166; "Eld. Grant's Injustice Toward Seventh-day Adventists," *RH Extra*, Apr. 14, 1874, pp. 1-4; *RH*, June 9, 1874, p. 204; *ST*, June 4, 1874, p. 8; *ST*, June 11, 1874, p. 16; *RH*, July 7, 1874, p. 30; *RH*, July 28, 1874, p. 54.

[33] *ST*, July 23, 1874, p. 40; *RH*, Aug. 4, 1874, p. 57; *ST*, Sept. 17, 1874, p. 55.

[34] *RH*, June 9, 1874, p. 204.

[35] *RH*, Aug. 25, 1874, p. 78; *ST*, Aug. 13, 1874, p. 48; *ST*, Sept. 17, 1874, p. 56; *RH*, Oct. 20, 1874, p. 134; *ST*, Oct. 22, 1874, p. 61; *RH*, Nov. 17, 1874, p. 166.

[36] *ST*, Jan. 14, 1875, p. 100; *RH*, Jan. 28, 1875, p. 38; *ST*, Feb. 11, 1875, p. 120; *RH*, Apr. 22, 1875, p. 132.

[37] JNL, diary, November 1874; JNL to Pacific Press Publishing Company, Jan. 13, 1880, m. 52, CAR; *PUR*, Nov. 15, 1906, p. 1; *PUR*, Nov. 22, 1906, p. 1; *ST*, Oct. 2, 1907, p. 637; McCumber, pp. 118, 119, 127, 131.

[38] *ST*, Aug. 13, 1874, p. 45; *ST*, Oct. 22, 1874, p. 63; *RH*, Oct. 27, 1874, p. 142; *RH*, Nov. 10, 1874, pp. 158, 159; *AUG*, May 10, 1977, p. 7.

[39] JNL to EGW, Dec. 23, 1874, m. 52, CAR; JNL to JSW, Nov. 5, 1874, m. 52, CAR; JNL, diary, Apr. 1, 1875; *RH*, Apr. 22, 1875, p. 136; *ST*, Apr. 29, 1875, p. 200.

[40] JNL, diary, April 1875; *RH*, Apr. 1, 1875, p. 112; *ST*, Apr. 1, 1875, p. 168; "Articles of Incorporation for the Publishing Association," *ST*, Apr. 8, 1875, p. 176.

[41] *RH*, Apr. 29, 1875, pp. 142, 143; *ST*, Apr. 29, 1875, p. 198; *PUR*, Dec. 13, 1906, p. 1; A. L. White, *Ellen G. White: The Progressive Years*, vol. 2, p. 478. For examples of Loughborough's "nagging" articles, see *ST*, May 27, 1875, p. 230; *ST*, June 3, 1875, p. 238; *ST*, June 10, 1875, p. 244; *ST*, June 24, 1875, p. 262.

[42] *ST*, Apr. 29, 1875, p. 200; *ST*, May 20, 1875, p. 224; *ST*, May 27, 1875, p. 232; *ST*, July 8, 1875, p. 280; *ST*, Sept. 2, 1875, p. 344; *RH*, Oct. 21, 1875, p. 124; *ST*, June

1964, p. 11; "Sisley, William Conqueror," *Ellen G. White Encyclopedia*, pp. 511, 512. William K. Loughborough, Orrin B. Jones, and William C. Sisley were the three most prominent SDA architects and builders at the end of the nineteenth century.

[43] That skeptic was Alma McKibbin's father, and she relates the story in *ST*, June 1964, p. 11.

[44] See JNL's series on "The Saints' Inheritance" in *ST*, July 9, 1874, p. 26; *ST*, July 23, 1874, p. 38; *ST*, Aug. 13, 1874, p. 46; *ST*, Sept. 17, 1874, p. 54; *ST*, Oct. 22, 1874, p. 59; *ST*, Nov. 12, 1874, p. 67; *ST*, Dec. 3, 1874, pp. 74, 75; *ST*, Dec. 17, 1874, pp. 82, 83; *ST*, Dec. 31, 1874, pp. 90, 91; *ST*, Jan. 14, 1875, pp. 98, 99; *ST*, Jan. 28, 1875, pp. 106, 107; *ST*, Feb. 11, 1875, pp. 114, 115; *ST*, Feb. 25, 1875, pp. 122, 123. For "Systematic Benevolence," see *ST*, Nov. 12, 1874, pp. 70, 71 and *ST*, Dec. 3, 1874, p. 78.

[45] See JNL's articles in *ST*, June 25, 1874, p. 24; *ST*, Dec. 31, 1874, p. 96; *ST*, Feb. 25, 1875, p. 124; *ST*, June 24, 1875, p. 258; *ST*, July 1, 1875, p. 266; *ST*, July 8, 1875, p. 274; *ST*, July 15, 1875, p. 282; *ST*, July 22, 1875, p. 290, 291; *ST*, July 29, 1875, pp. 298, 300; *ST*, Aug. 5, 1875, pp. 306, 307, 310; *ST*, Aug. 12, 1875, p. 314; *ST*, Aug. 19, 1875, pp. 322, 323; *ST*, Aug. 26, 1875, pp. 330, 334.

[46] See Loughborough's anti-Catholic articles in *RH,* April 29, 1875, pp. 138, 139; *RH,* Nov. 18, 1873, p. 182; *RH,* Jan. 27, 1874, p. 55; *RH,* Feb. 24, 1874, pp. 86, 87; *RH,* Mar. 3, 1874, p. 95; *RH,* Mar. 10, 1874, p. 102; *RH,* Mar. 17, 1874, pp. 110, 111; *RH,* Mar. 24, 1874, pp. 118, 119; *RH,* Mar. 31, 1874, pp. 126, 127; *RH,* Apr. 14, 1874, pp. 142, 143; *RH,* Apr. 21, 1874, p. 150; *RH,* Apr. 28, 1874, p. 159; *RH,* May 26, 1874, p. 191; *RH,* June 2, 1874, p. 199; *RH,* June 23, 1874, p. 15; *RH,* June 30, 1874, p. 23; *RH,* Aug. 18, 1874, pp. 70, 71; *RH,* Aug. 25, 1874, p. 79; *RH,* Sept. 22, 1874, pp. 105, 106; *RH,* Sept. 29, 1874, p. 115.

[47] JNL, "Something About Wheels," *RH,* June 6, 1871, p. 195.

[48] *ST*, June 17, 1875, p. 253; JNL, diary, March 1872-July 1875.

[49] JNL, *PUR*, Nov. 1, 1906, p. 1; JNL to Lucinda Hall, Dec. 4, 1873; JNL to Hall, Dec. 5, 1873; JNL to Hall, Dec. 18, 1873; JNL, diary, February and April 1874; *RH,* Feb. 24, 1874, p. 86.

[50] JNL, diary, May 1874, January-March 1875; *ST*, Apr. 1, 1875, p. 166.

[51] *YI*, Aug. 8, 1944, p. 13; *ST*, Apr. 8, 1875, p. 175; *RH*, Apr. 29, 1875, p. 7.

Chapter X

EVANGELIZING ALL THE WEST COAST (1875–1878)

"I have been looking over my life, especially in California. . . . I have, in many instances, been intemperate in labor. I have gone many times beyond my strength, and, at such times, with nervous power exhausted, I have not moved with that calm reflection becoming a minister of Christ. Words of impatience, savoring too much of scolding, have been spoken by me. . . . This was all wrong. . . . I do not ask you to excuse the wrong under the plea of overwork. . . .

"I am resolved, by the Lord's help, to be temperate in labor for the future, not only in amount of labor, but in kind."[1]

When J. N. Loughborough penned these words in March of 1875, he was grieving the death of his second wife, Maggie. To attain a balanced life, he needed a helpmate equal to him in intelligence, physical stamina, and organizational efficiency. As president of the Pacific SDA Publishing Company, John (43) had observed such qualities in an office secretary named Anna Driscoll (36), originally from New York State. During the fall of 1875 as Loughborough traveled around the conference, his business correspondence with Miss Driscoll became somewhat more personal and, by October, decidedly romantic in tone. Soon "pressing matters" required them to spend more time at the office. Shortly after Thanksgiving, John and Annie (as he called her) became engaged. On December 7 he took her to a San Francisco restaurant. Later that evening, James White married them and they spent their honeymoon night in the White's home. The following day, they returned to the office, for they had so much to do.[2]

A PROFESSIONAL PARTNERSHIP FORMED

Working together, John (as president) and Annie (as secretary) soon made the California Tract and Missionary Society (T&M) a highly efficient operation. They developed new office procedures, created new report forms, kept extensive records on local branches, and wrote articles in the *Signs* full of instruction for T&M officers. In "System," John emphasized the need for "conformity to order," for "a body without a head is a monster" (as a T&M society would be without officers doing their jobs). Such officers must be diligent recordkeepers and form fillers. Apparently most local T&M officers met these standards, for in 1875 John praised them for ending the year with their account books "all square." Another article explained the hierarchy of the T&M structure from its leaders in the local church to the highest official at the GC. Now everyone knew precisely who reported what information to whom. Every three months local and district officers convened for a quarterly meeting at Oakland.[3]

Given John's childhood fascination with decimals and multiplication, it should come as no surprise that he relied on statistical charts and tables to demonstrate the growth of the T&M work on the West Coast. Many of his articles read like actuarial reports. They measure growth in membership, number of *Signs* distributed, amount of money donated, and quantities of health almanacs sold from one quarter to the next. From the "missionary blanks" (forms) submitted by the local T&M secretaries, the office staff compiled statistical charts showing the progress of the literature program each quarter and year. When John was away from the office, Annie prepared the tables, which by 1878 showed that California, with 385 T&M members, boasted the second largest society in the denomination (behind Michigan's 1,542 members).[4]

As conference president, Loughborough followed the same approach in his annual camp meeting "Address," a speech sprinkled with numbers showing growth in church membership, Systematic Benevolence funds, literature distribution, church employees hired, and so forth. In 1877, for example, he reported that the California Conference had five ordained ministers and six licentiates (licensed ministers) serving 24 churches (up 50 percent from 1875), with more than 600 members (up 33 percent) who gave more than $5,500 in Systematic Benevolence offerings annually (up 33 percent).[5] As Loughborough would demonstrate in his books *Rise and Progress* (1892) and *The Great Second Advent Movement* (1905), statistics were a handy tool to show the progress of Adventism around the world and thereby testify to God's leading in the third angel's message.

Despite the negative effects of the Panic of 1873 (unemployment, bank closures, tight credit) in the U.S., California Adventists seemed "disposed to sacrifice and lift the harder," Loughborough declared. T&M members, like a "missionary army [with] good cheer and stability," redoubled their efforts to distribute Adventist literature. Following the example of the T&M Society in Rome, New York, they put up "tract distributors" (wooden racks) in railroad stations. Other groups donated books and pamphlets to the libraries of prisons and jails (the T&M even had members in San Quentin Prison).[6] Recognizing that alcohol abuse had led many inmates into a life of crime, the T&M societies sent out temperance tracts to counteract the influence of California's wine industry. After seeing an alcoholic suffering delirium tremors shot dead in a hotel for threatening a family, Loughborough told *Signs* readers, "There is temperance lecture enough for one day."[7]

Like his sister Minerva Jane Chapman,[8] John also boosted the Sabbath school program. As editor of the children's Sabbath school paper, the *Youth's Instructor,* from 1875 to 1879, Minerva published articles written by her brothers William and John. Loughborough urged Adventist ministers to promote Bible study and Sabbath schools in the churches. He also chaired the committee that formed a state Sabbath School Association in 1878. "What an opening [for public witnessing] is Sabbath-school work," he exhorted in the *Signs*. "Parents and guardians, learn the lessons yourselves; aid the youth and children to learn the lessons; encourage the school by your presence."[9]

In spite of those heavy responsibilities, however, John never forgot his first love—evangelism. He particularly liked preaching in San Francisco and Oakland (Ellen White called them "the two beehives"), seeing them as "the entrepôt of the nations" with hundreds of immigrants arriving each year. He also enjoyed visiting local churches (and after 1875 Loughborough calls them "churches," not "meetinghouses"). Such preaching forays, however, often presented unexpected challenges. While speaking in Visalia, he and William Healey contracted malaria, which gave them fever and chills for months. As Loughborough and Canright preached in Hollister, they faced competition from a noisy political gathering. Then an earthquake shook their tent and rattled the city jail, the "horrifying screams" of its inmates disrupting their services. In San Francisco heavy thunderstorms falling on sandy soil loosened their tent stakes while high winds tore the canvass top. Evangelism was never dull work.[10]

During their evangelistic series in San Francisco and Oakland, Loughborough and the Whites pioneered several creative techniques that later generations would call "saturation evangelism." Rather than scattering 50,000 handbills (with sermon outlines on one side and gospel songs on the other) throughout the city, the team focused on one square mile surrounding their tent. Prior to the meetings, "missionary workers" (volunteers) visited all 5,000 homes in this district four times, distributing posters, issues of *Signs*, and copies of the paper "The Tent Meeting." In addition, they placed ads in the San Francisco newspapers. Recognizing that the city was, in effect, "a cluster of villages" with diverse ethnic and immigrant groups, the team planned to move their 60-foot tent from one neighborhood to another. "To reach the people we must go where they are," Loughborough asserted, so "that a more thorough work can be done." Finding the usual practice of passing a hat or offering plate among the congregation "offensive," John created a "contribution box." Constructed of black walnut, the box (6" x 5" x 4"), with a sliding lid secured by a tiny lock, was screwed to the pulpit. On its face John glued a simple card labeled "Contributions" and beneath it, a sign that stated: "Those wishing to aid in the expenses of these meetings will please place their contributions in the above box." The plan worked: when the services ended, he had received sufficient funds to cover all his expenses.[11]

The results of such innovative approaches surprised even Loughborough. While some working and middle-class citizens attended their meetings, an even larger group of upper-middle-class educated and professional Whites (whom John called "an intelligent class of hearers") came. They requested issues of the evangelists' newspaper (which they considered "choice reading") and copies of the "rare pieces of music" printed on the handbills. As 1876 was the centennial of American independence and a hotly contested presidential election year, it fascinated them how the preachers tied the United States into Bible prophecy. The summer meetings resulted in the baptism of 34 converts. The previous December of 1875 Loughborough had dedicated the new San Francisco chapel that O. B. Jones had built.[12] Evangelistic meetings in Oakland in 1876 brought similar results, and Adventists there persuaded Jones to build them a church as well before he left for Battle Creek.[13]

By 1877 ministers had to pitch three tents to meet the demands for evangelistic series. But it presented a problem: the conference did not have enough ordained ministers to meet the demand. In his article "Calls for Labor," Loughborough suggested that in the interim, Adventists might distribute tracts, pamphlets, and copies of James White's lithograph "The Way of Life" to their neighbors. That spring John persuaded *Review* editor Uriah Smith (who almost never left his office) to come to California and hold meetings at St. Helena. Smith's lectures on Bible prophecy brought a "steady advance" in the truth there. When a rejuvenated James White began preaching in Oakland, John exclaimed: "Prospects were never more promising for the advancement of the cause in California than now." Indeed, he saw "a growth in grace and earnestness" among West Coast Adventists.[14]

The spiritual growth was especially evident at California's camp meetings. Lining up speakers for the Fairfax camp meeting in 1875, Loughborough informed James White that Parson Barnes, the local Baptist pastor, had declared that if "that little black-eyed woman [Ellen White] is not at the camp-meeting, there will be a great many disappointed." So the Whites agreed to come. Railroad and ferryboat officials boosted attendance by offering reduced fares. The North Pacific Coast Railroad even granted the use of their property for the encampment. Attendees brought their own bedding and tents, but found "food for man and beast" on site. In addition to its huge 96' x 60' main tent, the Fairfax convocation boasted 88 family tents and about 400 campers. Twelve more converts were baptized at its close.[15]

The Fairfax camp meeting is the first on record to feature special meetings for the children, 40 of whom came forward for prayer. Although in the 1850s James White had written Sabbath school lessons for children and youth (published in the *Youth's Instructor* in 1852), only a few scattered Adventist groups (in Rochester and Buck's Bridge, New York, and Battle Creek, Michigan) held Sabbath schools for young people. In the 1860s Adelia Patten and Goodloe Harper Bell had prepared some special lessons for the younger children in Battle Creek, where Bell taught a kindergarten class (later called "the Bird's Nest"). Loughborough's pioneering efforts to evangelize California Adventists' children led in 1877 to the formation of the first state Sabbath School Association. Within a year a dozen state Sabbath School Associations had organized, representing nearly 180 Sabbath schools with more than 5,800 members.[16]

Adventists who returned to Fairfax in 1876 experienced "a season of earnestness in preaching, in prayer, in confession and consecration" unseen at previous gatherings. Tear-filled confessions, social meetings with 70 testimonies an hour, thrilling altar calls, and youthful prayer sessions in the nearby woods (with adult supervision) brought a feeling of unity also reflected in the business sessions when motions passed unanimously. Again, about 400 Adventists camped in 66 tents and 1,500 people attended Sunday programs.[17]

Wishing to reach non-Adventists farther afield, California Conference leaders decided to hold two camp meetings in 1877: one at Yountville and the other at Lemoore. At Yountville 560 Adventists established a "cotton village" with more than 100 family tents pitched beneath shady oaks beside a stream. During social meetings, 100 gave their testimonies in 40 minutes. More than 1,000 local people attended Sunday services. The session resulted in the baptism of 57 converts. At Lemoore 115 campers in 22 tents attended services, and 33 were baptized. Such statistics demonstrate that by 1877 nearly every Adventist in the state came to camp meeting. Furthermore, those baptized included large numbers of German, French, Danish, Swedish, and Italian converts. Finally, growing numbers of non-Adventists joined the weekend services. They expressed "astonishment" at the lack of "noise and confusion" at Adventist meetings—a contrast with other camp meetings where the police made frequent arrests for disturbing the peace. Loughborough overheard several remark, "Well, this is a people in favor of order; I'm going to see what their ministers have to say."[18]

In the fall of 1878 leaders decided to hold three, weeklong camp meetings at Yountville, Lemoore, and Grangeville. Faced with hot weather (in an era when men wore black wool suits and women donned heavy ankle-length dresses), Loughborough got partway into his discourse at Lemoore and fainted dead away. As ministers carried his limp body from the platform, William H. Healey finished the sermon. After taking a cold bath the next day, John preached an hourlong sermon. But a day later, "weak from sweating," he cut his remarks short and took a nap.

Despite physical discomforts, Lemoore attendees raised $1,420 for the new British Mission Fund. Adventists at the Yountville camp meeting gave more than $4,000 ($100 of it in gold jewelry), while those at Grangeville collected $571 for the mission endeavor. In addition, the Grangeville crowd contributed 500 dimes to help build the Dime Tabernacle in Battle Creek. Then to Annie's surprise, they presented her with $50 in appreciation for her "faithful labors during the past year," calling her "a true helper" and noting that her account books were "free from error and a model for neatness." Delegates also resolved "that we earnestly recommend all our churches to use only unfermented wine in the communion [services], as being more in harmony with scripture and our faith than the use of intoxicating wine." At the Grangeville camp meeting Loughborough suffered another "fainting spell," so he cut his discourses short, took cold water baths, and napped more often.[19]

Thanks largely to Loughborough's enthusiasm for sacred music, Adventist worship services—at least in California—grew more polished, featuring the vocal talents of local members. Unfortunately, it was not the case in many Adventist meeting houses. Ellen White, who had preached in most of them, described the painful experience of hearing "untrained voices, pitched to the highest key, literally shrieking the sacred words of some hymn of praise." At such times, she admitted, "I long to stop my ears, or flee from the place, and I rejoice when the painful exercise is ended." To help musically untrained members sing in tune and in rhythm with one another, James White often "lined out the hymn," slapping his hand on his Bible as he marched down the aisle toward the front singing, "You will see your Lord a-coming" or "When I can read my title clear." Between themselves, James and his son Edson compiled 11 hymnals and songbooks. In many cases they borrowed tunes from popular secular songs that everyone knew and composed sacred texts for them (such as Uriah Smith's hymn "Land of Light," sung to the tune of Stephen Foster's "Old Folks at Home"). However, since Adventists, musically speaking, were heirs of the radical Reformation (Anabaptists, Mennonites, Moravians, etc.), a "plain people" who rejected the use of organs and all other instruments in sacred services, for decades they sang their praises to God a cappella. Thus in April 1876 at the dedication of the new San Francisco Central SDA Church, a choir performed two pieces, and the congregation sang two hymns. At camp meetings children's choirs usually gave several concerts, but without piano or organ accompaniment.[20]

Then at the historic Yountville camp meeting of 1877 J. N. Loughborough and Edson White conspired to introduce organ music to the congregation. After A. M. Goodnough, a Vallejo music dealer, loaned them a Smith pump organ, the two men hung a sign on the side of the crate that read "ORGAN" in huge letters. At the first service, John read Psalm 150 aloud to the congregation. When he reached verse 4, his voice rose, and with a flourish he exclaimed: "Praise him with the timbrel and dance: praise him with stringed instruments and [spelling the word out] O-R-G-A-N-S." Then, his eyes twinkling, he declared: "Why that is just the word that is on the back of that box, and in our very next meeting to-day we are going to have the organ out and praise the Lord with it, just as he has told us to do." Despite objections from three attendees (one of whom played the piano and another the violin), all agreed that the organ had "made a decided improvement in the melody and fervency" of the song services. Edson White, president of the California Sabbath School Association, introduced an organ at the next state convention.[21] Soon no evangelistic series was complete without organ accompaniment. During the 1878 San Francisco and Oakland campaigns, Edson White's fervent singing and his wife Mary's stirring organ playing attracted 500 citizens to the meetings at which Loughborough and M. C. Israel preached. Months later when John joined Ellen White, A. T. Jones, and I. D. Van Horn at the Salem, Oregon camp meeting, he introduced an organ at the first service. By the end of the week, most attendees could sing harmoniously.[22]

TRIALS AND EXPULSIONS

If the 1870s saw a growth in harmonious singing, however, the decade also witnessed an upsurge in criticism, backbiting, and rebellion among California's otherwise-minded Adventists. With characteristic candor, James White observed in 1875 that "in no State are ministers watched with a more suspicious eye" than in the Golden State. Sadly, he admitted that some Adventist ministers "with broken-down reputations" had fled to

California, bringing shame to God's cause, because "they did not succeed in leaving the devil on the other side [of the Rockies]." However, White felt that John's "correct deportment, indefatigable labors, and firm purpose for the right in times of trial, have given him favor with the people and with God."[23]

Yet if God approved Loughborough's course of action, some of His saints did not. Often personal discouragement, spiritual struggles, financial trials, transfers of members, deaths in the ranks, and a paucity of pastors sparked what John called "murmuring" in the ranks. With growing frequency, Loughborough chaired "church trials" and "meetings of investigation" to censure, suspend, or expel dissidents. His reports in the *Signs* indicate that most of the trials dealt with Adventists whose "evil lifestyles" (breaking the Ten Commandments) and "unsanctified spirit" (resistance to authority) had created "a very bad state of things . . . injurious to the cause." Often such meetings lasted past midnight as John pleaded with individuals to confess their wrongdoing and seek forgiveness. While most sessions involved spiritual wrongdoing (what John called "disaffection, discord, and Laodicean conditions"), sometimes "disorganizing elements" tried to "stab the cause and its friends," doing irreparable harm to the church's reputation. At one church such violence became real when one member shot another to death.[24]

As conference president, J. N. Loughborough took a redemptive approach to church discipline. "Our first care and interest should ever be the glory of God and the honor of his truth," he informed *Signs* readers. The second purpose was church unity. "Some have feared that discipline would injure if not break up the church," he explained. "[This is] a great mistake. Without it error and confusion are sure to come in, and the whole body [will] grow weak and sickly." A third goal sought to lead offending members to confess their sins, reconcile with fellow believers, and reform their lives. Only as a last resort should censure, suspension, or expulsion be employed to "check an evil in its rise." Loughborough discovered that in one congregation where "darkness and confusion" reigned and at another which he described as "a hopeless wreck," the selective use of expulsion brought unity. For that purpose, he recommended that church boards examine their membership lists once a quarter to weed out dissidents.[25]

As Loughborough frequently stated in his *Signs* articles, "Order is Heaven's first law." He compared the Adventist cause to an army of Christian soldiers "battling against sin" in the warfare with the devil. Soldiers always obeyed their generals' orders, because the officers saw the "bigger picture," he asserted. In the local church, ministers, elders, and deacons (the term "deaconess" had not yet entered the Adventist lexicon) constituted the "superior officers" whom members must obey to promote "proper order."[26] By the late-1870s Loughborough found many indications of unity and order within the Adventist ranks. "It is certainly encouraging to see and hear of the spirit of harmony and good cheer that comes in to take the place of the gloom that to some extent has seemed to hang over our cause in this State," he exclaimed. "On the whole I am gratified to find so firm a condition of matters in our churches."[27]

Annie Loughborough also did her part to promote peace in the ranks. When she learned that the Whites had taken offense at the way she had handled their finances, she hastened to apologize. In a letter to Willie (21) and Mary White (19), Annie (35) confessed that perhaps she had "conversed too freely" with them ("as with a younger brother and sister") in the past, presuming that they understood her feelings better than anyone else. (Annie and Mary had been press employees for two years when the teenager Willie White was a gofer transporting paper in his wheelbarrow. When promoted to president at 21 in 1876, the bachelor may have found it difficult to accept instruction from an older married woman.) Yet in a recent matter involving bank drafts from James White, she felt she had overstepped the bounds of propriety and interfered in family affairs. "I am astonished at my stupidity," she exclaimed. "Why I was so thoughtless I cannot understand." Willie had also taken offense at Annie's efforts to instruct him in a bookkeeping matter (despite her proven superiority in that field), and she apologized profusely, stating that when the matter had been presented to her "in this light, [I was] almost paralyzed." Recognizing that "selfishness lies so deeply rooted in my heart," she feared that her actions and words could jeopardize her "eternal interests." Therefore, she begged W. C. White's forgiveness and prayed for "God to be merciful" to her. In a subsequent letter to James and Ellen White, Annie apologized for her words and assured them that she had "no feelings of opposition" toward them. In closing, she added, "I pray God to forgive all my sins."[28]

Her remarkable letters reveal that, like her husband, Annie was a deeply sensitive, caring person with a ready capacity to apologize to those she felt she had offended. One may also see in them her deference toward a boss who, though 14 years younger, was nonetheless the son of two cofounders of the church and as such, one who probably felt entitled to direct others. If on the one hand the Whites could sometimes be hypersensitive concerning what they saw as personal sleights or implied challenges to their leadership, on the other hand, since both John and Annie believed in the divine inspiration of Ellen's visions, neither wanted to risk opening a rift in their friendship with the family. Consequently, as we have already seen, whenever John received a testimony of rebuke from Mrs. White, he hastened to apologize, seek forgiveness, and change his way of life. Moreover, as firm proponents of order, John and Annie did not want to say or do anything that might jeopardize church harmony or impede the progress of the Adventist program around the world.

STARTING AN OVERSEAS MINISTRY

As Americans celebrated their centennial, James White and J. N. Loughborough made a decision that, in the long run, would change the face of Adventist missions. After the Great Disappointment of 1844, Adventist witnessing had been stymied by the belief in the "shut door" (to 1851), the lack of centralized organization and specialized institutions, the paucity of funds and trained staff, and the conviction that the Second Advent was imminent. In 1874, however, the church sent its first official missionary—J. N. Andrews—across the Atlantic to Switzerland and France. In 1876 White and Loughborough decided to reach out to the islands of the Pacific. Prior to the 1890s, however, no steamship lines offered regularly scheduled voyages there. Packing Adventist books, tracts, and copies of the *Signs* inside a crate, the two entrusted them to a certain Captain Knowles, who took the crate on his ship the *St. John* and promised to drop it off at Pitcairn Island.[29]

Knowles kept his word, but the natives on Pitcairn, fearing this material might "poison their minds," kept it locked in storage. But one day some young people opened the crate and learned about the seventh-day Sabbath. Subsequently West Coast Adventists sent literature on the *Golden Hind* and the *Golden Fleece*, and the islanders examined the new material. Soon Mary McCoy began corresponding with White and Loughborough.

When John Tay, an Adventist carpenter on the *Pelican*, stopped in 1886, he gave Bible studies to the natives, and within five weeks the entire island had converted from Anglicanism to Seventh-day Adventism.[30]

Agreeing with Stephen N. Haskell that members should place Adventist literature aboard ships at all American ports, Loughborough called for volunteers to do it in San Francisco, where 50 ships embarked daily. In 1875 members of the California T&M Society distributed books, tracts, and papers aboard 62 vessels. Two ship captains converted as a result. Putting his money where his mouth was, Loughborough began donating $5 every quarter to the program. He challenged West Coast Adventists to give $1 to $25 each "to save sailors for God's kingdom." They responded enthusiastically, and during three months in 1876 T&M members placed 3,200 copies of the *Signs* on dozens of ships. In 1877 this regular Sunday ministry supplied the crews aboard 78 ships with reading material.[31]

The bulk of it, of course, came from the Pacific SDA Publishing Company in Oakland, where J. N. Loughborough was president and Annie, secretary. But in 1876 John resigned, telling the board of directors that he was "not acquainted with the printing and publishing business" and that "his labors [travels] will be so far from the Office much of the time that he cannot give it his immediate attention." The board chose W. C. White to replace him. As auditor of the publishing company, one of its five directors, and president of the state T&M Society, Loughborough continued to work closely with White in establishing a depository in San Francisco, increasing subscriptions to the *Signs*, and hiring employees. Occasionally, however, individuals had to be discharged. When Willie and Mary White left for Battle Creek College in 1877 and the board of directors reinstated Loughborough as president, he had to fire three girls for trying "to turn the folding room into a dance hall." But with press manager Edson White's expert assistance, the company soon acquired a stereotype machine, an electrotype machine, and a more rapid cylinder press that printed materials more quickly and therefore more cheaply.[32]

The new equipment soon filled the old publishing house "from garret to cellar," including the tank house and barn out back. So in 1878 the board began laying plans for a larger (30' x 85') two-story building bordering Twelfth Street. James White loaned the board $1,000 (almost one third of the projected $3,500 cost) to begin the construction. Work progressed rapidly, and that summer laborers transferred all the equipment from the old building to the new one.[33]

Another West Coast endeavor that James White enthusiastically endorsed was the Biblical Institute. Inaugurated in the spring of 1877, it brought together 50 ministers, licentiates, and Bible workers for three weeks of intense Bible study, lectures, and discussion. The first one at Oakland featured 64 presentations by James and Ellen White, Uriah Smith, J. H. Waggoner, and J. N. Loughborough. Despite having to sit through three intense sessions every day, attendees expressed gratitude for the "new light received on points not before clearly understood." At its close, two delegates received ordination credentials and six others received ministerial licenses.[34]

Yet a third project that White supported was the establishment of the Rural Health Retreat at St. Helena. Early in 1874, while Loughborough and I. D. Van Horn were visiting William Pratt's ranch in Pratt Valley, Van Horn hiked up the hill above St. Helena to Crystal Springs. When he returned, he told John, "I have found the ideal place for a health resort." When Loughborough returned three years later, he too felt that the warm climate, inspiring views, and fresh spring water on the 10-acre plot on Howell Mountain made it the perfect spot for a sanitarium. Shortly thereafter Mr. Atwood, Pratt's brother-in-law, asked Dr. Merritt Kellogg if he would like to run a sanitarium of his own near St. Helena. Kellogg agreed, and with the help of two other men raised $5,000 to make their dream a reality. On June 7, 1878, the Rural Health Retreat opened in a simple 28' x 72' frame building with 35 patients (some of whom camped out in tents). J. D. Rice, a patient who had arrived in a comatose state, testified that after 12 days, Dr. Kellogg's treatments had him able to rise from his bed and sit up.[35]

In his *Review* article "Beautiful California," James White also dreamed of retiring to California with its "green valleys" and "mild, beautiful climate." Despite the drunkenness, extravagance, and idleness of some citizens, he praised the Golden State for its chirping birds, rich farmland, pure air, delightful scenery, beautiful flowers, and majestic mountains. Every visit to the West Coast (by 1878 the Whites had crossed the U.S. nine times) rejuvenated him. Whenever James insisted on returning to their cabin in Colorado, Ellen (who felt her husband would be a burden to her there) reminded him of the health benefits of California—and she conspired with Loughborough to keep those benefits ever in her husband's mind. "[I want him to] take hold of [farm] matters as he did in Greenville [Michigan]," she asserted. Soon James was talking about cultivating flowers and fruits near Oakland.[36]

REACHING OREGON, WASHINGTON, AND NEVADA

Loughborough, warned by Willie White to seek his father's advice only "at times when he is feeling well and cheerful,"[37] rejoiced at James' recovery from his recent stroke. John needed the elder statesman's advice on a very important matter: Should he accept Isaac D. Van Horn's invitation to speak at a Portland, Oregon, camp meeting and help organize the Adventist advance in the Northwest? With his usual candor, James told John to go, because "Van Horn can no more run a camp-meeting than I can run the government of the United States."[38]

On October 10, 1877, J. N. Loughborough boarded the steamship *George W. Elder* at San Francisco for the three-day voyage to Portland, where Isaac Van Horn met him. Van Horn had scheduled John to preach at Portland and Salem, Oregon, and Walla Walla, Washington. As Walla Walla lay just up the road from the famous Whitman Mission, John recalled that in 1870 a Mrs. Husted had told him the story of the Whitman Massacre of 1847 in which she had allegedly persuaded Chief Wai-I-Lat-Pu to intervene and stop the "merciless" savages from further killing. Finding only a "weather-beaten board" to commemorate the event, John pleaded with local citizens to erect a suitable memorial. Shortly thereafter, at a service held at Whitman College, they unveiled a marble slab to honor the Whitmans.[39]

Having honored past memories, Loughborough turned his attention to future prospects. At a general meeting in late October at the Walla Walla Adventist Church, following John's hard-hitting sermon on order, unity, and harmony, 50 "backsliders" returned to the church. After prayer the 12 delegates formed the North Pacific Conference, the North Pacific Association, and the North Pacific T&M Society. They elected Van Horn as conference president, his wife Adelia Patten as secretary, and Alonzo T. Jones as treasurer. The new conference had two ordained ministers (Van Horn and Jones) and five licentiates. Attendees promised to purchase $5,000 worth of stock in the Pacific SDA Publishing Company and raise

$300 for the Missionary Fund. Grateful for Loughborough's guidance, delegates sang the Doxology with tears in their eyes.[40] Following this historic convocation, Van Horn led Loughborough on a whirlwind speaking tour across Oregon and Washington. In addition to preaching, John held T&M training seminars, gave temperance lectures (for men battling tobacco), ordained local deacons and elders, and presided over church trials. In 50 days Loughborough and Van Horn preached 64 times and chaired 10 business meetings. Exhausted but satisfied, in December John returned to San Francisco.[41]

But in February 1878 he was off again, this time by train to Nevada, where he boarded with the Fergusons and Baileys while preaching twice a day to the miners and their families. John found the people there "given to much pleasure seeking, such as horse racing, dancing, card playing, . . . drinking and all forms of gambling." Thanks largely to the efforts of local elder Jackson Ferguson, churches had begun in St. Claire and Stillwater, little towns on the edge of "the Great American Desert." Since the St. Claire church was too small to hold the 70 people who attended John's services, they met in the Churchill County Institute instead. During his monthlong series, Loughborough testified that "I never had better attention or better order . . . anywhere than I have had here." As a result, three requested baptism and 10 "signed the covenant" to keep the Sabbath. Church members also organized the SDA Association of Nevada with Loughborough as president, John Ferguson, secretary, and Jackson Ferguson, treasurer.[42]

That summer as Loughborough returned to Oregon and Washington with Ellen White, rough seas on the trip north made her seasick. The Salem campgrounds presented a striking color contrast: the 50-foot meeting tent decorated in red-and-blue bunting, 24 white family tents perched atop golden straw and set among a grove of 30 dark-green fir trees 150 feet tall, reaching to the azure sky overhead. About 200 Adventists camped during the week, and on weekends 2,000 local citizens came to hear Ellen White, A. T. Jones, J. N. Loughborough, and I. D. Van Horn preach. In addition, White spoke to the inmates in the state prison and gave a temperance lecture at the Methodist chapel. One man remarked that "he never saw a campground before that he would take his wife and daughters to," but after attending the first service he invited his family to join him.[43]

Since the new converts in Nevada had invited "the Rev. Mr. Loughborough . . . to visit us again at his earliest opportunity," immediately after the Salem camp meeting John took the Central Pacific Railroad to Reno. Apparently his reputation had preceded him, because his meetings were packed, with scores of listeners standing outside the tent. Because of speculation in worthless mining stocks, many families lived below the poverty line. When John arrived, public fears ran high due to nearby "Indian excitement" and the catastrophic fire set by angry Whites who destroyed Reno's Chinatown. Nonetheless, between 100 and 500 local people attended his 14 meetings. When Mrs. White joined him, 400 people listened with breathless silence as she delivered one of her favorite sermons, "Behold What Manner of Love."[44]

When the meetings ended, Loughborough organized 22 members into the Reno SDA Church. They formed a Sabbath school, a Bible class, and a prayer meeting. In addition, they elected as their church clerk a former Virginia slave who after the Civil War had drifted west to Nevada in hopes of striking it rich. Charles M. Kinney, a gregarious, talented young African American, would become secretary of the Nevada T&M Society at 26. Following further education at Healdsburg College in California, he would pioneer Adventism among Blacks in Kansas and the upper South, becoming one of the first ordained Black Seventh-day Adventist ministers. Loughborough and Kinney wrote regularly concerning a variety of topics.[45]

LOUGHBOROUGH'S WRITINGS AND DIARY

Judging from his submissions to the *Signs*, the one topic J. N. Loughborough enjoyed writing about most in the 1870s was the Roman Catholic Church. Between September 1875 and July 1877 he penned more than 30 articles attacking the papacy as the "Man of Sin," the "Lawless One," and the "Little Horn" of Daniel 3. Largely a rehash of his 1873-1874 series in the *Review*, the essays throttled popes past and present for their arrogance, pomp, power, greed, and cruelty. Loughborough also criticized the church for upholding traditions that mixed paganism with Christianity, advocating nonbiblical practices (such as worship of the saints, papal infallibility, purgatory, and transubstantiation), and presuming to forgive sins (confession to a priest, Mariolatry, penances). If his hard-hitting rhetoric resonated with Adventists, it probably found acceptance among California's White, middle-class Protestants as well. Indeed, Catholic-bashing had been a popular religious sport since the Reformation.[46]

Snatching time between his administrative and evangelistic duties, John penned occasional articles on other topics as well. Some focused on doctrinal subjects such as the two witnesses of Revelation 11, the state of the dead, signs of the world's end, and the Sabbath.[47] Others addressed issues related to Christian living such as telling the truth and showing proper reverence.[48] In his ever-popular "Questions and Answers" series, Loughborough tackled a wide range of queries both biblical (the identity of "seducing spirits" in 1 Timothy 4), health-related (the causes of diphtheria and rheumatism), and economic (whether Leviticus 11 permitted Adventists to raise hogs). Straddling the fence on the last topic, he felt that Adventists *could* keep pigs if they sold them to factories for lubricating oil (rather than to slaughterhouses for food) and that "to shun fevers and other evil diseases" they should locate their pigsties as far as possible from their houses.[49]

Although there was no pigsty anywhere near the Loughborough house, John and Annie did keep chickens for their eggs when the properties they bought had sufficient space for chicken coops out back. When that proved impossible, they purchased their eggs (at 25 cents per dozen) at the corner grocery, along with oranges (24 cents per dozen), pickles (50 cents per gallon), apples and peaches (a dollar per bushel), flour (10 pounds for 40 cents), fish (25 cents), and other commodities. On rare occasions John spent 20 cents on candy. As we saw in chapter 9, the Loughboroughs saved money by canning a wide variety of fruits and vegetables.

They also reduced expenses by not seeking professional medical help for themselves or for their children. Following the techniques he had propounded in his *Hand Book of Health*, John and Annie treated a wide variety of ailments with hot or cold water, rest, herbs, massages, dry or wet fomentations, and other folk treatments. In a typical year they cured colds, vomiting, diarrhea, rashes, toothaches, fevers, and headaches with natural remedies. Both tried to exercise regularly and get plenty of rest (through daily naps and sleep at night). Despite the many stressors in their lives, John and Annie took time to be together alone as well. If the frequency with which John drew ellipses with double X's (did the numbers such as "26" and "29" inside them indicate the number of hugs and kisses they exchanged?) in his diaries are any indication, Annie had clearly surpassed his former wives, Mary and Maggie, as his favorite.

Even entertainment cost them little. Every July 4 they watched the Independence Day parade in San Francisco and attended the fireworks display afterward. As their children grew, John and Annie invited their friends over for parties. When he was home, John took Delmer shopping at their favorite store—Pulcifer's Shop in San Francisco. Here John spent $36 (three weeks' salary) on a new suit of clothes in 1875. Occasionally Mr. Chittenden, a wealthy San Francisco entrepreneur, invited them aboard his large sailboat for excursions beyond the Golden Gate. On one such trip with a dozen friends, everyone except Ellen White got seasick because of choppy waves in the bay. The experience helped her describe more vividly the scene of Christ and His disciples on the Sea of Galilee during the storm, which she was then writing about and which would eventually be included in her book *The Desire of Ages.*[50]

Within weeks of that sailboat ride, John and Annie faced the prospect of making a trans-Atlantic voyage. The GC Committee on June 27, 1878, had resolved that "a mission in England be opened immediately." Noting that Loughborough "has labored successfully [for] the past ten years on the Pacific Coast, and under God has accomplished a great and good work," they decided that he "is the man to take charge" of the British Mission. James White started a campaign to raise the unprecedented sum of $100,000 during the next two years.[51]

The news that the denomination had chosen him to go to England did not come as a complete surprise to John, however. While he slept on the train to Reno, Nevada, in early July, an unseen hand had shaken him awake from his nap, and he had heard a voice in his mind saying, "Put up your household goods for sale and make your arrangements to go to the General Conference and to England." Dashing a letter off to Annie, he instructed her to sell all their furniture and household belongings at 50 percent off. In what the Loughboroughs saw as a providential act, within two days a bachelor about to get married paid cash for everything. With $2,300 in gold and currency, John and Annie stored their clothing and books with the sailor John Tay and left to make the rounds of California's three camp meetings.[52]

At the Yountville camp meeting Loughborough, after reviewing a decade of progress on the West Coast, exhorted his listeners to "trust in God. . . . Move in harmony with the General Conference and their decisions and efforts to help you." Then he closed with an apology: "I have made mistakes, as a result of these mistakes your feelings may have been injured, and perhaps in some things the cause would have been in a better condition to-day had I obtained more wisdom from God to guide my way. [But] I should have made more mistakes than I have had it not been for the counsel and instruction I received from the first by the gift of prophecy, as manifested through Sister White. Forgive my mistakes as I believe God has forgiven them. Ever remember that success in life does not consist in never making mistakes, but [in] avoiding the same mistakes a second time. I desire to learn by the past to seize ever the favorable present to do good, and wherever my lot may be cast, to be a faithful soldier of the cross of Christ."[53]

At Grangeville a choir premiered a special farewell hymn composed for the occasion:

"Farewell our brother, dear and true,
Farewell, may God thy footsteps guide.
Through tears for you we still can view
That meeting where no griefs abide.

"On us a faithful shepherd's care
With zeal thou ever hast bestowed,
And for thy care God will prepare
A crown beyond the narrow road.

"O may thy mantle on us fall,
Thy earnest zeal with us remain,
And may we all obey the call
To waken from our slumbers vain.

"The God of Israel, pilot, guide,
Will be thy guardian day by day,
Will speed thee on the mission wide,
Uphold thee in the righteous way.

"Farewell, our words and tears are vain
To show our soul's true earnest love;
Farewell, in God let hope remain—
A hope we all may meet above."[54]

On September 19, John (46), Annie (38), and Delmer (14) boarded the train for the 10-day journey to Battle Creek. There, reunited with Mary (17), they lodged with John's sister Minerva Chapman, dined with his brother William and William's wife, Eliza, and their daughter Lettie (now Michigan Sabbath School Association secretary), and visited old friends. At the General Conference session delegates sought John's advice at meetings of the Michigan Conference, Review and Herald press, Education Society, and T&M Society. He was also present when the delegates "voted that I should go to Great Brittain [*sic*]." (Once again the muse of spelling eluded him!) But he also found time to attend a ministerial confession meeting; to retreat to the woods with James White for a prayer session; to preach to the 3,000 attendees; to visit the new Dime Tabernacle (that held 3,200 members); and to take an "electric bath" at the sanitarium. Despite the pressures of his hectic life, John weighed in at 129 pounds—the most weight he would ever attain. After spending five days with Annie's parents in Hillsdale, Michigan, the three Loughboroughs (again Mary remained behind) boarded the train for New York City to catch their boat to Southampton, England. Yet through another series of what John saw as God's providences, they missed their boat—and thereby saved their lives.[55]

---

[1] *ST*, Apr. 1, 1875, p. 166.

[2] www.ancestry.com (accessed July 12, 2009); JNL, diary, September-December 1875 and 1915 (flyleaf).

[3] See JNL's reports in *ST*, July 29, 1875, p. 302 and July 8, 1875, pp. 277, 278; *RH*, Jan. 20, 1876, p. 23; *ST*, July 13, 1876, p. 240; *ST*, Mar. 28, 1878, p. 104.

[4] See JNL's reports in *ST*, July 8, 1875, pp. 278, 279; *ST*, July 22, 1875, p. 294; *ST*, Nov. 25, 1875, p. 23; *ST*, Jan. 6, 1876, p. 48; *ST*, Feb. 24, 1876, p. 96; *ST*, June 22, 1876, p. 22; *ST*, July 20, 1876, p. 248; *ST*, Jan. 11, 1877, pp. 21, 24; *ST*, June 21, 1877, p. 200; *RH*, Oct. 26, 1876, pp. 134, 135; *RH*, *Supplement* (between May 9 and 16 issues), 1878, p. 3; Annie Loughborough to WCW and Mary White, Feb. 21, 1878, m. 52, CAR.

[5] *RH*, Aug. 26, 1875, p. 59; *RH*, Oct. 19, 1876, p. 120; *RH*, Oct. 4, 1877, p. 105.

[6] See JNL's reports in *ST*, Sept. 6, 1877, p. 280; *ST*, Mar. 8, 1877, p. 88; *ST*, Apr. 5, 1877, p. 120; *RH,* Oct. 26, 1876, pp. 134, 135.

[7] JNL, *ST*, June 1, 1876, p. 197.

[8] It is worth noting that between 1875 and 1883 Minerva Jane (Loughborough) Chapman actually held *four* General Conference positions—GC treasurer, treasurer and secretary of the Review and Herald Publishing Association, and GC corresponding secretary—in addition to editing the *Youth's Instructor*. Like her workaholic brother John, she served the church for nearly half a century and died in 1923 at 94. See *RH,* Feb. 17, 1885, p. 103; *RH,* Sept. 26, 1985, p. 11.

[9] JNL, *ST*, June 6, 1878, p. 176; *ST*, June 27, 1878, p. 192.

[10] JNL, *RH,* July 15, 1875, p. 22; *ST*, Aug. 12, 1875, p. 317; *ST*, Nov. 25, 1875, p. 21; *ST*, Oct. 19, 1876, p. 344; *PUR*, Dec. 27, 1906, p. 1; H. McCumber, *Golden West,* p. 146.

[11] See JNL's reports in *ST*, Oct. 21, 1875, p. 382; *ST*, May 9, 1878, p. 144; *ST*, May 16, 1878, p. 152; *ST*, May 30, 1878, p. 168.

[12] See JNL's reports in *RH,* Nov. 11, 1875, p. 150; *ST*, Nov. 11, 1875, pp. 13, 16; *ST*, Nov. 2, 1876, p. 360; *ST*, June 13, 1878, p. 184.

[13] *ST*, Mar. 30, 1876, p. 136; *ST*, May 4, 1876, p. 168.

[14] See JNL's reports in *ST*, May 31, 1877, p. 176 and Jan. 25, 1877, p. 37; *RH,* May 31, 1877, p. 175; *ST*, Aug. 2, 1877, p. 240; JSW, *RH,* Nov. 22, 1877, p. 168; *ST*, Jan. 24, 1878, p. 32; *ST*, Mar. 14, 1878, p. 88; *ST*, June 6, 1878, p. 176. As the last article indicates, another reason for the success (or failure) of evangelistic meetings lay in the efforts exhibited by "tentmasters." A good tentmaster keeps the tent "neat and orderly" all the time, welcomes visitors, provides a moral example, exercises often, does not gossip with young women, but instead watches for opportunities to share present truth. Titus 2:6-8 challenged such men to be sober-minded, grave, sincere, and of sound speech. Throughout his ministerial career Loughborough was fortunate to have competent tentmasters.

[15] JNL to JSW, Aug. 10, 1875, m. 52, CAR; *ST*, Aug. 19, 1875, p. 328; *RH,* Sept. 2, 1875, p. 72; *ST*, Oct. 7, 1875, pp. 373, 374, 376; *RH*, Oct. 14, 1875, pp. 116, 117; JNL, *ST*, Oct. 21, 1875, p. 382; *RH*, Oct. 28, 1875, pp. 134, 135; JNL, *ST*, Aug. 17, 1876, p. 280.

[16] *ST*, Aug. 17, 1876, p. 280; "Sabbath School," *SDA Encyclopedia*, vol. 11, p. 508.

[17] *ST*, Oct. 5, 1876, p. 324; *ST*, Oct. 12, 1876, pp. 329-334; *RH,* Oct. 12, 1876, pp. 116, 117; *RH,* Oct. 19, 1876, pp. 121-123.

[18] *ST*, June 7, 1877, p. 184; *ST*, July 12, 1877, p. 213; *ST*, Sept. 27, 1877, pp. 290-294; *ST*, Oct. 4, 1877, p. 304; *RH,* Oct. 11, 1877, pp. 116, 117; *ST*, Oct. 11, 1877, pp. 308, 312; *RH,* Oct. 18, 1877, pp. 121, 122; *RH,* Oct. 25, 1877, p. 134.

[19] See reports in JNL, diary, September 1878; *ST*, Sept. 12, 1878, pp. 266-270; *ST*, Sept. 19, 1878, p. 277; *RH,* Sept. 26, 1878, p. 108; *PUR*, Feb. 21, 1907, p. 1.

[20] *ST*, Apr. 13, 1876, p. 144; JNL, diary, September 1876; EGW, *Evangelism* (Washington, D.C.: Review and Herald Pub. Assn., 1946), pp. 507, 508; Paul Hamel, *Ellen White and Music* (Washington, D.C.: Review and Herald Pub. Assn., 1976), pp. 17, 25, 78, 82; Lilianne Doukhan, *In Tune With God* (Hagerstown, Md.: Review and Herald Pub. Assn., 2010), pp. 210, 211.

[21] *ST*, Apr. 13, 1876, p. 144; JNL, diary, September 1876; *ST*, Sept. 27, 1871, p. 293; *PUR*, Jan. 10, 1907, pp. 1, 2.

[22] *ST*, June 27, 1878, p. 192; *PUR*, Jan. 24, 1907, pp. 1, 2.

[23] *RH,* Nov. 4, 1875, p. 138.

[24] *ST*, Jan. 20, 1876, p. 64; *ST*, Mar. 3, 1876, p. 104; JNL, diary, April and May 1876; *ST*, Apr. 27, 1876, p. 160; *ST*, May 1, 1876, p. 176.

[25] See JNL's reports in *ST*, May 25, 1876, p. 192; *ST*, June 8, 1876, p. 208; *ST*, June 15, 1876, pp. 213; *ST*, Oct. 26, 1876, p. 352; *ST*, May 17, 1877, p. 160; *ST*, May 31, 1877, p. 176.

[26] *ST*, Oct. 19, 1876, p. 342.

[27] *ST*, Oct. 19, 1876, p. 341; *ST*, Jan. 17, 1878, p. 24.

[28] Annie Loughborough to W. C. and Mary White, Feb. 22, 1876, m. 52, CAR; Annie Loughborough to JSW and EGW, Sept. 2, 1876, m. 52, CAR.

[29] *RH*, June 27, 1935, p. 14.

[30] *RH*, Nov. 13, 1986, p. 8; *RH*, Mar. 15, 1990, p. 17.

[31] See JNL's reports in *ST*, Nov. 16, 1876, pp. 366, 368; *ST*, Jan. 18, 1877, p. 32; *ST*, July 12, 1877, p. 216; *ST*, Apr. 25, 1878, p. 125.

[32] *ST*, Mar. 9, 1876, p. 112; *ST*, Apr. 13, 1876, pp. 141, 142; *ST*, Apr. 11, 1878, p. 112; JNL to WCW, Apr. 17, 1878, m. 52, CAR; JNL to WCW, Apr. 23, 1878, m. 52, CAR; *RH*, Apr. 25, 1878, p. 135; *ST*, May 23, 1878, p. 160; *ST*, June 13, 1878, pp. 180, 184.

[33] *ST*, June 13, 1878, p. 180; *ST*, July 4, 1878, p. 200.

[34] *RH*, May 3, 1877, p. 140; JNL, *PUR*, Jan. 3, 1907, p. 1. Also in the spring of 1877 J. D. Rice and Andrew Brossen converted John J. Ireland during their meetings in Pacheco. Ireland would marry Loughborough's daughter Mary and become a conference, union, and General Conference auditor.

[35] *ST*, July 25, 1878, p. 224; McCumber, *Golden West*, pp. 155, 156; *RH*, July 2, 1959, p. 20; "Pratt, William" and "St. Helena Sanitarium and Hospital," in *Ellen G. White Encyclopedia*, pp. 1121, 1122. Originally called Rural Health Retreat (1878-1882), then Crystal Springs Health Retreat (1882-1890s), after the 1890s it became St. Helena Sanitarium (and later the word "Hospital" was added).

[36] *RH*, Jan. 10, 1878, p. 12; Annie Loughborough to W. C. White, Apr. 23, 1878, m. 52, CAR; JNL to W. C. White, Apr. 25, 1878, m. 52, CAR.

[37] JNL to W. C. White, c. 1877, m. 52, CAR.

[38] James White, quoted in JNL to W. C. White, Apr. 23, 1878, m. 52, CAR.

[39] *ST*, Oct. 25, 1877, p. 328; *ST*, Nov. 1, 1877, p. 336; *RH*, Nov. 8, 1877, p. 150; *YI*, Apr. 29, 1913, pp. 3, 4.

[40] *ST*, Nov. 15, 1877, pp. 348-351.

[41] *ST*, Nov. 22, 1877, p. 360; *ST*, Nov. 29, 1877, p. 368; *ST*, Dec. 6, 1877, p. 376; *RH*, Dec. 13, 1877, pp. 190, 191; *RH*, Dec. 20, 1877, p. 195.

[42] JNL, diary, February 1878; *ST*, Feb. 14, 1878, p. 56; *ST*, Feb. 21, 1878, p. 64; *RH*, Feb. 28, 1878, p. 71; *ST*, Mar. 7, 1878, p. 80; *RH*, Mar. 14, 1878, p. 86; *RH*, Mar. 28, 1878, p. 103.

[43] JNL, diary, June and July 1878; *ST*, July 4, 1878, p. 200; *ST*, July 18, 1878, p. 216.

[44] *ST*, Mar. 7, 1878, p. 80; *ST*, July 25, 1878, p. 224; JNL, diary, August, 1878; *ST*, Aug. 1, 1878, p. 232; *ST*, Aug. 8, 1878, p. 240; JNL to EGW, Aug. 11, 1878, m. 52, CAR; *RH*, Aug. 15, 1878, p. 63; *RH*, Aug. 22, 1878, p. 71; Ellen G. White, *Testimonies for the Church* (Mountain View, Calif.: Pacific Press Pub. Assn., 1948), vol. 4, p. 296.

[45] *ST*, Aug. 22, 1878, p. 256; *ST*, Aug. 29, 1878, p. 264; *RH*, Sept. 27, 1951, p. 20; *PUR*, Feb. 28, 1955, p. 2; *RH*, Jan. 13, 1977, p. 6; G. Knight, *Lest We Forget*, p. 222; Louis B. Reynolds, *We Have Tomorrow: The Story of American Seventh-day Adventists With an African Heritage* (Hagerstown, Md.: Review and Herald Pub. Assn., 1984), pp. 173, 174. Given the prevailing White prejudice against Asians and Blacks, it is worth noting that the 22 SDAs in Reno crossed the color line in choosing their only Black member as their church clerk.

[46] See JNL's anti-Catholic *Signs* articles in Sept. 2, 1875, p. 338; Sept. 9, 1875,

p. 346; Sept. 16, 1875, pp. 354, 355; Sept. 23, 1875, p. 362; Dec. 9, 1875, p. 27; Dec. 23, 1875, p. 34; Jan. 6, 1876, p. 43; Jan. 30, 1876, p. 57; Jan. 27, 1876, p. 67; Feb. 3, 1876, p. 75; Feb. 10, 1876, p. 83; Feb. 24, 1876, p. 91; Mar. 16, 1876, pp. 116, 117; Mar. 23, 1876, p. 123; Mar. 30, 1876, p. 131; Apr. 13, 1876, p. 139; Apr. 20, 1876, p. 147; Apr. 27, 1876, p. 155; May 4, 1876, p. 163; May 11, 1876, p. 171; May 18, 1876, p. 179; May 25, 1876, p. 186; June 1, 1876, pp. 194, 195; June 8, 1876, p. 202; June 15, 1876, p. 211; June 29, 1876, p. 228; July 20, 1876, p. 241; July 27, 1876, pp. 249, 253; Oct. 26, 1876, p. 348; June 14, 1877, pp. 188, 189; July 12, 1877, pp. 214, 15; July 19, 1877, p. 224.

[47] See JNL's doctrinal articles in *ST*, Sept. 7, 1876, p. 297; Sept. 14, 1876, p. 305; Sept. 21, 1876, p. 313; Nov. 16, 1876, p. 362; Nov. 30, 1876, pp. 369, 370; Jan. 4, 1877, p. 16; Mar. 29, 1877, pp. 108, 109; June 7, 1877, p. 184; and Dec. 6, 1877, p. 373.

[48] JNL, "Lying," *ST*, Mar. 21, 1878, p. 96; "Keeping Silence," *ST*, May 30, 1878, p. 165. In the genre of practical living topics, his wife Annie wrote "Life's Discipline" for the *Signs of the Times* Literary Society in August 1877 (published in the October 4 issue of *Signs*). Curiously, she pointed out that life is earnest but short, and few people live to the age of 70. In fact, she would die at 67 in 1907 while John would live to 92.

[49] JNL, "Questions and Answers," *ST*, Jan. 3, 1878, p. 5; *ST*, Feb. 3, 1876, p. 79; *ST*, Aug. 8, 1878, p. 239.

[50] See JNL, diary, August 1875-August 1878; *RH*, Apr. 22, 1976, p. 5.

[51] *ST*, July 11, 1878, p. 208; *ST*, Aug. 15, 1878, p. 244; *RH*, Aug. 8, 1878, p. 52; *ST*, Sept. 26, 1878, p. 288.

[52] *PUR*, Feb. 14, 1907, p. 1.

[53] *ST*, Sept. 12, 1878, pp. 265, 266.

[54] *Ibid.*, p. 269.

[55] JNL, diary, September-October 1878; *ST*, Oct. 17, 1878, p. 308; "Four Battle Creek Meetinghouses," *Missionary Magazine*, August 1901, p. 367; *RH*, Oct. 17, 1878, p. 125.

CHAPTER XI

PIONEERING THE DENOMINATION IN ENGLAND (1878-1880)

"Now the field [of Great Britain] is ripe . . . and I [James White] think with God's help you [J. N. Loughborough] could sweep all [the Seventh Day Baptists in London] into the Seventh-day Adventist ranks. . . . If you wait until you have done all you may see to do on that [Pacific] Coast, you will never leave."[1]

Although the GC delegates in 1878 had voted to send J. N. Loughborough to England, he had serious reservations about going. In fact, he had sent the GC Committee a letter offering eight objections why they should delay his appointment. Patiently, James White and D. M. Canright answered each of his arguments. They reminded him that periodic changes in one's field of labor benefited both preachers and people. Tactfully, they pointed out to him that because he was 10 years older than when he went to California, "the best of your days for labor are behind you"—therefore, he should go to England now. They assured him that he would have the help of William Ings and Maude Sisley. Alluding to the Macedonian call, they said, "British souls are crying for help."

They also warned him that if he stayed another year "to complete what you say is 'begun,' you will find more 'begun' that needs to be finished than you see now." In short, he would never leave. Regarding his anxiety about the $10,000 for the Pacific SDA Publishing Company, they promised it would be raised at camp meetings, through the *Signs*, and by General Conference appeals. Moreover, if he remained in California, younger preachers would look to him for guidance and would not mature on their own. To his request to spend a year studying at Battle Creek College, they suggested hiring a tutor in England where he could learn more in a week than he could in a month in the U.S. The best way to study English customs, they asserted, "is right there on the ground, where you see the customs for yourself." Finally they told him that if he backed out now when the "general expectations" on both sides of the Atlantic favored his going, it would cause "general disappointment and great dissatisfaction." Instead, he should spend five years in Europe "while you have strength," and then retire to the U.S. "[to] be translated with them [the saints] when the Life-giver comes."[2]

In a letter to W. C. White, Loughborough raised another obstacle to his going to England: he had heard that Ellen White did *not* want him to go. If she had had a vision on the matter, he told Willie, then "I should not wish to go contrary to heavenly light." Should her objections not be based on a vision, however, then he suggested that the Whites consult with the GC Committee. Otherwise, John confessed, "I am a little perplexed to harmonize my own convictions of duty." But if everyone "agreed that it is England, so be it."[3]

Perhaps John was getting cold feet, but he need not have worried. In fact, the Whites had supported the idea of sending him to England for several years. Shortly after J. N. Andrews left for Switzerland, James had approached John about going to Britain. In June 1874 the two men had hiked through the brush above Oakland and spent several hours praying about the matter. Then, placing a hand on John's shoulder, James had asked, "You will go to England, won't you?" Loughborough told him that he "had no light [assurance from God] about England" yet. But Ellen White had that assurance, because Merritt Cornell recalled hearing her say, "If Elder Loughborough is faithful, his labors will yet be called for in England." The Whites saw Great Britain as a "prime target" for Adventist mission work for several reasons. Its peoples spoke English and read American literature. The Seventh Day Baptists there already kept the Sabbath and would no doubt be eager to accept other biblical teachings. Establishing a printing press in England would make it cheaper to distribute Adventist literature across Europe than mailing it from the U.S. Moreover, having an English publishing address would open doors for Adventist materials in Australia, New Zealand, South Africa, and the Pacific islands.[4]

However convincing such arguments might be, Loughborough confessed that after 10 years in sunny California "it was not [as] easy to 'let go' as one might think."[5] Yet in one sense, he really did not "let go": since Loughborough's ministerial credentials from 1878 to 1881 were issued by the California Conference (and *not* by the General Conference until after 1882), technically he was a missionary from California to Great Britain.[6] But "letting go" meant saying goodbye to family members, relatives, and old friends on the West Coast, in Michigan, and in New York, a task that took two months. Despite pain in his left lung, Loughborough also preached several times at Battle Creek and at Wellsville, Buffalo, Rochester, and Rome, New York. When the family reached Boston in mid-December, Annie and Delmer began packing steamer trunks while John bought tickets on the *Minnesota.* But three days later, the Warren Line steamship company transferred them to the *Homer.* When the *Homer*'s captain refused to take passengers, the company paid their train fare to New York City to board the *Nevada.* After the *Homer* sank with all hands, the Loughboroughs felt their delays in Boston had been providential.[7]

During the two-week voyage, John and Annie spent much of the time in bed, seasick as usual. John took advantage of the downtime to read an 800-page book, *The History of the English People*, gleaning as much information as he could about the history, customs, and religious background of the British Isles. On December 30 the ship reached Southampton, a city of 60,000 people and the third-largest English port (after London and Liverpool). From here the Pilgrims had set sail for America aboard the *Mayflower*; and here Isaac Watts had composed the stirring hymn "On Jordan's Stormy Banks I Stand" from the banks of the Itchen River. Grateful to be on land again, John wrote: "So ends 1878 in Old England the land of my progenitors."[8]

But as we saw in chapter 1, however, John's "progenitors" (the Loofboroughs) had most likely come from Ireland, and by the nineteenth century those who had immigrated to England seemed eager to leave. In fact, between 1870 and 1910, 11 of the 13 Loughborough households in Liverpool and Southampton (and most of the 66 Loughborough families in Middlesex, Surrey, Devon, Durham, and Yorkshire) departed for America. By 1881 J. N. Loughborough was one of only 15 people bearing his surname in all the British Isles.[9]

BACKGROUND OF THE ADVENTIST WORK IN BRITAIN

Just as Merritt Kellogg and J. W. Conkrite had prepared the way for Loughborough's missionary efforts in California, so scores of men and women had paved the way for his arrival in Great Britain. For more than two centuries, Seventh Day Baptists had been preaching the seventh-day Sabbath in London and elsewhere, occasionally suffering persecution for their efforts. During the Millerite Movement of the 1840s in America, biblical expositors in Britain had also proclaimed the imminent second coming of Jesus, converting about 2,000 people to that belief. Therefore, in a very real sense, Britons had already set the stage for the acceptance of the two cardinal doctrines—the Sabbath and the Second Advent—that Adventists advocated. In 1857 James White had sent some Adventist publications to Ireland, and three years later, to England as well. Then in 1874 en route to Switzerland J. N. Andrews had established contacts with Seventh Day Baptists in London and preached among them.[10]

But Ellen White felt that, for the most part, the church had ignored Britain. With J. N. Andrews in mind, she wrote: "Our American missionaries . . . have . . . passed by Old England to labor at much greater disadvantage among those with whose language [French] they were not well acquainted." Instead, she believed that "Elder Andrews' " time should be devoted some to Old England, and not confined to the French. But as chapter 12 shows, Andrews' failing health made it impossible for him to offer more than token help to the British Mission.[11]

Instead, three others would spread Adventist doctrines in Great Britain. After English sea captain George Drew heard Loughborough preach in San Francisco in 1870, he read his way into the message, devouring Uriah Smith's *Thoughts on Revelation* and all of Ellen White's *Testimonies*. When he returned to Britain in 1882, he pioneered the ship ministry in Liverpool. Born in Dorsetshire, William Ings had immigrated to America as a boy and married Jennie Husman in Iowa, where G. I. Butler converted them. Then from 1876 to 1879 they helped Andrews publish the Swiss paper *Les Signes des Temps*. In the spring of 1878, while visiting relatives in Southampton, William had distributed tracts door to door. After only four months he had 10 converts. Ings also visited the ships in Southampton's harbor, sending tracts with crews heading for Cyprus, Portugal, Bermuda, the Red Sea area, and the East Indies. "I was astonished to see the effect

[that] our publications had," he wrote in the *Signs*. During a period of several weeks he visited 200 families, and soon the demand for Adventist literature outstripped his supply. When many requested public lectures on Adventist beliefs, Ings appealed to the General Conference. "England needs one of our best ministers," he pleaded. "I hope the [General] Conference will send one here soon." Learning that Loughborough was coming, he responded: "I shall try . . . to prepare the way for Brother Loughborough, so that he may have a foothold."[12]

Yet establishing a foothold among the English proved challenging. First of all came the cultural hurdles. The Loughboroughs, who had traded with dollars and cents all their lives, now had to learn the complicated system of exchanging pounds, shillings, and pence. They also discovered that London's cab drivers charged by the hour, not by the distance covered (which made sense, given the capital's horrendous traffic jams). Deaf in one ear, John strained to understand the various English accents around him. A committed temperance advocate, he occasionally found himself forced to eat meat and compelled by social custom to drink tea with his converts. Over time, however, the family adjusted to English culture, as John's diary attests.[13]

But they could do nothing about the climate. Facing the Atlantic Ocean in southwestern England, Southampton was subject to windy, humid summers and bitterly cold winters that dumped seven feet of snow and irritated John's left lung, bringing frequent coughing fits. He soon discovered that Southampton's fog, rain, and high winds mildewed canvass and tore holes in his tent. Since the Anglican churches, Dissenting chapels, and schoolhouses were unavailable for evangelism, renting public halls, although more expensive in the short run, proved to be a long-term solution to this climatic problem. Moreover, Ellen White stated in 1887 that if ministers had used more halls instead of holding tent meetings, the work in England "might now be much farther advanced than it is."[14]

Furthermore, while the lower classes would come to tent services, the middle and upper classes shunned them. They would only attend meetings held in respectable public halls that cost more than Loughborough could afford. He despaired of ever reaching England's wealthy entrepreneurs and nobility whose mansions lay hidden behind locked gates and high walls. Moreover, while the working class welcomed the penny tracts

Adventists offered, the middle and upper classes refused them as suitable only for "poor sinners."[15]

On the religious front, members of the Church of England (many of them proud imperialists) distrusted foreigners in general and American Protestants in particular. Wedded to centuries-old traditions and customs, they had been reared to revere conformity and to fear change as deleterious to their beliefs and lifestyles. Their prejudice against Shakers (for celibacy) and Mormons (for polygamy) made them suspicious that Adventists advocated other undesirable beliefs and practices. Furthermore, since most Britons worked a six-day week, converting to Adventism often meant the loss of one's job or position. As Annie told Mary White, "It takes strong faith and a very large amount of moral courage and a good supply of noble independence for an Englishman to break away from the strong national customs and to come out frankly to keep the Sabbath."[16]

In spite of such obstacles, however, Loughborough and Ings found creative ways to foster Adventist evangelism in Britain. As he had done in America, Loughborough advertised his meetings in city newspapers and hired two men to attach large posters to every public notice board within a three-mile radius of their meeting place. On January 5, 1879—six days after arriving—John accepted an invitation from the Free Evangelists to speak to 150 people at Shirley Hall. It produced four converts to Adventism. As attendance increased, the two men rented Shirley Hall (which held 250 people), about a half mile from Stanley Cottage, their new home (a large five-room brick house with fireplaces in every room). Within a week, John had compiled a list of 200 individuals who wanted Adventist publications.[17]

Although the team purchased a Papyrographic Press to print short advertisements, tracts, and brochures, their main suppliers of SDA literature remained the Review and Herald and the Pacific SDA Publishing Company in America. The Review regularly mailed large batches (called "clubs") of the *Review and Herald* and various tracts and books, including Ellen White's writings, while the Pacific Publishing Company sent thousands of copies of *Signs of the Times*. Despite the depressed economy (due to bank failures, strikes, foreign conflicts, and heavy taxes), the demand for Adventist publications grew in inverse proportion to the scarcity of money. After John complained that "it is a grief to us to have the people literally begging for [tracts] when we have none for them," James White promised to send clubs of the *Signs* "such that no limits will be placed on the supply." Soon Adventists in America were mailing *Signs* to Southampton.[18]

In addition to Loughborough's preaching four nights a week and Ings' door-to-door canvassing, the two men visited 300 interested families in 10 days. Soon after purchasing government licenses for Southampton, Hampshire, and other nearby shires, the team distributed hundreds of copies of the *Signs, Review, Health Reformer,* and various tracts every month. Willie White, presuming that London was close to Southampton (it isn't) and that the two men had lots of spare time on their hands (they didn't), also asked John to investigate the number of cats in London! Graciously, John promised to do so, but in the meantime, he hoped to see a few of England's "castles, towers, and cathedrals."[19]

In fact, by early 1879 both men were so busy preaching, visiting, and distributing literature that they had no time for cats, castles, or cathedrals. Desperate for more staff, Loughborough begged the GC Committee to release Maude Sisley from Basel, Switzerland, to assist them. Born in England, Maude had immigrated to the U.S. in 1863 with her widowed mother and six siblings. She had worked in the composing room of the Review and Herald press for 10 cents per hour and became the first canvasser in the state of Ohio. Since 1877 she had been helping J. N. Andrews in Basel by setting the type for the first Adventist tract in Italian—a language she was still learning. In May 1879, however, the remarkable 28-year-old woman joined Loughborough and Ings as a Bible instructor and canvasser.[20]

This growing family of six full-time laborers (John, Annie, and Delmer Loughborough; William and Jennie Ings; and Maude Sisley)—besides other assorted guests—soon required larger quarters. John discovered a 17-room mansion at 252 Shirley Road called "Ravenswood Villa." For three years Ravenswood had been in Chancery Court (a high court of equity in England, presided over by the lord chancellor, with common-law functions), sitting vacant because it was allegedly haunted. At night neighbors heard moaning sounds in its cupola, doubtless the ghost of some unfortunate person murdered on the premises. As a result, a Chancery judge offered to rent it for $200 a year. The team transformed the ballroom into an auditorium with a rostrum and pulpit. The drawing room became a book depository and the other rooms dining and sleeping areas. During an inspection tour, John discovered that a pane of glass had broken in the cupola, allowing wind to "moan" through the crack. Once he had replaced the glass, the "Ravenswood Ghost" stopped troubling the neighborhood.[21]

Instead, a far different Spirit animated the creative efforts of this evangelistic team. Observing that health reform was "gaining ground" in Britain (John subscribed to the *Dietetic Reformer*), they joined with teetotalers in opening five cocoa rooms for the laboring poor. Responding to requests for deeper Bible study, Maude Sisley started Sunday Bible classes that focused on the history of the Sabbath. For the benefit of the children, she began holding three Sabbath school classes for 17 "scholars" as well. As the number of converts grew, Loughborough applied his carpentry skills to build an indoor baptistry in the basement of Ravenswood. Because rowdies throwing stones and brick bats had interrupted river baptisms by another denomination, Adventists baptized their converts inside Ravenswood.[22]

Long before they were ready for baptism, however, Loughborough put them to work distributing tracts, selling books, and assisting at meetings. "The interest in England far surpasses all our expectations," William Ings told *Review* readers. "Bro. and Sr. Loughborough are as busy as bees." True enough, but so was everybody else who stepped foot inside Ravenswood, for the evangelistic team found work even for non-Adventists to do. Every week the beehive of activity mailed 250 copies of *Signs* to interested readers across England, Wales, and Scotland. "The cause in 'Old England,' is still advancing," Loughborough declared, "if not as rapidly as we might desire, it moves nevertheless, and is getting hold of minds."[23]

The Adventist message certainly grabbed hold of Mrs. L. O. Neill's mind, inspiring her to write a poem about "The English Mission" to honor the Loughboroughs' sacrifices:

"Far across the mighty deep,
 God's faithful servants came,
From the New World to the Old,
 Glad tidings to proclaim;

To found a mission for the truth;
 God grant that it may be

Sustained of Heaven and fruit appear
  Throughout eternity.

"May those who hear, not idle stand,
  But cast the seed abroad,
And lend a faithful, helping hand
  In bringing souls to God.

"And may there be a harvest rich
  Yet found in English soil;
God bless the missionaries in
  Their ardent, earnest toil.

"Oh! may this glorious truth extend,
  With conquest, through the land,
And Sabbathkeepers soon appear,
  A strong and numerous band.

"We thank our friends with one consent,
  Beyond the rolling sea,
For sending help to lead us forth
  To light and liberty."[24]

TENT MEETINGS: SUCCESSES AND FAILURES

Yet while J. N. Loughborough brought new light to the English, he recognized that he had much to learn from them as well. Before holding tent meetings in the summer of 1879, he read books and interviewed other Christians seeking to understand "the ways and doctrines of the different sects . . . so as to know how to adapt our teaching to the circumstances and conditions of the people." He attended Church of England services (and noted that Anglicans believe in the Second Advent) and sat through two and a half hours of "chanting, singing, praying, [and] offering incense" with the followers of Edward Irving at Bedford Place (he described the "Irvingites" as a "Catholic Apostolic Church"). He left both services with a deeper admiration for the "reverence, dignity, and devotion" of their worshippers.[25] They would display the same reverence at his outdoor meetings.

Even before spring arrived, John had unwisely decided to hold tent meetings rather than to rent halls (and pay the extra $5 to $10 a night). He found a tentmaker who agreed to manufacture a canvass tent 60 feet in diameter with side curtains nine feet high and supply him with all the ropes, poles, and ground stakes for $425. The man even donated a flagstaff and a 15-foot-long Union Jack to fly above the tent. Loughborough then purchased a harmonium (a tiny organ) with "an excellent tone," lumber for benches (which came from Canada), kerosene lamps, a stove and pipes, coal (for the stove), and a carpet. He also crafted frames for his prophetic charts, a pulpit, and a "contribution box" (which he screwed to the pulpit). Altogether John had spent about $575—whereas in America, the canvass tent alone would have cost him $600. Euphoric, he sang for two solid hours![26]

When services began on May 18, 600 people crowded the tent. In contrast to Anglican services in which mainly choirboys sang traditional Christian hymns, attendees heard rousing gospel songs played by Delmer Loughborough on the harmonium and saw his dad, arms waving, lead the singing from the platform. The Anglicans, accustomed to brief prayers, short readings from the *Book of Common Prayer*, and pastoral homilies, listened in amazement to Loughborough's hourlong "expositions of Scripture," which resembled lawyers' arguments before the Court of Chancery.[27]

After 14 weeks and 74 lectures, the evangelistic team had sold more than $700 in books and tracts and received $735 in donations ($60 of that from the tent crowd alone). Nearly 40 listeners had "signed a covenant" to keep the Sabbath. Yet while the spiritual and financial outlook improved, the weather did not: weeks of cold rain caused the canvass to mildew and tear. Jealous ministers from other denominations also tried to stop the services by spreading rumors that Adventists were murderers. The story circulated that Loughborough had sacrificed his daughter! (Mary was safe in Battle Creek.) John, refusing to dignify such falsehoods publicly, declared that he would be like the blacksmith who refused to chase after lies, but would "stick to his business and hammer out a reputation on his anvil by doing honest work."[28]

Following such a course of action won Loughborough—and the entire evangelistic team—great respect among Seventh Day Baptists, whose history in Britain had taught them how to survive persecution. When J. N.

Andrews arrived from Switzerland that summer, he introduced Loughborough to William Jones, the leader of the Seventh Day Baptists at London's famous Mill Yard Chapel, established in the seventeenth century. During the next five years, as Jones and Loughborough preached at each other's services, stayed in each other's homes, and wrote each other letters, their friendship deepened.[29]

Because the inclement weather had nearly destroyed their tent, the team decided to start a new series of meetings that fall at Ravenswood. A real "fixer-upper," the old mansion needed lots of work to prepare it for services. Suffering from chills and fever and unable to do the work himself, Loughborough hired Mr. Judd, a jack-of-all-trades. While Judd did most of the painting, carpeting, wallpapering, and plastering, John installed the ventilators, mounted bells in the hallways, and painted the front door a bright red.[30] To ensure that the team had enough literature on hand to meet public demand, John engaged the services of Gatch and Box, the largest printer in Southampton, to print 2,000 sheets of a 76-page tract that the "Ravenswood family" laboriously folded to save money. John told W. C. White that English paper (which blended cotton and linen) was stronger than that made in the U.S. despite its "muddy shade, the Thames mud not being all filtered out of it." Nonetheless, "I wish we had a good hand press," he exclaimed. "We could print independent of these slow Englishmen." If John had understood little about the publishing trade when appointed president of the Pacific Publishing Company in 1874, his detailed discussion of printing costs, techniques, and technologies in Britain demonstrates that he had learned a great deal during the past five years.[31]

Despite cold, wet weather that fall, sizable crowds attended the meetings at Ravenswood. The fact that only a handful "signed the covenant" did not discourage Loughborough, for he recognized that "the people here move much more slowly than in America." Being of "a less excitable temperament," they were not so quick "to surrender their preconceived opinions" nor "so enthusiastic as their transatlantic brethren." Nonetheless, once convinced, they made "firm Seventh-day Adventists." Because Loughborough insisted on doing thorough work with his British converts, he indoctrinated them for several months in biblical teachings and Adventist practices. Finally, on February 8, 1880, he baptized the first six converts in the Ravenswood baptistry. Then, within a week, seven more were immersed.[32]

As spring meant the beginning of the "tent season," the evangelistic team retrieved their tent from storage and pitched it in a beautiful meadow near Romsey, a town of about 7,000 people approximately eight miles from Southampton. Reverend W. M. Jones (leader of the Mill Yard Seventh Day Baptists in London) and Reverend Carpenter (a former Seventh Day Baptist missionary to China), with their wives, spent several days listening to John's preaching. Feeling that "the general interests of the cause in Europe" required his presence in England, J. N. Andrews also joined Loughborough for the summer series. Unfortunately, his enthusiasm superseded his physical stamina, and coughing spells cut his discourses short. In fact, he spent a week in bed unable to preach, write, or read. But days after Loughborough anointed Andrews and prayed for his healing, he gained strength, began writing again, and shared the pulpit with his colleague. Nonetheless, Loughborough informed James White that Andrews' "true condition . . . is little known in America"—in reality, he was very ill (Andrews would in fact die of tuberculosis three years later). Recognizing that both men were exhausted, White praised them in the *Review*: "Time, toil, and care are making their marks upon these devoted pioneers of the cause. And while they are wearing out, we do not see men entering upon the work with the same devotion, self-sacrifice, and power that has characterized the ministry of these men."[33]

When a gale tore four sections from the top of their tent, the two men transferred their meetings to the Town Hall (a move the Whites heartily endorsed). The move attracted "a better class" of listeners who were generous givers, and by the close of the series, Romsey's citizens had paid all but 75 cents of the expenses. "We have a *deep, settled interest*" here, John informed White. He experienced equally rewarding results in Taunton, Somerset, where he preached for a month to a large audience of Christadelphians in the Market House Assembly Hall. Although physical weakness prevented Andrews from assisting him, he praised his colleague in the *Review*: "The work moves slowly, but there is no doubt that the truth is really taking hold of the people to a considerable extent. Bro. [Loughborough] is making a great effort for the salvation of men, and I believe that God will grant success." Loughborough's preaching and William Ings' door-to-door visitation soon brought the conversion of several Christadelphians who formed two Sabbath school classes with 25 members. By the autumn of 1880 25 converts had been baptized from the meetings at Southampton, Romsey, and Taunton. When Loughborough (with deep sincerity) showed how Sinn Fein violence in Ireland, Boer and British rivalry in South Africa, the "Eastern Question" (the Ottoman Turks in the Balkans), the rise in brutal crimes (Jack the Ripper would shortly become infamous in London), and Britain's 130 maritime losses all had their place in Bible prophecy, attendance grew. Interest ran so high, in fact, that by the end of the year the evangelistic team was holding two meetings every Sunday at Romsey and twice weekly services at Ravenswood.[34]

BEGINNING A SHIP MINISTRY

Although Loughborough's chronic seasickness may have prevented him from boarding ships in Southampton Harbor, he recognized early on the potential for spreading denominational publications via the sailors who daily embarked from the large port. Shortly after his arrival in 1879, he and Ings had shipped a box of tracts to Haiti aboard a German vessel. The steamship company had delivered the crate to the Episcopal missionary in Cap-Haitien, and he (with ecumenical fervor) had shared them with a Baptist minister, who distributed them to his congregation. As a result, two Jamaicans, Henry Williams and his wife, and Michel Isaac, a school principal, accepted Adventism.[35]

If the long-term benefits of ship ministry (Adventist converts around the world) were seldom as obvious as the short-term rewards (sailors and ship captains converted), Loughborough believed in sowing gospel seed and leaving the harvest to God. Within a year of his arrival, he and Annie had organized the British Tract and Missionary Society to disseminate Adventist material throughout the British Isles. As Great Britain constituted the hub of a vast empire on which the "sun never sets," however, he soon realized that by placing Adventist literature aboard ships, he could also reach Europe, Asia, Africa, and (via the recently completed Suez Canal) India and the Far East. Although the bulk of the church's publications existed only in English, a few books and papers (such as *Les Signes des Temps* and *Tiderness Tegn*) appealed to foreign language groups. Loughborough and Ings pleaded for more tracts in French, German, Russian, Norwegian, Danish, and Swedish to be sent them via Maurice's European Express Company, whose half-price shipping rates enabled Adventists to sell them cheaper in England. In addition, they begged James and Willie White to provide many more copies of the *Review, Signs,* and *Good Health* for public distribution.[36]

While Loughborough strongly supported the ship program, William Ings's enthusiasm for the program was boundless. In a letter quoted in the *Review* he told readers that during the past year he had boarded 339 vessels (and been tossed off only one), finding the ships' stewards eager for any sort of reading material to give their passengers and crew. On Sundays (when no ships sailed and shops closed) Ings did an especially brisk business selling tracts aboard ship. During one three-month period he had visited 97 vessels and sold or given away nearly 1,600 copies of the *Review* and *Signs* and 22,610 pages of tracts. Stewards on German steamships carrying 1,000 passengers each eagerly welcomed Ings aboard. "It takes longer here for people to weigh evidence than in America," he explained, "but a good foundation is being laid."[37]

It was indeed. By the spring of 1880 stewards and ship captains occasionally invited Loughborough and Ings to dine with them. One steward purchased six books. A captain who had read their tracts declared that Adventists preached the truth about the Bible and asked to be baptized. A Danish and a Norwegian captain promised to disseminate their literature at every port of call. "So steadily, the way is opening," Loughborough declared.[38]

The demand for Adventist literature throughout the British Isles was also growing—far faster than the supply of tracts and papers arriving from America. Even librarians at public libraries requested copies of Adventist books and papers for their patrons. When some clubs of *Signs* and *Reviews* failed to arrive six weeks after they had been promised, John fired off a petulant letter to W. C. White sarcastically inquiring whether he had sent them by sailing vessel around Cape Horn! The delay, he said, "has put a wet blanket" on the T&M work. Unless White could find a faster way to send the publications, "I think we will have a good chance to learn one part of the Third Angel's Message, 'HERE is the *patience* of the saints.'" After his blood pressure had dropped a bit, John wrote that "what can't be CURED should be ENDURED."[39]

The scores of letters pouring into Ravenswood every week helped John endure the delays and reassured him that Adventism in Great Britain was indeed progressing. In the summer of 1880 he learned that non-Adventists were selling Adventist tracts in Maidenhead, London, Corfe, Normenton, Derby, Yorkshire, Wolverhampton, and Bishop's Waltham. "So the truth is slowly but *surely* gaining ground," he assured *Signs* readers. He agreed with Andrews that the only way to cover the ground more quickly would be for the General Conference to establish a publishing house in Britain to print Adventist material on location. Since mildewed tents failed to draw the "better classes" of people and public halls cost too much, "a paper would add a hundred-fold to our strength," Andrews argued. Yet he too recognized that "our present poverty and feebleness of resources" made it impossible. Perhaps the best short-term solution would be to flood England with more than 2,000 copies of Adventist papers every month. While his suggestion may at first seem optimistic, in fact, during the last three months of 1880 the 30 members of the British T&M Society had distributed approximately 2,300 periodicals and visited nearly 2,000 families.[40] The Sceptered Isle was rapidly becoming a beehive of Adventist witnessing activity.

In the spring of 1880 Loughborough decided the time had come for him to witness to the Seventh Day Baptists. When Reverend and Mrs. Jones invited him to spend several days at their home at 15 Mill Yard, Goodman's Field in London, John eagerly accepted. When Jones asked him to preach at the Mill Yard Chapel, Loughborough's joy overflowed. "I was speaking in the place where noble defenders of God's Sabbath had proclaimed this sacred truth for the last two hundred years," he exclaimed. Afterward, Jones took him on a tour of Newgate Prison, Smithfield, Bunhill Fields, and other sites "sacred to the memory of martyrs." He also showed the astonished American his collection of 132 books published between 1600 and 1880—all advocating the seventh-day Sabbath. Having recently read Andrews' book *History of the Sabbath*, John could appreciate this treasure trove about the history of Sabbath observance.[41]

LOUGHBOROUGH'S WRITINGS AND DIARY

In spite of John's hectic schedule of traveling, preaching, and overseeing numerous administrative details, he still found time to write. Once settled in Southampton, he penned a series of 25 articles for Adventist children and youth entitled "From Sea to Sea." In effect, each article described one segment of the Loughborough family's journey from California to New York in 1878 and 1879. He also wrote articles about his trip to Europe. The fascinating travelogues amply demonstrate Loughborough's detailed observation of the geographical, geological, biological, historical, and cultural landscapes through which the family traveled by train, stagecoach, and boat.

Along the way he describes the mining of gold, silver, quartz, chalk, borax, quicksilver, and coal. He provides vivid descriptions of the Rocky Mountains, the Grand Canyon, a Nebraska prairie fire, and the "Mighty Mississippi" (which he mistakenly believed to be the world's longest river). To teach the value of vegetarianism, he provides gory details of Chicago's slaughterhouses. Regarding the transatlantic voyage to Europe, he re-creates the sights, sounds, and smells of life aboard a steamship, from the engine room to the 60-foot saloon (where, presumably, John spent very little time), including what it felt like to be crammed into the shelflike berths of a tiny (7' x 7') bedroom. We see Loughborough's fascination with mathematical and scientific data reflected in his explanations of how the sailors calculated the ship's latitude, longitude, and speed, and how they measured the ocean's depths.

But in describing the Native Americans they met along the way, J. N. Loughborough also mirrors the prejudices of his time. Just three years before in 1876 the Sioux at the Battle of the Little Bighorn River had annihilated General George Armstrong Custer's Seventh Cavalry. Across the Great Plains, detachments of the U.S. Army were hunting and killing both Indians and buffalo. Not long before, General Sheridan had allegedly asserted that "the only good Indian is a dead Indian." Consequently, it should come as no surprise that John saw the Paiute Indians as "a very inferior-looking race, not at all worthy of the old appellation, 'The noble Indian.'" Although they are "docile" and not "warlike," the Paiutes are also "whining" and lazy and "like all other Indians, do not like to work." But when facing starvation, they beg food from Whites, exclaiming, "We work. Heap-hog-a-die!" (meaning they are extremely hungry). Regaling readers of the *Youth's Instructor* with hair-raising tales of "savage Indians" who massacred Whites crossing the Plains by wagon train, Loughborough rejoiced that during his train trip east, "we could rest at night without fear of the wild savages." Then, with a brief notice of the polygamous Mormons and their "white slaves" (wives), John told readers that "we must leave the poor [Indians and Mormons], pitying them for their darkness."[42]

Fortunately for the future of the British Mission, Loughborough demonstrated greater tolerance and understanding for the English than he did for the Native Americans. In fact, the customs and culture of the British Isles changed John, Annie, and Delmer. Therefore, the Loughboroughs who left California in 1878 and the Loughboroughs who returned in 1883 were different in many ways.

Since the cold, wet climate of southwestern England did not favor fruit and vegetable gardening year-round as in California, the Loughboroughs occasionally ate meat. Likewise, since Queen Anne had switched from drinking ale to sipping tea in the early eighteenth century, the custom of observing tea time in the late afternoon often dictated that John and Annie drink tea as well when they visited the homes of converts. The Loughboroughs also learned to enjoy red currants (which they purchased by the gallon), dried apples (bought in 50-pound lots), and a wide assortment of nuts, raisins, and cakes that they often served at home parties (some attended by 25 guests). In addition, John developed a craving for black licorice, which he purchased by the pound and ate so often that he would later pay the price in dentist's bills. Likewise, when he gave his son Delmer "a treat," it was usually candy. Everyone in the family developed a "sweet tooth" rather early on.

The traditional celebrations surrounding an English Christmas also provided ample temptations to indulge one's appetite. Nineteenth-century American SDAs—following the "plain tradition" of contemporary religious groups such as the Quakers, Shakers, Mennonites, and Moravians—did not celebrate Christmas at all. But thanks in part to the influence of Queen Victoria's German husband Prince Albert, the English added decorated Christmas trees to their well-established customs of wassailing, gift giving, and eating roast goose and Christmas pudding. Deciding that when in England one should do as the English do (within reason, of course), the Loughboroughs celebrated their first Christmas in 1880 by exchanging wrapped gifts beneath a decorated tree and then devouring a huge dinner. As John's diaries reveal, they would continue to do so not only in Britain, but also after they returned to California.

Sharing a joint passion for history, John and Delmer wore out shoe leather seeing England's castles, towers, and cathedrals. During their frequent trips to London, they enjoyed visiting St. Paul's Cathedral, the Houses of Parliament, London Bridge, Westminster Abbey, Ludgate Hill, Spurgeon's Chapel, St. James' Palace, and especially the British Museum ("Oh! What a sight!" John wrote in his diary). Wherever they traveled, father and son looked for local museums and historical sites. Annie, somewhat less interested in history, preferred window shopping with Jennie Ings in Southampton and London. Somehow her penny-pinching husband managed to keep the family in the black at least eight months out of the year!

Surrounded by some of the world's most prestigious centers of learning, John vowed to improve himself academically. Shortly after landing in Southampton, he began studying French so that he could read (and perhaps write articles for) J. N. Andrews' paper *Les Signes des Temps*. Not content to study French from the dictionary he purchased, John engaged Monsieur Vögeli and Monsieur Veysey to teach him how to speak the language correctly. If the entries in his diary are accurate, Loughborough pursued the study of French *avec très bonne effort mais avec peut-être mois abilité* than his colleague J. N. Andrews. In short, although his vocabulary grew, he seldom provides proof that he could speak or write comfortably in the language.

As a bookworm from boyhood, however, John found England's free public libraries and YMCA reading rooms gold mines of information. He read histories (of the Celts, Anglo-Saxons, and Normans), biographies (of John Wesley and U. S. president James Garfield), and religious tomes (seeking to understand England's many denominations and sects). Loughborough bought an entire set of what he called the *National Encyclopedia* (possibly *Encyclopedia Britannica*). His personal library expanded so rapidly that he had to build several new bookcases (with glass fronts and brass trim) to hold all his books.

Although he publicly condemned the British class system, Loughborough traveled to Cowes to see the Duchess of Connaught and the Duchess of Edinburgh. Also he attended lectures by Lord Portman on the return of the Jews to Palestine, although given the Adventist position on end-time prophecy, he probably did not agree with Portman's views. John also carried on a written debate with Bishop Wilberforce on the state of the dead, although neither altered their views on that subject. Yet as these excerpts from his diary (and those that follow in chapter 12) indicate, life in Merry Old England had transformed John and his family in many ways.[43]

---

[1] James White to JNL, July 19, 1878, m. 53, CAR.

[2] JSW and D. M. Canright to JNL, July 19, 1878, m. 53, CAR; *PUR*, Jan. 31, 1907, p. 2.

[3] JNL to WCW, July 29, 1878, m. 52, CAR.

[4] *ST*, Aug. 1, 1878, pp. 228, 229; *PUR*, Jan. 31, 1907, p. 1.

[5] *PUR*, Jan. 31, 1907, p. 1.

[6] JNL's ministerial credentials, 1878-1882, DF 230, CAR.

[7] JNL, diary, November-December 1878; *YI*, July 21, 1880, p. 126; *RH*, Jan. 23, 1879, p. 32; *ST*, Feb. 13, 1879, pp. 52, 53; *ST*, June 12, 1879, p. 182.

[8] JNL, diary, December 1878; *RH*, Oct. 24, 1899, p. 689; Arthur McLarty, "Loughborough and the Founding of the English Mission, 1879-1883" (typed manuscript, Fall 1974), pp. 2, 3; *ST*, Feb. 13, 1879, pp. 52, 53.

[9] Ancestry.com, *The Loughborough Name in History* (2007, 2008), pp. 8, 9, 15, 32, 60, 71, 72.

[10] The most significant historiography on Seventh-day Adventism in England includes Hugh Dunton, "The Millerite Adventists and Other Millenarian Groups in Great Britain, 1830-1860 (Ph.D. diss., University of London, 1984); Harry Leonard, "Andrews and the Mission to Britain," in *J. N. Andrews: The Man and the Mission* (Berrien Springs, Mich.: Andrews University Press, 1985); Gideon D. Hagstotz, *The Seventh-day Adventists in the British Isles, 1878-1933* (Lincoln, Neb.: Union College Press, 1936); DF 4003-a, CAR; Nigel Barham, "The Progress of the Seventh-day Adventist Church in Great Britain, 1878-1974" (Ph.D. diss., University of Michigan, 1976); "Opening the British Mission," *Adventist Heritage* 9, No. 2 (1984):12-18; Denis Porter, *A Century of Adventism in the British Isles: A Brief History of the British Union Conference of Seventh-day Adventists* (Grantham: Stanborough Press, 1974); Rex Riches, *Establishing the British Mission of the Seventh-day Adventist Church, 1863-1887* (Greensboro, N.C.: for the author, 1997); and Hugh Dunton, Daniel Heinz, Dennis Porter, Ronald Strasdowsky, eds., *Heirs of the Reformation: The Story of Seventh-day Adventists in Europe* (Grantham, England: Stanborough Press, 1997). On Seventh Day Baptists in England, see Bryan Ball, *The Seventh-day Men: Sabbatarians and Sabbatarianism in England and Wales, 1600-1800* (Oxford: Clarendon Press, 1994).

[11] EGW to S. N. Haskell, Jan. 27, 1879, DF 4003-a-1, CAR.

[12] *ST*, Sept. 19, 1878, p. 277; *ST*, Nov. 7, 1878, p. 336; *RH*, July 11, 1878, p. 19; *RH*, Nov. 21, 1878, p. 168; *ST*, Sept. 19, 1878, p. 277; *PUR*, June 9, 1921, p. 6; *Missionary Worker*, July 25, 1924, p. 24; Hagstotz, *British Isles*, pp. 25, 36-38.

[13] JNL, diary, 1879-1883.

[14] *RH*, Sept. 9, 1880, p. 185; *GCB* (1895), p. 455; *ST*, Jan. 22, 1880, pp. 30, 31; Dunton et al., *Heirs*, p. 30; EGW to "Brethren" [D. A. Robinson and C. L. Boyd], June 18, 1887, GC Archives.

[15] *ST*, Jan. 22, 1880, pp. 30, 31; Leonard, "Andrews and the Mission to Britain," in J. N. Andrews, pp. 225-260; *RH*, Sept. 9, 1880, p. 185.

[16] Barham, "British Mission," p. 17; Annie Loughborough to Mary White, Apr. 4, 1880, m. 52, CAR.

[17] JNL, diary, January 1879; JNL to WCW, Jan. 11, 1879, m. 52, CAR; *RH*, Jan. 30, 1879, pp. 36, 40; JNL, *ST*, Feb. 13, 1879, pp. 52, 53; *YI*, Aug. 8, 1944, pp. 4, 13; Hag-

stotz, *British Isles*, pp. 42, 43, 52. The Ings and Loughboroughs lived in Stanley Cottage on Stanley Street near Shirley Road in Freemantle, a suburb of Southampton, England.

[18] JNL, diary, February 1879; *ST*, Jan. 16, 1879, p. 20; *ST*, Feb. 13, 1879, p. 56; *RH*, Feb. 13, 1879, p. 53; JNL, *ST*, Feb. 20, 1879, p. 61; *ST*, Feb. 27, 1879, p. 72; JNL to WCW, Mar. 30, 1879, m. 52, CAR.

[19] *RH*, Feb. 13, 1879, pp. 52, 53; *RH*, Feb. 27, 1879, p. 70; *RH*, Mar. 27, 1879, p. 102; JNL to WCW, Mar. 30, 1879, m. 52, CAR.

[20] JNL to WCW, Mar. 30, 1879, m. 52, CAR; *Adventist Review*, Mar. 3, 1994, pp. 12, 13.

[21] *ST*, Aug. 28, 1879, p. 262; *ST*, Sept. 20, 1921, pp. 12, 13; *Missionary Worker*, Oct. 4, 1922, p. 7; *Missionary Worker*, May 18, 1923, p.7; Denis Porter, "A Century of Adventism in the British Isles: A Brief History of the British Union Conference of Seventh-day Adventists" (n.p., 1974), pp. 5, 6; *LUH*, Nov. 18, 1969, p. 9; *PUR*, June 10, 1968, pp. 1-3; "Boyd, Maude (Sisley)," in *Ellen G. White Encyclopedia*, pp. 321, 322. Sarah Phipson, one of Loughborough's first converts, became treasurer of the Southampton Adventist Church. Mary Anne Warne and her husband, both illiterate, lived a while at Ravenswood where John taught them to read. Angelina Turney, her mother, and two sisters were expelled from their home by her father who was bitterly opposed to Adventism. As a result, Angelina and her mother found refuge at Ravenswood for about a year. Baptized in the homemade baptistry there when she was 15 years old, she and her mother helped the team mail copies of the *Signs* every Saturday night. Annie treated Angelina as her own daughter and Delmer, who played the organ for evangelistic meetings there, treated her as a sister. Regarding currency figures, Loughborough states that the British pound equaled $5 in 1879.

[22] JNL, diary, March 1879; *RH*, Feb. 27, 1879, p. 70; *RH*, Mar. 27, 1879, p. 102; *RH*, Apr. 3, 1879, p. 110; *ST*, Apr. 10, 1879, p. 119; *ST*, May 1, 1879, p. 142; Hagstotz, *British Isles*, pp. 47, 48.

[23] *RH*, Apr. 24, 1879, p. 135; *ST*, May 1, 1879, p. 142; JNL, *RH*, May 8, 1879, p. 150; *ST*, May 8, 1879, p. 150; *Missionary Worker*, July 25, 1924, pp. 9, 24.

[24] *RH*, Apr. 3, 1879, p. 110.

[25] *ST*, Apr. 24, 1879, pp. 130, 136.

[26] *ST*, Apr. 24, 1879, p. 136; *ST*, May 22, 1879, p. 166; JNL diary, April-June 1879; *RH*, May 15, 1879, p. 157; Hagstotz, *British Isles*, p. 44.

[27] *ST*, June 26, 1879, p. 199; *ST*, July 3, 1879, p. 206.

[28] JNL to JSW and EGW, July 17, 1879, m. 52, CAR; *RH*, July 24, 1879, p. 38; *RH*, Sept. 4, 1879, p. 86; *ST*, Oct. 2, 1879, p. 294; *Rise and Progress*, pp. 320, 321; Hagstotz, *British Isles*, pp. 45, 46.

[29] *RH*, July 17, 1879, p. 28; *ST*, July 24, 1879, p. 220.

[30] *RH*, July 17, 1879, p. 28; JNL, diary, September-November 1879.

[31] JNL to WCW, Dec. 15, 1879, m. 52, CAR; JNL to WCW, Dec. 23, 1879, m. 52, CAR.

[32] *RH*, Nov. 20, 1879, p. 166; *RH*, Mar. 11, 1880, p. 172.

[33] *ST*, June 3, 1880, p. 248; JNL, diary, July 1880; JNL, *ST*, July 1, 1880, p. 296; *RH*, July 8, 1880, pp. 40, 41; *ST*, July 15, 1880, p. 321; *RH*, July 22, 1880, p. 80; *ST*, July 29, 1880, p. 345; *ST*, Aug. 12, 1880, p. 356; JNL to JSW, Aug. 12, 1880, m. 52, CAR; *RH*, Aug. 26, 1880, p. 156.

[34] *YI*, June 2, 1880, p. 96; JNL to JSW, Aug. 12, 1880, m. 52, CAR; *RH*, Aug. 19, 1880, p. 140; *RH*, Sept. 16, 1880, p. 204; *RH*, Nov. 11, 1880, p. 316; *ST*, Dec. 16, 1880, pp. 564, 565; Hagstotz, *British Isles*, p. 53; *RH*, Apr. 22, 1880, p. 268; *Missionary Worker*, Aug. 29, 1906, p. 130. The Christadelphians denied the coeternality and full divinity of

Christ, the existence of both the devil and the Holy Spirit, the relevance of the Ten Commandment law for Christians today, and the reality of the resurrection for most people. As dispensationalists, they believed in a special probationary period for the Jews and an eternal kingdom in which mortals and immortals would comingle.

[35] *Columbia Union Visitor*, May 15, 1947, p. 1; E. Cooper, *The Great Advent Movement*, p. 229; *RH*, July 21, 1949, p. 24; *RH*, July 2, 1981, pp. 15-17.

[36] JNL, diary, January 1880; *RH*, Jan. 8, 1880, p. 26; *ST*, Jan. 8, 1880, p. 7; *ST*, Jan. 15, 1880, p. 20; *RH*, Feb. 5, 1880, p. 91; *ST*, Feb. 5, 1880, p. 54. John was president, Annie was secretary and treasurer, and Jennie Ings was librarian of the Hampshire district of the British T&M Society. There were 26 members in the British T&M Society's two districts (Hampshire and Somerset) by February 1880.

[37] *RH*, Mar. 25, 1880, p. 205; *ST*, Apr. 8, 1880, p. 165; *RH*, Dec. 16, 1880, p. 394.

[38] *RH*, Jan. 22, 1880, p. 60; *RH*, Feb. 5, 1880, p. 92; *RH*, Feb. 26, 1880, p. 140; *ST*, Mar. 4, 1880, p. 101.

[39] *ST*, Feb. 5, 1880, p. 54; JNL to WCW, Jan. 27, 1880, m. 52, CAR.

[40] *ST*, Mar. 11, 1880, p. 114; *ST*, June 17, 1880, p. 273; *ST*, Nov. 4, 1880, pp. 487, 488; *ST*, Nov. 18, 1880, p. 513.

[41] *RH*, May 20, 1880, pp. 332, 333; *ST*, May 27, 1880, pp. 236, 237. The Smithfield martyrs were sixteenth-century Protestants under Mary I, while those who died at Newgate and Bunhill Fields in the seventeenth and eighteenth centuries were nonconformists (including Seventh Day Baptists). Loughborough also visited sites sacred to John and Charles Wesley, although neither of them suffered martyrdom as his report seems to imply.

[42] See JNL's articles in *Youth's Instructor*, Feb. 19, 1879, pp. 29, 30; Feb. 26, 1879, p. 34; Mar. 5, 1879, p. 38; Mar. 26, 1879, pp. 49, 50; Apr. 9, 1879, pp. 57, 58; Apr. 30, 1879, p. 66; May 14, 1879, pp. 73, 74; May 21, 1879, pp. 77, 78; June 18, 1879, p. 94; July 2, 1879, pp. 105, 106; July 16, 1879, p. 114; Aug. 13, 1879, p. 130; Aug. 27, 1879, p. 138; Sept. 10, 1879, p. 150; Sept. 24, 1879, p. 158; Oct. 8, 1879, p. 166; Oct. 29, 1879, p. 178; Nov. 19, 1879, p. 190; Dec. 3, 1879, pp. 197, 198; Jan. 1, 1880, p. 2; Jan. 21, 1880, p. 14; Feb. 18, 1880, pp. 29, 30; Mar. 3, 1880, p. 42; Mar. 31, 1880, p. 54; Apr. 14, 1880, p. 66; July 28, 1880, pp. 129, 130; Aug. 11, 1880, p. 138; Aug. 25, 1880, p. 146; Sept. 8, 1880, p. 158; Sept. 22, 1880, p. 166; Oct. 20, 1880, p. 182; Nov. 3, 1880, p. 190; Nov. 17, 1880, p. 198; Dec. 15, 1880, p. 218. Of course, Loughborough ignores the very causes that precipitated such deplorable conditions among Native Americans: selling guns and alcohol to Indians, stealing their ancestral lands, killing the buffalo that the Plains tribes depended on, forcing them onto reservations where government agents cheated them out of food and clothing, and imprisoning or executing them for every act of disobedience or reprisal. For the most part, we can lay such at the doorstep of mercenary and immoral Whites.

[43] JNL, diary, January 1879-December 1880.

Four-generation photo of Minerva (Norton) Loughborough, son William Kerr Loughborough, granddaughter Lettie Estella (Loughborough) Marvin, great-granddaughter Edith (Marvin) Ashley, c. 1893

William K. Loughborough (1827-1912). John's older brother, a blacksmith and architect in New York and Michigan

Minerva Jane (Loughborough) Chapman. John's older sister (1829-1894)

John and his first wife, Mary J. (Walker) Loughborough, c. 1857

JNL-9

John and Mary Loughborough's home (1857-1866)
on 422 Champion Street, Battle Creek, Michigan

J. N. Loughborough, c. 1868, when he left for California at the age of 36

John's second wife, Maggie A. Newman (1840-1875), with little Delmer, about 1867

J. N. Loughborough in 1873, when he was California Conference president

J. N. Loughborough, c. 1880s

Loughborough family, c. 1884: Anna, Delmer, Mary, and John

Ravenswood, the SDA headquarters in Southampton, England, c. 1883 (front row, left to right: William Ings, J. W. Gardner, S. N. Haskell, J. N. Loughborough; back row, left to right: Mrs. Jenny Ings, Mrs. Jenny Thayer, Mrs. J. W. Gardner, Delmer Loughborough, Mary Loughborough, Anna Loughborough, H. L. Jones)

Delmer N. Loughborough (1864-1894). c. 1890

Mariah (Stewart) Loughborough.
Delmer's wife. c. 1880s

J. N. Loughborough preaching to students at Walla Walla College in 1910

Seven pioneer SDA ministers in 1915 (back, left to right: J. H. Rogers, J. O. Corliss, H. W. Decker, H. W. Cottrell; front, left to right: Stephen Haskell, J. N. Loughborough, George I. Butler)

J. N. Loughborough with his daughter Mary (Loughborough) Ireland in 1918

J. N. Loughborough in his 80s. c. 1918

J. N. Loughborough at the St. Helena Sanitarium. c. 1920

J. N. Loughborough at 90 in 1922, two years before he died in 1924

Final resting place of J. N. Loughborough; his second wife, Maggie (Newman); and his third wife, Anna (Driscoll), in St. Helena Cemetery in California

CHAPTER XII

SPREADING THE MESSAGE TO THE BRITISH ISLES AND BEYOND (1880-1883)

"No man has succeeded better as a preacher, pastor, and financier than Elder [Loughborough]. Probably his record shows greater success in all these branches of the work, than that of any other who has been connected with the cause of present truth. While he lives in the hearts of all his brethren, sanctified economy and caution have been his strength in building up the cause."[1]

This encomium, which James White wrote for the *Review* a few days before he died, demonstrates that he had a high opinion of John's talents and his accomplishments in England. Before the Loughboroughs left for Britain in 1878, Ellen White had also urged John to "settle into the work, make God your trust, and you will accomplish much." At the same time she had warned him that "you have too much self-sufficiency."[2]

During the Loughboroughs' first year abroad, John had apparently written Mrs. White a letter stating that he was "trying to become as English as possible." Shortly thereafter, she had an unsettling dream relating to his situation. As a result, she sent him a lengthy letter in 1879 urging him to "act out the American. No one expects you to act [like] an Englishman. . . . Just carry all the Americanism you can into your English Mission, and let England see you are not at all ashamed to stand under the stars and stripes." She cautioned John not to "ape English gentility" and reprimanded Annie for adding "ornaments" (broaches and pins) to her dresses, a custom Victorian women adopted with the money their husbands gave them (called "pin money") every New Year's Day.

Also in her letter, Ellen highlighted John's many "defects of character" and urged him "to keep close to Jesus Christ, or you will make some sad errors." After admonishing him that "you are not in possession of those qualities which will make you a successful missionary where you are not known," she mentioned several faults that could undermine his ministry. First, he sought praise: "You must have the credit of leading out in everything, and must keep everything under your jurisdiction." Second, he micromanaged: "You devote much time to little particulars, and the work that you can do which others cannot do you neglect." Third, he was not a team player: "You are so very particular to have everything done in a certain way . . . that it is next to impossible for anyone to work with you." Fourth, he failed as a preacher: "Your preaching is dry and has but little grace because your own soul is not drinking of the water of life." Fifth, he was vain: "You feel anxious about your personal appearance—in brushing your clothes and arranging your hair and having everything faultless so far as outward appearance is concerned." Sixth, he lacked grace: "Your soul is frequently snarled up and dusty and spotted. You need to seek God in prayer with penitence that His grace shall come into your heart before you come before the people. . . . You cannot accomplish much unless you pray much." Seventh, he criticized others: "Now if some of your exactness and criticism were exercised upon your own soul . . . angels of God would be round about you." Eighth, he had marital problems: "You and your wife should cultivate Christian courtesy, simplicity, openheartedness and frankness toward each other."

Then, after warning him that "there is no kingdom of God for you unless you exercise tender compassion and forgiveness toward others," she outlined the panaceas for his faults. He needed to seek God's grace daily: "Jesus in you, the hope of glory, will break down the cold, formal barriers that will be found in Europe." If he would spend more time in prayer, "angels of God would help you and break down the barriers which hedge up your way." Loughborough should throw away the dry discourses and write new ones under "the melting Spirit of God" that would become "new manna . . . to the hungry sheep." "What you need is more of Jesus and less of self," she told him. "Open your heart to the bright beams of righteousness."[3]

REACHING OUT TO OTHER GROUPS

Following Mrs. White's counsel gradually transformed J. N. Loughborough's ministry in the British Isles. His diary reveals that, at least in part because of more prayer and less criticism, greater teamwork, and less micromanaging, the evangelistic team at Ravenswood, like bees gathering pollen for the hive, began witnessing to new groups farther afield. During 1881 letters began arriving from Shropshire, Kent, Lincolnshire, and Lancashire indicating that others were reading their tracts, with Christadelphians, Wesleyan Methodists, and Plymouth Brethren greatly appreciating them. No doubt such gratitude mollified the group somewhat when they received one poison pen letter from an Anglican in London calling the *Signs* "ranting, dissenting trash" that the writer "burned . . . immediately."[4]

At least two dissenting groups, however, frequently invited Loughborough to speak to them: the Seventh Day Baptists in London and the Methodists in Darlaston. As we have already seen, John developed close personal and professional ties with the Baptist pastor William Jones. In the fall of 1881 the Wesleyan Methodists asked John to hold meetings in their chapel in Darlaston. Having just read biographies of John and Charles Wesley prior to the trip, Loughborough, knowing that an angry mob had carried Charles from Walsall to Darlaston and Wednesbury, retraced its route. Shortly after addressing 200 Sunday school scholars in the chapel, John began evangelistic meetings at the Public Hall with 100 people attending. He also spoke to 600 Primitive Methodist Sunday school teachers and pupils regarding Chinese "idol worship" in San Francisco. Although no mob assaulted him, a terrific gale sent roof tiles and loose bricks from toppled chimneys flying through the air. A "number of men" were killed. At sea the typhoon sank 90 ships. Doubtless this mayhem provided Loughborough apt illustrations for his discourses on end-time prophecy.[5]

In addition to preaching at several dissenting chapels, Loughborough participated in many social and professional organizations that had no direct bearing on his missionary activities in Britain. Like thousands of other Victorians, John was a "joiner." In Manchester, for example, he stayed with a Baptist friend so that he could attend meetings of the Vegetarian Society, in which he was an active member. Frank Spence, Esquire, the Honourable Secretary of the British Anti-Narcotic League, invited Loughborough to stay in his home for the annual meetings of that society.[6]

As a member of the United Kingdom Temperance Alliance, John joined delegates in Manchester in October 1881 to discuss ways to defeat Prime

Minister William Gladstone's local option bill (allowing citizens to vote for or against serving alcohol in local pubs). Then, standing before the 6,000 attendees, Loughborough proposed the following resolution: "That as non-smoking teetotalers are found to be five times less liable to break their pledge than teetotalers who smoke, [the society should] offer them the optional pledge against tobacco." When he pointed out that the British Bands of Hope had recently adopted the dual pledge, delegates passed his resolution. John also attended sessions of the Dietetic Reform Society. In addition, he avidly listened to lectures on phonography (or shorthand).[7]

By 1882 Loughborough had enough free time to join still more organizations. As an active participant in the Christian Temperance Missionary Society, he proudly wore the blue ribbon at meetings. From time to time his temperance friends asked him to plan and direct services for the local Band of Hope. Before they donned baptismal robes, Adventist converts were encouraged to sign at least the anti-rum and anti-tobacco pledges—and if they were willing, the teetotal pledge as well. Loughborough rejoiced that the number of converts signing the latter pledge was double the number of those signing the former two pledges.[8]

The growing ship ministry introduced Loughborough, Ings, and (by 1882) George Drew to many captains, stewards, and other naval officers. When they invited Drew to join the Mercantile Marine Association, he did so, happy in the knowledge that most of its members believed in the Second Advent and the conditional immortality of the soul. To demonstrate his support for the latter doctrine, Loughborough accepted an invitation from the Liverpool Conditional Immortality Association to address their delegates in Liverpool in 1883. Perhaps remembering how he had fainted during a vaccination in 1868, John also joined the Anti-Vaccination Society. After witnessing the forced vaccination of 1,000 steerage passengers (mostly lower class emigrants) bound for New York on the *City of Rome*, Loughborough wrote an impassioned article sharing the gory details with readers of the *The Vaccination Inquirer and Health Review*. "I turned from the scene of indiscriminate diseasing to scatter more of your anti-vaccination literature amongst the passengers on board," he exclaimed, "and resolved to do all I could to expose the mischievous delusion."[9]

Because the Salvation Army did not vaccinate, but sought to save the souls of Britain's lower classes, John became an enthusiastic advocate of the social gospel efforts of William Booth and his associates. In fact, his contacts with the Salvation Army influenced him to begin holding outdoor meetings (a relatively "new movement" since 1865) in the marketplaces at Great Grimsby and Louth in the fall of 1883. Belatedly recognizing that England's cold, wet weather mildewed and tore canvass, John sold the tent. "This [holding outdoor meetings] has been done to such an extent, and has worked so well, that it is looked upon with favor by all classes. . . . It seems to us like the most feasible thing we have tried in this Kingdom to reach the public ear." John expressed amazement at seeing hundreds of marketgoers standing quietly and listening intently to the discourses he and his associate A. A. John gave. British outdoor etiquette had improved markedly since the days of John and Charles Wesley! Loughborough especially loved the Salvation Army's stirring band music. Indeed, the words of his favorite gospel song—"Just the Same"—had been written by Colonel J. C. Addie, a Salvation Army officer.[10]

"When Moses and his people From Egypt's land did flee,
Their enemies behind them, And in front of them the sea;
God raised the waters like a wall, And opened up their way,
And the God that lived in Moses' time Is just the same today!

"When David and Goliath met—The wrong against the right,—
The giant armed with human pow'r, But David with God's might;
God's pow'r with David's sling and stone The giant low did lay,
And the God that lived in David's time Is just the same today!

"When Daniel, faithful to his God, Would not bow down to men,
And by God's enemies was hurled Into the lion's den;
God shut the lion's mouths, we read, And robbed them of their prey,
And the God who lived in Daniel's time Is just the same today!

"When sinners to the Saviour came, the weary ones found rest,
He pardoned and He healed them all, each one who came was blest,
O bring to Him your load of sin and come without delay
For the One Who welcom'd sinners then Is just the same today.

(Chorus) "He's just the same today, He's just the same today;
And the God that lived in Moses' time Is just the same today."[11]

Although encouraged by the fact that God remained the same, Loughborough received disturbing news in May of 1881 that J. N. Andrews, his old colleague and dear friend, was gravely ill. Dropping everything, he and Annie took the boat to Le Havre and the train to Paris, where they caught another train directly to Basel. Although their primary purpose in going was to nurse Andrews back to health, the couple took time to see some tourist attractions along the way. They visited Münster Cathedral, the Tomb of the Encyclopédiens, the Gates of St. John and St. James, St. Peter's Platz, and the military tournament ground (which John called *"cette trés belle promenade"*). In spite of their best efforts in Andrews' behalf, Annie correctly predicted that his "lung trouble" (TB) would soon kill him. But Andrews declared that their visit "was the occasion of much encouragement to us." When the GC Committee called for a day of fasting and prayer for Andrews' healing, Loughborough and the Swiss pastor James Ertzenberger anointed him and prayed for him (in French and English). "It was a solemn, heavenly place," Loughborough told *Review* readers. "Angels of God looked down upon the scene. The presence of God was here." After a refreshing night's sleep, Andrews sat up, ate his meals "with . . . relish," dictated a letter, and was soon taking short walks with John and Annie by his side. A letter from James White promising to visit him in Switzerland greatly cheered him.[12]

But when John and Annie returned to Southampton, a telegram awaited them. James White, the cofounder of the Seventh-day Adventist Church, was dead at 60 of malaria. "Our hearts were made sad indeed," John wrote. With tears in his eyes, he described White's "arduous labors in the past" to a gathering of British Adventists who had never known him. "His 'works'" (the many institutions he established) "will 'follow him,'" he said.[13]

EXPANDING THROUGHOUT THE BRITISH ISLES (1881-1884)

In January 1881 Loughborough had told James White that some British readers of the *Review* and *Signs* complained that they contained "too many reports and statistics" and "so little . . . pointing the sinner to the blood of Christ." In short, they preached "so much theory and so little heart work."

Thinking that a change of title might help, James suggested calling the *Review* "The Voice of Truth," "The Voice of the Prophets," or "The Prophetic Expositor." John advised him that Britons would find the first title "egotistical." The second would make them think its writers claimed to be prophets, while the third title "would hurt [us] here" because "prophecy does not draw attention here as it . . . does on your side of the waters." Tactfully, John hinted that it was not the *titles* but the *content* of the church's publications that needed changing.[14]

Despite such reservations, however, readers all over the British Isles requested so many copies of the *Review, Signs*, and *Good Health* that the Ravenswood team could not keep up with the demand. John informed White that they needed at least 300 copies of the *Signs* every week—but 1,000 would be better. In part, Ings and Drew had fueled the escalating demand. Their ship ministry in Southampton and Liverpool respectively surpassed all expectations. By the spring of 1881 they and other members of the British T&M Society had more than *tripled* their tract distribution from 300 copies a week to more than 1,000 copies a week. "The *Signs* . . . is becoming a regular visitor at many English firesides," Loughborough boasted.[15]

The avalanche of letters pouring into Ravenswood every week testified as to just how many people enjoyed reading Adventist literature. Their return addresses read like a study in British geography: Essex, Lincolnshire, Hampshire, Wales, the Isle of Wight, and Scotland. An especially large number of requests came from readers in London, Liverpool, Southampton, Glasgow, and Edinburgh. As a matter of fact, by 1883 catalogs of Adventist publications appeared in the Edinburgh *Scotsman*, the Glasgow *Weekly Mail*, and three other (unnamed) periodicals. Together they reached more than 200,000 readers weekly. "In a country where everything moves so slowly as in this kingdom," Loughborough commented, "we are glad to see indications of advancement in our work."[16]

Requests for Adventist publications kept people busy both in America and the British Isles. In the spring of 1881 Loughborough spent much of his time training "new hands" (both converts and non-Adventists) to send out 1,000 copies of the *Signs* every week. Even Delmer (now 17) learned to set type for short tracts and notices. In turn, the increased demand in Great Britain placed the shipping crew at the Pacific SDA Publishing Company under so much pressure that, instead of cutting the string that held the bundles together, they sliced their hands in their haste, leaving bloody fingerprints on some copies of *Signs of the Times*. Even the perpetually optimistic Loughborough, now 49, confessed, "I begin to feel the worse for wear." Nonetheless, he resolved "to wear out in the cause."[17]

The statistics that Ings and Drew regularly reported in the *Signs* concerning their work aboard ships indicated that they too were getting exhausted. In July 1881 alone they canvassed the crews of 88 ships at Southampton, Liverpool, and Hull, distributing hundreds of tracts and papers in English and 60 copies in Danish and Swedish. Realizing that their request for thousands of copies in Danish, Norwegian, Swedish, German, and Russian could not be immediately filled, they recruited A. A. John's wife, who could speak fluent Norwegian and Danish, to assist them in giving Bible studies to Scandinavian sailors.[18]

By the end of 1882 George Drew was visiting every ship that docked in Hull, finding among their crews "many warm friends" who received his papers (mostly *Good Health* and *Signs*) "with tears of joy." Once he sold $28 worth of publications in 10 days. Another time he spent an hour pleading with the sailors of the *Black Watch* to give their hearts to God. Days later off the coast of Wales, the ship sank in a gale and all hands drowned. "I was probably the last one who spoke to them on religious matters," he declared. Recognizing the urgency of reaching every individual for Christ, during the summer of 1883 Ings and Drew contacted the sailors on 660 ships: in short, they visited about seven vessels each day. But during one quarter that fall, they went aboard 1,080 vessels—an incredible 12 ships *every single day* (and one presumes their days were long ones indeed). As a result of their dynamic ship ministry, Adventist literature found its way to at least 15 foreign countries. By the end of 1883 letters arrived at Ravenswood from the West Indies, South America, South Africa, Australia, New Zealand, and the East Indies, where new converts expressed gratitude for the "Bread of Life" offered by Adventist publications.[19]

In addition to the spiritual bread of life, by the summer of 1881 the evangelistic team at Ravenswood also offered physical bread—or "bread gems" as they were called in America. To help English converts (many of them heavy meat eaters) adopt healthful, vegetarian lifestyles, John and Annie began selling milk, oatmeal, and bread at rock-bottom prices. While most British Adventists accepted health reform in theory, some struggled with its application. Loughborough loved telling the story of one man who, when asked how he was getting along with the new diet, replied, "Pretty well, I guess." "But tell me, Elder [Loughborough], would it be all right to cook the oatmeal before we eat it? I like it raw quite well, but my wife thinks she would relish it better if it were cooked."[20]

Far more palatable than dry oatmeal flakes, the bread gems were made from organic whole-grain (rather than white) flour and therefore packed with vitamins and minerals. The health fad so quickly gained the support of Britons that John and Annie could not keep up with the demand. Nearly every week during 1882 and 1883 they mailed the "Bread Pan Pattern," the gem pans, or copies of the recipe for baking "gems" all across the United Kingdom. Occasionally, Ravenswood must have resembled a factory, especially in weeks when its staff shipped four boxes of gem pans a day. For years after the Loughboroughs returned to the U.S., employees at the British Conference office shipped gem pans to Her Majesty's hungry subjects. So popular did the fad become that for decades British Adventists called wholesome bread "gems."[21]

The gems kept so well, in fact, that John brought some with him on his voyage to America to attend the General Conference of 1881. Once again, however, he nearly missed the boat—not because it left early this time, but because he, Delmer (17), and Mary (14) lacked the money. So John prayed about the matter and left it in God's hands. On the very day they needed to buy tickets, two letters arrived at Ravenswood. One came from an Adventist in northern England who sent in his tithe ($40) early because, he wrote, "I am so powerfully impressed that you are in need of this money now." The other envelope, containing $25, came from John's Baptist host in Manchester. Together the gifts covered all their travel expenses. "We recognized in this a direct answer to our prayers," he declared.[22]

As usual, shortly after the German steamship *Rhein* left the harbor, John parted with his breakfast. While Mary and Delmer devoured hearty meals, their father nibbled on bread gems and crackers, with occasional fresh apples and lemons. When a tempest struck the ship, the poor man endured a private purgatory. "Oh! What a time," he wrote in his diary. "I [am] not [going] to the table yet." After foolishly eating three meals on Thanksgiving Day (including ice cream for dessert), John faced another "rough night." The next day he nibbled on crackers and read copies of the *Good Health* magazine. But he survived the voyage, unlike one female passenger who was buried late one night at sea. When the *Rhein* reached New York City, the family took the train to Battle Creek. There they stayed at the home of John's sister Minerva Jane and her husband John Chapman.[23]

In addition to giving "a stirring discourse [about] the English Mission," highlighting its "obstacles," "peculiarities," "providences," and "prospect[s]," Loughborough attended an endless round of meetings and spoke to nearly every resolution brought to the floor. Delegates sought his counsel regarding the work of the T&M Society, the Health and Temperance Association, the Sabbath School Association, the Education Society, Battle Creek Sanitarium, Battle Creek College, the Review and Herald Publishing Association, the SDA Publishing Association, and the Missionary Society. He served on the Committee on Reading for Ministers that prepared a reading list of books totaling approximately 31,000 pages for all Adventist pastors to study and on the constitution committee that revised state constitutions and bylaws. Likewise, he was one of eight delegates who referred a motion to ordain women ministers back to the GC Committee (where it died a silent death). Afterward, old friends wanted him to preach in the magnificent Dime Tabernacle that held 3,000 worshippers. He chose as his subject "Be still and know that I am God." Perhaps the widow Ellen White, listening in the audience, found inspiration in his Christ-centered message.[24]

During a quick visit to the Review and Herald Publishing association, John met George King, whose stuttering prevented him from preaching, but whose zeal to witness made him an effective book salesman. King asked Loughborough what he thought about the idea of combining Uriah Smith's two books *Thoughts on Daniel* and *Thoughts on the Revelation* into one volume and then having canvassers sell 5,000 copies door to door. "Brother King," John replied, "my advice to you is to go ahead, and the Lord will prosper the undertaking." Loughborough's encouraging words helped launch a century of successful colporteur work by Adventist youth and adults.[25]

J. N. Loughborough's primary purpose in attending the 1881 GC session, however, was to recruit more staff for Great Britain. In this he was successful. The delegates voted to send A. A. John and his wife (then serving in Illinois) to assist Loughborough in evangelistic meetings. George R.

Drew (then in California) would take charge of the ship ministry at Hull and Liverpool (as the Ings returned to sunny California). Jennie Thayer, who, while still in her mid-20s, had served as secretary and treasurer both of the Michigan Conference Tract Society and the Health and Temperance Association, would help the Ravenswood team as a typesetter and proofreader and take charge of compiling and distributing the special British edition of *Signs of the Times* that the General Conference agreed to print.[26]

On January 9 John, Delmer, and Mary took the train to Rochester, New York. At Victor they spent two days visiting relatives before traveling to New York City to board the *Rhein* for the return voyage to England. But this time, no doubt cheered by the bright prospects before him, Loughborough wrote in his diary, "All [are] sick, I [am] well." Unfortunately for him, it didn't last long—he spent most of the voyage sleeping in his bunk. Mary Loughborough and Jennie Thayer, however, had a grand time walking about the ship's decks. When the *Rhein* docked at Southampton, John's only comment in his diary was "[I am] sick and cold."[27]

GENERAL EUROPEAN CONFERENCE[28]

He also discovered that because of his 10-week absence so much "accumulated business" awaited his attention he could neither report on the progress of the mission nor write articles for the church papers for the next four months. No sooner had John caught up, however, than he received an urgent summons to attend a general European conference at Tramelan (near Basel) Switzerland. The 10-day gathering (September 8-17) brought together 50 Adventist delegates and the church's five European leaders: J. N. Andrews of Switzerland; J. N. Loughborough, John and William Drew representing Great Britain; and John Matteson for Norway, Sweden, and Denmark. As the General Conference representative, Stephen Haskell presided over the session. After listening to each one describe the challenges he faced and the methods employed for overcoming them in his particular field, Haskell offered several observations. First, he noted that all the European fields faced similar difficulties and therefore they should seek similar solutions to their problems. Second, since "it is evident that more can be accomplished . . . by publications than by the living preacher," increasing the number of periodicals (rather than tracts, which were "distasteful" to Europeans) and publishing them in Europe rather than in

America would cut costs, mitigate prejudice, and show greater sensitivity for local customs. Haskell advised that in the very near future the denomination should publish a wide range of foreign language journals (particularly in Italian and German) and distribute them as widely as Andrews' *Les Signes des Temps* (which by 1882 had more than 1,000 subscribers).[29]

Convinced that a general organization tying the local churches to the General Conference would promote unity and efficiency on the continent, the delegates established the European Conference. Haskell, Loughborough, and Andrews wrote its first constitution (it contained only seven articles). Its three-man executive committee included Andrews, Loughborough, and Matteson, with A. A. John as elected secretary and Charles Andrews as treasurer. Delegates also voted to enlarge and adapt Matteson's Scandinavian *Tiderness Tegn* as a monthly periodical to serve the entire European field.[30]

But two thirds of the executive committee would not finish their terms. J. N. Andrews, weakened by tuberculosis, received anointing and special prayer as the delegates asked God to heal him. Although in the short term it appeared that "an angel of God [had] touched him and rebuked the disease," in fact he would die at Basel a few months later at age 54. Three months after the session, delegates at the General Conference meeting in Rome, New York, asked J. N. Loughborough to return to America. They felt that "in view of the wants of the cause in America, our Executive Committee [should] be instructed to make such changes in the English work as shall secure, as soon as consistent, the services of Elder Loughborough in the United States." They also decided that the time had not yet come to publish an English periodical in England, but hopefully someday soon that project could be funded (Jennie Thayer would, in fact, edit the British *Present Truth* two years later).[31]

LOUGHBOROUGH'S WRITINGS AND DIARY

As we have already seen, in addition to John's responsibilities as an administrator, preacher, husband, and father, he took seriously his duty to report in the American church the progress of Seventh-day Adventism in the British Isles. As time allowed, he also wrote articles for the *Review, Signs,* and *Youth's Instructor* on a wide variety of topics. After completing his series in the *Instructor* on the family's adventures from California to England,[32] Loughborough launched another series entitled "Ancient Britain." What his articles lacked in scholarly detail and historical accuracy, they made up for with human interest anecdotes and colorful descriptions. The 13 installments took readers on a whirlwind tour through Roman, Druid, Celtic, Irish, Anglo-Saxon, and Viking history—including their customs, religious practices, stone monuments, weapons, farming and mining, and political development.[33]

His historical survey must have elicited a positive response, for no sooner had it ended than he began another series on medieval England. With an emphasis on kings, military heroes, and political movers and shakers, Loughborough regaled youthful readers with stories about early Anglo-Saxon, Danish, and Norman figures from the time of Edward and Athelstane through Canute and William the Conqueror to Henry IV. Once again, he packed his articles with descriptions of weapons and battles, castles and cathedrals, and feudal customs, adding a generous dose of Adventist commentary on their superstitions and immoral behavior.[34]

If the majority of Loughborough's contributions to the *Review* from 1879 to 1883 consisted of progress reports, in 1882 the paper republished his three-part series on "The Two Witnesses" of Revelation 11 (the New and Old Testament). The articles focused attention on the 1260-year period (538-1798 A.D.) of papal supremacy and offered a black-and-white view of Medieval and Early Modern European history that praised the Waldensians and Huguenots and damned the Catholic powers (in Italy and France particularly) for their bloody persecution of dissenters. In general, Loughborough's narrative is long on blood, blasphemy, and bigotry and short on accuracy, balance, and context. Nonetheless, it makes fascinating reading.[35]

Less fascinating (but more accurate), the bulk of his articles for 1881 and 1882 appeared in the *Signs of the Times*. For the most part, they (recycling earlier ones) deal with theological issues. Once again, Loughborough preferred writing detailed Bible studies that, as we have already seen, would later become pamphlets or books. He penned three articles on the law of God and the Sabbath,[36] three on the devil's personality,[37] three more on hope in the Gospels,[38] and 15 on the punishment of the wicked at the end of the world.[39] Before leaving England, John penned another 15-part series dealing with his favorite topic: the saints' inheritance in God's everlasting kingdom.[40]

While waiting for the coming of God's kingdom, however, John and Annie found new ways to adapt to life in the United Kingdom. Sometimes it proved challenging, especially when expenses exceeded one's income. Major *monthly* expenses included rent for Ravenswood ($35), clothing for the family ($20), Annie's dental care and medicines ($30), food ($15), and coal or wood ($5). But even minor expenses such as books, furniture, transportation, and paying the hired helpers could add up, occasionally pushing the family over budget. John and Annie's trip to Basel, for example, set them back more than £10 ($50)—an entire month's salary—even though they restricted sightseeing activities along the way (they "saw Paris" on only 11 shillings—about $1.40). When food at Smith's Grocery cost too much, they ate oatmeal and milk or popcorn and apples (John even reduced his licorice intake). At least once, Annie walked two miles (to save the six cents' fare) to buy apples for two cents each. How thrilled they were when someone in the U.S. sent them a bushel of apples (John's favorite fruit).

Frugal in other areas of life as well, the Loughboroughs found inexpensive ways to entertain themselves. When not attending meetings of the professional societies mentioned above, John continued his ambitious reading program. With Monsieur Veysey's tutoring, he continued studying French. Because his Bible lacked the Apocrypha, he purchased a copy, and by the spring of 1881, began selling them for a dollar each (the Review and Herald Publishing Association printed them and Adventist authors occasionally cited the Apocrypha in their articles). His growing personal library contained books on theology, history, geography, science, and many other topics. By February 1882 Loughborough had crafted four bookcases to hold them all—and it took him three days to move his books onto the shelves. His diary also indicates that the family read two local newspapers, the *Daily News* and the *Independent*.

For physical exercise, John and Annie took vigorous walks around Southampton. They regularly went shopping (John still called it "trading") together, especially to Smiths' Grocery. Along the way, the couple gave six pence to one poor girl and two shillings to an unemployed man. On trips to London, Paris, and Basel, they visited historic sites and museums. When Del (Delmer) turned 18, John and Annie let him go sightseeing in London by himself. Shortly before Del left to attend Battle Creek College,

John and he spent four days visiting their favorite haunts (St. Paul's, Parliament, Westminster, the British Museum, and the Tower of London).

When the family was home, they invited friends over for teas, Christmas dinners, and birthday parties. In addition to eating, they enjoyed singing with their friends as Delmer played the harmonium. Also like Victorians everywhere, they sent copies of their silhouettes to their friends and requested silhouettes from them as well. When they could afford it, they went to a studio and had their pictures taken—or they invited the photographer to take a photo of the employees grouped in front of Ravenswood. These rare black-and-white photographs, in addition to the many letters, reports, and travelogue articles John wrote, constitute a valuable part of the Loughborough legacy in the British Isles.[41]

J. N. LOUGHBOROUGH'S LEGACY IN GREAT BRITAIN

Although one recent writer summarized Loughborough's five years in England as a failure,[42] Loughborough himself and most of his contemporaries provided a more nuanced assessment of his accomplishments. In a letter to James White in 1881 John recognized that "matters have not gone here [in England] as I expected nor as you expected—perhaps the fault is in me, but I have not been idle, but have done all my strength would admit." Given the "iron bonds of the Established Church and the ignorance and bigotry of the lower classes," he said, conversions had come more slowly in Britain than in America where a Republican government and strict separation of church and state had proved conducive to evangelism.[43]

Despite the obstacles, Loughborough's last report in 1883 provided much for which to be thankful: 49,140 families and ships visited; 21,708 letters mailed; 556 subscriptions to the *Signs* and the *Review*; approximately $2,750 in literature sold; and 100 new Seventh-day Adventists, returning approximately $2,100 in tithe annually.[44] After summarizing a lengthy list of obstacles facing Adventism in the British Isles, the GC Committee praised Loughborough's industry and efforts. They noted that he "has struggled hard against the many obstacles standing in his way to establish the [British] mission, and has practiced economy, and brought expenses as low as possible. He has a good degree of financial ability, which he has exercised to help the mission onward in its work, and save to the cause all he possibly could."[45] Six months later church leaders concluded that it would take *two* persons to replace Loughborough in England.[46] Perhaps the best assessment of his labors during his five years in Great Britain would be to say that despite a lack of overwhelming statistical results (baptisms, churches founded, etc.), his untiring efforts laid a firm foundation upon which future missionaries could build.

Two years after the Loughboroughs returned to America, A. A. John, hearing rumors that some were calling the program in Britain a failure, hastened to defend his former coworker: "The work in England is not a failure. God has already blessed the labors of Elds. Loughborough and Ings, and their families, and Sr. Thayer." He credited them with sowing the gospel seed that made it possible in 1885 for 10,000 British homes to receive the new paper *The Present Truth*.[47] Likewise, William Ings gave J. N. Loughborough credit for laying the groundwork for the growing congregation of 84 Adventists in Southampton by 1887.[48]

Despite harsh testimonies regarding John's personal faults, no one defended his accomplishments more adamantly than Ellen White. When she visited England in 1885, all that she saw favorably impressed her. Two years later, when Stephen N. Haskell wrote in the *Review* that the work in England from 1878 to 1887 had been a complete failure because not as much had been accomplished there as in the U.S. and Australia, she rebuked him for his misplaced pessimism. "There has been a good work done in Europe," she declared. "I think even in England a good work has been done. . . . Here is a good beginning made. Publications have been and still are doing a great work. Let not one grain of unbelief be sown." Then, placing the progress in the British Isles in a new context, she added, "When I think how slow the work has gone in New England and how little [has been] done in Massachusetts and Maine and many other places where they have all circumstances in their favor, we need not be discouraged in regard to Old England. . . . Because you do not see the same results in Old England that you did in Australia you should not demerit [demean] that which has already been gained . . . and notwithstanding the work may move slowly, nevertheless it moves, thank God for that."[49]

And in the years ahead, with new leaders at the helm, the Adventist cause in Great Britain would continue to progress. When John and Annie next visited the Sceptered Isle a little more than a decade later, they would be amazed at the changes they saw.

---

[1] *RH*, July 5, 1881, p. 24.

[2] EGW testimony, quoted in JNL to C. E. Holmes, May 2, 1920, m. 006529, CAR.

[3] EGW to JNL, Letter 40, 1879, CAR.

[4] JNL, cited in *ST*, Jan. 13, 1881, p. 24; *RH*, Apr. 12, 1881, p. 234.

[5] JNL, diary, October 1881; *RH*, Nov. 1, 1881, p. 282; *ST*, Dec. 1, 1881, p. 536; G. Hagstotz, *British Isles*, p. 167.

[6] JNL, *Rise and Progress*, p. 330; *ST*, Dec. 1, 1881, p. 536.

[7] JNL, diary, September-October 1881, October-November 1882; *Phonetic Journal* (1881), p. 540.

[8] *RH*, Dec. 6, 1881, pp. 363, 364; *ST*, Dec. 8, 1881, p. 549; JNL, diary, November 1882.

[9] *RH*, Sept. 4, 1883, p. 571; JNL, "Vaccination of Emigrants," *The Vaccination Inquirer and Health Review* 5, no. 60 (March 1884).

[10] *RH*, Sept. 18, 1883, p. 604.

[11] "Just the Same," words by Col. J. C. Addie and music by W. H. Jude. This author has so far discovered at least 13 different stanzas and two or three variations on the chorus for the song in various hymnbooks.

[12] JNL, diary, May 1881; Anna Loughborough to Mary White, Jan. 30, 1881, m. 52, CAR; *RH*, Aug. 23, 1881, p. 138; *RH*, June 7, 1881, p. 361; *RH*, July 19, 1881, p. 58; *RH*, Apr. 18, 1929, p. 10. In fact, the only French phrase J. N. Loughborough used frequently was "*Dieu Veuillant*" (often abbreviated as "D.V."), meaning "God willing."

[13] JNL to JSW, Mar. 16, 1881, m. 52, CAR; JNL, *ST*, Sept. 15, 1881, p. 416.

[14] JNL to JSW, Jan. 3, 1881, m. 52, CAR.

[15] JNL to JSW, Jan. 3, 1881, m. 52, CAR; *RH*, Jan. 11, 1881, p. 26; *ST*, Jan. 20, 1881, p. 32; *RH*, Feb. 15, 1881, pp. 107, 108; *RH*, Mar. 8, 1881, p. 154; *ST*, May 25, 1882, p. 236.

[16] *ST*, Mar. 17, 1881, pp. 128, 129; JNL, diary, July 1881; *ST*, Apr. 27, 1882, p. 201; *RH*, May 15, 1883, pp. 316, 317; *RH*, July 10, 1883, p. 443; *RH*, July 17, 1883, pp. 458, 459; *RH*, Oct. 9, 1883, p. 632.

[17] *RH*, May 31, 1881, p. 346; JNL to Mary White, Apr. 1, 1881, m. 52, CAR; JNL to WCW, Aug. 2, 1882, m. 52, CAR.

[18] *ST*, Aug. 18, 1881, p. 368; *RH*, May 16, 1882, pp. 316, 317; *RH*, July 11, 1882, p. 448; *RH*, Aug. 8, 1882, p. 507.

[19] *ST*, Dec. 14, 1882, p. 561; *RH*, Apr. 3, 1883, p. 218; *RH*, Aug. 14, 1883, p. 523; *RH*, Nov. 6, 1883, p. 694; *RH*, Feb. 9, 1886, pp. 93, 94; *ST*, Oct. 13, 1881, p. 464; *RH*, May 3, 1881, p. 284. Here and elsewhere I have converted sums involving pounds, shillings, and pence to their approximate value in U.S. dollars (at $5 per British pound).

[20] JNL, diary, June 1881; Richard W. Schwarz, *John Harvey Kellogg, M.D.* (Nashville: Southern Pub. Assn., 1970), p. 175.

[21] JNL, diary, July-September 1882, January, February, August, October 1883; *RH*, Oct. 27, 1885, pp. 667, 668.

[22] JNL, *Rise and Progress*, p. 330; Norma J. Collins, *Heartwarming Stories of Adventist Pioneers: Their Works Do Follow Them* (Hagerstown, Md.: Review and Herald Pub. Assn., 2007), p. 182.

[23] JNL, diary, November-December 1881.

[24] *RH,* Nov. 29, 1881, p. 352; *RH,* Dec. 13, 1881, p. 376; *RH,* Dec. 20, 1881, pp. 392, 393, 395; *GCB* (1881), pp. 196-208; *RH,* Jan. 3, 1882, pp. 6, 8, 10-12; JNL diary, December 1881.

[25] *RH,* July 15, 1920, p. 8; *NPUG,* May 9, 1933, p. 4.

[26] *RH,* Jan. 3, 1882, p. 9; *ST,* Jan. 12, 1882, p. 24; *AUG,* Sept. 25, 1940, p. 6; *RH,* Oct. 31, 1940, p. 23; Hagstotz, *British Isles*, p. 49.

[27] JNL, diary, January 1882.

[28] Although the terms "European General Conference" (1901-1903) and "General European Conference" (1904-1907) did not get officially adopted until two decades later, officials and many ministers in the late nineteenth century sometimes used those terms to refer to these general European gatherings.

[29] *RH,* Apr. 25, 1882, p. 267; *RH,* Oct. 10, 1882, pp. 632, 633; *RH,* July 18, 1882, pp. 456, 457.

[30] *RH,* Oct. 17, 1882, pp. 651, 652; *ST,* Oct. 19, 1882, p. 464.

[31] *ST,* Oct. 19, 1882, p. 464; *GCB* (1882), p. 222; *RH,* Dec. 26, 1882, pp. 786, 787; *ST,* Jan. 4, 1883, p. 8.

[32] His yearlong series came to an end in January 1881 with JNL's "Last Day on Shipboard," *YI,* Jan. 12, 1881, p. 7, and "Liverpool," *YI,* Jan. 19, 1881, pp. 9, 10.

[33] JNL, "Ancient Britain," *YI,* Feb. 9, 1881, p. 21; Feb. 23, 1881, p. 29; Mar. 16, 1881, p. 42; Mar. 30, 1881, pp. 49, 50; Apr. 20, 1881, pp. 61, 62; May 4, 1881, pp. 69, 70; May 25, 1881, p. 82; June 15, 1881, p. 94; July 6, 1881, p. 105; July 20, 1881, p. 114; Aug. 17, 1881, p. 130; Aug. 31, 1881, p. 138; Sept. 21, 1881, p. 150. While it is clear that Loughborough did extensive research to prepare the articles, it is equally obvious that he drew largely from sources that favored Celtic Christianity over Roman Catholicism and Anglo-Saxon culture over Norman customs. Given his SDA background and the fact that his own ancestors were Irish and possibly Celts, his innate bias is understandable.

[34] JNL's series on Medieval Britain appears in *YI,* Oct. 5, 1881, p. 162; Nov. 2, 1881, p. 178; Nov. 30, 1881, p. 194; Dec. 14, 1881, p. 202; Dec. 28, 1881, p. 210; Jan. 11, 1882, p. 6; Feb. 1, 1882, p. 18; Apr. 19, 1882, p. 62; May 3, 1882, p. 70; May 17, 1882, p. 78; June 7, 1882, p. 90; June 21, 1882, p. 98; and Aug. 16, 1882, p. 130.

[35] JNL, "The Two Witnesses," *RH,* Apr. 4, 1882, pp. 210, 211; Apr. 11, 1882, pp. 225, 226; and Apr. 18, 1882, pp. 242, 243. For example, the article repeatedly misspells Rousseau ("Rosseau") and falsely refers to him as "the apostle of the French Revolution" (Rousseau died in 1778). Loughborough's statistics are grossly exaggerated. He declares that 50,000 "pious Huguenots" died in the St. Bartholomew's Day Massacre in 1572 (the number probably did not exceed 3,000 in Paris and 10,000-15,000 throughout France); that 800,000 Huguenots fled France under Louis XIV's persecution (historians estimate the number at closer to 200,000); and that 1,022,351 people lost their lives during the French Revolution (the number probably did not exceed 40,000). His main source for the French Revolution is Louis Thiers, who focuses primarily on the radical elements during the revolution and highlights the bloodshed they caused rather than the restraint other individuals exerted.

[36] *ST,* Jan. 6, 1881, pp. 2, 3; Jan. 20, 1881, pp. 26, 27; and Feb. 3, 1881, p. 50.

[37] JNL, "Personality of the Devil," *ST,* Mar. 3, 1881, pp. 98, 99; Mar. 10, 1881, pp. 110, 111; Mar. 17, 1881, pp. 122, 123.

[38] JNL, "The Gospel Hope," *ST,* Oct. 13, 1881, pp. 458, 459; Oct. 27, 1881, pp. 470, 471; Nov. 3, 1881, pp. 482, 483. The series was then published as an 80-page pamphlet entitled "Hope of the Gospel," which sold for a dime. See *RH,* May 23, 1882, p. 335.

[39] JNL, "Is Sin Eternal?" *ST*, Mar. 24, 1881, pp. 134, 135; May 12, 1881, pp. 208, 209; June 2, 1881, pp. 242, 243; June 9, 1881, pp. 254, 255; June 16, 1881, p. 266; June 23, 1881, pp. 278, 279; June 30, 1881, pp. 290, 291; July 14, 1881, p. 302; July 21, 1881, p. 314; July 28, 1881, pp. 326, 327; Aug. 4, 1881, pp. 338, 339; Aug. 11, 1881, p. 350; Aug. 18, 1881, pp. 362, 363; Aug. 25, 1881, pp. 374, 375; Sept. 1, 1881, p. 386.

[40] These articles, although topically unified, appeared under various titles in *ST:* Nov. 10, 1881, pp. 494, 495; Nov. 17, 1881, pp. 505, 506; Nov. 24, 1881, pp. 518, 519; May 25, 1882, pp. 230, 231; June 8, 1882, pp. 554, 555; June 22, 1882, pp. 278, 279; June 29, 1882, pp. 290, 291; July 13, 1882, pp. 302, 303; July 20, 1882, p. 314; July 27, 1882, pp. 326, 327; 3 Aug. 3, 1882, pp. 338, 339; Aug. 10, 1882, p. 350; Aug. 17, 1882, p. 362; Aug. 24, 1882, pp. 374, 375; and June 14, 1883, p. 272.

[41] JNL, diary, January 1881-October 1883; JNL to Mary White, Jan. 30, 1881, m. 52, CAR; *ST*, Mar. 17, 1881, p. 132; JNL to WCW, Mar. 13, 1882, m. 52, CAR; JNL, quoted in Mary Colby Monteith, "California's First Tent Campaign," *RH,* Feb. 28, 1980, p. 10.

[42] Woodrow Whidden, *E. J. Waggoner: From the Physician of Good News to the Agent of Division* (Hagerstown, Md.: Review and Herald Pub. Assn., 2008), p. 110. In fact, with no footnote citation, Whidden states that "the earlier failures of J. N. Andrews and J. N. Loughborough in Europe, made evident the necessity for reform" (at the 1901 GC session).

[43] JNL to JSW, Feb. 3, 1881, m. 52, CAR.

[44] JNL, *Rise and Progress*, pp. 332, 335, 336; Hagstotz, *British Isles*, pp. 48-50.

[45] *RH,* May 1, 1883, p. 4.

[46] *RH,* Nov. 27, 1883, p. 741.

[47] *RH,* Aug. 4, 1885, pp. 490, 491.

[48] *RH,* May 17, 1887, p. 315.

[49] Ellen G. White, in George Knight, *Historical Sketches of the Foreign Missions of the Seventh-day Adventists* (Berrien Springs, Mich.: Andrews University Press, 2005), pp. 162-166; EGW to European Workers, Aug. 6, 1887, DF 4003-a-1, CAR; EGW to S. N. Haskell, Sept. 1, 1887, DF 4003-a-1, CAR.

Chapter XIII

A WIDE-RANGING WORK ACROSS AMERICA (1883-1888)

"[I] humbly seek God with confession and true contrition of heart. . . . [I want] a love for perishing souls . . . and a determination to work as never before for the advancement of the cause of truth. . . . Every man, woman, and child among us . . . can find some place in which to work for the advancement of the message."[1]

Shortly after the Loughboroughs returned to the United States from England, John participated in the 1883 General Conference session at Battle Creek, which he called "the best meeting of the kind I have ever attended." Reflecting on it afterward, he wrote the words quoted above in the *Review* as a testimony of his desire to preach the Adventist message with renewed zeal wherever church leaders asked him to go. Expecting to remain near church headquarters, however, John purchased the eastern half of Lot 580 in Oak Hill Cemetery (where his first wife, Mary, lay) so that five more family members could be buried there in due time.[2]

Instead, the GC Committee asked the Loughboroughs to go to New York, which still had not completely recovered from the spiritual and financial devastation caused by the defection of Conference president Nathan Fuller a decade earlier. While Loughborough and Kinne, living out of their suitcases, held revival meetings in the scattered churches, Annie and Mary, staying with the Harmon family in Newfane, sold religious publications. In addition to preaching "words of faith, hope, and love," John held quarterly meetings (Communion services) and helped establish inner-city missions in Auburn, Syracuse, Buffalo, Cortland, and New York City.[3]

Early in 1884, however, church leaders transferred the family to the Midwest, and John spent the winter perambulating among the churches in central and northern Michigan, where he held 20 revival meetings. For the first time in his ministry Loughborough began sharing his recollections regarding "the dealings of God with his people in the past . . . with the manifestation of the gift of prophecy among us." It would become the dominant theme of his preaching: God's providential leading in the rise and progress of the Adventist message from the Millerite movement to the present. His audiences (now composed of second-generation Adventists) found his personal experiences fascinating while his stories about Ellen White's visions "added evidence of [her] divine authority." One listener opined, "And how any one who has been troubled with doubts in the past could sit under the testimony borne and not have those doubts removed, is a mystery to me."[4] Instilling confidence in the veracity and divine origin of the Adventist message became one of Loughborough's primary goals. To that end, he encouraged members to subscribe to the *Review, Signs,* and *Youth's Instructor.* Realizing that as Adventists grew more prosperous, their children tended to "[drift] away into the world," John devoted more attention to such youth. Patting a boy or girl on the head, he would inquire, "Well, my boy [or girl], how are you getting along in the Christian life?"[5]

Once spring arrived in the Midwest, however, denominational officials asked Loughborough to return to California and share his successful revivalist approach with the rapidly growing churches on the West Coast. So John and Annie said goodbye to Mary (at Battle Creek College) and their many friends in Michigan. Once back in Oakland, John was appointed to the conference committee—which meant that he could now sign his own ministerial credentials.[6]

Without an administrative position, Loughborough was free to engage in evangelistic and revival meetings. Along with his old friends J. H. Waggoner, Ellen White, and her son Willie, the team chose Oakland for their first preaching effort. Public interest ran high, in part because of the recent enforcement of Sunday blue laws that had led to the arrest of more than 1,600 citizens in 1882 and 1883 (including Jews, Chinese immigrants, and Adventists). The authorities had jailed Waggoner, editor of the *Signs*, and closed Pacific Press. But Adventist leadership in the repeal of the state's blue laws brought the church favorable publicity.[7]

Rejoicing at the progress he saw all around him, Loughborough exclaimed, "The march of truth is on the scale of greatly accelerated motion." Since he had left six years before, the Oakland church had tripled in size; the Rural Health Retreat at St. Helena had doubled its capacity; and Healdsburg College had added new buildings to accommodate a growing student body. The conference also planned to publish a new health journal for the Pacific Coast, a project in which John would play a leading role. But aside from his few committee assignments, Loughborough (as W. C. White put it) "[is] not to be tied to one place, . . . but to help the churches." (The conference also gave Delmer, now 20, a colporteur's license, which meant that he was free to sell Adventist literature wherever he wished.)[8]

So J. N. Loughborough created a new role for himself: for the next four years he would be a minister without portfolio, free to hold evangelistic meetings wherever he wished and to visit old friends among the scattered churches at which he held revival services. Teaming up with old partners such as William Ings, M. C. Israel, and J. O. Corliss—and new ones such as J. G. Smith and N. C. McClure—John created his own schedule, mapped out his own travel routes, and preached and baptized to his heart's content. An avid PR man, wherever he went he promoted inner-city missions, the new *American Sentinel* and *Sunshine Magazine*, urban Bible readings, and the Sabbath school program. His reports testify that the interlude "was a heavenly season."[9]

While John lived out of a suitcase, boarding with church members, Annie desired a more permanent home. After living in several places, the Loughboroughs agreed to house-sit for Ellen and W. C. White during their three-year mission tour of Europe (1885-1887). In June of 1886, knowing that they would not return to the U.S. for at least another year, Willie offered to sell their Oakland home to the Loughboroughs, including land and fixtures (but not the furniture, which Ellen wanted to keep), for its original cost of $2,305. He informed John that when they returned to California, he and his mother would probably relocate to the Healdsburg area.[10]

Unlike his wife, John enjoyed being on the road, participating in what he called "the great second advent *movement*." He loved the smell of sawdust and canvass at camp meetings—and by the 1880s the California Conference hosted five of them every year. There he joined preachers such as

J. H. Waggoner and his son Ellet, William Ings, Sydney Brownsberger, J. O. Corliss, and, of course, Ellen White and her son Willie for approximately 10 days of meetings that usually began at 5:30 a.m. and sometimes continued past midnight. Since the Eureka campground was situated in an alder grove in sight of the Pacific Ocean, attendees heard the waves crashing on the shore. At Santa Ana, they pitched their tents beneath the shade of the fragrant pepper trees. Other camp meetings convened at Oakland, Fresno, and Woodland.[11]

Church officials in the Upper Columbia Conference (Oregon, Washington, and Idaho) also invited Elder Loughborough to be a featured speaker at the camp meetings at Walla Walla, Washington, and Portland, Oregon (1884) and at Milton, Oregon (1885).[12] A decade later, J. N. Loughborough stirred up a tempest in a teapot when he asserted that he had seen Ellen White receive her last open (daytime) vision at the 1884 Portland camp meeting. Based on information provided by W. C. White in Australia, however, Dr. Merritt Kellogg claimed that Mrs. White's last vision had occurred in 1879. But Ellen herself recalled that she might have received a nighttime dream, not a vision, at Portland.[13] If Loughborough was confused in this matter, it would not be the last time his recollections did not synchronize with everyone else's memories.

PRESIDENT OF THE UPPER COLUMBIA CONFERENCE

Fortunately, his friends in the Northwest did not hold his lapses of memory against him. Instead, at the Walla Walla constituency meeting in June 1884, delegates elected him president of the Upper Columbia Conference. Knowing that "the brethren in California" would be terribly disappointed if he accepted, he sent his name back to the nominating committee. The second time, the motion carried unanimously, and delegates rose to their feet to show their support for him. In response, Loughborough promised to give "strong reinforcement" to the work in the Northwest.[14]

Fulfilling his pledge proved both rewarding and discouraging. Conference presidents spent a lot of time traveling on coaches, trains, and boats, but John often saved the church money by walking to his destination. On one occasion he hiked 25 miles to keep an appointment. Even if it took him most of the day, he got lots of exercise and enjoyed the scenery. Less pleasant, however, were the occasions when he had to fire church employees for immoral behavior—as happened at the East Portland camp meeting in 1884 when the discipline committee asked him to expel two ministers. Another time he had to release a canvasser for laziness. When faced with such unpleasant situations, Loughborough quipped that he had "to lasso the elephant." At Salem and Scio, Oregon (two trouble spots), he and C. L. Boyd went door to door asking members to fill out forms describing their spiritual condition. Shortly thereafter, President Loughborough reported that "the cloud of discouragement that has hung over the cause . . . seems to be lifting. . . . It [the spirit of unity] is in such marked contrast with the state of things that existed one year ago that we can only say, 'What hath God wrought.'"[15]

As he traveled around his three-state district, John saw signs that the cause of Adventism was "fermenting" (an odd choice of words for a teetotaler, it meant changing or growing). "Our cause is an aggressive one," he boasted. Then, paraphrasing Ben Franklin, he added, "The Lord helps those who try to help themselves." He saw particular evidence of "fermentation" in the growing number of baptisms and in the aggressive efforts of the T&M societies to spread Adventist literature.[16]

When Loughborough learned that Adventists in Milton, Oregon, had begun sending their Sabbath school offerings to foreign missions (rather than buying supplies with them), he recommended the practice to C. H. Jones, director of the GC Sabbath School Association. Remembering that in 1883 Ellen White had suggested that the Sabbath school offering become "a thank offering to the mission work," Loughborough spearheaded a campaign to raise $700 for the new Australian Mission in 1885. Members should pay for supplies out of their own pockets, he suggested, for they were not "'the most needy field.'"[17]

Another innovation Loughborough supported was the holding of Biblical Institutes similar to those that he, the Whites, and Uriah Smith had sponsored in Oakland. Willie White assured John that such institutes would "give impetus to the work in that [Upper Columbia] Conference" and would "work up the spirit of missionary labor." He added, "I do not think that we shall ever be able to arouse our people to the importance of Bible study, without holding institutes of this kind." During the summer of 1885, Biblical Institutes convened at the Upper Columbia and the North Pacific conference camp meetings. While church officials required ministers, licentiates, Bible workers, and colporteurs to attend, they also encouraged regular church members to come. With the cooperation of the denomination's leading theologians, Loughborough would convene Bible Institutes across the United States in the 1880s and 1890s.[18]

W. C. White also gave enthusiastic support to two other projects in which John would invest much time. In the spring of 1885 Willie encouraged John to bring his growing collection of "Spiritual Songs" (gospel melodies) to the Pacific Press Publishing Company board (which White chaired) for publication as an Adventist songbook. In addition, he backed the idea of starting a new paper called *The Pacific Health Journal and Temperance Advocate* (printed at the Rural Health Retreat in St. Helena), and wanted John to promote that endeavor. In time Loughborough would become an editor of the publication.[19]

RURAL HEALTH RETREAT AND *PACIFIC HEALTH JOURNAL*

In fact, after the Rural Health Retreat board of trustees chose John as their president and his wife Annie as auditor in 1885, their responsibilities regarding the sanitarium and its health journal mushroomed. Not only did it fall on John's lot to adjudicate personal rivalries among the staff and to keep the patients happy, but it also seemed that everyone looked to him to make decisions concerning the health retreat's daily operation. As his "laboring days" grew longer, John concluded that getting more exercise and taking regular hydrotherapy treatments would be beneficial. Meanwhile Annie, already busy caring for a "family" of 13 persons (four Loughboroughs and nine boarders), told Mary White that she felt "buried" by her financial duties at the health retreat. With the help of a German girl, Annie soon had everything running smoothly at home. After spending months straightening out the financial records at the office, she looked forward to brighter days ahead in 1886.[20]

Thanks largely to John and Annie's efforts the Rural Health Retreat did see better days the next year. Ever the promoter, John knew that for the sanitarium to prosper, the public must learn about its location, services, and health benefits. In June 1885 the staff launched the *Pacific Health Journal and Temperance Advocate* (*PHJ*), a 24-page bimonthly journal. In addition to health-related articles, it carried advertisements bragging about the health retreat's outdoor setting: its natural spring, stunning landscape, colorful flower beds, and broad piazza. Indoors patients could enjoy wholesome food in a spacious dining room; relax in the elegant parlor; wash away their aches with a variety of baths (Galvanic, Faradic Electricity, hot, cold, and tepid); use its exercise equipment that strengthened lungs, muscles, vital organs, and chest. They asserted that following a variety of healthful diets guaranteed that "most invalids . . . rapidly recover." The institution had a competent director (Loughborough), two experienced physicians (Drs. J. S. Gibbs and W. P. Burke), and two female attendants—and none of them were "cranky vegetarians and grahamites [followers of Sylvester Graham's ascetic dietary reform]." Therefore, the ad boasted that the Rural Health Retreat's "natural advantages surpass those of any other health resort."[21]

Although Dr. John Harvey Kellogg found such rhetoric "in bad taste" and feared it would give the medical societies the impression that the Rural Health Retreat was "a quackish institution," the ads attracted so many new patients that within months after opening the tiny institution had 76 patients and could hold no more. When two wealthy patrons loaned the health retreat $30,000, the board voted to erect a three-story main building, to build a two-story laundry, and to enlarge the hydrotherapy rooms. In addition to supervising the building projects, Loughborough's overexertion in planting 100 trees (beechnut, almond, lemon, orange, fig, butternut, and gum) left him with a badly bruised leg and a pinched sciatic nerve that put him on crutches for two weeks. Thanks to Annie's treatments, however, he soon recovered. Likewise, because of her competent financial management, John could brag that the Rural Health Retreat, which in 1885 had been in "a precarious condition," was now "prospering."[22]

Indeed it was. That summer Annie told the board that income had exceeded expenses by about $3,500 and that the health retreat had a net value of almost $15,000. Delighted with John and Annie's efforts, the board reelected them as director and auditor respectively. Yet in some respects, Ellen White felt that such prosperity had come at too high a price. The staff had cut corners by hiring untrained girls, many of them lazy or sick, rather than employing competent helpers. Get rid of them, she told Loughborough, and hire strong Swedish girls who, even if they spoke little English, worked harder for the low wages the sanitarium paid.[23]

Unfortunately, by the spring of 1887 the Rural Health Retreat's labor problems had grown more acute. Dr. Burke (whom Ellen called a "troublemaker") clashed with Dr. Gibbs and with the board. He blamed Gibbs for not consulting him and the board for not supporting him. But when he received a letter of rebuke from Mrs. White, Burke packed his bags and left to establish a private practice in St. Helena—a move that Ellen and Willie applauded as "for the best." Indeed, shortly after Burke's departure, the number of patients at the health retreat rose sharply. Nonetheless, Loughborough blamed himself for not being able to negotiate a truce. "I pity him, and have prayed much for him," he wrote Ellen White. "[I] have tried to handle his case tenderly."[24]

Loughborough soon had good reason to pity Dr. Gibbs as well. If the doctor's amiable nature and cooperative attitude made him the darling of the board, such traits also attracted undue attention from the opposite sex. Furthermore, his "progressive" views regarding the use of certain medications clashed with Dr. Maxson's reliance on natural remedies. When the board met in January of 1888, Gibbs read a "testimony of confession" acknowledging his "imprudence and folly in his attention to girls and women" and then promptly resigned. The following day, Dr. Maxson and his wife also tendered their resignations. To make matters worse, by the end of the month the board had to fire Dr. Rice for mismanagement—although he vowed to fight his termination in the courts. "He [has] inherited some of the 'cast iron' that is in his makeup from some of his immediate ancestors," John quipped. "May the good Lord give us wisdom [as to] what to do, and how to go."[25]

Despite the unfortunate situation, the health retreat continued to succeed. At its annual meeting in 1887, the board reported a net gain of almost $5,000 over 1886. The sanitarium—described as a "large and flourishing" institution—was now valued at nearly $21,400. By the spring of 1888 the value of stock sold had doubled from $50,000 to more than $100,000. During its first four years approximately 1,000 patients had sought healing there, and the *Signs* boasted that "the greater number . . . have gone away cured." In the fall of 1888 the board drew up an ambitious $20,000 expansion plan to build a chapel and several cottages. Seeking competent nurses, Dr. Stewart decided to hold a training school and advertised for "the best girls" to apply.[26]

As chairman of the Rural Health Retreat board, J. N. Loughborough got a room of his own at the sanitarium. When his life as an evangelist and administrator grew too stressful, he found rest, relaxing massages and baths, and delicious food there. It is possible that the healthful diet at the sanitarium convinced him in 1886 to abandon meat altogether, even while traveling. For the rest of his life Loughborough followed a strict vegetarian regimen. Henceforth, when aboard a ship he asked the stewards for fruit, vegetables, and grains, and they readily complied (doubtless glad that an eccentric passenger's diet saved them money).[27]

HEALDSBURG COLLEGE

About the same time that J. N. Loughborough was elected to serve on the board of the Rural Health Retreat, he was also elected to the board of Healdsburg College, an Adventist institution which by 1909 was located near Angwin, California. Although it bore the title of "college," in the 1880s the teachers taught primarily high school pupils. Indeed, in 1886 the campus had only five classrooms devoted to college-level instruction. Instead of receiving sabbaticals to do research, the school expected its faculty to spend each summer recruiting new students and to supervise the work-study program (and teach five or six classes each) during the school term itself. If this made some teachers unhappy, one can imagine how the students felt when the board shortened their vacations and scheduled required religion classes at the end of the year to keep them from leaving early. But Healdsburg's financial statements show that the college needed every student it could get. In 1883 the treasurer had only $11.30 on hand, and a year later he had $18.47. In short, Healdsburg College was tuition-driven and operated on a shoestring budget.[28]

To save money, the board voted to follow the "boarding or *house system*" of lodging students in the homes of nearby faculty and church members. To keep costs to a minimum, its members required students to work part of their way through school by laboring in campus industries such as gardening, laundering, catalog printing, and tent manufacturing. On the other hand, to improve science instruction, the seven directors voted to spend $300-$500 (an enormous sum when the campus' net worth stood at $22,600 in 1888) on "philosophical apparatus" (people then referred to science as "natural philosophy").[29]

As he did with every institution on whose board he sat, Loughborough took a proprietary interest in the teachers, students, and programs at

Healdsburg College. He dropped by for student recitations and regularly attended graduation exercises. Students enjoyed hearing him speak, because, unlike other Adventist ministers, he did not stand at the pulpit and read his notes. Instead, he told stories and personal experiences, dashing from one side of the rostrum to the other. Waving his arms and raising his voice, the "little preacher" could easily be heard by every listener in the hall. One of his favorite icebreakers was to ask a student how he or she had become a Seventh-day Adventist. Those who credited him with influencing their decision found their names recorded in a "book of converts" that Loughborough kept.[30]

But if students' adulation boosted Loughborough's ego, Ellen White's letters humbled him. While in Europe she wrote him several lengthy testimonies. In 1885, after she had admonished him for his tendency "to bear down hard on those . . . in the wrong," he wrote to assure her that "I think I have made some advancement towards the right since." "I shall seek God's grace that I may deal tenderly while trying to reclaim the erring."[31]

A circular letter to J. H. Waggoner, E. J. Waggoner, A. T. Jones, and Loughborough in April 1886 urged them to show greater sensitivity toward E. P. Daniels, a minister who had predicted Christ's second coming in five years and who liked to make money on the side giving elocution and music lessons. Describing him as "a man of not the deepest judgment," she nonetheless believed that he needed wise counselors rather than harsh critics. "God works in and through frail instruments," she said, reminding them that they themselves needed "to study more thoroughly in the school of Christ and be sure that self and personal feelings do not mingle with your judgment of the work of God." She advised them not to prevent Daniels from preaching, despite his eccentricities.[32]

While in Christiana, Norway, Ellen expressed concern for John's spiritual life: "I feel deeply, more than I can express for you, who have grown gray in the work, and in the cause of God. The joy, the peace, the perfect trust in Jesus you ought to have, and never rest until you do have it. Self, let it be hid behind Jesus, for you need more spiritual discernment, or you will fall into Satan's deceptive snares. Get Christ in your own soul, drink of the living fountain day by day. Let the voice be softened, less sharp and rasping. Let the heart be melted with the love of Jesus, and you will melt your way. Jesus will be far more to you than he is now, if you will let him into your heart. Come lower, lower, my brother, at the foot of the cross if you would have distinct views of the love of Christ, and His willingness to bless you."[33]

Responding to her July 6 testimony (and a subsequent one on August 12, 1886), John thanked Mrs. White for "all the wholesome words of reproof and counsel and good advice" she had given him. "It saved us, humbled us, and helped us," he exclaimed. He promised, "I am earnestly seeking the Lord that he may give me a more full sense of my condition and need" so that he could "bear fruit to the glory of God." Then he added: "I accept all your words of counsel . . . I want so much of the Spirit of Jesus in my heart . . . I want to be nearer to God." One indication of the genuineness of Loughborough's confession is the fact that he actually read White's rebuke before hundreds of camp meeting attendees.[34]

That J. N. Loughborough took Mrs. White's counsel to heart and acted upon it seems evident when one reads his letter to her in January 1887. "I have shared some rich blessings from God in the last few months," he assures her, "and [this] makes me long for more." He had been "putting away the rough boisterous manner and talking tenderly and with sympathy." If in the past he has "done so much work that was cold and lifeless," he now longs "for the spirit of weeping and tenderness . . . that I may be more fully converted to God. . . . Oh! I want my soul filled with the love of God. . . . I want to get all the spirit of criticism and fault-finding out of my heart . . . to reflect the image of Jesus, my precious Savior, in all I do and say." Apparently, he felt his soul filled with God's love, because two days later he told Ellen that "the Lord is good and his love is infinite like a mighty deep."[35]

ORGANIZER AND ADMINISTRATOR

If White sometimes found Loughborough lacking in spiritual virtues and interpersonal skills, church leaders appreciated his talents for bringing order, efficiency, and progress to the work. One area that benefited from his oversight was the frontier territory of Nevada, populated during the 1880s by miners, ranchers, lumberjacks, and Chinese immigrants. Once convinced, however, its independent-minded citizens became "warm-hearted and enthusiastic" Adventists, "liberal toward the cause." In the fall of 1885

Loughborough partnered with W. A. Colcord, Briggs, and E. R. Jones to hold camp meetings at Carson City and Dayton. For weeks preceding them, colporteurs had canvassed the communities, selling Adventist magazines and books. Consequently, public interest ran so high that in addition to the 50 Adventists in 20 tents in "cotton town," between 400 and 500 citizens poured onto the campgrounds at Carson City—including the state's governor and several attorneys and judges. Insisting that Adventists hold another camp meeting there in 1886, citizens raised $400 to pay expenses. At the end of the week a company of 32 converts were organized. During social meetings at Dayton, "hearty confessions were made, and earnest testimonies borne, accompanied by freely flowing tears." Once again, about 50 Adventists and hundreds of local citizens attended. When the week ended, the latter insisted that the meetings continue for another week, so the Colcords remained behind to follow up the interest. As a result, 24 signed the covenant to keep the Sabbath, and three requested baptism.[36]

Seeking to build up the denomination's presence in the state, Loughborough returned in 1887. He preached in St. Claire, where in spite of the hay harvest hundreds flocked to the evening services, and in Reno, where members had erected a substantial "house of worship." In September approximately 200 Adventists filled the church during a camp meeting that featured special children's Bible classes taught by the dynamic Jessie Waggoner (Ellet J. Waggoner's wife). During these meetings, Nevadans lived up to their reputation for generosity by raising more than $70 for a sick woman's care, $40 for African missions, and $35 for Italy's poor laborers. At the close, ministers baptized nine converts in the Truckee River. The next year, when Ellen White joined Loughborough and others at Reno, she spoke on the subject of temperance for a Decoration Day gathering of hundreds of local citizens. After she had preached for an hour and a half, the women of the WCTU begged her to speak for another hour. Although Adventists disapproved of games such as chess and checkers, at Reno they invented a Bible game. Someone suggested a topic, and participants searched their Bibles for texts about that subject, then people compared their lists. So popular did the activity become that it occupied four meetings. Loughborough concluded that the people of Reno really liked gaming.[37]

Yet Nevada's camp meetings paled beside those held in California. At the 1886 convocation at Woodland 1,000 people, including 700 Adventists, attended services—"by far the largest camp-meeting ever held in this State," Haskell boasted. It required 180 to 190 tents to shelter them from the hot sun. The preaching extravaganza showcased the rhetorical talents of A. T. Jones, E. J. Waggoner, G. W. Colcord, S. N. Haskell, and J. N. Loughborough in 29 discourses. Again attendees proved generous, raising hundreds of dollars for several worthy causes—including $100 for a member whose horse had died on the grounds.[38]

Next to sharing stories about the rise and progress of Adventism at camp meetings, John enjoyed establishing new congregations and holding revival meetings. One new church he founded was located in Selma, a community of big-hearted Nebraska transplants. Eager to host a camp meeting, Adventists there put up nearly 60 tents for more than 300 campers who attended services in the spring of 1887. Desiring to please both man and beast, they created a restaurant on "the mutual benefit plan": a dining tent for people and an alfalfa field where horses could eat to their hearts' content for seven cents a day. After visiting a dozen Adventist churches, John exclaimed, "I am happy to report a spirit of good cheer among our people all along the line."[39]

When his enthusiastic news reached the ears of church leaders, they reversed a quarter-century pattern by deciding to hold the next General Conference session (1887) in Oakland rather than in Battle Creek. As the recently elected president of the California Conference and one of its seven delegates, John served on several committees, including those on religious services, religious liberty, and National Reform (to block Senator Blair's efforts to introduce a Sunday blue law in the U.S. Congress). In addition, delegates sought his advice concerning the establishment of a new health institute at Mount Vernon, Ohio, and building a ship for mission activity in the islands of the Pacific. Since John's sister Minerva Jane Chapman was corresponding secretary of the GC and his niece Winnie Loughborough was secretary of the International Sabbath School Association, the "Loughborough lobby" played a prominent role in the deliberations of that particular GC session.[40]

Certainly no one consulted it more frequently than W. C. White. White loved receiving letters from the Loughboroughs because they included the gossip that he wanted to hear. If his mother's epistles probed individual's faults and spiritual shortcomings, Willie's letters read like the gossip column of a local newspaper. The two men also shared letters that others had passed along (a common practice within high church circles) and asked each other's opinions about the qualifications of church employees. When Willie inquired what he should do regarding several incompetent ministers, John replied, "If they won't do thorough work in ministry, then let them return to farming!"[41]

If White wanted some pet project promoted, he often asked Loughborough to boost it. In the spring of 1888 Willie mailed John 1,200 tiny "missionary boxes" and urged him "to make a strong pull for our missions" at every meeting. He also encouraged Loughborough to share his ideas regarding the training of future administrators. "It seems to me that we are goners if we do not hurry to train someone to be managers and matrons of our boarding houses [or dormitories, a relatively new institution for Adventists]." On the other hand, if Willie wanted a secret kept or a rumor suppressed, he asked John to help him (he once asked him not to spread the word regarding a certain resolution passed by the GC Executive Committee). Indeed, Willie was not above using his friend to manipulate his mother. "It might do no harm for you to tell Mother how they will feel about her not attending the Reno [camp] meeting," he wrote in 1888. "I would be glad if she attended that meeting." John wrote, and Ellen did attend.[42]

As both W. C. White and J. N. Loughborough were now based in California, they often worked together as members of the same councils and committees. Prior to the reorganization of the denomination at the 1901 General Conference session, the Adventist church consisted of a number of "interlocking directorates" with the same men serving on the boards of different institutions. Consequently, the bond between W. C. and John grew during the 1880s as they rubbed shoulders on the California Conference committee, the Pacific Press publishing committee, the boards of the Rural Health Retreat and Healdsburg College, and many others.[43]

Sharing their ideas often resulted in innovative practices within the church. One of them involved the holding of workers' meetings (for ministers, licentiates, missionaries, and canvassers) a week prior to the camp meetings. Another was convening "Ministers' Councils" to discuss everything from E. J. Waggoner's views on the two covenants in Galatians 3 (for nine days) to the wayward course of E. P. Daniels (for three days).[44]

Loughborough felt relieved when in 1888 the California Conference "released [him] from other duties and labors, so that his entire time [could] be devoted to the actual supervision of the ministerial and other work of the Conference, visiting the churches, and attending to the general wants of the cause, and the spread of the truth." Consequently, although delegates reelected him conference president, the resolution released him from any obligation to represent California at the 1888 GC session in Minneapolis. Instead, the delegates chose S. N. Haskell, A. T. Jones, E. J. Waggoner, W. C. White, C. H. Jones, and M. J. Church to represent the state. Therefore, John would not be present at one of the most contentious gatherings in Adventist history.[45]

LOUGHBOROUGH'S WRITINGS AND DIARY

The above resolution not only gave President Loughborough freedom to visit local churches, but also provided him with more time to write. Since his sister Minerva Chapman and niece Winnie Loughborough were co-editors of the *Youth's Instructor*, they welcomed John's articles. He obliged them by sharing lessons he had learned by observing a Dominick hen in his chicken yard.[46]

But since John's nephew E. C. Loughborough worked at the Review and Herald, which published nearly all of John's books, he felt an obligation to write for the *Review* as well. While most of his contributions took the form of reports on his work for the church, between 1885 and 1888 he sent the *Review* articles about prophecy, God's thrones, the new *American Sentinel Magazine*, and Israel's 430-year sojourn in Egypt.[47]

To keep his friends on the West Coast happy, President Loughborough wrote for the *Signs* as well. "The Lord's House and Our Own Houses" asked readers if they took as good care of their church buildings as they did of their private homes. "Reverence" suggested that ministers kneel in prayer before they stand in the pulpit. In "Revelation vs. Imagination," John contrasted the "sensual appetites" of the Enlightenment philosophes with the self-denying lives of God's people.[48] Loughborough also penned two short book reviews. He called Uriah Smith's *Thoughts on Daniel and the Revelation* a magnum opus on Bible prophecy, "the most interesting work I have ever read." He found volume four of Ellen White's *Spirit of Prophecy, The Great Controversy,* "so deeply interesting, and profitable" that he was "exceedingly desirous to see it extensively circulated."[49] In the years ahead, Loughborough would play a significant role as the denomination's leading promoter of books in Adventist publications.

He also sent a few manuscripts to the short-lived periodical *The Gospel Sickle*. In the main they consisted of recycled articles from the *Review* and *Signs* (such as "Hope of the Gospel" and the series on "The Saints' Inheritance"). "The Purchased Possession," however, creatively answers the question Who owns the earth? God created it; humans sinned and lost it to Satan; but Christ's death at Calvary redeemed it and signified that the devil's lease is about to expire at the Second Advent.[50]

The lion's share of John's time, however, he devoted to the *Pacific Health Journal*, which he edited. Between 1886 and 1888 he penned more than 35 articles for it. Incorporating material from his *Hand Book of Health* (1868) and Dr. John Harvey Kellogg's *Home Handbook* (1880), Loughborough's articles focus on the wonders of the human body, blood circulation, the musculature and nervous systems, proper diet and nutrition, and ways to avoid disease.[51]

Curiously, they also show that in the 1880s J. N. Loughborough (like most other Adventists) still remained wedded to vitalism. "The Physical Man" is replete with phrases such as "vitality," "vital operations," "vital properties," and "vital economy." According to vitalists, "vital power" is "placed in the human body, at its birth, which will enable the body, under favorable circumstances, to live to a certain age." John warned readers "to manifest the greatest care" not to "overtax" their energies, waste their "life force," and thus shorten their days.[52] Loughborough also sprinkles his prose with phrenological terminology. In "Active Brain and Health" he explains that "the surface of the brain is arranged in various winding elevations, which constitute the phrenological organs of the prevailing system of mental philosophy of the present day." His descriptions of the brain's hemispheres, the cerebellum, the arachnoid membrane, and the mental powers of the mind rely on phrenological sources a generation old.[53]

Three other articles of a more pragmatic nature reflect Loughborough's personal experiences in England and the U.S. "Liquor Sellers' Asylum," which links TB with alcoholism, he based on his visits with dying alcoholics in Southampton. "Defective Drainage," which warns that poor barnyard drainage causes cholera, reflects the horrible conditions he witnessed in Basel. In "Seasickness" (a subject on which John was an expert), while disagreeing with the German pastor who said, "All you need to do is shust to keep your mind off the subject," John recommends instead getting lots of rest and consuming lemons and oranges "to cleanse the stomach" two or three days before sailing. Those suffering from *mal de mer* should avoid smokers, consume hot water, and lie on their backs until it passes.[54]

John's diary reveals, however, that in addition to his steady stream of articles for Adventist periodicals, he also found time to write for the secular press. A railroad buff since childhood, John penned an article for the *Railroad Gazeteer* in the summer of 1888. He also sent occasional letters to the San Francisco *Chronicle* reacting to news reports that had caught his interest (an avid "scrapper," he pasted the clippings in his scrapbooks). As we have seen, he was a "joiner": he attended the meetings of the temperance, vegetarian, shorthand, antialcohol, and antivaccination societies to which he belonged. Among the Cornhuskers at the Selma, California, camp meeting in 1887, he even organized a new "Rivulet" society.

But when the pressures of life built up, John also knew how to rest and recreate. One of his perks as president of the Rural Health Retreat board (besides a room of his own) was the massages and baths that relaxed him after exhausting days on the road. When at home, he and Annie loved to go "trading" (shopping), take buggy rides, and sing hymns together. For physical exercise he chopped wood, weeded the flower garden, harvested vegetables, and trimmed the yard. When he could get away, he loved hiking Bandy Canyon, walking up Howell Mountain, and exploring caves (his tiny frame gave him a distinct advantage). Every July 4 he and Annie took in a parade or attended a carnival in Oakland. Then every December 25 they attended "Christmas exercises" in St. Helena. When the budget permitted, they dined at one of Oakland's restaurants. John's use of double X's inside ellipses with the French word *bon* ("good") testifies that their love for each other intensified as they grew older.

Love was also in the air for the Loughborough children. In December 1887 John had the privilege of marrying his daughter Mary, now 26, to John J. Ireland, a recent convert and conference auditor. As Ireland chose Delmer, now 23, as best man, and Maria Steward, the woman Delmer could hardly keep his eyes off and whom Delmer would shortly marry, as maid of honor. When the Irelands moved to Healdsburg, they kept a bedroom for Loughborough (although his diary shows he paid them for their hospitality). As his duties took him farther afield in the late 1880s and 1890s, J. N. Loughborough would come to appreciate this quiet retreat.[55]

---

[1] JNL, *RH,* Jan. 8, 1884, p. 26.

[2] *Ibid.*; Oak Hill Cemetery Right of Burial, Oct. 26, 1883, ASC m. L92, CAR. Those five would probably be John's mother, Minerva; his wife Annie; his son, Delmer; his daughter Mary; and himself.

[3] *RH,* Mar. 4, 1884, p. 156; JNL, diary, December 1883; *PTB*, May 1884, p. 14; *RH*, Jan. 1, 1884, p. 15.; *RH,* Mar. 18, 1884, p. 189. Inner-city missions, a pet project of Dr. John Harvey Kellogg's, offered free food, cheap lodging, Adventist literature, jobs, laundry service, counseling, and other amenities to poverty-stricken citizens in many American cities and towns from the 1880s through the 1910s.

[4] *RH,* Jan. 22, 1884, p. 63; *RH*, Mar. 18, 1884, p. 189.

[5] *ST*, Mar. 27, 1884, p. 203; *PTB*, June 1884, p. 29; *ST*, Mar. 19, 1885, pp. 184, 185; *RH,* Oct. 4, 1928, p. 19.

[6] *RH,* Mar. 11, 1884, p. 176; JNL's ministerial credentials, DF 230, CAR.

[7] *ST*, Apr. 17, 1884, p. 256; *RH*, Apr. 1, 1884, p. 224; *RH,* May 27, 1884, pp. 349, 350; D. Morgan, *Adventism and the American Republic*, p. 41.

[8] *RH,* May 27, 1884, pp. 349, 350; *ST*, Oct. 9, 1884, pp. 597, 600-602; *ST*, Oct. 16, 1884, pp. 618, 619. Almost immediately local denominational leaders appointed Loughborough to the committees on nominations, credentials, fields of labor, and resolutions, and, of course, the executive committee for the California Conference.

[9] *ST*, Oct. 16, 1884, p. 624; Oct. 30, 1884, p. 650; Nov. 6, 1884, p. 667; Jan. 1, 1885, pp. 10, 11; May 7, 1885, pp. 282, 283; Oct. 8, 1885, pp. 598, 599, 602, 603; Nov. 12, 1885, p. 683; Nov. 26, 1885, pp. 715, 720; Dec. 3, 1885, p. 731; Feb. 11, 1886, p. 95; Mar. 25, 1886, p. 186; June 10, 1886, p. 342; June 24, 1886, p. 378; July 15, 1886, p. 425.

[10] WCW to JNL, Apr. 19, 1886; WCW to JNL, June 4, 1886; WCW to JNL, June 7, 1886; WCW to JNL, Aug. 23, 1886, WCW Letter Books, CAR. However, five months later, desperate for ready cash to pay off his debts, W. C. White doubled the asking price, requesting $4,500 for the house. See WCW to JNL, Nov. 30, 1886, WCW Letter Books, CAR.

[11] *ST*, Aug. 21, 1884, p. 512; *ST*, July 16, 1885, p. 431; E. R. Jones, *RH*, Sept. 1, 1885, p. 557; *ST*, Oct. 29, 1885, p. 656; *RH*, Nov. 10, 1885, p. 700; *ST*, Aug. 26, 1886, p. 528; *RH*, Sept. 7, 1886, p. 572; *ST*, Feb. 25, 1886, p. 128.

[12] *ST*, Apr. 3, 1884, p. 224; *ST*, Apr. 17, 1884, p. 254; *ST*, Apr. 23, 1885, p. 271; *ST*, May 14, 1885, p. 303.

[13] *GCB*, 1893, pp. 19, 20; Doug R. Johnson, *Adventism on the Northwestern Frontier* (Berrien Springs, Mich.: Oronoko Books, 1996), p. 65; M. G. Kellogg to J. H. Kellogg, June 3, 1906, cited by Ellen G. White Estate, *A Critique*, p. 85; Arthur L. White, *Ellen G. White: The Lonely Years* (Hagerstown, Md.: Review and Herald Pub. Assn., 1984), vol. 3, pp. 255, 256.

[14] *ST*, June 26, 1884, p. 400; *ST*, July 3, 1884, pp. 408, 410.

[15] JNL to WCW, July 2, 1884, m. 52, CAR; *ST*, July 17, 1884, pp. 426, 427; JNL to WCW, July 22, 1884, m. 52, CAR; *ST*, July 31, 1884, p. 459; JNL, quoted in Johnson, *Adventism on the Northwestern Frontier*, pp. 67, 68. It is worth noting that while most

of Ellen White's letters to JNL were testimonies focusing on his spiritual shortcomings and those of James White dealt primarily with church business, W. C. White's are full of personal news concerning individuals' actions and misbehavior. Repeatedly, Willie states: "We are always glad to hear from you because you have a faculty of telling us those things which we want to know." In short, both men were blue-ribbon gossips! See, for example, JNL to WCW, Sept. 12, 1884, m. 52, CAR.

[16] *ST,* Aug. 21, 1884, p. 511; *RH,* Aug. 19, 1884, pp. 533, 534; *RH,* Oct. 7, 1884, p. 635; *ST,* Oct. 9, 1884, p. 602; *ST,* Feb. 12, 1885, pp. 106, 107.

[17] JNL, quoted by Faye Eagle in "The Sabbath-school—Past and Present," *SWUR,* Apr. 14, 1908, pp. 6, 7.

[18] WCW to JNL, Feb. 25, 1885 and Mar. 16, 1885, WCW Letter Books, CAR; JNL, *ST,* June 25, 1885, p. 394; JNL, *ST,* July 16, 1885, p. 430.

[19] WCW to JNL, Mar. 10, 1885, WCW Letter Books, CAR; *RH,* July 28, 1885, p. 469.

[20] JNL to WCW, May 22, 1884, and July 24, 1885, m. 52, CAR; Annie Loughborough to Mary White, Dec. 7, 1885, m. 52, CAR; *ST,* May 14, 1885, p. 304.

[21] *PHJ,* June 1885, pp. 3, 4, 24; *PHJ,* June and July 1886, pp. 6, 7; *ST,* May 21, 1885, p. 320. The *PHJ* did tell readers, however, that "the meat into which the devils went [pigs or pork], and out of which there is no proof they ever came, is held in especial disfavor" at the Retreat, which, like Battle Creek Sanitarium, was a vegetarian institution.

[22] JNL to WCW, Jan. 17, 1886, and Feb. 2, 1886, m. 52, CAR; JNL to EGW, Feb. 16, 1886, m. 52, CAR; WCW to JNL, Feb. 17, 1886, WCW Letter Books, CAR; *RH,* May 18, 1886, pp. 312, 313; *ST,* July 1, 1886, p. 394. Of course, Willie White thought that Dr. Gibbs himself was "a little quackish" and wished both Gibbs and Burke would show more "first class style" (professional élan) in their work.

[23] *RH,* June 1, 1886, p. 349; EGW to JNL, Feb. 11, 1887, letter 34a, 1887, CAR.

[24] EGW to Dr. Gibbs, Dr. Rice, and JNL, Mar. 16, 1887, letter 2, 1887, CAR; WCW to JNL, Apr. 1, 1887, WCW Letter Books, CAR; JNL to EGW, Apr. 4, 1887, m. 52, CAR; JNL to EGW, May 8, 1887, m. 52, CAR. Incidentally, the May 8 letter is apparently the first one J. N. Loughborough composed on a typewriter. He told Mrs. White, "I am a 'raw' hand with the typewriter, but I thought it might be easier to read than my writing." However, since he typed it all in capital letters and single spaced it, that is debatable.

[25] EGW, diary, January 1888, ms. 22, 1888, CAR; JNL to EGW, Jan. 23, 1888, m. 52, CAR; JNL to EGW, Jan. 24, 1888, m. 52, CAR.

[26] *RH,* May 31, 1887, p. 349; WCW to JNL, Mar. 5, 1888, WCW Letter Books, CAR; *ST,* Mar. 23, 1888, p. 191; JNL, *ST,* Sept. 7, 1888, pp. 554, 555.

[27] JNL, diary, February 1888; *Life and Health,* March 1915, pp. 109, 110.

[28] *ST,* May 29, 1884, pp. 330, 331; *ST,* July 1, 1886, p. 394; JNL, diary, January 1888. Even after six years of operation, the college taught primarily Bible, history, singing, spelling, physics, and calisthenics classes.

[29] *ST,* May 7, 1885, p. 280; *ST,* May 28, 1885, p. 331; *ST,* May 13, 1886, p. 282; *RH,* May 22, 1888, p. 336.

[30] *ST,* May 7, 1885, p. 280; *ST,* Mar. 31, 1887, p. 208; *PUR,* Mar. 4, 1968, p. 3.

[31] EGW, December 1886, ms. 74, 1886; EGW, diary, February 1887, ms. 29, 1887, CAR; JNL to EGW, Dec. 6, 1885, m. 52, CAR.

[32] EGW to JNL, J. H. Waggoner, E. J. Waggoner, A. T Jones, c. April 1886, letter B-076, 1886, CAR; EGW to JNL, Feb. 5, 1887, letter 34, 1887, CAR. Daniels eventually abandoned his five-year Advent idea. As Gilbert Valentine explains in *The Prophet and the Presidents* (Nampa, Idaho: Pacific Press Pub. Assn., 2011), p. 127, Mrs. White often sent "general circular letters" to multiple recipients to be read publicly in churches or at con-

ference sessions and camp meetings to focus attention on wrong decisions or attitudes. Such letters, which frequently named specific individuals, undoubtedly caused them embarrassment, yet the practice in the past "had helped create strong motivation, if not an imperative, for making changes."

[33] EGW to JNL, July 6, 1886, quoted in JNL to C. E. Holmes, May 2, 1920, m. 006529, CAR.

[34] JNL to EGW, Sept. 3, 1886, m. 52, CAR.

[35] JNL to EGW, Jan. 17, 1887, m. 52, CAR; JNL to EGW, Jan. 19, 1887, m. 52, CAR.

[36] E. R. Jones, *ST,* Oct. 1, 1885, p. 586; JNL to WCW, Oct. 8, 1885, m. 52, CAR; JNL, *ST,* Sept. 30, 1886, p. 601; G. W. Colcord, *RH,* Oct. 19, 1886, p. 654.

[37] *ST,* Aug. 11, 1887, pp. 489, 490; *ST,* Aug. 25, 1887, p. 526; *ST,* Sept. 29, 1887, p. 601; *ST,* June 15, 1888, p. 361.

[38] S. N. Haskell, *RH,* Nov. 2, 1886, pp. 680, 681.

[39] *ST,* Mar. 10, 1887, p. 154; *ST,* Mar. 17, 1887, p. 176; *ST,* Apr. 21, 1887, p. 250.

[40] *GCB,* 1887, pp. 338, 339, 348-350, 361, 372, 373; *RH,* Nov. 29, 1887, p. 744; *RH,* Dec. 6, 1887, p. 761; *RH,* Dec. 13, 1887, p. 777; *ST,* Nov. 24, 1887, pp. 710, 711, 720; *Gospel Sickle*, Dec. 15, 1887, p. 191.

[41] WCW to JNL, Jan. 26, 1888, WCW Letter Books, CAR.

[42] WCW to JNL, Mar. 30, 1888; WCW to JNL and John Fulton, Apr. 4, 1888; WCW to JNL, May 14, 1888, WCW Letter Books, CAR. Missionary boxes were special containers for collecting foreign missions offerings during the 1880s and 1890s.

[43]*RH,* May 22, 1888, p. 336.

[44] *ST,* July 27, 1888, p. 462; JNL, diary, September 1888.

[45] *ST,* Oct. 19, 1888, pp. 634, 635.

[46] *YI,* Nov. 30, 1887, p. 231.

[47] In 1884 the Review and Herald published Loughborough's books *Home of the Saved* (82 pages for 10 cents) and *Hope of the Gospel* (80 pages for 10 cents); JNL, "That 'Chart of Days,'" *RH,* July 14, 1885, p. 448; "Two Thrones," *RH,* Apr. 13, 1886, p. 231; "The 'Sentinel' Tracts," *RH,* July 5, 1887, p. 432; "The Sojourn of Israel in Egypt," *RH,* July 10, 1888, p. 436; *YI,* Dec. 16, 1947, p. 5.

[48] *ST,* Jan. 29, 1885, p. 74; *ST,* May 7, 1885, p. 280; *ST,* Jan. 20, 1887, p. 34.

[49] *ST,* Sept. 18, 1884, p. 574; *ST,* Jan. 29, 1885, p. 80.

[50] *Gospel Sickle*, Feb. 1, 1886, pp. 2, 3; *Gospel Sickle*, Mar. 15, 1886, p. 31. "The Saints' Inheritance" fills 12 issues of *Gospel Sickle* from June 15 to December 1, 1886.

[51] See JNL's health articles in *PHJ*, August-September 1886, pp. 27-29, 47; October-November 1886, pp. 59, 60, 62, 63-65; December 1886-January 1887, pp. 91-95; February-March 1887, pp. 123-127, 133; April-May 1887, pp. 155, 156; June-July 1887, pp. 187-191; August-September 1887, pp. 219-221, 236, 237; October-November 1887, pp. 251-253, 266, 267; January 1888, pp. 1-3; February 1888, pp. 33-35, 37, 38; March 1888, pp. 65-68, 70; April 1888, pp. 97-99; May 1888, pp. 129-131; June 1888, pp. 161-163, 180, 181; July 1888, pp. 193-195; August 1888, pp. 225-228; October 1888, pp. 289-291.

[52] JNL, "The Physical Man," *PHJ*, June-July 1886, pp. 1-3.

[53] *PHJ*, September 1888, pp. 257-260.

[54] JNL, "Liquor Sellers' Asylum," *PHJ*, October-November 1886, p. 72; "Defective Drainage," *PHJ*, June-July 1887, pp. 202, 203; and "Seasickness," *PHJ*, January 1888, pp. 16, 17.

[55] JNL, diary, January 1885-October 1888.

CHAPTER XIV

FINAL ACCOMPLISHMENTS ON THE WEST COAST (1888-1891)

"Seeing these old places called up many scenes of the past, with the trials, conflicts, and victories connected with the first meetings."[1]

J. N. Loughborough filled his last years as president of the California Conference (1888-1890) with visits to local churches, growing administrative responsibilities, camp meeting tours, and editorial and writing duties. As the above quotation attests, nostalgia tinged those years as he recalled the triumphs and tragedies of his ministry on the West Coast.

President Loughborough loved nothing better than visiting the scattered Adventist churches in California, Oregon, Washington, Idaho, and Nevada, sharing personal experiences about the rise and progress of Adventism, and telling children stories about the lighthouses he had seen in 32,000 miles of ocean travel. Occasionally he teamed up with old preaching partners such as E. P. Daniels, Isaac Sanburn, and William Healey. More often, though, he hit the gospel trail alone, spending weekends in the homes of Adventist believers. He described the quarterly meetings, revival services, and ministerial institutes he attended as "precious" seasons blessed by the Spirit. And he found comfort in knowing that many prayers ("like sharp sickles") followed his footsteps.[2]

Yet as the Advent Christian preacher Miles Grant had dogged Loughborough's footsteps in the 1860s and 1870s, presenting a very different view of the Adventist past, so in the late-1880s Adventist dissident Dudley M. Canright—another of John's former preaching partners—shadowed him. Having recently completed his exposé *Seventh-day Adventism Renounced,*

Canright had traveled from Michigan to California, itching for a debate with any Adventist minister brave enough to take him on. In February 1889 the Ministers' Union scheduled a series of debates between Canright and William Healey (with Loughborough coaching him) at the Healdsburg College church. After Canright lectured on "The Mistakes of Adventists," Healey rebutted with "The Mistakes of Dudley Canright," using Loughborough's two-column chart showing Ellen White's statements in one column and "the falsity of Canright's claims" in the other. Healey and Canright spent 10 days debating Mrs. White's writings, the nature of man, and the true Sabbath. Although no extant account of the debates exists in published sources, it is evident from Loughborough's diary that he and Healey argued for the divine inspiration of Ellen White's writings, in favor of the conditional immortality of humankind, and for the seventh day as the biblical Sabbath. Canright, on the other hand, claimed that White had plagiarized her writings from contemporary authors, that the soul was inherently immortal, and that Sunday was the Lord's Day for worship. Reacting to the charge of plagiarism, Loughborough contacted Mrs. White immediately and the two spent a couple days preparing a response. John's diary shows that he burned the midnight oil writing his manuscript "Plagiarism" (no longer extant) and coaching Healey for further debates with Canright in St. Helena.[3]

Although the debates ended with no clear victory for either side, both Loughborough and Healey recognized that Canright had raised some serious issues concerning the nature of Ellen White's prophetic gift (what part was divine and what part human?) and the process by which she wrote her books (how significant were extrabiblical sources and what role did her secretaries play?). For days after Canright left, Healey sought to reverse the negative impressions Dudley had created by giving lectures on Canright's unstable career and defection from Adventism, while Loughborough spoke on Ellen White's divine inspiration to the college students and faculty. In addition, John's diary shows that he spent many hours counseling with Mrs. White and church leaders about "the Canright matter." In truth, the questions Canright had raised and the charges he had leveled against Mrs. White would provide both sides ample fodder for debates in the century ahead.[4]

If the attacks of one former preaching partner (Canright) made John defensive and angry, the death of another evangelistic teammate, John Harvey Waggoner, brought him deep sorrow. While "running the tents" with M. E. Cornell in Wisconsin, Loughborough had met Waggoner in 1853. Abandoning a promising career in the newspaper business, Waggoner had preached the Adventist message in the Midwest, on the West Coast, and in Europe. In addition he had edited the *Signs*, the *American Sentinel*, and the *Pacific Health Journal*. His death of a heart attack in Basel in 1889 shocked Loughborough. At the memorial service in Oakland, John praised his departed friend for his "active, earnest, unselfish labors." A true pioneer, Waggoner "knew what it was to go forth without purse or scrip to advance the truth." Calling him "a veritable tower of strength," Loughborough asserted that "his equal in reasoning and logical powers was rarely found."[5] Having exceeded the average 45-year lifespan for nineteenth-century Americans, Loughborough would now face the passing of friends with greater frequency.

GROWING ADMINISTRATIVE RESPONSIBILITIES

It is perhaps remarkable that the administrative burdens J. N. Loughborough shouldered did not kill him as well. In addition to his preaching and writing activities, he served as president of the California Conference, president of the Rural Health Retreat (St. Helena Sanitarium) board, president of the California Health and Temperance Society, and president of the California Tract and Missionary Society. In addition, he sat on the General Conference Committee, on the board of trustees for Healdsburg College, and on the board of directors at the Pacific Press Publishing Company. Each position brought with it a host of responsibilities that seemed to grow with each passing year.[6]

For example, as a member of the GC Committee, Loughborough spent much of his time at GC sessions serving on committees (credentials and licenses, education, nominations, resolutions, pastoral, and publishing, to name a few). With growing frequency, the chairmen (they were *always* men in those days) asked him to open meetings with prayer, consulted him to clarify ambiguous issues, and listened closely when he proposed motions or spoke concerning resolutions on the floor. If he was not always the oldest minister in attendance, his nearly 40 years of service to the church still added weight to his words.[7]

As California Conference president, Loughborough was the CEO of a three-person team (including a secretary and treasurer) who supervised all aspects of the denomination in the state. They assigned ministers, licentiates, and canvassers their territories and scheduled evangelistic series, camp meetings, biblical institutes, ministerial retreats, quarterly meetings, and other conference-wide activities. As president of the California Health and Temperance Society, John arranged for speakers, scheduled meetings, promoted health literature, and raised funds for temperance endeavors. "The principles of health reform, carried out in my life," he testified, "have saved me from a consumptive's [TB victim's] grave." By virtue of his position as president of the California T&M Society, Loughborough chaired the committees on resolutions (that planned the meetings' agendas) and nominations (that suggested names for various positions). In addition, he took the lead in promoting all Adventist books, tracts, and periodicals, compiling annual statistics on the society's activities, and fighting Senator Blair's proposed national Sunday blue law.[8]

In addition to the promotional (writing ads) and fund-raising activities (for a new chapel) associated with sitting on the Rural Health Retreat board, he was also one of three or four coeditors of its paper, *The Pacific Health Journal*. The position required him to solicit articles from qualified writers in the fields of health, temperance, and medicine—as well as to write such articles himself (with his wife Annie's help). His diplomatic skills were also required to settle internal quarrels among the sanitarium staff (as discussed in chapter 13).[9]

Fortunately, John's relationship with the administration, faculty, and students at Healdsburg College proved less onerous. Since Adventist college boards treated faculty like students and students like children, college campuses were peaceful oases of learning. Because Adventists in general saw their colleges as places to train church employees, the boards routinely rejected students "not disposed to submit to proper authority." As acting president of the board (in W. C. White's absence), John raised funds for new equipment, established new departments, and recruited dedicated faculty. Although Loughborough's formal schooling had ended with the eighth grade, he valued higher education. He occasionally visited classes, enjoyed dialoging with teachers and students, and read a lot of books.[10]

C. H. Jones (as president) and Loughborough (as vice president) also served together on the Pacific Press Publishing Company's board. In addition to hiring employees, shaping policies, and paying bills, John urged his colleagues to envision a global role for Pacific Press. With his encouragement, the board opened branches in New York City, Mexico, Australia, and England.[11]

While it may have been a pleasure for Loughborough to serve with his friend Willie White on boards and committees, their professional relationship created some frustration, especially when White was away and his letters made increasing demands on John's time. When GC president G. I. Butler resigned suddenly in 1888 and W. C. White was appointed acting president, he frequently asked John's advice about placing church employees, mailing the *American Sentinel* to professionals in the U.S., fighting Sunday blue laws, planning Bible institutes, and a host of other issues. In addition to being White's unpaid consultant, Loughborough served as a promotional agent for projects the acting president wanted him to push: city missions, Dr. Kellogg's books, and the "annexation" of Arizona, New Mexico ("a hard field costing more than it is worth"), and Utah ("that Mormon hell") by the California Conference.

Nor did White hesitate to twist John's arm for favors. One time he asked Loughborough to hire a Mr. Biter at the St. Helena Sanitarium and pay him "more than usual" for his experience. Another time he pleaded with John to "use your influence" to encourage better consultation among the directors of the Pacific Publishing Company and to bring "tighter unity" among ministers (such as E. P. Daniels, William Healey, and A. T. Jones) who were confusing church members by teaching that the seal of God was the new birth experience (not the Sabbath). Frequently, White begged for money, "because I am using up what little I have fast and shall be forced to forego the pleasure of giving for a while." In February of 1890 he asked John for a $300 no-interest loan from the California Conference, confessing that "[my financial] means are limited now and there is but little money at my command."[12]

Another man whose money problems gave Loughborough headaches was E. P. Daniels. By 1880s Adventist standards, Daniels was somewhat eccentric. Although all Seventh-day Adventists believed Christ's return was imminent, he set specific dates for the Second Advent, something that Ellen White had warned members not to do. While the church officially advocated vegetarianism, he publicly asserted that oysters "were the best kind of food." If most ministers managed to live on $12 a week, he supplemented his income by selling mining stock and giving lessons in "voice culture" (public speaking). Deeply concerned, Mrs. White in 1890 declared, "His case has been my special burden for years."[13]

Indeed, between 1886 and 1890, she had sent him and his wife a dozen letters highlighting various shortcomings and urging reform. Financially, they were "controlled by King Mammon," being poor money managers, loving extravagant attire, indulging in speculation and extortion, and sending their daughter Zua to Snell's Seminary, an expensive non-Adventist female finishing school where she learned to love novels and fashionable dress. Elder Daniels was guilty of hypocrisy for preaching healthful living while eating meat and drinking wine and tea. Spiritually, he suffered from pride, loved flattery, and neglected prayer and meditation. Instead, as pastor of the Fresno SDA Church, he employed his training in elocution to please the people and "mesmerize" large crowds with "witty things [and] amusing anecdotes," but "the Spirit of Jesus is not in it." Fearing for his eternal welfare, White begged him to repent and change his lifestyle. She assured him that "I am your friend because I tell you the truth." If he refused to heed her warnings, she predicted, "You will eventually have to leave the ministerial field." When the family not only ignored her counsel but publicly told lies about her, she authorized Loughborough to publish all of her testimonies to Daniels.[14]

In his correspondence with the minister, Loughborough clearly reveals the harsh side of his nature for which Mrs. White admonished him in many of her testimonies. However, subsequent letters show that once he was in possession of all the facts, John's kinder nature asserted itself.

In a November 1889 letter President Loughborough raked Daniels over the coals for a number of gaffes. His advocacy of oysters (rumor said that he held "oyster parties"—actually he bought them for his sick wife) went "directly against the teaching of Sister White, which she says is derived from what the Lord has shown her in vision." Therefore, he must not "go contrary to the Testimonies" in his health talks. His selling of "worthless mining stock" to gullible Adventists robbed the church ("It is the Lord's money after all"). For this risky activity he would not be allowed to "go scott [*sic*] free" but would instead face "an overhaul of this deal." What angered Loughborough most, however, was the fact that Daniels was giving voice lessons (20 lessons for $20) while on the conference payroll. Did he consider himself a minister or a businessman? After learning that Daniels had made $400 from 20 "scholars," John sarcastically declared: "It looked like so big a story that I could hardly credit it, for I did not think you had any information that you could consider of that value to them." After hearing some of the man's "lessons," he told him that the lessons were not worth a dollar apiece and insisted that E. P. either end this "voice culture scheme" or cease being an Adventist minister. The letter closed with John's hope that "you will still regard me as a friend, and not as an enemy."[15]

If Loughborough expected Daniels to comply with his demands, the latter's reply soon disabused him. Daniels defended his dietary views, selling mining stock, and giving voice lessons with some rather creative proof-texting from the Bible. Then, as if thumbing his nose at the conference president, he submitted an expense report for $80.55 to cover his hotel and travel expenses for November.[16]

Frustrated, Loughborough consulted Ellen White, who advised him "to protect our people from this scheming propensity of Elder Daniels." Fearing the result would be "the loss of his soul," she called him "a broken reed [whose] human influence is leading many astray." "I am pained to the heart over these things," she stated, especially after hearing that Daniels "rails out against the testimonies," which was equivalent to "despising the Lord who has given me my work." She attributed the "unsanctified admiration" that many showed for him as inspired by the devil.[17]

Following Mrs. White's counsel, Loughborough lowered the boom on Daniels. He was to cease giving voice lessons, stop selling mining stock, and go wherever the conference sent him. When the minister accused Loughborough of "meddling" in his affairs, John informed him that "we do not wish the Conference [to be] mixed up with this speculating scheme." If he refused to stop, he must turn in his ministerial credentials. Then he could "do his business" as he liked. In his next letter, Daniels submitted his credentials "for the sake of peace." Explaining that $12 a week was insufficient to feed four children and buy medicine for a sick wife, he added: "Since you have decided that I shall not be allowed to engage in anything not directed by your humble committee, I choose to go out alone with God."[18]

Once John understood Daniels' financial burden, the tone of his letters changed from accusatory to sympathetic. Expressing sadness that the man had chosen to submit his credentials, Loughborough offered to reimburse him for any documented expenses he cared to submit. In the meantime, as a gesture of good faith, he credited Daniels' account with $50. Grateful for Loughborough's generosity, he sent in his report and received his reimbursement.[19]

Ellen White felt that John's wife also needed to show "more love and less iron" in her actions toward others. In a lengthy letter to Annie in 1889, Ellen observed: "You can leave an impression upon the minds of the patients and guests [at St. Helena Sanitarium] that will be unfavorable to you and to the institution. Remember you are on missionary ground, and that your work is a work for the Master." Accusing Annie of showing "cold reserve," manifesting "manners [that were] forbidding" and leaving "a very disagreeable, unhappy influence upon the minds of others," Mrs. White asked if she could "break through this icy coldness and reserve" by allowing "the beams of the Son of righteousness" to warm her heart so that she could "reflect their bright rays to others." "Cherish [a] sunshine spirit," Ellen urged her. Then "joy, peace, love will be reflected in your countenance, in your words, and in all your [association] with others." If she followed this advice, her life would become "like a watered garden and like a spring of water whose waters fail not."[20]

Adventist camp meetings provided Annie and John time not only for warmhearted association with friends and fellow believers, but also ample opportunities to drink at that spiritual spring that renewed their Christian experience. Nineteenth-century Adventist camp meetings, which normally lasted one to two weeks, featured enthusiastic (if long) sermons, exuberant (but not always harmonious) singing, emotional (and short) personal testimonies, exciting mission stories from exotic places, and often scores of baptisms. It required much muscle and sweat to prepare the grounds, pitch the tents, cook the food, feed the horse teams, spread tons of straw, organize the services, and police the campsite. At old-fashioned camp meetings one heard bells ringing, children shouting, believers singing, and horses nickering in their stalls while smelling hot canvass, wet straw and hay, fresh manure, and nutritious (but not always delicious) meals cooking in the food tent. Depending on the location, one felt blistering sun, chilling wind, driving rain, or pounding hail. Looking around, one could see bearded, gray-haired ministers in black three-piece wool suits; women in snow-white blouses and dark ankle-length dresses; little boys in knickers and girls in skirts and hats. Camp meeting was a time for joyful reunions, tearful confessions, generous giving, and heartfelt commitments. In an era when paid vacations were unknown in America, Adventists joyfully took time off from their work to attend what J. N. Loughborough called "feasts of tabernacles."[21]

In several significant ways, President Loughborough shaped West Coast camp meetings, and many of his innovations spread throughout the denomination. As mentioned previously, in the late-1880s he began holding workers' meetings (for ministers, licentiates, canvassers, and Bible workers) a week prior to camp meeting and then business meetings (for elected delegates) afterward, so that matters relating to professional improvement and financial efficiency did not intrude on believers' spiritual fellowship. The California Conference may also have been the first to divide Sabbath school groups according to age, with "children's meeting[s]" (for those between 1 and 14), "young people's meeting[s]" (for those between 14 and 21), and adult Sabbath school classes (for those over 21). The camp meetings also featured daily classes in hygienic cooking, which soon became a popular feature at all West Coast convocations. If taking group photographs at camp meetings did not originate in California, not many Adventist ministers struck a Napoleonic pose (right hand inserted inside one's partially unbuttoned frock coat) as President Loughborough liked to do.[22]

Before he would preach 19 or more sermons "of a close, practical character" at each camp meeting, Loughborough would first show up in work clothes to help the grounds crew cut the grass, pitch the tents, and haul in the necessary supplies. His diminutive size and close attention to detail proved an advantage on at least one occasion when he discovered in the deep grass a greenback (paper money) with a silver coin wrapped inside at the Oakland camp grounds. The same attention to detail appears in his annual "Address," a speech chock full of inspiring statistics demonstrating the rise and progress of Adventism during the past year. Blending business reports and fund-raising appeals with calls for spiritual renewal, such speeches required weeks to prepare and hours to deliver.[23]

But preparing for camp meetings and fulfilling all his other administrative duties took a toll on his health. Although Loughborough was only in his late-50s, Ellen White told GC President G. I. Butler not to retain him as conference president another year. "The man is just about threadbare," she wrote; "his strength is about used up." Butler agreed with her that John was "all worn down." "[He] has . . . carried the many heavy burdens which are necessarily associated with it [conference administration]. . . . He has labored here [California], sparing no strength or thought to build up the cause."[24] During 1889 and 1890, *la grippe* (influenza) forced John and Annie to spend several days in bed and to seek hydrotherapy treatments at St. Helena Sanitarium. Occasionally he skipped Sabbath school and church services to sleep, after which he felt much better. By the fall of 1890 Butler concluded that the Loughboroughs would benefit from a change of scenery. Perhaps he could also find them some new project to support that would lift their spirits.[25]

LAUNCHING THE *PITCAIRN*

That special project proved to be a new mission ship called the *Pitcairn.* Nearly a century earlier in 1789, Fletcher Christian, master's mate of the HMS *Bounty*, had led a mutiny against the ship's commander, William Bligh, while docked in the Tonga Islands. Casting Bligh and 18 of his followers adrift, the remaining crew returned to Tahiti, where most of them decided to stay. Fearing the long arm of British retribution, however, Christian embarked with nine sailors and 18 Tahitians for Pitcairn Island. During the next 10 years, drunkenness and violence took the lives of every crew member except Alexander Smith. Recognizing that without moral order the tiny colony could not survive, Smith led his Tahitian colleagues in studying the Bible and the Anglican *Book of Common Prayer* until his death in 1829. Following several relocations, by 1864 the island had only 43 residents.[26]

In 1876 James White and J. N. Loughborough had sent a crate of Adventist materials to Pitcairn Island. Although the natives ignored it at first, eventually they studied the books and tracts, and when John Tay arrived a decade later, most of them converted and were baptized as Seventh-day Adventists. By 1888 the *Signs* reported that "the truth seems to be firmly established" on Pitcairn Island where "a happy people" worshipped God every Sabbath, singing hymns from *The Song Anchor* (a popular Adventist songbook) and sharing their faith with the passengers and crews of passing ships. The fact that the 106 Pitcairn Islanders did not smoke, drink alcohol, or eat meat even attracted the attention of the Sheffield (England) *Telegraph* and the *Encyclopedia Britannica*, in which writers praised them as "healthy, hospitable, and virtuous." Their two meals a day regimen of sweet potatoes, Indian corn, pumpkins, coconuts, pineapples, bananas, and eggs kept them in excellent health. It was said that their women had the strength of men and their men were as strong as horses![27]

The fascinating story of Pitcairn's conversion inspired Adventist leaders and church members to build a boat capable of carrying out mission advance among the Pacific islands. Since the denomination had no professional shipbuilders at the time, church officials hired Captain Matthew Turner of San Francisco and his workers in the Straits of Carquinez (30 miles north of Oakland) to build it. As their contract forbade them to work on the seventh-day Sabbath (and they never worked on Sundays), laborers referred to the missionary ship as "the five-day boat." About 100 feet long and 27 feet wide, the 120-ton vessel could accommodate 12 to 16 persons. Its international crew included sailors from England, France, Germany, Spain, and Scandinavia. When the time came to launch the ship on July 28, 1890, church leaders chose not to serve beer or wine to the workers, thus opting for a "dry launch" rather than a "wet launch." Instead, Adventist women provided them a wholesome lunch. After hours of singing, speeches, and prayers on the beach, the crowd of more than 200 people watched as the still unnamed vessel slid into the bay at high tide on a beautiful moonlit night.

All across America Sabbath school members gave their pennies, nickels, dimes, and dollars until they had raised almost $18,700 to pay for the boat. Boys and girls mailed more than 100 names for it, including "Glad Tidings," "Carrier Dove," "Angel of Mercy," "Gospel Steamer," "Joyful News," and "Island Visitor," but the winning entry was *Pitcairn*. Now that the vessel had a name, it could be dedicated. As Loughborough had offered a prayer at its launching, he was next asked to have opening prayer over the boat on September 25 when church leaders dedicated it. This time approximately 1,500 people showed up, and 600 of them had the opportunity to go aboard and inspect the ship. Again there would be no liquor served, no bottle of champagne broken over the bow. Instead, a male choir sang several numbers, M. C. Wilcox read his poem "The Sending Forth of the *Pitcairn*," appropriate speeches were given, and GC president O. A. Olsen preached a short sermon. With gratitude to God for the historic moment, the group sang the Doxology. A month later, on October 20, the *Pitcairn*, carrying the flags of five nations (the United Kingdom, France, Germany, Chile, and the U.S.), weighed anchor. When it reached its island namesake a month later, the crew found many islanders awaiting baptism, and before it left, 82 had been baptized. Loughborough's joy knew no bounds as he boasted of the wonderful missionary work "our ship" would soon accomplish.[28]

JOHN AND ANNIE'S ARTICLES

Back on the mainland, John and Annie fostered another missionary endeavor to promote good health among Adventists everywhere. While neither of John's previous wives had been writers, Annie had a gift for sharing homemaking tips in a down-to-earth manner. During the late-1880s and early 1890s, one finds her byline beside that of her husband in the *Pacific Health Journal*.

Once again, both Loughboroughs preferred writing short articles in a series focused on one topic, as John had done in the *Review* and *Signs*. While modern medical and nutrition specialists would disagree with some of their content, the articles emphasize the commonly accepted health ideas of a century ago. In a six-part series on the brain and nervous system, John warns against the dangers of "cramming" (it could be fatal), eating a monotonous diet (it induces insanity), nervous anxiety (it causes dyspepsia), and frightful experiences (which turned Marie Antoinette's auburn hair white overnight). For the best mental health, he recommended thinking analytically, eating good "nerve food" (whole-wheat flour, fruits and vegetables), avoiding harmful substances (tea, coffee, tobacco, alcohol), getting adequate sleep and exercise, and frequent bathing.[29]

His eight-part series on "Food and Nutrition" recommended returning to the diet of Adam and Eve in Eden: vegetables, fruits, grains, and nuts. A strict vegetarian himself, John warned against the dangers of eating meat (it "impair[s] the vital domain") and intemperance in food and drink (which destroyed the "barbarous" nations). Asserting that many people fed their poultry and cattle better than they do themselves, he urged readers to "accept the voice of the stomach, the brain, the nervous system" and not abuse them with stimulants, narcotics, condiments, and greasy foods. Just as the man who mainly ate meat got gout and the boy who only ate potatoes got rickets, so intemperance of any kind can induce dyspepsia. Once again showcasing his knack for storytelling and ethnic dialect, John told about the German bartender who offered a teetotaler a drink. "Vill you have sum brandy?" "No." "Then sum vine, or peer?" "No." "Den you take vun zigar?" "No." "Vot does you live on?" According to Loughborough, the correct answer was vegetables, fruits, grains—and water.[30]

In one 1890 series John highlighted the dangers of poor hygiene, improper drainage, faulty ventilation, and the misplaced drilling of wells (near cesspools, manure piles, etc.). Such carelessness (he calls it "physical sins") around one's property brought killer diseases such as typhoid, diphtheria, cholera, and bubonic plague. Loughborough then proceeded to give practical advice on how to protect one's family from such dangers.[31] Rounding out the year, John devoted five articles to the causes and prevention of kidney diseases (such as nephritis, diabetes, and kidney stones) and four articles to the symptoms and prevention of typhoid fever.[32]

If John's articles focus primarily on the dangers of poor health practices, Annie's one- and two-page entries offer housewives dietary, health, and time-saving suggestions to make their lives easier. In contrast to the negative, preachy tone of her husband's writing, Annie's articles reflect her positive, practical disposition. Like an Adventist Martha Stewart, she provides wholesome recipes, shares cooking and baking tips, offers advice on keeping dish towels "sweet," and gives shortcuts to save time and labor around the house. Her mantra is that "there is a right and a wrong way of doing everything, and the right way is always the better way." As every blue-ribbon housewife knows, "perfect order and system" and "promptness, economy, cleanliness, and carefulness are also essential qualifications for good house-keeping."[33]

Occasionally, however, illness entered even the best-kept household (including the Loughborough home), so Annie fills two articles with tips on how to care for invalids. They must have fresh air, clean bedding, and wholesome food to eat. In addition, they should drink rice water and toast water and eat their meals on the best china with spotless silverware. The fact that Annie would advise invalids to drink sugar and sweet cream in their coffee, inhale burning camphor-gum in fresh ground coffee ("wonderful in its invigorating effects"), and eat "the very best tenderloin [steak], delicately broiled, and served *hot*," probably indicates that most *PHJ* readers were neither vegetarians nor Adventists. She added, however, that the apple is "the prince of fruit" and should be frequently served in a variety of dishes, sauces, and pies.[34]

While John's diary does not indicate how often Annie baked him an apple pie, it does show that the Loughboroughs "walked the walk" when it came to living a healthful lifestyle. They followed a strict vegetarian diet, took walks, and regularly paid a Chinese man to keep their clothing and bedding clean. They rarely dined at restaurants in Oakland or San Francisco. Instead, they ate at home or with friends (especially Uriah and Harriet Smith when in Battle Creek). For exercise, they enjoyed hiking, riding horseback, and going for buggy rides. Doubtless the stressors in their lives as well as a lack of adequate rest brought on the occasional colds and bouts of flu they endured. Although John's diary indicates that by the late-1880s he dictated most of his business letters, it also shows that he had ceased taking naps. Lengthy committee meetings filled his days, and counseling sessions shortened his nights.

Consequently, the couple had little free time to get away from it all and simply have fun. But in July 1890 Annie and John took the train to Sacramento for eight blissful days all by themselves. On Sabbath afternoon they borrowed a horse and went sightseeing in the state capital. They visited Sutter's Fort, went camping on Mt. Diablo, hiked up the mountain and gazed at the moon through a telescope, and spent two lazy days playing quoits and writing postcards to family and friends. In effect, they enjoyed the honeymoon they had missed in 1878. John's diary indicates that although they were both "lame and tired," they enjoyed these "hot and lazy" days. Before getting back to work, they visited the San Francisco Mint and the Pioneer Museum and attended a travelogue on Russia.

NEBRASKA CONFERENCE PRESIDENT AND SUPERINTENDENT OF DISTRICT NO. 5

But their bucolic days in California were rapidly coming to a close. Acting on Ellen White's suggestion that the Loughboroughs needed a change of scenery, the GC Committee suggested that he become the next president of the Colorado Conference. W. C. White recommended that he live either in Denver or Colorado Springs where the climate would be better for his lungs. Because Joel Palmer (Colorado Conference president) lacked experience, White felt that Adventists there needed Loughborough's good judgment and firm leadership. The Adventists in Colorado, however, raised "considerable opposition" to his coming, for they did not want a "law and order" man such as Loughborough taking the reins. Although E. H. Gates (Superintendent of District No. 5) offered to "exert enough influence to elect him," GC secretary Dan Jones advised that in view of the opposition there, "We hardly think it would be wise to have him elected president."[35]

The warmhearted Adventists in Nebraska, however, recognizing that "things were in a bad state there . . . and that something should be done," were eager for Loughborough to preside over their conference. Before he had even set foot in the state, they elected him conference president "by a most unanimous and hearty vote." Yet Dan Jones commented that "it will be quite a revolution for them in Nebraska to have Eld. Loughborough come in and take charge of the Conference, but no doubt it will be an improvement, and they need a good, strong management there now." The GC Committee agreed that John should go. At the same time they appointed him Superintendent of District No. 5 (which in the 1890s included Kansas, Missouri, Colorado, Texas, Arkansas, Arizona, and Oklahoma). So in October 1890 John and Annie joined a dozen Adventists in a cozy Pullman sleeper for the journey from Oakland to Lincoln, Nebraska. Along the way, they saw the Mormon sites in Salt Lake City (where the church president had recently condemned polygamy), the Grand Canyon, Royal Gorge, and the Rocky Mountains.[36]

When the train pulled into Lincoln, President Loughborough hit the ground running. During his first six weeks in office, he reviewed all the previous reports for District No. 5, convened a general gathering of conference workers, preached five sermons, held canvassers' institutes, and laid plans for erecting a new college nearby. Despite deep snow and howling winds that December, he told *Review* readers, "I am happy to report an improvement in [my] health as a result of [this] change of fields, and a change in [the] kind of labor." Henceforth he would devote more time to preaching and teaching and spend less in "confining, perplexing, and sedentary labor" (office and administrative duties).[37]

Both John and Annie (who now held "Missionary Credentials" from the Nebraska Conference) resolved to get out among the churches rather than sit behind desks. They soon discovered that most church employees in the state were quite young (both in age and experience). Consequently, Nebraskans welcomed all willing, qualified persons to fill conference or local church offices irrespective of age or gender. In fact, in an era when men dominated the bureaucracy of the Adventist church, the Cornhuskers had elected Minnie Hennig as secretary and Mary Beatty as treasurer of the Nebraska Conference. Thus, for the first time in his life, Loughborough would be the "token male" in an administrative office.[38]

To all appearances, however, he adjusted well to his new environment. Shortly after his arrival, John preached at Omaha, Ashland, Blue Valley, Exeter, Fremont, Blair, Calhoun, Lincoln, and Decatur, sharing with the frontier folk the fascinating stories of his experiences in the rise and progress of the Advent message. One listener exclaimed, "The things [Loughborough] related were deeply interesting, and many of our brethren and sisters who might have been there, but were not, lost a rare treat." Everywhere he spoke, he gave believers a firm confidence in the ministry of Ellen White and in God's providential leading in the history of the Advent Movement. With growing frequency, church leaders began suggesting that he compile the stories into a book to instruct and inspire a new generation.[39]

---

[1] *ST,* July 15, 1889, p. 426.

[2] *ST,* Dec. 7, 1888, p. 752; *ST,* Jan. 14, 1880, p. 30; JNL, diary, February 1889; *ST,* Aug. 5, 1889, p. 475; *ST,* Nov. 25, 1889, p. 720; *RH,* Feb. 25, 1890, p. 124; *ST,* June 2, 1890, p. 331.

[3] JNL, diary, February-March 1889; Jud Lake, *Ellen White Under Fire* (Boise, Idaho: Pacific Press Pub. Assn., 2010), p. 57.

[4] JNL, diary, March 1889.

[5] *ST*, May 20, 1889, p. 294; *RH,* May 7, 1889, p. 304.

[6] *RH,* Oct. 30, 1888, pp. 684, 685; JNL, diary, November-December 1888; *ST,* Aug. 25, 1890, p. 463.

[7] *GCB*, 1889, pp. 8, 78, 79, 93, 111, 147, 150.

[8] *PHJ,* November 1888, pp. 339-341; JNL, diary, April 1889; *ST,* June 17, 1889, pp. 362, 363; *ST,* Oct. 21, 1889, p. 639; *ST,* Oct. 20, 1890, pp. 525, 526.

[9] *ST*, Dec. 28, 1888, p. 799; JNL, diary, January 1889; *ST,* July 15, 1889, p. 426; *ST,* June 2, 1890, pp. 330, 331. In 1889 J. N. Loughborough, Dr. Merritt G. Kellogg, and C. P. Bollman were coeditors of the *Pacific Health Journal.* See *RH,* July 9, 1889, p. 448.

[10] *ST,* June 10, 1880, pp. 347, 350; *ST,* June 9, 1890, pp. 346, 347.

[11] *ST*, May 6, 1889, pp. 266, 267; *RH,* May 14, 1889, p. 320; JNL, *RH,* July 16, 1889, p. 456; *RH,* July 23, 1889, p. 470.

[12] WCW to JNL, Nov. 20, 1888; Dec. 28, 1888; Feb. 12, 1889; Mar. 29, 1889; June 25, 1889; July 15, 1889; Aug. 28, 1889; Nov. 19, 1889; Feb. 1, 1890; Sept. 19, 1890. WCW Letter Books, CAR.

[13] Ellen White, "Elder Daniels and the Fresno Church" (n.p.: printed pamphlet, February 13 and 20, 1890), p. 6.

[14] Ellen White letters to E. P. Daniels, Aug. 6, 1886; Apr. 24, 1888; July 3, 1888; July 6, 1888; Aug. 1, 1888; Aug. 3, 1888; Aug. 10, 1888; July 28, 1889; Nov. 5, 1889; Feb. 13, 1890; Feb. 21, 1890; "Testimonies on the Case of Elder E. P. Daniels" (printed pamphlet, 1886-1890), 80 pp.

[15] JNL to E. P. Daniels, Nov. 28, 1889, m. 52, CAR.

[16] E. P. Daniels to JNL, Dec. 5, 1889, m. 52, CAR.

[17] EGW to JNL, McClure, and Owen, Dec. 10, 1889, letter 58, 1889, CAR; EGW to JNL, Feb. 11, 1890, letter 54, 1890, CAR.

[18] JNL to E. P. Daniels, Dec. 12, 1889; E. P. Daniels to JNL, Dec. 13, 1889; JNL to EGW, Dec. 17, 1889, m. 52, CAR.

[19] JNL to E. P. Daniels, Dec. 19, 1889; JNL to E. P. Daniels, Jan 12, 1890; E. P. Daniels to JNL, Jan. 14, 1890; JNL to EGW, Jan 15, 1890, m. 52, CAR.

[20] EGW to Annie Loughborough, letter 6, 1889, CAR.

[21] *ST,* July 15, 1889, p. 432; JNL to WCW, May 27, 1899, GC Archives.

[22] *ST,* Nov. 16, 1888, p. 704; *RH,* Apr. 3, 1975, p. 3; *ST,* Jan. 21, 1889, p. 47; WCW to JNL, Feb. 18, 1889, WCW Letter Books, CAR; *ST,* Mar. 4, 1889, p. 143; *ST,* Apr. 22, 1889, pp. 251, 254; JNL, diary, May, August, September 1889; JNL to WCW, Sept. 11, 1889, m. 52, CAR.

[23] *ST*, Sept. 16, 1889, p. 571; *ST,* Nov. 11, 1889, p. 688; *ST,* Oct. 14, 1889, pp. 617-619; JNL, diary, April 1890.

[24] Ellen White, "Talk Before the General Conference Committee at Goguac Lake Near Battle Creek, Michigan," July 14, 1890, ms. 19b, 1890, p. 2; *RH,* Nov. 4, 1890, p. 682.

[25] JNL, diary, August 1889; January and March 1890.

[26] Herbert Ford, *The Miscellany of Pitcairn's Island* (Mountain View, Calif.: Pacific Press Pub. Assn., 1980), pp. 6-8.

[27] *ST,* July 20, 1888, pp. 442, 443; Sheffield *Telegraph* and *Encyclopedia Britannica,* cited by *PHJ,* October 1889, pp. 304, 305; Ford, *Miscellany,* p. 8.

[28] *Church Officers' Gazette,* April 1916, pp. 8, 9; *ST,* Aug. 11, 1890, pp. 448, 507; *YI,* June 6, 1922, pp. 11, 12; *RH,* Aug. 19. 1890, p. 501; *RH,* Oct. 14, 1890, pp. 636, 637. Ironically, although the lion's share of funding to build the *Pitcairn* came from the United States, its crew did not include a single American.

[29] For JNL's mental health articles in the *PHJ,* see November 1888, pp. 321-323; December 1888, pp. 353-356; January 1889, pp. 1-3; February 1889, pp. 33-35; March 1889, pp. 65-67; and April 1889, pp. 97-99.

[30] For JNL's "Food and Nutrition" articles in the *PHJ,* see May 1889, pp. 129-132; June 1889, pp. 161-163; July 1889, pp. 193-195; August 1889, pp. 225-227; September 1889, pp. 257-259; October 1889, pp. 289-291; November 1889, pp. 321-323; and December 1889, pp. 353-355.

[31] For JNL's "Prevention Better than Cure" articles in *PHJ,* see January 1890, pp. 1-4; February 1890, pp. 33-36; and March 1890, pp. 65-67.

[32] For JNL's articles on "Kidney Diseases" in *PHJ,* see April 1890, pp. 97-99; May 1890, pp. 129-131; and June 1890, pp. 161-163. For his "Diabetes" articles, see July

1890, pp. 193-195; and August 1890, pp. 225-227. For his "Typhoid Fever" articles, see September 1890, pp. 257-259; October 1890, pp. 289-291; November 1890, pp. 321-323; and December 1890, pp. 353, 354.

[33] For Annie Loughborough's housekeeping tips, see *PHJ,* May 1889, p. 150; July 1889, p. 214; August 1889, p. 246; September 1889, p. 278; October 1889, p. 310; November 1889, p. 342; December 1889, p. 374; January 1890, p. 22; February 1890, p. 54; March 1890, p. 84, 85; April 1890, p. 118; May 1890, pp. 148, 149; June 1890, pp. 180, 181; July 1890, pp. 211, 212; August 1890, pp. 243, 244; September 1890, p. 277; and November 1890, pp. 339, 340.

[34] See Annie Loughborough's "Hints for the Sick-Room" and "Drinks for Invalids" in *PHJ,* February 1890, p. 54; December 1890, pp. 369, 370; and "The Apple" in October 1890, pp. 307, 308. A frequent theme in GC president O. A. Olsen's letters to the Loughboroughs is their health. Shortly after they moved to Nebraska he wrote, "I hope you are paying regard to your health and strength. I know you find much to do, much more than your vitality can stand" (OAO to JNL, Nov. 19, 1890; Aug. 20, 1893, GC Archives).

[35] Dan T. Jones to E. H. Gates, Aug. 25, 1890, GC Archives 21, Box 3, Secretariat Letter Book 4; WCW to JNL, Sept. 5, 1890, WCW Letter Books, CAR; *RH,* Sept. 16, 1890, p. 576. Loughborough replaced E. H. Gates (who left aboard the *Pitcairn* to work among the Pacific islands) as superintendent of District No. 5.

[36] Dan T. Jones to G. I. Butler, Sept. 19, 1890 and Dan T. Jones to L. C. Chadwick, GC Archives 21, Box 3, Secretariat Outgoing Letter Box 4; Dick, *Founders,* p. 295; *GCB* (1889), p. 90; JNL, diary, October 1890; O. A. Olsen, *RH,* Oct. 14, 1890, p. 631; JNL, *RH,* Dec. 9, 1890, pp. 765, 766.

[37] *RH,* Dec. 9, 1890, pp. 765, 766.

[38] "Record of Credentials Given to Elder J. N. Loughborough (1861-1924)," DF 230, CAR; O. A. Olsen, *RH,* Oct. 14, 1890, p. 631; *RH,* Oct. 28, 1890, p. 669; *RH,* Dec. 9, 1890, pp. 765, 766.

[39] JNL, diary, November 1890; H. Shultz, *RH,* Nov. 25, 1890, p. 730; L. A. Hoopes, *RH,* Dec. 23, 1890, p. 795.

CHAPTER XV

REINTERPRETING THE PAST: WRITING *RISE AND PROGRESS OF THE SEVENTH-DAY ADVENTISTS* (1891-1894)

"I say let Elder Loughborough do a work that is suffering to be done in the churches. The Lord would have his voice heard as was John's [the revelator], telling the things which he himself has experienced in the rise and progress of the third angel's message. . . . Do not bind him down to any one conference. Let him go here and there, and everywhere, telling what he has seen, and known and handled in the rise of the third angel's message."[1]

The present chapter will briefly interrupt the narrative of J. N. Loughborough's life to examine his first major work on Adventist history. In his book Loughborough pioneered a particular view of church history that shaped Adventist apologetics for decades to come. This chapter will analyze his purposes, sources, and writing techniques, as well as a few of the errors in *Rise and Progress*.

In her letter to GC president O. A. Olsen quoted above, Mrs. White not only hinted at Loughborough's next major assignment (writing the first history of the SDA Church), but also provided him with the title he chose: *Rise and Progress*. Previously, she had urged him to share his faith-building stories at camp meetings for the benefit of new converts. "You have an experience valuable to the cause of God," she declared. "It must be made to tell for its full value." His experiences and his "firm position on [Ellen White's] testimonies" should "serve the cause of God in a wider sphere," she added, dissipating the "unbelief and doubt and skepticism" in the church.[2] During his long career as an Adventist preacher, he had seen her in vision many times and witnessed numerous miracles. Who could tell that story better than the man who had participated in the church's growth for four decades?

Yet unlike such nineteenth-century historical narratives as George Bancroft's *History of the United States of America* (1885) and Francis Parkman's *Montcalm and Wolfe* (1884), Loughborough's *Rise and Progress* was not scholarly (it had no footnotes, index, or bibliography), nor was it intended to be entertaining. Instead, notices in the *Signs* and *Review* gave it the subtitle "Tokens of God's Hand in the Movement." In fact, it resembled the genre of providential histories penned by Puritans such as Cotton Mather and Jonathan Edwards. The book emphasized God's guidance in "the progress of the work," highlighted the "difficulties and triumphs of the message," and demonstrated the "advance steps and greater spiritual strength" imparted by Ellen White's gift of prophecy. Its "graphic account of the struggles and difficulties" of those who with "unwavering faith in God, and . . . unfaltering loyalty to the cause" pressed forward against all obstacles, was "soul-cheering and . . . cannot fail to quicken the faith of both old and young."[3]

Urging Adventists to buy, read, and distribute it to their neighbors, GC foreign missions secretary W. A. Spicer declared: "It would seem impossible for anyone . . . to read this book without feeling the conviction that God is indeed in this work."[4] William Ings, Loughborough's preaching partner in England, asserted: "If you are old in the faith, you need it. If you are young in the faith, you surely ought to read it. If you need encouragement, this book will give it to you."[5] C. A. Hall of Topeka, Kansas, reflected the view of many readers that Loughborough's " 'early recollections' of . . . the sacrifices and privations of the pioneers . . . brought vividly to the minds of our older brethren and sisters, their own experiences in the earlier days of the work, and awakened in the younger members a greater degree of confidence in the message, and more faith in its divinely directed progress and final triumph."[6]

In the preface Loughborough stated that he wrote the book to promote "the cause of Christ in many hearts," to show the divine nature of White's visions and ministry, to share personal experiences, to strengthen the faith of new converts, and to relate events never before published. To accomplish this, he reread the *Signs of the Times, Advent Herald,* and *Midnight Cry* (1843-1844); *Present Truth* (1849), *Advent Review and Sabbath Herald*

(1850-1890), the *Youth's Instructor* (1850-1890), and other SDA periodicals. He also skimmed his personal diaries (from 1853 to 1890) and Ellen White's *Life Sketches, Experience and Views, Testimonies*, and many of her letters, articles, and published visions. In addition, he consulted notes from interviews conducted in the 1850s and 1860s with Joseph Bates, Hiram Edson, James White, J. N. Andrews, and other (primarily male) pioneers. Finally, he consulted newspapers, magazines, and books (especially those written by Uriah Smith, Merle D'Aubigné, and James Wylie).[7]

But John did not accomplish the herculean task alone. Although his wife's name does not appear on the cover of *Rise and Progress*, it is evident from his diaries that Annie provided invaluable assistance in preparing the 400-page book. In the winter of 1890-1891 she helped gather materials and took notes on many of the sources. A former schoolteacher in Hillsdale, Michigan, Annie was a good grammarian and a blue-ribbon typist. As John finished each chapter in longhand, she typed it on a manual typewriter. Then they read them aloud, making corrections as they went along. During the seven-month period (January-July 1891) in which John did the research and writing for *Rise and Progress*, Annie typed *four copies* of the original 480-page printed manuscript—a total of almost 2,000 pages! With wry wit, John exclaimed, "That job of hers was not simply a matter of recreation."[8] His diary also reveals the incredible speed with which he and Annie churned out the chapters in *Rise and Progress.* Although preaching and administrative duties frequently interrupted him, with few exceptions John wrote each of the book's 29 chapters in only two to four days—some of them in only *one day*. Thus fewer than eighteen months elapsed between January 1891 when John began his research and September 1892 when *Rise and Progress* rolled off the press.[9]

As a result, *Rise and Progress* is more of a chronicle than a history book. It is full of exciting anecdotes, human interest stories, lengthy speeches and quotations, and faith-building homilies, but short on objectivity, analysis, and (in some cases) accurate interpretation of the facts. It is what historians call "a scissors-and-paste" approach to research: stringing one's notes together without explaining what they mean. In short, Loughborough's prose focuses on the who, what, when, and where of Adventist history but seldom on the how (causation) or why (reasons) behind it. Yet given his eighth-grade education, lack of Adventist historical models to follow, and pressing responsibilities, he probably did the best job he could at the time. Despite his hectic pace of writing, the book contains very few factual errors.[10]

More serious for the scholar, of course, are the subtle spins and deliberate omissions that permeate the book. We will mention only a few here. Convinced that the Millerites were "the most humble, God-fearing, conscientious members" of the mainstream churches, he portrays the rest (especially Advent Christians) as partygoing, bazaar-sponsoring Laodiceans, conveniently glossing over much of the fanaticism within post-Millerite ranks (William Gorgas, George Storrs, and the Maine spiritualizers). He has only praise for William Miller, Joshua Himes, Josiah Litch, and Charles Fitch—despite their mistakes of prophetic interpretation, he never criticizes them once. On the other hand, he has nothing positive to say about his former friends in the Advent Christian movement, whom he blames for spreading shut-door views (no more mercy for sinners) in 1844 (in fact, Sabbatarian Adventists—and Ellen White herself—believed in the shut door until 1851). His claim that many Advent Christian preachers "used mesmerism to gain adherents" is not supported by extant sources. His allegation that spiritualism in 1848 "threatened the moral overthrow of the American people" is also exaggerated.

Current research has also disproved his statement that William Foy "sickened and died" soon after refusing to share his third vision in 1844. In fact, Delbert Baker's biography *The Unknown Prophet* (1987) proves that Foy preached for another half century. (Loughborough in fact follows a pattern of condemning dissidents like the *Messenger* Party, the Age-to-Come Party, and the Marion Party to inevitable splintering, insanity, or early deaths.) Likewise questionable (due to a lack of primary support) are his assertions that Charles Litch received letters from 1,000 atheists who converted to Christianity after his prediction of Turkey's fall on August 11, 1840, and his statistic regarding the active ministry of 3,000 Advent preachers worldwide in 1844.

Loughborough covers some parts of the Adventist past in great detail, but ignores other events altogether. For example, he devotes one third of the book to the Millerite movement (probably because of its crucial importance to SDA prophetic interpretation and the ministry of Ellen White). Yet he completely ignores the Minneapolis GC session of 1888. For more than a century, Loughborough and M. E. Olsen would be the only Adventist historians to ignore the contentious conference. Is it possible that because he had close friends on both sides of the debates (righteousness by faith, the law in Galatians 3, prophetic interpretations in Daniel), he did not wish to offend them? When GC president G. I. Butler was pushed into early retirement after that session, Loughborough gave as the reason his failing health with no hint that the leader's doctrinal conflicts with Jones, Waggoner, and White had contributed to his demise.[11]

Regarding the prophetic ministry of Ellen White, Loughborough's descriptions of the physical phenomena while she was in vision (three shouts of "Glory," superhuman strength, no breath, a vacant stare, quoting texts from a heavy Bible without looking at it, etc.) became the church's official view of her divine inspiration for more than a century. In both *Rise and Progress* and his later history book *The Great Second Advent Movement* (1905), Loughborough claimed to have seen Mrs. White in vision nearly 50 times—more often than any other pioneer besides her husband, James. As a firsthand witness, therefore, his testimony regarding her visions received great weight in the Advent movement well into the twentieth century. Furthermore, the exhaustive indexes he compiled near the end of his life to all her published books and *Review* articles, the long lists he typed up of more than 100 of her fulfilled predictions, and the fascinating stories he related in his books and at camp meetings helped to shape future generations' views of Ellen White.

Although more than a century old, Loughborough's apologetic writings supporting Ellen White's divine inspiration are still being cited today. For example, Jud Lake's recent book *Ellen White Under Fire: Identifying the Mistakes of Her Critics* (2010) cites Loughborough's letters, stories, actions, and arguments numerous times throughout its 350 pages.[12] As the epilogue to this biography attests, so have writers of articles in Adventist periodicals during the past century.

ILLINOIS CONFERENCE PRESIDENT

In addition to sharing his apologetic version of Adventist history in book form, John followed White's advice to "go here and there and everywhere" speaking about the "rise and progress" of the Adventist message and the divine inspiration of her visions. During the 1890s Loughborough became an ambassador for Adventist history whose passport opened doors for him all across America.

His speaking appointments from 1891 to 1894 took him to camp meetings in the West (Colorado, Texas, Arkansas, Kansas), the Midwest (Ohio, Michigan, Indiana, Illinois), the South (Tennessee), and the East (New Jersey).[13] Each summer he traveled to a new camp meeting site every two weeks, living out of his suitcase, sleeping on a cot in a tent, and preaching without the aid of a PA system to hundreds and even thousands of people at one time. (M. E. Kern described the camp meeting at Lansing, Michigan, in 1892, with approximately 3,000 Adventists living in 379 tents, as the largest gathering of Sabbathkeepers "for centuries.")[14]

Dressed in black wool pants, a black alpaca coat reaching to his knees, a starched long-sleeved white shirt with a celluloid collar and a black bowtie (which he made himself), wearing spit-polished black buttoned shoes and carrying a well-worn Bible, Loughborough looked every inch the dignified preacher and conference president. But his singing, preaching, and storytelling electrified his audiences. Hearing one congregation sing the old hymn "I Am Bound for the Land of Canaan" in a halfhearted manner, he stepped to the pulpit and held up his hand for silence. "Brethren," he exclaimed, "you don't seem to sense the importance of these words. If you did, you could never sing this song in that way." He told them how early Adventists shouted "Hallelujah!" when they sang such songs, for Jesus' coming was near. "It was real to us in those days," he declared. "We truly were bound for the land of Canaan, and our hearts thrilled at the thought. Brethren, put your hearts into the singing of these themes. Let the world know that we believe the Lord is coming soon." The congregation sang the rest of the hymn with such fervor that many had tears in their eyes.[15]

J. N. Loughborough's preaching was equally enthusiastic. Abandoning the dusty old notes of his doctrinal discourses (as Mrs. White had urged him to do), he told stories and related personal experiences that mesmerized his audiences. One listener expressed the views of thousands when he said, "Being the oldest minister in point of service among us as a people, [Loughborough's] early experiences and reminiscences are very interesting, and are calculated to inspire faith in the message and the spirit of prophecy that attends it."[16] In the 1890s it was normal for Adventist services to last for two or three hours. After a lengthy song service, an hourlong sermon could be followed by an hour of tear-filled testimonies and praise. One service in Lansing, Michigan, lasted for *five hours*! John said he had not seen such indications of "the power of God manifested" since the Millerite movement.[17]

In addition to preaching, praise, and prayer, Loughborough occasionally employed humor to make a point. Sharing some advice about preaching, he told the story of the young man who came to his pastor with the news that God had called him to preach. "How do you know?" the pastor asked. The youth replied "that as he was plowing in the field he saw in the heavens the three letters GPC, and that meant 'Go Preach Christ.'" Given the opportunity to preach, the fellow failed miserably, so the brethren advised him that he had misread the letters in the sky. In reality, they meant "Go Plow Corn."[18] A blue-ribbon storyteller, Loughborough always invited the children occupy the front benches so he could be near them when he shared experiences about Ellen White and her visions. One of those children recalled decades later how Loughborough's "face was always shining when he recalled with enthusiasm the details of [Mrs. White's] visions. . . . He made everything so clear and convincing even to us children," she said.[19]

Loughborough brought that same knack for clarity into his administrative duties. He liked to see efficiency in every branch of God's work, and as a leading church official, he had his fingers in many pies. At approximately 60, when many men begin to lay aside heavy duties, John accepted even more responsibilities. As president of the GC Association Executive Board and a member of the Board of Foreign Missions, he served on key committees dealing with the selection and distribution of church employees around the world. His work on the Executive Committee of the International Tract and Missionary Society involved promoting the publication and global distribution of Adventist literature. As president of the Board of Trustees for the SDA Education Society, he fostered the founding, funding, and future growth of the church's early colleges, academies, and elementary schools. A seat on the GC Committee of Finance provided him the opportunity to allocate $255,000 each year to church institutions around the world. In 1892 Dr. Kellogg (who disdained Adventist ministers as poorly educated, meat-eating hypocrites) appointed Loughborough to the board of trustees of the newly formed SDA Medical Missionary and Benevolent Association to promote "pure Christian philanthropy."[20]

As superintendent of District No. 5 (1891-1893), Loughborough attended the conference business meetings in Kansas, Missouri, Colorado, Texas, Arkansas, and Oklahoma ("Indian Territory" at the time). Then as superintendent of District No. 3 (1893-1895), he attended sessions in Michigan, Ohio, Indiana, and Illinois. At each one he customarily served on two key committees—Nominations and Credentials and Licenses—that chose the names of candidates to be elected to each position and determined which church employees received ministerial credentials and missionary licenses. GC president Olsen felt that John's influence on such committees and at church officers' institutes was crucial, enabling him to shape the future growth of each conference. The statewide gatherings also provided him opportunities to compile the lengthy statistical reports he enjoyed sharing at business sessions and camp meetings.[21]

By virtue of his position as president of the Illinois Conference, John inherited a number of responsibilities that he shouldered as best he could. As president of the state T&M Society he planned the conference-wide canvassers' institutes. In support of Dr. Kellogg's social gospel work, John helped establish city missions in Chicago, Springfield, and Bloomington, Illinois. He and Annie actually lived at the Chicago Mission (at 28 College Place). In preparation for the great Chicago Columbian Exposition of 1893, he chaired the Committee on the World's Fair, seeking ways to enhance the Adventist presence on the grounds. Because his administrative duties generated mountains of paperwork, Loughborough was fortunate to have his friend Charles Welch (who could take shorthand dictation at more than 100 words a minute) as his personal secretary. When George B. Thompson (another friend whom John had ordained as a pastor) appeared reluctant to accept a mission call to South Africa, Loughborough encouraged him to go by reminding him that "it was no greater distance to heaven from Africa than from Illinois."[22]

John, however, intended to prepare for heaven in Illinois. During the 1890s the family put down roots in Chicago. He and Annie became active members in the South Side SDA Church, regularly attending prayer meetings, missionary gatherings, and Sabbath school and church services. Annie, a competent accountant, was elected auditor of the Illinois Conference every year between 1890 and 1895.[23]

Meanwhile, their son Delmer, now in his late-20s and recently married to the beautiful and brilliant Maria Steward of Chicago, was also engaging in ministry. As an assistant to M. G. Huffman and George Thompson, Illinois Conference evangelists, Delmer pitched the tent, led the song service, and gave Bible studies as they traveled across the state. Although troubled by the early symptoms of TB, he rose in the ranks to become District No. 1 director of the Illinois T&M Society. His wife, Maria, who was the state T&M corresponding secretary and secretary and treasurer of the Illinois Sabbath School Association, was the only woman (among four men) serving on the state's executive board (which J. N. Loughborough chaired). In 1892 the Illinois Conference gave ministerial licenses to both Delmer and Maria.[24]

During the winter of 1892-1893 Delmer began holding evangelistic meetings on his own, retracing his father's footsteps through northern Illinois and Indiana more than a quarter century earlier. In this "old battle ground," the son won new victories for Adventism, baptizing converts and raising up new churches as his father had done in the 1860s. The family's accomplishments were rewarded at the Illinois Conference session in 1893. The delegates reelected John as conference president and his wife Annie as conference auditor. His son Delmer became president of the Illinois Sabbath School Association and daughter-in-law Maria became conference secretary and treasurer as well as secretary and treasurer of the State Sabbath School Association. With John's sister Minerva Jane holding down several positions at the GC, his brother William active in the Michigan Conference Sabbath School Association, and his niece Winnie editing the *Youth's Instructor*, one could speak of a "Loughborough Dynasty" within the denomination.[25]

THE LOUGHBOROUGH LEGACY IN CHICAGO

While it would be impossible to describe all the accomplishments of this remarkable family, the Loughborough legacy includes three innovations that we should mention. In the fall of 1891 John prepared some brochures for what would become the Central Bible Training School for Foreign Missions (commonly called the "Chicago Bible School"). The institution brought together church employees (ministers, teachers, canvassers, and Bible instructors) for approximately three months of instruction by the denomination's leading scholars, evangelists, and administrators (including E. J. Waggoner, A. T. Jones, and J. N. Loughborough). The Chicago Mission provided students bed and board. "Our house [is] full of people," John informed GC president Olsen, but all lived together as "a happy family." As the school's popularity grew, its attendance tripled from about 15 in 1891 to 50 in 1892. At the same time its active outreach won dozens of converts. By 1893 the Chicago School had spawned one-week Bible Training Institutes in large cities across the Midwest. To provide attendees with reading material, Pacific Press created the *Bible Students' Library*, a collection of 118 pamphlets and tracts (in 1894) costing between two cents and half a dollar each (members of the *Bible Students' Library* who paid a dollar a year received its publications free).[26]

Loughborough, like W. W. Prescott, also sponsored monthlong ministerial institutes. Believing that "some steps should be taken to elevate the standard and guard the sacred office of the ministry," a committee met in 1891 to explore ways to improve the knowledge and skills of Adventist clergy. Nearly half a century before the establishment of the denomination's theological seminary in Washington, D.C., these institutes provided required courses of "study and self-improvement" to enhance pastors' professional development. The first institute, held in Battle Creek Tabernacle in the late fall of 1891, drew 155 ministers from all over the Midwest to hear lectures by A. T. Jones, O. A. Olsen, W. W. Prescott, J. N. Loughborough, S. N. Haskell, R. A. Underwood, R. C. Porter, and Dr. Kellogg. Their presentations covered church ministry, mission work, church history, medical and health programs, and Bible doctrines. Just as the Chicago Bible School had spawned Bible Training Institutes, so the Ministerial Institutes inspired Canvassers' Institutes and Teachers' Institutes beginning in 1892.[27]

President Loughborough's work among Chicago's ethnic groups also deserves attention. As a teenager in Rochester, John had been surrounded by Irish and German immigrants, and the experience prepared him for the Windy City's multicultural environment. In an era when Adventist ministers preferred working for their own kind (English-speaking, middle class Whites), John bridged racial, ethnic, and language boundaries. Not only did he offer financial support to Black preachers such as Charles Kinney and James Buster when they fell on hard times, but he also selected tracts and leaflets to be translated into Spanish for America's Hispanic population. In Chicago he spearheaded the Adventist work among the Chinese, establishing a mission school for Chinese boys directed by Mr. and Mrs. Brand. As its reputation grew, the directors of two other Christian Chinese missions asked Adventists to manage their schools, because they taught the Bible only and acted like genuine Christians. By 1894 the Adventist school had 60 Chinese students, 14 of them regularly attending church services. When his schedule permitted, John enjoyed visiting the schools and talking with the teachers and students—he and Annie even invited them home for dinners.[28]

DISSIDENTS, FAITH HEALINGS, AND DEATHS

Some aspects of Loughborough's work, however, did not bring him pleasure. His high positions, like lightning rods, sometimes drew the ire of angry constituents and dissatisfied dissidents. To meet accusations that he had amassed a fortune of $10,000, he pointed out that since selling his home in Santa Rosa in 1874, he and Annie had owned no property except two burial plots. Instead, they had lived in rented rooms. How does one become wealthy, he inquired, on $4-$15 a week? He challenged accusers to provide deeds, mortgages, or checks proving that he was worth $10,000, "as the cause [is] in need, and I [desire] to make a donation."[29]

In the late-1880s and 1890s John and Annie (and Ellen White) found themselves enmeshed in an ugly lawsuit brought by William Walling of Colorado, who had married Mrs. White's niece May. In a civil lawsuit William charged Ellen, John, and Annie with "wrongful alienation of the affections of his two daughters" and demanded $1,500 damages. In reality Walling had abandoned his daughters, Addie and May, and the Whites and Loughboroughs had taken them in. Treating the non-Adventist girls as family, they had fed, clothed, and educated them free of charge for 10 years. Annie had taught Addie typesetting and proofreading skills at Pacific Press. During her apprenticeship the girl had become an Adventist, further angering her father. Both daughters (and their brother Fred), upset at their father's past mistreatment of them, opposed his efforts to make them return to Colorado. Through the intervention of Harmon Lindsay (who called Walling "a desperate character, verging on the insane"), a cash settlement brought closure to the case, which induced a great deal of unwelcome distress and anxiety to Ellen White. By 1895, as legal adults, May and Addie chose to live apart from their father.[30]

If the Walling lawsuit threatened Loughborough's wallet, the case of Anna Phillips (later Rice) challenged his understanding of prophetic inspiration. In 1891 Phillips, with her adoptive father's help, began printing and distributing copies of visions she claimed to have received from God. Some church leaders (notably A. T. Jones) found Anna's "testimonies" remarkably similar to those of Ellen White (who was absent in Australia). Jones read passages from the writings of both women in the pulpit of Battle Creek Tabernacle, asking the congregation if they heard God's Spirit speaking through each. Loughborough, doubting the genuineness of Anna's claim, began a three-year correspondence with her in October 1891. He sent copies of their letters (as well as the "testimonies" she mailed him) to various church leaders. By 1894 John had concluded that the two "voices" were *not* the same. Instead, "the Gift of Prophecy which has been manifested among us for 50 years [Ellen White] should be listened to (especially as it is still a living testimony) before taking too firm grounds on some new thing [Anna Rice]." He concluded a letter to GC secretary Leroy Nicola with the prayer that God would "save his people in this hour of perplexities." During the next three decades Loughborough would invest much time and effort in combating Rice's alleged influence in the church.[31]

If Anna Rice appeared to counterfeit White's visions, the phenomena Loughborough encountered at the Mount Vernon camp meeting in August 1891 raised questions concerning the nature of faith healing. At the end of a week in which E. R. Jones, J. N. Loughborough, W. W. Prescott, and A. T. Jones had preached sermons about biblical types, the Year of Jubilee, righteousness by faith, and the rise of Adventism, church leaders conducted a praise service. A. T. Jones asked those who were sick or handicapped to approach the platform. Thirty came forward. After reading James 5, Jones anointed their heads with oil. Then he and Loughborough placed their hands on them and prayed for healing. Instantly, all 30 were restored to health. Astounded, John wrote GC president Olsen: "We have had a glorious camp meeting here." He told *Review* readers: "I can bear witness that the Ohio camp-meeting was the nearest approach to a pentecostal outpouring of the Spirit of God I have witnessed since 1844. Praise be to his [God's] holy name!" He called the Mount Vernon camp meeting "a green spot in the heavenly journey." Similar instantaneous healings occurred two weeks later at the Decatur, Illinois, camp meeting where Jones spoke.[32]

As previous chapters have shown, Sabbathkeeping Adventists recognized faith healings (the cure of disease by supernatural means through faith in divine power) as biblically sound doctrine according to James 5:14, 15. From its very beginning, the *Review* frequently described incidents of instant healing following prayer, carried articles about the Bible principles of faith healing, and warned against counterfeits. As a boy during the Millerite movement, John had witnessed miraculous healings in the 1840s. During the 1850s and 1860s he had seen Adventist pioneer workers instantly restored to health following prayer and anointing in New York, Michigan, Wisconsin, and California. Although in the 1890s some Adventists (perhaps conflating faith healing with the holy flesh movement in Indiana) suspected that such miracles might be a form of fanaticism, Loughborough remained firmly convinced that they were the work of the Holy Spirit.[33]

Although Loughborough had been instrumental in bringing healing to others, his own health deteriorated in 1891. The symptoms were mysterious: chills, fever, fainting spells, dizziness, aching, and an inexplicable weariness. On May 24, 1892, John fainted on the street in Bowling Green, Ohio. Seeking an explanation, he explored the cellar beneath the mission house. There he discovered that the "earthen sewer" (made of stones and clay) had burst during the recent rainstorms, turning the basement into "a trap for the filth to pour in." After he installed iron pipes and connected them to the sewer system under the street, the mysterious symptoms disappeared. "It is a wonder to me that half of us did not get the cholera or some other diseases," he wrote Olsen. "Thank the Lord that is cured." He also thanked his thrifty wife for paying the hefty $150 repair costs from the room rents she charged boarders at the mission (what John called "that little scheme" of hers).[34]

If the Loughboroughs had been spared from a painful death, however, they mourned the passing of others whom they loved. In a letter to Ellen White in 1893 John bemoaned the fact that "those associated with us in preaching the truth when I started out [in the 1850s] are ALL gone now, but you and I [*sic*]."[35] That fall, Merritt E. Cornell, John's partner in evangelism from Maine to California, died of an internal hemorrhage at 66 while caring for his paralyzed wife. Then Mary Haskell, one of John's earliest converts in Maine whom he had baptized in 1866, died of a stroke at 81 in 1894.[36]

The harshest blow, however, came that fall when 30-year-old Delmer was admitted to Battle Creek Sanitarium with typhoid fever contracted at a camp meeting. Attributing his son's illness to overwork during his recent evangelistic series in Indiana and Illinois, John left for meetings in southern Illinois. He wrote Ellen White, "I hope he will be better soon." But Delmer did not get better—instead, on October 8 he died in his sleep of inflammation of the bowels. A. T. Jones, W. W. Prescott, and G. C. Tenney presided at his funeral in the Battle Creek Tabernacle, and GC president Olsen sent his condolences. The *Review* described his brief life as "a bright and growing one." "A large circle of friends who loved him" would now miss him.[37]

Exactly one week later John's last living (family) link to his childhood in Victor, New York, disappeared when his 93-year-old mother Minerva Rowley died at her daughter Minerva Jane Chapman's home in Battle Creek. Reared as a Methodist, she had accepted the Millerite message of Christ's soon return in 1844. Then a few years before she died, she had converted to Seventh-day Adventism. "The calm expression of peace on her face in death," G. C. Tenney informed *Review* readers, "was an index of her peaceful life." Once again the family gathered at the Battle Creek Tabernacle, where the same three ministers who had served at Delmer's funeral now presided at his grandmother's service. Days later John and Maria selected tombstones for the two graves, sharing the expense between them.[38]

LOUGHBOROUGH'S WRITINGS AND DIARY

Given Loughborough's increased administrative duties, he had little time for writing books (other than *Rise and Progress*) and articles for church periodicals. John and Annie had stopped preparing material for the *Youth's Instructor* and the *Pacific Health Journal* by 1891. Nonetheless, his *Hand Book of Health* (1868) and his numerous articles on medical and health issues in the *PHJ* had not escaped the notice of medical professionals. Although Loughborough may not have been informed of it, in 1893 the Pan-American Medical Congress compiled a list of "Medical Journals to Which the Official Bulletins of the Congress Were Regularly Furnished." The list described the editor of the *PHJ* as "Dr. J. N. Loughborough." It was his only honorary doctorate.[39]

Between 1891 and 1894 John penned only six articles for the *Review*, and their positive, cheerful tone reflected the growing spiritual experience of a man who longed for the righteousness of Christ in his life. In a letter to Ellen White in 1893, he confessed, "I never had such clear views of the love of God, or felt that heaven was so near to me. . . . I want all there is of me to be used as he wills. . . . I am so glad that He has borne so long with my errors and wrongs and mistakes. I know He has taken some of the IRON out of my nature. Oh! I want it all taken out and [I want] to be a meek, humble lamb at His feet. It is His righteousness and His character that I claim by faith. In HIM I live." In his *Review* articles he urges readers to praise God often, trust Him more, love their neighbors, and return their tithes and offerings.[40]

One of John's most creative articles (inspired by Bunyan's *Pilgrim's Progress*) that appeared in the *Signs* told the story of "Do-Little" and "Do-Too-Much," two church workers in the "Middle States" who never attended services or gave money to the cause, preferring to follow their "religion . . . of convenience" instead.[41] More didactic in tone, "Bible Readings" in *The Home Missionary* gave readers a 10-step procedure to use in "imparting religious instruction to inquiring minds," incorporating a formula he had used hundreds of times in his own ministry.[42]

In fact, anyone who reads John's diary would conclude that his entire life followed a formula. The daily regimen of this very choleric man included set times for rising (5:00 a.m.), writing letters or manuscripts (6:00 a.m.-3:00 p.m.), holding committee meetings (3:00-8:00 p.m.), and retiring (9:00 p.m.). On a weekly basis he now took at least one bath and one nap, and his health was the better for it. Yet he managed to get by with a haircut every three months!

Now in his early 60s, John was showing signs of slowing down. Instead of climbing mountains, he and Annie took walks. Because John earned $25 a week, they could afford travelogues on India and China, meetings of the Swedish Society, knickknacks at the Chicago Exposition, and visits to the Mormon Temple at Kirtland, Ohio. They also purchased an organ (which John probably played, since he gave lectures on the organ). A rising income enabled them to enjoy such items as lemons and almonds that had been too expensive before. On the July 4 holidays, the couple joined friends for picnics at Petoskey Bay and Goguac Lake, where on a blistering day in 1892 John actually "bathed" (he couldn't swim) in the lake.[43] He would have been surprised to learn that within two years he would visit many more lakes all across Europe.

---

[1] Ellen G. White to O. A. Olsen, 1890, quoted in JNL, *The Great Second Advent Movement*, p. 485.

[2] EGW to JNL, in *Testimonies* (Mountain View, Calif.: Pacific Press Pub. Assn., 1948), vol. 7, p. 288; EGW to JNL, letter 46, 1890, DF 230, CAR; EGW to O. A. Olsen, fall 1890, cited by JNL to C. E. Holmes, May 2, 1920, m. 006529, CAR. Some of that "unbelief and doubt and skepticism," in fact, emanated from conference presidents who in the mid-1890s had believed unfavorable reports regarding Ellen White's ministry that led a few of them to invalidate her divine gift of prophecy. Some conference officers had declared that they "would not receive the testimonies" she wrote. Mrs. White, seeing this as part of "a strong confederacy" against her, urged GC leaders to send Loughborough to camp meetings across the U.S. to counteract this prevailing atmosphere of doubt and skepticism. See G. Valentine, *Prophet and Presidents*, p. 108.

[3] *ST*, Jan. 9, 1893, p. 157; *RH*, Sept. 20, 1892, p. 608; *RH*, Feb. 2, 1897, p. 78; *RH*, Dec. 21, 1897, p. 818. Because of the intervention of GC president O. A. Olsen, the manuscript was first approved by the GC Theological Committee and published by the GC Association rather than by the Review and Herald or Pacific Press (O. A. Olsen to JNL, Dec. 22, 26, 1892, GC Archives).

[4] *Home Missionary*, October 1892, p. 219.

[5] *RH*, Feb. 21, 1893, p. 128.

[6] *RH*, Nov. 3, 1891, p. 685.

[7] JNL, *Rise and Progress*, "Preface," pp. iii, 114; JNL, diary, June and December 1890; speech typescript manuscript (n.d.), CAR; EGW to JNL, Feb. 21, 1890, letter 120, 1890, CAR; A. L. White, *Ellen G. White: The Early Years*, vol. 1, pp. 92, 93; Vande Vere, *Windows*, p. 29. Loughborough did interview some women, including Ellen White's mother, Eunice Harmon, and her older sister Sarah Harmon in addition to Mrs. Haines, Drusilla Lamson, Mrs. Truesdail, and Ira Abbey.

[8] JNL, *The Great Second Advent Movement*, pp. 485, 486; "Individual Experiences," p. 3.

[9] JNL, diary, January 1891-September 1892. John received the first published copy of his book on September 11, 1892.

[10] Some factual gaffes worth noting include Voltaire's prediction of the Bible's demise during the French Revolution of 1789-1799 (he died in 1778); the Reign of Terror lasting from 1792-1795 (instead of 1793-1794); Miller's death in 1848 rather than 1849; James and Ellen White wed in 1846, not 1845; Bates' first trip to Jackson was in 1849, not 1851; White's first health reform vision occurred on June 6 (rather than June 3), 1863; and Jupiter and Saturn could not be inhabited because those planets have neither oxygen nor water to sustain life.

[11] JNL, *Rise and Progress*, pp. 30, 71, 119, 120, 127, 131, 139, 147, 156, 318; "Apostolic and Adventist Experience," pp. 21-33; "The Shut Door," *BTS*, March 1904, pp. 146-148; EGW to JNL, Aug. 24, 1874, DF 230, CAR; JNL, *Home Missionary*, May 1894, p. 99; A. L. White, *Ellen G. White: The Lonely Years*, vol. 3, p. 396. For a succinct summary of the factual and interpretational errors in Loughborough's *Rise and Progress* and *The Great Second Advent Movement*, see Brian E. Strayer, "When Loughborough Got It

Wrong: An Analysis of John Norton Loughborough's Historical Writings" (typed manuscript, 2011).

[12] See, for example, J. Lake, *Ellen White Under Fire*, pp. 40, 45, 57, 70, 164, 165, 302, 305.

[13] See JNL's camp meeting reports in *RH,* Mar. 17, 1891, p. 174; July 21, 1891, pp. 462, 464; Sept. 29, 1891, p. 604; Mar. 8, 1892, p. 155; Apr. 26, 1892, pp. 266, 269; May 10, 1892, p. 302; May 17, 1892, p. 317; June 7, 1892, p. 363; June 28, 1892, p. 415; July 12, 1892, p. 446; Aug. 30, 1892, pp. 553, 556; Oct. 25, 1892, pp. 667, 668; Apr. 4, 1893, p. 219; June 27, 1893, p. 414; July 18, 1893, p. 461; July 25, 1893, pp. 477, 478; Aug. 22, 1893, pp. 539, 540; Aug. 29, 1893, p. 556; Sept. 12, 1893, pp. 588, 589; Oct. 3, 1893, p. 628; Oct. 17, 1893, p. 655; July 17, 1894, p. 462; in *ST,* Sept. 26, 1892, p. 733; Oct. 3, 1892, p. 749; Sept. 24, 1894, p. 732; in the New York *Indicator*, Mar. 7, 1894, p. 2; and in his diaries for August 1892, September 1893, and August 1894.

[14] *RH,* Oct. 11, 1892, p. 635.

[15] *RH,* Mar. 1, 1973, p. 21; *RH,* July 23, 1950, p. 242.

[16] *RH,* July 21, 1891, p. 462.

[17] *RH,* Oct. 11, 1892, p. 635; JNL to G. B. Starr, Oct. 18, 1892, m. 52, CAR.

[18] *RH,* Mar. 5, 1959, pp. 4, 5.

[19] *PUR*, May 27, 1968, p. 1.

[20] *RH,* Mar. 24, 1891, p. 192; *RH,* Oct. 20, 1891, pp. 653, 656; *RH,* Mar. 29, 1892, p. 205; *RH,* Mar. 14, 1893, p. 169; GC Committee Minutes, July 27-October 15, 1891, pp. 24, 32, 36-38, 51-53; GC Committee Minutes, 1894, p. 100; *GCB*, 1891, pp. 9, 23, 24, 175, 218, 249, 252, 254; *GCB,* 1893, pp. 475, 491; *Home Missionary*, April 1891, p. 74; minutes of the Foreign Mission Board, July 27, 1892-October 25, 1893; *ST*, Aug. 22, 1892, p. 651. GC president Olsen frequently summoned him to Battle Creek for GC business meetings. See Olsen to JNL, Sept. 15, 1891, GC Archives.

[21] See JNL's reports in *RH,* Nov. 17, 1891, p. 717; Sept. 6, 1892, p. 572; Oct. 18, 1892, pp. 651, 653; Oct. 17, 1893, p. 660; Oct. 24, 1893, pp. 670, 671, 674; Oct. 31, 1893, p. 687; Mar. 6, 1894, p. 155; JNL, *ST,* Dec. 18, 1893, p. 108; JNL, diary, February 1893; Olsen to JNL, Nov. 11. 1891, GC Archives. As an example of Loughborough's love of statistics, see his "Illinois Conference Address," Aug. 24, 1892, pp. 1-6, m. 015951, CAR.

[22] *RH,* June 9, 1891, p. 365; *RH,* Mar. 31, 1891, p. 205; *RH.* June 16, 1891, pp. 379, 380; *RH,* July 24, 1930, p. 28; *RH,* Nov. 14, 1974, p. 22; *RH,* Oct. 13, 1927, p. 16; *ST,* Apr. 10, 1892, p. 365; GC Auditor's Statement, 1894. Although J. N. Loughborough taught himself to type on a "calligraph" sometime in the 1880s, he was never a very fast, accurate typist, as his letters reveal.

[23] *RH,* Oct. 23, 1894, p. 671; *RH,* Oct. 20, 1891, p. 653.

[24] For reports by and about Delmer and Maria Loughborough in the *RH,* see May 26, 1891, pp. 331, 332; Aug. 18, 1891, pp. 523, 524; Nov. 10, 1891, pp. 701, 702; Dec. 1, 1891, p. 750; July 26, 1892, pp. 475, 476; Aug. 30, 1892, p. 556; Sept. 20, 1892, p. 605; Sept. 27, 1892, p. 620; Sept. 19, 1893, pp. 604, 605; and in the *Sabbath School Worker*, January 1892, p. 2; January 1893, p. 2; October 1893, pp. 170, 191. Although Maria received a ministerial license in 1892, in 1893 the conference gave her only a missionary license.

[25] For reports by and about Delmer and Maria Loughborough in the *RH,* see Nov. 1, 1892, p. 683; Oct. 17, 1893, p. 654; July 24, 1894, p. 477; Sept. 19, 1893, p. 604; and in *Sabbath School Worker*, February 1894, p. 26; and *LUH*, June 3, 1914, p. 6. Interestingly, in 1891 Ellen White blocked Delmer's and Maria's appointment to the Cleveland

Mission on the grounds that "their experience was not equal to the responsibility." See O. A. Olsen to JNL, Aug. 27, 1891, GC Archives.

[26] For information on the Central Bible Training School, see reports in *GCB* (1891), p. 218; JNL, diary, September 1891, November 1892, flyleaf and December of 1893; WCW to JNL, Nov. 17, 1891, WCW Letter Books, CAR; JNL to O. A. Olsen, and Dec. 12, 28, 1892, JNL Folder, Box 2, General-Historical Miscellaneous Records, General Conference Archives; JNL to O. A. Olsen, Apr. 24, 1893, m. 006529, CAR; JNL to EGW, May 7, 1893, m. 52, CAR; *RH,* Mar. 1, 1892, pp. 140, 141; Nov. 29, 1892, pp. 748, 749; Jan. 31, 1893, pp. 75, 76; and *Sabbath School Worker*, March 1894, p. 56. Bible institutes met in Battle Creek, Cleveland, Indianapolis, Springfield, West Salem, Kankakee, Rockford, Aledo, and Ottawa between October 18 and December 27, 1893.

[27] EGW, "Remarks at Presidents' Council," February 25-27 and March 2-4, 1891, ms. 91, 1891, CAR; *RH,* Dec. 15, 1891, pp. 780, 781; *ST*, Mar. 6, 1892, p. 274; *RH,* Apr. 12, 1892, p. 236; *RH,* May 3, 1892, pp. 284, 285; *RH,* June 21, 1892, p. 397; *RH,* Feb. 7, 1893, p. 88; JNL, diary, February 1894.

[28] On Loughborough's support of Black pastors, see Douglas Morgan, *Lewis C. Sheafe: Apostle to Black America* (Hagerstown, Md.: Review and Herald Pub. Assn., 2010), p. 128. Loughborough would later ordain Sheafe to the ministry. Regarding his work for Hispanics, see GC Minutes, July 7, 1893, p. 67. For Loughborough's support of Chicago's work among the Chinese, see *RH,* Apr. 26, 1892, p. 266 and Apr. 10, 1894, p. 237; *GCB*, 1893, pp. 268, 505; GC Minutes, Mar. 19, 1893, p. 49, and Apr. 2, 1894, p. 15; JNL to O. A. Olsen, "Report for District No. 3," Apr. 30, 1893, CAR; *ST,* Mar. 5, 1894, p. 285; and JNL, diary, May 1893 and September-October 1894.

[29] JNL, *Rise and Progress*, pp. 374, 375.

[30] Annie Loughborough's affidavit regarding the Walling Case, 1891, m. 52, CAR; EGW, "Statements Concerning the Walling Suit," Jan. 23, 1895, ms. 2b, 1895, CAR; JNL, "Statement Regarding the Walling Case," 1891, m. 52, CAR; Valentine, *Prophet and Presidents*, p. 87.

[31] JNL, diary, October-November 1891; January, April, and May 1893; JNL to Leroy Nicola, Feb. 24, 1894, CAR. Actually, Rice had very little influence in the church after 1894.

[32] *RH,* Sept. 1, 1891, pp. 552, 553; *RH,* Sept. 15, 1891, p. 571; *RH,* Oct. 6, 1891, p. 619; *RH,* Oct. 13, 1891, pp. 636, 637; JNL, diary, August 1891; JNL to O. A. Olsen, Aug. 25, 1891, CAR. For another interpretation of Adventist faith healings in the context of the "Receive ye the Holy Ghost" movement of the mid-1890s, see Gary Land's biography of A. F. Ballenger, *Seeker After Light* (Berrien Springs, Mich.: Andrews University Press, 2000). GC president O. A. Olsen also rejoiced "that the Lord wrought for you there [at Mt. Vernon]" (Olsen to JNL, Aug. 26, 1891, GC Archives).

[33] "Healing, Faith," *SDA Encyclopedia*, vol. 10, pp. 675, 676.

[34] JNL, diary, May 1892 and January 1894; JNL to O. A. Olsen, Dec. 12, 1892, m. 006529, CAR; Olsen to JNL, Dec. 13, 29, 1892, GC Archives.

[35] JNL to EGW, Dec. 3, 1893, m. 52, CAR. It was not quite true, for Uriah Smith, J. O. Corliss, S. N. Haskell, G. I. Butler, and a handful of other Adventist ministers still lived and continued to preach at a slower pace.

[36] JNL, diary, November 1893; *RH,* Jan. 23, 1894, p. 63; *ST,* Feb. 12, 1894, p. 237.

[37] JNL to EGW, Sept. 4, 1894, m. 52, CAR; JNL, diary, October 1894; *RH,* Oct. 30, 1894, p. 687; O. A. Olsen to JNL, Oct. 23, 1894, GC Archives.

[38] JNL, diary, October 1894 and flyleaf of 1894 diary; *RH,* Oct. 30, 1894, p. 687.

[39] See *PHJ*, January 1891, pp. 1, 26; "Transaction of the Pan-American Medical Congress," 1893, in the author's possession.

[40] JNL to EGW, Dec. 3, 1893, m. 52, CAR; for JNL's *RH* articles, see Jan. 27, 1891, p. 50; Feb. 24, 1891, pp. 115, 116; Mar. 3, 1891, pp. 129, 130; Mar. 10, 1891, pp. 147, 148; Dec. 5, 1893, pp. 758, 759; and Jan. 9, 1894, p. 18.

[41] JNL, *ST,* Mar. 14, 1892, p. 301.

[42] JNL, *Home Missionary*, March 1892, pp. 62, 63.

[43] JNL, diaries, January 1891-October 1894.

CHAPTER XVI

NEW CHALLENGES AND HEALTH PROBLEMS (1894-1897)

"Often do I call to mind former days when your father, mother, and myself were traveling together. . . . I try to do . . . what I can each day . . . to keep at it. . . . [So] the old man has got over some ground yet. . . . I seek to use what there is of me to His [God's] glory. . . . I share much of the sweet presence of the Lord by day."[1]

Despite the fact that in his letter to W. C. White, J. N. Loughborough, now 63, called himself an "old man," his extensive preaching tours and growing administrative duties in the mid-1890s demonstrated that he could still "get over some ground yet." Refusing to let physical afflictions curtail his activities, John "kept at it," sometimes by sheer grit and determination. During 1895, for example, he traveled 13,600 miles by train to preach 176 sermons (averaging more than three each week) and attend 607 meetings (almost two a day) in nine states stretching from Michigan to Texas. Two years later he logged 29,600 miles, preached 246 sermons (about five a week), attended 400 meetings (more than one a day), and made 134 visits in 11 states and England. He had trimmed his portfolio of sermons to five topics: the fulfillment of Ellen White's visions, the rise and progress of the SDA cause, the sealing message, prophetic signs of the end of time, and the health message. Because he knew such topics by heart, he did not need notes to preach. Consequently, he could roam the platform, waving his arms and projecting his deep voice so that those up to half a mile away could hear him.[2]

With 45 years of active service, Loughborough was by 1897 the longest-serving minister in Adventist ranks. As a result, he enjoyed a celebrity status comparable to that of Billy Graham in the twentieth century. He was in demand at church dedications and baptisms. People did not consider a camp meeting a success without "dear Brother Loughborough" on hand to tell stories about the early years of the Advent movement. Congregations from coast to coast greeted his mantra—"The cause is *advancing*"—with hearty "Amens!" He was as popular in the North as in the South, in the East as in the West. His charisma surmounted barriers of ethnicity and language: he preached in churches in which the members spoke Swedish, Norwegian, Danish, German, or Chinese, and the experience of working with translators would stand him in good stead during his European tour of 1896-1897.[3]

MOVING TO KANSAS

It also proved valuable for his next assignment—Kansas—where German-speaking Adventists held their own camp meeting. At the General Conference session in the spring of 1895 church officials reassigned the Loughboroughs from District No. 3 (the Midwest) to District No. 5 (the West and Southwest). So John and Annie moved to Topeka to be centrally located within their territory. They spent the month of May unpacking, hanging curtains, hauling books upstairs, making window frames and screens, laying carpet, and wallpapering the rooms of their new home at 815 West 5th Street.[4]

But before they settled in, speaking invitations began arriving. John rushed to Texas to give the dedicatory address at the new Keene Industrial School with its 180 teenaged students. His summer filled quickly with church workers' councils, youth convocations, and camp meetings (10 of them, including Kansas, Oklahoma, Arkansas, Texas, Missouri, Nebraska, and Colorado). Despite the grueling travel schedule, bouts of illness, and the oppressive heat (102 degrees in the shade at the Oakland Park camp meeting), Loughborough kept going. Perhaps telling stories to fidgety kindergarteners gave him renewed energy. At the German camp meetings in Kansas and Oklahoma he learned how to pause so that interpreters could catch up with him. But John returned home after the last meetings in Lincoln, Nebraska, "sick with [a] cold and fever." Despite the hugs and handshakes, conversions and baptisms, multiple camp meetings took their toll on mind and body.[5]

If camp meetings brought glamour, however, administrative duties required grit, and because ecclesiastical calculus equated aging with experience, church leaders put Loughborough on many committees. As one of eleven men on the GC Executive Committee and a "delegate at large" at GC sessions, he occasionally chaired plenary meetings. The denomination required his expertise on ministerial credentials and licenses committees, committees on resolutions, and committees on nominations. His voice was often heard at meetings of the Committee for Education, the Battle Creek Sanitarium Improvement Corporation, the SDA Publishing Association, the Foreign Mission Board, the Committee on Camp Meeting Arrangements, and the Medical Missionary and Benevolent Association, to mention a few. When he proposed resolutions and made motions, delegates listened with respect, then passed them unanimously. Yet whatever other gifts they possessed, his fellow ministers were well endowed with that of gab, and consequently GC meetings lasted for hours. After one lengthy service, John wrote in his diary: "My head feels sore. I am weary with so much sitting." The next day he played hooky and visited his old Millerite acquaintance Joshua V. Himes at the sanitarium.[6]

Every fall, of course, Superintendent Loughborough made the rounds of his territory to attend business sessions in each state. In District No. 5, at least, it required the patience of Job and the wisdom of Solomon, for few of the region's rugged individualists saw eye to eye on anything. Although most Adventists followed the tithing plan (adopted in 1878) and passed the offering plate in church on Sabbath, the Adventists in Arkansas still adhered to the Systematic Benevolence plan (begun in 1859) and collected offerings door to door on Sundays in the 1890s. In such situations John found it wise to "give counsel" without laying down the law. Considering Loughborough's near reverence for Ellen White's writings, the objection some had to creating an index to her works (thus making them "books of reference" rather than devotional study guides) may have surprised him. While he respected the view, toward the end of his life John would compile numerous indexes (both handwritten and typed) of Mrs. White's books and articles for his own use. Meanwhile his wife Annie, who delighted in teaching the kindergarten Sabbath school at Topeka, served as the secretary of the Kansas Sabbath School Association and president of the state's Christian Help Bands.[7]

If Loughborough's preaching and administrative duties made huge demands on his time, his hectic travel schedule took its toll on his health. Even at the end of the nineteenth century, traveling by boat or train in the U.S. involved many hazards and inconveniences. With a frequency that would astound twenty-first-century travelers, paddle wheelers ran aground on sandbars or impaled their hulls on sunken boulders and rotting trees. Riverboats and Great Lakes steamships burst their boilers and burned to the waterline or sank in storms. Trains collided, plowed into buffalo herds, or hit washed-out sections of track or collapsed bridges and derailed, and hundreds of people died in such tragic accidents every year. John's diaries describe hours-long delays due to train wrecks and washed-out track, railroad stations clouded with cigar smoke, and roads rendered nearly impassable by huge snowdrifts or axle-deep mud.

Despite his vegetarian regimen, regular baths, and frequent naps, Loughborough's childhood bout with malaria occasionally returned to afflict him. To combat the headaches, fevers, and chills, he drank hot lemonade, wrapped himself in a hot dry pack (sweat towels), took hot sponge baths, purged himself with enemas, and (as a last resort) swallowed quinine pills. At the Hutchinson, Kansas, camp meeting in 1895, John's illness so depleted his strength that it left him prostrated for a week. The ministers convened at his bedside. His weak lungs also predisposed him to catch frequent colds during the winter, and he began complaining of rheumatic pains in his right shoulder as well. Although the cause of Adventism was progressing, John's health was regressing, at least temporarily, as he neared his mid-60s.[8]

THE EUROPEAN TOUR OF 1896-1897

Loughborough's 1892 book *Rise and Progress of the Seventh-day Adventists* had sold so well in America by 1895 that GC president Olsen asked him to revise it for a foreign language edition. In January of 1896 John spoke (through an interpreter) with German students at Union College in Lincoln, Nebraska. Subsequently he and Annie devoted several weeks that winter and spring to revising and editing the manuscript. By the time they had added 80 pages of new material (on foreign missions) and finished the index, the German edition had 382 pages. Ignoring the tornado that threatened their home in Topeka, John and Annie finished proofreading the manuscript the day before he left for Battle Creek on the first leg of a nine-month tour of Europe. The next year the Adventist publishing house in Hamburg, Germany, published his book *Entstehung und Fortschrift der Siebenten-Tag-Adventisten.*[9]

In April of 1896 President Olsen had invited Loughborough to visit Adventist institutions in Europe. Consequently John had only three weeks to complete the revisions on the German edition of *Rise and Progress*, settle administrative matters in his district, pack his bags, and take the train to New York to catch the *City of New York* to Southampton. With him were Sophia Walberg, the baker Joseph Smith (headed for Basel), and Elder and Mrs. F. I. Richardson (missionaries to South Africa). Unfortunately the Richardsons became separated in the melee. While Mrs. Richardson boarded the steamer, her husband did not. Confronted with a hysterical woman, John wrote in his diary, "Oh! dear, she quieted down after [the] boat got over the bar." While Mrs. Richardson spent most of the voyage in bed pining for her absent husband, John enjoyed the most pleasant transatlantic crossing of his life. "I [was] not sick a particle," he wrote. En route, he polished the three sermons that church leaders had asked him to present on the continent (Ellen White's divinely inspired ministry, the sealing message, and the rise and progress of Adventism) and placed them in his trunk beside the manuscript of "Spiritual Gifts" he was preparing for the *Bible Students' Library*.[10]

Unfortunately, when the *City of New York* arrived in Southampton and the Adventist party took the train to London, John's trunk did not follow them. Since England had not yet adopted the American system of checking luggage on the train, railway officials in London dumped the trunk at Waterloo Station. After Loughborough and J. O. Corliss had spent three fruitless days searching for a suitcase with "Topeka, Kansas" written on it, they returned to William Spicer's home. During a 30-minute nap on the sofa by the hearth, however, John had a peculiar dream. In it a voice assured him that he would find his trunk in Sweden. Sure enough, when the boat docked in Gothenburg, there was his steamer trunk sitting on the wharf. How it got there remained a mystery, one that he attributed to God's answer to his prayer.[11]

During his European tour Loughborough would attend 372 meetings, preach 273 sermons, and make 70 visits to Adventist believers.[12] He spent

June and July traveling with E. J. Waggoner and H. P. Holser in Norway, Sweden, and Denmark, attending ministerial councils, dedicating churches and schools, baptizing new converts, preaching in tiny churches, and staying in the homes of scattered believers in villages whose names he frequently misspelled. Although Scandinavian camp meetings were smaller than those in America (the one at Frederiksstad, Norway, featured 50 Adventists staying in 10 tents), believers responded to his preaching with equal enthusiasm. "It was a heavenly sitting together for us all," John exclaimed. In Copenhagen, Denmark, two dozen of them prepared a picnic for him in the woods at the park near the royal palace. Probably the highlight of his first Scandinavian trip came in Sweden when he had the opportunity to interview several men and women who, as children and young people, had preached and prophesied in 1843. One of these young persons declared: "Yes, I had to preach. I had no devising in the matter. A power came upon me, and I uttered what I was compelled by that power to utter." Called *rapare* (those who speak with divine power), nearly 40 children (from toddlers to teenagers) had quoted Bible texts, related visions, preached imminent judgment, and called for repentance. When Lutheran prelates and King Oscar I's officials threatened them with arrest, beatings, or confinement at Orebro Prison, they fled into the forest. Excited to be "in the midst of 1844 [history]," John visited the prison and other sites connected with the child preachers.[13]

In late July Louis R. Conradi, leader of the church in Germany, met Loughborough, Waggoner, and Holser in Hamburg. After touring the city on foot in the rain for several hours John preached to 225 church employees from all over Europe. At the close of the two-week conference delegates speaking 12 different languages gave "spirited" testimonies at a social meeting. Loughborough baptized five of them and ordained R. G. Klingbeil to the gospel ministry. Mixing pleasure with church business, John visited Hanover, Frankfort-am-Main, Mayence, and the Luther sites in Worms and Wittenberg before taking the train to Strasburg and Basel (where he visited the graves of J. N. Andrews and J. H. Waggoner).[14]

At Yverdun (the home of the famous educational reformer Pestalozzi), Loughborough spent 11 days preaching in a grove of poplars near beautiful Lake Neuchâtel. More than 200 Adventists had gathered to hear him share stories of the rise of Adventism in America. Since half of them spoke

French and the other half German, they met in separate tents. At times interpreters would stand on each side of John, simultaneously translating the message. Scores of local citizens attended, and eight of them asked for baptism. Following the camp meeting, Waggoner and Loughborough hiked several miles into the Jura Mountains for a stunning 200-mile vista of the majestic Alps before hastening on to visit the Institut Sanitaire and the Adventist school at Peterlen (near Bienne), with Swiss evangelist Albert Vuilleuimier and his son Luc.[15]

As Waggoner left for Turkey, Loughborough returned to Denmark in August and for the next three months traveled across Scandinavia with Elder Johnson, holding meetings in tents, halls, and private homes; baptizing new converts; and ordaining deacons and elders. Along the way, John visited Viking museums, chatted with Laplanders in their huts, and preached at the royal palace in Stockholm (where he boldly touched His Majesty's throne and sat in the king's seat in the government chamber). After filling 16 appointments in Sweden (including an invitation to speak to 200 Methodists), Loughborough returned to Denmark for a series of 26 talks to the students at the Frederikshavn Höjskole (an SDA high school). At this point in the tour he informed *Review* readers that he had given 110 discourses with interpreters translating them into five languages. "I have had no opportunity as yet to give a straight English discourse, without an interpreter, on this side [of] the water [Atlantic Ocean]." Seeking solitude with his (English) thoughts, John gathered colorful leaves for Angelina Cornell (the widow of Merritt Cornell) and wandered the beach collecting pretty shells.[16]

Returning to Hamburg in November, Loughborough spent the next four weeks visiting Adventist groups in Prussia (with Conradi translating into German) and Holland (with Klingbeil translating into Dutch). For the most part he preached in the homes of scattered believers, except in Amsterdam (a city of 400,000 with approximately 30 Adventists) and Rotterdam (a city of 250,000 with 40 believers), where each group had small church buildings. Ever the history buff, John visited the tourist sites in The Hague, Haarlem, Magdeburg, and Halle. He also gained added appreciation for the military might of the Second Reich when he saw 60,000 of Kaiser Wilhelm II's troops massed along the border between East Prussia and Russia.[17]

His merry-go-round itinerary took him back to Scandinavia yet a third time in December for the dedicatory address at the Adventist high school at Frederikshavn. Then he spent a month visiting scattered bands of believers throughout Norway, preaching and baptizing new converts. Along the way, he gathered more shells on the beaches, saw a 60-foot whale in the North Sea, and visited Trondheim Cathedral where Swedish kings had been crowned rulers of Norway in the eleventh century. Here he also witnessed the "shortest days of sunshine" he would ever see in his life: it lasted two hours (from 11:00 a.m. to 1:00 p.m.)! After logging 1,157 miles in seven months on the continent, during which he gave 200 sermons (one a day) to 16 different language groups, Loughborough returned to London on December 30, 1897, relieved that he could finally preach in English without an interpreter.[18]

During the month of January, in addition to speaking in London, Bristol, Bath, and Southampton, John revisited some of his favorite haunts. He toured St. Paul's Cathedral; bought a new suit at Hope Brothers (a men's clothing store); visited the Roman baths at Bath (drinking its famous mineral water); and strolled the London docks. In Southampton John walked 120 miles to visit old friends. When Waggoner, Holser, and Loughborough held a weeklong conference for denominational staff at the chapel on Duncombe Road in Holloway, London, John was thrilled to learn that the British Conference now had nearly 80 Bible workers and canvassers, whereas in 1883 there had been only one. Before leaving for America he returned to Southampton and delivered 10 discourses to about 100 Adventists gathered in the tiny chapel on Shirley Road, a stone's throw from Ravenswood where the Loughboroughs had lived nearly two decades earlier. Now "Old England" had more than 500 Seventh-day Adventists.[19] Boarding the *New York*, he returned to the U.S. After arriving, he exclaimed, "Thanks be to God for his fatherly care, and for good health, in the travel and labors of the past eight and one-half months of my absence from America."[20]

General Conference president Olsen had sent Loughborough on his exhausting tour to report on the progress of the work in northern Europe, and John accomplished it by sharing his detailed observations concerning Adventist churches, conferences, and institutions in private letters and through several articles published in the *Review*. But he did far more. His sermons and personal visits strengthened the faith of scores of new converts, many of whom he personally baptized; his advice (often sought) helped make Adventist institutions more efficient and cost-effective; and his genial humor and high work ethic promoted a positive bond between European and American church leaders who would long cherish memories of Loughborough's good will tour.

If J. N. Loughborough hoped for some respite before tackling his administrative duties, he was disappointed. Once the 1897 GC session got underway in late February and March, he found himself swept up in its business meetings. Once again he served on several key committees. In addition, delegates appointed him to the board of trustees of the new Haskell Home for Orphans in Battle Creek. As always, he took an active part in the deliberations of the Medical Missionary and Benevolent Association, the Education Society, Battle Creek College, and several other organizations. Weary of sitting, he retreated to his brother William's workshop to craft wooden cases to hold his growing coin and shell collections. He also took time to visit old friends such as Angelina Cornell, Permelia Lane, and Linnie Caviness, and enjoy "popcorn feasts" with his brother William and wife, Eliza, his niece Winnie, and his sister Minerva. At the end of March, he returned to Topeka, Kansas, to the loving wife who had not seen him in nearly a year.[21]

LOUGHBOROUGH'S WRITINGS AND DIARY

Because of Loughborough's peripatetic lifestyle in the mid-1890s, he had little time to write more than cursory reports during his travels. Aside from revising *Rise and Progress*, between November 1894 and January 1897 he wrote only 17 articles for church publications. We see his lifelong fascination with geography reflected in "Not Heard of God," a short piece in the *Signs* explaining the modern locations of biblical Tarshish, Pul, Lud, Tubal, and Javan.[22] "The Latter Rain," an article he sent to the *Home Missionary*, likewise demonstrates his deep interest in end-time events and how Adventists should prepare for them.[23]

The *Review* printed John's other 15 articles, some of which had appeared before in other periodicals. For example, his three-part series on the "Personality of the Devil," first published in three March 1881 *Signs* issues, now went out for a new generation to read.[24] John's only foray into fiction—the five-part series on "Uncle Elkins and His Nephews," penned from Frederikshavn, Denmark—featured a rather preachy uncle sharing Adventist history stories with two prim and proper nephews who visited him each week (one wonders how real boys and girls responded to its wooden style).[25] Loughborough's sermonic style dominates his short pieces dealing with disobedience ("Fruits of Fearfulness"), unbelief ("Witnesses of Faith"), harmony ("One"), sinful hearts ("The Root"), and keeping covenants with God ("Vows").[26]

As he reflected on his Adventist past, John expressed gratitude that "My Old Friend" (the *Advent Review and Sabbath Herald*) had been a part of his life for 44 years. James White had once nicknamed the *Review* "his 'oldest child,'" while Loughborough called it "my oldest friend in this cause," adding, "I am glad to welcome this old friend every week." By 1897 Loughborough was perhaps the only Adventist pioneer still living who had actually read every issue of the *Review* from 1850 on. "I cannot do without it," he declared. "It ought to be in the home of every family that professes the present truth." He urged readers to "keep the ball rolling, and get all you can to take our church paper."[27]

Indeed, John's diary shows that when fatigued with household labor, he relaxed in the parlor with his "old friend" the *Review*. And in Topeka, Kansas, there was *always* work to do. Thanks to his childhood training in carpentry and blacksmithing, John did most of it himself. As his diary attests, even in his 60s John could make window screens, put new bottoms in rocking chairs, dig a root cellar, repair a pump organ or a stove, and craft bookcases, candle stands, and shelves. He and Annie washed the windows in their home, did their laundry, and planted and weeded the vegetable garden.

Weary from "choring around the house," Annie and John found relaxation in a variety of social activities. They attended Thanksgiving "festivals" and Christmas celebrations, often at other Christian churches, then distributed food to the needy. On trips they went sightseeing, visited museums, and toured Chicago's Columbian Exposition. And they shopped for groceries and clothes. When in Battle Creek, they dined with their friends Uriah and Harriet Smith and Dr. John and Ella Kellogg. In 1895 they attended a banquet there reuniting 75 to 100 friends and church workers from the Empire State. John regaled them with stories about "The Birth and Infancy of the SDA Cause in New York," after which Dr. Kellogg dragged them all to the gym for a lecture on health and hygiene that lasted until midnight. Back in Kansas one hot summer's day, after eating ice cream at a friend's home, they bought an icebox and ordered ice so that they could enjoy the new treat more often. Perhaps the promise of ice cream attracted even more friends (especially the gossip Florence Luther, whom John labeled "that talker") to their door for refreshments.

As a conference president and district superintendent, Loughborough was expected to provide bed and board for traveling church employees to save them the expense of lodging and meals at local hotels and restaurants. In his travels John frequently stayed with church members—and his diary proves that he scrupulously tithed the benefits of food and lodging he received. Although Loughborough firmly believed that one can never outgive God's blessings, his generosity defies belief. On a salary of $800-$1,000 a year (roughly $16-$20 a week depending on his administrative duties and the current rate of remuneration), he not only returned a tenth of that to the church, but he also gave generously to a wide range of causes. For example, in 1897 (when he was 65), he pledged more than $100 (six weeks' wages) for the Keene Industrial School, the Oakwood Industrial School (for Blacks), the Graysville Industrial School (for Whites), the Guadalajara (Mexico) Sanitarium, the medical missionary program in India, and a new building in Jamaica. In addition, he pledged $50 (two weeks' income) for the ship *Pitcairn*. Furthermore, half a century before credit cards existed, the Loughboroughs *always* paid cash—and they *always* ended each year in the black (for example, in 1897 John's salary was $1,026 and the family's expenses totaled $992, so they finished the year $34 ahead). In fact, during the Panic of 1893, when railroad magnate J. P. Morgan had loaned the U. S. Treasury tens of millions of dollars to keep the Federal Government afloat, J. N. Loughborough provided the nearly bankrupt General Conference $500 without interest to help it meet its fiscal obligations around the world. Like the heroes of Horatio Alger's rags-to-riches novels, the "boy preacher" of Victor who had once worn borrowed clothing several sizes too large had grown up to become rich enough to bankroll a global church. Following the dictum of the Methodist preacher John Wesley—"Earn all you can; save all you can; give all you can"—the fiscally conservative Loughborough was in great financial shape to think about retirement.[28]

---

[1] JNL to WCW, Dec. 10, 1895, m. 52, CAR.

[2] JNL, diary, flyleaf for 1895 and 1897. Those states included Illinois, Michigan, Texas, Missouri, Kansas, Arkansas, Iowa, Minnesota, North Dakota, South Dakota, Tennessee, Alabama, Georgia, Oklahoma, Colorado, and Nebraska.

[3] *ST,* Nov. 5, 1894, p. 828; *RH,* Nov. 13, 1894, p. 716; *ST,* Jan. 10, 1895, p. 28; *RH,* Jan. 22, 1895, pp. 59, 60; *RH,* June 11, 1895, p. 383.

[4] *RH,* June 11, 1895, p. 383; JNL, diary, May 1895; *RH,* May 7, 1895, p. 303.

[5] For reports of these camp meetings and speaking engagements, see *SWUR,* Jan. 6, 1914, p. 4; *RH,* June 4, 1895, p. 362; *RH,* June 18, 1895, p. 395; JNL, diary, July-October 1895; *RH,* Aug. 6, 1895, p. 511; *RH,* Sept. 3, 1895, p. 570; *RH,* Sept. 24, 1895, p. 617; *RH,* Oct. 1, 1895, p. 633; *RH,* Oct. 15, 1895, p. 668.

[6] *GCB,* 1895, pp. 49, 176, 221, 249, 275, 276, 316, 341, 353, 372, 424, 444, 487; minutes of the Foreign Mission Board, 1892-1896; GC Minutes, Mar. 7, 1895, p. 43 and May 2, 1895, pp. 79, 80; GC Minutes, Feb. 20, 1896, p. 1, and Mar. 10, 1896, p. 26; *RH,* Feb. 12, 1895, p. 111; *RH,* Feb. 19, 1895, p. 128; JNL, diary, March 1895; *RH,* Mar. 12, 1895, p. 171.

[7] *RH,* Sept. 17, 1895, p. 604; *RH,* Nov. 5, 1895, p. 717; GC Minutes, Feb. 20, 1896, p. 1 and Mar. 18, 1896, pp. 58, 124; JNL to WCW, Dec. 10, 1895, m. 52, CAR. Delmer Loughborough's widow did not follow John and Annie to Kansas. Instead she resigned from all of her administrative positions in Illinois and moved to Battle Creek to study medicine at American Medical Missionary College.

[8] JNL, diary, June, August, November 1895.

[9] JNL to WCW, Dec. 10, 1895, m. 52, CAR; JNL, diary, January-May 1896. It is possible that Louis R. Conradi translated Loughborough's *Rise and Progress* into German.

[10] JNL, diary, April-May 1896; *RH,* May 26, 1896, p. 336; JNL, "Spiritual Gifts," *Bible Students' Library* 16 (1895-1899), pp. 3-38.

[11] JNL, diary, June 1896; *RH,* Feb. 18, 1937, p. 10; *RH,* June 6, 1940, p. 9.

[12] JNL, flyleaf of 1896 diary.

[13] JNL, diary, June, July, September 1896; *RH,* June 2, 1896, p. 351; *RH,* Aug. 4, 1896, p. 492; *RH,* Aug. 11, 1896, p. 506; *RH,* Oct. 27, 1896, pp. 686, 687; JNL, *The Great Second Advent Movement,* pp. 140-145. Loughborough actually met Ole Boquist and Mr. Walham, both of whom had been sent to Orebro Prison as teenagers for preaching without government or church permission.

[14] JNL, diary, July-August 1896; *RH,* Aug. 25, 1896, p. 541.

[15] JNL, diary, August 1896; *RH,* Sept. 8, 1896, p. 574; *RH,* Sept. 22, 1896, p. 606.

[16] JNL, diary, August-October 1896; *RH,* Oct. 6, 1896, p. 637; *RH,* Oct. 13, 1896, pp. 655, 656; *RH,* Nov. 3, 1896, p. 704; *RH,* Nov. 10, 1896, p. 719.

[17] JNL, diary, November 1896; *RH,* Dec. 8, 1896, p. 782; *RH,* Dec. 15, 1896, p. 799; *RH,* Dec. 22, 1896, pp. 814, 815; *RH,* Dec. 29, 1896, p. 834.

[18] JNL, diary, November-December 1896; *RH,* Jan. 5, 1897, p. 11; *RH,* Jan. 12, 1897, p. 27; *RH,* Jan. 26, 1897, pp. 59, 60.

[19] JNL, diary, January 1897; *RH,* Feb. 16, 1897, p. 107; *RH,* Feb. 9, 1897, p. 87; *RH,* Feb. 23, 1897, p. 123; G. Hagstotz, *British Isles,* p. 59.

[20] *RH,* Feb. 23, 1897, p. 123.

[21] JNL, diary, February-March 1897. Loughborough's diary shows, however, that he regularly wrote letters to Annie throughout his extensive tour of Europe.

[22] *ST,* Dec. 3, 1896, pp. 758, 759.

[23] *Home Missionary,* April 1896, pp. 83, 84.

[24] *RH,* July 16, 1895, pp. 451, 452; *RH,* July 23, 1895, pp. 466, 467; *RH,* July 30, 1895, pp. 482, 483.

[25] See *RH,* Dec. 15, 1896, pp. 790, 791; Dec. 22, 1896, p. 806; Dec. 29, 1896, pp. 822, 823; Jan. 5, 1897, p. 2; Jan. 12, 1897, p. 18.

[26] See *RH,* Nov. 27, 1894, p. 738; Feb. 5, 1895, pp. 82, 83; May 14, 1895, pp. 306, 307; Aug. 13, 1895, p. 516; Nov. 19, 1895, p. 739; Nov. 26, 1895, pp. 755, 756.

[27] *RH,* Aug. 4, 1896, p. 496.

[28] See JNL's diaries, November 1894-February 1897; New York *Indicator*, Mar. 20, 1895, p. 1; G. Valentine, in *Prophet and Presidents*, pp. 86, 125, quotes GC Treasurer L. T. Nicola in 1896 as stating that the treasury was empty and GC president George Irwin as declaring in 1897 that on some days "we have not a dollar in the treasury" but live "from hand to mouth, so to speak."

CHAPTER XVII

RETIRED—OR NOT? (1897-1901)

"I do not believe my work is done yet. I believe the Lord wants me to speak a word to his people, and thus I am free to go from place to place." "I was released from district and local work [in 1897], that I might be free to go and bear my testimony of the rise of the cause, etc., wherever the providence of God may indicate, and such labor be called for."[1]

Although J. N. Loughborough turned 65 in January of 1897, he had no thoughts of retiring in the conventional sense of that word. Aside from minor health complaints, he still felt strong enough to write articles and books, to preach in local churches, and to travel to camp meetings. Besides, the Adventist Church—whose members in the 1890s still believed in the imminent return of Jesus—had given little thought to providing for its aging pioneer workers. Not until shortly before World War I would the General Conference create the Sustentation Fund for retired employees. Consequently, one kept working until disabilities forced one to resign. Then one lived with relatives or entered a sanitarium for one's remaining days.

As the above quote reveals, the General Conference officers in 1897 started John on the path to retirement by releasing him from most of his administrative responsibilities. After that date he became a delegate-at-large at GC sessions. Although still on salary, he held no conference positions, and leadership gradually reduced his committee appointments. It left him free to fulfill what he called "my commission"—his mandate from Ellen White "to go here and there and everywhere" sharing his faith-building stories about Adventist history and her prophetic ministry. From May to December 1897 Loughborough traveled 29,600 miles, attending 400 meetings and preaching 246 sermons in 11 states and Great Britain. In his first year of semiretirement (1898) he logged 13,500 miles, attended nearly 200 meetings, preached 222 sermons, and made 150 visits in 13 states. In short, he showed no signs of slowing down. Borrowing a metaphor from Joseph Bates, he compared himself to an old horse that could no longer pull the plow but was permitted to "keep the collar on" and walk beside the team.[2]

John's hectic speaking schedule gives the impression, however, that he was still in the harness. During the summer of 1897 he shared his four signature sermons—the parallels between biblical prophets and Ellen White, the rise of Adventism, the fulfillment of end-time prophecies, and signs and wonders in the heavens—at a dozen camp meetings in Iowa, Minnesota, North Dakota, South Dakota, and Nebraska. He spoke under canvas tents pitched in shady groves; at the "Corn Palace," a large public hall in Mitchell, South Dakota; on the Chautauqua grounds in Beatrice, Nebraska; and at the State Fairgrounds in Des Moines, Iowa. And he slept in tents and in clay houses with two-foot-thick walls, plastered dirt floors, and ovens heated by sheep or cow manure. Thousands heard him preach and scores requested baptism.[3]

After his "extended and active camp-meeting tour," the *Review* informed readers that Loughborough was "resting" in Battle Creek. Actually, he was laying plans for an even more ambitious tour of the American South with GC president George Irwin and R. M. Kilgore, superintendent of District No. 2 (soon to become the Southern Union). As they traveled deeper into Dixie, they discussed how the church should relate to "the color line" (race relations) in an era when the lynching of Blacks was rising across the South. In Tennessee John gave $100 (seven weeks' salary) for the Southern Industrial School at Graysville (for Whites), then led its 100 students and faculty on a three-mile hike up the mountain where amid the stunning fall colors he talked with them about God's goodness. Then in Alabama he preached three times at the Oakwood Industrial School (for Blacks), picked cotton with its 27 students, and visited the Alabama State Agricultural and Mechanical College for Negroes in nearby Huntsville. Ever the history buff, Loughborough took time between his preaching appointments to tour the

Civil War battle sites, museums, and cemeteries at Chattanooga and Atlanta. During his time in Florida he visited a pineapple warehouse, witnessed a lunar eclipse, and recorded the lynching of "a colored man" in Tampa. Going to South Carolina (then virgin Adventist territory), he rejoiced when three listeners in Spartanburg requested baptism. As his preaching circuit came to an end in New Orleans, he told *Review* readers that it had been "a season of refreshing at every point."[4]

When his summer 1898 speaking appointments took Loughborough to camp meetings in the East (District No. 1), he visited many historic sites along the way. In Philadelphia he saw the Liberty Bell, Franklin's press, and the house where Jefferson had written the Declaration of Independence. At Washington, D.C., he toured the Library of Congress, the U.S. Senate and House chambers, Ford's Theater, the Smithsonian buildings, the National Museum, the Federal Mint, and the Washington Monument (at 66, he climbed all 912 steps to the top). As he and Elder Kimball entered the Metropolitan Methodist Episcopal Church, they saw President William McKinley worshipping there. Visiting New York City, he toured the Navy Battery, a Staten Island sanitarium, and an aquarium. If the waving tentacles of the octopus mesmerized him, John's habit of jubilantly singing the Salvation Army hymn "Just the Same Today" left a lifelong impression on one Brooklyn boy who saw him lead the singing.[5]

Loughborough returned to Battle Creek for five days' rest before heading to Wisconsin for another month of camp meetings. Once again his European experience of speaking through interpreters came in handy as he preached to German, Danish, Norwegian, and Swedish congregations around the state. Then he spent a week at the Grafton, West Virginia, camp meeting proudly displaying his "wonders in the heavens charts" (huge full-color, hand-painted sheets that John and his brother William had created to illustrate how astronomical phenomena fulfilled end-time prophecies). The unique depictions of bizarre celestial events would also appear in his forthcoming book *Last-Day Tokens* (1904) which correlated specific Bible texts with unusual lunar, solar, and planetary events to prove that Jesus' second coming was near. Wherever Loughborough went, his dynamic preaching and those dazzling charts won scores of converts. Speaking for many, one man declared: "This all fits together like clockwork, and with me this matter . . . is *settled* and *clinched*."[6]

During Loughborough's eastern and southern tours he had several dreams about returning to California. When he finally reached Oakland that fall, however, demands for his sermons and colorful charts soon uprooted him again. For the next several months he spoke at camp meetings, church workers' institutes, and other gatherings in California, Washington, and Oregon. Despite the frigid weather, Loughborough's fervent preaching at the Milton, Oregon, camp meeting in 1899 led 40 persons to request baptism—nearly 10 percent of those attending. In spite of incessant rain in Portland, pentecostal preaching followed by anointing and prayer brought instant healing to a dozen gravely ill believers. Although John found the cures "remarkable," he accepted them as genuine manifestations of God's miraculous power.[7]

SUPPORT OF BLACKS, YOUTH, AND WOMEN IN MINISTRY

Despite John's spot-on imitation of Black dialect (as well as Irish, German, Chinese, and Native American speech patterns), he strongly supported the ministry of Blacks in the church. As we have seen, for many years after Charles M. Kinney's 1878 conversion in Reno, Nevada, John wrote him encouraging letters and sent him money to help insure his success as an evangelist. Likewise, at the 1899 GC session held in South Lancaster, Massachusetts, Loughborough participated in the ordination of Louis C. Sheafe, who, although a recent convert to Adventism, had for more than a decade been a successful Baptist pastor in the Midwest and South. Sheafe would become the denomination's leading Black evangelist in the early twentieth century.[8]

Loughborough also longed for Adventist youth to become successful church workers. Although he felt that many of them "are inclined to don the garments of Babylon" (pursue secular pleasures), others had the potential to become "burden-bearers in the church." Wherever he saw signs of "worldly conformity" among them, John prayed "that Satan shall not capture the young with his worldly baits." In the winter of 1901 he shared 13 of his "rise and progress" talks with more than 50 church employees and students at Healdsburg College, seeking to affirm their faith in the ministry of Ellen G. White and in God's leading in the development of the church.[9]

Loughborough's firm conviction in her divine inspiration may have opened his mind to the possibility that God could call other women to gospel ministry. In 1881 he had been a member of the General Conference Committee when the motion to ordain female ministers was first proposed and then sent to a subcommittee (of which he was a member) for reconsideration, where it apparently died. Yet during his travels around the United States John had met some of the church's outstanding female preachers and Bible instructors (such as Angelina Cornell, Sarah A. Hallock Lindsey, and Lulu Wightman). In 1898 he and Sarepta Myrenda Irish Henry (a nationally famous WCTU lecturer recently converted to Adventism) shared the same camp meeting circuit. As he listened to her "practical talks" on temperance, family life, and receiving the Holy Spirit, John was convinced that she had a talent for oratory as well as tremendous God-given gifts. Wherever she preached, spiritual revivals followed. Before long they became fast friends, spending hours chatting together and sharing materials. John dubbed her "Our Lady Henry" and gave her books *The Abiding Spirit* and *The Lord Gave the Word* glowing reviews, calling them what "the mass of the people need at this very time." He hoped that they would "find [their] way to tens of thousands of homes."[10]

While on the Wisconsin camp meeting circuit, John met Ida A. Higbie, whom he nicknamed the "white-ribbon evangelist" (perhaps because she preferred wearing white rather than black outfits as most Adventist preachers did). Ida returned the compliment, declaring that Loughborough's "simple but comprehensive statement of facts and incidents" proved that the "testimony of Jesus" was indeed "the spirit of prophecy" that the Adventist Church possessed.[11] On his eastern tour Loughborough met the formidable L. Flora Plummer from Iowa, whose delightful use of stories and practical discourses on witnessing (then called "home missions") charmed him.[12]

No doubt inspired by the example of such women, Loughborough translated inspiration into action in 1899. On a return trip to California when the train stopped for an hour in Albuquerque, New Mexico, he attended his first Salvation Army meeting led by a female preacher and enjoyed it greatly. Back in the Golden State, he celebrated New Year's Day by ordaining Leta Silkwood as a local elder in the Santa Ana SDA Church. By the end of the year he was also urging *Review* readers to pray for the women who constituted a majority in many Adventist churches in the British Isles.[13]

John's praying, in fact, impressed listeners as much as his preaching. Later generations would have described him as "a prayer warrior." Recognizing that Loughborough was the oldest active pioneer minister in the denomination, church leaders routinely called on him to offer invocations and benedictions at GC sessions. His prayers regularly opened meetings of the SDA Publishing Association, the SDA Education Society, the International Sabbath School Association, as well as key committees on which he sat. Described as "touching," "appropriate," and "spirited," Loughborough's prayers are full of gratitude (for Christ and for the ministry of Ellen White), supplication (for wisdom and blessings on church leaders and laborers), confession (of past wrongs), and resolutions (to do better in the future), and they often mention the needs of specific individuals by name.[14]

John's prayers, which illustrate the highly concrete and literal nature of his beliefs, are almost poetic in their visual imagery, as at the GC session of 1899 when he painted a word picture of the Second Coming: "And when the Lord shall come, a little way in the future, when the conflicts are over, when the battle of life shall have been passed, when Christ shall come with the chariots of angels to bear all his children home, O Lord, may we each then have our eyes open to see our guardian angel coming to gather us up, and place us in a chariot, that we may be borne up to the city of God, and join in that song of triumph; and when the gates shall be opened that the righteous nation that have kept the truth shall enter in, and when they shall cry, Who is this King of Glory? and when the portals of the gates of the city shall be thrown open, O Lord, grant that we may be among that company that shall pass triumphantly through, singing, The Lord God of Hosts, he is the King of Glory."

Following his prayer, the kneeling delegates stood to their feet and sang the Doxology.[15]

Just as meaningful as his prayers, Loughborough's dreams continued to guide his thoughts and actions. He told the delegates at the 1897 GC session how God had led James White through dreams, giving him instructions on where to labor and which banks were safe places (in an era of "wildcat banks") to deposit church funds. Then he related how God had given him dreams prior to leaving for California in 1868 and Scandinavia in 1896: when he arrived, he saw places and met people he had previously seen in his dreams. Such dreams convinced him that church leaders needed to seek guidance from God more than from committees, for "individuals are in His hands, not committees."[16]

To the delegates at the 1899 GC session, he commented, "I don't know but [what] you will say the dreamer is coming again," John related two recent dreams. In the first, he had seen 40 delegates at a railroad station waiting to buy tickets. At a nearby table sat a beautiful woman guarding foot-high piles of money, some in $20 stacks and others in $50 stacks. He interpreted this to mean that if the delegates would "start out in faith," then "plenty of money will come in" for foreign missions. In the second, he and C. H. Jones encountered a garden of dwarf peas engulfed in sand. John said to his companion, "It is too bad to have these nice peas left in such a condition. *You can help this situation.*" A voice informed him that the American Religious Liberty work (and especially the *Sentinel,* its printed organ) needed both men's assistance.[17]

In June of 1901 Loughborough had another "impressive dream" in which he saw the Battle Creek Sanitarium and Battle Creek College surrounded by "a glorious silvery light" with a vividly colored rainbow arching overhead. A "voice spoke from heaven" declaring "that [the sanitarium] is my institution, and [it] is destined with its branches to accomplish a vast amount of good in the world. What is needful to insure its success in the work is a constant, living connection of the workers with heaven. If they have this, they will not fail of success." In the final scene he saw Dr. Kellogg with tears flowing down his face. Despite Loughborough's positive interpretation of his dream, eight months later in February of 1902 the Battle Creek Sanitarium burned to the ground. The "silvery light" had become flames of destruction, and Kellogg's joyful tears had become ones of sorrow. Dreams, whatever their source of inspiration, could be tricky things to decipher.[18]

One's daily health could be equally unreliable, especially if (as in Loughborough's case) one were in one's late 60s. During the latter part of the late-1890s John suffered from occasional colds, dizzy spells, sore lungs, and fever. He confided in his diary: "I am still quite weak from overwork. [I] must have rest." For the most part, however, he found rest only when illness forced him to bed. On his tour of the South in 1898 he preached seven or eight times a week in spite of congestion in his chest that left his lungs "in a somewhat wearied condition." Instead of swallowing pills or potions, he took hot fomentations or cold compresses, ate oranges and grapefruit, and slept most of the day. Also he adopted two habits that undoubtedly improved his health and lengthened his life: daily naps and a daily cold bath. Probably his visits to Scandinavia (where he saw saunas, hydrotherapeutic baths, and massages) had won him over to the benefits of bathing. By 1901 he frequently took "treatments" (salt glows, hot and cold sprays, and massages) at St. Helena Sanitarium. In addition, regular brushing and trips to Frank Lamb's dental clinic in San Francisco helped repair the damage caused by English licorice and American ice cream.[19]

CLOSER RELATIONS WITH ELLEN WHITE

As John adopted habits conducive to his physical health, he also developed a closer relationship with Ellen White despite the fact that from 1891 to 1900 she lived in Australia. Perhaps, as the old saying goes, "absence makes the heart grow fonder," for judging by their letters, the two old friends became mutually supportive pen pals. As Mrs. White's progress reports of the denomination in Australia and New Zealand frequently ended with appeals for money, Loughborough found ways of obtaining funds to finance activities in the Land Down Under. As her money manager, he helped transfer $1,000 from the Bible Mission in Chicago to Australia and sent her regular investment checks. And as her fund-raiser, he asked wealthy friends to loan her $1,000 at low interest rates and promised to raise $500 more in Battle Creek. In his diary John revealed the magnitude of his own generosity: in 1898 he sent her $200 (three months' salary) to build a new church and school (later called Avondale College). The next year he gave her an interest-free loan of $500 (eight months' wages) to build sanitariums in Sydney and Newcastle. That same year, he sent 80 percent of his annual sacrifice offering to Australia and the other 20 percent to England. When in 1900 he sold the copyrights to his books *Rise and Progress* and *Hope of the Gospel* to the General Conference for $1,000, John tithed the money and gave the rest to Adventist institutions around the world (including $300 to Australia)—he did not keep a dime for himself.[20]

Ellen and W. C. White repeatedly expressed gratitude for his fund-raising efforts. Thanking him for sending $1,000 in 1897, Ellen added, "I wish

I could see you, and have a long visit with you. . . . The Lord bless you and keep you spotless till His appearing is my prayer."[21] A year later Willie, calling John "my very dear brother," told him that he and his mother "appreciate you [*sic*] abundant liberality towards the work we are so earnestly struggling to establish here."[22] In 1899 Mrs. White assured him that "not one dollar of this money have I invested for my own personal use." Instead, every dollar had gone to develop the work "in newly planted fields." She challenged Adventist institutions and laborers in well-developed areas of the world to sacrifice to support the work in new fields, something she called "the law of restitution."[23]

EUROPEAN TOUR OF 1899-1900

Because of Loughborough's generous support of missions and his pioneer experience in Great Britain, the GC Committee in March 1899 asked him to go on another preaching tour of Europe. John's wife, Annie, and his granddaughter Fannie Ireland would accompany him to England. For only the second time on a transatlantic voyage, John did not get seasick. Instead, he spent the week reading, strolling around the deck, and attending gospel services. After the *St. Paul* docked in Southampton, the Loughboroughs' friends welcomed them warmly.[24]

Yet some of the old-timers inquired why Loughborough "[moved] about so often." He responded by citing his commission from Ellen White that he should be free to "go from place to place, telling of the rise of the message." Others, concerned about his health, suggested that at 67 he should now rest. "Bless your soul," he replied, "I'm resting all the while."[25]

But his hectic pace over the next 15 months put the lie to that. In fact, he had grown so thin (he weighed only 115 pounds compared to Annie's 140 pounds) that before he left for Europe, he stopped at Hope Brothers in London to buy a new suit and underwear. Then he, W. W. Prescott, and Drs. Daniel and Lauretta Kress were off to camp meetings in Bristol and Liverpool. Despite torrential rain that sometimes forced John to stop speaking until the storm passed, he shared his four sermons in seven English cities and in Cardiff, Wales. Huge crowds gathered in six different halls to hear him speak. Between appointments he and Annie walked for miles, visited old friends, and shoveled coal to heat their rented rooms. Perhaps in memory of his deceased son, Delmer, John took a group of boys on a tour of London; he and Annie went Christmas shopping; and they ate cauliflower for the first time. They celebrated the holiday with many friends and abundant food.[26]

In January Loughborough joined Louis Conradi, president of the European General Conference, and Henry Schuberth, secretary of the German Conference, for a whirlwind tour of nine churches in Germany and three in Switzerland. He spoke to the students at the newly opened school in Friedensau (where he gained weight eating the dark German bread); to the staff of the Institut Sanitaire in Basel (where 10 percent of the patients converted to Adventism); and to the employees of several Adventist vegetarian restaurants. Along the way he toured the Luther sites in Erfurt, explored castles in Heidelberg, hiked along Lake Geneva, and visited the graves of St. Boniface, J. N. Andrews, and J. H. Waggoner.[27]

When he returned to England, Loughborough met with leaders of the British Conference in London to lay plans for starting an Adventist school (eventually named Newbold College). He also attended cooking classes offered by "Mrs. Dr. Kress" (as he called her). That spring he and British evangelist E. E. Andross met with E. J. Waggoner, the editor of *Present Truth*, to express their concerns regarding his extreme views of sanctification and healthful living. Both men felt that Waggoner's assertions that "every meal was a sacrament in which believers ate the body and drank the blood of Christ" and that those who followed his "new gospel of health" would never get sick again prefigured the pantheistic views later expressed in Kellogg's book *Living Temple*. Following this meeting, Waggoner modified his views—at least temporarily.[28]

Then Loughborough visited his ancestral land of Northern Ireland, preaching to tiny congregations in Belfast, Portadown, Banbridge, and Baleyborough. Traveling by steamship, donkey, and on foot, he addressed hundreds of people in large halls and handfuls in home parlors. Along the way, he visited an Irish fair and toured a linen factory, amazed at how its 10,000 spindles created such exquisite cloth.[29]

The summer saw him back on the continent, once again traveling with Conradi and Schuberth through Germany, Switzerland, and Scandinavia. He preached at church workers' gatherings, gave his testimony at social meetings, offered counsel at European General Conference sessions, and spoke at camp meetings. After a camp meeting in Germany, he quipped:

"I think the Germans can endure more meetings than any other people I ever met. It was almost a continuous meeting from six o'clock in the morning till nine o'clock at night, and everyone was as loyal as can be in attending." In Christiana (modern Oslo) he visited King Oscar II's palace; in Switzerland he went mountain climbing with E. E. Andross and baptized a convert in Lake Geneva; and he began learning German from a German New Testament. In addition, he collected colorful leaves and mosses and attached pretty flowers to a card given him at Friedensau. When he reached Basel, his weary mind and sore muscles welcomed the compresses, shampoo baths, electric baths, sprays, and massages the sanitarium staff provided. Afterward, he slept for hours and dreamed of being in California.[30]

But first he had to return to England to collect his wife, who had not seen him in months. On the way to Southampton, he stopped in London to buy yet another suit at Hope Brothers and to visit Osborne House (one of Queen Victoria's many homes). In mid-September John and Annie once again said farewell to their English friends and boarded the steamer *New York* for the rough voyage back to America. Although the mountainous waves and the pitching of the ship gave Annie headaches and seasickness, John was bragging that he could still eat hearty meals when a heavy tenterhook fell on him, giving him a nasty cut on the head and "a rough night."[31]

THE 1901 GENERAL CONFERENCE SESSION

In the spring of 1901, however, Loughborough looked forward to attending the GC session in Battle Creek. As a delegate-at-large, he stood on the platform next to Ellen White, Uriah Smith, Stephen Haskell, George Butler, and A. C. and D. T. Bourdeau. John "stood out" as the shortest in stature, and "his clothes sometimes appeared a bit ancient." But at 70, his booming voice could still fill any hall, and during the debates that followed about reorganizing the church, he intended to make his views heard.[32]

For several years church leaders had recognized that the organizational structure of the 1860s no longer fit the needs of a rapidly expanding denomination. Like an infant that had long since outgrown its diapers, the global Seventh-day Adventist Church found itself constricted by garments that tied it to its provincial past. Its ecclesiastical structure—with local congregations at the bottom, state conferences in the middle, and the General Conference at the top—had remained virtually unaltered since 1863 (save for the addition of six loosely organized "districts" supervised by "superintendents" after 1889). Consequently, its three GC officers (president, secretary, and treasurer) found themselves stretched to the breaking point. When the GC proved inadequate in responding to needs in the field, a host of independent organizations (the General Sabbath School Association, the SDA Education Society, the Health and Temperance Association, the Medical Missionary and Benevolent Association, the Foreign Mission Board, the National Religious Liberty Association, and the International Tract and Missionary Society) evolved in the 1880s and 1890s to fill the void. Their directors, trustees, and leading stockholders—like those in America's business corporations or trusts—became interlocking directorates with the same individuals sharing similar ideas and passing similar policies. All too frequently the various organizations duplicated services and worked at cross purposes with the General Conference. Furthermore, although the church had grown in membership (nearly 300 percent between 1888 and 1900) and territory (entering 38 new countries), it had failed to add links to the chain connecting scattered congregations to the General Conference or to expand its representational base. Thanks to the pioneering efforts of A. T. Robinson (who transformed auxiliary organizations into conference and union departments in South Africa in 1892 and later in Victoria, Australia in 1898), delegates at the 1897 GC session voted to create union conferences to link state conferences to the General Conference.[33]

Yet at both the 1897 and 1899 GC sessions sharp differences of opinion regarding the various approaches to reorganization and the allocation of personnel and funds had split the delegates into basically two camps. Progressives such as Ellen White, A. T. Jones, O. A. Olsen, W. C. White, and W. W. Prescott viewed innovation as both positive and essential to adapt the administrative structure of the church to changing times and circumstances. On the other hand, conservatives such as Uriah Smith, S. N. Haskell, George Irwin, and George Butler defended the model of church organization established in the 1860s as God-ordained: if it was good enough for the founders of the church, it should be good enough for their descendants today. Nonetheless, delegates in 1897 voted to divide the General Conference into three sections (U.S. and Canada, Europe, and Australasia); form union conferences in the U.S. and Europe similar to those already established in Africa and Australasia; and increase the number of members sitting on the GC Committee.[34]

In 1899 Loughborough had voted for biennial GC sessions (exclaiming that since Christ's second coming "is right upon us," quadrennial sessions "may be too late") and favored expanding "numerical representation" on GC committees, but he balked at making further changes to the denominational machinery. Because the General Conference structure had been "established in the providence of God" in 1863, current leaders had "better let it alone." For him, providential guidance trumped "political reasons" every time. "I want to take a straight-forward course," he told the delegates, and "come out a triumphant conqueror."[35]

Although Loughborough took an equally "straight-forward course" at the 1901 GC session, changing circumstances in the interim caused him to join the progressives this time. The fact that Ellen White (recently returned from Australia) spoke out boldly in favor of organizational reforms helped John see the providential dimension in her suggestions. In addition, he wanted to show his support for her authority in the face of what he considered "slitting remarks" against her writings made by E. J. Waggoner and W. W. Prescott. John also saw the revised GC constitution as an effective means of combating the congregationalist tendencies of P. T. Magan, E. J. Waggoner, and A. T. Jones (which he would effectively counter six years later in his book *The Church: Its Organization, Order and Discipline*). His positive stance got him appointed to the Committee on Organization, which asked him to review the history of church organization and the growth of independent entities from the 1850s to the present for the benefit of the delegates. Following vigorous discussions, the delegates voted to make the International Sabbath School Association, the SDA Education Association, and the Foreign Mission Board as departments of the General Conference. They also admitted several new union conferences and missions worldwide, voted to transfer health and educational institutions from GC to union ownership, and further expanded membership on the GC Executive Committee to 25.[36]

LOUGHBOROUGH'S WRITINGS AND DIARY

Loughborough's deep concern about growing opposition to Mrs. White's authority and church order clearly dictated the choice of subject matter for his articles in the *Review* between 1897 and 1901. One lengthy series explained how the Holy Spirit guided individuals, inspired prophets (especially Ellen White), defeated fanatics, and brought peace, holiness, and harmony throughout the history of the Christian church.[37] Another series in the *Review* (reprinted in the *Pacific Union Recorder* in 1901) on church order, liberally buttressed by biblical texts and Ellen White quotations, discussed the dangers of schism and the blessings of unity while citing numerous examples from Adventist history.[38]

As it had so often done in the past, the Review and Herald press reprinted John's sermons and articles as pamphlets and books. In 1898 his lectures on celestial phenomena that fulfilled end-time Bible prophecies appeared as a 130-page booklet entitled *Last-Day Tokens* (which the press sold for a dime as part of its *Words of Truth* series).[39] The following year the press recycled his series on the Holy Spirit and the Spirit of Prophecy as the 40-page tract "Spiritual Gifts" (no. 156 in the *Bible Students' Library*). Greatly expanded in 1901, *The Prophetic Gift in the Gospel Church* became a 120-page booklet (available for 15 cents as no. 164 in the *Bible Students' Library*).[40]

No doubt because Loughborough's pamphlets and books "sold like hotcakes" (to use a Victorian expression), leading Adventist authors asked him to endorse their works, thinking perhaps that his Midas touch would boost sales. In 1897 he described A. T. Jones' book *The Empires of the Bible* as "a rare treat" that had provided him not only with "much light on the Scriptures," but also "a clearer idea of the empires of the world for the time thus covered." He recommended it for "all who wish to study the true history of those early times of our world."[41] His review of Edson White's *The Coming King* in 1898 was even more glowing. "It is written in a manner to rivet the attention of the reader," Loughborough declared, "and is one of those books that, when you begin to read [it], you are not satisfied until you have read it all. . . . It should have a wide circulation."[42] A few months later, in a "Personal Letter to Every Seventh-day Adventist" printed in the *Review*, he promoted Ellen White's recent book *Steps to Christ*, urging Adventists to buy the 50-cent booklet and place 50,000 copies in homes all across America. It was indispensible for ministers, he added, "even if they had to sell their overcoats" to buy it. Likewise, every Adventist pastor should carry a copy of *The New Webster Dictionary and Vest-Pocket Library* with him, because, as John asserted, "it contains much more than I ever saw in a work of its character, brought into so small a compass."[43]

Perhaps Loughborough's own diminutive size led him to prefer small things. In addition to the pocket dictionaries he carried, each of his diaries (the "Field Laborers' Daily Record" available from the General Conference)—with their tiny, cramped handwriting— easily fit inside a shirt or jacket pocket. Even his tattered brown leather wallet is small by today's standards. Nonetheless, it held the coins with which he purchased huge bunches of bananas (at 40 cents each), oranges (for 28 cents a dozen), apples (a nickel apiece), and lemon drops and licorice (at 10 cents a bag). Also he kept in it the greenbacks he so liberally gave to the cause he loved: $200 (more than three months' wages in 1901) to help institutions in Norway, Brazil, and England and to assist Blacks in the South, Indians out West, and orphans at the Haskell Home in Battle Creek. In addition to money, John gave gifts in kind wherever they would do the most good. For example, he sent boxes of books to build up the library at the new Keene Industrial School in Texas.

Furthermore, he generously shared his time, especially with family members. He and Annie took walks, went shopping together, and attended Epworth League concerts. Grandpa Loughborough loved spending time with his granddaughters Nellie, Fannie, and Jennie, and they in turn enjoyed playing with his collies in the backyard. John bought them pet birds, took them to parades and fireworks displays, and led them on long walks. During a train trip to Los Angeles with Jennie, John read her the exciting story of Pitcairn Island. Although Delmer's widow, Maria (now studying medicine at Battle Creek Sanitarium), had married Sanford Edwards in 1899, she and John kept in touch through letters and visits. They especially enjoyed gazing through her telescope at the night sky. As the new century dawned, Loughborough (now pushing 70) probably anticipated spending even more time with his family, friends, pets, and garden. But circumstances he could not foresee would change that.

---

[1] *GCB* (1901), p. 460; *ST*, May 13, 1897, p. 300.

[2] JNL, flyleaves of 1897 and 1898 diaries; *RH*, Mar. 2, 1897, p. 142.

[3] For 1897 camp meeting reports, see JNL, diary, May-October, 1897; *RH*, May 11, 1897, p. 303; *RH*, June 29, 1897, pp. 411, 412; *RH*, June 8, 1897, p. 366; *RH*, July 13, 1897, p. 443; *RH*, Aug. 10, 1897, p. 510; *RH*, Aug. 17, 1897, p. 526; *RH*, Oct. 5, 1897, p. 637; *RH*, Nov. 16, 1897, p. 733; *RH*, Dec. 14, 1897, pp. 796, 797.

[4] For details on JNL's Southern tour, see the *Review* reports for Aug. 3, 1897, p. 496; Oct. 26, 1897, p. 687; Dec. 7, 1897, p. 780; Dec. 14, 1897, p. 795; Dec. 28, 1897, p. 833; Jan. 4, 1898, p. 16; Feb. 8, 1898, p. 96; Feb. 15, 1898, p. 112; Mar. 1, 1898, p. 144; Mar. 8, 1898, p. 161; JNL, diary, November-December 1897 and January 1898.

[5] JNL, diary, June-July 1898; *ST*, July 21, 1898, p. 459; *RH*, Aug. 23, 1898, p. 542; *PUR*, Nov. 11, 1968, p. 1.

[6] See reports in *RH*, Aug. 23, 1898, p. 542; July 12, 1898, p. 450; July 26, 1898, p. 482; Aug. 9, 1898, p. 514; Sept. 13, 1898, p. 591; Sept. 20, 1898, p. 608; Oct. 4, 1898, p. 641; Oct. 11, 1898, p. 654; JNL, diary, September-October 1898.

[7] See Western reports in *ST*, Oct. 27, 1898, p. 682; *RH*, Jan. 3, 1899, p. 12; *RH*, June 13, 1899, p. 382; *RH*, June 20, 1899, p. 401; *RH*, July 4, 1899, p. 432; *ST*, Dec. 15, 1899, p. 800; *California Missionary*, Nov. 5, 1900, p. 1; JNL, diary, November-December 1898 and May 1899.

[8] *GCB* (1899), p. 145; *California Missionary*, Jan. 20, 1901, p. 2. Douglas Morgan's recent book *Lewis C. Sheafe: Apostle to Black America* will long remain the definitive biography of Lewis C. Sheafe.

[9] *California Missionary*, Jan. 20, 1901, pp. 2, 3; *California Missionary*, Feb. 3, 1901, p. 2; *RH*, Jan. 22, 1901, pp. 13, 14; *RH*, Feb. 19, 1901, p. 14.

[10] JNL, diary, May-June 1898 and February-March 1899; *RH*, July 5, 1898, p. 431; *RH*, July 19, 1898, p. 463; *RH*, Mar. 21, 1899, p. 191; *RH*, June 6, 1899, p. 367. Perhaps the fact that both Loughborough and Henry had Irish backgrounds helped their friendship along as well.

[11] *RH*, July 19, 1898, p. 463.

[12] JNL, diary, July and September 1898.

[13] JNL, diary, January and March 1899; *RH*, Dec. 19, 1899, p. 825.

[14] Regarding the frequency of JNL's public praying, see *RH*, Mar. 16, 1897, p. 172; *GCB* (1897), pp. 106, 230; *RH*, Feb. 21, 1899, p. 128; *GCB* (1899), pp. 2, 28, 185, 186; *ST*, Mar. 15, 1899, p. 182; *RH*, Mar. 21, 1899, p. 187; GC Minutes, Oct. 11, 12, 14, 15, 1900, pp. 57, 61, 62, 67; and *Training School Advocate*, February 1901, p. 18. Because recording secretaries, like GC delegates, normally knelt in prayer with heads bowed and eyes closed, only two of Loughborough's prayers have been transcribed word for word: his invocation at the 1899 GC session and his prayer at Ellen White's funeral in July 1915.

[15] *GCB* (1899), p. 185.

[16] *GCB* (1897), pp. 199-204. Loughborough had similar dreams in August 1898 telling him that he would soon embark on another European tour, which he did in 1899-1900. See JNL, diary, August 26 and 30, 1898.

[17] JNL, diary, February 26 and March 4, 1899; *GCB*, 1899, p. 116.

[18] *RH*, July 30, 1901, p. 491.

[19] JNL, diary, February, March, and December 1898, April and June 1899, March 1900, and September 1901; *RH*, Mar. 29, 1898, p. 207.

[20] EGW to JNL, Dec. 19, 1897, letter 92a, 1897, CAR; WCW to JNL, June 6, 1898, WCW Letter Books, CAR; WCW to JNL, Oct. 22, 1898, WCW Letter Books, CAR; JNL to EGW, Dec. 18, 1898, m. 52, CAR; EGW to JNL, Feb. 19, 1899, letter 35, 1899, CAR; EGW to JNL, Feb. 19, 1899, WCW Letter Books, CAR; JNL to EGW, Dec. 14, 1899, m. 52, CAR; WCW to JNL, Jan. 18, 1900, WCW Letter Books, CAR; JNL to WCW, Apr. 24,

1900, m. 52, CAR; *RH,* July 24, 1900, p. 12; *Gospel Herald*, November 1900, p. 100. Loughborough told Mrs. White, "We try to practice economy in our family so as to save all possible for the cause" (JNL to EGW, Dec. 14, 1899, m. 52, CAR). However, in 1900 W. C. White insisted on giving Loughborough a 5 percent interest rate on his loan in recognition of his "experience as one of God's stewards" (WCW to JNL, Jan. 18, 1900, WCW Letter Books, CAR). In 1899 Mrs. White, who routinely suffered from chronic insomnia in Australia, was writing letters full of hyperbole and satire to GC and Review and Herald press leaders calling them allies of "his satanic majesty" in robbing her of her royalties and ignoring her testimonies. Consequently Loughborough's unfailing support and generosity buoyed her spirits considerably. See G. Valentine, *Prophet and Presidents*, pp. 44, 45, 324-230.

[21] EGW to JNL, Dec. 19, 1897, letter 92a, 1897, CAR.

[22] WCW to JNL, June 6 and Oct. 22, 1898, WCW Letter Books, CAR.

[23] EGW to JNL, Feb. 19, 1899, letter 35, 1899, CAR; EGW, quoted in *Gospel Herald*, December 1899, p. 109.

[24] GC Minutes, Mar. 5, 1899, p. 17, CAR; JNL, diary, July 19-26, 1899.

[25] *RH,* July 18, 1899, p. 468.

[26] JNL, diary, August-December 1899; *RH,* Aug. 29, 1899, p. 560; *RH,* Sept. 26, 1899, p. 624; *ST,* Oct. 4, 1899, p. 651; *RH,* Oct. 10, 1899, pp. 655, 656.

[27] JNL, diary, January 1900; *RH,* Mar. 13, 1900, p. 13; *ST,* Mar. 21, 1900, p. 187; *RH,* Apr. 17, 1900, p. 12. It appears that Annie Loughborough remained in England as John frequently wrote her letters during his European travels.

[28] JNL, diary, February-April 1900; Gilbert M. Valentine, *The Shaping of Adventism: The Case of W. W. Prescott* (Berrien Springs, Mich.: Andrews University Press, 1992), p. 136.

[29] JNL, diary, May 1900.

[30] JNL, diary, May-August 1900; *RH,* Aug. 21, 1900, pp. 11, 12; *RH,* Nov. 6, 1900, p. 13; *Atlantic Union Conference Record*, Oct. 1, 1900, p. 2.

[31] JNL, diary, August-September 1900; *Missionary Magazine*, November 1900, p. 527.

[32] Arthur W. Spalding, *Origin and History of Seventh-day Adventists* (Washington, D.C.: Review and Herald Pub. Assn., 1962), vol. 3, p. 45; Ernest J. Lloyd, "Memories of Elder J. N. Loughborough," *RH,* Nov. 8, 1962, pp. 6, 7. In all the photographs of church pioneers that this author has seen, it would appear that only Ellet J. Waggoner was shorter than J. N. Loughborough.

[33] Valentine, *Prophet and Presidents*, pp. 39, 40; G. Knight, *Organizing to Beat the Devil*, pp. 75-83; Barry Oliver, "Principles for Reorganization of the Seventh-day Adventist Administrative Structure, 1888-1903: Implications for an International Church" (Ph.D. diss., Andrews University Seventh-day Adventist Theological Seminary, 1989), pp. 69-73, 82-90.

[34] Oliver, "Reorganization," pp. 132, 143; Knight, *Organizing to Beat the Devil*, pp. 87-90.

[35] JNL, *GCB* (1899), pp. 98, 154, 185; Valentine, *Prophet and Presidents*, pp. 138, 221.

[36] *GCB* (1901), pp. 27, 66, 460, 499; W. Whidden, *E. J. Waggoner*, pp. 246-250; Valentine, *Prophet and Presidents*, pp. 39, 40; Oliver, "Reorganization," pp. 162, 173; Knight, *Organizing to Beat the Devil*, pp. 105-117. Loughborough's recitation of the half-century history of denominational organization is largely accurate except for his blooper concerning the location of the *Review and Herald* press in Rochester from 1852 to 1855 as being at "124 Mountain Top Avenue" instead of 124 Mount Hope Avenue.

[37] On the Holy Spirit's work, see JNL's *RH* articles for Sept. 27, 1898, pp. 614, 615; Oct. 18, 1898, pp. 662, 663; Oct. 25, 1898, pp. 678, 679; Nov. 8, 1898, p. 710; Nov. 15, 1898, p. 740; Nov. 22, 1898, pp. 747, 748; Nov. 29, 1898, p. 763; Dec. 6, 1898, p. 778; Dec. 13, 1898, p. 794; Jan. 3, 1899, p. 2; Jan. 31, 1899, pp. 66, 67; Feb. 7, 1899, p. 82; Feb. 14, 1899, pp. 99, 100; Feb. 21, 1899, pp. 113, 114; Apr. 18, 1899, p. 242; Apr. 25, 1899, p. 258; May 2, 1899, p. 274; May 9, 1899, p. 290; May 16, 1899, pp. 306, 307; May 23, 1899, p. 322; May 30, 1899, p. 338; June 6, 1899, p. 354; July 18, 1899, p. 454; July 25, 1899, p. 470; Aug. 1, 1899, p. 486; Aug. 8, 1899, p. 502; Aug. 15, 1899, p. 518; Aug. 22, 1899, p. 534; Aug. 29, 1899, p. 550; Sept. 5, 1899, p. 566; Sept. 12, 1899, p. 582; Sept. 19, 1899, p. 598; Sept. 26, 1899, p. 614; Oct. 3, 1899, p. 630; Oct. 10, 1899, p. 646; Oct. 17, 1899, p. 662; Oct. 31, 1899, pp. 698, 699; Nov. 7, 1899, pp. 714, 715; Nov. 14, 1899, pp. 730, 731; Dec. 5, 1899, p. 782; Dec. 12, 1899, p. 798; Dec. 19, 1899, p. 814; May 1, 1900, p. 276.

[38] On church order and schism, see JNL's *RH* articles for Aug. 24, 1897, p. 538; Aug. 31, 1897, p. 547; Feb. 21, 1899, pp. 113, 114; Feb. 28, 1899, p. 130; Mar. 7, 1899, pp. 146, 147; Mar. 14, 1899, p. 162; Mar. 21, 1899, p. 178; Apr. 4, 1899, supplement, pp. 1, 2; Apr. 11, 1899, p. 226; June 13, 1899, p. 370; June 20, 1899, p. 390; June 27, 1899, p. 406; July 4, 1899, p. 422; July 11, 1899, pp. 438, 439; Nov. 21, 1899, p. 750; Nov. 28, 1899, p. 766; Dec. 25, 1900, pp. 11, 12; Feb. 19, 1901, pp. 10, 11; Apr. 9, 1901, pp. 10, 11; Apr. 16, 1901, pp. 11, 12; May 7, 1901, pp. 12, 13; May 28, 1901, pp. 8, 9; June 11, 1901, pp. 10, 11; June 18, 1901, p. 11; June 25, 1901, pp. 2, 3; July 2, 1901, pp. 1, 2; July 9, 1901, pp. 2, 3; July 16, 1901, p. 2; Aug. 6, 1901, pp. 2, 3.

[39] *RH,* May 24, 1898, p. 338; *RH,* Aug. 2, 1898, p. 499; *RH,* Aug. 9, 1898, p. 515. *Last-Day Tokens* was also printed and sold widely in Norway, Denmark, and Germany. Loughborough sold his original color paintings to his friend Louis Conradi for $10. See JNL, flyleaf of 1900 diary.

[40] *ST,* Jan. 25, 1898, p. 79; *RH,* June 25, 1901, p. 15; JNL, *Prophetic Gift in the Gospel Church* (Oakland, Calif.: Pacific Press Pub. Co., 1901).

[41] *RH,* Apr. 13, 1897, p. 239.

[42] *RH,* May 17, 1898, p. 323; *Gospel Herald,* March 1899, p. 67.

[43] *RH,* Nov. 1, 1898, p. 706; *RH,* Mar. 14, 1899, p. 175.

CHAPTER XVIII

PREACHER WITHOUT PORTFOLIO (1901-1904)

"The cause needs the help of the old hands, the aged workers, who have had years of experience in the cause of God; who have watched the development and the progress of the message in its various lines; who have seen many go into fanaticism, cherishing the delusion of false theories." "Elder Loughborough can still use his abilities and his gifts in God's work. He has stood faithful amid storm and trial."[1]

At 70 J. N. Loughborough certainly qualified as one of the "old hands" and "aged workers" whom Ellen White had in mind when she penned the preceding exhortations. Including his stint as a "boy preacher" in the Advent Christian movement, by 1902 he had given nearly 53 years to the gospel ministry—longer than the average lifespan in America at that time. Yet despite his age, he fully intended to "use his abilities and gifts in God's work" as long as he received invitations to preach. And since Adventist camp meeting crowds loved to listen to his faith-building stories, the invitations kept coming—and he kept accepting them.

From his home at 1228 Chestnut Street in Oakland, Loughborough contemplated his itinerary for the summer of 1901. It included six camp meetings in 10 weeks: three in Utah (Ogden, Salt Lake City, and Bountiful), two in Montana (Bozeman and Missoula), three in Washington (Spokane, Walla Walla, and Seattle), one in Idaho (Weiser), and one in California (Red Bluff). Although his audiences ranged from 65 to more than 250 people, and the spectrum of weather he encountered varied from hot and humid to cold and stormy, John was in his element. At the Bountiful camp meeting, a "large audience of Mormon friends gave good attention" as he shared stories of the rise and progress of the Advent movement in four daily services. Afterward six converts requested baptism in Rattlesnake Creek. Despite his rigorous itinerary, Loughborough exclaimed, "I came out in even better health than when I started."[2]

When the camp meeting season ended that fall, Loughborough turned his attention to strengthening the faith of Adventist youth, a growing burden on his heart. For several weeks in December 1901 and January 1902 he spoke to nearly 200 students in chapels at Walla Walla College. His sermons on the "evidences of the truthfulness of God's Word," the "rise and progress" of Adventism, and the divine inspiration of Ellen White's visions brought fervent revivals and emotional testimony meetings. Twenty-three students were baptized, with more requesting baptism. In January he spoke to the students at Healdsburg College and led them in a canvassing foray with White's new book *Christ's Object Lessons.*[3]

Although he had never been to Asia, John's curiosity about foreign cultures and his deep interest in history made him eager to learn more about exotic lands. In Fresno he listened spellbound as Georgia Burrus, one of the denomination's first female missionaries in India, talked about her work among India's poorest castes. Loughborough then visited Fresno's Chinese Sanitarium operated by Dr. Charles Kimm (a Chinese man) with his Japanese helpers. After dinner they taught John to sing in Japanese. At the time he did not know that in Kobe, Japan, Mr. Yamazaki, a highly educated scholar who had purchased a secondhand copy of *Rise and Progress,* had recently converted to Seventh-day Adventism. John also ordained C. E. Leland as the newest missionary sent by the Pacific Union Conference to Hawaii Territory.[4]

Because he had been appointed assistant pastor of the Oakland SDA Church in 1902, Loughborough accepted only three speaking engagements that summer: at Grand Junction, Colorado, and in Petaluma and Los Angeles, California. Once again large crowds came to hear him share his experiences. After much prayer, however, he concluded that he should not have accepted the pastoral position in Oakland. Instead, he declared, "My mind . . . has been much impressed that I should go out somewhere among our people, telling them of those things which I 'have seen, known, and handled' in our experience as a people in the rise of the third angel's message." In dreams he had viewed himself "going from place to place, east of the Rocky Mountains, holding meetings."[5] So when Kit Carson Russell invited him to spend several months attending meetings in the Central Union Conference, John saw it as a call from God. "From the very day that I decided to go," he said, "I have gained in health and strength."[6]

During the summer of 1903 his camp meeting itinerary took him to Colorado, Nebraska, Kansas, Iowa, and Missouri. At many of them he spoke (via translators) to large gatherings of German, Danish, Norwegian, and Swedish Adventists. One month he preached in 98 meetings to groups ranging from 150 to more than 1,000 people. Everywhere he went, he observed that his preaching seemed "to have a cheering and confirming effect upon our people." Listeners described Loughborough's talks as "searching and practical," of "a straight, plain, decided nature." They "made us all feel that we must have more of the old-time spirit of sacrifice and earnestness." As for himself, John explained that "the recounting of these mercies of God is like living them over again." His "stirring sermon[s]" were calls for revival, and the unconverted responded in droves. That summer Loughborough helped baptize more than 200 converts.[7]

Doubtless the baptism that meant the most to him personally, however, came the day after New Year's in 1904. Between the Sabbath school and church services at the Oakland SDA Church, Grandpa Loughborough had the privilege of baptizing his granddaughter Nellie Ireland and her friend Edna Shull, a compositor at the *Signs* office. Following this solemn rite, they celebrated Communion together.[8]

VENERABLE COMMITTEE MAN

Ellen White's 1902 testimony (quoted at the beginning of this chapter) warned against placing "the old standard-bearers . . . in hard places." Instead, she declared, they "are ever to be honored and respected. . . . [As] God's workmen." She added, "Let them [church leaders] give them [aging pioneer laborers] an honored place in their councils."[9] Loughborough's half century of experience in the Adventist movement certainly qualified him to share his wisdom with church officials and delegates at all administrative levels. Consequently, he received invitations to serve on numerous committees.

When the Pacific Union Conference[10] organized in 1901, its officers (including Loughborough's son-in-law J. J. Ireland as auditor) invited John to attend annual constituency meetings as a delegate-at-large representing the General Conference. He did so regularly, and delegates routinely assigned him to the Committee on Plans, the Committee on Counsel, the Licenses and Credentials Committee, and the Education Committee. Given his vast experience in evangelism, the delegates at the 1902 session put him on the Plans and Evangelistic Work Committee, and because of his age and retirement status, they added him to the new Plan for Caring for the Aged Workers Committee. Likewise, John participated in the process of organizing the North Pacific Union[11] after 1904. Furthermore, after the forming of the Southern California Conference in 1902, John attended its annual sessions and usually served on the Committee on Credentials and Licenses. At the 1904 session Loughborough and J. O. Corliss were the oldest, longest-serving ministers to receive credentials.12

When the General Conference Fall Council convened at Oakland in October of 1902, John chaired the "Entertainment Committee" charged with finding accommodations for all the delegates in the homes of local Adventists (church employees, lacking travel budgets, rarely stayed in hotels). He was also appointed to the Committee on Delegations. In addition, the church's new president, Arthur Grosvenor Daniells (whose last name John habitually misspelled) invited him to caucus with the GC Executive Council for six hours concerning the formation of a new British Union Conference. At the spring 1903 sessions the officers asked Loughborough to open several meetings with prayer. When he heard G. I. Butler refer to him as one of "the old hands" who "can remember . . . some things that most of these brethren [the 76 delegates] cannot, as sure as you live," John modestly replied, "True!"[13]

At the 1903 GC session when delegates discussed further plans to reorganize the world church, sharp differences of opinion arose between advocates of individualism and independent thought such as A. T. Jones, E. J. Waggoner, and Dr. Kellogg on the one side and proponents of organizational unity such as A. G. Daniells and W. W. Prescott on the other. As tempers flared and voices rose, Loughborough calmly listened to the debates. Then he stood and shared with the delegates some of the "battles we went through" in the 1860s to establish the Adventist Church. Reminding his listeners that opponents of organization had used some of the same language then as certain ones were using now, he cited the parallel examples of the Advent Christians (who, lacking organization, rapidly declined) and Seventh-day Adventists (whose tight-knit global structure promoted growth and efficiency). To reverse the accomplishments of decades would precipitate a situation "where you don't have any constitution or any order at all." Like Ben Franklin appealing for unity among the Founding Fathers in 1787, he reminded the delegates that in drawing up the new constitution of 1903, they all needed to hang together or assuredly opponents would "hang" them separately in print. Also like Franklin, he assured them that he was praying daily for God's guidance in the matter. His logical appeals and fervent prayers helped to bring progress at the session. If the vote to place the medical and health programs under the direct supervision of the General Conference displeased Kellogg, Jones, and Waggoner, they (at least temporarily) persuaded delegates to adopt a constitution referring to Daniells as the "chairman" rather than as the "president" of the GC.[14]

But a far different spirit animated those who attended the 1905 GC session in Takoma Park, a suburb of Washington, D.C. To those waiting for the Holy Spirit to descend, John replied, "If the Spirit of God was not here on this ground yesterday afternoon when Sister White spoke to us, when do you expect to receive it?" As one of only five founders of the 1863 General Conference still living (the others were Isaac Sanborn, C. O. Taylor, Washington Morse, and Ellen White), he reminded them that in the early days of the Advent Movement "the mighty power of God went with that message like a tornado, and seemed to move independently of human agencies." Assuring his listeners that God wanted to pour out His Spirit today just as He had then, he declared: "It is [essential] for us to keep our cups right side up" to receive His blessings. Apparently many of the delegates experienced spiritual blessings, for at the session's close, Loughborough told them that it had been "the best General Conference that I have ever attended." Undoubtedly, having his photograph taken with President Theodore Roosevelt at the White House also made the session a memorable one for him.[15]

At their biennial session delegates paused to remember two of the pioneers who had passed away in 1903: Uriah Smith, writer, scholar, and longtime editor of the *Review*, and Abraham La Rue, the denomination's first missionary to Hawaii and parts of Asia. Loughborough had known them both intimately: Smith from the earliest years of the Adventist movement in Rochester and Battle Creek, and La Rue in California during the 1870s and 1880s. As old friends shared stories about the men's contributions to the cause, John remembered La Rue as a very generous individual. When Jesus came again, Abraham had told his friends, he wanted to have only 25 cents in his pocket.[16]

GENEROUS DONOR AND DEFENDER OF THE FAITH

Although he would never have admitted it, Loughborough himself had become one of the denomination's major donors. His diaries bear ample proof of his sacrificial giving. Not only did he return to the church 10 percent of his salary, but he also tithed his book royalties, the gifts he received, and every act of hospitality (bed and board) extended to him. In the fall of 1902 he gave a sermon at the Oakland SDA Church on the blessings of giving a second tithe. One can *never* outgive God, he assured his parishioners. Glued into one pocket of his well-worn wallet was a faded, typed copy of Psalm 41:1-4: "Blessed is he that considereth the poor: the Lord will deliver him in time of trouble. The Lord will preserve him, and keep him alive; and he shall be blessed upon the earth" (verses 1, 2). He informed *Review* readers that James White used to say: "Giving is a trade, to be learned just as well as any other trade."[17]

The 5-year-old boy from Victor who had once refused to buy candy so that his allowance could provide a New Testament for a child in Africa grew up to become a man who had mastered the "trade" of giving. In fact, John and Annie paid most of their household bills with coins and gave their dollars to mission work around the world. Incredible as it may seem, an analysis of John's 1902 diary shows that while his total income was $1,073, he returned to the Seventh-day Adventist Church $698 in tithes, offerings, and other donations—almost 65 percent of his earnings—and that he and Annie lived on the remaining $375. By raising their vegetables and fruit, keeping chickens for eggs, and wearing their clothes until they wore out, they lived comfortably but frugally. Occasionally, they even bought malted nuts, lemon drops, and licorice.[18]

As prodigal in the choice of projects he supported as he was in his benevolence, John spread his material blessings everywhere. A few examples will suffice. Between 1902 and 1905 he donated to several Adventist schools; to the San Francisco Medical Missionary and Benevolent Association; to the Chicago Medical Mission; and to the Prisoners' Fund. He also gave generously to build Adventist churches in Washington, D.C., and Port-of-Spain (Haiti), and to start a school in Iowa. John supported the new publication *The Gospel Herald* and was the third-highest individual contributor to the One Hundred Thousand Dollar Fund. Yet he still had enough money to offer the General Conference a $500 loan at 5 percent.[19]

Once a well-meaning Sabbath school secretary tried to give Loughborough a copy of the lesson quarterly, telling him, "Oh, you needn't pay for this; none of us pay for them; they are paid for out of the contributions [Sabbath school expense offering]." After reading her the small print on the back page, "The contributions this quarter are for the most needy fields," he added, "I beg to state that I am not the 'most needy field.'" Then he handed the woman a nickel to pay for his quarterly. Likewise, after spending three exhausting days helping Healdsburg College students sell copies of *Christ's Object Lessons* door to door, John refused the commission offered him—instead, he gave it to a sick friend in the Santa Rosa Church. His motto: Freely you have received, freely give.[20]

Loughborough's generosity and loyalty made it difficult for him to understand or sympathize with those who criticized the church, its leaders, or its mission. His previous experience combating the influence of offshoot movements such as the *Messenger* Party, the Age-to-Come Party, and the Marion Party as well as debating dissidents such as Moses Hull and Dudley Canright made him defensive toward those he perceived as undermining the rise and progress of Adventism. Remembering how the alleged visions and false testimonies of Anna Rice and Anna Garmire had deceived some church leaders (including A. T. Jones), Loughborough continued speaking and writing to counteract their lingering influence. Beginning in 1902, John added to his standard repertoire of sermons on the rise of Adventism, the prophetic wonders in the heavens, and the divine inspiration of Ellen White a fourth discourse on "the fate of opposition parties" in the history of Adventism. By explaining such "apostasies and how they came out," he hoped to fortify his listeners against future deceptions and ground them in Adventist truth. As future chapters will show, combating heresies in the church would become an all-consuming passion with J. N. Loughborough to the very end of his life.[21]

Without doubt, Loughborough's zeal in fighting heresy and dissidence in the church was inextricably linked to his passionate devotion to Ellen White and his desire to promote her visions and disseminate her writings as widely as possible. To his mind, a reverence for the divine inspiration contained in Mrs. White's testimonies, coupled with a correct understanding of the "rise and progress" of Adventism and its prophetic last-day message, constituted the surest bulwark against apostasy in the ranks. Like most Adventist ministers at the turn of the century, John studied her writings and quoted them frequently in all of his sermons and articles in denominational publications. But he did even more. By the late 1890s he began hand copying or typing (as he gained proficiency on his "calligraph") large portions of her testimonies on specific topics for his own study and to share with others. In 1901 he commenced a mammoth project that would consume his time and energy for the rest of his life: preparing indexes to *all* of Ellen White's published writings—her testimonies, her other books, and even her *Review and Herald* articles. In the fight against fanaticism, it was essential to have one's ammunition organized and categorized.[22]

BUILDING A HOUSE AT 72

Defending the faith also required strength of body and mind. If Loughborough, now in his 70s, remained mentally strong, he felt himself slipping physically. Occasionally he suffered from bad colds, rheumatism, fainting spells, eye strain, and an aching back or knee. Refusing pills and potions, he headed for the nearest sanitarium. There he enjoyed hot fomentations, baths (electric thermal, sweat, and ice), sprays (cold and salt glow), massages and oil rubdowns, and shampoos—all of which cleansed, relaxed, and restored him. Although no extant photographs show Loughborough wearing glasses, his diary attests that in 1903 he went to an optician to be fitted for a pair of spectacles. Perhaps even he was experiencing difficulty reading his tiny, cramped handwriting.[23]

John's rigorous camp meeting tours also seemed to be tonics to improved health. After traveling 6,370 miles, attending 175 meetings, and preaching more than 100 times during the summer of 1903, he exclaimed, "I have come home with better health than when I left."[24] A year later, one camp meeting attendee remarked, "Though well advanced in years, our brother [Loughborough] is still quite vigorous, and enjoys good health for one of his age."[25] When asked for the secret of his good health, John would reply: "I thank the Lord for the benefits I have experienced in health reform, and still I am reaching out for more."[26]

As far as Loughborough was concerned, good health depended on beginning the day with vigorous exercise and a proper breakfast. So when he was a guest of the Harmon family in Fallon, Nevada, John woke their two boys every day at dawn and challenged them to a half-mile *barefoot* race. Although the boys usually beat the 70-year-old preacher out on the quarter-mile stretch, he always passed them on the way home because, as he put it, he "had worked up an appetite and had to hurry back to breakfast."[27]

Probably the greatest proof of Loughborough's good health lies in the fact that at 72 he built a new house from basement to roof. After 30 years in Oakland (1874-1904), the Pacific Press Publishing Association transferred its headquarters to Mountain View, then a tiny village of 800 people. John and Annie decided to move there also "to get the benefit of a more congenial climate for our declining years," adding that as I am "well into my seventy-third year, more rest is required than in the earlier days of [my] California experience."[28]

But rest would elude them both, at least for awhile. In July of 1904 John resigned his position as assistant pastor of the Oakland SDA Church. He and Annie packed their worldly goods in a horse-drawn wagon and days later unpacked them inside the large tent in Mountain View that would be their home for the next four months. In the first two weeks John put in an outdoor latrine, made sawhorses and a work bench, built a chicken coop, and drew up blueprints for their house. Then on a warm evening in July he went for his first automobile ride. During August, he, A. O. Tait, and Mr. Beeman dug the cellar, poured concrete, hauled redwood lumber and bricks, nailed down the wooden floors, raised the walls, finished the roof, laid the brick sidewalk, and framed the back porch. In the process, John's hands and arms got "fired with poison oak" and filled with splinters, making his nights an agony of "burning and itching."[29]

During September, John shingled the roof and back porch, finished the floors, lathed the walls, put in partitions, and built lots of shelves. He let a plumber install the pipes and asked Owen Tait to wire the house for electricity (it would be the Loughboroughs' first home with electric lights). Then, in his spare time, John fixed a flower bed for Annie's geraniums, made two clothes presses, and built another chicken coop (Annie's favorite Plymouth Rock hen had just hatched eight chicks). On September 7 the couple ate their first meal in the newly finished basement. Two weeks later they slept in the bedroom for the first time. Annie, weary of tenting, began moving things into the house, dodging the plasterer, plumber, and electrician as she did so. October witnessed the completion of a cesspool, the installation of drain pipes, the papering of the walls, and the painting of nearly every surface in sight indoors and out. Finally, after 110 days of living in a tent, they moved into their new home.[30]

It had been three decades since John had sold the last house he owned in 1874. Since that time, he explained, "I have sojourned in various climes, in different parts of the world, at times comfortable, and at other times very uncomfortable, oftener the latter." All he wanted now, he said, was a cottage and a little garden "for the closing days of my earthly pilgrimage." Thirty years before he had entrusted $500 from the sale of his home to the Medical Missionary and Benevolent Association (MMBA), hoping that in the near future he could pay a contractor to build his retirement home. But the MMBA (possibly facing fiscal constraints itself) would not return his funds, making it necessary for him to "take the saw and hammer and go to work with my hands." Looking on the bright side of this disappointment, however, he asserted that building a house had been "a physical benefit." Indeed, he added, "now I can do quite a day's work without overfatigue."[31]

Although the Loughboroughs had moved into their new home, it required a couple more months of labor to make it livable. In November John and Mr. McCorckle laid carpets, dug holes for 125 fence posts, put in the carriage steps and a hitching post, and hauled 61 wheelbarrow loads of firewood. That December, John and Annie planted scores of strawberry plants, grapevines, rosebushes, and fruit trees (apricot, apple, plum, pear, peach, cherry, and fig)—and John hauled the eighty-second wheelbarrow load of firewood onto the property. Tired and dirty, he took the first hot bath he had enjoyed in five months. Days later, he and Annie celebrated the first Christmas in their new home.[32]

Apparently a few sour saints accused the Loughboroughs of extravagance in building their own home, but Ellen White would not hear of it. In a sermon preached in Mountain View, she defended the right of "those that have been working hard all their lives, like Elder Loughborough, [to] have a little home." Thanking him for devoting his physical strength and money to building up the Adventist cause, she said, "Let not your heart be troubled [by these rumors]." She urged believers everywhere to "esteem them ["the aged ministers"] very highly for their works' sake."[33]

LOUGHBOROUGH'S ARTICLES AND BOOKS

One of the "works" for which J. N. Loughborough was most esteemed, of course, was his articles and books. As the panoply of periodicals expanded after 1900, so did John's contributions to them. For example, his series "The Church," which had earlier appeared in the *Review,* was reprinted in the *Recorder* (the official publication of the Pacific Union Conference) beginning in the fall of 1901.[34] Meanwhile the *Review* continued carrying Loughborough's on-going series defending the "Prophetic Gift" and drawing parallels between the ministry of biblical prophets and Ellen White.[35]

When invited to do so, John also wrote articles for other Adventist papers. His short piece "How About Sunday Buying?" in the March 1902 *Sentinel of Christian Liberty* emphasized that the Bible condemns both buyers and sellers who break the Sabbath, not just the former as most Sunday blue laws did. In "Fifty" he congratulated the *Youth's Instructor* on reaching its golden anniversary. After reviewing its history, he said that "the growth of the paper in merit has afforded [me] the greatest pleasure," calling it "the *best paper* I know for the youth of this evil time." His article "Seeing the King" contrasted earthly coronations with Christ's second coming, which, he said, will include a glorious rainbow and angels blowing trumpets. For the *Union Conference Record*, John penned a two-part series on the history of Adventist canvassing and the qualifications of a good colporteur.[36]

Of all the new periodicals, however, Loughborough's clear favorite was the *Bible Training School*, a magazine edited by his friends Stephen and Hetty Haskell in New York City (1901-1903) and South Lancaster, Massachusetts (1903-1919). Its subtitle—"A Monthly Journal Devoted to the Interest of House to House Bible Work"—meant that its market encompassed literature evangelists, Bible instructors, and Sabbath school teachers. Largely written by the Haskells, Ellen White, and Loughborough, each issue contained several Bible studies on a variety of topics.[37]

Beginning with the December 1902 issue, John submitted an article nearly every month until the magazine's demise in 1919. His choice of subject matter covered the spectrum from biblical parables to end-time prophecies. Starting in 1903, his lengthy series on "The Great Second Advent Movement" gave readers a synopsis of his forthcoming book by that title. Just as Loughborough's Bible studies reflected traditional Adventist exegesis, so his historical sketches projected a conservative picture of the past. But John occasionally fractured his facts. For example, in the June 1904 article he informed readers that the British had impressed Joseph Bates into their army (rather than navy) and had imprisoned him in the dreaded "Black Hole of Calcutta" in India (rather than at Dartmoor Prison in England).[38]

Many of Loughborough's article series found new life between the covers of books, a standard practice at Adventist publishing houses in those days. The series on "The Saints' Inheritance" he had written for the 1861 *Review* reappeared as an 88-page pamphlet in 1903 and as the Sabbath School Lesson Quarterly in 1904.[39] The lengthy articles on the gift of prophecy became a 120-page booklet entitled *The Prophetic Gift in the Gospel Church* in 1901 and part of the *Bible Students' Library* until 1911.[40] His popular presentations connecting bizarre heavenly phenomena to end-time Bible prophecies found their way into both English and German editions of the book *Last-Day Tokens*, an approximately 200-page tome that sold for a quarter and included 24 reproductions of 34 scenes of John and William Loughboroughs' full-color charts. Those who questioned whether all of these "inexplicable" planetary, stellar, lunar, and solar events had been "produced by the direct power of the Lord" and therefore had prophetic significance were simply "illiterate" (in the eyes of the author) and thereby fulfilled another prophecy concerning the increase of "scoffers" in the last days.[41]

Unfortunately, one of Loughborough's most popular books—*Rise and Progress of Seventh-day Adventists*—originally published in 1892, could not be reprinted. On December 30, 1902, fire engulfed the Review and Herald Publishing association in Battle Creek and burned it to the ground. Consequently, the same flames that destroyed the manuscript for Dr. Kellogg's controversial pantheistic book *The Living Temple* also melted the well-worn plates for Loughborough's *Rise and Progress*. Along with Uriah Smith's *Thoughts on Daniel and the Revelation*, *Rise and Progress* had for years been a textbook for seventh- and tenth-grade pupils at Adventist schools. It was also required reading for college students who became summer canvassers. But now it was out of print and unavailable (except in German) to an Adventist market that had come to depend on it. Yet like the fabled phoenix of Greek mythology, from the flames in Battle Creek would emerge a revised and expanded version of *Rise and Progress* that by 1905 would bear the title *The Great Second Advent Movement*.[42]

---

[1] EGW, *Testimonies for the Church*, vol. 7, pp. 286, 287; EGW letter 47, 1902, DF 230, CAR.

[2] *GCB* (1902), p. 602; JNL, diary, August 1901; *PUR*, Aug. 1, 1901, p. 6; *PUR*, Sept. 12, 1901, pp. 4, 6, 16; *RH*, Oct. 1, 1901, pp. 11, 18; *ST*, Oct. 2, 1901, p. 637; *PUR*, Oct. 10, 1901, pp. 3, 4; *RH*, Oct. 29, 1901, pp. 11, 12; *PUR*, Oct. 24, 1901, pp. 5, 6; JNL, *PUR*, Nov. 7, 1901, pp. 4, 5.

[3] *ST*, Dec. 4, 1901, p. 781; *RH*, Dec. 31, 1901, p. 13; *PUR*, Jan. 16, 1902, p. 3; *YI*, Jan. 30, 1902, p. 36; *ST*, Jan. 1, 1902, p. 13; *ST*, Jan. 29, 1902, p. 77; *YI*, Feb. 27, 1902, p. 68; *RH*, July 22, 1902, p. 20.

[4] *PUR*, Dec. 5, 1901, p. 5; *YI*, Sept. 26, 1922, pp. 3, 4; *ST*, Mar. 5, 1902, p. 157.

[5] *RH*, July 28, 1903, p. 18; *PUR*, July 17, 1902, pp. 6, 7; *RH*, July 22, 1902, pp. 17, 18; *PUR*, Oct. 9, 1902, p. 4.

[6] *RH*, July 28, 1903, p. 18.

[7] *ST*, Nov. 25, 1903, p. 749; *Echoes From the Field*, Aug. 5, 1903, p. 4; JNL, diary, September 1903; *RH*, Sept. 3, 1903, pp. 13, 14; *Echoes From the Field*, Sept. 16, 1903, p. 4; *Workers' Bulletin*, Sept. 15, 1903, p. 38; *Workers' Bulletin*, Sept. 29, 1903, p. 46; *RH*, Oct. 8, 1903, pp. 18, 19; *RH*, Oct. 1, 1903, p. 17; *RH*, Nov. 12, 1903, p. 19; *RH*, Nov. 19, 1903, pp. 20, 21; *PUR*, June 2, 1904, p. 7.

[8] *ST*, Jan. 13, 1904, p. 29.

[9] EGW, *Testimonies for the Church*, vol. 7, p. 289.

[10] When formed in 1901, the Pacific Union Conference included California, Oregon, Washington, Idaho, Montana, Utah, Nevada, Alaska, Hawaii, and British Columbia. The denomination added Arizona in 1902.

[11] When established in 1906, the North Pacific Union included Oregon, Washington, Idaho, Montana, British Columbia, Alaska, and the Hawaiian Territory.

[12] JNL, diary, March and September 1902; *PUR*, Mar. 27, 1902, pp. 1, 4; *RH*, Nov. 4, 1902, p. 17; *PUR*, Mar. 24, 1904, p. 11; JNL, diary, May 1904; *PUR*, June 30, 1904, p. 7; *RH*, Aug. 4, 1904, pp. 15, 16.

[13] JNL, diary, October 1902; EGW, ms. 194, Feb. 9, 1903, p. 3, CAR; *GCB* (1903), pp. 1, 17, 29, 37, 66, 129, 161-164, 196; *RH*, Mar. 31, 1903, p. 24.

[14] *GCB* (1903), pp. 17, 161-164; B. Oliver, "Reorganization," pp. 182-209; G. Knight, *Organizing to Beat the Devil*, pp. 114, 115.

[15] *GCB* (May 11, 1905), pp. 6, 7; GCB (May 18, 1905), pp. 23, 25, 28. Loughbor-

ough was one of 40 delegates handpicked to meet briefly with Theodore Roosevelt in the White House in May 1905.

[16] JNL, *GCB* (1905), p. 24.

[17] JNL, diary, October 1902; JNL, *RH*, Feb. 17, 1903, p. 9; JNL, *RH*, Dec. 10, 1903, p. 19. The Center for Adventist Research at Andrews University has one of Loughborough's black leather wallets (c. 1890s), which has four tan-colored pockets for bills, notes, and coins. Besides the copy of Psalm 41:1-4, it contains a perpetual calendar for all dates from 1865 to 1900.

[18] JNL, flyleaf of his 1902 diary.

[19] For examples of JNL's giving, see *RH*, Apr. 1, 1902, p. 11; *RH*, June 10, 1902, p. 20; *PUR*, July 31, 1902, p. 13; *Life Boat*, September 1902, p. 223; JNL, diary, November 1902; *Life Boat*, February 1903, p. 55; *RH*, Feb. 10, 1903, p. 14; *RH*, Apr. 14, 1903, p. 17; *AUG*, Nov. 25, 1903, p. 543; *Workers' Bulletin*, Dec. 8, 1903, p. 88; *PUR*, Dec. 3, 1903, p. 4; *RH*, Apr. 28, 1904, p. 20; GC Minutes, Apr. 1, 1904, p. 71; *RH*, Dec. 22, 1904, p. 19; and *Gospel Herald*, February 1905, p. 8.

[20] *Union Conference Record*, Oct. 15, 1903, p. 6; *PUR*, Apr. 24, 1902, p. 6; *AUG*, May 7, 1902, p. 204.

[21] See, for example, JNL, diary, May 1902 and October 1903 where he mentions the cases of Anna Rice and Anna Garmire and preaching against opposition parties.

[22] See, for example, JNL, diary, November-December 1901, January 1902 and November 1903.

[23] JNL, diaries, February and April 1902; March, May, June, August, and December 1903; February and June 1904.

[24] *RH*, Nov. 26, 1903, p. 19.

[25] *RH*, June 30, 1904, p. 17.

[26] *Columbia Union Visitor*, Aug. 26, 1903, p. 3.

[27] *PUR*, May 6, 1968, p. 2.

[28] *RH*, June 16, 2011, pp. 10, 11; *PUR*, July 7, 1904, p. 3.

[29] JNL, diary, July-August 1904.

[30] JNL, diary, September-October 1904.

[31] *RH*, Oct. 20, 1904, p. 15. However, after John sent two personal letters to Dr. Kellogg in July and September 1907, Kellogg mailed him a check for $600 ($500 plus 6 percent interest) in November 1907. Loughborough, like most Adventists at the turn of the century, distrusted banks, having seen hundreds of them fail during the Panics of 1837, 1857, 1873, and 1893. Consequently, for decades he entrusted his surplus funds to various publishing and health institutions. See JNL to JHK, July 18, Sept. 19, and Nov. 10, 1907, Carton 251, Box 9, File 14, CAR.

[32] JNL, diary, November-December 1904.

[33] EGW, sermon at Mountain View, California, Jan. 22, 1905, ms. 189, 1905, p. 2, CAR.

[34] See JNL's "The Church" series in *PUR*, Oct. 10, 1901, p. 2; Oct. 24, 1901, pp. 2, 3; Nov. 7, 1901, pp. 2, 3; Nov. 21, 1901, pp. 1, 2; Dec. 5, 1901, pp. 3, 4; Dec. 19, 1901, pp. 4, 5; Jan. 2, 1902, pp. 1, 2; Jan. 16, 1902, pp. 1, 2; Jan. 30, 1902, pp. 1, 2; Feb. 13, 1902, pp. 2, 3; Mar. 13, 1902, pp. 2, 3; Apr. 10, 1902, pp. 1, 2; Apr. 24, 1902, pp. 2, 3; May 8, 1902, pp. 2, 3; May 22, 1902, pp. 2, 3; June 5, 1902, pp. 2, 3.

[35] For JNL's "Prophetic Gift" series, see *RH*, Jan. 21, 1902, p. 15; Feb. 18, 1902, p. 3; Nov. 18, 1902, pp. 9, 10; Dec. 9, 1902, pp. 8, 9; Apr. 21, 1903, pp. 8, 9; Apr. 28, 1903, pp. 7, 8; May 19, 1903, pp. 9, 10; June 30, 1903, pp. 7, 8; July 14, 1903, pp. 9, 10; July 28, 1903, pp. 8, 9; July 21, 1903, pp. 9, 10; Aug. 4, 1903, pp. 10, 11; Sept. 10, 1903, pp. 7, 8.

[36] *Sentinel of Christian Liberty*, March 1902, p. 228; *YI*, Aug. 7, 1902, p. 249; *Bible Training School*, Jan. 1906, pp. 115, 116; *Union Conference Record*, Dec. 15, 1904, p. 4; *Union Conference Record*, Jan. 15, 1905, p. 4.

[37] *Columbian Union Visitor Supplement*, Feb. 11, 1903, p. 2; see any issue of the *BTS*.

[38] For examples, see JNL's articles in the *BTS* between December 1902 and 1919.

[39] *ST-A*, June 8, 1903, p. 11; Sabbath School Lessons, July 1904.

[40] JNL, *The Prophetic Gift in the Gospel Church*; *Bible Students' Library* (Oakland, Calif.: Pacific Press Pub. Co., 1900-1911), vol. 7, pp. 5-100.

[41] JNL, *Last-Day Tokens* (Mountain View, Calif.: Pacific Press Pub. Co., 1904); *RH*, Sept. 23, 1902, p. 2; *RH*, June 9, 1904, p. 18; *Workers' Bulletin*, Oct. 4, 1904, p. 56; *Workers' Bulletin*, Dec. 6, 1904, p. 92.

[42] JNL, diary, Dec. 31, 1902; JNL, *RH*, Dec. 10, 1903, p. 19; *RH*, Mar. 17, 1903, p. 20; *PUR*, Sept. 8, 1904, pp. 5-7; *PUR*, Sept. 29, 1904, pp. 6, 7.

CHAPTER XIX

PREACHING THE PAST: WRITING *THE GREAT SECOND ADVENT MOVEMENT* (1904-1907)

"The record of the experience through which the people of God passed in the early history of our work must be republished. Many of those who have since come into the truth are ignorant of the way in which the Lord wrought. The experiences of William Miller and his associates, of Captain Joseph Bates, and of other pioneers in the advent message, should be kept before our people. Elder Loughborough's book should receive attention. Our leading men should see what can be done for [its] circulation."[1]

When the fire that burned the Review and Herald in 1902 destroyed the plates for J. N. Loughborough's popular book *Rise and Progress* (1892), a growing demand by Adventist youth, literature evangelists, and ministers dictated the production of an updated edition. In her letter (quoted above) to George I. Butler, president of the newly created Southern Union Conference, Ellen White urged: "We must study to find out the best way in which to take up the review of our experiences from the beginning of our work, when we separated from the churches and went forward step by step in the light that God gave us."[2]

Yet Loughborough recalled hearing a rumor in 1899 that Mrs. White regretted the publication of *Rise and Progress*. Troubled, he had written Willie White asking if that was true. "You well know it was no job of my seeking writing that [1892] book," he said. Now that church officials wanted a revised, expanded edition, he feared that "if it was wrong to write and print the book first, I do not wish to increase my offense any more in the matter." Willie had assured him that "I have never heard her [Mrs. White] express the opinion that its publication was a mistake, or that it ought not to have been written." But he had heard his mother say "that she was sorry that you had made her so prominent in the work," giving her a greater role in the early years of Adventism than she deserved. Obviously, despite the fact that Marion Davis, Ellen's assistant, had received a copy of the manuscript of *Rise and Progress*, Mrs. White (then in Australia) had not read it until the book came from the press.[3]

In preparing the revised edition, Loughborough made amends for that oversight by taking portions of his manuscript to her at St. Helena. Ellen wrote her son Willie on February 15, 1904: "He wishes to call my attention to some points. I could do nothing about the matter to-day, but will try to go over the points with him to-morrow."[4] In addition to interviewing Ellen White, John cross-checked his facts with the aging pioneers George Butler and Stephen Haskell.

The footnotes for *The Great Second Advent Movement* clearly reveal that John also consulted a wide array of primary source material. In addition to frequent quotations from the Bible and the writings of Ellen White, he cites the works of Protestant Reformation historians (especially Wylie and D'Aubigné), Enlightenment philosophers (particularly Voltaire and Rousseau), Millerite leaders (Miller, Fitch, Litch, Himes, Snow, and Marsh), and prominent Adventist leaders (including James White, Uriah Smith, and L. R. Conradi). He and Annie reread reams of yellowing Millerite papers (*Signs of the Times, Midnight Cry, Voice of Truth,* and *Advent Herald*). They also scanned tattered copies of *Present Truth, Advent Review and Sabbath Herald,* and *Signs of the Times.* Since many pioneers had died, John exhumed the dusty notes of previous interviews he had conducted with Joseph Bates, James White, J. N. Andrews, D. H. Lamson, Hiram Edson, Heman Gurney, and Uriah Smith. To his credit, Loughborough interviewed more women for *The Great Second Advent Movement* than he had consulted in writing *Rise and Progress* in 1892. In addition to Ellen White, he sought verification of facts and anecdotes from Elizabeth Haines, Drusilla Lamson, Eunice and Sarah Harmon, Frances Howland, and Mrs. Truesdail, to mention a few female sources.[5]

By far the most significant source for *The Great Second Advent Movement*, of course, was Loughborough himself. At 73, he had witnessed the development of the Second Advent movement from its Millerite roots to its global mission outreach. As he continually reminds his readers, he knew all about Joseph Marsh's Age-to-Come theories; the post-Disappointment mockery; the rise of fanatical groups within Adventism; the establishment of institutions; the formation of churches, conferences, unions, and the General Conference; and the development of overseas missions. In a very literal sense, during 60 years of public ministry he had "been there and done that." No one was more qualified to write about the Adventist past than he, and he intended to complete this revision quickly.[6]

Quickly, perhaps, but not alone. As with the research and production of *Rise and Progress* in 1892, Annie's assistance in gathering materials, taking notes, typing multiple drafts, and proofreading the manuscript proved invaluable. Although her name does not appear anywhere in the pages of *The Great Second Advent Movement*, John testified years later that "the faithful wife was on hand again to help make this book just as complete as it could be with our facilities."[7] An excellent typist, grammarian, and proofreader, she helped him complete the manuscript for *The Great Second Advent Movement* between November 1903 and April 1904—an astonishing five months' time—despite the fact that *The Great Second Advent Movement* was 50 percent larger than *Rise and Progress* had been. The manuscript for *The Great Second Advent Movement* was typed on the same 1888 "calligraph" (typewriter) that she had used to produce the manuscript for *Rise and Progress*.[8] After officials at Nashville's Southern Publishing Association sent them the galley proofs, Annie and John marked and mailed them back within four weeks, then compiled an index for the book.[9]

Although Annie's superb copyediting skills guaranteed that the text of *The Great Second Advent Movement* would be virtually free of spelling and grammatical errors, a comparison of the 1892 and 1905 books demonstrates that John did not do his part to prevent factual errors in *Rise and Progress* from finding their way into *The Great Second Advent Movement*.[10] Far more serious for the scholar, of course, are the errors of interpretation or "spins" that Loughborough uses to portray a positive view of the Adventist past. For the most part, in his treatment of the Millerite movement (to which he devotes *half* of the chapters in *The Great Second Advent Movement* as opposed to *one third* in *Rise and Progress*) and the early Sabbatarian Adventists, he makes not a single critical remark about their leaders, publications, or activities. Bypassing any mention of fanaticism, setbacks, or unwise decisions, he focuses instead on the positive aspects that support his "rise and progress" theme. Debates about theological, organizational, or personal issues find no place in *The Great Second Advent Movement*. The only exception to this rule is when Loughborough traces the unfortunate ends of those who opposed White's visions.[11]

Yet church leaders had not asked Loughborough to write a scholarly history book. Instead, *The Great Second Advent Movement* sought to show "the supernatural origin" and "divine origin" of the Adventist movement from its Millerite roots to the present. Whereas the Pacific Press Publishing Company had intended *Rise and Progress* to reach an Adventist audience, Southern Publishing Association marketed *The Great Second Advent Movement* to the non-Adventist market as well. Indeed, all the state Tract and Missionary Societies in North America sold the book. Church leaders' recommendations reveal its evangelistic purpose. George Butler believed that its "thrilling, wonderful, and soul-inspiring" stories, facts, and statistics would provide "valuable . . . instruction" for "younger people, and those not conversant with the great advent movement." He felt that it would also "greatly strengthen and quicken the warmth and piety of those who are in discouragement, or depression, [in a] cold or backslidden [state], and fire their hearts with new zeal." O. A. Olsen agreed, asserting that "the perusal and study of this book would greatly strengthen faith and courage, and . . . lead to a fuller consecration to the work."[12]

Adventists especially needed to read this "inspiring narrative" because it contained "all the facts connected with the early rise of this great advent movement." In addition, it provided answers to the "slurs, innuendoes, and falsehoods" regarding Millerism and Adventism. A blurb in the *Review* describing its author as one who "speaks with authority" on church history, and asserted that his "deep insight" into Ellen White's ministry "will do much to stem the tide of unbelief in the Testimonies which is coming in among us."[13]

To stem the tsunami of criticism flooding the church (especially Dr. Kellogg's pantheism and A. T. Jones' antiestablishmentarianism), church leaders urged young people to read *The Great Second Advent Movement*. In 1905 the Sabbath school lessons referenced it for a series of studies: "The Gift of Prophecy." The next year Arthur W. Spalding, chair of the English Department at Emmanuel Missionary College, wrote a quiz for the book. Then in

1907 M. E. Kern, chair of the GC Missionary Volunteer Department, created the "Standard of Attainment" in SDA history that required Adventist youth to study Loughborough's book and pass an exam on its contents, if they desired to take the exam. One reason for doing it was to "strengthen [their] faith and confidence in the great advent movement." Widely advertised as "a complete account" of Adventist Church history, "a grand storehouse of knowledge," and "a most important book for our people and others," *The Great Second Advent Movement* promised to make those who read it "settled, grounded, rooted, and established" in the Adventist faith. It was also part of the Missionary Volunteer Reading Course of inspiring books that "all young people should study."[14] Within a few years *The Great Second Advent Movement* had hit the "best seller" list of SDA publications. For a half century it would remain the leading Adventist history textbook.

Despite receiving high marks for its fascinating anecdotes, detailed statistics, and faith-building stories, however, *The Great Second Advent Movement* has come under attack for its apologetic tone, biased prose, and factual inaccuracies (see endnote 10). Toward the end of his life Loughborough engaged in an acrimonious exchange of letters with Adventist apostate E. S. Ballenger concerning his interpretation of early Adventist history, especially regarding the "shut door" doctrine and the prophetic role of Ellen White (see chapter 12). Consequently, although Loughborough deserves to be remembered as the preeminent chronicler of the nineteenth-century Adventist movement, on the other hand his historical interpretations of those events shaped (some would say "warped") Adventist historiography for generations. His "disciples" (primarily Arthur W. Spalding, LeRoy Edwin Froom, F. M. Wilcox, and C. Mervyn Maxwell) continued writing apologetic histories "the Loughborough way," emphasizing mainly the progressive, inspiring stories of the past in their books and articles. Only during the past 40 years have scholars begun taking a more critical look at Adventist sources and reinterpreting the past more objectively.

CELEBRITY SPEAKER

Nonetheless, the publication of *The Great Second Advent Movement* enhanced Loughborough's reputation as a something of a celebrity. With growing frequency, church leaders ascribed to him titles indicative of the esteem he now enjoyed within Adventist ranks. In 1905 before John preached at the dedication of the new Pacific Press buildings in Mountain View, M. C. Wilcox, president of the board of directors, called him "a pioneer in this [publishing] field."[15] The *North Pacific Union Gleaner* dubbed him "the venerable brother." The *Missionary Worker* lauded him and Haskell as "old standard bearers of the work."[16]

Indeed, no camp meeting roster was complete without Lougborough's name on it. Yet as his fame grew, John found himself in the awkward position of having to turn down invitations to many convocations. Instead, he concentrated on meeting appointments in the West. In 1905 he attended the California and Nevada conference sessions, serving on their credentials and licenses committees, and with Ellen White and George Irwin, he preached at five camp meetings on the West Coast. His sermons focused on early Adventist history, spiritual gifts, sacrificial giving, and dissident groups and "how they came out."[17]

The following year, as a delegate-at-large, he represented the General Conference at the Pacific Union Conference session in Portland, Oregon. His summer camp meeting appointments for 1906 took him to California, Texas, Arkansas, and Oklahoma (where, after preaching in the German tent, he taught them the rousing gospel song "Gideon Marching Out to Fight"). Everywhere he went, listeners reported that he spoke with "clearness and power" and that his talks were "productive of much good in confirming and establishing the faith of the people in the spirit of prophecy and work of Sister White in these times of doubt and apostasy." He returned to California with empty pockets, but many warm memories. Then, catching the train for Battle Creek, John attended the three-week General Conference session in 1905. In addition, he preached seven times at the Battle Creek Tabernacle and twice at the elementary school, and he shared thrilling stories with the "old people" (his term) at the James White Memorial Home. Between meetings, he visited with his old friends Harriet Smith, George Amadon, A. C. Bourdeau, and Isaac Van Horn.[18]

Except for one trip to Denver to attend the Colorado Conference session, however, Loughborough remained west of the Rockies for 1907. He accepted invitations to speak to the patients at the Adventist sanitariums in Glendale, Loma Linda, Paradise Valley, and St. Helena, where his talks on early Adventist history packed the parlors. John met several times with the students at Fernando Academy (San Fernando Academy after 1914), and they listened to his stories of adventure with wide-eyed wonder. Paying most of his expenses, John confessed to GC President Arthur G. Daniells that he had returned home with only 20 cents in his pocket.[19]

His cash shortage was due, not to John's extravagant spending, but to his benevolence. As his diaries demonstrate, his and Annie's annual income always exceeded their expenses (often by more than $100). Thanks in part to their frugality as well as to the royalties from John's books, the Loughboroughs could afford to give to a wide variety of causes. They helped the struggling Menominee SDA Church in Michigan's Upper Peninsula; gave a $10 goldpiece, which provided 500 copies of the *Signs* for an exposition at Jamestown, New York; and sent $10 for the "poor child widows and caste-enslaved Aryans of India."[20]

Despite humorous renditions of Negro dialect and occasional use of the N-word in private letters, Loughborough cared deeply about Edson White's work for southern Blacks and gave liberally to support the Southern Missionary Society (SMS) in an era when some General Conference officials and Edson's own brother Willie seemed reluctant to do so. In addition, he regularly sent money to erect new church and school buildings for Black Adventists in Greenville, Mississippi, and Atlanta, Georgia, and to build a baptistry at Louis Sheafe's African-American church in Washington, D.C. (John also financially supported Sheafe's evangelistic efforts in the nation's capital when few GC officials lifted a finger to help him). Loughborough's example inspired his granddaughter: In April 1907 Jennie Ireland, then a student at Healdsburg College, gave $6.41 to the SMS—$1.41 *more* than her uncle William Loughborough gave that month. Within a few years Jennie would become something of a pioneer herself, teaching inner-city Black children in Los Angeles.[21]

INCREASING HEALTH ISSUES

Having passed the biblical lifespan of three-score and 10, John began experiencing a number of health issues that depleted his energy and restricted some of his activities. Despite daily naps and cold baths, his weak left lung made him more susceptible to respiratory afflictions such as colds and flu (then called "la grippe"). Coughing spells would shake his feeble body for up to an hour at night. For these ailments, he visited the nearest sanitarium for hot and cold fomentations, electric baths, salt glows, and oil rubs (massages).

The strain on his vocal cords from speaking for hours at a time also meant that he sometimes returned home exhausted and hoarse. In addition, he occasionally suffered "a fiery time" with hives, perhaps induced by something he had eaten or touched at camp meetings. Whatever the cause, some of the attacks lasted for an hour and proved so debilitating that he nearly fainted from the pain. His yen for licorice and lemon candy also paved the way for painful trips to the dentist to have decayed teeth extracted and false teeth inserted in their place. Impulsive dietary decisions—eating too many beans or a combination of fresh onions and strawberries—gave him stomach cramps.[22]

When he returned from his camp meeting circuit in 1907, having preached at 42 meetings in five weeks, Loughborough weighed only 110 pounds. The junket had required "more labor than I had put forth in the same length of time [during any period] in [the past] ten years," he confessed in the *Review*. "I was much exhausted in strength," he said, adding philosophically, "Well, this earth is waxing old, as well as the people upon it."[23]

One incident he felt that proved that the earth was "waxing old" occurred on April 18, 1906, when a catastrophic earthquake struck northern California, leveling large sections of San Francisco. Even roughly 30 miles south at Mountain View, the trembler toppled the walls of the Pacific Press building. Yet only three blocks away, Annie and John's cottage sustained only $1 in damages—mainly small cracks in the ceiling—while nearby houses lost their chimneys or roofs. "Well, God must smile on you," one man remarked to John, who replied that although he did trust in God, he was "no better than others" whose homes had sustained severe damage.[24]

LOUGHBOROUGH'S WRITINGS

Without question, earthquakes, as did meteor showers and comets, provided grist for the mills of Adventist preachers and authors who saw them as fulfillments of end-time prophecies. Loughborough, like other Adventists of his generation, firmly believed that "we have come to the generation which shall not pass off the stage of action until Christ himself shall come." In *The Great Second Advent Movement* he had declared that *this generation*—those who saw the stars fall in 1833, the comet of 1844, and other "wonders" portrayed in *Last-Day Tokens* (1904)—would witness the Second Advent that the Millerites had anticipated more than 60 years before.[25]

Explicating end-time prophecies also became the focus of a lengthy series John wrote for the *Review* between 1905 and 1907. Covering topics such as the 18 sins of earth's last generation, the 144,000, and the 1290- and 1335-day prophecies of Daniel 12, the articles read like shortened versions of sermons or Bible studies for new converts. In each one, he cites many Bible texts, quotes Mrs. White's writings, and offers examples from experience and history to support his points.[26]

Thanks to Hetty and Stephen Haskell's editorial generosity, John enjoyed carte blanche to explore a wide spectrum of subjects in the *Bible Training School*. His short articles cover the gamut from early Adventist history to end-time prophecies. They discuss the open and shut doors in the heavenly sanctuary, the ministry of angels, the symbolism of Jewish feasts, and the spiritual meanings of "heart" and "tongue" in the Bible. One article raises the question as to whether the Bible forbids shaving—then concludes that while it was practiced by "Heathen Indians," shaving might not be recommended for Christians. Then for about a year (1906-1907) he explored all of the biblical references to the number three.[27]

His fixation on pet topics appears in other church periodicals as well. For example, in 1905 Loughborough devoted five articles in the *Pacific Union Recorder* to Melchizedek. After quoting Mark Twain's quip about science ("I do like science; you can get so much theory from so few facts"), he squeezed as much meaning as he could from a handful of Bible texts (and Josephus' works) regarding Melchizedek's name, identity, roles, and larger symbolic meaning.[28] That same year, another series began in the *Signs of the Times* focused on spiritual gifts in the church.[29]

If *The Great Second Advent Movement* constituted Loughborough's most important historical work, *The Church, Its Organization, Order, and Discipline* (1907) is arguably the most significant policy manual he ever produced. Just as the former became the leading denominational history textbook for nearly half a century, the latter became the unofficial procedural handbook until GC vice president J. L. McElhany wrote the *Church Manual* in 1931. Indeed, some administrators preferred John's handbook well into the 1950s.[30]

The publication of *The Church* marked a major turning point in SDA history. Back in 1882 the GC Committee had asked W. H. Littlejohn, J. O. Corliss, and H. A. St. John to prepare some guidelines on church order. The *Review* had printed them in a three-month series between June and August 1883, but due to significant opposition, the General Conference had never officially adopted them. As GC president G. I. Butler explained, "The Bible contains our creed and discipline. . . . What it has not revealed relative to church organization and management, the duties of officers and ministers, and kindred subjects, should not be strictly defined and drawn out into minute specifications for the sake of uniformity, but rather be left to individual judgment under the guidance of the Holy Spirit."[31]

Consequently, Loughborough's booklet, which reflected decades of personal experience in establishing new churches, conferences, and institutions, originally appeared as a series of articles in the *Review* in 1899-1900 and then as a private typewritten manuscript that he made available upon request to local church officers. But as an expanding church faced administrative challenges around the world, the need for some kind of policy manual became readily apparent. Consequently, a rising demand brought John's private manuscript to the attention of the Review and Herald press, which published it in 1907.[32]

Loughborough devotes half of the 30 chapters to explaining the biblical foundation for the church's authority, the spiritual duties of its leaders, and the necessity of order, unity, and discipline in the church. Quoting freely from the Bible and the writings of Ellen White, he portrays the church as a building erected on Christ as the foundation; its officers are undershepherds and Jesus is the Great Shepherd; its members are branches and Christ is the Vine. He devotes four chapters to a discussion of order, service, and submission in the apostolic church and three chapters to the rise of apostasy and how the apostolic and Adventist movements dealt with it. Chapters 20-25 deal with church finances; legal incorporation; forming local congregations, conferences, and unions; numerical representation; and the duties of committee members. Finally, chapters 26-30 contain warnings and advice, historical precedents, and answers to frequently asked questions.[33]

A few of his answers to queries show how attitudes in the church had changed during the past century. For example, asked whether church bodies should follow strict parliamentary rules, he asserted that "they would probably make greater progress in seeking the Lord for His guidance than of being too strenuous," because "the presence of one angel in our church councils would expedite church matters more rapidly than an armful of parliamentary rules." Regarding the purchase of insurance, he recommended that local churches purchase property insurance, but advised members to trust in God rather than buy life insurance. For the most part, however, the twenty-first-century SDA Church still follows most of the specific procedures originally printed in Loughborough's book a century ago.[34]

The Church met with the hearty endorsement of church officers combating the divisive influence of Alonzo T. Jones's congregational and antiestablishmentarian views. A. Nelson, in the *Southwestern Union Recorder,* hailed it as "present truth for this time."[35] The *Northern Union Reaper* called it "a publication for the times" that would "do much toward fortifying our people against any suggestion from any other source which will tend to poison their minds against our present system of organization" which was "the perfect system."[36] In the *Review* George Butler praised the book as an "invaluable treatise" that would combat current congregational and independence movements within the church.[37]

Although Butler mentioned no names, he undoubtedly had in mind the extreme views advocated in the 1890s by A. T. Jones, E. J. Waggoner, and others. Arguing that since Christ was the true Head of the church that all other human-originated titles and positions of authority constituted "Babylon," Jones promoted a "radical individualism" based upon the ideal of total equality among members ("the priesthood of all believers"). From his perspective, to call someone "president" represented apostasy; parliamentary procedures were "from the devil"; and the only biblical form of organization was "gospel order" or congregationalism wherein each member had as much authority as every other member. Given these views, therefore, it is somewhat ironic that Jones agreed to become president of the California Conference in 1901 and president of Dr. Kellogg's Battle Creek College a few years later. Nonetheless, at the 1903 GC session he tried to block acceptance of the new GC Constitution substituting the term "president" for "chairman" (a title adopted in 1901). When he published his incendiary *One-Man Power* pamphlet in 1903, the GC responded with *A Statement Refuting Charges Made by A. T. Jones Against the Spirit of Prophecy and Plan of Organization of the Seventh-day Adventist Denomination* (1906). A year later, Loughborough's book *The Church* also appeared to combat Jones' influence.[38]

The book made Loughborough an instant authority on matters relating to church policies and practices, at least in the eyes of some members who saw the aged pioneer as a sort of ecclesiastical "Dear Abby." Soon John began receiving letters seeking advice on a wide range of issues. F. M. Burg in British Columbia wanted to know if being single disqualified one for being a church elder. "Charles X" asked if marriage was only for producing children, or if a certain amount of "sexual indulgence" was OK. James Garmire of Seattle argued about a host of doctrinal issues (the cleansing of the heavenly sanctuary, the two-horned beast, the sealing work, and the third woe of Revelation) and disagreed with Adventist practices relating to the eating of swine's flesh, divorce and remarriage, and how to live a perfect life. Louis R. Conradi, now president of the European General Conference, debated with John over the church's interpretation of "the daily" and the 1335-day prophecy of Daniel 8. Meanwhile, women requested his photograph and deaconesses wanted his recipe for making Communion bread.[39]

LOUGHBOROUGH'S DIARY

John's diaries seem to indicate that the 300 Loughborough letters that exist today in Adventist archives probably represent less than 5 percent of his total correspondence, which may have exceeded 6,000 letters during his lifetime. The diaries also show that he and Annie frequently stepped back from their professional duties to spend time together. For example, they took breaks from reading the galley proofs for *The Great Second Advent Movement* to set out blackberry and loganberry bushes; plant almond, orange, and lemon trees; and create colorful pansy, aster, geranium, and morning glory beds around their cottage and outhouse. Ever the handyman, even in his 70s John could build kitchen cupboards, sink drawers, and chicken coops; modify the electrical wiring throughout the house; install a new oil stove; and make his own bow ties. He was still cutting and hauling wood for the kitchen stove, painting the picket fence, collecting eggs from his wife's Rock Island Reds, and planting a huge garden every summer. The cornucopia of vegetables the Loughboroughs ate suggests that their garden may have covered several acres. What they did not consume fresh they sold or canned for the winter.

But life wasn't all work. For example, they enjoyed attending evening concerts when the Pacific Press Orchestra performed at Olympia Hall. They especially loved visiting with their friends and neighbors Ellen and Willie White, Sarah McEnterfer, Dr. Merritt G. Kellogg, and H. A. St. John. Traveling church employees—especially ministers, missionaries, and teachers—found a warm welcome in their home. We see John's love for children reflected in his teaching both a girls' and a boys' Sabbath school class in the Mountain View SDA Church. In addition to attending Sabbath school, church, testimony, and prayer meetings there, John and Annie went to the services of a local Presbyterian Church. Lacking a crystal set (radio), Victrola (record player), and a telephone, they spent quiet evenings reading to each other in the parlor. Clearly they hoped to enjoy this peaceful life for many years to come.[40]

Probably they would have done so had it not been for the intrusion of the Grim Reaper. As had happened before in John's life, death knocked twice at their door. In 1867 he had lost his wife Mary and one stillborn daughter on the same day; in 1894 his mother and his only son Delmer had died within a week of each other. Then in June of 1906 John learned that Eliza Norton, the wife of his brother William, had passed away from cancer at 79. Former Millerites who converted to Sabbatarian Adventism in the 1840s, William and Eliza Loughborough had moved to Battle Creek in 1868 where they had raised three children. One daughter became an editor of the *Youth's Instructor*; another served as a nurse-administrator at Glendale Sanitarium; and their son became a pressman at Pacific Press. John's former preaching partner Isaac Van Horn preached at Eliza's funeral in Battle Creek.[41]

In May 1907 Annie began experiencing severe asthma attacks that convulsed her body in coughing fits. At first two physicians diagnosed her affliction as rheumatic fever combined with neuralgia—too late they discovered that the problem was heart trouble. John stayed by her side during the day, preparing meals and giving her medicines. Each night a rotating shift of church women sat with her. At sunset on Friday, May 31—a date John would mark in his diaries until the day he died—Annie passed away from pericarditis at 67. Converted to Sabbatarian Adventism at 18 by the preaching of Bates, Waggoner, and Cornell in 1857, Anna Mariah Driscoll had studied business and accounting at Albion College before becoming a public high school teacher in Hillsdale, Michigan. Then in 1875 she moved to California, where she became secretary and treasurer of Pacific Press. After marrying John in 1878, she served as a missionary to England, matron of the St. Helena Sanitarium, matron of the Bible school and mission in Chicago, and secretary of the State Sabbath-School Association in Kansas. Unlike her famous husband in 1924, Annie would have not one but *two* funerals: the first at Mountain View SDA Church and the second at St. Helena Sanitarium.[42]

Just as Annie had given generously to Adventist missions in life, so in death her benevolence continued. As she lay dying, she asked John to forward a check for $20 to the India Mountain Mission Home so that Adventist missionaries laboring in the subcontinent's tropics might enjoy a cool mountain retreat away from the "debilitating and health-destroying heat of the lowlands." Furthermore, her last will and testament (which they both signed) directed her husband "to place all of the belongings of the deceased in the treasury for the advancement of the [SDA Church's] work." That fall, John sold Annie's household goods—and most of his own—and then moved in with his daughter Mary and her husband, John Ireland, in Healdsburg.[43]

Writing to his good friend Willie White, John confessed, "I am not discouraged or cast down by the bereavement that came upon me, but the shock on my nerves has left me very weak physically. I have no special pain or sickness, but I lack in strength to do much of anything."[44] However, despite the sudden death of his third wife, J. N. Loughborough in his late 70s and 80s would travel farther and accomplish more than he could possibly have imagined.

---

[1] EGW to G. I. Butler, letter 105, 1903, in Ellen G. White, *Manuscript Releases* (Silver Spring, Md.: Ellen G. White Estate, 1993), vol. 17, p. 344.

[2] *Ibid.*, p. 345.

[3] WCW to JNL, Nov. 20, 1899, WCW Letter Books, CAR. Thus, Andrew Mustard's assertion in *James White and Seventh-day Adventist Organization* (1987) that Loughborough "ascribed a more crucial role to Ellen G. White's leadership in the development of SDA Church organization than we have discovered in this study" is supported by Ellen White.

[4] EGW to WCW, Feb. 15, 1904, letter 87, 1904, CAR.

[5] Author's compilation of sources consulted in *The Great Second Advent Movement* (2010).

[6] See, for example, JNL's personal experiences cited in *The Great Second Advent Movement* (Washington, D.C.: Review and Herald Pub. Assn., 1905), pp. 505-507, 526, 527.

[7] JNL, "Individual Experiences," p. 4, published in 1919, about 12 years after Annie's death.

[8] JNL, diary, November 9, 1903-April 1, 1904; *PUR*, Nov. 4, 1968, p. 8. Although the published *Rise and Progress* (1892) had 392 pages, *The Great Second Advent Movement* (1905) had 473 pages and included three appendices not found in the 1892 edition. Consequently, although both books had about the same number of chapters (29 in *Rise and Progress* and 28 in *The Great Second Advent Movement*), the chapters in the 1892 book averaged 11 pages each whereas those in the 1905 revision averaged 17 pages each.

[9] JNL, diary, January-February and October 1905.

[10] For example, that Voltaire (who died in 1778) predicted the abolition of the Bible during the French Revolution (1789); that Foy (who lived into the 1890s) "sickened and died" soon after refusing to relate his three-step vision in 1844 (p. 147); that Advent Christians (not SDAs) believed that the "shut door" meant "no more mercy for sinners" (p. 234) between 1844 and 1851; and that EGW herself never believed it (pp. 222, 223); that Louis Philippe of France (who was a "citizen king," not an emperor) had fled from a Paris surrounded by walls in 1848 (they had been torn down during the French Revolution—p. 271); that EGW's health vision in 1863 occurred in a tent (rather than in Aaron Hilliard's home in Otsego—p. 358); and that Bates first went to Jackson, Michigan, in 1851 (instead of in 1849).

[11] See, for example, *The Great Second Advent Movement*, pp. 463, 469-472, 570 and JNL, "Chronological Outline Traced in *The Great Second Advent Movement*" (typewritten manuscript, n.d.), m. ASC000303, CAR.

[12] *West Michigan Herald*, July 5, 1905, p. 4; *RH*, June 22, 1905, pp. 5, 6; *ST*, July 12, 1905, p. 444; *Union Conference Record*, Apr. 13, 1908, p. 8.

[13] *RH*, Mar. 1, 1917, p. 2; *RH*, Feb. 8, 1906, p. 2.

[14] JNL, diary, July 1907; *YI*, May 30, 1905, p. 7; *Union Conference Record*, Oct. 21, 1906, p. 8; *RH*, Apr. 25, 1907, p. 2; *RH*. June 6, 1907, p. 2; *ST*, July 19, 1907, p. 450; *NPUG*, Oct. 23, 1907, p. 8; *Columbia Union Visitor*, Oct. 23, 1907, p. 2; *RH*, Aug. 22, 1907, pp. 9, 10; *RH*, Oct. 24, 1907, p. 2; *Echoes From the Field*, Oct. 30, 1907, p. 1; *RH*, Nov. 7, 1907, p. 21.

[15] *PUR*, May 4, 1905, pp. 2, 3.

[16] *NPUG*, Nov. 29, 1906, p. 1; *Missionary Worker*, June 7, 1905, pp. 90, 91.

[17] JNL, diary, June-July 1905; *PUR*, July 27, 1905, p. 2; *RH*, Aug. 10, 1905, p. 19; *PUR*, Feb. 8, 1906, pp. 2, 3.

[18] *ST*, Feb. 28, 1906, p. 141; *PUR*, Mar. 1, 1906, p. 1; JNL, diary, July, August, and October 1906; *SWUR*, July 17, 1906, p. 1; *SWUR*, Aug. 21, 1906, p. 4; *SWUR*, Aug. 28, 1906, pp. 2-4; *RH*, Sept. 20, 1906, p. 18; *RH*, Nov. 15, 1906, p. 19.

[19] JNL, diary, December 1906; *RH*, Jan. 3, 1907, pp. 19, 20; *Northern Union Reaper*, Oct. 29, 1907, p. 8; *Echoes From the Field*, Sept. 11, 1907, p. 3; JNL to A. G. Daniells, Oct. 1, 1906, CAR.

[20] *West Michigan Herald*, Feb. 21, 1906, pp. 3, 4; *ST*, June 13, 1906, p. 356; *ST*, June 26, 1907, p. 415.

[21] *PUR*, Sept. 14, 1905, p. 8; *Gospel Herald*, July 1906, p. 27; *Gospel Herald*, August 1906, p. 32; *RH*, Sept. 21, 1905, p. 24; *Gospel Herald*, October 1907, p. 40; *Gospel Herald*, November 1907, p. 43; JNL to WCW, July 22, 1884, ms. 52, CAR; D. Morgan, *Lewis C. Sheafe*, p. 286; *Gospel Herald*, June 1907, p. 23. According to G. Valentine's *Prophet and Presidents*, p. 229, for a while "an intense animosity" existed between Edson and Willie

that manifested itself in an open "dislike and lack of respect" for each other that brought pain to Ellen White's heart.

[22] JNL, diary, June 1904, November-December 1905, January-February 1906; JNL to Mrs. H. F. Randolph, Feb. 17, 1907, m. 006529, CAR; *RH,* Aug. 29, 1907, p. 18; *ST,* Oct. 2, 1907, p. 637.

[23] JNL, diary, August 1907; *RH,* Feb. 21, 1907, p. 17.

[24] *RH,* Oct. 11, 1906, pp. 18, 19.

[25] JNL, *The Great Second Advent Movement*, pp. 93-98. According to an ad in the *Sabbath School Lessons* for July 1904, p. 40, *Last-Day Tokens* contained 24 full-color plates (reproductions of those painted on cloth by John and William Loughborough) depicting "the marvelous sights seen in the heavens during the last fifty years," all of which John saw as "tokens" of Christ's imminent return.

[26] See JNL's *RH* series on last-day prophecy in July 13, 1905, p. 9; Nov. 16, 1905, pp. 12, 13; Nov. 23, 1905, pp. 9, 10; Jan. 11, 1906, p. 9; June 14, 1906, pp. 8, 9; June 21, 1906, pp. 8, 9; Oct. 18, 1906, pp. 8, 9; Mar. 28, 1907, p. 10; Apr. 4, 1907, pp. 9, 10; Oct. 31, 1907, pp. 9, 10; Nov. 7, 1907, pp. 9, 10; Nov. 14, 1907, p. 10.

[27] See JNL's *BTS* articles in February 1904, pp. 130-132; April 1904, pp. 164, 165; February 1905, pp. 130, 131; April 1905, pp. 162, 163; May 1905, pp. 179, 180; July 1905, pp. 19, 20; August 1905, pp. 37, 38; October 1905, pp. 66, 67; November 1905, pp. 82, 83; December 1905, p. 104; January 1906, pp. 115, 116; February 1906, pp. 130, 131; March 1906, pp. 147, 148; April 1906, pp. 163, 164; May 1906, pp. 179, 180; June 1906, pp. 194, 195; July 1906, pp. 18, 19; August 1906, pp. 42, 43; September 1906, pp. 50, 51; October 1906, pp. 67, 68; November 1906, pp. 83, 84; December 1906, pp. 98, 99; February 1907, pp. 131, 132; March 1907, pp. 146, 147; April 1907, pp. 163, 164; May 1907, pp. 180, 181; July 1907, pp. 18, 19; August 1907, pp. 34, 35; September 1907, pp. 53, 54; and November 1907, pp. 82, 83. As photographs prove, both Stephen Haskell and J. N. Loughborough wore well-trimmed beards all their lives.

[28] JNL, "Melchisedec," in *PUR*, Oct. 19, 1905, p. 1; Oct. 5, 1905, pp. 1, 2; Oct. 26, 1905, pp. 1, 2; Nov. 2, 1905, p. 1; Nov. 9, 1905, pp. 1, 2. Ironically, these innocuous (if esoteric) articles raised the hackles of some readers who thought Loughborough was "attacking" the author of a similar series published in the *Signs of the Times*. See *ST,* Dec. 6, 1905, p. 784.

[29] See JNL's series on spiritual gifts in *ST,* Nov. 22, 1905, pp. 741, 750; Apr. 11, 1906, p. 2; Oct. 16, 1907, pp. 659, 660.

[30] N. Collins, *Heartwarming Stories of Adventist Pioneers: Their Works Do Follow Them*, p. 183; F.D.N., *RH,* Feb. 14, 1963, pp. 12, 13; Walter R. Beach, *RH,* Aug. 30, 1979, pp. 12, 13. The many similarities in organization and content between Loughborough's booklet and McElhany's manual in fact show that the latter followed the pattern set by the former quite closely.

[31] *RH,* Nov. 27, 1883, quoted in *RH,* Aug. 8, 1974, p. 10.

[32] *RH,* Apr. 11, 1907, p. 2.

[33] JNL, *The Church*, chaps. 1-30, pp. 1-184.

[34] *Ibid.*, chapter 30. However, Loughborough's list of 16 questions for baptismal candidates (first used at the North Side Swedish SDA Church in Chicago) has considerably shortened through the years. See JNL, *The Church*, pp. 175, 176 and *Workers' Bulletin*, Oct. 15, 1907, pp. 1, 2.

[35] *SWUR*, Apr. 23, 1907, p. 7; *SWUR*, June 4, 1907, p. 6.

[36] *Northern Union Reaper*, Apr. 30, 1907, p. 8.

[37] *RH,* May 9, 1907, p. 2.

[38] G. Knight, *Organizing to Beat the Devil*, pp. 86-96, 106-115, 117-122. Jones also

contributed to the apostasies of Adventist evangelists Lewis Sheafe and E. E. Franke early in the twentieth century.

[39] JNL, diary, January 1907; JNL to Elder F. M. Burg, Jan. 15, 1906, CAR; JNL to Mr. Charles X, Apr. 21, 1907, m. 52, CAR; JNL to "Dear Brother," Apr. 21, 1907, m. 006529, CAR; James Monroe Garmire, "Reply to Elder J. N. Loughborough's Reply to 'Open Letter,' No. 2" (n. p., c. 1906), pp. 3-31, CAR; L. R. Conradi to JNL, c. April 1907, DF 201c, CAR. In one instance Loughborough claimed that he got the recipe for the Communion bread from John I. Tay, but in another statement he said that he had adapted it from the practice of the Jews in making unleavened bread for the Passover. The recipe (1 pint water, 4 cups fine flour, 1 tablespoon butter, all well mixed, baked in a hot oven for 15 minutes, then cut into squares 9/16ths of an inch in diameter), which can be found in JNL's 1906 diary, appeared in several Adventist periodicals, including *The Missionary Worker*, Mar. 28, 1906, p. 56, and *North Michigan News Sheet*, Oct. 8, 1907, p. 2.

[40] See JNL's diaries, January 1905-July 1907.

[41] *West Michigan Herald*, June 27, 1906, p. 4; *RH*, July 5, 1906, p. 23.

[42] JNL, diary, May-June 1907; *RH*, June 20, 1907, p. 23; *PUR*, June 6, 1907, p. 5; *AUG*, June 19, 1907, p. 212; *Northern Union Reaper*, June 18, 1907, p. 8.

[43] JNL, diary, September 1907; JNL to WCW, July 30, 1907, m. 52, CAR; *ST*, Aug. 14, 1907, pp. 525, 528. Ironically, the *ST*, conflating John's second and third wives, reported the death of "Mrs. [Annie] [Newman] Loughborough" instead of Annie Driscoll Loughborough. In this biography I have consistently spelled Annie's maiden name as "Driscoll" rather than "Driscol" because John always spelled it that way in his diary. If a husband doesn't know how to spell his own wife's name, then who does?

[44] JNL to WCW, July 30, 1907, m. 52, CAR.

Chapter XX

GLOBAL CELEBRITY (1907-1910)

"Voted, That, while we appreciate the offer of Elder Loughborough to visit Australia, on account of his advanced age and the great risk to his health incurred in making such a long journey at this season of the year, as well as the change in climate which would necessarily result in visiting Australia at the present time, we deem it inadvisable that he accept [Australasian Union president O. A. Olsen's] invitation."[1]

Although at 76 J. N. Loughborough certainly qualified as a person of "advanced age," his extensive speaking itinerary between 1907 and 1910 aptly demonstrated that he saw no "great risk" to his health in accepting invitations to preach at camp meetings and constituency sessions up and down the West Coast. Furthermore, as previous chapters have shown, at times of loss, John typically buried his sorrow in travel and work. After his first wife Mary Walker died in 1867, John left for California with his new wife Maggie Newman in 1868; and after Maggie died in 1875, he married Annie Driscoll, and then left for England in 1878. While he did not remarry after Annie's death in 1907, he did keep traveling. If the GC Committee felt that it was too risky to send him to Australia, he would prove them wrong in 1908-1909 by taking a global tour of Adventist institutions on three continents.

But first he had appointments to fill in the Northwest. During the winter of 1907-1908 John shared his faith-building stories with church members in Salem and Portland, Oregon, with patients at the Salem Institute and the Seattle Sanitarium, and with students at the Laurelwood School and

Walla Walla College. Wherever he went, people snapped his picture as if he were a celebrity, which, in a way, he was. One announcement boasted that "this will be one of the greatest treats . . . in a long time. . . . For such as Elder Loughborough is, doesn't come very often."[2] As a delegate-at-large at the Pacific Union Conference session in 1908, he enjoyed the preaching of his friends Ellen White, W. W. Prescott, and A. G. Daniells. John described the gathering as "one of the most powerful and harmonious meetings that we have witnessed in California." "The spirit prevailing, especially in connection with the preaching services, to me seemed to be much [like] the power attending the message of 1844." At its close, he participated in a special farewell service for China-bound missionaries. If his spelling of exotic places was poor and his knowledge of geography faulty, Loughborough did, in fact, know the names and locations of every SDA foreign missionary, and he followed each one with deep interest.[3]

Summertime, of course, meant camp meetings, which for John represented the "dessert course" on the menu of preaching opportunities. Widely billed as the "pioneer of the Third Angel's Message," "a veteran of the cross," and "the Lord's venerable servant,"[4] Loughborough welcomed every invitation to hit the sawdust trail. During the summer of 1908 he joined Ellen White, J. O. Corliss, and Stephen Haskell (billed as "the oldest, active pioneers in this cause") to speak at camp meetings in Lodi and Melrose, California, and Reno, Nevada.[5]

During an extensive tour of the eastern United States in 1909, Loughborough filled several speaking engagements in South Lancaster, Massachusetts, Rochester, New York, and Takoma Park, Maryland, where he attended the General Conference session. On his way back to California, he stopped in Battle Creek, where 3,500 people packed the Dime Tabernacle to hear him preach. Former Review and Herald pressman George Amadon, who felt that his discourses "were a Godsend to us," described them as having "the good old-time ring of the early [eighteen-] fifties." By the time John returned to Lodi, he had covered 47,500 miles, attended 580 meetings, and preached 358 sermons in 16 months, and he showed no signs of slowing down.[6] After a brief rest, he joined his old friends Hetty and Stephen Haskell to deliver doctrinal discourses at the Healdsburg and Armona Bible Institutes. During John's lectures church workers listened with rapt attention.[7]

In addition to attending the Pacific Union Conference sessions with his son-in-law, John Ireland (secretary of the conference), every year, Loughborough accepted invitations to speak at a variety of venues. During 1910 alone, he preached at colporteur book institutes, weeks of prayer, religious liberty conventions, health institutes, and constituency meetings in California. "I know of no better 'rest' at this time than to labour on as the Lord gives [me] strength," he wrote in the *South African Missionary.*[8]

One of John's favorite ways of laboring, of course, included telling stories to children, academy youth, and college students, and he accepted nearly every invitation from an Adventist school that came his way. "The Elder seemed to enjoy talking with boys and girls," one pupil recalled decades later. Between 1907 and 1910 Loughborough shared his boyhood experiences with elementary pupils in Lodi and Chico, California; with academy students in Lodi and San Fernando, California, Gaston, Oregon, near Vancouver, Washington, and South Lancaster, Massachusetts; and with young adults at Walla Walla College in Washington and Pacific Union College in Angwin, California. As a father and grandfather, he knew how to tweak his presentations to meet the ability levels of his young listeners, who always found them "intensely interesting" and "instructive." As a rule, students not only gave him "earnest and marked attention," but they also *took notes* while he talked! Even when he did not have invitations to speak, John regularly attended Young People's meetings (after 1907 called Missionary Volunteer meetings) to sing and pray with them.[9]

In at least one respect, John was similar to the boys and girls he associated with, for both had vivid nighttime dreams. If the children's dreams reflected visual stimuli, wish fulfillment, or snacks eaten too late at night, Loughborough believed that many of his dreams came from God and were intended to prepare him for a change in ministry. As we have seen, months before leaving for California in 1868 and England in 1878 he had received dreams in which he saw himself traveling to these places and speaking with people he had not met. Sometimes, as in the fall of 1907, he witnessed specific venues where he would be asked to speak days or even weeks before the official invitation arrived in his mailbox. In those circumstances, he felt that God was not only alerting him to the work He wanted him to do, but also encouraging him. Although Loughborough never called them "visions," he firmly believed they emanated from the same divine source as Ellen White's visions, but with a particular application to his own life. In fact he saw these dreams as the fulfillment of Mrs. White's 1862 testimony telling him that in the future, God would "lay out" (make clear) to him the fields in which he was to labor.[10]

Between 1897 and 1901, for example, Loughborough had received "scores" of dreams in which he saw himself in Australia; a dozen such dreams had come to him in 1899-1900 alone. In a letter to Ellen White, he said: "[M]y mind has been impressed that it would yet be my duty to visit the Australian field." Although he had seen no need for him to go in the 1890s while Ellen and Willie White and Stephen Haskell were there, after their return to the U.S. the impression began growing on him that he needed to "bear a testimony there of the rise of the message and the leading hand of God in the work." When GC president George Irwin had asked him to go in 1901, he decided to take Annie with him at his own expense, feeling that "at our age I don't think an ocean should be between us." In 1897 Mrs. White had favored sending Loughborough to Australia, but in 1901 she told him that he was needed in the U.S. to counteract the influence of Jones and Kellogg, so he stayed.[11]

Seven years later, however, Ellen and Willie White, Stephen Haskell, and O. A. Olsen (president of the Australasian Union Conference) felt that the time had come for him to spend a year in the antipodes. So in the summer of 1908 John wrote to GC president Daniells requesting permission to visit Australia. He assured the president that since in his dreams he had not seen himself dying in the Land Down Under, he fully expected to return to America whenever church leadership wished him to do so. (However, in case he was wrong, John told Daniells that he had saved $300 for burial expenses and left a will with his daughter Mary.) Daniells took the matter to the GC Committee, who declined Loughborough's request on the basis of his age, health, and presumed inability to adapt to Australia's winter climate. Friends also tried to dissuade him from going, but believing that his call had come from a higher Source, John would not be deterred.[12]

LOUGHBOROUGH'S WORLD TOUR

Consequently, the GC Committee reversed itself and gave him permission to go, not just to Australia, but on a global tour of Adventist institutions. During his 16-month junket Loughborough traveled 30,000 miles by sea and 17,500 miles on land, attended 500 meetings, and preached 352 times in churches, missions, schools, and sanitariums in Australia, New Zealand, South Africa, Northern Europe, and Great Britain. He later declared: "I was never sick a day or missed a meal. I tripped the deck each day and felt like a boy." His diaries, however, provide a more nuanced version of his adventure.[13]

In preparation for sailing from Vancouver to Sydney, John packed three steamer trunks with clothing, books, papers, and personal items (including crackers, almonds, and malted nuts). Although the Pacific Ocean, initially "smooth as a floor," soon sported "white horse waves," he had felt not a twinge of seasickness or "the least sense of weariness." Cracking nuts with his teeth, however, may have caused the loss of his left incisor. As the ship steamed past the Hawaiian, Wallace, and the Fiji islands, he watched for flying fish in the morning, napped in the afternoon heat, enjoyed evening band concerts, and attended Episcopal services on the weekends. In addition, for the first time in his life, he ate alligator pears, papaya, and coconuts. "I am gaining in health every day," he assured readers. "The trip thus far has been a rest and recreation."[14]

All that changed, however, once he reached Australia. During the train ride to Wahroonga Sanitarium, John learned that he had two preaching appointments the next day. That August and September he spoke numerous times at the sanitarium, in scattered churches, at Missionary Volunteer meetings, and to students at Avondale College. In addition, he attended several committee meetings, taught an Adventist history class at the college, gave worship and chapel talks, told stories to children's Sabbath school classes, and delivered the baccalaureate sermon at the college's graduation exercises. During his free time he toured "Sunnyside" (the White's home in Australia) and hiked for miles into the bush. October found him preaching at the New South Wales camp meeting, sharing his experiences in the rise of the Advent movement, and showing children his colorful "Wonders in the Heavens" charts.[15]

According to the official reports, Loughborough's visit brought a breath of fresh air into an atmosphere choked with skepticism in Australia. After hearing him speak at the Australasian Union Conference session at Cooranbong, one man praised his "stirring incidents" regarding Ellen White's ministry and the "interesting anecdotes" he shared about Adventist history.

Then he commented that Loughborough's "implicit faith in the Word of God" and his "perfect confidence . . . that the Lord would fulfil every word of prophecy" stood in a stark contrast to "the scoffing infidelity" so popular in the Land Down Under. The *Union Conference Record* declared that "his counsel and talks" had been "interesting, instructive, and profitable," "a fountain of help and blessing to us, and our souls have been watered and refreshed." President Olsen informed *Review* readers that "I have never before seen him enjoy such freedom and power in speaking as the Lord has given him during the time of our union conference."[16]

In November Loughborough and Olsen visited western Australia, traveling by ship and train to churches in Adelaide, Freemantle, Perth, Heidelberg, and Melbourne. En route to Albany, the steamship *Kanonna* encountered rough seas, and John lost a couple meals over the railing. But he quickly discovered that there existed no better way to promote his books than to go on the speaking circuit, for everywhere he went, believers snatched up copies of his *The Great Second Advent Movement*. From Melbourne the two men sailed for Tasmania aboard the *Loongana*, and once again rough seas kept John awake, pacing the deck, and reading his new Authorized Version of the Bible. At the camp meeting in Moona (a suburb of Hobart), the "oldest minister of the message" preached to an attentive crowd of approximately 200—save for one "old lady belching out all through [the] discourse." Nineteen converts requested baptism. As Gilbert Valentine has stated, "Camp meetings became a particularly successful strategy for growing the Australian church." By the time he returned to Wahroonga Sanitarium—counting all the hares he saw along the way—he had traveled 10,200 miles, preached 100 times, and baptized dozens of new believers.[17]

In December 1908 a combination of stress, loneliness, and blistering summer heat took their toll on the septuagenarian. He experienced a series of bizarre dreams loaded with fearful imagery and devoid of divine inspiration. In one dream his deceased brother William asked him to care for Isaac and Adelia Van Horn who had been poisoned as William (in the dream) claimed he had been. Another nightmare took him to William's blacksmith shop in Rochester to fight off malaria-carrying mosquitoes on the Erie Canal; in still another he battled huge ants, killing eight of them. After eating spoiled fruit, he dreamed that James White, John Waggoner, and he had marched together in the procession at Martin Luther's funeral! To make matters worse, when he sailed for New Zealand, an albatross followed the badly leaking ship *Warrimoo* across rough seas.[18]

But he made it safely to Wellington. Despite suffering from colds and nosebleeds, he preached daily at the Linwood camp meeting. During his New Zealand tour he told stories to the children at the Pukekura and Auckland schools, preached at Christchurch, and visited with the staff at Papanui Sanitarium (they gave him an expensive leather briefcase as a memento). Returning to Sydney aboard the *Wimmena*, John celebrated his seventy-seventh birthday by tossing some old clothes overboard and donning a lifejacket as the ship plowed through storm-tossed waves.[19]

During February and March church officials kept John busy speaking to students at Avondale College, attending conference business sessions, and preaching at camp meetings in Box Hill (near Melbourne) and Alberton (near Adelaide). Persistent mosquitoes and the drunken revelry of several men who kept him awake until midnight marred the Alberton gathering. By the end of his tour, John had preached at seven different camp meetings in Australia and New Zealand. And contrary to the GC Committee's dire prediction, he had adjusted so well to the Southern Hemisphere's climate that the persistent lung trouble he'd had when he arrived had disappeared by the time he left in March. As a reporter in the Australian *Signs of the Times* boasted, after traveling approximately 21,500 miles by sea and rail, attending 331 meetings, and preaching 177 sermons, "the oldest Seventh-day Adventist minister in the world" had been "fully restored to health." Loughborough attributed it to God: "I have enjoyed much of the blessing of God in my labours in Australia," he wrote in the *Record*, "and have had an interesting time in my associations with our people in this field." He would leave "carrying a very pleasant memory of my stay among you." The editor of the *Record*, speaking on behalf of Australia's Adventists, stated that John's "labours have been much appreciated and of inestimable value to this field."[20]

After six months in Australia, Loughborough boarded the steamship *Medic* to sail from Melbourne to Hobart, Tasmania, where he spent several days preaching and visiting church members before leaving for South Africa. During the rough approximately monthlong voyage, while his shipmates played games topside, John quietly read his Bible below decks. One woman, noticing that he ate no meat, exclaimed, "And you are alive yet!" "Yes, madam," he replied, "I am very much alive." When the ship reached Durban, he began a tour during which he attended 44 meetings in 30 days, speaking at 40 of them.[21]

As racial segregation had not yet become the official policy in South Africa, John was free to preach in Black and White, Afrikaner and English churches everywhere he went. Taking full advantage of the privilege, he visited sanitariums in Durban, Maritzburg, and Plumstead and spoke to Black students at the Maranatha Mission near Bethlehem and to Whites at Claremont College near Cape Town. In addition, he preached to Black and White congregations in Durban, Heisterbad, Johannesburg, Bloomfontain, Maranatha, and Cape Town, among others. The *Review* explained that at "the two Kafir [native black] churches at Salt River and Parow," it required two interpreters to convey his message to the diverse crowd. Despite strong opposition from Catholic and Dutch Reformed ministers, Loughborough's preaching brought "an awakening" among the Boers (settlers of Dutch descent). J. H. de Beer reported that as a result of hearing his inspiring talks, "our courage was revived, and our confidence settled in all points of the great threefold message." As he traveled, John saw several poisonous puff adders, scores of long-horned Cape buffalo, and hundreds of ostriches. A consummate tourist, he visited the Kimberly Diamond Mines, climbed Table Mountain, and met Peter Wessels, the Adventist millionaire. Other highpoints of his African experience included carriage tours of Mr. Lorenz' 1,000-acre farm near Bethlehem and of Albert W. Staples' 1,500-acre pineapple and banana plantation near Grahamstown. Eating such delectable fruit, along with other Dutch and English delicacies, added nearly 10 pounds to his slender frame.[22]

After attending 118 meetings and giving 108 sermons in South Africa, John boarded the steamer *Goorkha* toward the end of July to sail for Europe, where 1,400 Seventh-day Adventists waited to hear him preach. During the two-week voyage he compiled the first of many lists of the promises in God's Word. He kept a sharp lookout for whaling vessels, French battleships, and flying fish. In the evenings he attended the captain's Church of England services.[23]

Once again the relaxing lifestyle ended as soon as his feet hit land. With the assistance of interpreters Louis Conradi (German) and Mr. Curdy (French),

John preached at the Swiss-German camp meeting near Yverdon and the Swiss-French camp meeting near Vergese, besides attending the Roman-Swiss Conference session, where delegates found his talks "encouraging, helpful, and upbuilding." Along the way he took time to visit the chateaux of Louis Napoleon, Mme. de Staël, and Arouet de Voltaire (in whose living room at Ferney he ate three meals). In addition, he toured the Roman baths, the Temple of Diana, and the Coliseum at Nîmes as well as the sites near Vienne where Herod Agrippa died and Pontius Pilate allegedly drowned.[24]

Then, taking the train for Calais, John sailed for England, stopping long enough in London to purchase yet another suit at Hope Brothers. Once again church leaders had his itinerary planned in advance. During September he attended the South Scottish Conference sessions in Glasgow, speaking seven times. Following that session he preached in scattered Adventist churches in England (Manchester, Southampton, London, Ludgate Hill), Scotland (Perth), and Wales (Cardiff). The *Missionary Worker* marveled at how "the Lord's venerable servant" could meet all these appointments and still remain "in such good health and able to show so much vigour . . . in his advanced age." In fact, John was gaining in weight but shrinking in height, so he had his new pants let out a bit and his overcoat shortened. The Cadbury bars and the licorice sticks that tasted so sweet in the mouth were expanding his waistline.[25]

When he left for the U.S. on the *Arabic*, the *Missionary Worker* summed up the impact his visit had had on the Adventist cause in England. "The Lord used His aged servant to greatly encourage all hearts and confirm the faith of any who may have been in doubt as to spiritual gifts."[26] Despite the rough voyage to New York, John, avoiding seasickness, attended daily orchestra concerts and enjoyed a "jolly time with [the] passengers." Catching the train for Washington, D.C., he attended the General Conference session, where, for the first time in his life, he played only a minor role as a "general delegate," chairing no meetings, making no speeches, and serving on no committees. Instead, he gave lectures to the students at Washington Missionary College, to overseas workers at the Foreign Mission Seminary, and to the staff at Washington Sanitarium. But when he could, he attended concerts by the Review and Herald Orchestra and a stereopticon (an early version of the slide projector) program on India given by Elder Ingersoll. Before returning to California, John preached in the new church in Rochester, New York, and spoke to students in South Lancaster and to the nurses at Melrose Sanitarium in Massachusetts. Demonstrating his ecumenical spirit, he also attended services at the Grace Methodist Episcopal Church in Rochester, New York, and at the synagogue in Concord, Massachusetts. Loughborough found it helpful to know what the competition was teaching.[27]

But when the Adventist globe-trotter returned to California, he must have felt a bit like Rip Van Winkle when he discovered that his "home" had shifted once again. Having sold the house that John and Annie had built in Mountain View, the Irelands had since moved. When they invited John to live with them, he informed readers of the *Review* that his new address would be Box 13, RFD 4, Lodi.[28]

Although Loughborough returned from his world tour heavier and happier than when he had left, certain persistent health problems continued to plague him. Noticing that cool, damp air bothered his weak lungs, he chose not to preach in the evenings, particularly in the Northwest, where heavy rains and cold winds exacerbated his condition. Attending the camp meeting at Denver, Colorado, however, did his lungs a world of good. The crisp dry air, the high altitude, and God's blessing, he felt, had cured him of la grippe. Given the strain on his vocal cords that extended preaching tours entailed, he explained to *Review* readers in 1908: "I can not hold a long series of meetings in new fields, as in former years."[29]

Ironically, John's world tour in 1908-1009 proved that in fact he *could* hold meetings in new fields—if he ate well, rested often, and adapted to the climate. During his time in Australia he had bragged that he was enjoying "the best health I have had in many years." He attributed it to Australia's cool, dry climate; the delicious fruit (especially strawberries) and vegetables; and, of course, to God's blessings. At no other time in his life had John gained 10 pounds in six months as he did in the Land Down Under. Thanks in part to all the great Adventist cooks he encountered, J. N. Loughborough returned to the United States 14 pounds heavier than he had been the year before. One old friend said, "We hope that his life may be spared for many years yet."[30]

LOUGHBOROUGH'S WRITINGS

So long as he had life, John intended to keep writing as well as preaching, and as the years went by and more Adventist periodicals appeared, he submitted articles to many of them. Between 1907 and 1910 the *Review* printed several articles dealing with Adventist history, including John's five-part series "Things That Differ," his 17-part series on the publishing program (1844-1864), and his eight-part series on Christ's two thrones. Occasionally, however, John simply liked to play around with numbers, as in his article about the use of "40" in the Bible.[31]

Likewise, a growing number of Adventist papers promoted Loughborough's books, especially his *The Great Second Advent Movement*, the required textbook for those studying for the Missionary Volunteer Standard of Attainment in Adventist history. Numerous ads and articles in the *Review, North Pacific Union Gleaner, Youth's Instructor, West Michigan Herald,* and *Kansas Worker* (to mention a few) urged new converts, seasoned Adventists, academy and college youth, colporteurs, and nurses to read it not only for information but also for inspiration, "to realize as never before what God can accomplish through a weak but willing people." His textbook also became the basis for Sabbath school lessons, an Missionary Volunteer reading-course book, and a series in the paper *Der Jugendbote* ("Youth's Messenger"). Likewise, publications from the Indiana *Reporter* to the global *Signs of the Times* urged church officers to acquire Loughborough's book *The Church* to answer their questions and solve problems related to church policies, practices, and discipline.[32]

During John's stint in Australia and New Zealand the *Union Conference Record* reprinted his *Review* series "Early Experiences in the Publishing Work" and "The Two Thrones," as well as a new six-part set of articles dealing with Bible prophecies in Daniel 8 and 9, Hebrews 9, and Revelation 10 and 14, all relating to the sanctuary.[33] In addition, in 1908 the Australian edition of *Signs of the Times* carried four autobiographical articles entitled "Some Personal Experiences," "Serving from Principle," and "Wisdom and Understanding."[34] If Loughborough was a star in the antipodes, his celebrity status in Great Britain likewise insured that several of his articles focusing on the Adventist past and the new earth restored would appear in the British *Present Truth*.[35]

John's favorite venue, however, continued to be the *Bible Training School*, published each month by his friends Hetty and Stephen Haskell. With clocklike regularity, he submitted tightly written Bible studies dealing with ancient Israel, the Second Advent, the book of Joel, and contemporary applications of biblical parables. He also wrote a 13-part history of the rise of Seventh-day Adventism from the Millerite movement, obviously condensed from his popular *The Great Second Advent Movement*. But his August 1910 study entitled "Taking Away the Daily" touched a raw nerve in some Adventist circles.[36]

Just as eighteenth-century philosophers mocked the theological debates of Medieval clerics by asserting that they argued over how many angels could dance on the head of a pin, so contemporary Christians reading the highly charged debates of early Adventists about the meaning of "the daily" in Daniel 8:11-13 and 11:31 might conclude that it was "a tempest in a teapot." Yet as Gilbert Valentine has accurately pointed out, "a community [of faith] impassioned by a conviction of the nearness of the impending end-time, motivated by a strong sense of urgency, and shaped by a clear sense of identity and mission could hardly avoid conflict," especially in the area of doctrinal beliefs.[37]

The debate pitted aging pioneers such as Uriah Smith, Stephen Haskell, George Butler, and J. N. Loughborough against church scholars such as W. W. Prescott and Louis Conradi. While the "pioneers" claimed that the removal of the daily sacrifice from the sanctuary referred to Antiochus IV Epiphanes' taking away Jewish sacrifices in 167-164 B.C. or pagan Rome's destruction of the Jerusalem Temple services in A.D. 70, the "scholars" saw "removal of the daily" as pointing to the papacy's substitution of penance and the Eucharist in 508 A.D. for Christ's death at Calvary and ministry in the heavenly sanctuary. Although both groups quoted the Bible, the "pioneers" also cited the writings of William Miller and Ellen White to buttress their arguments, whereas the "scholars" employed a host of historical sources in defense of their position. Mrs. White, caught in the middle, reprimanded both sides for their harsh attitudes, for misusing her writings, and for ignoring more important issues such as mission outreach.[38] Her sermon at Loma Linda Sanitarium in July and her circular letter of August 3, 1910, chastised those who made "the daily" a "test question," for it had nothing whatsoever to do with eternal salvation. She declared: "This is not a subject of vital importance. . . . I see no need for the controversy. Regarding this matter . . . , silence is eloquence." The debate had brought confusion in the ranks at a time when the church needed to be united in preaching the gospel.[39]

But for more than three years Loughborough had been following a course that ran directly contrary to her advice. In April 1907 he had written an article on the 1335-day prophecy for the *Review* that upheld Uriah Smith's view of "the daily" as paganism. Eight months later, however, when he submitted his manuscript "Taking Away of the Daily" to the *Review*, editor W. W. Prescott turned him down flat. Filling his letter with quotes from Mosheim, Neander, Hume, and other historians, Prescott reminded John that the date A.D. 508 had little significance insofar as Christianity replacing paganism in Britain was concerned. In fact, Augustine of Canterbury did not reach England until A.D. 597. "After reading the testimonies from these histories," Prescott said, "I hardly think you would wish me to publish your article in the REVIEW, as it would open the way for criticism which we should be unable to meet. We are being attacked on various sides now, and I desire to use all care not to give anyone standing ground upon which to successfully make warfare upon our teachings."[40]

Nonetheless, publication was exactly what Loughborough *did* want. Listening to Prescott deliver a four-hour tirade concerning "the daily" before a group of ministers gathered at Mrs. White's home at Elmshaven in January 1908 merely served to strengthen John's resolve to get the "old view" before the Adventist public.[41] Seeing himself as a "defender of the faith," Loughborough spent seven months in 1910 researching and writing another manuscript on "the daily." The Haskells accepted it for publication in the August issue of *Bible Training School*—only days after Mrs. White's Loma Linda sermon and letter warned leaders not to agitate the matter.[42]

Why did Loughborough and the Haskells ignore counsel from a woman they all believed to be inspired by God? Three possible answers surfaced a couple years later in 1912 when John submitted yet another manuscript on "the daily" to the *Bible Training School*. In addition to assuring his old friend that "I believe in the principles you set forth," Haskell stated that "God [has] opened [the matter] up to you." Loughborough's argument, he believed, would leave "Brother Prescott and others [particularly the higher critics] without excuse." Then Stephen added: "May the Lord save His people is my prayer." In short, the "pioneers" saw their view of "the daily" as an inspired landmark doctrine. Abandoning it would lead the church down the slippery slope of compromise in other doctrinal areas, while defending it helped counteract the deleterious effects of higher criticism in the church. In fact, between 1909 and 1913 the "old guard" lobbied W. C. and Ellen White (whose book *Early Writings* they saw as supporting their "old view") to help them remove Prescott and GC president A. G. Daniells from office in order to "save the church." The Whites refused to help them.[43]

LOUGHBOROUGH'S DIARY

If J. N. Loughborough was conservative and to some extent backward-looking in his theology, his diary reveals that he was forward-looking and progressive in adapting to modern life. As improved technology came along, he adopted it if he saw that it would improve his life. In previous chapters we noted that he had learned to type in the 1880s, and as better manual typewriters came along, he purchased them so that he could type letters to friends, articles for church papers, and indexes to Mrs. White's writings. He had his picture taken more often so that he could send these "ambrotypes" (as he called photos) to his many friends around the world. Although no extant photographs show Loughborough with eyeglasses, his diaries reveal that he wore spectacles for reading. Acquiring a telephone was such a significant event in his life that he recorded the date (January 5, 1908) and subject matter (Mrs. Frisbie's funeral) of his first phone conversation.

The "Little Philosopher" who as a boy had built every device in his physics textbook remained fascinated with machines throughout his life. In 1910 he spent two hours in Pacific Union College's noisy sawmill watching students turn logs into lumber, then, noticing that the grandfather clock in the assembly hall was not working properly, he grabbed some tools and repaired it. No matter what the subject matter, he loved stereopticon programs, especially travelogues on Germany, Mexico, and South America. While he mostly traveled by horse and buggy, trolley cars, and trains, J. N. Loughborough *never* turned down an opportunity to go for a ride in a horseless carriage. In 1910 automobiles were a rich man's toy. While noisy, unreliable, and dangerous to drive, John loved them. As an active octogenarian during the 1910s, he could often be seen in the passenger seat of a neighbor's auto whizzing down the dusty streets of Lodi at breakneck speeds approaching 15 mph. After all he wanted to be a part of the great Advent *movement!*

---

[1] GC Minutes, June 4, 1908, p. 118.

[2] JNL, diary, December 1907; *NPUG*, Dec. 18, 1907, pp. 2, 3.

[3] *PUR*, Feb. 6, 1908, pp. 1, 2; *PUR*, Feb. 13, 1908, p. 3; *AUG*, Feb. 19, 1908, p. 58; *PUR*, Sept. 30, 1968, p. 1.

[4] *Missionary Worker*, Aug. 18, 1909, p. 136, *Missionary Worker*, Sept. 1, 1909, p. 138; *LUH*, Oct. 20, 1909, p. 5; *Kansas Worker*, May 11, 1910, pp. 1, 2.

[5] *PUR*, May 7, 1908, pp. 6, 5; *PUR*, June 4, 1908, p. 2; *PUR*, July 2, 1908, pp. 4, 5; *RH*, July 9, 1908, p. 17; *RH*, July 16, 1908, p. 17.

[6] JNL, diary, November 1909; *LUH*, Nov. 24, 1909, p. 4; *RH*, Jan. 27, 1910, p. 11.

[7] *PUR*, Dec. 9, 1909, p. 4; *PUR*, Dec. 16, 1909, pp. 2, 3; *PUR*, Jan. 20, 1910, p. 2.

[8] *PUR*, Feb. 10, 1910, p. 1; *South African Missionary*, Feb. 28, 1910, pp. 2, 3; *PUR*, Apr. 7, 1910, p. 10; *RH*, May 12, 1910, p. 16.

[9] *PUR*, Apr. 1, 1968, p. 1; *NPUG*, Dec. 18, 1907, p. 3; *NPUG*, Jan. 1, 1908, pp. 1, 2; *ST*, Feb. 19, 1908, p. 124; JNL, diary, March 1908 and February and April 1910; *PUR*, Apr. 2, 1908, p. 4; *AUG*, Oct. 27, 1909, p. 336; *PUR*, Mar. 3, 1910, p. 6; *PUR*, Mar. 17, 1910, p. 4.

[10] *NPUG*, Jan. 1, 1908, pp. 1, 2; JNL to Arthur G. Daniells, July 23, 1908, m. 52, CAR.

[11] GC Committee Minutes, Mar. 24, 1897, p. 49; JNL to EGW, Oct. 4, 1901, m. 52, CAR. Annie called her husband's dreams "dreams of duty." "You dream to the mark," she once told him, "because your dreams do not deal in symbols; but all seem to come out literally." See JNL to A. G. Daniells, July 23, 1908, m. 52, CAR.

[12] JNL, diary, May 1908; *RH*, Aug. 6, 1908, p. 32; WCW to JNL, July 12, 1908, WCW Letter Books, CAR; JNL to A. G. Daniells, July 23, 1908, m. 52, CAR; JNL, Will of Aug. 3, 1908, m. 006529, CAR; Oakland *Tribune*, Mar. 12, 1914, p. 7.

[13] GC Minutes (online), June 16, 1909, p. 136; E. Robinson, *Lighter of Gospel Fires*, p. 168; *RH*, July 19, 1951, p. 13.

[14] JNL, diary, July-August 1908; JNL to WCW, July 23, 1908, m. 52, CAR; *PUR*, Aug. 20, 1908, p. 6.

[15] JNL, diary, August-October, 1908; *Union Conference Record*, Jan. 4, 1909, p. 7.

[16] *ST-A*, Sept. 28, 1908, p. 614; *Union Conference Record*, Oct. 19, 1908, pp. 4, 5; *Union Conference Record*, Nov. 2, 1908, pp. 3, 4; *RH*, Nov. 12, 1908, pp. 16-18.

[17] JNL, diary, November-December 1908; *Union Conference Record*, Nov. 16, 1908, p. 8; *Union Conference Record*, Nov. 23, 1908, p. 7; *Union Conference Record*, Dec. 7, 1908, pp. 7, 8; *Union Conference Record*, Dec. 28, 1908, pp. 5, 6; G. Valentine, *Prophet and Presidents*, p. 212.

[18] JNL, diary, December 1908.

[19] JNL, diary, January 1909; *Union Conference Record*, Feb. 1, 1909, pp. 7, 8.

[20] JNL, diary, February-March 1909; *Union Conference Record*, Jan. 25, 1909, p. 7; *Union Conference Record*, Feb. 22, 1909, p. 7; *Union Conference Record*, Mar. 22, 1909, pp. 7, 8; *PUR*, Mar. 25, 1909, p. 6; *Union Conference Record*, Mar. 29, 1909, p. 8; *Union Conference Record*, Apr. 5, 1909, pp. 4, 7; JNL, *Union Conference Record*, Apr. 19, 1909, p. 4; *ST-A*, Apr. 19, 1909, p. 252; *ST*, May 12, 1909, p. 301.

[21] JNL, diary, April 1909; *PUR*, May 20, 1909, p. 6; *Union Conference Record*, May 24, 1909, p. 8; *RH*, Apr. 29, 1909, p. 24; *Union Conference Record*, June 7, 1909, p. 8; *PUR*, June 10, 1909, p. 6; *RH*, July 8, 1909, pp. 18, 19; *Life and Health*, March 1915, pp. 109, 110.

[22] JNL, diary, April-July 1909; *RH*, July 15, 1909, p. 16; *RH*, Sept. 23, 1909, p. 17.

[23] JNL, diary, July-August 1909; *RH*, Sept. 23, 1909, p. 17.

[24] JNL, diary, August 1909; JNL, notes on tour sites, m. 006529, CAR; *PUR*, Sept. 9, 1909, p. 5; *RH*, Oct. 21, 1909, pp. 13, 14. It is more likely, however, that the emperor banished Pilate to Spain.

[25] JNL, diary, August-September 1909; *Missionary Worker*, Sept. 15, 1909, pp. 145, 146; *Missionary Worker*, Oct. 13, 1909, pp. 162, 164.

[26] *Missionary Worker*, Sept. 29, 1909, p. 153; *PUR*, Oct. 28, 1909, p. 4.

[27] JNL, diary, October 1909; *GCB*, 1909, p. 330; *RH*, Oct. 21, 1909, p. 24.

[28] *RH*, Nov. 11, 1909, p. 22.

[29] *NPUG*, Jan. 15, 1908, pp. 4, 5; *RH*, Jan. 23, 1908, pp. 17, 18; *RH*, Apr. 30, 1908, p. 17.

[30] For reports concerning JNL's health, see *PUR*, Nov. 26, 1908, p. 6; *PUR*, Dec. 24, 1908, p. 6; *PUR*, Feb. 25, 1909, p. 6; *RH*, Apr. 29, 1909, pp. 14, 15; *RH*, Aug. 12, 1909, p. 16; *South African Missionary*, Feb. 28, 1910, pp. 2, 3; and *ST*, Feb. 8, 1910, p. 96.

[31] For JNL's "Things That Differ," see *RH*, Oct. 31, 1907, pp. 9, 10; Nov. 7, 1907, pp. 9, 10; Nov. 14, 1907, p. 10; Nov. 28, 1907, p. 11; Dec. 12, 1907, p. 11; Dec. 19, 1907, pp. 10, 11. For JNL's series on SDA publishing, see *RH*, Apr. 16, 1908, pp. 21, 22; May 14, 1908, pp. 18, 19; May 21, 1908, pp. 18, 19; June 4, 1908, pp. 19, 20; June 18, 1908, p. 19; June 25, 1908, p. 19; July 30, 1908, pp. 20, 21; Aug. 20, 1908, pp. 18, 19; Sept. 17, 1908, p. 29; Sept. 24, 1908, p. 21; Oct. 1, 1908, p. 21; Oct. 22, 1908, p. 22; Nov. 5, 1908, p. 21; Dec. 31, 1908, pp. 19, 20; Jan. 14, 1909, pp. 19, 20; Feb. 11, 1909, pp. 18, 19; Mar. 25, 1909, pp. 21, 22. For JNL's "Two Thrones" series, see *RH*, June 2, 1910, pp. 4, 5; June 9, 1910, pp. 5, 6; June 23, 1910, p. 4; June 30, 1910, pp. 4, 5; July 7, 1910, pp. 4, 5; July 14, 1910, pp. 4, 5; July 21, 1910, p. 4; July 28, 1910, p. 4. For his "40" in the Bible, see *RH*, July 23, 1908, p. 9.

[32] Regarding notices for *The Great Second Advent Movement*, see *RH*, Jan. 9, 1908, p. 2; *RH*, Apr. 2, 1908, p. 2; *RH*, Apr. 29, 1909, p. 2; *RH*, June 17, 1909, p. 6; *NPUG*, Dec. 4, 1907, p. 6; *NPUG*, Dec. 1, 1909, p. 5; *YI*, Dec. 31, 1907, p. 4; *YI*, Aug. 25, 1908, p. 4; *YI*, Sept. 7, 1909, p. 2; *West Michigan Herald*, Apr. 15, 1908, p. 4; *Kansas Worker*, Oct. 6, 1909, p. 2; *Kansas Worker*, Nov. 24, 1909, p. 3. For notices regarding *The Church* see *Indiana Reporter*, Feb. 5, 1908, p. 4; *ST*, July 29, 1908, p. 493; *Union Conference Record*, June 13, 1910, p. 8.

[33] *Union Conference Record*, Nov. 9, 1908, pp. 1, 2; Nov. 16, 1908, pp. 1, 2; Nov. 23, 1908, pp. 1, 2; Nov. 30, 1908, p. 1; Dec. 7, 1908, p. 1; Dec. 14, 1908, pp. 1, 2; Dec. 21, 1908, p. 1; Dec. 28, 1908, p. 1; Jan. 4, 1909, pp. 1, 2; Jan. 11, 1909, pp. 1, 2; Jan. 18, 1909, p. 1; Jan. 25, 1909, p. 1; Feb. 1, 1909, pp. 1, 2; Feb. 8, 1909, p. 1; Feb. 15, 1909, p. 1; Feb. 22, 1909, p. 1; Mar. 1, 1909, p. 1; Mar. 8, 1909, pp. 1, 2; July 12, 1909, pp. 1, 2; July 19, 1909, pp. 1, 2; July 26, 1909, pp. 1, 2; Aug. 2, 1909, pp. 1, 2; Aug. 9, 1909, pp. 1, 2; Aug. 16, 1909, pp. 1, 2; Aug. 23, 1909, pp. 1, 2; Aug. 30, 1909, pp. 1, 2; Apr. 5, 1909, pp. 1, 2; Apr. 12, 1909, pp. 1, 2; Apr. 19, 1909, pp. 1, 2; Apr. 26, 1909, p. 1; May 17, 1909, pp. 1, 2; May 13, 1910, p. 6.

[34] *ST-A*, Apr. 13, 1908, p. 237; July 13, 1908, pp. 441, 442; Aug. 17, 1908, pp. 513, 514.

[35] *Present Truth*-Great Britain, July 30, 1908, pp. 485, 486; Dec. 3, 1908, p. 771; Special 1910 issue, p. 12.

[36] *BTS*, December 1907, pp. 100, 101; January 1908, p. 120; March 1908, pp. 146, 147; May 1908, pp. 201, 202; June 1908, pp. 4, 5; July 1908, pp. 18, 19; August 1908, pp. 37, 38; September 1908, pp. 54, 55; October 1908, pp. 66, 67; November 1908, pp. 98, 99; December 1908, pp. 115, 116; January 1909, pp. 7, 8; February 1909, pp. 166, 167; March 1909, pp. 178, 179; April 1909, pp. 5, 6; May 1909, pp. 227, 228; June 1909, pp. 7, 8; July 1909, pp. 18, 19; September 1909, pp. 51, 52; October 1909,

pp. 68, 69; November 1909, pp. 84, 85; December 1909, pp. 14, 15; January 1910, pp. 134, 135; February 1910, pp. 152, 153; March 1910, pp. 162, 163; April 1910, pp. 2, 3; May 1910, pp. 213, 214; June 1910, pp. 7, 8; July 1910, pp. 34, 35, 38, 39; August 1910, pp. 50, 51; September 1910, pp. 66, 67.

[37] Gil Valentine, *Prophets and Presidents*, p. 267.

[38] R. Schwarz and F. Greenleaf succinctly summarize the debate over "the daily" in *Light Bearers*, pp. 608, 609. Those desiring a more detailed discussion should consult Valentine, *Prophets and Presidents*, pp. 281-284; Denis Kaiser, "Ellen White and the 'Daily' Conflict," in *Ellen White and Current Issues Symposium* 6 (2010): 10-21; *SDA Encyclopedia*, vol. 10, pp. 429-433; and especially Heidi Heiks, *The "Daily" Source Book* (Brushton, N.Y.: TEACH Services, 2008), pp. 3, 9-17, 23-35, 48, 54, 55, 71, 159-164, 177.

[39] EGW sermon at Loma Linda Sanitarium, July 31, 1910, ms. 11, 1910, CAR; EGW to G. I. Butler, J. N. Loughborough, S. N. Haskell, F. C. Gilbert, A. G. Daniells, W. W. Prescott, Aug. 3, 1910, cited by Arthur L. White, *Ellen G. White: The Later Elmshaven Years, 1905-1915* (Washington, D.C.: Review and Herald Pub. Assn., 1982), vol. 6, p. 259; the "daily" in *Ellen G. White Encyclopedia,* pp. 751-754.

[40] W. W. Prescott to JNL, Dec. 12, 1907, m. 52, CAR. See also G. Valentine, *Shaping of Adventism*, pp. 218, 223; Gilbert Valentine, *W. W. Prescott: Forgotten Giants of Adventism's Second Generation* (Hagerstown, Md.: Review and Herald Pub. Assn., 2005), p. 188; and A. L. White, *Ellen G. White: The Later Elmshaven Years, 1905-1915*, vol. 6, p. 247.

[41] See Valentine, *Prescott*, pp. 219, 220, concerning this contentious conference attended by Hetty and Stephen Haskell, Loughborough, C. C. Crisler, Ellen and Willie White, D. E. Robinson, A. G. Daniells, and W. W. Prescott.

[42] JNL, diary, January, May, July 1910.

[43] S. N. Haskell to JNL, Oct. 19, 1912, m. 52, CAR; Valentine, *Prophets and Presidents*, p. 281.

Chapter XXI

ACTIVE OCTOGENARIAN (1910-1915)

"There are but few of the old pioneer workers still living who saw the wonderful works that God did to confirm the truth—these old standard-bearers are to be respected. When new and strange theories are introduced, it is time to call a halt and to revive the past workings of the Lord's grace and power among us as a people. As I have seen the old standard-bearers fall one by one, I have longed, O so much, that some might be spared as was the disciple John, to declare the great works of the Lord. . . . We are ever to seek to keep the evidences of the past before us."[1]

In 1908 when Ellen White, then 80, penned the above words, she was deeply concerned about aberrant teachings in Battle Creek, theological attacks on "landmark" doctrines, and efforts to undermine her prophetic authority in the church. She also worried that only a handful of the pioneers remained to combat those threats—all in their 70s and 80s. As the number of standard-bearers declined and those of the dissidents grew, a new generation of leaders turned to men such as J. O. Corliss, G. I. Butler, S. N. Haskell, and J. N. Loughborough "to revive the past workings of the Lord's grace and power among us as a people."

Loughborough, who became an octogenarian in 1912, determined to promote unity and combat heresy by sharing his faith-building stories wherever invitations opened the way. Despite the fact that when he stood behind a conventional pulpit only his head and arms were visible to the audience, he could still preach an hour-long sermon with enthusiasm. Years later one listener recalled seeing the "little preacher" vigorously waving his arms, raising his voice, and pacing the platform, his black boots glistening beneath his dark pants. "He never put much emphasis on theology as it is known today [1968]," she recalled, "but he did preach 'Christ and Him crucified.' "[2]

Although John's preaching circuit had narrowed from global and national tours to West Coast venues, he still spoke at a broad spectrum of Adventist gatherings. As always, camp meetings took top priority with him, and between 1910 and 1915 he followed the sawdust trail to 15 convocations (about three each summer) in California and Utah.[3] His camp meeting tours proved both spiritually and financially rewarding, for in a typical summer Loughborough would baptize a dozen new converts and sell between 2,000 and 4,000 copies of his books (roughly $2,000-$4,000 in sales). As the number of Hispanic Adventists increased in the 1910s, California camp meetings featured Spanish services, and, with the help of interpreters, John preached to them as well. Hispanics, he discovered, liked hearing stories about Ellen White and seeing his colorful "Wonders of the Heavens" charts. In the days before PA systems, audiences had no trouble hearing every word Loughborough spoke, but at 83, he noted in his diary: "I [am] getting deaf; [I] hear only half of what other speakers say."[4]

As summers brought camp meetings, autumns featured Bible institutes, opportunities for John to meet old friends and mingle with professional colleagues. Between 1910 and 1915 he teamed up with Stephen and Hetty Haskell to speak at seven Bible and missionary institutes in California and Nevada, each lasting a week or more. At the Southern California Ministerial Institute he focused on early Adventist history and the development of Adventist organization, showing how Ellen White's prophetic gift had "saved [the church] . . . from shipwreck" at the hands of apostates. As John's talks typically minimized the pain that the pioneers had endured at the hands of such dissidents, many listeners wished "that the old, old times . . . might return."[5]

Another one of Loughborough's favorite speaking venues was Adventist sanitariums. Here the nurses and female staff members, who pampered the aged pioneer with rubdowns and massages, listened entranced as he told them anecdotes about the pioneers. Loughborough frequently visited the Adventist spas at Glendale, Loma Linda, and St. Helena, California, and on his way back from the 1913 General Conference session in Washington, D.C., stopped at Hinsdale Sanitarium in Illinois to give "lectures" to the sanitarium family.[3]

With his deep love for Adventist youth, John accepted every invitation to influence them that came his way. As the Irelands lived right across the road from the Lodi SDA Elementary School and Lodi Academy, John regularly visited their classrooms, attended their Missionary Volunteer meetings, spoke at their graduations, and shared early Adventist history with them. In addition, he traveled to Fernando Academy (after 1914 known as San Fernando Acacemy) to exhibit his "Wonders" charts. By combining his teaching and entertainment techniques, he insured that students were "amused, interested, and instructed by these old, old stories," which many never forgot. One listener recalled the "unusual power" with which the aged pioneer talked about "the past, present, and future of this glorious third angel's message and the people connected with it." On a more advanced level, John shared lessons from the Adventist past with teachers at Professor C. C. Lewis' summer schools. At Pacific Union College the students never tired of hearing the little man speak.[7]

Although Loughborough held no administrative positions, church leaders frequently invited him to attend conference, union, and General Conference sessions as a delegate-at-large. John especially enjoyed the statistical reports that demonstrated the "rise and progress" of Adventism around the world. In 1911 he traveled to Salt Lake City with his son-in-law John Ireland to attend the Utah conference sessions, then on to Phoenix, where he showed his charts and gave daily Bible studies. Ever the tourist, he attended an organ concert at the Mormon Tabernacle, visited the Saints' museum, saw Brigham Young's grave, and strolled down Temple Street. When he went to the Pacific Union Conference sessions, the octogenarian served on the Credentials and Licenses Committee just like "old times." At the 1913 gathering of Pacific Press stockholders in Mountain View, John regaled them with stories of the early days of Adventist publishing. When press manager C. H. Jones bragged that he had operated "the first power press [at PPPA] thirty-six years ago," John quipped, "I worked a power press sixty-one years ago [at Rochester in 1852], but I furnished the power."[8]

In fact, so ancient had Loughborough become that when he showed up at the 1913 GC session in Washington, D.C., several delegates were surprised to see that he was still alive. A friend told John's daughter that he checked the obituary columns in the *Review* every week to see if John had passed away! Secular newspapers and Adventist periodicals praised him as a living legend, calling him "this aged servant of God," the one "whom so many fields delight to honor as their pioneer," and "the venerable J. N. Loughborough." Reminding delegates that 1913 marked the golden anniversary of the establishment of the General Conference in 1863, John called himself "the last [living] relic of the organization of [that] conference." He told the attendees that of the 12 committee members in 1863, eight had since died, and four had apostatized. In fact, the only five individuals still living who had attended that meeting were Loughborough, Isaac Sanborn (who would pass away days later), Mrs. R. M. Kilgore, Ellen White, and her son Willie, then an 8-year-old water boy.[9]

Despite their doctrinal differences concerning "the daily," GC president Daniells seated Loughborough, G. I. Butler, S. N. Haskell, and O. A. Olsen beside him on the platform at the opening meeting. As one of 356 delegates, the 81-year-old minister offered several public prayers, exhibited copies of his colorful Wonders charts and Himes' 1843 prophetic chart, told pioneer stories at the morning meetings, and shared reminiscences at the funeral service for Isaac Sanborn. In addition, his prayer on behalf of Chinese missions inspired such generosity among attendees that the deacons had to collect the offering in wastebaskets![10]

Amazed at Loughborough's vitality, George Thomason commented that he was "eighty-two years *young*. A man is as old as his arteries. He [John] has soft arteries, and so he is young." Introducing him to the delegates, Thomason remarked, "I want you to take a good look at him, and see what a splendid representative he is of the principles we are enunciating."[11] Graciously John responded: "In those earlier years I had no thought that God would let me live to be a boy again, but in his providence he has permitted me to live to be over eighty-two years of age [actually eighty-one and four months]. I am living on God's time. Brethren, I am glad to be here." Turning on the Irish charm, he exclaimed, "If any of you think you are the happiest man on this camp-ground, you must have forgotten [that] I am here!" Adding a touch of humor, he related how in the 1850s people in the eastern United States used to mock Sabbathkeeping Adventists by saying, "Why, you are all Yankees. When you get into other countries you will all go to pieces." Pausing until the laughter died down, Loughborough punned: "They were right, you know. Some four years ago I went around [the world] to see some of the pieces, but thank God they were all stuck together and greatly increased in size."[12]

That Loughborough possessed a rollicking sense of humor is an aspect of his personality Adventists today know little about. Yet his contemporaries were aware of it, and they provided opportunities for him to showcase his Irish wit. Early twentieth-century camp meetings, with their curious blend of rousing gospel music, tear-filled testimonies, long-winded sermons, and sober business sessions could at times resemble variety shows that included humor. In 1914 at the age of 82 Loughborough created a one-man temperance act entitled "Mike and the Saloonkeeper" that was so side-splitting funny that it "brought down the house" (or, in his words, "caused a revolution") at the Sacramento and Fruitvale, California, camp meetings. So popular did his skit become that he had to repeat it several times. Naturally, John never told his audiences that the reason he could mimic Irish brogue so accurately was because he himself was Irish and had once been a Loofborough.[13]

John could also do spot-on imitations of Negro dialect, and in an era when blackface humor was extremely popular, his narrative of a fugitive slave escaping to Union lines during the First Battle of Bull Run was so memorable that the *Pacific Union Recorder* printed it. When Union officers asked the runaway who he was, he replied, "My name is Sam." "Sam what?" "No, no! not Sam Watt; my name is jus' Sam." "Who is your master?" "I ha'n't got any. When de war come, he's jus' clean done gone and runned away." "Who is your father?" "I ha'n't got any fadder. Never had any fadder." "Well, who are you, anyway?" "O, I'se jus' Sam. And when you see me, you see all there is of us."[14]

If Loughborough's ethnic parodies fall uncomfortably on modern ears, we must understand that his mimicry did not reflect ethnic or racial prejudices on his part. As a matter of fact, John not only gave liberally to support the Southern Missionary Society's activities among American Blacks, but he also subscribed to the *Gospel Herald*, a newspaper edited and printed at the Oakwood Manual Training School in Huntsville, Alabama. In the spring of 1913 he sent its Black editor a letter commending him and the staff for doing such a "neat" job on the paper. Recalling the situation on campus when he had visited in 1897 and found two dilapidated slave cabins, a two-story school building, and a crumbling mansion, he exclaimed, "[I] rejoice to learn of the advancement of the work in the Southern field." John even previously sent a check to pay for a second incubator for raising poultry. Furthermore, in his article "From an Old Pioneer," Loughborough revealed that every day on his knees, he prayed for specific Oakwood students *by name* and hoped that "they are making a success in the way to Zion."[15] While he subscribed to the popular belief that Negroes had dark skin because of climate, miscegenation, or various diseases, he reminded readers that "the Scriptures seem plainly to teach that there was but one parentage to the present races of mankind."[16]

PLACED ON SUSTENTATION

Because Seventh-day Adventists for more than half a century had believed that Christ would return to earth at any moment, the growing church had made no financial provisions for the retirement of its employees, most of whom (like Loughborough) continued working into their 70s and 80s if health permitted. But at the Autumn Council in 1910 the General Conference established the first retirement plan—called sustentation—to support sick, aged, and retired employees as well as the children of deceased church workers. At first it amounted to only a dollar a day, but within a year it had increased to two dollars a day.[17]

The day after the 79-year-old Loughborough received his first sustentation check on March 13, 1911, he fired off a letter to GC Treasurer W. T. Knox objecting, not to the *amount* of the check, but to the *implication* that he was now "retired." Indicating that he "did not take kindly" to the idea of being "sent out to pasture"; he compared himself to the old horse that, after having labored for years with its mate, had now been replaced by a younger horse and banished to the stables. But the old horse kept kicking the stable to pieces until the owner put a collar on it and allowed it to walk along beside the new team. Despite being placed on sustentation, John asserted, "I want to be permitted to keep the collar on."[18]

Although the sustentation program officially cut his salary in half, Loughborough's income actually grew thanks largely to increased revenue from his books' royalties (which he deposited at Pacific Press). Consequently, he was able to give just as liberally to a broad spectrum of church projects as he had before going on retirement pay. Besides giving his tithe (he called it "church dues") and offerings, John supported the building of churches and elementary schools from Maine to California; sponsored worthy students; and regularly gave to the Poor Fund. His enthusiasm for missions inspired him to donate to the Pitcairn Island Fund, the China Mission Fund, the Australian *Signs* Distribution Fund, and the China Famine Fund. His generosity helped pay for the first Adventist press in China. In 1908 Loughborough also championed the Birthday-Thank Offering by which children and adults gave an annual gift (matching their age in pennies) to open mission stations in new areas. When John sent a generous check to South Africa to sponsor two orphans at Claremont College, he explained that "my father died when I was seven years old, so I have been a half orphan since. Early in life I had to look out for myself, so I have a sympathy for orphans."[19]

However, Loughborough's deepest sympathy—and his greatest generosity—was extended to African Americans. He was immensely proud that his granddaughter Jennie Ireland, who had studied medicine under Dr. Kellogg at Battle Creek Sanitarium, chose (while still in her early 20s) to open a medical clinic in the "Furlong Tract" of Watts, a rough inner-city Black district in downtown Los Angeles. Thanks largely to her medical expertise, her classes in hygienic cooking, and her Bible studies in the homes of clients, by 1908 she had raised up a church of 28 members—the first Black SDA church west of Missouri. Until the Black pastor Louis Sheafe held evangelistic meetings in Watts in 1914, no Adventist minister—White or Black—had helped her. But Grandpa Loughborough did so with his money and prayers.[20]

He also gave systematically to the Southern Missionary Society to promote evangelism and education among poor Blacks in the South. His gifts (which often equaled a week's wages and put his name at the top of all donor lists) supported local churches, schools, and publishing efforts across Dixie. Even in 1909 while laboring in distant Australia, John sent checks to Eva Sharpe and Chanie Rowe, Black students in Yazoo City, Mississippi, reminding them that he prayed for them daily and hoped they were "making good progress in their studies and in the Lord's service."[21] Perhaps John's notation in his diary regarding the passing of financier J. P. Morgan (worth more than $500,000,000) in March 1913 should be understood as the silent cry of a man who wished he had been blessed with such wealth so that he could give even more.[22]

FACING DISSIDENTS WITHIN THE CHURCH

Just as Loughborough gave generously from his retirement income to support church projects around the world, he also invested huge amounts of time during his final years in combating apostasy in the church. Although he enjoyed telling Adventist audiences the sad stories of past apostates and "how they came out" (always badly, of course), it must have seemed to the octogenarian that dissidents were hiding behind every doctrinal tree. During the last decade of his life (1914-1924) Loughborough's diaries are full of references to the attempts of Dudley M. Canright, Anna Garmire, and the Ballenger brothers to undermine Adventism's landmark doctrines. Despite his valiant efforts to curtail their influence, however, apostasy, like the Hydra of Greek mythology, seemed constantly to take on new shapes and grow.

Although Canright and Loughborough had been preaching partners in the early years of the Adventist Church, Dudley's book *Seventh-day Adventism Renounced* (1889)—a vicious attack on key doctrines and church leaders and a formidable weapon in the hands of evangelical Protestantism's anti-Adventist arsenal—drew a line in the sand that John refused to cross. Instead, Loughborough prepared and distributed a typed manuscript entitled "Canright vs. Canright" that emphasized Dudley's contradictory doctrinal statements and hypocritical lifestyle. Even so, he and Canright remained on speaking terms, for in June 1913, Dudley dropped by to visit John in Battle Creek. Yet despite Loughborough's personal efforts to reclaim his old friend, when Canright died in 1919, he left behind a manuscript that was published posthumously as *Life of Mrs. E. G. White*, accusing her of fraud, lying, plagiarism, and being a false prophet.[23]

While Loughborough was absolutely certain that Ellen White was *not* a false prophet, he was equally sure that Anna Garmire of Michigan *was* an imposter. After reading her letters and testimonies, studying the accounts of her visions, and comparing them with those of Mrs. White, he concluded that the Holy Spirit had not inspired Anna's writings or motivated her life. Consequently, in 1911 John prepared materials exposing Garmire as a fraud.[24]

Dealing with Albion Fox Ballenger (and later with his brother Edward) proved a bit more difficult, however. Albion, the son of an Adventist minister, had served the church in the U.S. and Europe with distinction as a pastor, religious-liberty advocate, and director of the Irish Mission until he began expressing doubts concerning the Adventist position on the cleansing of the heavenly sanctuary in 1844. After church officials fired him in 1905 and stripped him of his ministerial credentials, he returned to America and in 1914 used *The Gathering Call* (previously edited by the Seventh Day Church of God) to propagate his views among Seventh-day Adventists until his death in 1921. Hearing Pacific Union Conference president E. E. Andross speak about the "Ballenger case" in 1911, Loughborough added Ballenger to his list of dissidents who deserved his attention. Beginning in 1915, John began answering a series of letters from Albion's brother Edward inquiring about a host of statements that Loughborough had made concerning early Adventist history in his *The Great Second Advent Movement* (1905). Although at first cordial in tone, the correspondence would become increasingly embarrassing to the old pioneer as Ballenger offered evidence that undermined some of John's alleged facts and interpretations.[25]

While Loughborough's diaries do not indicate that he expended the same amount of effort combating A. T. Jones' antiestablishmentarianism and Dr. Kellogg's pantheism, it is clear that he disapproved of both. After "carefully and prayerfully reading" J. H. Morrison's *A Straight Talk to Old Brethren* (an attack on Jones, Ballenger, and other church opponents), John's review, quoted in the *Central Union Outlook*, praised the book. "I consider it a complete refutation of the claims set up by those who are asserting that Seventh-day Adventists have so changed that they [the dissidents] have a message to call us out of Babylon." Furthermore, he felt that the " 'come out' movement, with its no organization and contradictory doctrines, is of itself a vindication of organization for a united and successful work."[26]

To better combat the influence of dissidents, Loughborough embarked on a related project that would occupy his final years: compiling indexes of all Ellen White's visions (and their fulfillments), *Review* articles, and published books. As none of his handwritten (and later typed) manuscripts exist today, only his diaries remain as mute witnesses to the enormous amount of time (literally days and weeks at a stretch) that he devoted to indexing. In the fall and winter of 1910-1911, for example, John reread more than 16,000 pages of White's *Review* articles and her nine-volume set of *Testimonies* in order to prepare indexes on them. Driven indoors by torrential rains in March 1911, he tried to "improve the time" by reading about 6,000 pages of her writings to compile a list of more than 100 predictions she had made that had been fulfilled. Also that spring, he wrote references to her books *The Desire of Ages* and *Christ's Object Lessons* in the margins of his new Bible. And from that same Bible he copied into his pass book every divine promise he could find—the list would eventually encompass 3,573 promises.[27]

His projects for 1911-1912 included indexing White's *Christ's Object Lessons, Patriarchs and Prophets,* the four-volume *Spirit of Prophecy* set, and her *Special Testimonies*. When Mrs. White sent him an autographed copy of her new book *The Acts of the Apostles* in 1912, he added that to the list of books to index. During 1912-1913, he typed up his handwritten indexes to her *Testimonies* and prepared an index for the 1911 edition of *The Great Controversy*. In 1913-1914 he updated, expanded, and revised his indexes, then sent a letter to the North American Division Committee asking church leaders to form a Bible and Testimony Study Club and Prayer League (the forerunner of Testimony Countdown half a century later). Without doubt, this blue-ribbon indexer would have made a superb library cataloguer.[28]

John was also a top-notch scrapbooker. Although few of his notebooks remain, the ones for 1911 and 1914 are crammed with what he called "Bits and Pieces": statistical lists, poetry, biblical texts, E. G. White quotations, stories, and newspaper clippings. Undoubtedly he mined his collections as he prepared his talks and sermons, as the 1911 scrapbook includes sermon outlines. Given his broad spectrum of interests, it should come as no surprise that his collection ranges from the significant (the history of SDA publishing programs and prophecies fulfilled in history) to the trivial (8,000 peace treaties between 1500 B.C. and A.D. 1860; liquor drinking on the *Titanic*) to the bizarre (dog funerals for $5,000-$14,000).[29]

John's diaries and scrapbooks also reveal his voracious reading habits. Incredible as it seems, at 83 he was keeping up with more than 20 Adventist publications from around the world.[30] As each one arrived, he placed it at the bottom of the growing pile beside his chair. "I am reading our [SDA] periodicals [today]" is a frequent refrain in his diaries. But he did not skim them: he literally read every word of every periodical from cover to cover, a fact that becomes evident from his letters to various editors in which he comments on specific points made by authors and corrects their factual errors. More graciously, he promised to pray for them. Also, he sent generous checks that usually put his name at the top of their donor lists.[31]

But Loughborough's reading included far more than Adventist publications. As war clouds formed over Europe in 1914, he regularly read *Collier's Magazine* to stay up-to-date on international developments, especially in Germany where he had many friends. For local and national news, he subscribed to the San Francisco *Daily Chronicle*. One gets the impression that, despite his poor spelling ability, Loughborough must have been a self-taught speed-reader. For example, he plowed through Himes' *Life and Views of William Miller* and the six-volume *Great Epochs in American History* set in a single month.[32]

LOUGHBOROUGH'S WRITINGS

Meanwhile, Loughborough's own books were garnering new readers and growing respect. His *The Great Second Advent Movement,* in addition to being a frequent "Gift Book," a required textbook in Adventist schools, and an absolute necessity for those wishing to pass the Missionary Volunteer Standard of Attainment exam, also served as the final authority for the *Signs*' "Question Corner" on Adventist history.[33] By the same token, his ecclesiastical manual *The Church* (1907) quickly assumed the same role for matters relating to church policies and procedures. As a matter of fact, in Resolution No. 6, the delegates to the 1910 session of the Central New England Conference declared that his book should be studied along with the Bible and Ellen White's *Testimonies*. In the *Atlantic Union Gleaner* C. L. Kilgore referred to it in answering readers' inquiries to his "Question Box." By 1911 local elders across the United States were using Loughborough's list of 16 questions in *The Church* to screen baptismal candidates.[34]

Yet Loughborough, refusing to rest on his laurels, continued writing articles for church papers at a remarkable pace. As *Review* editor Francis Wilcox quipped in 1911, "his pen . . . still writes for our profit."[35] It did indeed, for between 1910 and 1914 John sent an average of six articles a year to the *Review*, including his eight-part series on Christ's "Two Thrones," two articles on "Judas," and another 16-part series on the "Second Advent Movement." In addition, he penned doctrinal pieces on the Sabbath and the heavenly sanctuary and provided advice on how to give Bible readings, produce Adventist books, and hold Communion services. No matter what his subject, John's sources for these articles were the Bible and the writings of Ellen White, which in many cases, he quoted at length without critical analysis or commentary.[36]

On average, Loughborough submitted two articles each year to the *Signs of the Times*. As one would expect, they dealt primarily with biblical topics and end-time prophecies. But here John followed a "scatter-shot" approach, addressing a broad spectrum of subjects: Crucifixion chronology, the second coming of Christ, the new earth restored, the nature of humanity, and so forth. As with his *Review* articles, his contributions to *Signs* had become little more than Bible studies and book reviews with reams of texts and Ellen White quotations following one another in a cut and paste manner, signifying perhaps that his creative and analytical juices were drying up.[37]

Nonetheless, editors of many Adventist publications wanted John's conservative, faith-building articles in their periodicals. The Australian *Signs of the Times* printed his articles on "Prophecy in the Christian Church," "The Gospel Hope," and "The Way of Peace," in which he blended theological material with a devotional message.[38] In "Fearful Sights and Great Signs," the *The Life Boat* magazine summarized his talks about celestial wonders to the workers at Hinsdale Sanitarium, while in "Dead and Living Faith," John provided 10 "positive assurances" of a vibrant faith experience.[39] He gave a brief "Religious Liberty—Retrospective" for *Liberty* magazine in 1911 and shared memories of his life with *Life and Health* readers after his eighty-third birthday in "A Young Octogenarian."[40] His two articles in the *Church Officers' Gazette* instructed church leaders on how to act as Christ's servants and encouraged them to spread gospel literature.[41]

Loughborough's love of children and his knack for telling animal stories are evident in his articles "The Chicken Stepmother," "Intelligence of Animals," and "As Little Children" in the publication *Our Little Friend*.[42] For the *Youth's Instructor*—a paper John had read since its beginning in 1852—he shared stories about the training of children, ministers who preach with their hands in their pockets, the evils of tobacco, and the development of U.S. postal facilities.[43]

On the West Coast, subscribers to the *Pacific Union Recorder* enjoyed John's extended (more than 150 articles) series on his boyhood and youth, along with other stories he shared from his scrapbooks. One of those articles, however, struck a raw nerve with a woman who objected to his mentioning the "errors" of a distant relative of hers who had confessed his wrongs and received forgiveness. It would not be the last time that Loughborough's penchant for specificity got him into trouble.[44] The *North Pacific Union Gleaner* also refers to an article he wrote for F. C. Gilbert's *Yiddish Magazine*, but the article is no longer extant.[45]

Thanks in part to John's prolific pen, the *Bible Training School* continued to thrive in the pre-WWI era. His monthly articles covered a wide range of topics, including prophecy (the 1290- and 1335-day prophecies, the seven trumpets of Revelation), Adventist history, and biblical exegesis (of Joel and the Gospels), with a 12-part series on "The Pursuit of Knowledge" (in 1912-1913), to mention a few. After reading one book on ancient China, Loughborough summarized what he had learned in a short article entitled "Chinese History," which gave *BTS* readers fascinating (if not always accurate) insights into China's emperors, religion, and customs.[46]

LOUGHBOROUGH'S DIARY

When he was not preaching or writing, John usually spent his time hoeing in the vegetable garden or pruning the grapevines in the Ireland's two-acre vineyard. For an old man, he was in remarkably good health, even if his body was showing signs of aging. On his eightieth birthday he spent $22 at Dr. M. A. McElhany's office getting several bad teeth pulled and replaced with false ones.[47] In his "report on the teeth," he told Dr. McElhany that "they seemed at first to interfere with that 'magnifying tongue,' until it got used to the newcomers. Of the tenderness of the gums we expected it to take a little time for them to harden down to business."[48]

John's lungs also proved sensitive, and during the cold, rainy spring of 1914, he found himself "battling with a cold in [his] heart and throat." He lost the battle and contracted pneumonia. Dr. Myers and Nurse Barrett came regularly to give him mustard plasters, hot fomentations, massages, and kerosene rubdowns in bed—which soon had him sitting up, dressed, and "happy in the Lord."[49] He wrote Ellen White: "While my general health is comparatively good, I have not the strength for much public speaking."

In her reply she challenged him to "cultivate faith. Speak and pray faith. Walk humbly with the Lord. Grasp by faith the promises," and he would soon get well.[50]

Within days the phlegm had cleared from his lungs and his pulse, temperature, and blood pressure returned to normal. At 82 he boasted to a reporter for the Oakland *Tribune,* "I believe I am good for a hundred years" and told the man that he had the "arteries of a boy." Unfortunately, he had the lungs of an old man and was, as he was referenced to in the *Review*, "living on borrowed time." In 1915 another bout of pneumonia confined him to bed for two weeks as Dr. Myers, Nurse Hanson, and his granddaughter May nursed him around the clock. By the end of April he assured Willie White, "I am now as well as usual. . . . I get out to chore about a little when the winds are not too brisk." Learning, however, that his old friend Ellen White was failing, he told her, "We often think of you, and pray that the Lord will give you health and strength, and that He will prolong your days."[51]

But the days of many of John's family members were numbered, and with growing frequency, he began attending funerals. Maria Loughborough Edwards, his son Delmer's widow and a successful physician in Illinois, died of a brain hemorrhage at 45 in 1911.[52] The following year, William Loughborough, blacksmith, builder, and architect, passed away at 85 in Glendale, California. Sadly, John learned of his brother's death four days after the funeral.[53]

Many of the old Adventist pioneers Loughborough had worked with were also passing off the scene. His friend Robert Kilgore, Southern Union Conference president, died in 1912 at 73. When former GC president George Irwin (68) and Isaac Sanborn (91), Adventism's oldest preacher, died on May 23 and 24, 1913, respectively, General Conference delegates adjourned to attend their funerals. Loughborough, one of four church officials to eulogize Irwin before 4,000 mourners, described him as a godly man who would rise in the resurrection day. In 1915 former GC president Ole Olsen (70) died. Faithfully John recorded the passing of each of these pioneers in his diaries.[54]

He also noted that in February of 1915 Ellen White had fallen and broken her hip. A month later, Loughborough and six members of the St. Helena Sanitarium board visited her at Elmshaven for nearly two hours, and she spoke "words of cheer and courage." During the next three months, however, she grew weaker, and died on July 16. Her family and church officials planned three funerals: a private one on the lawn at Elmshaven (July 18) for 500 family members and friends; a public one at the Richmond campgrounds near Oakland (July 19) for about 1,000 attendees; and an even grander service in the Battle Creek Tabernacle (July 24), with nearly 4,500 mourners. As one of Mrs. White's dearest friends, Loughborough was asked to participate in the first two funerals. Standing beneath a shady canopy at Elmshaven, John gave a personal sketch of her prophetic career, focusing especially on the Holy Spirit's work in her life. The editor of the *North Pacific Union Gleaner*, delighted with his sketch, promised to reprint it (he never did). The following day Loughborough offered the invocation at her funeral in Oakland—and the *Gleaner* did print his moving prayer.[55] John also helped W. C. White prepare a memorial sermon to be sent to all Adventist churches in North America.[56]

Although his friends now lay silent in their graves, John had no intention of sitting still. Indeed, as one scans his diaries between 1910 and 1915, one would hardly guess that such a "man on the go" was in his 80s. During his free time he and his neighbor Mr. Gage donned their dusters, caps, and goggles and dashed down the dusty roads around Lodi frightening horses, scattering chickens, and waving to friends along the way. John also begged rides from Mr. McPharaon, from Mr. Fero's uncle, and from John and Mary Ireland (who purchased an auto in 1910). One Sabbath McPharaon's auto blew two tires, making them late to church.

Never one to turn his back on old technology, however, every year John applied for—and received—a discounted railroad permit granted by railway officials to active ministers. As mentioned above, in addition to wearing the hats of preacher, writer, and storyteller, John served as chief gardener on the Ireland estate. Every month of the year found him planting, hoeing, watering, harvesting, or canning the fruit and vegetables he raised virtually by himself. Once, at 82, he spent eight hours clipping and raking grapevines. When he took the time to "sit a spell," he preferred reading a book, listening to a concert, or attending a stereopticon program at Lodi Academy. In an article pointing out that during his lifetime he had witnessed the "perfection and commercialization" of telephones, phonographs, moving pictures, typewriters, street cars, trains, automobiles, and airplanes, the Oakland *Tribune* saluted him as one who "occupies a unique position, not only in religious circles, but [also] in the citizenship of the State [of California]." J. N. Loughborough was also unique in that he voted in every local, state, and national election during an era when many Seventh-day Adventists frowned on political involvement. Although he longed for heaven, he was determined to do good here on earth while he waited.[57]

---

[1] EGW, "Truth to Be Maintained," May 5, 1908, ms. 25, 1908.

[2] Brownie R. Owen, quoted in *PUR*, Nov. 18, 1968, p. 1. In his diary for January 1, 1911, Loughborough gave his height as 5'4", his hat size as 7.5", his collar size as 7.5", and his shoe size as 7. His weight varied from 110 to 120 pounds. Had he dressed in Irish green, he would have resembled a leprechaun.

[3] The camp meetings convened in San Diego, Berkeley, Visalia, Tulare, Stockton, Long Beach, Sacramento, Santa Rosa, Glendale, San José, Los Angeles, Fruitvale, Alhambra, Oakdale, and Chico, California, and in Salt Lake City, Utah. See JNL, diary, August-October 1910; May-July 1911; June-August 1912; July-August 1913; July-October 1914; June-August 1915; *RH*, Sept. 8, 1910, pp. 16, 17; *PUR*, June 8, 1911, pp. 1, 2; *PUR*, July 27, 1911, pp. 3, 5; *RH*, Oct. 5, 1911, p. 16; *RH*, Nov. 2, 1911, p. 15; *RH*, Sept. 26, 1912, pp. 16, 17; *PUR*, July 17, 1913, pp. 1-3; *PUR*, July 31, 1913, p. 1; *PUR*, Nov. 12, 1914, p. 5; *PUR*, May 6, 1915, pp. 2, 3.

[4] *RH*, Sept. 8, 1910, pp. 16, 17; JNL, diary, August 1913 and August 1915.

[5] The institutes convened at Reno and Fallon, Nevada, and in Turlock, Eureka, Oakland, Fresno, Sacramento, and Los Angeles, California. See JNL, diary, October 1910; *PUR*, July 21, 1910, p. 3; *PUR*, Oct. 20, 1910, p. 8; *PUR*, Dec. 8, 1910, p. 3; *RH*, Jan. 12, 1911, p. 16; *PUR*, Mar. 2, 1911, p. 12; *Southern Union Worker*, May 25, 1911, p. 167; *RH*, Apr. 11, 1912, p. 7; *PUR*, Jan. 26, 1911, pp. 2, 3.

[6] JNL, diary, February-March 1912; *PUR*, Mar. 7, 1912, p. 6; *PUR*, May 23, 1912, p. 4; *RH*, Aug. 8, 1912, p. 15; *Life Boat*, July 1913, p. 219.

[7] *RH*, Aug. 11, 1910, pp. 16, 17; *PUR*, Nov. 24, 1910, pp. 4, 5; *PUR*, Feb. 16, 1911, p. 5; JNL, diary, August 1911; January-April 1912; March-May 1914; *PUR*, Aug. 3, 1911, p. 7; *PUR*, Jan. 25, 1912, p. 6; *PUR*, Oct. 3, 1912, p. 4; *PUR*, Sept. 4, 1913, pp. 4, 5; *PUR*, July 1, 1915, p. 6. Fernando Academy (1906-1914) became San Fernando Academy after 1914. In 1906 the denomination renamed Healdsburg College Pacific Union College.

[8] JNL, diary, September 1911; *PUR*, Aug. 31, 1911, p. 8; *PUR*, Oct. 26, 1911, p. 8; *RH*, Jan. 4, 1912, p. 17; *PUR*, Apr. 18, 1912, p. 1; *PUR*, Jan. 30, 1913, pp. 1, 2; *Southern Union Worker*, May 29, 1913, pp. 177, 178; *PUR*, Mar. 26, 1914, pp. 1-8; *RH*, Apr. 29, 1915, pp. 17-19.

[9] *RH*, Aug. 31, 1911, p. 17; Mountain View *Register and Leader*, Jan. 24, 1913, cited in *Workers' Bulletin*, Feb. 11, 1913, p. 2; *Central Union Outlook*, Jan. 13, 1914, p. 4; July 23, 1914, p. 4; *ST*, Feb. 10, 1914, p. 76; *GCB* (1913), pp. 2, 6, 33, 117, 187, 192, 193, 297, 326; *ST*, Mar. 17, 1914, p. 148; *ST*, July 8, 1913, p. 410; *Northern Union Reaper*, May 20, 1913, pp. 1, 2; *RH*, May 22, 1913, p. 13; *SWUR*, May 27, 1913, pp. 1, 2; *RH*, June 5, 1913, pp. 5, 6; *AUG*, June 4, 1913, p. 6; *AUG*, June 11, 1913, pp. 3, 4; *PUR*, June 12, 1913, p. 8.

[10] *GCB* (1913), pp. 2-4, 18, 31-33, 50, 77, 117, 144, 186, 187, 192, 193.

[11] *GCB* (1913), p. 253.

[12] JNL, *AUG,* May 21, 1913, p. 3; *RH,* July 3, 1913, p. 19; *Southern Union Worker,* May 22, 1913, p. 169.

[13] JNL, diary, June 1914. Unfortunately, no copies of his rollicking act exist in the Loughborough Collection at the Center for Adventist Research at Andrews University and the author's attempts to find it online have proved futile. Ostensibly, John wrote the script himself and later threw it away.

[14] *PUR,* Apr. 25, 1912, pp. 3, 4.

[15] JNL, "From an Old Pioneer," *Gospel Herald,* April 1913, p. 31.

[16] *YI,* Mar. 3, 1914, pp. 6. 7.

[17] The first indication that Loughborough had begun receiving sustentation checks appears in a March 13, 1911, diary entry (for $30). By November, however, he was receiving $60 a month (see JNL, diary, Nov. 21, 1911). See also "Retirement Plans," *SDA Encyclopedia* (2nd rev. ed.), vol. 11, p. 440.

[18] JNL to F. C. Gilbert, Mar. 14, 1911, as indicated in JNL, diary, March 1911; *RH,* Nov. 16, 1944, pp. 4, 5; *RH,* Dec. 29, 1910, p. 21.

[19] JNL, flyleaves of 1910-1915 diaries; *Union Conference Record,* Sept. 21, 1908, p. 16; *AUG,* Mar. 23, 1910, p. 94; *ST,* Mar. 19, 1912, p. 191; *ST,* Apr. 18, 1911, p. 254; *ST,* Aug. 15, 1911, p. 511; *ST,* Aug. 29, 1911, pp. 542, 543; *South African Missionary,* Jan. 12, 1914, p. 8; *NPUG,* June 1, 1964, p. 2.

[20] D. Morgan, *Lewis C. Sheafe,* pp. 374-376.

[21] See JNL's giving record in *Gospel Herald,* January 1908, p. 4; March 1908, p. 12; November 1908, p. 43; January 1909, p. 3.

[22] JNL, diary, Mar. 31, 1913.

[23] See, for example, JNL's diary entries for June 1913 and August 1914. For a short summary of Canright's career, see R. Schwarz and F. Greenleaf, *Light Bearers,* pp. 614, 615.

[24] JNL, diary, July and September 1911.

[25] JNL, diary, July 1911; JNL to E. S. Ballenger, Jan. 6, 1915, Collection 87, Box 35, Folder 7, A. F. Ballenger and Mote Papers, CAR. For a succinct summary of A. F. Ballenger's career, see Schwarz and Greenleaf, *Light Bearers,* p. 618, and for a more complete biography, see Gary Land, *Seeker After Light* (Berrien Springs, Mich.: Andrews University Press, 2000).

[26] JNL, *Central Union Outlook,* May 25, 1915, p. 2.

[27] JNL, diaries, September 1910-February 1911 and note in Jan. 2, 1913, diary; *RH,* Apr. 6, 1911, p. 16.

[28] JNL, diary, April-October 1911, August and December 1912, November and December 1913, April and October 1914; JNL to EGW, Jan. 11, 1912, m. 52, CAR. The NAD Minutes for October 29, 1914, indicate that the NAD Committee discussed Loughborough's proposal—and then dumped it in the lap of the Committee on Plans, where it apparently expired without a whimper, despite some grassroots support from influential Adventists such as Florence Welthy Merrett.

[29] JNL, "Bits and Pieces," 1911 and 1914 Notebooks, m. 006529, CAR.

[30] They included *Review and Herald, Youth's Instructor, Liberty, Education, Sabbath School Worker, Good Health, Life and Health, Present Truth* (British), *The Missionary Worker, South African Missionary, Gospel Herald, Life Boat, Health and Temperance, Bible Training School, The Watchman, Signs of the Times* (weekly), *Signs Magazine* (monthly), *Our Little Friend, Pacific Union Recorder, The Liberator,* and the *Church Officer's Gazette.* While some of them were monthly, most were weekly periodicals.

[31] JNL, diary, February 1913 and flyleaf of 1915 diary. These tendencies are evident, for example, in his frequent correspondence with the *South African Missionary.* See July 25, 1910, p. 4; Aug. 1, 1910, p. 4; Nov. 7, 1910, p. 2; Sept. 11, 1911, p. 4; Dec. 18, 1911, p. 4; and Apr. 28, 1914, p. 4.

[32] JNL, diary, May and October 1912, January and October 1913, May 1915. In fact, page 19 of the first volume lists Loughborough as a "Patron" of the *Great Epochs in American History* set (published in 1912) for the State of California.

[33] *ST,* Aug. 30, 1910, p. 2; *PUR,* Dec. 7, 1911, p. 3; *NPUG,* Mar. 28, 1912, p. 4; *YI,* July 22, 1913, p. 5; *Field Tidings*, Feb. 25, 1914, p. 8; *Echoes From the Field*, Mar. 25, 1914, p. 3.

[34] *AUG,* Oct. 26, 1910, p. 338; *Northern Union Reaper*, Dec. 19, 1911, p. 6; *AUG,* Sept. 4, 1912, p. 2.

[35] *RH,* July 6, 1911, p. 9.

[36] See the conclusion of JNL's series "Two Thrones" in *RH,* July 14, 1910, pp. 4, 5; July 21, 1910, p. 4; and July 28, 1910, p. 4. For "Judas," see *RH,* Oct. 30, 1913, p. 7 and Nov. 20, 1913, pp. 4, 5. For his series "Second Advent Movement," see *RH,* July 9, 1914, pp. 3, 4; July 16, 1914, pp. 4, 5; July 23, 1914, p. 4; July 30, 1914, pp. 3, 4; Aug. 6, 1914, p. 4; Aug. 13, 1914, p. 5; Aug. 20, 1914, p. 6; Aug. 27, 1914, pp. 4, 5; Sept. 10, 1914, pp. 5, 6; Sept. 17, 1914, pp. 4, 5; Sept. 24, 1914, pp. 4, 5; Oct. 15, 1914, pp. 5, 6; Oct. 22, 1914, pp. 4, 5; Nov. 5, 1914, pp. 5, 6; Nov. 19, 1914, p. 4; and Nov. 26, 1914, pp. 5, 6. For "Elihu on the Sabbath," see *RH,* Jan. 4, 1912, p. 3. For "The Sanctuary," see *RH,* Dec. 12, 1912, p. 5. For "How to Hold Bible Readings," see *RH,* May 11, 1911, pp. 18, 19. For "Books," see *RH,* Nov. 30, 1911, p. 6. For "Communion Service," see *RH,* Dec. 28, 1911, pp. 3, 4; for "Order and Organization," see *RH,* June 26, 1913, pp. 3, 4.

[37] See *ST,* Feb. 11, 1913, pp. 85, 86; Feb. 18, 1913, pp. 101, 102; Mar. 11, 1913, pp. 149, 150; Dec. 16, 1913, p. 760; Jan. 13, 1914, p. 2; Feb. 3, 1914, p. 56; Feb. 17, 1914, p. 87; Dec. 1, 1914, p. 739; Feb. 23, 1915, p. 121.

[38] *ST-A,* July 24, 1911, pp. 474-476; Nov. 25, 1912, pp. 754, 755; Mar. 9, 1914, p. 155.

[39] *Life Boat*, July 1913, pp. 209-211, and March 1914, pp. 70-72.

[40] JNL, "Religious Liberty—Retrospective," *Liberty* 6, no. 1 (1911): 40-43; *Life and Health*, March 1915, pp. 109, 110.

[41] *Church Officers' Gazette*, July 1914, p. 5, and July 1915, pp. 1, 2.

[42] *Our Little Friend*, Mar. 21, 1913, pp. 98, 99; July 25, 1913, pp. 244, 245; Aug. 1, 1913, pp. 252, 253; Aug. 8, 1913, pp. 258, 259; July 16, 1915, p. 236; Aug. 1, 1913, pp. 252, 253.

[43] *YI,* Jan. 7, 1913, p. 12; Apr. 22, 1913, pp. 6, 7; Nov. 18, 1913, p. 13; Dec. 9, 1913, p. 5.

[44] *PUR*, Oct. 8, 1914, p. 3; *PUR*, Apr. 1, 1915, p. 10; *PUR*, June 10, 1915, p. 2; WCW to JNL, Jan. 28, 1912, m. 52, CAR, concerns his article no. 119 in *PUR.* For the autobiographical series (which covers his life from 1832 to about 1854), see the *PUR,* 1906-1914 or read E. Robinson's *Lighter of Gospel Fires*, largely based on that series.

[45] *NPUG*, July 15, 1915, p. 8.

[46] JNL, *BTS*, September 1910 to June 1915 monthly issues.

[47] JNL, diary, September 1910 and February 1912; *Life and Health*, March 1915, pp. 109, 110.

[48] JNL to Dr. M. A. McElhany, Mar. 3, 1912, Adventist Heritage Room, LLU Library.

[49] JNL, diary, January 1914; JNL to WCW, Jan. 12, 1914, m. 52, CAR.

[50] JNL to EGW and her response, Jan. 18, 1914, ms. 13, 1914, CAR.

[51] Oakland *Tribune*, Mar. 12, 1914, p. 7; *RH,* Mar. 12, 1914, p. 20; JNL, diary,

March-April 1915; JNL to WCW, Jan. 18, 1914 and Apr. 22, 1915, m. 52, CAR; WCW to JNL, Apr. 27, 1915, m. 52, CAR. See also JNL's articles "A Young Octogenarian," in *Life and Health*, March 1915, pp. 109, 110, and "Young Old Age," in *ST*, Feb. 13, 1912, p. 110.

[52] *PUR*, Mar. 16, 1911, pp. 5-7.

[53] JNL, diary, November 1912; *RH*, Jan. 23, 1913, p. 22.

[54] A. Spalding, *Origin and History*, vol. 3, p. 272; JNL, diary, May 1913 and January 1915; *Columbia Union Visitor*, June 4, 1913, p. 3; *PUR*, June 5, 1913, p. 3; *RH*, June 5, 1913, pp. 15-17; *Northern Union Reaper*, June 10, 1913, p. 8, reprinted from *GCB* (1913).

[55] JNL, diary, February, March, and July 1915; W. C. White, *Eastern Canadian Messenger*, Apr. 20, 1915, p. 2; WCW to JNL, Apr. 19, 1915, m. 52, CAR; Spalding, *Origin and History*, vol. 3, p. 283; *NPUG*, July 22, 1915, pp. 1, 2; *NPUG*, July 29, 1915, pp. 1, 2; *NPUG*, Aug. 5, 1915, pp. 1-3; *ST*, Aug. 24, 1915, pp. 516, 517; *Southern Union Worker*, Aug. 12, 1915, pp. 253, 254. Several editors of union papers felt that Loughborough's sketch of White's life should be published, but none did so.

[56] WCW to JNL, May 6, 1915, and JNL to WCW, May 12, 1915, m. 52, CAR.

[57] JNL, diaries, September 1910-January 1915; Oakland *Tribune*, Mar. 12, 1914, p. 7.

CHAPTER XXII

FINAL YEARS OF SEMI-INDEPENDENCE (1915-1917)

*"Loughborough . . . , who has weathered so many gales,
was present [at the Fall Council] giving his cheery testimony
that the old gospel ship was sure to enter the harbour."*[1]

Beginning with the war years (1914-1918), as Loughborough entered his mid-80s, he began turning down invitations to speak at camp meetings across the U.S. From now on, his "gospel ship" would only enter "harbours" in California. During 1915 he shared his faith-building stories with thousands of eager listeners at camp meetings in Los Angeles and Huntington Beach, and gave "interesting" and instructive talks to hundreds more at churches in Fresno, Armona, Bakersfield, and San Jose, and in the Watts district of Los Angeles, where his granddaughter Nellie had established a small African American church.[2]

Chosen as one of 10 delegates to represent the Pacific Union Conference at the Autumn Council session in Loma Linda, Loughborough joined Stephen Haskell, George Butler, J. O. Corliss, and others on the platform to share their memories of GC president O. A. Olsen and Ellen White, both recently deceased. "Although their heads are whitening with the years," the *Review* stated, "their hearts are still young, and their zeal unabated." In addition to offering prayers at several meetings, John preached "with fire and zeal, and . . . confidence" (according to one listener), emphasizing the importance of the writings of Ellen G. White in the history of the Adventist Church. During the session a photographer took a picture of the four "venerable counselors" (Loughborough, Butler, Corliss, and Haskell), perhaps sensing that it was the last time they would all be together.[3]

In front of the 150 delegates Loughborough said: "I praise the Lord for the Spirit of God, which is moving upon the Lord's people all over the world, and for the close cooperation of the holy angels with those who are called to be laborers together with God." Then he declared: "We know not . . . just when the Lord will come; but we know that event is right at hand, and I am of good courage. I believe we are almost home." Others joined him in testifying of their fervent belief in the imminent Second Advent.[4]

In the summer of 1916, as the war intensified across Europe, John preached at camp meetings in Hanford and Stockton. At the latter, "the oldest ordained minister in the denomination" (at 84) participated in an ordination service for two church elders. Then at the Northern California Conference session he served on the Credentials and Licenses Committee, a role that he had filled for more than half a century. Back home in Lodi he frequently walked across the road to tell stories to the boys and girls at the elementary school and to the Ministerial Club at the academy. Occasionally he joined the youth at Missionary Volunteer meetings and went with them on school picnics as well. On one such outing he met Edith Barnes, a science teacher and amateur nurse who would play a major role in his future life.[5]

If Loughborough was not standing behind a pulpit preaching, he could be found sitting in his chair reading. Although by 1916 he was reading less than before, he still managed to keep up with 16 church periodicals.[6] Once again, his frequent letters to editors correcting factual or chronological errors make it obvious that he examined each issue thoroughly. He also read his Bible through every year (a practice he had begun in 1852 at the age of 20), adding to his growing list of divine promises—3,044 in the Old Testament and 529 in the New Testament. For a change of pace, he started keeping a list of all the "threatenings" (curses) he found in Scripture. Eventually his tally reached 2,936 (with 353 yet to be fulfilled in the future). In addition, he continued rereading Ellen White's writings in order to update and revise his typed indexes. During 1916 and 1917 he indexed more of her articles in the *Review* and *Signs of the Times*. Perhaps to refresh his aging memory, John also perused the pages of his *The Great Second Advent Movement* from time to time, rereading it entirely at least five times during the last decade of his life. Pursuing his love of history and biography, he read Josephus's description of the Jewish Temple, a biography of the Duke of Argyll, Robinson's *History of Western Europe*, and a book on England's diplomatic and military relations with Turkey (Adventists had a deep interest in "the Eastern Question," or how Turkey fit into various eschatological prophecies).[7]

PEN PAL TO THE WORLD

But Loughborough was reading fewer books and periodicals than before primarily because he had more letters to answer. Decades before the *Youth's Instructor* and *Junior Guide* sponsored letter-writing clubs, nearly every prominent Adventist around the world who had met John saw him as their pen pal. For his eighty-fifth birthday alone (in January 1917), he received more than 200 telegrams, notes, cards, and letters. Even more remarkable, perhaps, is the fact that he tried to answer every one of them. His diaries list every communication he received and answered—dozens of letters every month (unfortunately, few are extant today). John regularly corresponded with A. G. Daniells (GC president), W. T. Knox (GC treasurer), W. C. White (in charge of his mother's archives), M. E. Kern (GC Missionary Volunteer director), E. E. Andross (Pacific Union president), M. C. Israel (missionary to Australia and New Zealand), Hetty Haskell (editor of the *Bible Training School*), and Dr. David Paulson (editor of *Life Boat*), to mention a few.[8]

But he also responded to letters from ordinary lay members who inquired about his health, asked him historical or theological questions, or requested copies of his books and pamphlets. For example, in August 1916 alone he mailed nearly 200 books and papers to James Harvey in Oakland, who acted as John's agent to redistribute copies of his works.[9] Given his age and experience, many members related to him as if he were an ecclesiastical "Dear Abby" or a pious guru whose vast knowledge could solve all their problems. He told one man who asked for copies of his dreams, "I do not wish to have them used as an exaltation of self above others, but as a token that the Lord is willing to guide in a personal duty, His servants who humbly trust Him. I have not taken my dreams as a dictation to other people, but have in their literal fulfillments been encouraged that I was moving in the line of duty."[10] Despite his caveat, some church officials, including R. A. Underwood (president of the Central Union Conference) and L. H. Christian (president of the Lake Union Conference), cited Loughborough's dreams in articles written for church papers to drive home moral lessons.[11]

Loughborough's responses always followed the orthodox line of thought he had laid down in his earlier books *Rise and Progress* and *The Great Second Advent Movement*. When one woman inquired about early Sabbatarian Adventists' beliefs in the "shut door," he assured her that only Joseph Turner and the Advent Christians had believed that this meant "no more mercy for sinners" after October 22, 1844. Neither James and Ellen White nor any other Sabbathkeeping Adventist had taught that no further sinners could be saved. Although on this issue John's "head was made up," E. S. Ballenger would later force him to "face the facts" by showing him documents proving he had been wrong about the pioneers.[12] Naturally John's most frequent correspondents were members of his extended family. When on the speaking circuit, he sent letters to his daughter Mary Ireland, to his sister Minerva Jane Chapman, to his cousin Bert Loughborough, and to his granddaughters May, Nellie, Jennie, and Winnie (unfortunately, not one of those family letters has survived). As a brother, father, and grandfather, Loughborough definitely believed it was important to keep in touch.[13]

LOUGHBOROUGH'S WRITINGS

Through reprints of his books and pamphlets and his articles in church papers, John also kept in touch with a growing circle of readers. If his old friend George Butler felt that *The Great Second Advent Movement* was "not being read as much as it deserves to be,"[14] that could not be said of his policy manual *The Church*. In addition to screening baptismal candidates by having them answer the 16 questions he had listed there, local church officers followed the book's suggestion to place "inactive members" (those who no longer attended services) on a "retired list." Doing so, however, stigmatized them as no longer "members in good and regular standing." One church official, anxious that such a list not become "a sort of 'Limbo,'" urged faithful Adventists to labor tirelessly "to revive or discipline such [inactive] members."[15]

To answer queries about the "sealing message" and the composition of the "144,000," Loughborough in 1916 compiled a 47-page pamphlet that he sold for a dime and largely distributed himself. Full of esoteric language and prophetic symbols, his unique tract sought to prove that the so-called sealing message undermined the "new light" apostasy that some had been advocating since the 1890s. Unlike John's previous work, however, his pamphlet relied far more heavily on quotations lifted from the writings of Ellen White, Joseph Bates, and other pioneers than it did on biblical texts. Today only the most determined readers would choose to navigate their way through its dense prose and convoluted arguments about spiritualism, the 144,000, the seal of God, the seven last plagues, the sealing work, and the last tribulation. Nonetheless, as an expression of the literalistic and legalistic mind-set of early-twentieth-century Adventism, the pamphlet is a gem. Although largely self-published, it received the endorsement of many church leaders, and ads for it appeared in several church papers.[16]

Although John was now in his mid-80s, Adventist editors pressured him relentlessly to write for their periodicals, as the Loughborough name boosted sales. To keep them happy, he adopted the practice of sending short pieces to selected papers that other periodicals then reprinted (an "Adventist News Network" decades before the concept became reality). For example, his article "Peace Beyond Understanding," printed in *Field Tidings* in July 1915, appeared five months later in the *Columbia Union Visitor*. Typically, union conference papers reprinted articles he had prepared for the *Review, Signs*, or the *Pacific Union Recorder.* After all, the *Review* had been lifting articles from other religious papers (and they from the *Review*) for half a century before copyright laws interfered with the practice.[17]

For the new *Church Officers' Gazette* (published since 1914 by Edith Graham and Matilda Erickson), John penned articles with tips about conducting church services, baptisms, and quarterly meetings (gradually being referred to as Communion services at which members washed one another's feet and shared the bread and grape juice).[18] Meanwhile, *Our Little Friend* continued to publish his delightful series on animal intelligence, packed with personal anecdotes from his childhood.[19] Somewhat more serious and moralistic in tone, John's two articles in the *Youth's Instructor* cited a wide array of ancient sources that buttressed the biblical Flood account and urged Adventist youth to stand tall for God's truth.[20]

Because his old friends Hetty and Stephen Haskell always extended him a blank check to write whatever he wished for their paper, his articles in the *Bible Training School* cover a wide range of topics. Between 1915 and 1917 he sent them Bible studies concerning apostasy, tithing, Flood geology, the cities of refuge, Bible "sovens," Tyre, and the unpardonable sin, as well as several articles explaining how the United States during the Civil War and Europe during World War I fit into end-time prophecies.[21]

MOVING INTO ST. HELENA SANITARIUM

Although bouts of pneumonia in 1914 and 1915 and influenza (*la grippe*) in 1916 had weakened Loughborough somewhat, the nicknames his ministerial colleagues assigned him must have made the octogenarian feel even feebler than he was.[22] The *South African Missionary* hailed him as "our oldest living Seventh-day Adventist minister," while the *Western Canadian Tidings* called him "one of the oldest pioneers in this message."[23] The *Northern Union Reaper*, employing a term applied in print to no other Adventist pioneer, praised him as "our venerable Elder J. N. Loughborough" (a word some old-timers felt too "Catholic"). In fact, John was so revered that the *Workers' Bulletin* declared that he had been "one of the very first to accept the [third angel's] message in the '[eighteen]forties'"—an obvious blunder since John did not convert to Sabbatarian Adventism until 1852.[24]

But his aging was also profitable—at least to others. To raise money for the new Ellen G. White Memorial Hospital in Los Angeles, Adventist women in southern California conceived the idea of selling photographs of the remaining pioneer ministers. For 50 cents, one could choose between two photos: one showing G. I. Butler, S. N. Haskell, and J. N. Loughborough in full white beards and long black frockcoats, beside a pool, and the other depicting seven pioneer pastors, all dressed to the nines with some holding their Bibles. For a dollar, one could buy both photographs. Judging by the fact that so many of them still survive, it must have been a very successful fund-raiser.[25]

Yet despite all the flattering nicknames, picture-taking, and praise, John's muscles and bones informed him that he was growing weaker. When he and George Butler met again shortly after their photo shoot, Butler described his friend as "feeble." As M. C. Israel, recently widowed, shared a tent with John at camp meeting, he too noted that "he is getting feeble."[26]

Then in the fall of 1916, when John Ireland accepted a call to Takoma Park (near Washington, D.C.) to join the General Conference auditing staff, Loughborough knew he had to make a tough decision: go east with his daughter Mary and her husband, or remain in California among friends he had known for decades. In his case, the "water" of friendship proved thicker than the "blood" of family ties. Choosing to stay, however, also meant drastically reducing his lifestyle. On September 27 Loughborough moved into a fifth-floor room at St. Helena Sanitarium. "I have arranged to spend the remainder of my days in this sanitarium," he told his friend C. E. Holmes, "being sustained here from the sustentation fund, which portion is furnished to me each month." Besides clothing and other personal items, he brought with him a few books, letters, and other artifacts, including his diaries (which he called "my relics").[27]

Those who came to know him there agreed that "his presence is a constant inspiration to the [sanitarium] family."[28] Always smiling and chipper, Loughborough refused to sit around in his room bemoaning his physical limitations. Instead, during the last eight years of his life, he wrote dozens of articles for church papers, mailed scores of letters and hundreds of books, entertained a constant stream of visitors, and made many new friends—one of whom ("Nurse Edith") would play a major role in his life after 1917, and by saving his 60 diaries after his death, she would greatly enrich the quality of this biography.

---

[1] *Union Conference Record*, Jan. 24, 1916, p. 2.

[2] JNL, diary, September-October 1915; *Union Conference Record*, Jan. 24, 1916, p. 2; *PUR*, Sept. 2, 1915, p. 8; *PUR*, Sept. 16, 1915, p. 5; *PUR*, Sept. 30, 1915, p. 5; *PUR*, Nov. 18, 1915, p. 4.

[3] GC Minutes, Nov. 7 and 10, 1915, pp. 82, 94, 95; *Columbia Union Visitor*, Dec. 16, 1915, pp. 3, 4; *LUH*, Dec. 8, 1915, p. 3; *PUR*, Dec. 2, 1915, p. 1; *RH*, Nov. 25, 1915, p. 24; JNL, diary, November 1915; Lewis H. Christian, *Pioneers and Builders of the Advent Cause in Europe* (Mountain View, Calif.: Pacific Press Pub. Assn., 1937), p. 32.

[4] *RH*, Nov. 25, 1915, p. 4; *RH*, Dec. 2, 1915, p. 4.

[5] JNL, diary, March, May, June 1916, January 1917; *PUR*, July 13, 1916, p. 1; *PUR*, July 20, 1916, p. 2.

[6] *Our Little Friend, Youth's Instructor, Gospel Herald, Signs of the Times* (weekly), *Review and Herald, Sabbath School Worker, Watchman, Good Health, Educator, Life and Health, Missionary Worker, Conference Officer's Gazette, Present Truth* (British), *Signs of the Times* (monthly), *Bible Training School*, and *Pacific Union Recorder.* See JNL, flyleaves of 1916 and 1917 diaries.

[7] JNL, diary, February, September, and November 1916 and February 1917; *RH*, Feb. 10, 1916, p. 20; *RH*, July 27, 1916, p. 5; *Missionary Worker*, March 1916, p. 6; *Life and Health*, April 1916, p. 188.

[8] JNL, diaries, December 1915, January, August, and October 1916, and January 1917; JNL to WCW, undated (c. 1915), m. 52, CAR; JNL to M. E. Kern, Sept. 26, 1915, m. 52, CAR; "Israel, Mendel Crocker," *Ellen G. White Encyclopedia,* pp. 423, 424.

[9] JNL, diary, August 1916.

[10] JNL to D. A. Parsons, Oct. 27, 1916, DF 230, CAR.

[11] See, for example, R. A. Underwood's "Which Train Are You Traveling On?" in *Central Union Outlook,* May 2, 1916, pp. 1, 2, and L. H. Christian, "A New Experience," *NPUG,* June 1, 1916, p. 1.

[12] JNL to Lissie Weekly, Mar. 16, 1917, Adventist Heritage Room, LLU Libraries.

[13] See JNL's diaries for 1915-1917 inclusive.

[14] *RH,* Aug. 17, 1916, pp. 9, 10.

[15] *Northern Union Reaper*, Oct. 5, 1915, pp. 4, 5.

[16] *Questions on the Sealing Message* (Lodi, Calif.: Loughborough, 1916; Bakersfield, Calif.: B. F. Gregory, 1916). See ads in *PUR,* July 27, 1916, p. 8, and *RH,* Dec. 14, 1916, p. 24.

[17] See, for example, *Field Tidings*, July 7, 1915, p. 7, and *Columbia Union Visitor*, Dec. 9, 1915, p. 6.

[18] *Church Officers' Gazette*, December 1915, p. 2; January 1916, pp. 1, 2; March 1916, p. 1; May 1916, p. 2; August 1916, pp. 1, 2, 7; October 1916, pp. 1, 2; December 1916, pp. 1, 2; January 1917, pp. 1, 2; February 1917, pp. 1, 2.

[19] JNL, "The Intelligence of Animals," *Our Little Friend*, Aug. 13, 1915, p. 267; Aug. 27, 1915, pp. 284, 286; Sept. 3, 1915, p. 292; Nov. 26, 1913, p. 388.

[20] JNL, "The Flood," *YI,* Dec. 14, 1915, p. 4; "One," *YI,* July 25, 1916, p. 8.

[21] See JNL articles in *BTS* between August 1915 and January 1917.

[22] Loughborough briefly mentions his physical afflictions near the end of his *Questions on the Sealing Message*, p. 41.

[23] *South African Missionary*, Nov. 1, 1915, p. 4; *Western Canadian Tidings*, Dec. 23, 1915, p. 7.

[24] *Northern Union Reaper*, Apr. 25, 1916, p. 8; *Workers' Bulletin*, Nov. 16, 1915, p. 1.

[25] See the promotion in the *RH,* Apr. 27, 1916, p. 20.

[26] *RH,* Jan. 25, 1917, p. 18; *Union Conference Record*, Aug. 14, 1916, p. 8.

[27] JNL to C. E. Holmes, Apr. 13, 1920, C. E. Holmes Collection 142-2, CAR. Fortunately for him, St. Helena Sanitarium had installed an elevator, although it did not always work properly.

[28] *Life and Health*, February 1917, pp. 58-60.

Chapter XXIII

LIFE AT ST. HELENA SANITARIUM (1917-1920)

"But if you have seen me in a spirit of fight, that I must drive things through, I want to confess it. I thought I was doing what God wanted done. I thought I had to force things through. And I ask some of you to forgive me. God has. I want to be right with this people. I do not expect to meet with you in another General Conference."[1]

When J. N. Loughborough spoke those words to the delegates gathered in San Francisco for the 1918 GC Session, he was already past 86 years of age. The globe-trotting missionary and nationally famous camp meeting speaker now lived in a single room at St. Helena Sanitarium. Although his mind remained sharp, his body had grown frail. While he boasted that a healthful diet had given him the arteries of a child, at 107 pounds he also had the body of a boy—but one with weak muscles and brittle bones. Unable to care for himself, John moved to the sanitarium to enjoy around-the-clock attention from its physicians and nurses. During the seven years he spent there (1917-1924) he also benefited from the services of a caregiver he called "Nurse Edith," a remarkable woman whose contributions to his private life lie buried in obscurity.

WHO WAS NURSE EDITH?

Edith Mary Barnes was born February 1, 1882, in Grand Island, Nebraska. As a girl, she watched her mother (a trained nurse) care for elderly patients in their home, and over time the girl learned how to give massages and hydrotherapy treatments. After the family moved to California, Edith paid her own way through the teacher-training program at the Western Normal Institute (later Lodi Academy) and Pacific Union College. For several years she taught at the Elmshaven School, then at the Lodi School, and later at Lodi Academy.

Although today we have no contemporary photographs of Miss Barnes (or "Aunt Great" as her pupils called her), Faye Jull, the five-year-old niece who used to visit her science classes at Lodi, remembers her as a bubbly, outgoing woman. Barely five feet tall, with dark eyes and brown hair gathered into a bun, this little dynamo enjoyed weeding in her vegetable and flower gardens, playing Chinese checkers and card games, and frolicking with students on school picnics. Deeply spiritual, she also sang hymns and read her Bible. Although she chose to care for her invalid mother rather than to marry, Edith preferred the moniker "maiden lady" to "old maid."[2]

For several weeks in the spring of 1916 as Loughborough recovered from the flu, Miss Barnes came to the Ireland's home to give him daily hot fomentation treatments. When Loughborough moved to the St. Helena Sanitarium six months later, Edith, then 34, quit her teaching position at Lodi to provide the special care he needed. Although she did not live at the sanitarium and never became a paid member of the staff, John's diary shows that she gave him regular massages and fomentation treatments. Each time she visited, they dined together, attended sacred and secular programs, walked to the "deer park" (nature preserve), and chatted for hours. When she was away visiting family in Glendale and Loma Linda, they corresponded regularly.[3]

As the years went by, the fun-loving masseuse and the witty preacher became very close friends. After one visit in June 1920 John (then 88) wrote in his diary: "Edith [then 38] came this eve. We had a good Christian love visit."[4] The juxtaposition of those two words—"love" and "Christian" —suggests that Loughborough, like a kind old uncle, treated Edith like one of his nieces rather than simply a caretaker. Faye Jull recalls hearing her Aunt Edith describe Loughborough as "a Christian gentleman," and no doubt he was. In fact, never once during his 75-year ministry did the whisper of a scandal taint his reputation. Despite the fact that the vast majority of his visitors at the sanitarium were women (as his diaries show), John treated each one as a Christian gentleman should.[5]

PUBLIC SPEAKING OPPORTUNITIES

If Loughborough could no longer visit Adventist camp meetings, thanks to the excellent care he received at the sanitarium he could accept local invitations to speak. In 1917 he attended the annual stockholders' meeting at the Pacific Press along with J. O. Corliss and W. C. White, then spoke to the students at Pacific Union College. Although invited to address the Fresno camp meeting that summer, he sent "a letter of cheer and confidence" instead, indicating "that while absent in the flesh he was present in the spirit." He assured attendees that even at 85 "I am not on the sick list, thank the Lord." Occasionally he preached at the Lodi SDA Church and attended children's and MV meetings at the school there. Also he shared his memories at Sabbath and holiday services in the sanitarium chapel.[6]

As World War I was grinding to a halt across Europe, Loughborough (now 86) received an invitation to attend the 1918 San Francisco GC session as one of 12 special guests. At first he sent a letter declining the invitation and promising to pray for the delegates. But they insisted that he join them. When two men carried him to the platform in a rocking chair, the temptation to speak proved too strong. Raising his trembling voice, he gave a "touching talk . . . relating the experiences of the message in its infancy." Before leaving the platform, he begged his friends not to shake hands with him as the physical strain would prove too much. Instead, he asked all those who would like to shake his hand to wave their hands toward him, and he did the same for them. Hailing him as one of the "faithful Calebs in the [Advent] movement," the delegates voted to renew his ministerial credentials. In addition to his fervent prayers, "ringing testimony," and short talk, John brought with him several artifacts of the Millerite and early Adventist movements that he exhibited in the hall.[7]

During his stay at the sanitarium, a surprising number of people wrote to him to request copies of these old Adventist materials and especially of his earlier books and pamphlets (such as *Prophetic Gift in the Gospel Church*). To keep them happy, John spent many hours each day wrapping materials and tapping out letters on his 1880s typewriter. The demand for his pamphlet *Questions on the Sealing Message* (1916), for example, reached phenomenal heights: at one point in the fall of 1917 the octogenarian was filling orders for 5,000 copies! Furthermore, his diaries indicate that Pacific Press mailed him literally hundreds of copies of his books to sell to customers (500 in June alone). At times his cluttered room must have resembled a bookshop.[8]

Those who visited him, however, saw it as a sanctuary. One sanitarium worker recalled a half century later how he "would almost tiptoe out of his [Loughborough's] room with the feeling that [he] had been with a man in tune with heaven." Matilda Erickson, assistant GC Missionary Volunteer director, was in awe as John wrote her some of his dreams concerning Adventist youth, one of which, she said, "is coming true" as hundreds of young people around the world "are rendering valiant service." The Nelsons, en route to India as missionaries, stopped by to see Loughborough's "relics" and have him pose for a picture in his shiny, well-worn Prince Albert frock coat. Likewise, John's friend C. E. Holmes loved to have him share copies of the five testimonies he had received directly from Ellen White.[9]

DEALING WITH DISSIDENTS

Defending the divine inspiration of Mrs. White's testimonies—especially when confronted with Margaret Rowen's spurious ones—occupied much of Loughborough's time. In 1916 Rowen, a 40-year-old recent convert living in Los Angeles, announced that God had selected her as His special messenger to take Ellen White's place. After interviewing her church leaders concluded that while her writings resembled White's, she provided no convincing evidence of a divine call. Yet her physical characteristics while in vision (which replicated White's precisely) convinced some ministers that God had indeed chosen her. In the 1920s, however, her false predictions, bizarre biblical exegesis, lies, greed, and attempt at murder proved her undoing, and she spent a year in San Quentin Prison.[10]

When Loughborough first encountered her writings in 1917, of course, none of those sad events had occurred. Remembering his notes decades earlier when Anna Phillips had claimed to be a prophet, John reread his comparison of her writings with Mrs. White's testimonies. Then he prepared a similar list matching statements from Rowen with those of White on similar topics. By the spring of 1918 he was certain that Rowen was a false prophet. Preparing a lengthy manuscript demonstrating it, he sent the document to Pacific Union Conference president E. E. Andross. In 1919 and 1920 he wrote further "testimonials" (as he called his written arguments) disproving her claims to divine inspiration and debunking her bizarre biblical interpretations (i.e., Christ created as an angel; the 144,000 saved would come only from the United States; God's final judgment to occur on July 23, 1919, etc.).[11]

If he could easily debunk Margaret Rowen's claims, the charges made by Edward S. Ballenger proved tougher. Like his brother Albion, Edward had been an Adventist minister until defrocked in 1914 for unorthodox views on the investigative judgment and the heavenly sanctuary. Thereafter he helped his brother produce the dissident paper *The Gathering Call*, becoming its editor when Albion died in 1921.[12]

Unfortunately for Loughborough, E. S. Ballenger knew some things about the Adventist past that John either did not know or refused to admit. For example, in his *Rise and Progress* (1892) and *The Great Second Advent Movement* (1905), John had stated categorically that neither Ellen White nor any of the pioneers had ever believed that the "shut door" meant "no more mercy for sinners" after 1844. Instead, he blamed that teaching on his former Rochester neighbor, the Advent Christian leader Joseph Turner. Moreover, Loughborough asserted that the founders of the Seventh-day Adventist Church had believed in 1844 that it was still possible for those "from the world" (non-Christians) to be converted and that by 1845 or 1846 they had entirely abandoned their belief in the "shut door" and embraced the "open door."[13]

Believing that Loughborough was either consciously deceiving his readers or ignorant of the facts, Edward sent him the first of many letters ostensibly seeking "to get all the details of those early days . . . while some of you old pioneers are still living." Cordial and inquisitive, Edward initially played the role of a student seeking wisdom from an experienced teacher of Adventist history. He asked his mentor to enlighten him concerning the authority of White's visions, the accuracy of her 1846 vision on astronomy, and her "shut door" views. It seemed innocent enough, but Ballenger had baited a trap. When John answered by citing his personal experience (rather than the Bible) in observing White in vision, quoted the nineteenth-century astronomer Herschel (rather than a modern one), and denied that White had taught "no more mercy for sinners," Ballenger sprang the trap.[14]

In a series of angry (but private) letters he accused Loughborough of twisting the facts, making false statements, and taking quotations out of context to deliberately deceive his readers regarding the pioneers' "shut door" views. Calling on the old man to "make this right by confession before you are called into the presence of the Judge of the world," Edward reminded John that his claim that he had read all Adventist literature from 1849 to the present meant that he could not plead ignorance of the facts. Instead, Ballenger accused him of making statements "so worded . . . that you lead the reader to believe a direct falsehood" and editing quotations to make it appear that the pioneers had abandoned belief in the "shut door" after 1845. Consequently, reading this "absolutely false" interpretation of Adventist history had brought "an awful shock" to Ballenger. "These things cannot be covered [up] much longer," he warned, implying that certain "enemies" were eager to "confess" John's deceit for him if he did not own up to it shortly.[15]

Maintaining the calm demeanor for which he was famous, Loughborough thanked Ballenger "for freely expressing your mind to me," saying that he regretted "the strong language" Edward had employed. Then, pleading old age, he added, "[but] you certainly could not expect a feeble man . . . to answer all you write about in a short letter." Wittily, he told Edward that perhaps he would "wait until they [his enemies] make the confession" and then "I can endorse it" and this would "make a shorter job for me." Then, citing several of his "old relics" (the *Voice of Truth*, an old almanac, letters), John used satire to debunk Edward's claim that the "shut door" *always* meant "no more mercy for sinners" to any of the pioneers except Marsh. Finally, the old man concluded: "This is none of my funeral. And I am not yet convinced that I am liable to loose [*sic*] eternal life over this case."[16]

Convinced otherwise, Edward informed John that he had found "no little disappointment" in his replies and would hold him accountable for his "deceptions" and "misrepresentations" concerning the "shut door." Citing several relevant documents, Ballenger asserted that the Advent Christians had not taught the "shut door" after April of 1845; that the *Voice of Truth* never propagated it; and that the *Present Truth* (May 1850) and various letters proved that James and Ellen White had believed it between 1844 and 1851. Once again calling on Loughborough to admit his errors, Edward provided him with a two-part confession to sign:

"A. I do not believe that Elds. James White or Joseph Bates ever taught the shut door doctrine after they accepted the seventh-day [Sabbath], and thus became [Seventh-day] Adventists; and I do believe that the First-day Adventists [Advent Christians] did teach the shut door doctrine after the Albany Conference, Apr. 29-1845.

Signed:__________________

"B. In preparing the manuscript for the *Great [Second Advent] Movement* I did not knowingly misstate any facts nor attempt to cover up any facts; neither did I attempt to mislead nor deceive in any way the prospective readers.

"Signed__________________"[17]

Refusing to sign the two statements, John instead took his case before the Adventist public in 1919 by publishing the 70-page pamphlet "Apostolic and Adventist Experience Compared" and the 99-page booklet "Some Individual Experience," both elaborate responses to Ballenger's charges that essentially reiterated what he had already said in his 1892 and 1905 books. In a subsequent letter, Edward wrote, "Again, I plead with you to either sign these statements or make a full and free confession." Instead, Loughborough called Ballenger "one out of six [people] that are going after 'the old man' in his 'declining days' for 'confession,'" all of whom had charged him with "knowingly and purposely" deceiving his readers. To all, he confessed that he had "a conscience 'void of offense toward God and man'" and signed himself, "Yours in hope of eternal life."[18]

So was Loughborough deceiving his readers or was he simply ignorant of the facts? Those were the two options Ballenger offered him. Yet between these polar opposites, a third possible explanation exists. The fact that Loughborough did not convert to Sabbatarian Adventism until the fall of 1852 seems relevant here. He told Ballenger that he had heard the "facts" about the "shut door" from the very "mouths" of pioneers such as Joseph Bates, James White, and Hiram Edson. True enough, no doubt, but by the time John interviewed them in the mid-1850s their views of the "shut door" had undergone a radical transformation from the "no more salvation for sinners" position of 1844 to an "open door" stance by 1851. Could it be, then, that in his writings Loughborough was simply doing what theologians call "eisegesis" (reading one's own opinions into the biblical text)? Is it possible that Loughborough (who had not participated in the internal doctrinal debates of 1850-1851) was so convinced that the pioneers had *always* held the beliefs they taught him in 1852 that he "read" those beliefs into the past? While he boasted of having read *all* the issues of *Present Truth* and the *Review* from 1849 onward, he was much less familiar with Adventist literature between 1844 and 1849. Finally, if one accepts his statement that his conscience was "devoid of offense against God and man" as proof that he was not being deceptive, then perhaps this third explanation (reading present beliefs into the past) sheds some light on a few of his historical misinterpretations.[19]

If Loughborough had not consciously deceived readers regarding the pioneers' views of the "shut door," when it came to interpreting his family genealogy, he was self-deceived. As mentioned in chapter 1, "Loofborough" is an Irish name meaning "town by the lake." Yet throughout his life John claimed to be the direct descendant of the nobleman Alexander Wedderburn, Lord Loughborough, the chancellor of George III in the 1780s. However, John either did not know or ignored the fact that Lord Loughborough never had children—and consequently no heirs—by his two wives. Yet after 1917 John wrote lengthy letters to his distant relatives Ross Loughborough (of Rochester, New York) and Alice Loughborough (of Los Angeles) seeking confirmation of what he believed were noble English roots. Frequently his diaries reveal that he devoted many hours to "working on the Loughborough and Norton pedigrees." If this harmless pursuit convinced few outside his family of the Loughborough's noble birth, no doubt it boosted his self-esteem in his declining years.[20]

Concerning his physical health, John described himself at 87 as "kindly cared for at this sanitarium" so that he was "free from bodily pains." Although "afflicted with the weakness of age" he told R. H. Kelley, "I sleep much, I do a little writing, responding to letters, and qestions [*sic*] of the past."[21] One visitor remarked in 1918: "His mind is still clear, active, and alert; his interest [is] still deepening and growing in the progress of the work of God; but he is weak in body."[22] After eating lunch with the patriarch, California Conference treasurer H. B. Thomas observed that John used a lot of olive oil, and perhaps that contributed to how well preserved John was.[23]

Yet even while John boasted that he expected to reach the age of 100, he made plans predicated on his mortality. In 1917 he drew up a will specifying that in the event of his death, his daughter Mary should receive the royalties from his books. After tithing them, she was to give half of the remainder to foreign missions and keep the other half for her own use. However, if she predeceased him, then the entire amount should go to foreign missions. In addition, he deposited $300 in an "Emergency Fund" to pay for his funeral and burial, which he insisted must be simple. "I do not wish more than an ordinary burial casket," he said, "and no tombstone. Simply a black redwood headboard painted white with [the] name J. N. Loughborough." Any money remaining in the fund after his burial should go to the sanitarium's foreign mission program.[24] Like other pioneer preachers, Loughborough chose to give most of his income to the church before he died.

By the end of World War I the number of those old preachers was shrinking rapidly. At the 1918 GC session in San Francisco, seven "Pioneer Workers"—J. H. Rogers, J. O. Corliss, H. W. Decker, H. W. Cottrell, S. N. Haskell, J. N. Loughborough, and G. I. Butler—had posed for a photograph. During the next few months, however, they began passing away. By the summer of 1918 both Rogers and Butler had died. Months later, Lewis Oswald Stowell, the Review pressman John had seen instantly healed after anointing and prayer in 1852, died at 89, the oldest Sabbathkeeper in the denomination.[25]

The passing of Hetty Haskell in 1919, on the day before the seventy-fifth anniversary of the Great Disappointment, however, brought Loughborough the deepest grief, for she had converted to Adventism after hearing his "Saints' Inheritance" sermon at the Oakland camp meeting of 1885. Active as a Bible instructor, a teacher at numerous Bible Institutes, and coeditor of the *Bible Training School*, Hetty had labored in England, Africa, and Australia with her evangelist husband, Stephen. During her short life (62 years) she had been miraculously healed half a dozen times in response to prayer. John wrote her obituaries in the *Review* and in the *Bible Training School* (which ceased publication in 1920).[26]

While John missed Hetty and her magazine, he still managed to keep up with about 17 weekly and monthly church publications in his late 80s. On a warm, sunny day, one could find him sitting in a comfortable chair under the oak trees that spanned the front lawn of the sanitarium, working his way through a huge stack of periodicals. As each one arrived in the mail, he opened it, laid it on the pile with the others, and as he had time, read every word from first page to last. Nothing pleased him more than following the progress of the Second Advent movement. To those who complained that they could not afford the *Review* and other church periodicals, he quoted a remark from H. L. Hastings: "If you want to economize, don't begin on your brains."[27]

LOUGHBOROUGH'S WRITINGS AND DIARY

To a surprising degree, Loughborough's books and pamphlets maintained their appeal to second- and third-generation Adventists. His *The Great Second Advent Movement* continued to be a best seller, in part because it was still required reading in many Adventist schools and for those wishing to pass the exam in SDA History for the Standard of Attainment Award. In the 1910s the GC Missionary Volunteer Society relied heavily on John's book for information concerning Adventist foreign missions and the education, health, and medical work in preparing its programs. According to evangelist B. G. Wilkinson and *Lake Union Herald* columnist C. A. Russell, the textbook could even win converts. "No one can read this book without having his faith more firmly rooted and grounded in the principles of the message," Russell wrote. "The many prophecies connected with the beginning of our work, as well as its growth and progress, surely point . . . to the fact that this is God's message for this time."[28] In addition, demand for reprints of *Saints' Inheritance* (1859) and *The Church* (1907) remained high, especially in Australia.[29]

As Loughborough had read every *Review* for 67 years, so he continued writing for it in his late 80s. His nine articles and ads from 1917 to 1919 discuss tithing, God's providential leading, making vows, showing love for others, Mrs. White's Civil War predictions, the sealing message, and how to face trials. As usual, each one reads like a Bible study or homily and is packed with biblical and Ellen White quotations.[30] During the same period, John penned articles for other church papers such as the *Atlantic Union Gleaner* (Ellen White's prophecies), the *Missionary Leader* (Rachel Preston and early Sabbathkeepers), the Australian *Signs of the Times* (Jonah and the whale), and (via the *Bible Traning School*'s contributions) the *Columbia Union Visitor* (conversion).[31]

No doubt believing that recycling material was a practice that should be sanctioned in one of advanced age (perhaps to save vital force), Loughborough either sent similar manuscripts to several church papers or they simply agreed that copying his articles would be acceptable. For example, the *Columbia Union Visitor* frequently reprinted articles he originally wrote for his favorite publication, the *Bible Training School*. Between January 1917 and January 1920 he wrote more articles (32) for *BTS* than for all other church papers combined. As usual, they covered a wide range of topics dealing with doctrine (spiritualism, speaking in tongues), successful Christian living (righteousness by faith), prophecy (Zionism, end-time predictions), and a final 10-part series on "Providence." Curiously, in his final article "Disappointed," he quoted from The Wisdom of Solomon (an apocryphal book found in Catholic Bibles), a practice most Adventist preachers had abandoned decades earlier.[32]

In the preface to his *Questions on the Sealing Message*, Loughborough provided a succinct answer for those who wondered why a man approaching 85 felt compelled to write so much. He quoted a testimony from Ellen White, then applied it to himself: "As those who have spent their lives in the service of God draw near the close of their earthly history," she wrote, "they will be impressed by the Holy Spirit to recount the experiences they have had in connection with His work."[33] It was this "commission" (as he called it) that impelled him to write. Moreover, the realization that, even though he was confined to a room at the sanitarium, he could still make a positive contribution to the future of his denomination drove the feeble octogenarian to mail *hundreds* of copies of his books, pamphlets, and sermons to Adventists around the world every month. At times it must have been exhausting work.[34]

During such times, the frail little man simply grabbed his cane and headed outdoors. In the warm California sunshine he gathered the acorns scattered across the sanitarium lawn, and when his bag was full, he walked up the hill to the "deer park" (or nature preserve) where a herd of deer awaited the treats he brought them every week. On other days he and Edith hiked to the reservoir for a chat in the shade. If inclement weather prevented such treks, John exercised in the sanitarium's gymnasium. In the evenings he and Edith attended religious services, band concerts, and stereopticon programs. Noticing that many of John's suits (which he wore every day) had a greenish sheen from too much wear, Edith chided him that the time had come to replace his threadbare Prince Albert suit (his favorite from Hope Brothers in London). After taking her teasing all summer, in September 1919 John consented to buy a new suit—the first gray serge he had ever owned. During his final four years at the sanitarium, Loughborough would demonstrate that despite his age he could still adapt to changing times.[35]

---

[1] JNL to delegates at the 1918 GC session, *GCB* (Apr. 12, 1918), p. 162.

[2] *RH*, Oct. 10, 1974, p. 31; Faye Jull to Brian Strayer, Feb. 20, May 26, and June 16, 2011.

[3] *PUR*, Oct. 21, 1974, p. 4; JNL, diary, March-April 1916, March, August, December 1917; April, October 1918; flyleaves of 1919 and 1920 diaries.

[4] JNL, diary, June 11, 1920.

[5] See JNL's diaries, September 1916-March 1924.

[6] JNL, diary, May and September 1917, February-March, November-December 1918, July 1919; *PUR*, Mar. 8, 1917, p. 1; *RH*, Mar. 22, 1917, p. 16; *PUR*, June 14, 1917, p. 1; *RH*, July 26, 1917, p. 17; *PUR*, Oct. 24, 1918, p. 2; *RH*, June 12, 1919, p. 28; *PUR*, June 5, 1919, p. 2.

[7] *RH*, May 9, 1918, p. 24; *Northern Union Reaper*, Apr. 23, 1918, p. 2; *GCB*, 1918, pp. 1-3, 148, 160, 179; GC Minutes, Feb. 5, 1918, p. 20; *YI*, May 28, 1918, p. 7.

[8] JNL, diary, June 1917, August 1918; *RH*, Sept. 13, 1917, p. 18; *PUR*, Nov. 4, 1968, p. 8; JNL to George A. Campbell, June 5, 1917, m. 006529, CAR; JNL to Wilfrid Balleau, Mar. 25, 1918, DF 230, CAR.

[9] Ernest Lloyd, *PUR*, Mar. 18, 1968, p. 1; Matilda Erickson, *YI*, Dec. 23, 1919, p. 3; JNL to C. E. Holmes, Apr. 29, 1920, C. E. Holmes Collection, 142-2, CAR; Mrs. Arthur E. Nelson, in *PUR*, July 1, 1968, p. 1.

[10] For a summary of Margaret Rowen's career in Adventism, see R. Schwarz and F. Greenleaf, *Light Bearers*, pp. 618, 619.

[11] JNL, diary, July 1917, May-June 1918, March and December 1919, January 1920.

[12] For a summary of the Ballengers' careers in Adventism, see R. Schwarz and F. Greenleaf, *Light Bearers*, p. 620.

[13] See, for example, Loughborough's statements in *The Great Second Advent Movement*, pp. 533, 536, 540-543, 552.

[14] E. S. Ballenger to JNL, Feb. 6, 1917, and JNL to Ballenger, Feb. 15, 1917, Ballenger-Mote Collection, C. 87, B. 35, F. 7, CAR.

[15] E. S. Ballenger to JNL, Aug. 25, 1918, Ballenger-Mote Collection, C. 87, B. 35, F. 7, CAR.

[16] JNL to E. S. Ballenger, Sept. 10 and 26, 1918, Ballenger-Mote Collection, C. 87, B. 35, F. 7, CAR.

[17] E. S. Ballenger to JNL, Oct. 27, 1918, Ballenger-Mote Collection, C. 87, B. 35, F. 7, CAR; JNL, "Individual Experience," p. iv.

[18] JNL, "Apostolic and Adventist Experience," pp. 1-48; "Individual Experience," pp. 7-9, 49-95; E. S. Ballenger to JNL, Dec. 25, 1918, Ballenger-Mote Collection, C. 87, B. 35, F. 7, CAR; JNL to E. S. Ballenger, Dec. 31, 1918, Ballenger-Mote Collection, C. 87,

B. 35, F. 7, CAR. See also JNL, *The Great Second Advent Movement*, pp. 488-511.

[19] Whichever viewpoint (deceit, ignorance, eisegesis) one accepts, Adventist historians and theologians for the past half century have known that Ballenger was correct on many points (including the pioneers' views on the "shut door") and that Loughborough was misinformed on this and many other points relating to the nature of Adventism in the 1840s and 1850s.

[20] See JNL, flyleaf of 1917 diary, October 1917, January 1918, November 1922.

[21] JNL to R. H. Kelley, Dec. 23, 1919, DF 230, CAR; see also *RH*, June 12, 1919, p. 32.

[22] *RH*, Apr. 18, 1918, p. 24.

[23] *PUR*, May 6, 1968, p. 2.

[24] JNL, final will and testament, Sept. 26, 1917 (to PPPA), and Oct. 8, 1917 (to St. Helena Sanitarium), m. 006529, CAR.

[25] Photo of seven "Pioneer Workers," *RH*, Apr. 11, 1918, p. 3; JNL, diary, July 1918; *RH*, Oct. 17, 1918, p. 12.

[26] JNL, diary, October 1919; *BTS*, November 1919, pp. 116, 118; *RH*, Nov. 20, 1919, pp. 24, 25. In the November 1919 issue of *BTS*, business manager Irene J. Cady stated: "On account of the death of the editor's wife . . . it has been decided to discontinue publishing the BIBLE TRAINING SCHOOL with the January [1920] number." However, the office in South Lancaster remained open a while longer to sell tracts, charts, books, and materials for the blind. It is also interesting to note that on the last page of the final issue, the Haskells placed an ad for JNL's book *Questions on the Sealing Message*. See *BTS*, January 1920, p. 33.

[27] JNL, flyleaf of 1918 diary; E. Robinson, *Lighter of Gospel Fires*, p. 169; *PUR*, Sept. 20, 1917, p. 3. The 17 periodicals Loughborough read in 1918 included *Review and Herald, Youth's Instructor, Liberty, Signs of the Times, Life and Health, Church Officers' Gazette, Literary Journal, Watchman, The Life Boat, Missionary Worker, Good Health, Present Truth* (British), *Sabbath School Worker, Bible Training School, Present Truth* (U.S.), *Gospel Herald,* and *Pacific Union Recorder.*

[28] *Church Officers' Gazette*, April 1917, p. 16; *Columbia Union Visitor*, May 24, 1917, p. 1; *YI*, Apr. 16, 1918, p. 14; *Missionary Worker*, August 1918, p. 6; C. A. Russell, *LUH*, Dec. 3, 1919, p. 11.

[29] *Union Conference Record*, Sept. 24, 1917, pp. 4, 6; *ST-A*, Sept. 23, 1918, p. 607.

[30] For JNL's *RH* articles, see Sept. 6, 1917, pp. 6, 7; Sept. 13, 1917, p. 9; Dec. 13, 1917, p. 9; Jan. 17, 1918, p. 6; Feb. 7, 1918, p. 1; Mar. 7, 1918, pp. 11-13; July 10, 1919, pp. 1, 2; and Oct. 16, 1919, pp. 9, 10.

[31] *AUG*, Nov. 7, 1917, pp. 1, 2; *Missionary Leader*, April 1918, p. 6; *ST-A*, July 15, 1918, pp. 442-444; *Columbia Union Visitor*, May 9, 1918, p. 4, and Oct. 17, 1918, p. 5.

[32] See JNL's *BTS* articles between January 1917 and January 1920. See "Disappointed," *BTS*, January 1920, pp. 11, 12, in which John quotes Wisdom of Solomon 5:1-5 to show that in the final day of judgment, the wicked and the righteous will have very different ends.

[33] EGW, *Testimonies for the Church*, vol. 7, p. 288.

[34] See, for example, JNL, diary, April and November 1917.

[35] See JNL, diary, April 1917-September 1919; Faye Jull to Brian Strayer, Jan. 25, 2011.

CHAPTER XXIV

THE LAST OF THE PIONEERS (1920-1924)

"People seem to have a strange idea of me. . . . As a sample here is a letter from Madison, Tennessee, which says. 'When you are in the East we would be pleased to have you call on us.' Just as though I was scouring the country as before I was laid up here. My sister [Minerva Jane Chapman] wrote me that one person wrote her that I 'was well, but doing nothing.' I think when he reads the seventeen articles which I have been working on for the last three years . . . that man will conclude that his 'Nothing,' is indeed 'Something.' "[1]

Although Loughborough left the sanitarium only three times between 1918 and 1921, as he told F. C. Gilbert, secretary of the GC Jewish Department, he had not been idle. While physically unable to attend camp meetings and constituency sessions, he still gave brief talks to local groups whenever invited to do so. To mark his eighty-eighth birthday in 1920, the Pacific Union Conference awarded him an "Honorary Ministerial Credential"—and he intended to make good use of it.[2]

In 1920 he rode in a friend's auto to Pacific Union College, and sitting in his rocking chair, spoke to the summer school teachers for half an hour about the beginnings of Adventist education while Harriet Sherrill, the art teacher, painted his portrait. Although he enjoyed the experience, he confessed that "it took me several days to recover."[3] He preferred speaking in the sanitarium or its immediate vicinity. Typically he would take a few minutes to share stories about the early years of Adventism at vespers and prayer meetings, in church worships and Communion services, and with Sabbath school classes. Often when Pastor Nelson had finished his

Sabbath sermon, Loughborough would rise from his easy chair at the front and share a story or two from the past that supported the pastor's topic. Likewise, even in his 90s, John occasionally assisted Nelson with special anointing services for the sick. His unblemished record for Sabbath school attendance won him blue ribbons every quarter, placing him on a list of only 16 Adventists in California who had achieved perfect attendance. "What an inspiration it is to Sabbath school members," the *Pacific Union Recorder* enthused, "to know that one of our oldest pioneers believes in regular and prompt attendance at the Sabbath school."[4]

When the 1922 GC session convened in San Francisco, church leaders sent greetings to the 90-year-old pioneer and informed him that they had appointed him a delegate-at-large and an honorary member of the GC Committee. The letter included his updated ministerial credentials signed by GC president William A. Spicer and GC Secretary Arthur G. Daniells. At one session, Daniells opined: "How I wish our dear Brother Loughborough, up there in St. Helena Sanitarium [50 miles away], could be down with us this morning."[5]

Instead, he sent greetings and an apology: "I have less physical strength than in January. I am getting so deaf that if I were in the meeting, I would hear but very little of what is said." He begged their permission to remain at the sanitarium and follow the proceedings in the *Bulletin* and the *Review*. "Be assured that my prayers will daily ascend to God," he told them, "that He may guide in the doings of the conference and in the plans for the rapid extension of this last message of mercy to the world."[6] But his prayers were not sufficient: they demanded his presence. They sent European Division president Louis Conradi with his wife and son to persuade John to attend the Sabbath services, and he agreed to go. Following the sermon, Spicer invited him to speak for five minutes. Instead, he talked for 20 minutes sitting in a rocking chair as the delegates, many with tears in their eyes, shouted hearty "Amens." Ignoring Edith Barnes' warnings that he was endangering his health, he declared, "I have a message for this people; I must deliver it."[7]

The delegates, however, did not know that for years John had been battling depression. In 1913 he had nearly succumbed to discouragement after listening to "one of the lies that the devil has been trying to tell me for a number of years. That lie was that the brethren did not want to hear from me. He would say, 'You keep still; they do not want to hear you.' . . . The devil tells me I have got old and had better keep still. He has told me that a thousand times, I suppose, . . . but if I understand that [White's] testimony, I can say something once and a while that will encourage the people."[8]

Ellen White's encouraging words at the 1913 GC session and the invitations from delegates at the 1918 and 1922 sessions had reassured the old man that he still had something worth sharing with third- and fourth-generation Adventists who needed to know about their past.

GENEROUS GIVER TO THE END

Living in retirement on a fixed income should have restricted John's financial ability to give to the church, but it did not. Indeed, his diaries and donor lists in Adventist publications demonstrate that he actually *increased* his giving in the 1920s. After sharing with Madison College president Edward A. Sutherland that someone had recently told him, "You seem to want a part in every enterprise that comes up," he said he wanted "to add my mite" to many good causes. In addition to tithe and Sabbath offerings, he gave to provide the poor with coal, distribute Adventist publications, send medical missionaries abroad, build rural schools for southern Blacks, and keep inner-city Rescue Homes operating. His last contribution of $13.20 four weeks before he died went for tithe, foreign missions, a church school, and the poor fund.[9]

Since the *Life Boat* raised funds primarily to assist the poor, Loughborough regularly supported its efforts. In 1924 its editor told readers that for "several years" John had furnished "a ton of coal each month for the five winter months to keep our girls and babies warm in the Home."[10] Clifford Howell, who had received only 60 cents for his first term of teaching in rural Tennessee, wept when Loughborough sent him a check for $5. It "made us feel that our work bore a very close relation to the rise and progress of the message," he recalled years later.[11] In addition to giving, John told a friend at Madison College: "Those who are feeble in health can pray for those in active labor. . . . Madison is on my daily prayer list."[12]

Yet as Loughborough approached his ninetieth year, those who visited him at the sanitarium expressed surprise at his mental acuity and physical health. One found him "enjoying a good degree of health, and for a man of his age [89] is quite active. . . . He is contented and happy, rejoicing in the blessed hope, which ever cheers his heart and buoys him up as the days go by."[13] When Eric and Matilda Andross visited him, "his hands trembled with age," but "his keen eyes shone with added luster" as he showed them some of his "relics."[13] Grateful to God for prolonging his life, John gave *two* birthday thank offerings each year: one for his natal day in 1832, the other for his conversion day in 1852, which he called "my twice-born day."[15]

On January 26, 1922, the members of the Pacific Union Conference Committee surprised Loughborough by sending him a generous check and a congratulatory letter for his ninetieth birthday. Expressing "pleasure that God has lengthened your life, that He has used you in the work of the third angel's message [for] so many years, and that you still live at this advanced age [when the average life span was about 55 to 60]," they sent him their "sincere love and esteem." Adding that "we reverence things that are old," they assured him that as "one who has exceeded the three score and ten [years] mark," he was "worthy of greater esteem and reverence." The letter closed with a promise: "We want you to know that while you live you are never forgotten."[16]

When F. C. Gilbert asked the secret of his longevity, John replied: "I have to live by [the] rule. To keep up I have to get just about so much sleep. [I] select a diet that I know has in it a good supply of the real nutritive elements, and then [I] do a thorough grinding of the food in my mouth, so that it shall be mingled with the saliva before it goes into the stomach. It is better to do the grinding in the mouth, than to increase the work of the stomach."[17] The fact that John still had all but three of his adult teeth certainly helped with the "grinding."

Reaching such an advanced age caused Loughborough to reflect on his life, and as he did so, he asked God to bring to mind any offense he had committed so that he could seek forgiveness. Suddenly, he recalled an incident from 1909 when he was preaching on "The Saints' Inheritance" at the Healdsburg SDA Church. Near the wood stove sat two boys, Alonzo Baker (15) and Bennie Grant (13), and as John waxed eloquent describing what life would be like in the "surbubs" of the New Jerusalem, the boys burst out laughing. Annoyed by the interruption, he had reprimanded them. "I wish that Lonnie Baker and Bennie Grant . . . would cease their whispering for I am saying some things I think they need [to hear] in order to be better Christian boys." He had warned them that if they did not behave, they would never be able to live even in the "surbubs" of that heavenly city. At the time, many of the hundreds of worshippers had turned in their seats and stared disapprovingly at the two delinquents.

Now, feeling that he had been too hard on the boys, John apologized for being "unnecessarily harsh and severe with you. . . . I humiliated you two boys in front of all that large congregation, a thing I should not have done. I am now reviewing my entire life to prepare to meet the Lord someday, and the episode . . . came vividly into my mind. I ask you . . . to forgive me. I have already asked God's forgiveness for this grievous thing I did. . . . I hope my rebuke did not discourage you two boys in your Christian experience, for I want to meet you both in the kingdom of heaven."[18]

Years later Alonzo Baker, then a leading Adventist historian in his own right, confessed that "we deserved his rebuke. It did both of us much good." Nonetheless, they saw in his humility "a sign of greatness of character."[19]

In part at least, John's character had grown stronger through the years by his choice of good reading, and having reached the age of 90, he was determined to continue the practice. Sitting in a wheelchair, spectacles on his nose, he enjoyed reading Adventist periodicals in the sanitarium's solarium (on rainy or cool days) and on the front lawn (on sunny days). At 91 he still managed to keep up with a dozen periodicals every week.[20]

Once a young nurse, seeing him reading the *Review*, remarked, "I hear that you have read every *Review* that has ever been printed." With a mischievous twinkle in his eyes, John replied, "No, sister, that is not true." Then, seeing the disappointment in her face, he added, "After I have finished reading this one, then I will have read them all!"[21]

In addition, he had read the entire Bible through every year since his conversion in 1852. Describing it as "a loving letter from our Heavenly Father," a reprinted letter to a friend showed readers of the *Youth's Instructor* that a few weeks before his ninetieth birthday that "[he] started [his] seventieth reading of the Old Testament, and [his] seventy-first reading of the New Testament." In fact, by the time they died, the three oldest Adventist pioneers had read their Bibles a total of 216 times (J. O. Corliss, 67 times; S. N. Haskell, 73 times; and J. N. Loughborough, 76 times).[22] Not content simply to *read* the *words* of Holy Writ, each time he studied his Bible, John kept a pen and pad of paper nearby so that he could add to his lists of divine promises and fulfilled prophecies.[23] He followed the same procedure with Ellen White's writings: he not only annotated them, but also compiled indexes and lists of fulfilled predictions. In less than three weeks in February 1922 he finished White's *Acts of the Apostles, Steps to Christ,* and *Christ's Object Lessons,* truly a reading marathon.[24]

LOUGHBOROUGH'S LAST WRITINGS

In addition to his remarkable feats of reading, John churned out manuscripts for church publications at an amazing rate. In 1920 the General Conference Fireside Correspondence School (later Griggs University) asked his help in preparing lessons, quizzes, and tests to accompany an Adventist history course that used *The Great Second Advent Movement* as a textbook. The GC Missionary Volunteer Department also appropriated some of his questions on its exam for the Standard of Attainment in church history. The *Youth's Instructor* introduced a regular question-and-answer column with historical teasers taken from his book. Then John (who would have made a great game show host) created a 17-part series called "Questions and Answers" focusing on aspects of Adventist history ("Shut Door" for $50, please?). In 1923 and 1924 the junior and senior Missionary Volunteer devotional books were based on *The Great Second Advent Movement*—as were several MV programs. In fact, one could still purchase the 20-year-old textbook in both cloth and paper editions.[25]

Partly this was due to John's popular writing style, which his three most successful imitators—Ernest Lloyd, LeRoy E. Froom, and Arthur W. Spalding—described as "distinctly his own." Unlike "the more solid and sometimes ponderous" compositions of other Adventist writers, Loughborough filled his books with "incident and anecdotal illustrations." Thus when compared with the weighty and often dry prose of pioneers such as Joseph Bates, James White, John Andrews, and Uriah Smith, Loughborough's contributions "stood out in sunny relief" for their brevity, variety, and use of narrative techniques.[26]

John's submissions to the *Review* in the 1920s reflect this sunny disposition. In contrast with his doctrinally oriented Bible studies of the 1850s and 1860s, his later work focuses more on helping believers get to know Jesus better (his four-part series "Walking With God" in 1920) and appreciate His leading in the Adventist past (the 11-part series "Second Advent Movement" in 1921). To help ground the "Flapper Generation" in Adventist history, the *Review* printed this "Second Advent Experiences" series in 1923.[27]

Originally, however, Loughborough had prepared a 17-part series on Adventist history for the *Review*. Consequently, editor F. M. Wilcox's letter explaining why he could not print seven of the articles came as quite a shock to the old man. Tactfully, Wilcox told John that while readers loved his stories, the articles focusing on the pioneers' "shut door" views flew in the face of recent evidence showing that, in fact, James and Ellen White (among others) did believe that after October 22, 1844, there was "no more mercy for sinners," and that many did not abandon this stance until 1851. If the paper published those articles, Wilcox warned (no doubt with Ballenger in mind), "it would call forth considerable protest." Instead, he suggested that his staff could edit the 17 articles down to 10 in such a way that no one would know the difference. "I do not dispute your conclusion," the editor said, "but when you present arguments on one side, and leading brethren present arguments on the other side, it seems to me that until the questions are harmonized the only thing I can do is to keep out of the controversy so far as the church is concerned."[28]

Loughborough's response to this masterpiece of diplomacy indicated that, since the Holy Spirit had inspired him to write the articles on the "shut door," he hoped that the *Review* would print them in full and that the Review and Herald press would publish them as a pamphlet to counteract charges D. M. Canright had made against the pioneers in his books. If neither chose to do so, then he wanted his 17 articles returned. Unfortunately, his letter reached the *Review* too late to stop the presses. Three weeks later Wilcox apologized profusely for printing the 10-article version against Loughborough's wishes. Assuring the aged patriarch that "anything you may write will have most faithful consideration," Wilcox added, "[but] I do not feel that the *Review* is a forum in which this matter [the "shut door"] should be thrashed out."[29]

Loughborough's contributions to other church periodicals proved far less controversial. Between 1920 and 1924 he sent 12 articles to the *Lake Union Herald* (autobiographical sketches), two to the Australian *Signs of the Times* (the Sabbath, Jonah), and one to the *Western Canadian Tidings* (tithing miracles), in addition to his ads boosting the *Watchman Magazine* in several union papers.[30]

While John's stories kept memories of the pioneers alive in the minds of Adventist readers, by the 1920s most of the church founders had passed from the scene. To commemorate them, the GC Home Missionary Department in 1921 produced the first "Pioneers Calendar," a large wall calendar with portraits and biographical sketches of 14 early church leaders. It also included important dates in Adventist history, North American sunset tables, weekly prayer and missionary meeting appointments, and inspiring quotations. "May it call us all to the earnestness, consecration, and faithfulness in service for God shown by these worthy examples," ads exhorted.[31]

In the summer of 1920 fellow pioneer Stephen Haskell had dropped by the sanitarium to visit with John. The two bearded patriarchs, dressed in their black frock coats and holding Bibles in their hands, had posed for the camera as they sat in rocking chairs enjoying the warm California sun. The following spring, they once again donned their black suits, black bow ties, black vests, and held their black Bibles as they posed for the camera. Then they talked about old times and had "a praying season" together. It would be their final visit. On October 10, 1922, John wrote in his diary: "Elder S. N. Haskell died at ten o'clock last night."[32] A few months earlier M. C. Israel, the pioneer evangelist and missionary to Australia and New Zealand whom Loughborough ordained in 1878, had also passed away.[33]

The harshest blow fell on April 25, 1923, when a telegram arrived informing him that his sister Minerva Jane (Loughborough) Chapman (almost 94) had died in Battle Creek. Although her husband Oscar Chapman had never converted to Seventh-day Adventism, they had moved to Battle Creek in 1866, and she began work as a typesetter at the Review and Herald press. Between 1866 and 1889 she had served the church as treasurer and secretary of the SDA Publishing Association, treasurer and corresponding secretary of the General Conference, and editor of the *Youth's Instructor*, before retiring in 1893. Feeling weary while doing housework, she had lain down to rest and never woke up. GC secretary A. G. Daniells praised her as "an earnest, tireless home missionary, a faithful member of the Sabbath school, a lover of mankind, and a Christian whose life won the confidence of all who knew her." The *Review* called her a woman of God, faithful in all her service.[34] Her death severed John's last living link to his boyhood in Victor.

A few months later Loughborough's longtime preaching partner J. O. Corliss died in September of 1923, and once again John noted another passing in his diary. Weeks before his death, however, Corliss had sent an article to the *Review* that appeared posthumously. In it, he described Loughborough as "whole-hearted," "an efficient laborer" for the truth, "a close observer . . . [with] a retentive memory" who was now "passing into suitably ripened years."[35]

LOUGHBOROUGH'S DIARY

At times, however, John felt "overripe" as the physical limitations of aging gradually restricted his movements. Both his eyesight and his hearing had diminished markedly by 1920. Although he refused to pose for photos with his glasses on, he wore them constantly to read periodicals, write letters, and type manuscripts on his new Smith Premier Typewriter. Just as his trusty hickory cane had become his right-hand fulcrum, so Edith supported his left arm whenever they left the sanitarium. On sunny days one could see them walking to the laundry, the store, or the post office; ambling across the bridge and up to the waterfalls; down to the food factory; or up the road to feed acorns to the deer (now only a buck and two does).

Despite poor hearing, John loved chatting with old friends, and during his last four years at the sanitarium he entertained a constant stream of them. His most frequent visitors included W. C. White, C. H. Jones, Eugene Farnsworth, and F. C. Gilbert. Occasionally PUC students stopped by to visit. Despite their doctrinal differences, E. S. Ballenger now and then dropped in for a chat. Likewise, Loughborough's frequent visits with and letters to Arthur W. Spalding, F. M. Wilcox, and L. E. Froom in 1922-1923 may indicate that the aged "Elijah" was passing the mantle of writing apologetic history to the "Elishas" of a new generation. Through the 1960s the three men followed the "Loughborough model" of portraying the history of the church in a positive light.

Although his daughter Mary and her husband John Ireland had lived on the East Coast since 1916, they came once a year and spent several days with him as well. But as John's infirmities increased after 1920, he leaned on his caretaker Edith Barnes for assistance. In addition to going on walks with him, Edith (who stayed in the nurses' dorm) took him on scenic drives to Lodi, to July 4 celebrations, and to the polling places to cast his vote. Back in his room at the sanitarium, she read to him, mended his clothing, and helped him make neckties and repair his typewriter. Edith probably assisted him in August 1923 when, at age 91, Loughborough presided at the marriage of John Schroder and Esther Miller in the sanitarium parlor. It would be his last wedding service.[36]

Getting from his fifth-floor room to the parlor for meals was becoming increasingly difficult, especially on days when the elevator was not working. At such times he had to hobble down five flights of stairs, his left hand gripping the railing while using his right to keep the cane balanced. It was quite a feat for an old man. On May 21, 1923, he slipped and fell, wrenching his back. For the next five weeks he was confined to his bed or a wheelchair. Nurses gave him hot fomentations and monitored his progress around the clock. Although ambulatory by the end of June, he did not make a full recovery, but gradually grew weaker.[37]

Unable to keep his diary up to date, he dictated the words to Davis, who wrote most of the entries for the last half of 1923. Then, perhaps fearing that some of his letters and manuscripts might fall into the wrong hands after he was gone, John began "tearing up old papers." He even instructed "a young nurse" to destroy his diaries after his death—but she later refused to do so, thereby earning the gratitude of this biographer and hundreds of future readers.[38]

Deluged with a tsunami of get-well cards and queries, Loughborough requested the *Review* to instruct readers not to write to him. Editor Wilcox complied, stating that "owing to the increasing infirmities of old age, he has been confined to his bed, with a nurse in attendance." While "cheerful and hopeful as ever," he "is in no condition to consider or reply to questions that are sent to him by correspondents. He therefore makes earnest request that he shall not be troubled with letters from any quarter, as he is unable to answer them." Wilcox further suggested "that we shall permit him, in the closing days of his life, to have that restful repose, free from all needless care and burden, which surely is his due after his long years of service."[39] In that spirit, in February and March of 1924 many old friends and family members rallied to relieve John of financial burdens by secretly paying his bills at the sanitarium and any other outstanding debts.[40]

THE LAST OF THE PIONEERS

Relieved that his bills had been paid, the 92-year-old patriarch could face the future unafraid. Within five years, the nation would be engulfed in a Great Depression. A decade later, the world would be at war for the second time—but those events were not part of *his* future. For him, the future ended at 9:20 a.m. on Monday, April 7, 1924, when he lost consciousness and passed to his rest. The funeral, presided over by his old friends A. G. Daniells, W. C. White, and M. C. Wilcox, took place in the St. Helena Sanitarium chapel, where his body lay in a simple redwood casket, his right hand holding a bright-red rose over his heart, and on his chest a plaque declaring, "My trust is in Christ, the Rose of Sharon [Song of Solomon 2:1]."[41]

John had been surrounded by Adventist friends in life, and so he would be in death. Today more than 400 Adventist graves cluster around his burial spot in St. Helena Cemetery. Although he had asked that only a simple wooden board with his name on it mark his final resting place, his friends in the St. Helena SDA Church, at Pacific Union College, and on the General Conference Committee decided in 1967 that he deserved something better than that. Following a fund-raising campaign spearheaded by the Graves for Pioneers Committee, they purchased a small marble stone and installed new cement curbing around the plot. The marker reads: "John N. Loughborough, 1832-1924. First Seventh-day Adventist minister in California, 1868. Wife Maggie A., died Mar. 24, 1875. Wife Anna M., died May 31, 1907, and Baby [Eliza Eunice] Loughborough." Then on May 20, around 150 people gathered for a memorial service during which Arthur White gave a sketch of J. N. Loughborough's life—just as Loughborough had read a life sketch of *his* grandmother Ellen White half a century earlier.[42]

Tributes to Loughborough the year before his death had called him "the oldest living pioneer of the third angel's message" and "the only living representative of the early pioneers."[43] Immediately following his death, Adventist leaders and periodicals hailed him as "our esteemed [or revered] brother," "a faithful soldier of the cross," "one of the princes in our Israel," and "the last link binding us to the early days of this movement."[44] Those who knew him best called him "a beautiful example of faith, zeal, steadfastness, and self-sacrifice." Many praised him for his "earnestness and consecration and simplicity," while others remembered his calm demeanor, dynamic preaching, and sense of humor.[45]

The fact that J. N. Loughborough was "the last of the pioneers," however, created a doctrinal dilemma for many of his contemporaries. For decades they had taught that Christ's words in Matthew 24:34 ("This generation shall not pass, till all these things be fulfilled") referred to those who had seen the "falling of the stars" (meteorite shower) in 1833 and the comet of 1844. Loughborough, who had been a year old in 1833 and 12 years old in 1844, represented "this generation" who should live to see the Second Coming of Christ. The fact that before he died Loughborough had compiled a list of 20 pioneers who had gone through "the 1844 Movement" (and a longer list of 22 preachers in 1858 who had not) shows that he, too, was thinking about the fulfillment of Christ's promise. In 1913 the *Workers' Bulletin* had stated that "the whitened heads of some of these pioneers . . . gives us some idea of the shortness of time." But time had continued another decade and all the pioneers of "this generation" had died. Harsh reality forced many to search for a new understanding of the meaning of "this generation" and to redefine the word "soon" in relation to the Second Advent.[46]

But that debate would continue without him. His main concern was that Jesus had written his name on that heavenly list known as the Book of Life or "God's Album."

"There is another album,
Filled with leaves of spotless white,
Where no name is ever tarnished
But forever pure and bright,
In the Book of Life—God's album,
May your name be penned with care
And may all who here have written
Write their names forever there."[47]

---

[1] JNL to F. C. Gilbert, Mar. 29, 1921, Adventist Heritage Room, LLU.

[2] JNL to Lida F. Scott, Sept. 20, 1921, Adventist Heritage Room, LLU; *PUR,* Feb. 26, 1920, p. 1.

[3] *PUR,* July 8, 1920, p. 8; *RH,* Apr. 27, 1922, p. 24; *PUR,* Apr. 15, 1968, p. 2. Dr. G. F. Wolfkill stated in 1968 that the portrait hung on the wall in PUC's library.

[4] JNL, diary, May, September, November-December 1920; December 1921; March-April, July-August, December 1922; February 1923; *PUR,* Apr. 22, 1968, p. 1; *PUR,* Jan. 18, 1923, p. 5; *PUR,* Feb. 8, 1923, p. 4.

[5] GC Minutes, May 7, 1922, p. 79 and Oct. 9, 1923, p. 225; *RH,* June 5, 1922, p. 29; *GCB* (1922), pp. 13, 306, 333; JNL's ministerial credentials (1922), CAR. Benjamin McArthur, author of a forthcoming biography of A. G. Daniells, suggested to me with tongue in cheek that probably Daniells wanted Loughborough to attend the GC session because he needed his vote and his influence to get reelected as GC president. If that was indeed part of Daniells' "hidden agenda," it did not bring him the success he sought.

[6] JNL to GC delegates, *GCB* (1922), p. 13.

[7] JNL, diary, June 1922; *GCB* (1922), p. 224; *Church Officers' Gazette*, August 1944, pp. 8-10.

[8] JNL to delegates at 1913 GC, *RH,* June 12, 1913, pp. 5, 6.

[9] *The Life Boat*, February 1920, p. 50, and September 1920, pp. 270, 271; JNL to E. A. Sutherland, July 6, 1920, CAR; JNL, flyleaf of 1921 diary and November 1921; flyleaf of 1922 diary; offering receipt from St. Helena SDA Church, Mar. 2, 1924, CAR.

[10] *The Life Boat*, May 1924, p. 154.

[11] Clifford G. Howell, *Columbia Union Visitor*, Apr. 6, 1933, pp. 1, 2.

[12] JNL to Lida F. Scott, July 20, 1920, m. 006529, CAR.

[13] Andrew Nelson, *RH*, July 22, 1920, p. 21.

[14] Matilda Erickson Andross, *Story of the Advent Message* (Washington, D.C.: Review and Herald Pub. Assn., 1926), p. 75.

[15] L. Schmitke, *Heavenly Visions*, p. 2.

[16] PUC Committee to JNL, Jan. 26, 1922, DF 230, CAR.

[17] JNL to F. C. Gilbert, Jan. 7, 1923, m. 006529, CAR.

[18] JNL to Alonzo Baker and Bennie Grant, 1923, quoted in N. Collins, *Heartwarming Stories*, book 2, p. 185, and in *PUR*, Aug. 26, 1968, pp. 1, 2. I am also grateful to Robert Johnston for sharing Alonzo Baker's version of the incident that he heard many years ago at a faculty banquet at Andrews University. The term "suburbs" was then just coming into common usage and, as we have seen, Loughborough never met a new word he couldn't misspell or mispronounce.

[19] *PUR*, Aug. 26, 1968, pp. 1, 2.

[20] These included *Signs of the Times, Our Little Friend, Watchman Magazine, Medical Evangelist, Review and Herald, Youth's Instructor, Church Officers' Gazette, Liberty, Gospel Herald, Pacific Union Recorder, Asiatic Outlook,* and *The Life Boat.*

[21] A. V. Larson told this story in *PUR,* Dec. 9, 1968, p. 2, as did Collins in *Heartwarming Stories*, book 2, p. 186.

[22] These phenomenal statistics are verified in *Central Union Outlook*, Oct. 26, 1920, p. 1; *YI,* May 16, 1922, p. 4; *NPUG*, Dec. 31, 1940, p. 4; *RH*, Oct. 2, 1952, p. 6.

[23] Eventually, Loughborough tallied 3,573 Bible promises and concluded that 85 percent of all Bible prophecies had been fulfilled by 1924. See *PUR*, Mar. 3, 1937, p. 10; *RH,* Oct. 21, 1954, p. 13; *RH*, May 21, 1970, p. 20.

[24] JNL, diary, February 1922.

[25] JNL, diary, January 1921; *Eastern Tidings*, Aug. 15, 1920, p. 4; *Missionary Worker*, Aug. 18, 1920, p. 8; JNL, "Q&A," typed manuscript, c. 1921; *YI*, Apr. 3, 1923, p. 16; *YI*, Apr. 10, 1923, p. 16; *YI*, Apr. 17, 1923, p. 2; *Church Officers' Gazette*, October 1923, p. 11; *Eastern Canadian Messenger*, Feb. 12, 1924, p. 7; *Church Officers' Gazette*, August 1924, p. 8; *NPUG*, Nov. 20, 1924, p. 2.

[26] A. Spalding, *Origin and History*, vol. 1, p. 211; LeRoy E. Froom, *The Prophetic Faith of Our Fathers: New World Recovery and Consummation of Prophetic Interpretation*, vol. 4 (Washington, D.C.: Review and Herald Pub. Assn., 1954), p. 1106; Ernest Lloyd, "Memories of Elder J. N. Loughborough," cited by L. Schmitke, in *Heavenly Visions*, p. 1.

[27] For JNL's "Walking With God" series, see *RH,* Apr. 8, 1920, pp. 8, 9; Apr. 15,

1920, pp. 7, 8; Apr. 22, 1920, pp. 11, 12; May 6, 1920, pp. 10, 11. For his "Second Advent Movement" series, see *RH,* July 28, 1921, pp. 7, 8; Aug. 4, 1921, p. 7; Aug. 11, 1921, pp. 6, 7; Aug. 18, 1921, pp. 4-6; Aug. 25, 1921, pp. 5, 6; Sept. 1, 1921, p. 7; Sept. 8, 1921, pp. 4, 5; Sept. 15, 1921, p. 5; Oct. 13, 1921, pp. 7, 8; Oct. 20, 1921, pp. 6, 7; and Oct. 27, 1921, pp. 5, 6. For the reprise of "Second Advent Experience," see *RH,* June 7, 1923, p. 8; June 14, 1923, pp. 7, 8; June 21, 1923, pp. 5, 6; June 28, 1923, pp. 9, 10; July 5, 1923, p. 5; July 12, 1923, p. 18; July 26, 1923, p. 5; Aug. 2, 1923, p. 6.

[28] F. M. Wilcox to JNL, Sept. 29, 1921, m. 013983, CAR.

[29] JNL to F. M. Wilcox, Oct. 10, 1921, and F. M. Wilcox to JNL, Oct. 30, 1921, m. 013983, CAR.

[30] *ST-A,* Aug. 21, 1922, p. 135; *ST-A,* Mar. 10, 1924, pp. 11, 12; *Church Officers' Gazette*, January 1921, pp. 1, 2; *LUH*, almost weekly between June 20 and September 26, 1923; *Western Canadian Tidings*, Oct. 24, 1923, p. 3. For blurbs on *Watchman Magazine*, see *Southwestern Union Record*, July 3, 1923, p. 1; *Northern Union Reaper*, July 10, 1923, p. 6; *Central Union Outlook*, July 10, 1923, p. 7; *Field Tidings*, July 18, 1923, pp. 1, 2; *Columbia Union Visitor*, July 19, 1923, p. 1; *Atlantic Union Gleaner*, Aug. 22, 1923, p. 3.

[31] *RH,* Nov. 17, 1921, p. 23; *NPUG,* Nov. 17, 1921, p. 2.

[32] *RH,* May 6, 1926, p. 6; JNL, diary, April, May, and October 1922; *ST*, Aug. 21, 1923, p. 9.

[33] *Union Conference Record*, Apr. 3, 1922, p. 2.

[34] JNL, diary, April 1923; "Chapman, Minerva Jane Loughborough," in *SDA Encyclopedia*, vol. 10, p. 320; *RH,* May 10, 1923, p. 24; *RH,* Jan. 3, 1924, p. 22.

[35] JNL, diary, September 1923; J. O. Corliss, *RH,* Nov. 29, 1923, p. 9.

[36] JNL, diaries, February 1920-December 1923.

[37] JNL, diary, May-July, October 1923; *RH,* July 5, 1923, p. 24.

[38] JNL, diary, March 1922; *PUR,* Aug. 19, 1968, p. 8; Eldyn Karr, *RH,* June 1, 1972, pp. 16, 17. This biographer suspects, however, that Loughborough might have had posterity in mind, because from time to time his diary entries seem to be addressing someone other than himself. See entries for January 18, 1921 ("Excuse the blunder"); April 13, 1921 ("Reading papers of our denomination"); October 22, 1922 ("Wrote to my sister Jane"); April 25, 1923 ("My sister Jane died 8 AM").

[39] *RH,* Feb. 7, 1924, p. 24.

[40] St. Helena Sanitarium receipt for $30 to Elder A. Nelson, Mar. 2, 1924; St. Helena Sanitarium receipts and bills for March and April 1924, m. 006529, CAR; Mrs. J. J. Ireland to H. G. Childs, and Mrs. J. J. Ireland to E. R. Palmer, Dec. 1, 1924, m. 006529, CAR.

[41] *RH,* Apr. 17, 1924, p. 24; *NPUG,* Apr. 17, 1924, p. 8; JNL, funeral note, Aug. 20, 1918, m. 006529, CAR; *PUR,* June 19, 1924, p. 6; GC Minutes, Apr. 7, 1924, p. 67.

[42] Photo of J. N. Loughborough's tombstone, CAR; GC Minutes, July 13, 1967, p. 18; *PUR,* July 17, 1967, p. 1; *PUR,* June 3, 1968, p. 1; *RH,* Nov. 28, 1968, p. 3.

[43] *Western Canadian Tidings*, Apr. 11, 1923, p. 4; *LUH,* June 20, 1923, p. 12.

[44] *AUG*, Apr. 16, 1924, p. 8; *Union Conference Record,* June 2, 1924, p. 8; *RH,* Apr. 17, 1924, p. 24; *RH,* May 27, 1926, p. 14; GC Minutes, Apr. 7, 1924, p. 67; M. Olsen, *Origin and Progress*, pp. 728, 729.

[45] *RH,* June 19, 1924, pp. 17, 24; memories of Loughborough originally published in the *Pacific Union Recorder*, DF 230, CAR.

[46] *Workers' Bulletin*, May 27, 1913, p. 3. Curiously, Loughborough's two lists were printed in the *Review and Herald,* Sept. 18, 1924, p. 63.

[47] Loradale, "God's Album," c. 1893, JNL Notebooks, CAR.

EPILOGUE

THE LOUGHBOROUGH LEGEND AND LEGACY

"I greatly desire that the old soldiers of the cross, those grown gray in the Master's service, shall continue to bear their testimony right to the point, in order that those younger in the faith may understand that the messages which the Lord gave us in the past are very important at this stage of the earth's history. Our past experience has not lost one jot of its force. . . . The testimony of the aged ministers will ever be a help and a blessing to the church."[1]

When Ellen White spoke those words as part of her "charge to the aged pioneers" at the 1913 GC session, only about 12 "soldiers of the cross" remained. Barely half a dozen "aged ministers" mustered out for a photo shoot at the 1918 GC session, and by 1922 only Haskell, Corliss, Loughborough, and Allen Moon remained. In 1926, when the GC *Bulletin* printed a montage of 10 pioneer preachers, not one of the 10 remained alive.[2]

In every group photograph this biographer has seen depicting nineteenth-century Adventist pioneers, Loughborough (at 5'4" and 110 pounds) "stands out" as the shortest and thinnest minister in the denomination (with the possible exception of Ellet J. Waggoner, who was barely five feet tall). But if Loughborough was physically a leprechaun among men, the lengthening shadow of his influence after death made him a giant among his peers. While a few of the pioneers were memorialized in brick and stone long *after* they died (i.e., the James White Home for the Aged in Battle Creek, the Ellen White Memorial Hospital in Los Angeles, the Bates Memorial High School in Trinidad, and the J. G. Matteson Institute of Evangelism in Norway), Loughborough received tangible honors even during his lifetime.

In 1897 J. E. Fulton, missionary to Fiji, christened his newest boat *The Loughborough*. Thirty feet long with a 10-foot beam, mainsail, jib, and hatchway, this magnificent craft plied the waters among the 80 inhabited islands of Fiji for many years.[3] The alumni association of Pacific Union College established in 1926 a museum containing 35 curios, including the 1880s typewriter that Annie and John used to type the manuscript for *Rise and Progress* and the *The Great Second Advent Movement*. For decades after that, an oil portrait of Loughborough hung on the wall of Pacific Union College's library, and the pulpit in which he had preached adorned the platform of the St. Helena Sanitarium SDA Church. General Conference president R. R. Figuhr at the 1962 GC session received a gavel created from a wooden block Loughborough had brought back from Panama on his trip to California in 1868.[4]

With every passing decade, the reputation of this tiny man seemed to grow larger in the collective Adventist psyche. A. V. Farnsworth considered him one of the "faithful apostles" in 1929; J. E. Fulton invoked his "sacred" memory in a sermon on sacrifice in 1932; and H. F. Brown called him "a good prophet" in 1934. Even Alonzo Baker, whom as a boy Loughborough had publicly rebuked, praised him as one of the "dauntless heralds of the remnant church." Reminiscing about their friendship, Dr. Daniel Kress hailed John as one of those "men of God, . . . whom I revered." In 1950 Adventist author and editor Raymond Cottrell identified S. N. Haskell, W. C. White, and J. N. Loughborough as "apostles of the message." Nearly a half century later *North Pacific Union Gleaner* editor Ed Schwisow compared Loughborough (who in life had avoided *all* sports) to a "small forward" on a basketball team who, with the help of "great centers" such as James White, "power forwards" such as J. N. Andrews, and the "team psychologist visionary" (Ellen White), had led the "team" (church) to "championship glory."[5]

Still other Adventists such as Dr. Owen Parrett recalled Loughborough's amazing memory for details. Once during Parrett's student days at the College of Medical Evangelists (now Loma Linda University), he passed John on the sidewalk. Pointing to a flowerbed, Loughborough had remarked that a year ago a certain kind of flowers had been planted in that plat, but since then they had been removed. During the previous year he had been all over Europe, meeting dozens of people, preaching scores of sermons, and traveling hundreds of miles, yet he still remembered what flowers had been planted in which flowerbeds on campus![6]

THE APOCRYPHAL LOUGHBOROUGH

As previous chapters have shown, however, John's memory sometimes failed him, and it occasionally led him to make statements that cannot be buttressed by the facts. Repeatedly throughout his writings, for example, he claimed to have seen Ellen White "in open vision" (daytime public visions) "fifty times," "nearly fifty times," "more than forty times," and "forty times" (the number diminished toward the end of his life). Yet in his "Comprehensive Index" to Loughborough's *Rise and Progress*, Ronald Graybill tallied only 40 visions referred to in *Rise and Progress*—and Loughborough indicates that he was present at only 14 of those. Although the section on "Visions" in the three-volume *Comprehensive Index to the Writings of Ellen G. White* indicates that she had about 100 visions between 1852 (when John first met her) and 1868 (when he left for California), the fact that the two of them were often miles (even states) apart would have made it nearly impossible for him to have witnessed her in vision 50 times. Moreover, it is somewhat curious that a blue-ribbon list-maker who revered Mrs. White as a prophet of God never seems to have compiled a list of the dates, places, and subject matter of those experiences he had observed (as he did with the fulfillments of her predictions).[7]

Loughborough also invoked White's authority after 1917 to encourage Adventists to buy and read the *Review*. In 1919 he stated that "not long before her last illness" in 1915 Mrs. White had declared: "To those who fail to read the *Review* and keep track of the progress of the work, the loud cry of the message may come, and they [will] not know it." Between 1917 and 1939 that quote, which appeared 17 times in six different Adventist periodicals, probably sold many subscriptions to the *Review*—especially since prominent church figures loved to repeat it. Seeking to give the statement some historical cachet, E. R. Corder declared in 1930 that it appeared in the May 6, 1862 issue of the *Review*. But that issue contains no articles, reports, or letters by Loughborough and only one article by Ellen White ("The Cause in Northern Wisconsin"), which does not contain the above quote.[8]

In fact, the White Estate has informed this biographer that Mrs. White never made such a statement. What John *probably* heard her say (about 1881) was that "those who consent to do without the *Review and Herald* lose much. Through its pages Christ may speak to them in warnings, in reproofs and counsel, which would change the current of their thoughts and be to them as the bread of life." Four decades later, however, John may have conflated White's statement about not reading the *Review* with his current research on the "sealing message" and come up with the "Loud [but false] Cry" instead.[9]

To help the "Loughborough legend" along, others have made claims concerning the last of the pioneers that defy chronology and logic. For example, in 1955 one woman had "an early impression" of hearing him describe the "falling of the stars" as he remembered seeing the event in 1833—but little Johnny was not quite 2 years old when those meteors crashed to earth! In an article entitled "The Young Guard" in 1977 the author asserted that John had been only 17 when he converted to Sabbatarian Adventism when in fact he had been almost 21. Then in the 1980s the church rejoiced to hear that Adventist Historic Properties, Inc., (AHP) had purchased the Loughboroughs' 1854 home in Battle Creek and would soon restore it. A few years later, however, AHP was forced to admit that, due to inadequate deeds research, they had bought the *wrong house*—and that wreckers had demolished the *real* Loughborough house![10]

Had he been alive, of course, John could have prevented that gaffe, yet in his own lifetime he made plenty of mistakes (historical and otherwise). Nonetheless, the "Loughborough legend" ascribed to him an aura of accuracy he sometimes did not deserve. Church leaders wishing to sell more copies of his *The Great Second Advent Movement* (1905), for example, described it as one of the "reliable sources" and its author as "an authority" on Adventist history. As late as the 1950s those writing articles for Adventist publications continued to cite John's book.[11]

But a few strident voices—both inside and outside of the church—felt the time had come to dispense with Loughborough's view of history. In "An Open Letter to Seventh-day Adventists" in 1934, W. H. Brown asserted that the editor of *The Gathering Call* mistakenly suggested that *The Great Second Advent Movement* should be "revised" by being "cast [into] the flames" as it "is so unreliable that it ought to be entirely discarded."[12]

A decade later the rising church historian Arthur W. Spalding openly questioned some of Loughborough's assertions concerning the Millerite movement (although he followed the pioneer's anecdotal and apologetic approach to history in his books). Everett Dick, a Union College history professor, began charting a more scholarly course for Adventist history with his *Founders of the Message* in 1939, widely advertised as a "reference book for ministers, teachers, and all others who may be interested in refreshing, scholarly glimpses into the lives of the sturdy characters who played such prominent parts as founders of the advent message." Unfortunately, Dick's critical-analytical approach to the past did not set well with some church leaders. Consequently, they refused to publish his dissertation on the Millerite movement.[13]

Yet the growing demand for John's history books during the next half century amply demonstrates that for most Adventists, there was only *one way* to write SDA history, and that was Loughborough's. Well into the 1960s, the *Review*, many foreign SDA periodicals, and many union conference papers in North America printed repeated requests for copies of Loughborough's works. GC departments, book and Bible house directors, SDA Theological Seminaries, foreign missionaries, evangelists, librarians, historians, academy and college teachers and students, recent converts, and antiquarians—all clamored for copies of Loughborough's out-of-print works.[14]

As in the field of economics, a rising demand must be met with increased supply. If Loughborough's and M. E. Olsen's books were no longer available, some other writer must fill the gap. That author proved to be Arthur W. Spalding, the former head of the GC Home Commission. For several days in 1946 he traveled 1,100 miles through upstate New York researching early Adventist history. Subsequent trips through the New England states led to his writing a number of books on the Adventist past, including the four-volume set *Origin and History of Seventh-day Adventists* (1961-1962). Because his apologetic, anecdotal style mimicked Loughborough's, Adventist periodicals advertised his books as "the best source for stories from denominational history." For years Adventists worldwide would buy them at Book and Bible Houses and camp meetings.[15]

But church scholars, historians, and antiquarians thirsting for "classic Loughborough" refused to settle for these "diet Spalding" imitations: they demanded the real thing. In 1993 they got an appetizer when Loma Linda University (LLU) reprinted John's *The Great Second Advent Movement*. The main course became available a year later when LLU produced a CD-ROM containing many of the writings of 10 Adventist pioneers, including J. N. Loughborough.[16]

Likewise, for decades after his death, Missionary Volunteer societies around the world stayed loyal to Loughborough. His *The Great Second Advent Movement* remained the sine qua non for junior and senior devotional reading; it was indispensible for planning meetings focused on Adventist history; and it was still required for those desiring to pass the Standard of Attainment exam in church history until the 1940s. In addition, GC Missionary Volunteer secretary Alfred Peterson argued that reading Loughborough's stories led to "a strengthening of faith and a learning of advent doctrine which formed a framework for the thinking of these youth as they grew into sturdy Adventist men and women."[17]

THE LOUGHBOROUGH LEAGUE

Just as church leaders urged Adventist youth to read Loughborough's writings to strengthen their faith, they also cited his Bible reading record to encourage young people to study God's Word more faithfully. In 1925 A. E. Green of the Central California Conference, introducing the Bible Year Plan, invoked the name of J. N. Loughborough who "read the Bible through seventy times." Three years later Frank Yost of the Northern Union Conference also boosted Bible study by asserting that Loughborough had "read the Bible through some 70 or 75 times." By 1940, however, the unknown author of "Everyone Should Read the Bible" accurately credited J. O. Corliss with reading his Bible through 67 times, S. N. Haskell, 73 times, and J. N. Loughborough, 76 times. As late as 1949 one could still examine John's well-marked Bible at the General Conference Missionary Volunteer Department in Washington, D.C.[18]

Then in the fall of 1951 the conference Missionary Volunteer secretaries of Michigan, Wisconsin, Indiana, and Illinois brought to Lake Union Missionary Volunteer director John Hancock a proposal "whereby encouragement could be given to the young people to read their Bibles more." Remembering the Morning Watch of 1907 (which Loughborough himself had followed), someone suggested calling the new plan "the Loughborough League" and promoting it with the slogan "Read the Bible Through in '52." Soon the Missionary Volunteer leaders in the North American Division and General Conference supported the idea, and after Theodore Lucas, associate secretary of the GC Missionary Voluntary Department, launched the plan at a youth rally at Emmanuel Missionary College in January 1952, it spread like wildfire. Those who signed the pledge agreed to read three chapters every day (and 10 on Sabbath) in order to finish studying their Bibles by December 31.[19]

Promoting the Bible study plan around the world, Lucas reminded Adventist youth that exactly 100 years ago the 21-year-old pioneer had begun reading his Bible through every year, and had done so 76 times by the time he died.[20] "Was not that the secret of the spiritual power which characterized the great men who pioneered this movement?" G. W. Chambers asked. "Do we not need the same power now?" In Australasia Alfred Peterson boosted the league as "a new Missionary Volunteer fellowship" to prepare young people for "the last great conflict between truth and error." Victor H. Cooper promoted the League in Great Britain. Meanwhile, across North America, book and Bible houses struggled to meet the escalating demand for Bibles.[21]

The Loughborough League proved so popular around the world in 1952 that church leaders decided to keep it going for at least another five years. In 1953 the GC Missionary Volunteer Department issued multicolored ribbons (bookmarks) that it awarded to those who had read their Bibles through one to five times (by 1957). A youth rally in Lexington, Kentucky, that year launched the Missionary Volunteer Legion of Honor, and one enterprising fellow (imitating the game-show craze on American TV) created the Loughborough League Bible Quiz Program.[22] In 1955 Missionary Volunteer leaders in the Southwestern Union informed Adventist youth that in order to avoid "spiritual starvation," they must "join the Loughborough League . . . and read the Bible through as he did."[23] Although top-level advocacy for the Loughborough League disappeared from Adventist publications in 1954, as late as 1958 the *Instructor* offered colorful bookmarks to those who read their Bibles in a year.[24]

Beyond merely reading the words of Holy Writ, however, the *Instructor* told young people that Loughborough had made lists of the divine promises he found in the Old and New Testaments, finding 3,573 promises. Then on the flyleaf of another one of John's many Bibles he had tallied 5,891 promises in God's Word! In the 1960s and 1970s Adventist revivalist Elder Glenn Coon decided to stick with the shorter list when in his meetings he preached about the "ABC's of Bible Prayer."[25]

Certainly another posthumous legacy of the "little preacher" is the numerous converts whose lives that his sermons, articles, books, Bible studies, and visits transformed. From the 1890s and into the 1940s nearly every issue of the *Review* (as well as many North American union conference papers) contained obituaries mentioning the fact that the deceased had been converted, baptized, married, or ordained by Loughborough. The last to do so was Louraine Mitchell, an African American whom Loughborough had baptized during his retirement years in California. Mitchell, who had begun Adventist work among Blacks in the Oakland-San Francisco area, died in 1995 at the age of 104. Other obituaries invoked John's name as a pioneer who had preached in the church or visited the home of the deceased. Although Loughborough kept many different kinds of lists, there exists no extant tallies of his Adventist converts, but doubtless the number would reach into the thousands. Indeed, one boy who claimed that J. N. Loughborough had "helped to make a Seventh-day Adventist of me" grew up to become James Lamar McElhany, the General Conference president from 1936 to 1950.[26]

LOUGHBOROUGH MEMENTOS AND MONUMENTS TODAY

Given the major impact Loughborough had on the global Seventh-day Adventist Church during his lifetime, it is perhaps surprising that no one attempted to write his biography until three decades after his death. In 1955 Ella M. Robinson, the daughter of W. C. White and granddaughter of Ellen White, wrote *Lighter of Gospel Fires*, a narrative biography covering Loughborough's childhood, youth, and Adventist ministry. Based largely on John's autobiographical articles in the *Review*, *Youth's Instructor*, and the *Pacific Union Recorder* as well as on her memories of hearing Loughborough speak, the little book received wide promotion in church periodicals. Feeling a burden to pass along some of John's "soul-inspiring stories" to the younger generation, Robinson had largely excerpted (and polished) most of the anecdotes from his childhood and youth in New York. Until the book went out of print in the 1970s, church papers touted it as a great graduation gift for boys (girls were to read the biography of Ana Stahl, missionary to Peru). Although as a storybook, *Lighter of Gospel Fires* lived up to its billing as "fascinating" and "inspiring" reading, by omitting the last 70 years of his life, it created a need for a scholarly biography.[27]

Like most American denominations, the Seventh-day Adventist Church has never fostered the development of amusement parks to celebrate the legacy of its founders and pioneers (for example, Disneyland for Walt Disney and Dollywood for Dolly Parton). Except for a handful of restored pioneer homes in New York and New England and Historic Adventist Village (which recreates the life and teachings of the pioneers of Battle Creek), there are no "Whitewoods" or "Bateslands" anywhere in the world. If one wanted to establish a theme park to honor J. N. Loughborough, however, they need look no farther than Merced, California. In 1968 the members of the Merced SDA Church named the quarter-mile stretch of road that divided their 12-acre property from the new shopping mall "Loughborough Street." Three years later, they built a multipurpose auditorium-gymnasium behind their church and christened it "Loughborough Memorial Auditorium." Then in 1972 when the members erected a new elementary school, they named it the "Loughborough SDA School." Loyalty to Loughborough runs deep in Merced![28]

Another school near London commemorates Loughborough's contributions to the Adventist Church in the British Isles. In the fall of 1980 church leaders purchased a former Roman Catholic high school in Tattenham, a London suburb, and renamed it the John Loughborough School. Britain's first private Black school, the large, 12-classroom complex featured two labs, a library, an assembly hall, a fully equipped cafeteria, and one of the best gymnasiums in north London. Here 17 teachers taught 340 mostly Black students—all of them dressed in maroon-and-white uniforms, Loughborough's favorite colors. In 1984 when its students passed O-level exams three times better in math (and passed O-level exams twice as well in English compared with the six nearest comprehensive schools), members of the House of Lords took notice. The next year their lordships established a commission to discover the reasons for such phenomenal success rates, hoping to apply the same methods to other inner-city Black schools. Throughout the 1980s the media praised the Loughborough School's students "for achieving high standards in education among the London Afro-Caribbean community."[29]

In 1963 church leaders of the Greater New York Conference purchased a 280-acre country club at Wingdale, New York, and renamed it Camp Berkshire. Developing its ample acreage for summer camp meetings and youth retreats, conference officials in the 1980s erected three- and four-bedroom suites with shared bathrooms. Perhaps because the units were small and rented for only $9-14 a day, they became known as "loughboroughs."[30]

A LOUGHBOROUGH RETROSPECTIVE

The vast majority of Adventists who knew and loved J. N. Loughborough during his lifetime bequeathed warm memories to the next generation of church leaders, writers, and preachers, who in their books, articles, and speeches created glowing images of the man for the next generation. One man, whom John first met in Brooklyn and whose name he still knew 15 years later when they met again, praised his phenomenal memory in 1919.[31] In the 1920s J. O. Corliss recalled Loughborough's unflappable calmness in the face of emergencies.[32]

His preaching partner Eugene Farnsworth declared in the 1930s that John had been "more of a field laborer. . . . He was on the front lines battling most valiantly for the propagation of the truth." Yet at the same time this mighty warrior had been "a humble, devout man of God . . . who prayed most devoutly, earnestly, and often." Like S. N. Haskell, Loughborough had been "filled and running over with the Scriptures," and from "this inexhaustible storehouse they had gained their inspiration and power."[33] Praising the sacrificial lives of the pioneers, the *Union Record* stated that Loughborough "knew nothing of the luxuries in life" and often "seemed to be denied its necessities." Yet he had possessed "a lion's heart and knew his blessed Bible." The article quoted John's words that "it pleases the Lord to use small men with a big message."[34]

In his writings during the 1940s and 1960s Arthur Spalding called Loughborough "a disciple," "an apostle," "the right hand" of James and Ellen White, "the dean" of Adventist pioneers, and compared him to "John . . . the beloved disciple of Jesus" who outlived all his companions. Spalding portrayed Loughborough's "genial and sprightly nature" and the "gentle, kindly, vitalizing spirit of his life." At St. Helena Sanitarium he remained "an agreeable companion, . . . a thorough caretaker and an indefatigable worker."[35] Retired GC president W. A. Spicer remembered Loughborough as a man "of quiet temperament, unassuming in manner," but "ever active as a soul winner."[36] D. A. Delafield agreed, stating that although Loughborough had been "a diminutive little preacher," he had possessed "a big heart and a wise mind," making him "a consecrated, godly man."[37]

In the 1950s retired GC president James L. McElhany described Loughborough as a "dauntless . . . self-sacrificing" man, "hardy, courageous, filled with a spiritual vision of a great work to be accomplished." He was one of several who "laid the foundations for the development of the Advent cause."[38] North Pacific Union Treasurer J. C. Kozel agreed, praising Loughborough as one of the pioneers who made sacrifices for the cause.[39]

In 1964 the world-famous artist Harry Anderson created a memorable oil painting depicting George Butler and John Loughborough standing behind a pulpit at the California camp meeting in 1874 as eager Adventists come forward with their gold coins, gold bars, bags of gold dust, and jewelry to help launch the *Signs of the Times* and the Pacific Press Publishing Association.[40] The portrait sealed forever in the Adventist memory an image of J. N. Loughborough that endures today. While that image portrays one aspect of his life, it is hoped that this biography has presented a more balanced and nuanced interpretation of the complex life of one of Adventism's earliest historians.[41] How did Loughborough shape the Adventist movement both during his lifetime and long after his death?

THE LEGACY OF J. N. LOUGHBOROUGH TO SEVENTH-DAY ADVENTISM

When he died in 1924 at age 92, J. N. Loughborough was widely hailed as "the last of the pioneers." The term is appropriate for the man who had pioneered Adventist evangelism in new territories such as the Midwest in the 1850s, California in the 1860s and 1870s, and the British Isles in the 1880s. In addition, he sent the first boxes of tracts to Pitcairn Island and Haiti in the 1870s and helped launch the ship *Pitcairn* in 1890. His preaching tours across Europe, Australasia, and Africa between 1896 and 1910 greatly strengthened Adventist mission programs in those areas.

Loughborough also pioneered many organizational innovations. In the 1860s he played key roles in selecting the official name, incorporating the Review and Herald Publishing Association, organizing scores of local churches (he wrote the covenant they followed), forming the General Conference, writing state conference constitutions, contributing to the first health journal (*The Health Reformer*), and convening the first SDA camp meeting in Pilot Grove, Iowa (1866). During his 70-year career he filled numerous administrative positions, in many of which he was the pioneer official. In the 1860s he was Michigan Conference president, a General Conference Executive Committee member, and president of the first denominational health institution. During the 1870s he served as California Conference president, president of the Pacific SDA Publishing Association, president of the California Tract and Missionary Society, president of the California Sabbath School Association, and president of the British Tract and Missionary Society. Then in the 1880s he became president of the St. Helena Sanitarium and served on the board of Healdsburg College (later PUC). Finally, in the 1890s he became in turn president of the Nebraska and Illinois conferences as well as superintendent of two multistate districts stretching across America's Midwest and Southwest. At the same time he also served on the Foreign Mission Board, the International Tract and Missionary Society, the SDA Education Society, and the SDA Publishing Association. Even after he officially retired in 1897, Loughborough remained active: he helped reorganize the General Conference in 1901, form the British Union Conference in 1902 and the Pacific Union in 1906, and served as the assistant pastor of the Oakland SDA Church well into his 70s.

We should also remember Loughborough for many famous "firsts" in Adventist history. In the 1850s he was the first to use tents for evangelistic meetings; the first to sell Adventist tracts to the public; the first to keep Sabbaths from sundown to sundown; the first to suggest a tithing plan known as Systematic Benevolence. During the 1860s he was first to persuade Michigan's governor and the U.S. Government to grant SDA men noncombatant status during the Civil War; first to advertise public meetings in local newspapers; the church's first fund-raiser for its first sanitarium; and he—not Dr. Kellogg—wrote its first medical book (*Hand Book of Health*). Then in the 1870s Loughborough pioneered big-city gospel efforts in San Francisco; promoted methods for "saturation evangelism" in urban centers; started the ship ministry and Biblical institutes; and created the first recipe for Communion bread and persuaded West Coast members to substitute grape juice for wine. Next, in the 1880s he drew up the first ministerial reading list (31,000 pages); held the first workers' meetings one week prior to camp meetings; and pioneered the children's storytime at worship services. Finally, in the 1890s he led in establishing the first inner-city missions, the Chicago Bible School, and canvassers' and teachers' institutes. After he retired, John popularized the Birthday-Thank Offering in 1908. He actually gave separate offerings each year to mark his birthday and his conversion day.

Loughborough also deserves recognition for advancing Adventist music. Trained in choral singing as a boy, he served on the GC Hymnbook Committee in the 1860s that developed the earliest songbooks. In the 1870s he sponsored singing lessons for California's Sabbath school leaders, convened quarterly music conferences, urged local churches to install pump organs, encouraged children's choirs to sing at camp meetings, and was the first to print musical scores on one side of his evangelistic handbills with sermon outlines on the other. Against some opposition, Loughborough brought organs and harmoniums into camp meeting tents and public halls wherever he preached. Pacific Press in 1885 published his collection of "spiritual songs" as a new songbook.

Besides promoting musical harmony, Loughborough's successful encounters with fanatics, dissidents, and false prophets throughout his career brought spiritual harmony to the church. In the 1850s he helped to combat Case and Russell's "age-to-come" fanaticism and Gilbert Cranmer's attacks on the Whites in Michigan as well as Stephenson and Hall's *Messenger* Party defection in Wisconsin. During the next decade he had a major role in defeating fanaticism in Maine and the Snook and Brinkerhoff apostasy in Iowa. During the 1870s he successfully used public church trials to defeat defection in California. With voice and pen he combated false prophets such as Anna Garmire, Anna Phillips, and Margaret Rowen, and publicly debated dissidents such as Dudley M. Canright, A. T. Jones, and E. S. Ballenger even during his retirement years.

Although some Adventists in his day considered faith healings to be fanaticism, Loughborough did not. As a boy during the Millerite movement he had witnessed miraculous healings. He saw Adventist pioneers instantly restored to health in response to prayers and anointing in New York, Michigan, Wisconsin, and California in the 1850s and 1860s and again when A. T. Jones preached at the Mount Vernon, Ohio, and Decatur, Illinois, camp meetings in the 1890s. He remained firmly convinced that it was the work of the Holy Spirit.

The future church leaders Loughborough converted or trained constitute yet another significant legacy of his 70-year ministry. In the 1850s he converted John Matteson (future missionary to Scandinavia), Moses Hull (his future preaching partner in New England), George I. Butler (a future General Conference president), and Nathan Fuller (a future New York-Pennsylvania Conference president). For the 1870s his converts included William Healey (a future missionary to Hawaii and North Pacific Union Conference president) and Charles Kinney (one of the first ordained Black pastors who worked successfully in the South). Then in the 1890s Loughborough ordained Louis Sheafe (an outstanding Black evangelist in the West and South). Loughborough and W. C. White also pioneered the ordination of several female church elders in California.

Above all, J. N. Loughborough deserves to be remembered as the preeminent chronicler of Adventist history. Not only did he personally know most of our church's pioneer workers; not only did he participate in many of the watershed events that shaped our church's future; but his historical interpretation of those events shaped Adventists' views of the past for more than a century. His autobiographical articles in the *Advent Review and Sabbath Herald*, the *Youth's Instructor*, and the *Pacific Union Recorder*, and his path-breaking books *Rise and Progress of the Seventh-day Adventists* (1892) and *The Great Second Advent Movement* (1905) created the apologetic style of writing Adventist history followed by his disciples Arthur W. Spalding, LeRoy Edwin Froom, and F. M. Wilcox. Not until the rise of a new generation of professionally trained historians in the 1970s would church scholars probe the Adventist past with a greater degree of objectivity. Until then, however, pastors, teachers, and church officials continued to write history "the Loughborough way," emphasizing primarily the divinely led, progressive, inspiring stories of the past. During his retirement years, he also helped to shape future generations' views of Ellen White by compiling extensive indexes to all her published books and articles, by drawing up lists of more than 100 of her fulfilled predictions, and by sharing fascinating stories about her life and visions.

Consequently, for his evangelism in new territories, his outstanding leadership, his creative innovations, his encouragement of music, his combating fanaticism, his promotion of spirituality, his training of future church leaders, and his interpretation of the past, John Norton Loughborough deserves to be remembered as one of our church's outstanding pioneers.

---

[1] *RH*, June 12, 1913, p. 5.

[2] *GCB* (1926), pp. 7, 14. The 10 pioneers pictured are J. N. Loughborough, J. O. Corliss, S. N. Haskell, Joseph Bates, Uriah Smith, Hiram Edson, H. H. Wilcox, Frederick Wheeler, J. H. Waggoner, and J. G. Matteson.

[3] *RH*, Oct. 19, 1897, pp. 668, 669; *ST*, Nov. 4, 1897, p. 683; *Home Missionary*, June 1897, p. 120.

[4] *PUR*, Nov. 4, 1926, p. 8; *PUR*, Mar. 27, 1961, p. 3; *GCB* (1962), p. 45.

[5] *Western Canadian Tidings*, Feb. 5, 1929, pp. 4, 5; *PUR*, Mar. 10, 1932, pp. 1-4; *SWUR*, Apr. 11, 1934, pp. 2, 3; *GCB* (1936), pp. 79, 80; *RH*, June 10, 1941, pp. 249, 250; *Union Conference Record*, Aug. 21, 1950, pp. 3, 6; *NPUG*, Jan. 17, 1994, p. 2.

[6] *Life and Health*, January 1962, pp. 26, 27.

[7] *Union Conference Record*, Nov. 28, 1955, p. 12; Ronald Graybill, "Comprehensive Index" to J. N. Loughborough's *Rise and Progress of the SDAs* (Wheaton, Md.: n.p., 1985), pp. 53, 54. Furthermore, Arthur White's claim that Ellen White had "approximately 2,000 visions" during her lifetime is a statistical guess based on his "feeling" that she "averaged" a vision every two weeks, which the White Estate has never verified in print. See "Q&A," File 43-J-3, CAR.

[8] *PUR*, Sept. 20, 1917, p. 3; *RH*, July 31, 1919, pp. 14, 15; see also *NPUG*, Jan. 15, 1929, p. 10; May 21, 1929, p. 3; May 28, 1929, p. 7; May 8, 1934, p. 2; Oct. 10, 1939, p. 6; *Columbia Union Visitor*, Aug. 18, 1927, p. 3; June 19, 1930, p. 5; July 30, 1931, p. 8; *SWUR*, Feb. 5, 1929, p. 3; *Eastern Tidings*, July 1, 1934, p. 8.

[9] William Fagal (an associate director of the Ellen G. White Estate) e-mail to Brian Strayer, Jan. 4, 2010; EGW, *Testimonies for the Church*, vol. 4, p. 599.

[10] *Union Conference Record*, June 6, 1955, p. 2; *NPUG*, Apr. 18, 1977, p. 7; *RH*, July 8, 1982, p. 24; *RH*, Sept. 7, 1989, pp. 28-31.

[11] *ST-A*, July 5, 1926, pp. 8, 9; *Union Conference Record*, May 6, 1940, p. 2; *Union Conference Record*, Sept. 2, 1940, pp. 2, 3; *ST*, Sept. 9, 1941, pp. 8, 9; *GCB*, 1946, pp. 70-75; *ST*, Nov. 8, 1949, pp. 12, 13; *ST*, October 1958, pp. 14, 15.

[12] "An Open Letter to Seventh-day Adventists," *The Gathering Call* (1934), cited by *NPUG*, Jan. 9, 1934, pp. 2-6.

[13] A. W. Spalding, "Charting the Course," *YI*, Apr. 4, 1944, pp. 5, 13; Everett Dick, "Chronicler of Pioneer Days," *YI*, Aug. 8, 1944, p. 4, 13; Everett Dick, *Founders of the Message*, advertised in *SWUR*, Nov. 15, 1939, p. 5; Gary Land, preface to Everett Dick, *William Miller and the Advent Crisis* (Berrien Springs, Mich.: Andrews University Press, 1994).

[14] For a cross-section of these requests, see *PUR*, Dec. 11, 1924, p. 8; *AUG*, Mar. 10, 1926, p. 8; *NPUG*, July 13, 1926, p. 7; *PUR*, Feb. 3, 1927, p. 8; *ST-A*, Apr. 17, 1933, p. 16; *NPUG*, Apr. 9, 1940, p. 4; *Columbia Union Visitor*, Mar. 4, 1943, p. 6; *PUR*, Feb. 28, 1945, p. 2; *NPUG*, Aug. 20, 1946, p. 5; *Union Conference Record*, Aug. 5, 1946, p. 7; *Southern Tidings*, July 30, 1947, p. 4; *NPUG*, Dec. 9, 1947, p. 1; *PUR*, May 12, 1958, p. 3; *NPUG*, Apr. 13, 1959, p. 2; *LUH*, Jan. 10, 1961, p. 14; and *PUR*, Aug. 5, 1963, p. 4. It remains a mystery to this author why the Review and Herald did not keep *The Great Second Advent Movement* in print, at least until Spalding's historical works came along.

[15] *AUG*, Nov. 1, 1946, p. 3; *Union Conference Record*, Apr. 2, 1951, p. 7.

[16] *Columbia Union Visitor*, Mar. 15, 1993, p. 21; *RH*, Jan. 27, 1994, p. 7.

[17] *Southern Tidings*, June 6, 1934, p. 3.

[18] *PUR*, Apr. 9, 1925, p. 3; *Northern Union Reaper*, Jan. 3, 1928, p. 4; *NPUG*, Dec. 31, 1940, p. 4; *RH*, Sept. 8, 1949, p. 12.

[19] *LUH*, Jan. 29, 1952, p. 3; *LUH*, Dec. 11, 1951, p. 7; *Southern Tidings*, Dec. 26, 1951, p. 3; *YI*, Jan. 29, 1952, pp. 21, 22. Actually the Loughborough League entailed four parts: The Morning Watch (reading specified Bible texts each day), *In the Morning* (a devotional commentary), The Bible Year (reading the Bible through in a year's time), and the Character Classic plan (reading character-building books).

[20] *LUH*, Jan. 1, 1952, p. 8.

[21] G. W. Chambers, *NPUG*, Jan. 7, 1952, p. 1; *Union Conference Record*, Mar. 3, 1952, p. 4; *Union Conference Record*, Sept. 15, 1952, p. 7; *SWUR*, Sept. 10, 1952, pp. 3, 4; *SWUR*, Oct. 22, 1952, p. 4; *Columbia Union Visitor*, Nov. 13, 1952, pp. 2, 3; *PUR*, Dec. 22, 1952, pp. 3, 4; *YI*, Apr. 7, 1953, p. 10. Coincidentally, the inauguration of the league in 1952 commemorated both the 120th anniversary of Loughborough's birth in 1832 and the 100th anniversary of his conversion to Sabbatarian Adventism in 1852.

[22] *YI*, Jan. 6, 1953, p. 6; *SWUR*, Jan. 28, 1953, p. 6; *Southern Tidings*, Apr. 1, 1953, p. 9.

[23] *SWUR*, Jan. 19, 1955, p. 2.

[24] *Union Conference Record*, Jan. 4, 1954, pp. 5, 6; *LUH*, Feb. 16, 1954, p. 6; *RH*, May 26, 1954, p. 41; *RH*, May 31, 1954, pp. 113, 114; *YI*, Apr. 8, 1958, p. 16.

[25] *YI*, July 6, 1954, p. 4; *Union Conference Record*, Sept. 6, 1997, pp. 10, 11; Glenn Coon, *The ABC's of Bible Prayer* (Dynamic Bible Living Publications, 1966).

[26] E. J. Westman obituary for Mary June Strader, *Western Canadian Tidings*, Feb. 2, 1932, p. 7; *AR*, December 1995, p. 6; *PUR*, June 26, 1930, p. 5; *Union Conference Record*, Oct. 27, 1952, p. 2.

[27] *PUR*, Mar. 28, 1955, p. 3; *YI*, May 10, 1955, pp. 11, 18; *NPUG*, May 21, 1962, p. 4; *NPUG*, June 2, 1975, p. 27.

[28] *PUR*, Nov. 25, 1968, p. 3; *RH*, Dec. 19, 1968, pp. 19, 20; *PUR*, Sept. 27, 1971, p. 3; *PUR*, Oct. 23, 1972, p. 3.

[29] *Messenger*, Dec. 19, 1980, pp. 1, 4; *RH*, Feb. 12, 1981, p. 18; *RH*, May 24, 1984, p. 11; *RH*, July 19, 1984, p. 19; *RH*, May 30, 1985, p. 23; *RH*, Mar. 23, 1989, p. 20.

[30] *AUG*, Apr. 12, 1983, p. 7.

[31] *RH*, Aug. 21, 1919, p. 26.

[32] *RH*, Nov. 29, 1923, p. 9.

[33] *Church Officers' Gazette*, August 1931, p. 7.

[34] *Union Conference Record*, Aug. 7, 1939, p. 2.

[35] A. Spalding, *Origin and History*, vol. 1, p. 211; *ST*, May 24, 1949, pp. 8, 9, 14, 15.

[36] *RH*, Jan. 15, 1942, pp. 9, 10.

[37] *Missionary Leader*, February 1949, pp. 3, 4.

[38] *GCB* (1954), pp. 7, 8.

[39] *NPUG*, Nov. 9, 1959, p. 1.

[40] Harry Anderson painting, depicted in *ST*, June 1964, pp. 1, 3.

[41] Among those who wrote about SDA church history, Joseph Bates preceded Loughborough, while M. E. Olsen followed him chronologically.

INDEX

C

G

M

N

O

P

T

Y